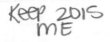

NIGHT TALES FROM LONG AGO

Michael Jay Katz

JASON ARONSON INC.
Northvale, New Jersey
London

The Night Tales Trilogy

Night Tales from Long Ago is Volume III of ***The Night Tales Trilogy*** by Michael Jay Katz. Volume I, *Night Tales of the Shammas,* contains Alef, Bet, and Gimel in the story cycle. Volume II, *Night Tales Remembered: Fables from the Shammas,* continues with Dalet, Hey, and Vav. *Night Tales from Long Ago* concludes with Zayin, Het, and Tet.

Cover artwork, maps, and bookplate for the trilogy were drawn by Nancy A. Burgard of Cleveland Heights, Ohio.

Hebrew letters by Jay Seth Greenspan.

This book is set in 11 pt. Schneidler by Lind Graphics of Upper Saddle River, New Jersey, and printed by Haddon Craftsmen in Scranton, Pennsylvania.

10 9 8 7 6 5 4 3 2 1

Library of Congress Cataloging-in-Publication Data

Katz, Michael Jay, 1950–
Night tales from long ago / by Michael J. Katz.
p. cm.
Vol. 3 of the Night tales trilogy.
ISBN 0-87668-590-4
1. Legends, Jewish. 2. Jews–Germany–Rhineland–Miscellanea.
I. Title.
BM530.K378 1993
296.1'9–dc20 92-40322

Manufactured in the United States of America. Jason Aronson Inc. offers books and cassettes. For information and catalog write to Jason Aronson Inc., 230 Livingston Street, Northvale, New Jersey 07647.

CONTENTS

Good evening, Rabbi. Of course–please sit here by the stove; the late-night fire helps me to become sleepy also. I look into the warm white glow and my mind floats far away. I find myself rolling along, traveling old country roads and mountain lanes and weedy riverside paths–and then before I know it I have nodded off. Now that I am old, I am always musing and napping, dozing and traveling, just like the old rabbi that my grandmother loved so much, the mystic writer Achselrad of Cologne.

This was Rabbi Abraham ben Alexander who headed the Jewish community of medieval Cologne in the last half of the twelfth century. Rabbi Abraham was a student of Eliazer ben Judah, the mystic rabbi of Worms, and Abraham ben Alexander was somewhat of a mystic himself. But even in those far distant days, the ordained rabbi–the *semikhah*–concentrated first on scholarship. The rabbi was the head of a medieval Jewish university; his primary task was to interpret the holy written and oral literatures. Still, old Achselrad was magic.

I mean no disrespect to you rabbis by this. In those days there was more magic abroad, even in the synagogue. Why, the youngest schoolboys in the yeshivas could recite a verse from the Holy Scriptures and make the pages in their prayerbooks shiver when there was not the slightest breeze at all. Rabbi Eliazer ben Judah had actually made a Golem, and Rabbi Achselrad slowed the day in order to stretch out a Friday Sabbath eve. . . . You do not know about Achselrad's stretched-out Sabbath eve? Well, let me tell you exactly what my grandmother told to me:

This particular Sabbath eve began with a *ki tov* dawn. It was early one Friday morning. The world seemed young and fresh. Yes, Rabbi, it was very early in the morning, one day long, long ago, in old medieval Cologne. The sun was out and no one was about at the old yeshiva. Rabbi Abraham Achselrad stood up. He walked through the main prayer hall; he looked out the front door. Old Achselrad took a deep breath. It was the great *ki tov* dawning of the day.

Ah, Rabbi, are dawn colors purer and clearer and finer than sunset colors? It certainly looks that way to me. The dawn colors glow in the opposite order of the evening colors: at sunrise there are the reds, then come the oranges, and finally God's brilliant golden yellows glow from behind the clouds. Old Rabbi Achselrad looked up into the Almighty Lord's yellow sky, and he looked down at the Almighty Lord's dust-brown dirt. The Rabbi looked around him. Where were all the people? Rabbi Abraham Achselrad stood still for a moment. Then he stepped out into the courtyard. Was the world empty of all mankind? How could this be? It felt so bright and so warm.

But it was not just people in general that the Rabbi wondered about. No, Rabbi Abraham was thinking specifically of one man: he was thinking about Samuel ben Abdon ha-Kohen. Samuel was a relative of Petahiah ben Jacob, Achselrad's childhood friend. Samuel was thin, and he tilted his head when he talked. Samuel had about him a certain feel–it was the feel of Petahiah himself–and old Achselrad liked Samuel for childhood reasons that no one could ever put into simple words.

Samuel ben Abdon was returning from Dusseldorf. He had been due in Cologne yesterday, but he had not yet arrived. Where was he now? Was he lost? Was he delayed? Rabbi Abraham did not know, but he was worried. And well he might have worried, because a wicked little demon kept waylaying poor Samuel. It was already Friday morning. A Jew should not travel after the Sabbath had begun on Friday night. Would Samuel make it to Cologne for the Sabbath night? The Rabbi wondered and worried, and he shook his head.

Far to the north, at just that hour, Samuel too was looking at the dawn. Wherever he found himself, Samuel tried to be one of the pious *early risers.* He would awaken before dawn. He would watch for the first rays of the sun; then he would match his *Shema* prayer with the very first light. Why did he do this? It was because he followed Psalm 119, which says:

I wake before dawn's gate
  And pray to You, my Guide,
Then I set my daily fate
  On the answers You provide,
And also I have studied late
  Through the dark night hours
So that I may meditate
  On the Laws, Your holy flowers.

Samuel was in Ohligs in the early morning, and in Ohligs the sky was cloudy. Somewhere the sun was rising brightly–perhaps far to the south in Cologne–but Samuel could not see the dawn. Had he guessed properly? Had he said his first prayers just as the great *ki tov* dawn arose and turned the sky red with her wispy pink fingertips? Samuel did not know, and a wicked little demon hissed and whispered in order to make Samuel shake his head, doubtful and worried.

Back in Cologne, old Rabbi Abraham sighed and returned to his study room. He sat at his desk. The morning moved on. Prayers followed study, and study followed prayers. Planning, explaining, reading, and all manner of rabbinical chores whisked the hours by. The sun was high; it was getting later and later, and the Sabbath was fast approaching. A tense feeling was in the air. Were storm clouds gathering somewhere to the north?

Meanwhile, Samuel had dressed hurriedly. He left Ohligs, and he followed the River Rhine south. Yesterday he had begun in Dusseldorf and had passed through Neuss. There the dark little demon had first found Samuel and had detained him with thunderstorms. Now Samuel was a day late on his planned schedule. Samuel ben Abdon was uneasy: Had his morning prayers been on time? Should he have eaten breakfast? The wagon axle was clicking–what if it broke? Samuel's mind rolled these things around and around. The wagon wheels kept sticking in the mud from yesterday's rains. Time and again Samuel got down from his seat to push. Would he never see the town of Hitdorf?

At last Hitdorf came, and then it went. The road was endless. The horse plodded along with slow tired steps. It seemed to take hours to reach the trees that Samuel saw up ahead. By midafternoon Samuel had come only to the town of Reindorf, where the River Wupper enters the River Rhine. Once, when he was little, Samuel had traveled up the River Wupper through small towns and hamlets far above the Rhine and into the hills by the town of Opladen. But today as Samuel crossed the River Wupper his thoughts were only on Cologne.

And what was happening in Cologne, in the old Jewish yeshiva behind Judengasse Street? The aging scholars were sitting on the wooden benches along the wall, and they were discussing Samuel. White-haired Baruch ben Jacob said, "My friends, I fear for Samuel. It is not like him to be late."

A younger scholar, Elisah ben Samuel, said, "We must think only good thoughts, Baruch – the Lord will provide."

"True," said Joshua ben Eliezer. "However, a prayer would not be amiss. We might offer some comforting verse from the Holy Scriptures."

The other scholars nodded, and Lewe ben Anselm said, "Well, from the Book of Exodus, I might say this":

With love and care and Grace
You guided Israel –
You saved that ancient race,
Leading them safe and well
To the gentle resting place
Where You shall ever dwell.

"Amen," said Reb Baruch.

Menahem ben Joel said, "Amen, also. And now gentlemen, I would repeat those holy words from the Book of Numbers":

Almighty Lord rise up anew
Protect us at Your side,
And may our enemies too
Be scattered far and wide,
And as to those who scorn You –
Dissolve them like an ebbing tide.

"I hope these traveler's prayers will help Samuel in some little way," said Moyses ben Nathan. "In addition it would not hurt to offer a general verse of protection":

Terror and dread fell upon them
And through the might of Your right arm
They all stopped, stone-still
While Your people passed safe from harm
Through the danger–by Your will,
Amen.

And Old Shimshon ha-Zaken coughed and said, "I am certain that Samuel will be safe. He is a good and pious man, and God always accompanies the pious traveler."

The worried sages nodded and stroked their beards and said many "amens." But the sun was low in the sky and Samuel ben Abdon ha-Kohen was only nearing Mulheim. Samuel was hungry and he was tired. And if Samuel felt this way, then how did his horse feel? But Samuel did not stop. He pushed on to Kalk, where he turned west in order to cross the River Rhine into Cologne.

It was still light. The demon laughed and hissed and it waved a hairy arm. The horse stumbled. A box dropped off the back of the wagon; it broke–Samuel's turnips spilled onto the road. Samuel stopped. He took a rope and he patched the box as best he could. He picked up the turnips; they were muddy from the road. Then he put the box back on the wagon. Next, Samuel went over to look at the horse. The horse seemed to be limping, and Samuel rubbed its left back leg. Samuel felt very tired. He climbed onto the wagon. Slowly, they started on their way again.

Meanwhile in Cologne the seven sages looked at one another. Rabbi Abraham was sleeping at his desk. The old men shook their heads. They stroked their beards. They muttered quietly among themselves. Just then, there was a noise outside, and Rabbi Abraham awoke. Old Shimshon ha-Zaken looked at the Rabbi and he asked, "And what is *your* opinion, Rabbi?"

Abraham Achselrad looked a bit confused. "What is my opinion?" he asked.

"Yes, Rabbi," said Shimson. "What do you think? Why is Samuel ben Abdon late?"

Rabbi Abraham sat up in his chair. He pushed a book back on his desk. "What do I think? Why is Samuel late?" he repeated. Old Achselrad stroked his beard and he looked at the wall. He nodded as if listening to a far-off voice. It was spring and the days were lengthening and distant sounds floated into Cologne from other lands and from ancient times. "Travel is always a risk," said the Rabbi slowly. "But outside settled communities the dangers are the greatest. A companion would help. Unfortunately we cannot get to Samuel now – so perhaps we need an amulet."

The Rabbi reached into his desk and he removed a small piece of kosher parchment. On one side he wrote the *Shema* followed by seven mystical words. On the other side, he wrote:

Go, my prayers, and wish to all
Flowers in the garden and meat in the hall
A bin of wine, a spice of wit
A house with lawns enclosing it –
A living river by the door
A nightingale in the sycamore
Warm friends, laughter, and children –
And the traveler coming home again,
Amen.

The Rabbi reread the charm and he nodded and smiled. Then he rolled the parchment into a tight scroll. He tied the scroll with seven white threads and in each thread he put seven neat knots. Next, he walked down the alley and out into Judengasse Street. Rabbi Abraham set the parchment in the center of the street, pointing north toward Dusseldorf, and he said seven mystical names of the Lord God Almighty (blessed be He). Passersby looked at old Achselrad and they shook their heads. Rabbi Abraham was a strange man, and sometimes he did strange things.

Now the day seemed interminable. The afternoon shadows had almost stopped in their tracks. But how long could time be held in check? The three evening stars swirled about in the great cosmic tides of the Almighty Lord God: they were getting restless, pushing and jostling one another, trying to peek through the blue nighttime shroud at the edges of an endless afternoon sky. The old men in Cologne looked at one another. They raised their eyebrows. They shook their heads. Where was poor Samuel now? they wondered.

To the north, Samuel ben Abdon had finally reached the edge of Cologne. The afternoon shadows lengthened and turned blue-gray. The air was cooling; the sun was setting. Samuel crossed the broad River Rhine along the Roman bridge at the town of Deutz. And then into Cologne came Samuel ben Abdon ha-Kohen.

The Cologne streets were winding and tortuous. Buildings crouched in the shadows. Dark doorways seemed fierce and angry. People milled about, they shouted, they rushed here and there. Samuel was deep in the marketplace. Pigs and chickens, vegetables and baskets, cloths and clothes were for sale along every wall. Cutlery filled the open carts. Woven silks hung from small wooden fences. People pushed and talked and ate. Barrels of wine and casks of herrings were piled in corners. The city seemed to whirl and twirl, and Samuel stopped a moment to get his bearings.

The Dom, the grand Catholic Cathedral, stood to the north. In front of Samuel was the town hall, the *Rathaus.* Samuel turned south. Crowds were everywhere. He pushed through the Alter Markt district and then through the Heu Markt and past the church of Saint Maria im Capitol, the oldest church in Cologne. Finally, Samuel found Hohestrasse Street. Soon the cathedral of Saint Albans was on his left, with its statue of a Roman soldier carrying a sword and a cross.

Noise rolled over him like waves, and Samuel felt dizzy. He was weak and hungry and tired. His arms and his head ached. His horse limped. Where was the Juden Viertels? And what was this? Was Samuel already at the southwestern walls of the city? Samuel turned right and went north on Hohestrasse Street. He found Buddengasse Street, but which way should he turn? He had been in Cologne just a few weeks before. Why could he not remember? The dark little demon laughed and hissed and it whispered "left," so Samuel turned west, away from the Juden Viertels again.

In the yeshiva, white-haired Baruch ben Jacob said, "Samuel is still gone, and the Sabbath is coming."

Elisah ben Samuel shook his head. "Nighttime is the time for evil spirits," he said gloomily.

Joshua ben Eliezer said quickly, "Elisah, one must not say such things aloud, especially not in the synagogue."

Lewe ben Anselm nodded and he said, "Once a man has set upon a journey, he must think only good and hopeful thoughts."

"Amen," said Menahem ben Joel.

Moyses ben Nathan nodded. "Keep the Lord ever before your eyes, I say."

"Exactly," said old Shimshon ha-Zaken. "The Lord is our guiding shepherd, amen."

The Rabbi tilted his head. To what was he listening? He stroked his beard; he tapped his chin. Shammas Chayim came in. "The sky is darkening," he reported.

In the eastern sky, the second evening star had already appeared. And as to Samuel? He was now in the northwest corner of Cologne. He had reached the old walls. But how could this be? Was he still lost? Again he turned his wagon. He passed the church of Saint Gereon, which was dedicated to the early Christian martyrs, the Theban Legion (the "Thundering Legion") led by Saint Maurice, where some of the martyrs were buried in the old crypt inside. Then – could it be? Yes, Samuel had once again found Hohestrasse Street and Budengasse Street. And here was Judengasse Street! Bearded Jews hurried along. Samuel waved. The men looked surprised. The evil little demon hissed and coughed and whispered, but either Samuel did not listen or he could not hear. His body was calm and happy and comfortable. His clothes felt loose and cool. The Sabbath spring evening had begun to take hold.

It was early in the spring. The evening sky was a darkening blue. The third night star was still hidden somewhere in the cosmic tides of God's great Celestial Heaven. Samuel and his horse and wagon rolled south on Judengasse Street. They went faster and faster. They crossed Engegasse Street on the right. They reached the alley, parallel to Engegasse Street, leading into the courtyard of the synagogue. Samuel stopped the wagon and jumped down. He reached for his satchel. But again the dark little demon hissed, and with one last whisk of his dark and demony hand the demon broke the handle of the satchel. Three stars were beginning to shine in the evening sky. Samuel grabbed his satchel in both arms, he set a gold coin on the wagon for the evil little demon, and he ran, ran, ran down the alley and into the front door of the synagogue building, just as Chayim the shammas was about to close and to lock it for the Sabbath evening service.

Samuel slipped off his shoes in the anteroom. He took a deep breath. He walked into the main prayer hall, which was filled with wooden benches. He passed the twelve stained-glass windows with their colored lions and snakes. The room glowed in a quiet warm candlelight. Samuel looked up at the Holy Ark made of stone and with a deep sigh he sat down on the front bench as all the assembled men raised their eyebrows. Old Rabbi Abraham Achselrad had his eyes closed, but he nodded and smiled a warm and holy smile. And then the welcoming Sabbath prayers began anew again.

Ah, good evening again, Rabbi. Yes, I know – it is always hard to sleep during the new moon. The night is so absolutely dark. It is as if a black shroud has been laid upon the heavens by the great angels and now the only light that slips through trickles in like a fine powder between the tiny stitching. Is that how it will be in the grave? . . . I do not know either. . . .

Well, I did not mean to bring up such gloomy matters. Let me push the coals back in the stove. There is nothing like the white glow to wash away the cares of a hard day. . . . What? A story from me? Rabbi, all I know are the children's tales, the grandmother fables. You need something new and fresh to keep your mind keen. Otherwise you will become a dreamy old man like me and you will find yourself constantly musing and dozing and nodding off in front of the stove. . . .

What do you mean you are already an old man? Do you really think that sixty years is old? You are still a child. When you reach eighty, *then* you will be old. You doubt that you will live to see eighty years? Well, then you will never grow old. . . . All right, all right, I know no special stories but mentioning shrouds reminds me of a tale my grandmother told about the quiet death of Salomo ben Uri, "the Regulator" of Cologne:

Once upon a time, began my grandmother, in medieval Germany along the wide River Rhine, there lived a pious and somewhat mystical scholar named Abraham ben Alexander, Achselrad of Cologne. Rabbi Abraham had a yeshiva, and one of its poor but faithful members was a man named Salomo ben Uri ha-Bahur.

Salomo lived alone. He was a cranky old man, and people called him "the Regulator" because he was always trying to get the community to pass rules. Salomo watched everyone carefully. Were any children out too late? Did each man contribute to the poor box? Were the bare ankles of any young women peeking out from beneath their skirts? Did every family light the Sabbath candles? Salomo had no family or relatives in Cologne, but he acted as if he were the stern father of the entire community. And as he got older and older his conversations became increasingly sharp. His talk was filled with pointing fingers and with accusations. He pecked and he scolded; even the Rabbi was not immune.

Then one day, Salomo died suddenly. One neighbor reported to the next, and finally word reached Rabbi Abraham. The Rabbi went and found Etan ben Jacob in his woodshop–Etan's wife was the head of the Burial Society. "I am sorry, Rabbi," said Etan, "my wife is in Duren with a sick sister." The other members of the Burial Society were also unavailable: the widow of David ben Aram was ill, and Aaron ben Samuel's oldest daughter could not be located. Rabbi Abraham sighed–he would have to go and prepare the body himself.

It was a cold day in the spring month of *Nisan.* Old Rabbi Achselrad put on his hat and his coat. The morning lesson would have to be set aside. "Tell the boys to report to Reb Shimshon," said the Rabbi to one of his pupils, Hasadiah ben Joseph ha-Levi. "Why, Rabbi?" asked Hasadiah. "What has happened?"

"Well, Hasadiah," said the Rabbi, "Old Salomo has died–I must go prepare the body."

"The Regulator has finally died?" asked Hasadiah. "Why is the Burial Society not taking care of things?"

"Somehow, no one is available," said Rabbi Abraham, and he

began to walk out the door. Hasadiah hesitated; then he said, "Rabbi–just a moment . . ."

Rabbi Abraham stopped and he turned around. "Yes?"

"May I come and help?" asked the boy.

The Rabbi looked at him for a moment. "Yes, I suppose so–well, just a moment, Hasadiah. You are a Levite," he said slowly. "The Torah says":

> The *Levite,* the high priest, shall not enter into a place where any man's dead body lies–not even for the funeral of his father or his mother.

Rabbi Abraham tapped his chin. "Some people object to any Levite preparing a dead body," he continued. "But–well, Hasadiah, my feeling is that this applies only to the highest religious officials, officials even higher than us common rabbis." The Rabbi was silent a moment. "Very well," he said finally, "come along."

The two Jews walked from the synagogue. They went down the alleyway and out along Judengasse Street. Soon they came to Salomo's house. The door was partly opened. A neighbor, Jacob ben Martel, was sitting quietly inside. The house had a damp, unpleasant smell, and Jacob was happy to leave when the Rabbi arrived. Hasadiah felt frightened and uncomfortable.

Salomo was slumped in a chair. The Rabbi carried him over to his cot. He laid the body down and smoothed it out as best he could. Jewish burial rites are not very elaborate, nonetheless there are a number of important steps. Hasadiah watched as old Rabbi Achselrad removed Salomo's clothes and closed Salomo's eyes. The Rabbi straightened each finger. Then he reached into his own pocket and took out one of the synagogue keys, which he put under Salomo's head.

"Would you get me some salt?" the Rabbi said to Hasadiah.

Hasadiah found a wooden box of salt in the pantry. The Rabbi sprinkled salt lightly over the whole body. He took a clean cloth and wet it with salt water and he washed the body from head to toe. Next the Rabbi looked through Salomo's belongings. He found two prayer shawls. One he wrapped around the body; the other he set aside. Folded in with the prayer shawls was a clean linen cap, and this the Rabbi put on Salomo's head.

"Someone must stay with the body at all times," said the Rabbi to

Hasadiah. "I will wait here. Would you go back to the synagogue and check with Shammas Chayim? I left instructions for him to get a casket; you can help him to bring it here." Hasadiah nodded and left. Now the Rabbi was alone with old Salomo.

Abraham Achselrad looked down at the silent old man. What could he remember about Salomo ben Uri ha-Bahur? The Rabbi remembered a bent old complainer. He remembered a man who would say: *takkanot* before he would say *sholom.* Those *takkanot,* the myriad ordinances that a Jewish community was always inflicting on itself, were Salomo's whole life. Rabbi Achselrad closed his eyes and leaned back in the chair. He remembered the time that Salomo had tried to pass a *takkanah* prohibiting shaving. Another time, Salomo pushed a resolution forbidding Jews from prosecuting other Jews in the Christian courts. Salomo "the Regulator" had gotten a rule passed to restrict gambling and also a rule that fined men one gold coin if they dared to dance with a woman who was not their wife.

And was it Salomo who thought of the idea of requiring ten men at all weddings? Yes, undoubtedly it was, thought Rabbi Abraham. Certainly Salomo had instigated the *takkanah* forbidding secular singing on the holidays and also the *takkanah* requiring our charity money to be used here in Cologne before it was given out to other needy communities. The Rabbi smiled. Once, Salomo ben Uri had attempted to get the congregation to pass a "May his" *takkanah:* Salomo wanted anyone excommunicated if he did not add "May his life be long!" after Jewish names on official documents. What a vast number of strange constraints has passed through our community, thought the Rabbi. Fortunately, to be kept alive most *takkanot* required yearly reapproval. And all *takkanot* had a limited life span–automatically they quietly faded away after five years. How many of these strictures had come and gone? Old Achselrad sighed again. Now Salomo too had come and gone.

The Rabbi opened his eyes; he stretched his arms. Hasadiah was returning with two men. The men carried a coffin made of rough white wood and smelling of pine and cut forests. Rabbi Achselrad spread Salomo's second white *tallit* inside the wooden box, and then into this casket they gently folded the body in the position of an unborn child so that someday Salomo might roll smoothly like a round, round bottle into the Holy Land beyond the grave. Old

Salomo's hands were put at his sides. Spices were sprinkled over his body. The Rabbi touched Salomo's forehead and he said a silent prayer.

The Rabbi sent Hasadiah to search the house: every bit of water must be poured out. Old Achselrad straightened up the household. The two other men agreed to sit with the body through the night, and finally Hasadiah and the Rabbi left.

The next day was the funeral. The weather was cold; the ground was wet. Would ten men be found for the burial ceremonies? The Shammas went down the street to the house of Hiyyah ben Jacob ha-Levi. Hiyyah was piling wood in his yard. Yes–he would stop and put on his good clothes and come to the funeral, for attendance at a funeral is the best of good deeds. Etan ben Jacob also agreed to come. The old sages from the yeshiva would walk along. So, there were ten adult Jews after all, ready to accompany Salomo on his last journey from Cologne.

Jews were buried in the *Am Toten Juden.* Slowly the small group of mourners followed the coffin south toward the cemetery. (They walked *behind* the body because of the talmudic injuction: "and no living man shall go out first." As you know, Rabbi, evil spirits are set free by a death, and they fly in front of the coffin waiting to pounce on anyone who should walk ahead of the body.) The men held their coats tightly against the cold air. They listened and nodded as the Shammas repeated Psalm 91 seven slow times, beginning:

You who enjoy God's protectiveness
Resting in His Heavenly shade,
Admit that He is your strong fortress
Your refuge and your barricade.

The Holy One will soon subdue
The fiercest gales that rainstorms bring
And He is continuously guarding you
In the shelter of His mighty wing.

and ending:

"When he calls to Me, I will answer:
I will help him in his strife,
Then I will bring him lasting honor
And will give to him long life.

"So a good and humble person–
He who trusts and follows Me–
Will enjoy My full salvation
Through a glorious Eternity."

The procession reached the southern gate, the Bonn Gate, in the Cologne walls. Just beyond was the *Am Toten Juden.* Formally, the cemetery was in the Parish of St. Severin and it was leased for four gold coins a year from the knight Orlivus of the monastic Chapter of St. Severin. The Jewish cemetery was almost forty thousand square meters, and it was surrounded by four walls, each two hundred meters long, with its east wall extended along the Bruhl road. In the good weather many Jews visited the *Am Toten Juden*–it was a calm refuge, a shady sheltered park with trees and bushes and a small stream.

Into the cemetery walked the mourners. They passed grave upon grave. The oldest graves were covered with flat slabs of rock, and the stones were set like tents and held together with mortar. Other graves were simply covered with piles of odd-shaped stones and marked with flat headstones. The Rabbi chose a spot along the Bruhl wall. The men took turns digging. It was still between the winter and the spring and the earth was hard and the dirt was clumped. Gray-brown gromwell leaves were scattered among the rocks; dried grass stems lay flat and cold.

The digging was slow work, but finally there was a hole the size of the casket. Four men set the wooden box into the grave, with Salomo's head to the west and with his feet to the east. It is true that the Talmud says: "monuments are not erected to the pious, their words are their memorial," but this is not a rule that forbids headstones. Rabbi Abraham told his congregation, "This simply means that in talmudic times headstones were not necessary: the eloquent words of those famed scholars were a sufficient remembrance. Today, however, most of us are not that well-spoken." Therefore the Rabbi had brought a pine board for Salomo's gravemarker. The Rabbi kneeled on the ground. With a knife, he engraved:

Salomo ben Uri ha-Bahur
Who cared for his community
Died 10 *Nisan* 4926

Later, Old Achselrad would arrange to have the board replaced by a stone slab.

There were rites and prayers and silent thoughts, and then Rabbi Abraham tore up a tuft of brown grass and dirt and he tossed it behind his back.

"Why did you do that, Rabbi?" asked Hasadiah.

The Rabbi pulled his coat around him. "Well," he said, "I will tell you: At death, Dumah, the black angel, comes down. He whisks the soul away to the farthest celestial reaches of Heaven, and there it passes through the Final Court of the Omnipotent Lord God (blessed be He) – then the soul learns what will be its place in the Great Hereafter.

"However, the soul must return for the burial. It slips down from those distant reaches of Heaven and it accompanies the empty body to the grave. But, Hasadiah, the soul cannot simply leave after the ceremony. It must stay in the cemetery until the congregation of the living gives it permission to return to Heaven. In fact, sometimes the souls of sinners are condemned by the congregation to remain on earth in cemeteries, wafting, wavering, and wandering about near their old bodies."

The Rabbi looked down at the grave. "I have just tossed a bit of grass and dirt behind my back. It is a signal to the soul. 'Go back to Heaven; rest in peace,' I have said. 'Enjoy your eternal rest in the warm arms of the Lord, in the bosom of Abraham, in the gentle *Gan Eden* forever.' "

Again Rabbi Achselrad looked down at the newly covered grave. "Now," he said to Hasadiah, "the soul of Salomo has flown back to rest in Heaven, while the body of the old man is resting, finally and forever, in the *House of Life – The Living Garden of the Jews.*"

The Rabbi nodded to himself. It was getting late. The other men had already left. Now these two Jews – old Abraham and young Hasadiah – also left, walking back into Cologne from the cemetery. A wind arose, and neither said anything more. The sky was gray. The entire day seemed to have disappeared. Was the day itself forgotten, or had it flown off to rest in Eternity along with Salomo's soul?

Hasadiah and Abraham walked through the darkening streets of Cologne. They rounded the corner of Obenmarspforten Street. The warm scent of oatcakes and sourbread slipped by suddenly – then it was gone.

The sky was dark. The hour was late. The two Jews reached the synagogue at the end of the alley that led back from Judengasse Street. Hasadiah walked down the alley to the yeshiva with the Rabbi–but now he should be going home. The Rabbi's legs hurt. He had a headache. Old Rabbi Achselrad was tired and hungry. He felt old, and he felt weak. He put his hand on the synagogue door. Then he took a deep breath, and he turned and he patted Hasadiah on the shoulders. "Thank you, my friend," said the old man. Hasadiah smiled, he looked down at his feet, and then he turned to go home. Rabbi Abraham ben Alexander stood and watched Hasadiah until the boy had disappeared completely into the darkening night. It was late. It was a cold springtime evening in the Juden Viertels of medieval Cologne. The Rabbi went into the well-regulated Jewish community's wooden yeshiva and he closed the door behind him.

Good evening, Rabbi. It is rather late for you to be here. Are you cold? Sit down on the bench – I will stoke up the oven. There, now you can see the spirits. . . . What do I mean? It is simply that the spirit is like a flame. Why else do we see flickering lights in cemeteries at night? And why do candles and night fires keep away demons? It is because demons are weakened by the warmth and the light and the goodness of the spirits that are in the flames. Old Ephraim ben Jacob of Bonn described Jews as golden candle flames surrounding the Great Throne of Glory. . . . You do not know about Ephraim ben Jacob? He was a medieval Jewish scholar from Bonn, and once upon a time he came to Cologne – Ephraim came in the spring, that most hopeful spirit-filled season of the year.

It was the twelfth century, and in the city of Bonn there lived a Jew named Ephraim ben Jacob. Ephraim was not a rabbi – at least not formally – but he loved the Talmud and he absorbed languages like cotton soaks up water. Ephraim was such a fine writer that people spoke well of him as far away as Prague and Paris. He wrote responsa, he wrote essays on the standard prayers and on the circumcision ceremony, and he wrote a commentary to the holiday prayer book. In addition, Ephraim ben Jacob wrote religious poems. Ephraim is especially remembered for his famous poetic hymn, now known as the "Bonn Benediction," which is repeated in German synagogues during the last week in *Adar,* the week before the *Hahodesh* Sabbath that consecrates the month of *Nisan.* The "Bonn Benediction" is:

May the Almighty Holy Being
(Our welfare is His concern)
Grant us the lasting joy of seeing
The Jews of Exile finally return.

May He bless us from above
And rain down joy and comfort–
May we feel His warmth and great love
In the Temple, in His holy fort.

May He lead us from the dead
Lands filled with gloomy shadows,
And may He then enshroud instead
Our enemies and our mortal foes.

May He fulfill with all due swiftness
The promise of our first birthright:
"The people who walked in bleak darkness
Shall once again see a wondrous light."

May He light our nighttime eyes
As written in the holy Word:
"Though darkness floods through all the skies
God's radiance soars like Heaven's bird."

God burns like a golden flame, alit
Like the sun in Heaven's dome–
And Jews are glowing pious spirits,
Golden candles round His holy throne.

So may He grant you a warm sun-ray
From the sunshine of His glorious day
And at night moonglow from the Milky Way
And holy light from where angels play.

Ephraim wrote this hymn many, many years ago, in the days when Abraham ben Alexander was the Chief Rabbi of Cologne. One time, the two men actually met and talked in person. It was on a mild springtime evening in the last week of the month of *Adar.* Rabbi Abraham was studying alone, and that evening a thin traveler, a wanderer, found his way to the alley leading from Judengasse street to the Cologne yeshiva. Into the synagogue building walked the stranger. He stepped in the front door, and he removed his shoes in the anteroom.

On stockinged feet, the man padded through the sacred building. He entered the main prayer hall, which was filled with wooden benches. He passed the twelve stained-glass windows with their colored lions and snakes, he looked up at the Holy Ark made of stone, and he walked to the door of the back study room. There, Rabbi Abraham was bent over a book, lost in his reading.

"Rabbi . . ." said the stranger quietly.

Abraham Achselrad looked up. "Yes?"

"Good evening, Rabbi. My name is Ephraim ben Jacob. May I come in?"

"Certainly, certainly," said Rabbi Abraham, pushing aside his book. "Please come in and sit down." The Rabbi stared at the traveler. "I do not recognize you. Are you from the Rhine regions here?"

Ephraim sat down on one of the worn benches. He put his knapsack on the floor by his feet. "Well, Rabbi, now I live in Bonn. Earlier, I lived near Konigswinter."

Old Rabbi Achselrad looked at the wall, picturing the city of Bonn, for he had been there many times. Bonn is on the left bank of the River Rhine south and east of Cologne; it has villas and gardens and it is interlaced with narrow streets. In his mind's eye Rabbi Abraham saw the huge Roman Catholic Munster Church, a grey stone monument with five tall towers. Rabbi Achselrad thought of Bonn, and he was lost in his musing. After a moment, Ephraim said, "Excuse me, Rabbi. Is everything all right?"

Rabbi Abraham's eyes had closed. Now he opened them again, and he smiled. He was tired from his writing and his thinking. He took a breath. He sat back. "Yes, yes, young man – everything is fine," he said. "You must tell me your story. I have plenty of time, so begin at the beginning and end at the end."

Ephraim raised his eyebrows. "Well, if you wish . . ."

Rabbi Abraham nodded. Ephraim settled back on the bench. "All right, Rabbi," he began, "it is like this: I have lived in Bonn for perhaps fifteen or twenty years, but I was born farther south, near Konigswinter. Konigswinter is a magical place–there is a castle on the Drachenfels Hill behind the town, and somewhere in the Hill is the cave of the dragon that Siegfried killed."

Ephraim smiled. "When we were little we used to find sharp white stones that once were dragon's teeth–at least that is what my friend Shmulik told me, and who knows if he was right?

"But in those days, things were very unsettled everywhere; it was a sad time. Between the evil King Henry and the Crusades–well, we suffered immensely. Jews were robbed and beaten. We did not dare to go out at night, and during the days we had to walk together in groups for protection. When I was thirteen, we heard that bands of Jew haters were moving toward us from the west. So, my family paid ten gold coins for me and my three cousins to hide in the tower of Wolkenburg."

"Was that the Wolkenburg Castle?" asked Rabbi Abraham. "I thought it belonged to the Archbishop here in Cologne."

"Yes, it does," said Ephraim. "But the Archbishop was sympathetic to us Jews. He said nothing about the 'guests,' and quietly we were allowed to live in Wolkenburg through the spring and the summer."

Ephraim sighed. "I have some fine memories of that beautiful place," he said. "We walked every day, even in rainy weather, with water dripping from the trees like a waterfall. In the mornings, I tramped out through the thick forest, among the pines and the larches. There are seven great hills along the River Rhine. I have been up and down the whole Rhinelands and no part is more wonderful than Wolkenburg–it has dark green slopes and castles and sudden wild views, with crags and cliffs and the tops of trees as far as the eye can see.

"On some days, Joshua–my oldest cousin–and I would slip down to the town below. We stood in the background, along the walls and in the corners of the marketplace. And we heard terrible stories about Jews being killed and tormented. It was the time of the Second Crusade. The Mohammedans were the main enemy. But we Jews are

Semitic too. If the Mohammedans were planning to invade all of Europe, then, argued the Germans, the Jews must be their advance agents. In the Holy Lands the Mohammedans had already retaken the major cities, such as Edessa and Jerusalem. Mohammedans were coming across the Mediterranean from Africa into Spain. It was only a matter of time before they appeared in Germany, and then the Jews would join them – or so we heard."

Ephraim nodded to himself. "There was a secret society of young Jewish fighters, and Joshua and I joined them. When synagogues were attacked, when stores and farms were burned, we Jews fought back. Usually we only angered the Gentiles further. We lost most of the battles. We were outnumbered, and we had poor weapons. Of course officially we could not own weapons because we were supposedly 'protected citizens.' So we stole. We took swords and knives; one boy even had a crossbow and arrows. And, Rabbi, I must confess that at times we fought on the Sabbath. . . . But it was never exciting or glorious. No – instead it was terrible. When I look back, all that I remember is a sad, sad time. I saw much and heard much and I cannot get the visions out of my mind, especially late at night. I tried to write some poems, some laments about those days. I thought that they might make me feel a bit better, but they do not really help. Here, this is one of my verses":

If I were filled with endless tears
And my eyes were bottomless wells
Then I could weep throughout the years
For the sad story our history tells.

My heart bitterly groaned aloud
As cruel terrors flared around me;
Children and gray old men unbowed
Were wounded and cut down brutally.

Now for Abraham's sons I weep,
The Hebrew people of Israel
Are swept aside in a lifeless heap
Like dry leaves in the bleak cold fall.

And so we stand and remember them –
But will God save *us* someday?
Will our bodies be sung a requiem
While our souls fly up to Heaven to stay?

Ephraim rubbed his chin and he looked down at his knee. "In Bonn," he said, "we still sing laments at all the fasts and feasts. . . . But sometimes, Rabbi, I do not know whether it is better to remember or to forget."

Good evening, Rabbi. Are you having difficulty sleeping again? Put your feet up on the side bench and I will open the stove door. Let me push this coal back; the white glow will wash away all the cares of your hard day. . . .

No, let's just sit here quietly. You and I are too old to have to talk, talk, talk in order to communicate. We can just enjoy each other's company. We are like an old married couple. Of course it is different with newlyweds: Talk to your bride, I tell young men. Who knows what strange thoughts she might have in her head? That is good advice for middle-aged couples too. As the Talmud says: "If your wife is tall, then stand on a chair and talk to her." (What? Yes, yes, the Talmud also says: "If your wife is short, then bend down and whisper in her ear.") How else can one know what another person is thinking? Ideas do not float about magically like leaves in the wind, you know.

Ah, what strange ends come from unspoken ideas. Jerahmeel is a good example. . . . This was Jerahmeel ben Moses ha-Levi, a quiet man of Cologne; he lived in the days of old Rabbi Achselrad. Jerahmeel did not talk very often, and certainly he never said a word about what he was feeling. Nonetheless, he was a good man—he was pious and charitable, and he went to the synagogue every day.

Jerahmeel had been married for twelve long years, but he and his wife, Rechlin, still had no children. The Talmud says: "If a man marries and if he waits ten years and if the couple still has no children, then the man need wait no longer. After ten years, he may divorce his wife and remarry." It also says: "A childless person is accounted as dead." Jerahmeel knew these things and one day he said suddenly to Rechlin: "We should get divorced."

Rechlin stood still. Then she sat down. How could Jerahmeel say such a thing? But he *had* said such a thing–Rechlin had heard it quite clearly–and now that he had said it out loud, then perhaps it must come to pass. Rechlin felt that a river was sweeping her along. All that she could say was: "Very well."

Were things then decided? It was so sudden. Whatever could have been the cause of these problems? I myself think that it was demons, Rabbi. Undoubtedly it was Ashmedai himself, the prince of demons, the evil spirit of anger and lust and marital problems and the plague of King Solomon. Ashmedai once said:

> Among mortals, I am called "Ashmedai." And as to my business? It is to plot against married couples, especially the young and the newly-wedded. I give them calamities, I sever their ties with one another, I break their spirits, and especially I estrange their hearts.

Ashmedai whispered in Jerahmeel's ear; so the good but quiet man of Cologne decided to divorce his wife. First, however, he went to the old yeshiva at the end of the alley off Judengasse Street. Jerahmeel went into the synagogue building, he walked through the empty prayer hall, and he came to the back study room. The spring weather was still cool, and the small stove in the study room was hot. The Rabbi was bent over a book. A group of scholars was sitting talking quietly.

"Gentlemen," said Jerahmeel, "I am thinking of divorcing my wife."

The old men raised their eyebrows, they looked at one another, and there was silence. Jerahmeel sat down. "You see," he continued, "we have had no children. Undoubtedly it is my fault, and I would like to free her to marry again."

Still there was silence. "Do you have any counsel?" asked Jerahmeel, looking around.

White-bearded Baruch ben Jacob looked at his companions, and then he said, "It is true, Jerahmeel–the purpose of marriage is to have a family."

The sages nodded. A younger scholar, Elisah ben Samuel, said, "Ideally, you will have many sons and sons-in-law who are trained in the Torah."

"Exactly, Elisah," said Joshua ben Eliezer. "The Talmud reminds us":

> He who loves his wife as himself, who honors her more than himself, who leads his sons and daughters in the path of the Lord, who arranges for their educations and their marriages–it is he who shall finally know that his tent is at peace.

"Amen," said Lewe ben Anselm.

"Therefore," continued another sage, Menahem ben Joel, "if you marry and if ten years pass without a child, then you may divorce. In this way each person can try again to found a family."

Again the men nodded. Moyses ben Nathan said, "Yes, Reb Jerahmeel, the Book of Deuteronomy clearly allows for divorce under appropriate circumstances–and all rabbis agree that childlessness is an appropriate circumstance."

The scholars stroked their beards and muttered, and old Shimshon ha-Zaken coughed and cleared his throat and he said, "You know, of course, Jerahmeel, that both the man and the woman must agree to the divorce."

"Well," said Jerahmeel, "both my wife and I agree to a divorce."

Rabbi Abraham had been listening quietly; he frowned. "Let me add a word here, gentlemen," he said. "Rabbinical rules require that you–the husband–also make an acceptable settlement payment to your wife. A *ketubah,* a marriage settlement, is necessary."

Jerahmeel said, "What should I pay her?"

"I leave that up to you to decide," said the Rabbi. "However, it must be acceptable to your wife."

Jerahmeel frowned. "I do not have much money at the moment,

and I have few goods. As you know, I am a coal merchant. How about a large load of coal?"

Rabbi Abraham raised his eyebrows. He tapped his chin. "Ask your wife," he said, and he looked down again at his writing.

Jerahmeel waited a moment. No one else spoke, so Jerahmeel left the yeshiva and went home. Rechlin was working in the kitchen. "Wife," said Jerahmeel, "the sages agree that we can get divorced. Rabbi Abraham says I must make a payment, a marriage settlement with you. Will you accept a load of coal?"

Rechlin kept working; she said nothing–she only nodded.

Jerahmeel returned to the yeshiva. "Rechlin has accepted my offer," he announced. The Rabbi was writing. A few minutes of silence passed. Then Rabbi Abraham sighed. "Well," he said looking up at Jerahmeel, "tomorrow is Thursday. A *Bet Din* will be convened and we will have three rabbis. Please return then."

Thursday morning after two other matters were settled, the shammas declared, "Now it is time for the divorce of Jerahmeel and Rechlin."

Rabbi Abraham asked whether Jerahmeel wished to divorce Rechlin. Jerahmeel stood, and he said, "Yes, I do."

The Rabbi turned to Rechlin. "Do you wish to divorce Jerahmeel?" he asked.

"I do," answered the woman.

The Rabbi stepped to the almemar–the synagogue reading desk–and he began to write a Bill of Divorcement. The Rabbi wrote thirteen neat lines of print with each of the letters interlaced so that no additional words could be inserted. Rabbi Abraham wrote slowly and deliberately: the final paper must have absolutely no errors. Minutes passed in silence. The Rabbi finished writing. Gently he blew on the parchment to dry the ink. He read the paper again, and then he passed it to the two other rabbis.

Each rabbi read the entire document and signed it at the bottom. Rabbi Abraham signed underneath. Jerahmeel signed the paper. Rechlin signed the paper. The Rabbi folded the parchment document in half. Jerahmeel took the document and put it into Rechlin's outstretched hands. A tear was in her eye. Rechlin took the paper and she gave it back to Rabbi Abraham, who cut it into two pieces. Then the

Rabbi put the pieces in the bottom drawer of the almemar–and I am sure that Ashmedai smiled and smiled.

"I now declare you divorced," said old Achselrad quietly. "Rechlin, you will be free to remarry in three months time."

Rechlin turned. She walked from the main prayer hall, and, after a moment, Jerahmeel followed.

Jerahmeel was very sad. He sold his coal business the next week, he packed his belongings, and he left town. No one was certain where he went–perhaps he lived for a time in Dusseldorf with a cousin. Meanwhile, he had arranged for a workman to deliver the load of coal. When it arrived, Rechlin found a sack of money hidden inside.

Rechlin's friends told her that she must go on with her life. But how could she earn money–what sort of business could she run? "I only know housekeeping," she said. "Well," they told her, "start an inn." An inn? Well, why not? So with the money from the load of coal, Rechlin bought an old house. At one time the house had been a Christian hostel called the Inn of St. Julian, the patron saint of travelers. Rechlin renamed the house the Inn of Elijah. She cleaned and decorated the five sleeping rooms and the large eating hall. Rechlin became the cook, and she hired two maids and a stableboy to help. Rechlin was serious and neat and hardworking; in fact, she was hard-nosed and practical. Soon the business was prospering.

The days came and the days went. The seasons turned. One year disappeared and then the next, and suddenly twelve long years had passed. What had happened to Jerahmeel? Rechlin thought of him often. She even asked about him, but no one had any news.

Then one day, Jerahmeel found himself back in Cologne. He was in the middle of a trip to Bonn. He was tired, he was alone, and now he was also poor. Jerahmeel had had difficult times and he was embarrassed to see his old friends, so he stopped at a new inn, the Inn of Elijah. The maid took his satchel. But what was this? It cost a gold coin for two days and four meals? That was too much money for him to pay. Jerahmeel took his bag from the maid, and he turned to leave. He started out the door. On the steps was a woman–it was Rechlin, coming in from the market. Rechlin stopped, she opened her eyes wide, but she said nothing. Jerahmeel rubbed his fingers against one another. He looked down at the ground. His hands were warm and gritty. His throat felt uncomfortable.

Finally, he said, "Hello again . . ."

"Hello."

There was silence.

"How are you?"

"All right–how are you?"

"I am all right too."

Again there was silence, and then: "Did you send me the money in the coal?" asked Rechlin.

"Yes," said Jerahmeel.

Rechlin raised her eyebrows. "Why? I thought that you did not like me any longer."

"No . . . I always loved you very much."

"Then why did you divorce me?" asked Rechlin.

"We had no children," answered Jerahmeel. He shrugged. "It was my fault. Anyway, I hope that you have remarried and that now you have a big family."

"No," said Rechlin, "I am still alone." Then she was quiet.

After many minutes, Rechlin went on: "Perhaps you can stay here for the night."

"I am afraid I cannot afford your luxury rates."

"I can make an exception–I do owe you something. . . . In fact, in a sense, I guess that this is your inn too."

"Well," said Jerahmeel, "I would not mind staying here."

So Jerahmeel stayed that night and many nights thereafter. And one day a few weeks later, the couple went to the Rabbi.

Jerahmeel and Rechlin went to the old synagogue behind Judengasse Street. As usual, Rabbi Abraham was bent over a book in the back study room, and seven sages sat on the worn benches along the wall. The couple stood in the doorway. White-haired Baruch ben Jacob looked up. He raised his eyebrows; then he said, "Jerahmeel–why are you here?"

Jerahmeel looked at Rechlin. Rechlin looked at Jerahmeel, and Jerahmeel said, "Gentlemen, Rechlin and I wish to remarry."

The sages were quiet for a moment. Then the youngest sage, Elisah ben Samuel, said, "Ah, Jerahmeel, your first wife is always your best-loved wife. As the Talmud says: 'When a man's first wife dies, it is as though the Temple had been destroyed in his lifetime.' "

And Joshua ben Eliezer said, "The Talmud also says: 'When a man's first wife dies, the whole world becomes dark for him.' "

"How true," said Lewe ben Anselm.

Menahem ben Joel nodded and said, "The Talmud goes on to say: 'If a man marries another woman after his first wife, then he will always remember most fondly the deeds of the first.' "

"Amen," said Moyses ben Nathan.

Finally, old Shimshon ha-Zaken nodded and he said, "It is the same with all our first loves–they never lose their magical glow."

The many sages muttered and nodded and stroked their beards. Jerahmeel turned to Rabbi Abraham. "What do *you* think, good Rabbi?" he asked.

Old Abraham Achselrad woke with a start. "What?" he asked. Then he said, "What do I think? Well–I think that one should always trust in the Lord."

Rabbi Abraham squinted and he blinked his eyes. He tapped his fingers on a linen tablecloth lying on the edge of his desk. Then he stroked his beard and he smiled and said, "My friend, the world does not stand still. The good Lord God, blessed be He, whirls and twirls our little earth in His holy palm."

Jerahmeel looked puzzled. Rabbi Abraham stood up; he walked over and patted Jerahmeel on the back and said, "By all means, Jerahmeel, you should definitely remarry." And so the couple was betrothed.

Two weeks later, at dawn on a Friday in the springtime month of *Nisan,* the Rabbi and the shammas went to the inn and formally called Jerahmeel to the *meien* ceremony. With the Rabbi leading the way, a group of men walked into the courtyard of the synagogue. The men carried candles and they chanted a prayer; then Jerahmeel and the Rabbi remained in the courtyard while the men went back to the inn.

Now the men escorted Rechlin along Judengasse Street and down the alleyway into the synagogue courtyard. Jerahmeel came forward. He took Rechlin's hand; it felt cool and light. Rechlin smiled. She looked very young in her white cap and white dress. The men tossed wheat into the air and it settled down ever so gently, like feathers or a summer snow, over the heads of the bride and the groom. White-haired Baruch called out, "Be fruitful and multiply! Be fruitful and multiply! Be fruitful and multiply, amen!" Jerahmeel and Rechlin smiled and took seven long even steps and walked to the door of the synagogue.

Without a word, Rechlin and Abigail, the wife of Menahem ben Joel, returned to the inn. Rechlin put on her wedding outfit. She set an embroidered white headband around her cap. She put an embroidered white shawl over her shoulders. She tied an embroidered white belt around her waist. Abigail gave Rechlin a last hug and said, "Sister–may you grow into thousands of myriads!" Rechlin laughed and hugged Abigail.

The women returned to the synagogue. The morning prayer service had ended. People stood waiting for the wedding, and when Rechlin arrived they hung a flower necklace on her shoulders. Then the bride and the groom stood together under the groom's Sabbath *tallis* as a wedding canopy. The Rabbi sang the blessings. He said the Seven Benedictions. He gave a sip of wine to Jerahmeel and then to Rechlin. Jerahmeel took the glass and threw it against the wall; the glass shattered and the company cheered. Finally, Rabbi Abraham recited the "to a newly married couple" verse from the Book of Numbers:

> How finely your tents have stood,
> Wondrous homes at gentle ease,
> Like rows of shady palm tree hoods
> Like rich and fragrant river trees
> Like God's tall gracious eaglewoods
> Like cedars in the evening breeze;
> And now your smooth cool waterjars
> Shall always overflow,
> And you'll have children like the stars–
> Bright, numerous, and aglow.

So Jerahmeel and Rechlin were married once again. And, Rabbi, my grandmother heard that eventually Jerahmeel and his wife Rechlin had a child–but whether it was their own or whether it was an adopted orphan she did not know and no one has ever told me either.

Good evening again, Rabbi. You look tired. . . . What is that? Old? You are not so old–but what if you were? It would be a blessing: old men give wise counsel. As they say: "An old man in a house is good for the household."

I know what you are thinking: one can be wise at any age. Of course there is some truth to that. Young men can be thoughtful too. However, wisdom comes with age, even for those who are slow to learn, if only they continue to grow. It is like Reb Markus. Everyone admits that he is slow. But Markus is serious. He pauses before he smiles and he hesitates before he frowns. Each year, he reads a little more of the Holy Scriptures. He listens, and he taps his chin and he creases his forehead when you talk.

Although he is slow, Reb Markus is steadfast. Once a bit of knowledge has settled in his mind it puts down firm roots, it takes a tenacious hold, it never lets go. Just yesterday I was amazed when I heard him talking to Reb Anton. "The daily prayers are modified for half the year," began Reb Markus. "And why is this? Well," he continued, "it is because the Jewish year is divided into the days of sun (beginning on the first day of Passover) and the days of rain (beginning on the eighth day of the Feast of *Sukkot*)." Now I ask you: Where did old Markus learn this? . . . Well, I do not know either, but wherever it came from, the idea certainly stuck fast. Ah, steadfast old Reb Markus – he reminds me of steadfast old Manasseh, the dairyman. . . . You have never heard of Manasseh? Then let me tell you his story:

Steadfast old Manasseh was a dairyman. His full name was Manasseh ben Asher ha-Kohen. He was devout and he was serious. He was a good man and well liked, and he lived at the time of Rabbi Abraham ben Alexander, the mystic Achselrad of Cologne. Manasseh had a horse but no cart. He carried his butter, cheese, eggs, and milk in a sack on his back, and he rode from village to village in the countryside west of Cologne. Manasseh's horse was a beautiful peastalk animal, the color of a pike and the shape of a slick black salmon.

Manasseh was well known for his cheese. And what was his secret? After all these years, I can tell you, so listen carefully: Manasseh would take the evening's milk and set it aside. The next morning, he skimmed off the cream. He warmed it. And then what did he do? Why, he added the warm cream back to the old milk, of course.

Next, Manasseh put in new morning milk and he added his special ingredient, a bit of the crumblings from his best earlier cheeses. Manasseh warmed this mixture. He added carrots (which he had already softened by boiling them in milk). Stirring, stirring, stirring, he mixed and he heated, and soon the whole vat became thick and curdled. The mix stood, the cheese curds sank, and Manasseh poured off the liquid. Now he squeezed together the cheese bits: he pressed and kneaded them into a solid loaf. He set the cheese loaves in a salt bath and let the water dry away. Finally, he washed the cheese and put it into wooden boxes to age and to flavor. Manasseh was in no hurry, and his orange-colored cheeses – three, six, and even nine months old – were prized throughout the River Rhine valley.

This was steadfast old Manasseh, the cheeseman, who lived in the town of Stommeln. Outside this village, there lived a rockborn demon, a harsh evil spirit that nursed an enduring grudge, a long-lasting ill will, toward the Jewish dairyman. The demon was eternally angry. Was it jealous of Manasseh's cheese? Or was there something else? Ah, Rabbi – does even the good Lord God know why a demon has its strange and evil feelings?

Every day the demon muttered to itself. It hissed and it coughed, and it sat and it waited. The demon sat in a tree, watching evenings and mornings for Manasseh to come by at just the right spot along the River Rhine. The demon wanted to catch Manasseh. But it was not at *any* time that the rockborn demon wanted to catch the Jew–this demon wanted to catch Manasseh when the water was rushing and when the rapids were fierce and when the streams and eddies were treacherous whirlpools.

This demon was an archer, a bowman, a marksman. The demon was as old as the hills, and it had learned archery even before the Egyptians, who were the first famous archers. The Egyptians had used bows as tall as a man with arrows as long as your arm. In Manasseh's day, after the first Crusade, Europeans used crossbows, fierce and accurate because of their weight and high tension. But the rockborn demon still used the longbow. It made its bows from yew trees, with wood from the Mediterranean coast, wood that had been seasoned for thirty-three years. It made its string from strands of hemp interwound thirty-three times and dressed with glue. And daily, the demon made a new pile of wicked arrows, a handful of strong sharp arrows turned neatly from oak wood. The arrowheads were steel, they had little sparrow-tail feathers on the ends, and the tips were dipped in a reptiles's black venom.

Now, Rabbi, it was the night, a greening wet springtime night, when the river was rushing and roaring. Old and steadfast Manasseh was riding by, riding along the broad dark River Rhine. . . . What is that? Well, I will tell you: "Rhine" means clear–*Rhine* comes from *Rein,* the river's name in distant days when the entire valley of the *Rein* was occupied by Celtic tribes, and when the *Rein* was a vast clear waterway cutting through the heart of Europe. But that was a millennium before Manasseh. It was before Charlemagne. It was even before the Ancient Roman Empire–it was when the rockborn demon had been young and carefree.

Now, however, it was springtime in the German Middle Ages, and Manasseh followed the River Rhine. As he rode on his dairy route, Manasseh felt the force of the ancient river–it swept from Heaven to the sea, from the highest Alps to the mud banks of Holland. It ran through every possible landscape, through reed-filled inlets, wild rocky cliffs, and jostling boat-filled ports, the great cities of Europe. At Coblenz the valley of the River Rhine widens suddenly: it is almost four hundred meters across. Then the hills close in again at Andernach, deep ravines appear past the Siebengebirge Mountains, and beyond

Bonn and Cologne the banks flatten in the lands through which Manasseh rode and rode and rode.

Manasseh lived and worked in the gently hilled countryside near Cologne. Here, on that wild springtime night, Manasseh rode along the flat bank of the river. The River Rhine raged from yesterday's rains. Tonight was clear–but it was Walpurgis Eve, the night before the month of May began. This was the night when evil demons felt bold and energetic and when they held wild revels. Yes, it was Walpurgis Eve, and the watcher, the rockborn demon archer, felt wild and bold. It laughed and jumped and it took the straightest arrow from its pile. It chose the best shaft, steel tipped and poison dipped. Then, it aimed the arrow at the center of Manasseh's heart.

The demon took aim and let fly the arrow. But, by the Grace of the good Lord God, the arrow curved; it flew up to the sky and it split a cloud, with the sound of a distant wind. The demon shot a second arrow–but this one went down into the Earth below and it split a rock, with a great crashing crack. Ah, but the third arrow went straight, it flew straight into the horse. Poor Manasseh's wonderful peastalk horse stumbled and it fell at the edge of the river.

And then Manasseh himself fell too. He tumbled right into the water. Manasseh turned straight into the raging waves. In fact, he went in and under for six full minutes. Manasseh was washed down to the depths, below the River Rhine where it rolls and rushes among the large gray basalts. Steadfast Manasseh curled himself into a round ball, like a tiny infant in his mother's womb. He rolled along the bottom. He was pushed and tumbled by the tide. He swept through the rocks. Manasseh drifted, and the open expanse of the river caught him up and carried him along. Finally, he uncurled and he managed to catch onto a floating log. Manasseh raised his hands above the dark waves and he took a deep, deep breath from the air of the nighttime sky.

Manasseh took one breath of nighttime air, and then he took another. He breathed and he prayed to the Lord God Almighty, just as one does on the last day of *Sukkot,* the Feast of the Huts:

> I call to You, Lord: Rescue me now!
> I ask of You, Lord: Give me success!
> I beg of You, Lord: Honor Your vow!
> I pray to You, Lord: Look down with kindness!

And, on His far-off Golden Throne of Glory, the great Lord God heard Manasseh. The moon was a white pottery plate low in the sky, and the Almighty Lord of Heaven looked down from behind the moon. All the dairy products had spilled from Manasseh's pack. The cream swirled in round, round pools. The orange cheeses floated like golden islands in the River Rhine. And the eggs had broken, and little bits of yellow shone and glittered like river stars in the moonlight: they gleamed with their own pale light, mirrors of God's golden stars in the sky. Then God waved His mighty arms, and Manasseh ben Asher ha-Kohen saw the shore, the home edge of the River Rhine, and he paddled over and he breathed a deep and restful breath, a heavy sigh of relief.

Manasseh ben Asher ha-Kohen climbed onto the bank. He leaned against a tree, and he sat and rested. He squeezed out his coat and his pants. Little shining pools formed at his feet. Manasseh reached to the right and picked up a small rock and he put it in his pocket. Then he stood and walked tiredly away from the water. Manasseh found his horse–it was alive and it was well, for the arrow had only grazed a bone. And he hugged his peastalk horse, a fine young mare, the color of a pike and the shape of a slick black salmon. Then steadfast Manasseh the dairyman climbed onto its back, and he rode home again to his dairy farm in the little medieval town of Stommeln. . . .

Why, yes, Rabbi–that is the whole story; there is no more to tell.

Rabbi, I am glad to see you here tonight. Sit down – I will rake the coals in the oven. Here, my friend, watch this: I reach into the glowing sea, flowing with warm tides, and I roll over the souls of the coals, just like the old-time sea witches. . . . You do not know what I am talking about? Have you never heard tales of the sea witches, dragging the ocean waves with their long iron rakes? They pull and they tug, fishing out the souls of those who have been lost at sea. The old witches pole their long cold rakes down, down, down into the murky depths. Then they pull out dripping pieces of weedy souls, and some pieces float, some pieces sink, and some pieces roll and flow through the depths. . . .

What? Well, I cannot believe that you know nothing of this. Did you never have a grandmother? Oh? Then she must have kept her stories to herself; for I first heard about these witches from my grandmother. I think that her tale came originally from old Rabbi Petahiah. Let me see . . . yes, I remember – it was from one of Petahiah's letters. As you recall, Petahiah ben Jacob was the brother of Rabbi Isaac ben Jacob ha-Lavan (Yizchak the White, also known as Isaac "the Wise") of Prague, who wrote a profound commentary on several talmudical treatises. Petahiah was a wanderer, in fact he toured the entire world.

Petahiah traveled through Poland, Russia, the land of the Khazars, Armenia, Media, Persia, Babylonia, and Palestine, and then he wrote about his adventures in a book called *Sivuv ha-Olam (Around the World).*

Rabbi Petahiah's travels were at the end of the twelfth century, in the days of old Achselrad and well before Asher ben Yehiel was the Chief Rabbi of Cologne. Why do I introduce Rabbi Asher? It is simply this: when he was the leading scholar in Cologne, Asher spent most of his time writing and reading. Rabbi Asher studied the Torah and the Talmud, and he always worked in the little back room of the yeshiva; this was the room where the Cologne rabbis had passed endless hours working and thinking and arguing with themselves. Above the back study room was a loft for storage. One spring morning–a day he felt should be devoted to organizing and to piling papers, to dusting off books, and to setting things in their neat and orderly places, a day with little time for difficult thought–on that gentle, dreamy springtime day, Asher ben Yehiel was rooting around among the manuscripts in the loft. After a while, he found an old letter from Rabbi Petahiah of Regensburg to Rabbi Abraham ben Alexander, Achselrad of Cologne.

"*My dear Rabbi Abraham–*

"I have just met a fine young man, a Jew from Heidelberg. He has agreed to carry this letter to my good friend Rabbi Baruch ben Dan of Mannheim who I am certain will then arrange to transport it to you. I write to wish you and you family well, to convey my fondest greetings to all the Jews of your blessed community in Cologne, and to praise the good Lord God (blessed be He) and His Almighty Name for ever and ever, amen.

"I will not trouble you with the details of my many wagon rides and sea voyages. Suffice it to say that these travels safely brought me here to the Oriental regions, regions that are so near to the great Holy Land where someday the Messiah shall return and deliver us and resurrect all souls and rebuild the Temple on Zion, amen. I write now in order to record for you some details of the lands and the peoples that I have seen in these old and foreign realms. The bright and glorious hand of the good Lord God is visible everywhere, if only we look–praise the Lord Yahweh-Elohim.

"As I mentioned, my old friend, I have had many, many adventures in arriving here. I hope–with the good Lord willing–to relate these events to you in person. For now, let me just say that after touring the Holy Lands of Palestine, I turned north again, and now I am in the city of Antioch.

" 'Antioch? Which Antioch?' you may ask, for I am told that there were once as many as sixteen cities with this name sprinkled throughout Asia. Well, Abraham, this is the most famous one. It was founded by the Greeks, not long after the golden days of Athens with its famed philosophers, Socrates, Plato, and Aristotle. This Antioch was the center of all Syria: the two easiest routes east from the Mediterranean, through the gorge of the River Orontes and through the Beilan Pass, both converge in the plain of Lake Antioch, and in its day Antioch was a center of commerce rivaling Damascus to the east and Alexandria to the west.

"Antioch is on the banks of the River Orontes. It is watched over by a high hill, Mount Silpius. At the top of this hill is a well, and the well water flows down to the city through underground aqueducts. There is a well-keeper whose sole job is to keep the water flowing. He lives in a stone house encircled by a brick wall overlooking the city. Two days ago, we climbed to his house, where we were warmly received. All afternoon we sat on the wall and talked. The city below is laid out like a gridiron, in imitation of the great city of Alexandria. Two streets lined with columns intersect in the center. The eastern sector of the city is enclosed completely by a wall. Just beyond the city, to the north, a large island floats in the River Orontes, with its own separate walls. Throughout the main city there are many gardens, and the western sector borders a park with woods and small lakes and a Greek temple.

"The Romans came to Antioch after the Greeks, and Antioch became a provincial capital of the original Roman Empire. It was in Antioch that the Roman general Germanicus died suddenly and mysteriously, in the Christian year 19. Germanicus loved travel. He was fascinated by strange lands and by exotic people and customs, and he was on his way to Egypt when he died–it was rumored that he had been poisoned by enemies who hid among his many travel companions. Germanicus's body was carried back to Antioch, and it was burned in the central forum; his ashes were then taken to Rome by his widow, Agrippina, and were spread on the grave of his patron, the Emperor Augustus Caesar.

"Fifty years later, after the Roman siege of Jerusalem, the young Roman general Titus stole statues of cherubim from the Temple in Jerusalem and he then set them over the main gates in Antioch. But over the years, Jews moved into Antioch. In the sixth century, many Jews lived here. Their lives were restricted; Jews could not be government officials, they were not allowed to hold positions of honor, and they were forbidden to build new synagogues. A sad massacre of Jews occurred in the Christian year 507. During the annual athletic games, a drunken mob formed in the park to the west of the city. It was a Sabbath afternoon. The crowd was wild and angry. Hoodlums surged into the town, they destroyed the main synagogue and its yeshiva, and they murdered the worshipers.

"Throughout the following centuries, Antioch was held by various Mohammedan powers. Finally, the Crusaders established a capital here, and for three generations this has been the center of an outlying Latin province ruled by European princes with the family name Bohemund.

"Today, Antioch is an agricultural trading center–the markets are filled with maize, cotton, and liquorice, wool, wheat, and mulberries, and oranges, almonds, and raisins. After arriving, I wandered past the open shops, talking with all manner of traders. I quickly found that even five centuries after the massacre there remain bad feelings toward Jews, and in fact, I have located only about ten Jews, all of whom are glass manufacturers. I was well received by this close and quiet little group. One night, we sat talking late in the cool air after dinner. The eldest Jew, an old man named Karash, told me a very strange story about three rabbis who had passed through here not long ago; the other listeners nodded in agreement and assured me that this was exactly what they too had heard:

"A few generations ago," said Karash, "three Babylonian rabbis, Rabbi Gamliel, Rabbi Eliezer, and Rabbi Joshua, were traveling in the countryside not far from here. They were coming north, returning from the city of Tripolis. It was spring, the weather was warm, and late one afternoon, the men found themselves near a small village. They stopped and were welcomed by a hospitable Jew named Aaron ibn Shelomi.

"The evening meal was set out. A quiet blessing was said. But then, before he ate or served his guests, Aaron stood and carried every single dish into a small room off the pantry. The three Rabbis looked at one another. Soon Aaron returned. He sat down and began to eat. The three Rabbis raised their eyebrows. Rabbi Gamliel looked at Rabbi Eliezer. Rabbi Eliezer looked at Rabbi Joshua. Rabbi Joshua looked back at Rabbi Gamliel. Finally, Rabbi Gamliel said to Aaron, 'My good sir, what does this mean?'

" 'Yes,' continued Rabbi Eliezer, 'exactly what are you doing? Have you added something to the food?'

"Rabbi Joshua nodded. 'Or,' he asked, 'are you perhaps bewitching the meal?'

" 'No, no, my friends,' said Aaron quickly. 'It is my father, Shelomi.'

" 'Your father?' asked the three rabbis.

" 'Yes,' said their host, 'it is my father. You see, I am feeding him dinner, but he has taken a vow: he will never leave his room until three Jewish sages come and release him from his torment.'

"Again the rabbis looked at one another. 'Ah, this is no coincidence, Aaron,' said Rabbi Gamliel.

" 'The Lord preordains all,' said Rabbi Eliezer. 'In fact, my friend, *we* are three Jewish sages.'

" 'So tell us: Exactly what is tormenting your father?' asked Rabbi Joshua.

"Aaron put down his spoon. He sat back in his chair. 'Well, gentlemen, I will tell you,' he began. 'I have been married for twelve years.'

"Aaron smiled and nodded. 'It has been twelve years, and it is a fine marriage,' he continued. 'My wife is a good and responsible woman. But sadly, I have no children. My father believes that he cannot die in peace until he sees his grandchildren here on this earth. It is his last and only wish. It is all that he thinks about. And now every day I wonder: Have I been cast under an evil spell? Am I here merely to be the torment of my old father? Is this the will of the Almighty Lord God–or has He been busy elsewhere and has a demon intervened? In any case, not long ago, my father learned in a dream that three Jewish sages will come and help him with this problem.'

" 'Very well,' said the rabbis. 'Let us talk with your father.'

"Aaron stood and walked into the small room off the pantry. The rabbis heard two voices talking back and forth and back and forth. Eventually, Aaron returned. 'Please follow me, gentlemen,' he said, and the three sages went in to see Aaron's father.

"Shelomi was lying in his bed. His hair was thin and white, his beard was long and gray, his skin was old and wrinkled. He was wearing many robes and he was also wrapped in a blanket. Shelomi's voice was high and shaky. He bemoaned his fate. He told every single detail of his life and of the life of his son. He said that he could not sleep at night. He had no appetite. His hands shook. The room was always cold. The sky was always gray. He would die soon, he said, and his life would have been totally empty, for there were no grandchildren and perhaps there would never be anyone at all to carry on a new generation.

"The rabbis stood patiently. Then they sat on a bench. Rabbi Gamliel tapped his foot. Rabbi Eliezer stroked his beard. Rabbi Joshua rubbed his fingers. It became dark outside and candles were lit. The rabbis listened and they thought. They listened some more. Then they talked quietly among themselves. They prayed and they read the Bible. They talked again. Finally, Rabbi Gamliel said to old Shelomi, 'Yes, there is no doubt–your son has been bewitched.'

" 'I knew it,' said the old man. 'Now there is no hope at all. A man from the neighboring village had a bewitched son. One day the old man died, and later his grave just disappeared. This will happen to me too.'

"Rabbi Gamliel looked at Rabbi Eliezer. Rabbi Eliezer looked at Rabbi Joshua. Rabbi Joshua looked back at Rabbi Gamliel. 'I would not feel so hopeless,' said Rabbi Gamliel. 'We have a plan.'

" 'Plans are good for young men,' said Shelomi, 'but I am old and I need actions, not words.'

"Rabbi Eliezer said, 'Keep calm, Mar Shelomi–tomorrow night we will take action.' Rabbi Joshua nodded, and the three rabbis left the room.

"Rabbi Gamliel turned to Aaron. 'Young man,' he said, 'will you allow us the freedom of your house?'

"Aaron shrugged his shoulders. 'Do as you must, gentlemen,' he said.

"The next night, the three rabbis went into the pantry. Far in the back, Rabbi Gamliel found a small jar with black seeds. These he handed to Rabbi Eliezer. Rabbi Eliezer planted the seeds in the garden behind the house. Rabbi Joshua patted the soil and repeated many mystical incantations. Aaron ibn Shelomi followed the Jewish sages, and he watched and waited, mystified and somewhat worried.

"In two days, a strange twisted plant had grown. The plant had a short stem and oval leaves; a thin brown runner wound from its root and slid across the dirt. The three rabbis waited until it was the dead of the night. They went out into the garden and they took hold of the plant and the root and the runner. They pulled with all their strength. Up came another tangled root from deep within the sandy soil. The root was gray and brown and hairy, and it was shaped like a gnarled, wrinkled, hairy old woman: this was a Mandrake woman, an old sea witch, and she was the demon who had cast the spell.

"Rabbi Gamliel held the demon woman by the hair. Rabbi Eliezer tied an amulet around her wrist. Rabbi Joshua said the nine mystical Names of the Almighty One Himself. The demon hissed and shivered and began to change its shape. Rabbi Gamliel felt weak. His legs were stiff; his hands shook–but he took heart in the Lord, and he held onto the demon with all his might. And what was this? The demon was suddenly a miniature lion. Now it was a serpent, then a leopard, and next a boar. It became a tree, a flame, and running water. However, somehow the rabbi managed to hold fast through all these changes.

"At last, the demon returned to its usual hairy, evil form, a shriveled, ugly old woman. She hissed and she spat. She shivered and she shook, and she called out, 'All right, all right, I give in, you cruel men–I will tell you what you want to know.'

"There was a silence. Then the demon woman nodded twice and she said in a dusty rasping voice, 'Yes, you Jewish sorcerers, it was *me* who cast the spell on Aaron and his wife. But now the spell is sunk deep into the bottomless blue depths of the sea. It is far from your grasp, and you cannot undo it.' And she laughed and she coughed and she hissed, and the night got darker still.

"The three rabbis raised their eyebrows, and then they put the root demon into a sack and tied the sack with seven knots. The sea witch churned and thrashed in the sack, but she could not get out. Then Rabbi Gamliel, Rabbi Eliezer, and Rabbi Joshua carried the sack to the edge of the sea, and Aaron ibn Shelomi followed along, wide-eyed and frightened. The rabbis came to the edge of the vast black ocean topped by powdery stars. The holy men set the sack on the sand and stood back. They recited the nine mystical Names of the Almighty Lord God. They chanted mystical *zirufim.* And then they untied the sack and they commanded the root woman to fetch the spell so that it could be destroyed.

"The demon woman shook and she hissed, but she took an iron rake and she walked out upon the waves and sank up to her waist in the water. The sea witch dragged the pole one time with the flow of the current. She pushed a second time against the current. She pulled a third time at a slant. And this time she pulled up a muddy sheaf of grain in the iron rake. But was it really grain? No, actually it was a small piece of the spell. The sea witch flung the bit of the spell back onto the beach. Again and again the demon woman dipped the rake into the current, along, against, across. Each time she pulled a piece of the incantation from the depths–until finally she had retrieved the spell in all its sixty times sixty slimy pieces.

"The sea witch was wet and tired. She returned to the shore and laid the pieces out on the sand. The pieces of spell were all manner of odd shapes. They were covered with muck and seaweed. They smelled like fish and they looked like mud and sticks and stones. The root woman looked at the rabbis. She hissed and she frowned, but she arranged the parts into their original order. The rabbis had brought two jars. Rabbi Gamliel opened the first jar and he poured oil on the spell. Rabbi Eliezer opened the second jar and he poured honey on the spell. Rabbi Joshua bent over and he breathed his warm breath along the edges of the spell. Magically the entire spell knit together. It began to quiver gently, and then suddenly the evil incantation rose up into one misty cloud. Quickly, the three rabbis caught the spell in the sack, and they burned the sack, chanting":

Be split, be accursed, be broken and be banned–
You son of mud, you demon from an evil land.

"The three rabbis had to work carefully and quickly. For a moment they took their eyes from the root woman. As they did, she jumped and she hopped, and she ran off into the night. And although this particular spell was destroyed, I am afraid that the root demon is still at large somewhere, far off in the wilds of our vast uncharted world.

"The rabbis searched the sand and the shore, but they could not find the demon anywhere that night; so eventually they returned to the village. Inside the house, each of the three rabbis set his hands on Aaron's head. Rabbi Gamliel said, 'May the Lord always guard you – praise God.' Next, Rabbi Eliezer said, 'May the Lord lead you to perfection – praise God.' Finally, Rabbi Joshua said, 'And may the Lord grant you the happiness of both worlds – praise the good Lord God.' Then one year afterward, a child was born to the villager Aaron ibn Shelomi and his wife, and they named the boy Judah, meaning 'praised.'

"And that is the end of the story from Antioch, so I will end my letter too. As I do, I close my eyes, Abraham. I can see you reading this in your holy study in Cologne. I think of you often, old friend – do you think of me also? Do you remember how once *we* dug roots on the banks of the wide River Rhine, happy as the grass was green in the light of our blue-skied childhoods? I remember, and I know that someday we shall be together again in the *Gan Eden* digging in the rooty soil, eternal childhood gardeners once more, playing in the warm black dirt where only gentle angels wind their hairs around the stems and roots of all the wondrous tangled plants of the Lord's great Garden of Paradise – praise the good Lord God, amen.

"Your childhood friend,
Petahiah, the son of Jacob"

Hello, Rabbi, I will be with you in a moment–I cannot leave until every tablecloth is folded, otherwise the day has not ended properly. . . . There, now I am finished at last and I can sit next to you by the stove. So, the holy Sabbath begins again, "gently raining down joy upon our peaceful resting faces." It is a time when all the glorious white lighthearted angels of Heaven slip and slide down from the clouds; they float along, they dance, and they follow the Sabbath queen–praise the great Lord God, amen, amen.

The Sabbath is a day of rest and peace; it is a day of angels and poetry. Do you know the Sabbath poem:

Finally comes the Friday night
And Sabbath tiptoes up the stair
You sit and rest in quiet light
And fleecy sheepskins whisper bare
While light gray nighttide clouds of air
Are cool white Sabbath robes you wear
And rocking in an evening chair
A sleepy child is curled there
Inside your lap without a care
You tell her now of angel's hair
And sing her soft a song or prayer
And give her gentle hugs to spare.

What a holy, restful Sabbath picture. Are you falling asleep? No? I am not sleepy either. But I am relaxed because I enjoy these poems about Sabbaths and children and angels. . . . That poem? I first heard it from my grandmother when she told me about the angel Barkiel, who lived for a time in medieval Coblenz. Actually, grandmother's tale was really a story within a story, and it began north of Coblenz in old Cologne:

It was a springtime day, said my grandmother to me – it was a fine afternoon once upon a time in Cologne along the dark medieval River Rhine. It was the day before the Sabbath, and old men were sitting, talking idly in the rabbi's little study room.

Yes, Rabbi, it was the gentle, restful springtime. The windows were open, a light cool breeze blew in, and it felt to the men as if holy spirits and Sabbath angels were washing through the worn wooden yeshiva. One of the scholars, old Shimshon ha-Zaken, said, "The Lord of Hosts is the Lord of all the angels and the planets and the stars."

Why did he say this out of the blue? No one knew. But the other sages smiled and nodded and murmured. Then, Lewe ben Anselm said, "Yes, He is the Lord of the angels, the stars, *and* the sun and the moon and all the armies of Israel – *these,* then, are the full contingent of hosts."

The men nodded again and stroked their beards and they said many "amens."

Next, old Reb Joshua said, "Mainly, though, it is angels, my friends – today there *are* no more armies (that is, no more *Israelite* armies) – but there are always angels. There are angels forever unto eternity."

And a younger scholar, Elisah ben Samuel, said, "Definitely, Reb Joshua – the world is thickly populated with angels. Every single thing on earth, animate and inanimate, from man through all the other things of God's great Creation – the birds and beasts, trees and brooks, even to the last blade of grass – each has its own angel. Houses and cities, winds and seasons, months and hours and days, each star above, each speck of dust underfoot – why no thing in nature or even in our imaginations exists independently of its *memuneh,* its heavenly appointed deputy angel."

Joshua ben Eliezer nodded. "Ah, my friends," he said, "you are right. Sometimes we forget that these angels are the deputies of everything. *They* are the celestial actors. *They* are the agents through whom the entire universe operates."

Lewe ben Anselm stroked his beard. "Well, Joshua, you should be more accurate." Joshua ben Eliezer raised his eyebrows as Lewe continued: "Angels are not mere intermediaries: they are guardians and defenders too. It is a well-known fact, Joshua, that no person and no nation can be defeated until its deputy angels have fallen or disappear or at least are won over to the other side."

The other scholars began to mutter among themselves. Menahem ben Joel said, "It is true that every person here on earth is watched over by a guardian angel. But then the angels themselves are represented by the stars above." Menahem looked up at the ceiling. "In fact," he said, "that is how the stars guide a man's fate."

"It is good to have defenders," said Moyses ben Nathan. "Our angels represent us. They speak for us in the great Court of Heaven, when they are not busy conveying messages to earth from the holy Final Court."

And old Shimson ha-Zaken coughed and rubbed his cheek and he said, "I am glad that you mentioned 'messages,' Reb Moyses, for, gentlemen, we must never forget that first and foremost angels are *malakhim:* they are the messengers of the Lord."

The men in the little back room nodded quietly, rocking gently back and forth, each thinking his own holy angelic thoughts. After a few minutes, white-bearded Baruch ben Jacob said, "Ah, the Lord of Hosts–He is the Lord of all the angels. He is the First Guardian and the Prime Messenger. He is the Master of the stars. Is this not what *you* always say, Rabbi?"

The scholars looked to the Rabbi–but the Rabbi was asleep. Old Rabbi Abraham had been writing all night in his book of mystic Kabbalistic lore, the manuscript entitled *Keter Shem Tov.* (As you know, Rabbi, this work has never been printed; to this day it remains hidden in the loft above the rabbi's little study room in the yeshiva of Cologne.) Rabbi Abraham ben Alexander was breathing slowly and heavily and his eyes were closed, so after a while Elisah asked loudly, "And what do *you* think, good Rabbi?"

Achselrad awoke with a start. "What do I think?" he asked. The Rabbi looked around him. He winked and he blinked and he said, "I think we must always trust in the good Lord God (blessed be He), amen."

The Rabbi looked at the men sitting on the worn benches. The old scholars murmured "amen," but they seemed a little puzzled. Had the Rabbi been listening? Was he fully awake now? Elisah ben Samuel said gently, "And as to angels and guardians and messengers and stars, Rabbi?"

"Of course, Reb Elisah," said the Rabbi, "I was just coming to that. The sages tell us that when the time comes for a righteous man to die, the deputy of the reigning star – the particular holy angel who is ruling at the moment – begs that the man not die just then. Otherwise, the angel will be held accountable for his death, and any death weighs heavily on an angel.

"So, my friends, the angels try to restrain Death and plead our final cases before the Almighty Judge. Of course, the angels are always interceding for us, even in small daily affairs. We mortals pray, but if our prayers are to be answered then our angel must repeat them directly before the Great Throne of Glory. You see, your angel listens to you morning, noon, and night. Then, he flies up past the mountaintops. He slips among the white clouds. He glides along the endless wispy edges of the beard of the Holy One, blessed be He, and whisking lightly up, up, up through the day and the night and the stars and the planets, past the sun and the moon and the great blue celestial tides of forever, this glorious angel falls at the feet of God in the radiance of His *Shekhinah.*

"Then the angel pleads the case for the mortal, who waits hopefully somewhere far below on our dusty earth like a speck, a tiny, tiny speck. And God listens and nods His head and decides. Of course, you do not *have* to pray. Many people choose to act completely on their own, and in this case God gives you free will. Why, men and angels *both* have free will: we can, if we desire, set our own courses.

"Do not look so surprised, gentlemen – even angels have free will. They, like we, have the choice to follow or to ignore the Holy Laws and the rules and the dictums of the Lord."

Rabbi Abraham ben Alexander nodded and smiled and he looked somewhere far, far away. "For example," he continued, "let me tell you something that occurred in the town of Coblenz many years ago. It was when the angel Barkiel was a shammas. . . .

"What? You gentlemen are surprised? Well, it is true–the holy angel Barkiel actually served as a shammas for thirty years in Germany, and this is how it came about:

"Once upon a time, many years ago, soon after Rabbi Amram (may a blessing be forever on his name, amen) had left this community and floated by boat up to Mainz where finally he was buried next to his parents, it came to pass that the Lord God Almighty sent the angel Barkiel to take away the soul of a widow in Coblenz.

"Barkiel bowed to the great Lord Almighty, he flew down from Heaven, and he went to the widow's house. The woman was sick and weak, but she was nursing two young twins, two tiny little boys. They were round as potatoes and pink and wrinkled, and they were very, very hungry.

"The angel watched the mother and her children. How could he take the soul of this woman? Barkiel was invisible. He sighed, and he spread a gentle warm breeze like a blanket over the house; then he flew away. And the angel Barkiel returned to Heaven without having carried out the Lord's command.

"Barkiel returned alone. The Lord was puzzled. 'Why have you not brought Me the soul of the widow?' He asked.

"Barkiel looked down at his feet. 'It was for the sake of those two children, O Lord. I simply could not take the life of their mother.'

"God was angry. He frowned. Thunder clouded His awesome brow. Lightning flashed from His eyes. The mountains shook. Great winds arose and the seas raged. 'My angel,' said the Lord, 'I want you now to dive down into the deepest sea.'

" 'I should go to the bottom of the sea?'

" 'Yes, you should,' said God. 'Go down to the deepest ocean depths. And from the bottom, Barkiel, bring Me a certain stone. You will recognize it by its sparkling green color. You will know it by its absolutely smooth surface. You will see its glowing golden sheen. It sits at the mouth of a great sea serpent with two white fangs and with eyes that never close.'

"Barkiel raised his eyebrows, but he said nothing. Instead he plummeted down to the bottom of the deepest ocean. When Barkiel had found the stone and had returned to Heaven, the Lord told him, 'Now, angel–break it in half.'

"The archangel lifted his right hand and he split the stone. Inside the stone, Barkiel found two little blue worms, alive and thriving. Then the great Lord God said, 'Now, Barkiel, Who feeds these worms inside the stone at the very bottom of the deepest sea?'

"Barkiel answered, 'Obviously, it must be You.'

"And the Lord said, 'Of course it is Me. And if I can feed two tiny blue worms inside a rock at the very bottom of the deepest sea, do you dare to imagine that I would have the slightest difficulty feeding two fine young boys in the midst of a busy city on the surface of the earth?'

" 'I suppose not, O Lord,' said Barkiel.

" 'You *suppose* not?!' roared the Lord. And He shook His head and sent Dumah, the black angel of Death, to take the soul of the widow. Then the all-knowing and inscrutable Lord God condemned the angel Barkiel to serve as a shammas for thirty long years."

The men in the yeshiva in Cologne stroked their beards. They shook their heads. They murmured many words among themselves. Rabbi Achselrad waited for them to become quiet, and then he continued:

"Yes, gentlemen, the Lord God Almighty condemned the angel Barkiel to serve for thirty years as a shammas to the Chief Rabbi of Coblenz. Barkiel was to care for the yeshiva, for the congregation, and for the Rabbi himself.

"Hearing this decree, Barkiel laughed. 'I am an angel – in fact, I am one of Your chief angels. Should I now be a servant, a shammas, a caretaker of a small wooden yeshiva?'

" 'You are a messenger and a guardian,' answered the Lord. 'Moreover, because you have dared to laugh, you must take this job with complete and solemn seriousness. You are not to laugh or even to smile for thirty long years. And at the end of thirty years you must whisk away the soul of old Rabbi Godescalcus and then carry his soul back here to My Throne of Glory on high.' So the Lord spoke, and so it came to pass. Thus, the angel Barkiel flew down to earth to become the humble, meek, obedient, and humorless servant of Rabbi Godescalcus ben Mordecai of Coblenz.

"As God had decreed, Barkiel stood one day in the doorway of the synagogue in Coblenz. The angel appeared as a thin, white-haired, unsmiling man. Rabbi Godescalcus listened to his story and took him on for a trial period as the shammas, the synagogue beadle.

"Immediately the Rabbi was astonished at this quiet man's abilities. The shammas read Hebrew perfectly: he could correct a reader's errors in the Holy Scriptures or in the Talmud or in any prayer book. The shammas understood all the details of the many rituals for every single holiday. He had a vast memory, and instantly he learned the names of all the local Jews and all their families and even their distant relatives. When it came time to summon a person to the *Bet Din,* the Jewish court, the shammas knew exactly where to find that person at any time of the day or night–and when called by this shammas, people always came on the first request. Moreover, in some inexplicable way, the shammas always knew what the Rabbi needed, even before the holy man had said anything aloud.

"Frequently, Rabbi Godescalcus shook his head in surprise. The shammas is a quiet man and a serious man, thought the Rabbi, but he is also a remarkable man. Everything he does is smooth and efficient. Everything is absolutely correct. He knows every single religious rule. He even seems to know what will happen in advance–somehow he knows when we will have to make a last-minute search for the tenth man for a prayer service or when the Jewish bakers will have difficulty finding flour or if we are in for a period of new taxes and fees. And yet he always remains quiet, reserved, and even solemn. Nothing angers him, nothing excites him, and he never smiles. Again the Rabbi shook his head.

"And so it went for thirty years, and in all that time no one saw the shammas laugh or smile even one single time."

In Cologne, the old sages raised their eyebrows and they looked at one another, but Rabbi Achselrad did not seem to notice. Old Achselrad was staring off into space as he talked. "Now, my scholarly friends," he continued dreamily, "one time near the very end of the thirty years, Rabbi Godescalcus said to Barkiel, 'My good shammas, please go and buy me a pair of shoes. But do not buy the very cheapest: I would like a pair that will last at least one year.'

"Barkiel seemed to cough a moment and then he could not stop himself–the shammas laughed. Rabbi Godescalcus was taken by surprise. 'Is something happening to the mind of our shammas?' he wondered. 'He has always been such a serious and steady man.'

"The Rabbi stared at the shammas. Rabbi Godescalcus was worried, so quietly he asked one of the old congregants to accompany the shammas, to watch him, and perhaps even to protect him.

"In those days, Coblenz was a comfortable town for Jews; it was under the jurisdiction of the Archbishop of Trier, who tolerated Jews and Jewish businesses. Perhaps you have not been to Coblenz, gentlemen. So let me describe it: The city is triangular, and it is protected like a fortress. The River Rhine is on one side, the River Mosel is on another side, and strong walls form the third side. Barkiel walked from the Jewish Quarter, near the walls, toward the marketplace, near the rivers; the congregant followed the shammas at a distance.

"At the edge of the markets, a poor man sat on a large stone. He was begging. 'Give me alms!' he called. 'Have pity on me. I am weak and practically blind. I have no money. How will I eat?' Again Barkiel seemed to cough a moment–but what was this? The angel shammas was not coughing, he was laughing–laughing at the sad fate of the beggar! The old Jewish congregant watched and shook his head: something was seriously wrong with the shammas.

"Barkiel continued on through the marketplaces. The church of St. Castor stood ahead, with its four solemn stone towers. In the shadow of the towers people jostled one another. Animals and carts filled the streets. Piles of wood and barrels and rags lined the walls. A fancy carriage rolled past. Inside sat two wealthy men: one was the Parnas of the congregation, the other was a rich Jewish merchant, a banker who was an advisor to the local duke. The angel stepped back, and he laughed and laughed and laughed. Tears came to his eyes. People turned to stare.

"Finally, Barkiel took a deep breath and he regained control of himself; then he managed to walk toward the shoe stalls. As the angel shammas was looking around, he noticed a small dark man who darted past the edge of a pottery stand. Why, the man was running off with two earthenware pots! The old Jewish congregant was appalled, but Barkiel practically fell to the ground laughing. A guardsman said roughly, 'Here, here, you troublemaker, let's have a bit of quiet! Otherwise, go someplace else!' Barkiel apologized and rubbed his eyes.

Eventually, the angel shammas bought a pair of shoes for the Rabbi, and then he headed back to the Juden Viertels.

"Barkiel returned to the yeshiva. He gave the shoes to the Rabbi, and he went into the main prayer hall to sit quietly and to compose himself. Meanwhile, the old congregant slipped into the back room. He took the Rabbi aside. Softly he recounted the whole strange trip to and from the marketplace. 'I am worried,' he said to the Rabbi. 'Our shammas has never behaved like this before–and the things that he laughed at were not at all funny.'

"Rabbi Godescalcus was worried too. He walked into the main prayer hall, he went over to the shammas, and he said, 'My friend, let us have a talk. What is going on here? What does all this laughter mean?' The Rabbi sat down. He looked intently at the shammas. 'For thirty years you have been serving me,' said Rabbi Godescalcus, 'and you have done a wonderful job. You are a blessing to this congregation: you are a gift of God. But all this time, while you have been endlessly helpful, you also have been endlessly meek, quiet, solemn, and very serious. In fact, I have never seen you smile. Today, suddenly I find you laughing–in fact, you laughed three or four times.'

"The angel nodded. 'This is true, Rabbi,' he said. Barkiel paused a moment. 'Tomorrow is the Sabbath,' he said. 'I will tell you everything tomorrow morning after prayers.'

"The Rabbi raised his eyebrows. Then he stood. 'All right, my friend,' he said, and he walked back into his study room.

"The next morning, after the prayers, the angel shammas sat down in the rabbi's small study room where Rabbi Godescalcus was standing, reading a book. 'Now I can tell you the full truth, Rabbi,' he began. 'The essential fact is this: I am the angel Barkiel.'

"The Rabbi put down his book and opened wide his eyes. The heavenly shammas continued: 'Yes, Rabbi, it is true: I am an angel. Watch–' Barkiel became invisible and he reappeared sitting on the other side of the room. Calmly he went on: 'Once, my friend, many years ago, I was sent by the Almighty Lord God (blessed be He) to Coblenz to take the soul of a widow. When I arrived, I found that she was nursing two tiny children.

" 'Well, Rabbi, I simply could not bring myself to take her life. I returned to Heaven empty-handed. The Omnipotent One was angry. He sent me here to serve as your shammas for a period of thirty years.

When first He told me, I laughed at the idea–therefore, the great Lord God, in His infinite wisdom, also required that I remain completely serious for the entire time.'

"The Rabbi stood speechless.

" 'Now,' said Barkiel, 'the thirty years finally have passed. Today, I am to take your soul and to accompany it to Heaven, where you will have a place of luxury. Good Rabbi, you will dance and you will sing. Then you will sit forever on satin cushions beside the many white-bearded, curly haired rabbis who feast among the angels in the *Gan Eden,* the great and glorious Hereafter of Eternity.'

"Godescalcus ben Mordecai stood with wide eyes. He hardly breathed. Barkiel smiled at the Rabbi. 'Yes,' he repeated, 'today the thirty years have come to an end. Thirty years of smiles and laughs have been hidden away inside of me. So today I laughed for small reasons–and I will tell them to you:

" 'First, I laughed when you asked me to buy you a pair of shoes, shoes that were to last for a year. My thirty years have ended–and so have yours, Rabbi: at the moment, you have less than one day to live on this earth.'

"And Rabbi Godescalcus looked at the angel in amazement. Finally, he could stand no longer. He sat down heavily on a bench.

"Barkiel stood and walked over to the Rabbi. He patted Rabbi Godescalcus on the shoulder. 'Do not feel afraid, old man,' said the angel. 'I will come with you.'

"There was silence in the room. Barkiel walked over to the desk and then he walked back. He turned to Rabbi Godescalcus. 'Would you like to hear about my other laughs? . . . Good–then I will tell you. Although we angels are mainly *malakhim*–messengers–and watchers, we have many powers. We can fly. We can change our shapes. We can appear and disappear at will. We can intercede with the Great and Holy One Himself (blessed be He for ever and ever). And we can see through stone and earth. That, in fact, is why I laughed a second time. As we walked through the marketplace, I heard a beggar asking for alms. I looked and I stared, and I saw that this poor man was sitting right over the spot where a cache of money was buried and now forgotten. Had he dug just a hand's breadth below his feet, he would have been rich for the rest of his days.' "

Rabbi Abraham ben Alexander paused. He had been looking up at the ceiling. Now he opened wide his eyes, as if he could see through stone and earth, beyond the ceiling and the walls. The seven sages of Cologne began to murmur among themselves. They looked at one another. Was their Rabbi an angel too? Was he staring through wood and earth and stone? Eyebrows were raised and beards were stroked.

The Rabbi blinked and he looked again at the old sages. "Yes, gentlemen," he continued, "once the angel Barkiel began to tell his story he told it all: beginning, middle, and end."

Rabbi Achselrad stopped his story for a moment. "Beginning, middle, and end," he repeated quietly. He stroked his beard; then he went on:

"The angel Barkiel looked straight at Rabbi Godescalcus. He smiled and he said, 'Then, Rabbi, I laughed for a third time when I saw the two rich men riding about together. These were the same twins that I had seen thirty years ago–the twins that started me on this strange earthly mission! They were actually the sons of the widow on whose behalf I had been punished. Imagine, seeing them together and healthy and exactly at the end of my term as a shammas here on earth! . . . Well, perhaps it does not seem so funny now–but at the time, I could not control myself.

" 'In any case, I walked on. Then suddenly in front of me was a thief: I saw a man steal two clay water jugs. Into my mind came the passage in Genesis':

> Then the Almighty Lord God (blessed be He) formed a man from the dust of the ground, and He breathed into his nostrils the holy breath of life. Thus, the man of dust became a living creature.

'The thief was clay, the pottery was clay, and in a flash I saw that it was merely clay stealing clay.'

"Barkiel shook his head and he almost laughed again. Rabbi Godescalcus remained silent. 'You men are clay,' said the angel, 'although, of course, you are fine and wondrous clay at that. But your souls, Rabbi–your glorious souls are holy and immortal. So, my good friend, do not worry that your final time has now come. Prepare yourself, and gently we will journey to see the Great Lord Almighty.'

"Then," said Rabbi Abraham, "the old Rabbi, Godescalcus ben Mordecai, nodded and he closed his eyes, and the angel Barkiel quickly whisked the silvery soul from out of the head of the Rabbi. It was a beautiful morning in the warm springtime month of *Sivan,* and the two spirits flew on light, warm Sabbath breezes up to Heaven in the great and wondrous celestial regions of forever and ever and ever; there the Rabbi danced and sang and the golden light played all around, all around–and the green grass grew all around."

Good evening, Rabbi. . . . Of course, of course, sit here by the stove – the night fire helps me to become sleepy also. You and I are not blessed like old Reb Elbaum; once again he nodded off during the last prayers this evening. He has learned to sway piously even while asleep. Undoubtedly he acquired some magic from the mystic Achselrad. Well, Rabbi, we too could use a dose of Achselrad tonight – my grandmother said that he could put men into a sleep trance by waving a gold coin before their eyes.

As you remember, Achselrad was a pupil of Eliazer ben Judah, the mystic of Worms. Strange and mystical visions visited old Rabbi Abraham in the synagogue of Cologne. I doubt whether he would be tolerated nowadays. But my grandmother said that Rabbi Abraham was also a scholar; he always claimed that his visions came from devout and pious study. In any case, many an astonishing event took place in his yeshiva – or so my grandmother was told.

Rabbi Achselrad was proficient in visions and dreams. He had much experience with sleep. He napped frequently, and he understood dream divination. Although the Talmud claims: "Dreams are only a sixtieth part of prophecy," Rabbi Achselrad could see the future clearly in dreams. In fact the old rabbi often said that nothing happens to a man before he has seen some hint of it in a dream.

Dreams are transmitted by angels, said Achselrad. They are arcane views of the real world. In a dream you are in the midst of strange people: their language is difficult to understand, and their dress and their manners are unusual and exotic. Nonetheless dreams have rules – there is an order and a meaning to things – but these rules make no simple sense. For example, in a dream a white horse is good but a red horse is bad. All liquids in a dream are good omens, except for wine. Full grape vines predict a healthy new child and all other fruits are good, except for dates. Roots and vegetables (excluding turnip heads) foretell a good future, and, in particular, wheat signifies peace and barley means that sins will be forgiven.

Old Rabbi Achselrad wrote this and much other dream lore in his set of Kabbalistic tomes. One morning, in the early dawn light, the Rabbi was writing about dream symbols in one of these books, the *Keter Shem Tov.* Suddenly he heard a noise and he looked up. There in the doorway he saw the dejected figure of a wealthy Jew from Cassel – it was Manis ben Avigdor ha-Kohen.

Why had Manis come to see the Rabbi and why was he so discouraged? Well, I will tell you:

In the days of Rabbi Achselrad, there lived in Thuringia a duke named Otto. Otto was a restless man filled with energy. He tapped his feet and he drummed his fingers. He wanted to do things continually – to build castles, to move armaments, to collect artworks, to organize noblemen and merchants. Project after project rolled through his mind, and Otto needed money to carry all of them out. The normal taxes were insufficient. Therefore, Otto was always concocting special levies and fines, and most of these extraordinary fees fell on the Jews. One day, Duke Otto issued a proclamation instituting two new taxes: Jews must pay a defense fee for their protection; in addition, they must pay a new yearly fee for each house that they owned.

The order went out on a Tuesday morning. A guard delivered the proclamation to the shammas of each major synagogue. In Cassel, the shammas gave the letter to the Rabbi, who showed it to the elders of the congregation. What was this? they moaned. How could the Jews of Cassel pay still *more* tax money? The Rabbi declared a week of mourning. The Jews of Cassel prayed to God. They tore a rip in their clothes. Then the Rabbi sent a delegation to the Duke.

Three old Jews appeared in the court of Duke Otto. The eldest Jew stepped forward. He began by quoting from the Book of Deuteronomy, where God's Law says:

> When one of your fellow-countrymen becomes poor, do not be hard-hearted or close-fisted. Instead, be open-handed and lend him the money that he needs.

Duke Otto frowned. "Listen here," he said, "I know a bit of the Bible, too, my friends. In the First Book of Kings, the Jews are warned by their tough-minded king, King Rehoboam":

> I am your master, and I am strong. My little finger is thicker than my father's thighs: my father laid a heavy yoke on you – but I will make it even heavier.

"Now, old men, I am afraid that I must repeat that warning to you: my lightest tax will be heavier than the taxes of my predecessors."

Then Otto continued: "Of course, I do not do this with a mean spirit. Times change, gentlemen. In the past, you received our help and protection without contributing sufficiently. But those days have passed. Frankly, you are not really Germans. Do you think you can live free in our land? I am afraid that you will have to pay your own way from now on."

The Jews were devastated. Each man and woman felt that his days had turned gray. Money could not be squeezed from the walls. It did not drop from the clouds or the trees. It could not be dug from the hard earth. The community chest was empty. From where would help come? Neighboring Jewish communities had the same taxes and the same impossible financial pressures. The men of Cassel reviewed every possibility. What could be sold? Who can we borrow from? Is there anywhere to turn for advice? One man mentioned Rabbi Abraham. Ah, the mystical, magical Achselrad – some men shook their heads, but others said that even magic must be considered in such a crisis. So the Jews of Cassel sent a messenger, a prominent local merchant named Manis ben Avigdor ha-Kohen, to see Rabbi Achselrad in Cologne. Manis packed his satchel, he set off on Thursday, and he arrived very early on Friday morning, the day of the Sabbath eve.

Manis ben Avigdor stepped in the front door of the synagogue of Cologne. He went through the anteroom, and he walked into the main prayer hall, passing the twelve stained-glass windows with their colored lions and snakes. Manis looked up at the Holy Ark made of stone. He walked to the back study room. There, the Rabbi was bent over a book, and a group of scholars was seated on the worn benches along the wall.

Manis stood for a moment in the doorway. Then he bowed slightly and said, "Gentlemen, let me introduce myself. My name is Manis ben Avigdor. I live in the town of Cassel. Normally, we Jews manage to get along with the local authorities in Cassel. But now, my good friends, we are in a terrible quandary. We need your advice."

Old Shimshon ha-Zaken nodded. "Welcome, Reb Manis," he said, staring at the merchant from Cassel. "We can see that you are unhappy."

"I am more than unhappy," said Manis, and he sat down heavily. "I am devastated."

Manis shook his head. He clasped and unclasped his hands.

"Things cannot be as bad as you think," said white-bearded Baruch ben Jacob. "Whatever are your difficulties–have faith, for the Lord will provide."

"Amen," said another sage.

"Ah, if only that were true," sighed Manis. "Certainly, the good Lord God protects us. He gives us inner strength. He gives warm breezes and quenching rains. He makes plants grow and animals become fat and healthy. But can He rain down money?" Manis shook his head, and his shoulders sagged.

"Tell us more details, Reb Manis," said a younger scholar, Elisah ben Samuel. "What exactly is your problem?"

"It is like this, my friends," answered Manis. "Our local Duke has instituted yet another tax that applies only to Jews. As it is, most Jewish families are buying food on credit. Everyone is poor, and we have no extra money to pay these new fees. But the Duke has set a deadline: we have one month to raise the funds. If we do not, then our property will be confiscated. We merchants are like everyone else – we have bought on credit. I myself have promised to pay my suppliers as soon as I sell my cloths and utensils. Until then, I have no available money. What can I do? I will be ruined! I am certain that the Duke is using the new fees as an excuse. He wants to force the Jews to leave town; then he himself will take over all the Jewish belongings."

Joshua ben Eliezer shook his head sadly. "We have heard such stories before," he said. "But remember the old saying: "There is nothing so bad that it does not contain some good.' "

The many sages sitting on the benches nodded and stroked their beards, but they said nothing for many minutes.

Finally old white-haired Baruch said, "Ah, Joshua, goodness always comes from the Lord. We must pray and then await His divine help. Take comfort in the Proverbs, my friend":

> The Almighty turns His radiant head,
>   Standing aloof from the wicked crowd;
> But the good Lord listens closely instead
>   To the prayers of the righteously endowed.

And Elisah ben Samuel added, "Exactly, Baruch – and there is also the Proverb":

> Never rob a defenseless man –
>   Instead, aid him selflessly,
> And never scorn a hungry man
>   Nor plague his family.
>
> God is our Protector
>   He shields the humble and the weak;
> He punishes the wicked braggart
>   Then He redeems all the meek.

Again the other scholars nodded. Joshua ben Eliezer said, "And there is the hopeful verse from Psalm 76":

You are like a mountain
  Towering strong and tall,
You overshadow men;
  At the rumble of Your call
The warriors fall and scream,
  And fainting dead away
All begin to dream
  Of Your final Judgment Day.

Manis listened politely and he said, "I do take comfort in the Holy Scriptures, gentlemen, but is there anything more practical that you can suggest?"

"Pray," said Reb Lewe.

"Fast," said Menahem ben Joel.

"Repent for your sins," said Moyses ben Nathan.

"Be patient," said old Shimshon ha-Zaken.

Manis nodded slowly, but he looked quite sad. He stared at his feet. The old men of Cologne were muttering among themselves. Manis felt tired. There was no more magic in Cologne than there was in Cassel, he thought.

After a moment, Rabbi Achselrad opened his eyes and he cleared his throat. Had he been asleep? The old Rabbi said, "Reb Manis, our scholars here have reminded us of Psalm 76." Rabbi Abraham nodded two or three times to himself. "This holy verse has given me a flash of insight."

Rabbi Abraham opened his eyes even wider, and he stared at Manis. "I have had a vision from the Psalms–I have seen a dream," said the Rabbi.

Manis looked at the Rabbi, who seemed to be peering straight through the merchant. "There is always hope," said old Achselrad, "and we must not spoil the peace of the Sabbath with any sad thoughts. Stay here in Cologne until tomorrow night. I have an idea–but it must wait. So, for now, try and put your fears aside. Remember, my friend, God never abandons the righteous."

Again the Rabbi nodded to himself. Then he looked down, and he began to write in his ever-present manuscript. The other scholars were talking quietly among themselves. Manis looked about him, and after a few minutes he left the yeshiva.

That evening the bright white Sabbath came in peace and restful ness and she trailed behind her a host of gentle angels. There were prayers and there was eating. There was laughter and relaxation. And then, the next evening, the Sabbath left as quietly as she had come. As the Sabbath slipped out, Manis was praying with the congregation. Rabbi Achselrad finished blessing the departing Sabbath Bride; he bowed his head and he recited:

Ancient Guard of the Covenant
Our Mighty Fount of Grace
Preserve Your faithful servants
Protect the Hebrew race
And command Your golden angels
Who watch over all our sleep
To work Your holy spells
Through the dreams that they keep.

"Amen," said the worshipers.

"Amen," repeated the Rabbi, and the congregants began to leave the synagogue. Old Achselrad turned to the seven sages and to Manis ben Avigdor ha-Kohen and he said, "Gentlemen, it is night and it is the time for dreams. Elisah, please get a long rope–then, my friends, we shall solve Reb Manis's problem."

The Rabbi put on his hat and his coat. The other men stood and got their coats also. Elisah returned from the courtyard with a strong rope. Everyone was silent, and Manis watched carefully. The Rabbi nodded and walked out of the old wooden synagogue; the seven sages of Cologne and the merchant of Cassel followed behind.

Out Judengasse Street they walked and through the streets of the Jewish Quarter–they walked down the winding Cologne streets and out the southern gate. The late-night procession passed the *Am Toten Juden,* the Jewish cemetery, where the tombstones reached like fingers toward the black night sky, and then the walkers went into the fields beyond. At last, the Rabbi stopped. He stood next to a deep water well. Knotroot grass was tangled along the edges. Rabbitwood shoots climbed among the broken stones. Bellwind shimmered in the cool late-night breezes. Rabbi Abraham spoke many mystical words; then he said, "Now, lower the rope to the bottom of this well and hold tightly to the end."

Elisah let down the rope. Manis and the old men of Cologne held on to the very end of the rope.

"All right, my friends – pull!" said Rabbi Achselrad.

The men began to pull the rope back up. It was heavy, amazingly heavy. Up came the rope, slowly, hand after hand. It rubbed against the stone edge of the well. It groaned as if it would break. And what was this? As the men pulled the rope out of the well they almost let go, for at the end was tied a bed! Yes, Rabbi, there was a magnificent wooden bed dangling from the end of this rope, and asleep on the bed was Duke Otto of Cassel.

The men lifted the bed over the stones and set it on the ground. Rabbi Abraham walked up to the sleeper. He shook the Duke, who woke with a start. "So," said old Achselrad, "you are the man who is oppressing the Jews of Cassel."

"What?" said the Duke. "Where am I?"

"It does not matter where you are, Duke," said the Rabbi. "What matters is that God can find you wherever you are. And, Duke, He expects more honorable behavior from His rulers."

"I am a duke," said Otto rubbing his eyes. "I make the rules. If the Jews are suffering, then it is their own fault. They do not contribute enough to the local community – they are selfish and they care only for their own kind."

"Duke, you must face the facts: the Jews are taxed beyond their means," said the Rabbi.

But the Duke answered, "As I said, old man: I make the rules."

"Well, Duke," answered old Achselrad, "perhaps you make the rules in Cassel, but here it is a different matter. Now get up."

The Duke hesitated; then he got out of bed. His face was pale. His legs were weak. His hands shook. Rabbi Abraham took off his hat. "If you want to return to Cassel," he said, "then I expect you to empty this well with my hat. You have until dawn."

Then the Rabbi crossed his arms over his chest and he stood waiting.

The Duke looked at the hat. He held it up and he could see the nighttime stars through the loose weave. "I cannot carry water in this hat," said the Duke. "Not only is it too small to empty the whole well, it has holes and it will leak. This is a totally unfair request."

"Ah," said the Rabbi, "I see that you have a bit of insight after all.

Can you collect grapes from thistle plants? Can you wash a blackbird white? Can you catch the wind in a fishing net? Can you make cheese from chalk? Certainly not. Then why do you insist on the impossible in Cassel? These poor Jews have no more money. It is impossible to squeeze any more taxes from them – give them a reprieve."

The Duke looked down. These old men were Jews. Why were they tormenting him? Would they actually harm him? Finally he said, "Yes, yes – all right, perhaps I can change my mind for the moment. I will withdraw my command if you spare my life and let me go back to Cassel."

"Your life is not in my hands, Duke Otto," said the Rabbi. "Only the great and Almighty Lord God (blessed be He) deals in life and death. My task is smaller: I try to make the lives of people a bit easier here on earth."

The Duke was silent.

"Now," said Rabbi Achselrad, "sign this document and then give me your signet ring and your shoes as a token of our agreement."

From out of nowhere the Rabbi produced a parchment and a pen; the paper said:

> I, Duke Otto of Cassel, agree to rescind all new and extraordinary taxes and fees that have been imposed on the Jews of our city. In the future, they shall pay only their fair share as equal citizens with the other townsfolk, Christian or otherwise.

The Duke read the paper and he hesitated. Rabbi Abraham frowned. Duke Otto was alone in the nighttime countryside, far from home: he took a deep breath, he reached for the pen, and he signed his name. Then he gave his ring and his shoes to the Rabbi. Rabbi Abraham handed the paper, the ring, and the shoes to Manis. "Now," said old Achselrad to the Duke, "get back in your bed and close your eyes."

The Duke climbed into the bed. He pulled up the covers, and he closed his eyes. The Rabbi touched Duke Otto on the head, and the Duke seemed to fall asleep. Then the Rabbi nodded once and the men lowered the bed and the sleeper back down into the well. In a moment, they pulled the rope up again – now it was bare and empty and wet. The men looked at one another but they said not a word; then they coiled the rope and they all returned to Cologne. Manis left for Cassel the next day.

In his mansion in Cassel, the Duke awoke the following morning. He looked around. The world seem ordinary and normal. "Strange," he thought. The details of his nightmare were still clear in his mind. "What a frightful dream that was," he shuddered. "Fortunately, dreams are nothing but cobwebs and featherstitching, and they dissolve completely in the bright morning light." The Duke shook his head, and he dismissed the matter from his mind.

A week passed. Then two weeks came and two weeks went. One day, it was time for the Jews to bring the new tax money to the Duke. The Rabbi of Cassel said, "Manis, it is up to you to save us." Manis took a deep breath. He packed his satchel, and he set off early in the morning to call on the Duke.

Cassel–which used to be called Cassala–lies along the hills and the woods on both sides of the River Fulda. Manis crossed the central stone bridge going from the Jewish Quarter in the east to the wealthy Gentile section in the west. Manis walked along Konigstrasse Street until he came to the Duke's palace. Then he hesitated. Manis was alone. He looked up to Heaven and quietly he recited the protective verse from the Book of Exodus:

> Terror and dread fell upon them
> And through the might of Your right arm
> They all stopped, stone-still
> While Your people passed safe from harm
> Through the danger–by Your will,
> Amen.

Then Manis walked into the busy courtroom of the Duke.

People were talking. Officials stood in uniform with swords at their sides. Manis was ignored. Manis ben Avigdor stood for one hour and then for two. He leaned against a wall. He stood with his weight on his left foot and then on his right. His legs grew tired; his back ached. Finally, he whispered to a guard. "May I have just a moment with the Duke?" The guard frowned and walked away. It seemed like another hour, but eventually the guard spoke to an official and the official spoke to the Duke. Manis was escorted to a fancy wooden desk at the far side of the room. The Duke looked up, he tapped his finger on the desk, and he looked back at his writing.

"Excuse me, Duke," began Manis. "Perhaps you will recall that one night a few weeks ago you promised to reduce the special Jewish taxes."

"I do not recall any such thing," said the Duke, still writing.

Manis raised his eyebrows. "Did you not make this promise in a dream?" he asked quietly.

One of the guards laughed. The Duke frowned. He opened his mouth to say something–then he hesitated. How did the Jew know about the nightmare? Was he some kind of sorcerer? The Duke stared at Manis. Manis waited a moment, and then he opened his satchel and he took out the signed parchment and the Duke's signet ring and his shoes. Where did he get those things? wondered the courtiers. Duke Otto's face turned red. People began to whisper. The Duke took a deep breath and said in a shaky voice, "Never mind those trifles. I have been thinking for some time that it would be a noble gesture for me to give the Jews another chance. Of course I expect them all to contribute more to our general funds–but I will give you Jews a grace period of, let us say, one year, before we consider new taxes."

Duke Otto went back to his writing. Manis said quietly, "Thank you, sir." And he turned and left. Manis reported immediately to the community elders. The Jews spread the word. Men and women thanked the good Lord that they had been given a reprieve. Then Manis and the other merchants quickly bought even more goods on credit and they built up their stocks and stores. Who knew what the future would bring–and as the old saying goes: "When your foot is in a shoe, *then* is the time to run and then, too, is the time you may safely step on thorns."

So the days seemed brighter now and the Jews of Cassel were happy. Businesses flourished and, not long afterward, Manis ben Avigdor ha-Kohen found himself in Cologne on a buying trip. He visited with friends and then he stopped in at the old yeshiva to report his success and to thank the Rabbi. Rabbi Abraham Achselrad was in the back study room. He looked up from his writing. He listened to Manis. He smiled and he nodded, but he had a faraway look in his eyes. "Was that really magic?" asked Manis after a moment. Rabbi Abraham stroked his beard and tapped his chin but he said nothing.

Perhaps he had not heard Manis. Or if he had heard, it did not seem that he was about to answer. Manis waited patiently, but the Rabbi sat back in his chair and stared absently at the ceiling. Slowly, he closed his eyes. His breathing became heavy and regular. Then old Rabbi Achselrad nodded his head. Had he fallen asleep? If so, he was dreaming his holy magical dreams once again.

Ah, good evening again, Rabbi. It is always hard to sleep on the night of a bright half-moon. Put your feet on the side bench here and I will open the stove door. Let me push the coals back – the white glow will wash away all the cares of your hard day.

I could not help overhearing your conversation with Reb Anton, and I was like Sarah. . . . Yes, exactly – I mean Abraham's wife. Sarah eavesdropped on the Patriarch Abraham as he talked with the three angels, and then she laughed. (That was when she heard that she – an old, old woman – would soon have a child, a son named "Isaac.") I eavesdropped and I laughed too, Rabbi. . . . No, not about Sarah – I laughed about bartering and negotiating. . . .

Do you not recall the conversation? Reb Anton was puzzled: How could old Abraham dare to bargain with the Lord? The Book of Genesis relates:

> "If there are only forty-five good men in the city of Sodom," asked the Patriarch Abraham, "then will You spare the city?" And the good Lord God (blessed be He) said that He would. "But suppose," continued Abraham, "that there are only thirty good men – would You then kill

> the good and the bad together?" And God said that he would spare the city for thirty good men.
>
> Still, Abraham did not give up; he continued: "Now, I hardly presume to speak to the great and almighty Lord God–dust and ashes that I am–but, O Lord, suppose that there are just ten upstanding men in Sodom. Would You hold back Your wrath for the sake of ten good men?" Again the Lord God (blessed be He) agreed. "Yes, yes–for the sake of the ten, I will not destroy Sodom," said the Lord.

It was at this point, Rabbi, that I laughed. And why did I laugh? Well, I pictured Abraham. He is a bent old man with a long white beard. The thin hair on his head is blown askew by the wind. He looks down at his feet, and he tilts his head a bit. "How much do I dare say?" he wonders. He cannot believe his own brazenness–here he was, bartering and negotiating with the awesome Lord God Himself! Obviously, God must have been holding His celestial temper in check, for with a flick of His right hand He could topple mountains or carve out seas or devastate forests, fields, and farmlands. To me, it was a comical picture and, for a moment, the Lord God seemed (excuse my saying this, Rabbi) almost human.

Ah yes, yes–I know, it is just as you always tell us, the old tales, even in the Bible, are told in human terms. They have human emotions and they are built on a human scale so that we can all relate to them. The Holy Scripture is human so that each person, small or humble as he is, can be a part of the greatest and most wondrous Night Tale of them all. . . .

What is that? A Night Tale from me? Rabbi, I know only children's stories, the old grandmother fables. You need something new and fresh to keep your mind keen; otherwise you will become a dreamy old man like me, and you will find yourself constantly musing and dozing and nodding off in front of the stove.

What do you mean you are already an old man? Do you really think that sixty years is old? You are still a child. When you reach eighty, *then* you will be old. You doubt that you will live to see eighty years? If so, Rabbi, then you will never grow old. . . . All right, all right, I know no special stories, but speaking of eavesdropping has reminded me of a tale that was told to me by my grandmother. Now, where shall I begin? Well, I suppose I should begin at the beginning:

In the beginning of the Jewish communities in Germany, said my grandmother to me, there lived in Cologne, on the River Rhine, a pious scholar named Saul ben Josiah. Saul was a farmer with a generous heart and a very quarrelsome wife.

It was a year of little rain and poor crops, and it was the day before *Rosh Hashanah.* Saul was in the marketplace–his wife had sent him to buy some bread for the holiday. A poor man stood next to the bakery; he was thin and weak and very hungry. Saul walked past the man. "I cannot ignore this sad character," he thought, so he walked back and gave the beggar a gold coin. Then Saul returned home without any bread.

When Saul's wife, Krasna, heard what happened, she said, "What is this, Saul? We work hard for the little money that we have. (Of course *you* could certainly spend more time working and less time talking with your friends in the yeshiva–but as for me, *I* work day and night.) We have barely enough money for food. And do we have any treats at all for the table? No, of course we do not. And now, my friend, you go and give away all of our money! If they need food, then other people can work too, you know."

Then Krasna listed all the things that they would not have for the holidays. She pointed out that each year they put off celebrating properly so that they could save for the next year. At this rate, they would die before they had one decent *Rosh Hashanah.* Of course, said Krasna, even though she was younger than Saul, she would probably die first. And why was this? It was because of all the aggravation that Saul caused. If only Saul took more responsibility for things around the house. You would think that after all these years he would finally grow up and become a responsible adult. You would think that a fifty-year-old man would be capable of a little restraint and a little financial planning–and on and on and on.

Poor Saul had no answers. Eventually, he walked out of the kitchen and out of the house. He did not want to talk to anyone and he was tired of listening, so he went to the cemetery. At least he could spend a night in peace among the silent graves. Medieval Jewish cemeteries were pleasant well-tended parks, far from Jewish homes; in

Cologne, the *Am Toten Juden* cemetery was a peaceful place outside the town limits, beyond the southern walls, and formally within the parish of St. Severin.

Saul walked south, down the dark streets of Cologne. He passed through the old southern gate. No one was around when Saul arrived at the *Am Toten Juden.* The Persians call their cemeteries "The Cities of the Silent," but we Jews call our cemeteries "The Gardens of Life"–and the Cologne *Garden of Life* was a fine, restful, and happy park. Saul found a soft spot sheltered by some bushes and trees, and he lay down. Little breezes kicked and skittered. It felt to Saul as if spirits were tickling him. Saul shifted his shoulders, he bent his knees, and he put his hands under his head as a pillow. He breathed easily. Things became vague and quiet, and Saul fell asleep. Suddenly he was awakened. He sat up. What was this? Apparently, two girl spirits were talking.

The first spirit was saying, "Ah, nighttime at last. Come with me, my friend, let us fly over the world. Perhaps we can hear what is being said from behind the curtain of Heaven. After all, today is *Rosh Hashanah,* when the yearly plan is set. I wonder what fortunes and misfortunes are in store for the living during the next year."

A light breeze shifted the leaves in the bushes around Saul. Soon he heard the second spirit. "I am sorry," she said sadly. "I cannot go with you. You see, I was buried in a straw shroud. Imagine how I would look among the golden angels; I am ashamed to go to Heaven in such clothes. You go on alone–when you return, you can report everything to me."

There was silence. Had the first spirit left? Saul rested quietly. Night winds rolled in the trees. The stars shifted. Time passed. Then as he was about to fall asleep again, Saul heard the second spirit say, "Well, my companion, what have you learned?"

"I will tell you everything," said the first spirit. "I sped up to Heaven. It is a glorious trip, past snow-white mountaintops and into the ocean of the blue nighttide depths. Then, I slipped behind the curtain of the Great Court of Glory. I opened wide my eyes. I listened with my softest and tiniest ears. And I heard that a late hailstorm will destroy any crops planted too early, before the month of *Ivar.* It will be a very dramatic event. The angels could talk of nothing else; then I was afraid of being discovered, so I quickly flew back down to earth."

Well, Rabbi, these spirits were like Sarah and me: they loved to eavesdrop–and of course old Saul ben Josiah was eavesdropping too. (Do you know why we say "eavesdrop," Rabbi? Well, I will tell you: Once upon a time, it was called "eavesdrip," and it referred to people who stood close enough to a house to hear the voices inside and also close enough to get wet from water falling off the eaves.)

Saul ben Josiah was within "eavesdrip" of the spirits, and he heard the prediction. The spirits became quiet again, and Saul fell back to sleep. The next morning, he returned home. "Aha," said Krasna, "have you been at the inn all night? It is a good thing you had no money; otherwise, you would be drunk on a holiday. Now you will probably want to go straight to the synagogue without helping me clean up the house"–and on and on and on. Saul frowned, he shook his head, and he went to the synagogue.

Later that year, when sowing time came, Saul waited. "Why do you let everyone else get a head start on you?" asked Krasna. "Do you think you know more than the other farmers? Do you think people are out planting now because they have nothing better to do? I have never seen such a lazy man." Even the neighbors thought, "Old Saul must be getting lazy." Weeks passed. Finally, Saul began to plant–and as usual he set out peas, beans, buckwheat, and flax. Just after he had finished all his planting, the weather turned cold and there was a terrible hailstorm. The young plants in the neighbors' fields were damaged, but Saul's plants had not come up yet and they remained safe and sound.

"So," said Krasna, "our gardening is working this year. At last you are listening to me. How many times have I told you: plant in even rows. Finally you are doing things more carefully. You see–it pays off. And you have added more ash to the soil. I do not know how many years I have said this to you–why are you only starting that now? Honestly, Saul, if you had only listened a bit more and not felt that you knew everything yourself, we would have been better off long ago." Saul shook his head and left for the evening prayers in the synagogue.

Things went on this way all year. The summer came and went, and suddenly it was the night before *Rosh Hashanah.* Various matters came up between Saul and Krasna, and again Saul felt the need for a peaceful sleep. He walked from the house and through the streets of Cologne. Out the southern gate went Saul; then he stepped into the old

Am Toten Juden. He took a deep breath of fresh air. He stretched. He lay down in the same spot as he had last year. Saul shifted his shoulders. He bent his knees, and he put his hands under his head as a pillow. He began to breathe easily. His mind rolled gently over all manner of nothings. The world became vague and quiet, and Saul fell asleep. Suddenly he was awakened by the voices of two girl spirits.

The first spirit said, "Well, my old friend, here it is *Rosh Hashanah* again. We should slip up to Heaven and find out what the new year will bring."

A light breeze shifted the bushes around Saul. "As you know," said the second spirit sadly, "I cannot go up to Heaven with you. I have nothing to cover myself but a pale straw shroud. You go alone–then report to me what you have learned."

There was silence. The first spirit sped along the edges of the clouds up to Heaven. She whisked beyond the nighttime celestial blue tides, and she slipped behind the curtain of the Great Court of Glory. There, she opened wide her bright, bright eyes and she listened well with her softest and tiniest ears; then she flew back down to earth.

Saul lay very quietly. The winds rolled through the trees. The stars shifted, time passed, and eventually Saul heard the second spirit say, "And what have you learned in the High Court of Heaven?"

"Well," said the first voice, "again I heard a report about the weather. This time a hot, dry, sunny spell is due. Apparently, vegetable plants had best be well along in their growth before that time in order to be strong enough to survive. In fact, those farmers who sow their fields late, after the month of *Ivar,* will have their still-tender crops burned completely by the sun."

"Well, that is quite different from last year," said the second spirit.

"Yes, the good Lord God (blessed be He) seems to be alternating the weather. It is just as it was in the biblical story of Egypt, where Joseph predicted to Pharaoh: 'There are to be seven years of great plenty throughout the land, but after them will come seven years of famine.' In those days, good years were followed by bad and one type of weather was followed swiftly on the heels by its exact opposite."

"Ah, so it was then and so it is now," sighed the second spirit.

Saul heard the prophecy. He raised his eyebrows and lay back; soon he fell asleep with the words of the two female spirits ringing in his ears. The next morning Saul returned home smiling. "Why are you so happy?" asked Krasna. "Undoubtedly you can smile because at least you knew where *I* was last night. Of course I had no idea whether *you* were alive or dead. And now it is the holiday already–you have come home just in time to do nothing useful but spend all day eating and relaxing in the synagogue"–and on and on and on.

The high holy days slipped by, and then the winter passed. Saul was out in his fields as soon as the frosts were over. He planted his seeds extraordinarily early; in fact, Saul set out the peas, the beans, the buckwheat, and the flax in the month of *Nisan,* well before all his neighbors. The other farmers looked at one another. "Whatever has gotten into Saul this year?" they wondered. "Why does he have this sudden spurt of energy? Perhaps he needs an excuse to get out of his house and away from Krasna. But he is taking his chances–we may still have a killing frost or spring floods or cold rains." However, the spring passed uneventfully, and when the hot weather arrived, Saul's crops were already well-grown, strong, and firmly rooted. In contrast, his neighbors' plants were still small and weak and easily scorched, and many farmers lost their entire crop in the hot summer drought.

"Ah," said Krasna, "now you are finally listening to me. Did I not say that you should plant earlier this year? And of course now that you have, you are having a bit of success. If only you had listened to me earlier in our marriage, then we might have saved enough money to get by in our old age."

And Saul answered, "Listen to you? If I had listened to you, my ears would be broken by now."

"Well, I see that I can expect no appreciation from you, old man," said Krasna. "Clearly you are jealous of my advice. *You* do whatever happens to fall into your empty head at the moment. But *I* think about things. I use common sense–and I combine that common sense with what I learned of farming from my father (may he rest forever in peace and may I be a continuous atonement for his sins, amen)."

"Your advice is not worth a dried pea," said Saul.

"Oh? And I suppose that you just decided to plant early because a bird told you to do that," said his wife.

"Well, in a way I did," said Saul.

"What?! You go listening to birds and not to your wife?" said Krasna. "You are more of a fool than I thought."

"It was not a bird, woman – it was a spirit," said Saul, and he told her the whole story.

Saul's wife raised her eyebrows, but for a moment she said nothing. Then she shrugged her shoulders and said, "At least it was the advice of female spirits. We women know a thing or two about the world, old man. You would do well to listen to us more often." Then Saul left the room and went to the synagogue to pray.

Well, Rabbi, as you might imagine, Krasna quarreled with everyone around her. Several months later, she was arguing with the mother of one of the dead girls. "Come now, admit it," said Krasna, "your daughter lies buried in a shroud of straw. She is too embarrassed to go to Heaven; in fact, she just wanders the cemetery sadly at night, complaining to her friends."

"That is a terrible thing to say! It is a sacrilege!" cried the mother. "We have done our best. How can you speak to me in this unholy way of the dead? Are you now suggesting that we go and dig up her grave?!" And, shouting angrily, the woman slammed the door as she left Krasna's house.

Ah, Rabbi, this put Krasna in a foul mood indeed. It was the day before *Rosh Hashanah,* and Saul and his wife got into an argument. "You would not believe how rude Moshe's wife was to me," began Krasna.

"Oh yes I would," said Saul. "You could drive anyone to rudeness."

"Why do you always defend other people?" yelled Krasna. "I have feelings too, you know. I try to be sympathetic to *you,* even when things are your fault – need I mention the money you lost buying worthless spice boxes? And it takes a saint to put up with your eating habits. Do you ever offer food to me first? No, of course you do not. Always, you just reach out and take the main portion first. But do I say anything about it? No – I keep silent: I hold my tongue. And another thing, my upstanding husband . . ." and on and on and on.

Saul shook his head and he went to spend the night in the cemetery. Saul ben Josiah walked south, down the dark streets of Cologne, and he passed through the old southern gate. No one was about when Saul arrived at the *Am Toten Juden.* He found the same soft grassy spot sheltered by bushes and trees, and he lay down. Little breezes kicked and skittered, like spirits lightly tickling Saul's back and riffling his hair. Saul shifted his shoulders, he bent his knees, and he put his hands under his head as a pillow. A gentle calm settled over the world, things became vague and quiet, and Saul fell asleep. Suddenly he was awakened; again, he heard the two girl spirits talking.

The first spirit said, "I would like very much to hear a report on the new year. But I suppose that once more I will have to go to Heaven alone."

There was a sigh in the wind, but otherwise Saul heard no answer. Had the second spirit nodded her misty wispy head? A light breeze shifted leaves in the bushes around Saul. Saul lay very still. The stars slid along their tracks. Time passed. Winds rolled high in the trees.

The gentle rustling continued for minutes and minutes, and eventually Saul heard a voice. It was the second spirit asking: "And what have you learned, my friend?"

"Ah, may the good Lord bless me, I learned that someone has been eavesdropping. Someone has secretly listened in on the conversations of the angels and the Great Lord Almighty Himself! That is all that they could talk about in Heaven: apparently, some earthly farmer seems to know in advance exactly what the weather will be."

"Heaven defend us!" cried the friend fearfully. "If there are eavesdroppers in Heaven, then there could be eavesdroppers anywhere. We had best keep our own mouths shut. I tell you, it is shameful–one cannot say anything in private."

"Yes," said the first spirit, "the least little leaf pricks up its ears at the sound of a quiet talk. Everyone wants to hear everything. Even walls have ears, and they seem to hear our thoughts before we have said them aloud. It is as the Holy Scriptures say in the *Song of Songs*":

> My bride–my lovely little lady–
>   Sitting in the garden green,
> What is it that the other men
>   Listen to beside the stream?
> Is it your light and gentle voice
>   Whispering behind the soft moonbeam?

The second spirit sighed. "It is night," she said. "We are behind a moonbeam. In fact, we are in a cemetery. But I suppose that even here we are not safe. Everything that we talk about is carried off on some breeze or another. Very likely at this moment someone is eavesdropping on us." The first spirit nodded and shook her head, and the two spirits wavered and drifted in the nighttime breezes. Then neither spirit said another word–and they have remained silent from that day until this.

Saul stroked his beard and he shrugged his shoulders. Then he settled into a little hollow in the ground, and he fell fast asleep. Early the next morning, he awoke and he walked home. "Well," said Krasna, "here he is at last, back from the dead."

"Ah, the dead know more than you, old woman," said Saul.

"Perhaps," said Krasna, "but will they tell what they know?"

Then Saul shook his head, he put some cotton in his ears, he ate his breakfast, and off he went to the synagogue to pray.

Good evening, Rabbi. Sit down and get warm. Next to the oven it feels as if we have stepped into some warm southern clime–it is like one of those Mediterranean lands where Jews first walked the earth and where we have always flourished. I close my eyes and wonder: Are we suddenly in the suntanned Holy Lands again? Or is it perhaps some spot nearer to home, such as Spain or southern France–could we have slipped into old Narbonne?

Ah, Narbonne–now *there* was a bustling Jewish center, at least in the Middle Ages. Narbonne is on the vine-growing plain near the Mediterranean. Once it was a beautiful, warm, freethinking Jewish hometown–late in the Dark Ages, King Charlemagne himself granted a third of the city to the Jews, and in medieval times we had schools and synagogues and a famous university there. . . .

What? Oh, I was thinking of Narbonne because my grandmother would tell stories about it–although I do not know if she ever saw that old French city herself. In its golden days, Jews lived there quietly and happily. They were farmers and honey traders and wine growers and merchants. The Narbonne Jews manufactured bricks and tiles, and of course they were the premier importers and exporters.

In the Narbonne yeshiva, the Jews studied and wrote, and the

Jewish literature of southern Europe foreshadowed the Renaissance. For many years, the local Christian patrons supported all forms of science, arts, and poetry, and they believed in independence and in free speech, even about religion. With this freedom, the local Jews wove Judaism together with the surrounding cultures. Jews became translators and purveyors of foreign literature and stories, and it was in Narbonne that the famed Berachiah ben Natronai ha-Nakdan grew up. . . .

Why, Rabbi, I do not understand how a well-educated man such as yourself could never have heard of Berachiah ha-Nakdan. Ha-Nakdan was a fabulist, second only to Rabbi Meir of Palestine. . . . Well then, old man, I will tell you about him:

Berachiah was born in Beziers and later he moved to Narbonne. For a time, the old community of Beziers had accepted Jews and they lived harmoniously with the Christians. However, one day a new bishop came to Beziers. On Palm Sunday, he preached an angry sermon against the Jews: he charged that the Jews had murdered Christ. Afterwards, the young men attending the service roamed the city with stones and sticks. They attacked Jewish houses and schools. They broke doors and furniture, and Jews were beaten – and this was repeated for three years in a row. Finally, in the month of *Iyar* of the year 4920, a new cleric, Bishop William, banned the mob attacks on Palm Sundays. He even threatened to excommunicate priests who spoke out against the Jews, and, in return, the Jewish community pledged to contribute four pounds of silver to the Church every year on Palm Sunday.

Berachiah ha-Nakdan grew up in Beziers, and he remembered the fearful Palm Sundays of his childhood. But, Berachiah was a trusting and optimistic man – he had no doubt that the righteous would triumph in the end. Did not the Book of Proverbs say:

Kind deeds, both generous and brave,
  Protect the righteous-spirited,
But selfish rogues will be enslaved –
  By their own fierce greed they'll be misled.
Yes, the pious man is saved
  From disasters he would dread,
While wicked men who misbehave
  Drown in those selfsame griefs instead.

Berachiah believed this with all his heart. In fact, he wrote this very proverb at the end of a fable in a letter to Rabbi Abraham ben Alexander, the mystic Achselrad of Cologne. Old Achselrad then recorded the fable in his Kabbalistic tome the *Keter Shem Tov,* a work that is sprinkled with ancient tales.

You see, Rabbi, Abraham ben Alexander was a great admirer of fables. He listened closely to the many storytellers who came through Cologne, and he was especially fascinated when ha-Nakdan himself stopped in the Rhinelands. That was on a mild springtime morning. The sun was yellow and gentle, the sky was blue and cool, and a stranger, a traveler, a wanderer, walked into the back room of the Cologne yeshiva, where Abraham Achselrad was working. As you know, in those far-off days all manner of pious pilgrims came through Germany each week. They came from the East, from the Mediterranean shores, and from the Holy Lands, and it was not unusual for strange men to appear suddenly at odd hours of the day and night in the Cologne yeshiva.

It was morning. Outside, a splash of golden yellow washed through the sky. It shone through the windows of the old wooden synagogue, and gently it settled on the parchment in front of Rabbi Abraham, who was writing at his desk. Was there a noise? The Rabbi looked up. There in the doorway stood a man whom Rabbi Abraham did not recognize.

"Hello?" said the Rabbi.

"Are you Rabbi Abraham?" asked the stranger.

"I am,"answered Achselrad.

"My name is Berachiah ben Natronai ha-Nakdan. May I come in?"

Rabbi Abraham raised his eyebrows. Ha-Nakdan was a name that he had heard before. Berachiah's father, Rabbi Natronai ha-Nakdan, was a talmudical scholar from southern France. Berachiah's brother, Samuel, had written a number of books on grammar and on talmudic commentary. Berachiah himself had followed in his family's scholarly tradition. He was the author of the "Compendium" *(Sefer ha-Hibbur)* and the "Masref" *(Sefer ha-Matzref),* two ethical treatises written in Hebrew. Berachiah was also a translator: he had translated Adelard's *Quaestiones Naturales* (known in Hebrew as *Dodi Venehdi,* the "Dialogue between the Uncle and the Nephew") from French into

Hebrew, and he had translated into Hebrew the Latin "Lapidarium," a treatise on minerology that described seventy-three gemstones.

These were Berachiah's academic achievements. However, Rabbi, only a small part of the world really enjoys such esoteric scholarship. The language and the detailed ideas of the academics are far from our common, direct, day-to-day experiences: few people live intimately with such abstract language and with such distant contrived ideas. The strange constructions of philosophy, economics, and science are technical, specialized, and largely invisible. On the other hand, we all tell stories. People continually recount adventures and myths and Night Tales. We common people talk in anecdotes–and Berachiah ha-Nakdan was a common person. Berachiah was a storyteller, and he wrote a collection of Hebrew "Fox Fables," the *Mishle Shualim,* which he dedicated to Rabbi Meshullam ben Jacob of Lunel.

Berachiah, the son of Natronai ha-Nakdan, was simply a storyteller, and he became the most famous fabulist of the Middle Ages. . . . What? Yes, "ha-Nakdan" does mean "punctuator." Biblical copying was quite specialized in those days, and some medieval families were trained specifically to add the correct Masoretic notes and punctuations, the vowels and the accents. The title ha-Nakdan–"the punctuator"–was appended to the families of copyists and commentators who were experts in the detailed word structure and the grammar of the Bible, and such was Berachiah's family. And on that spring morning in Cologne, Rabbi Abraham said, "Ha-Nakdan, the punctuator–please, come in and sit down."

Berachiah stepped into the small back room. He set his pack on the floor, and he sat down on one of the worn wooden benches. Berachiah smiled at the Rabbi and said, "Ah, Rabbi, it is true–my family is a family of punctuators. But as for me? I am simply a storyteller."

Rabbi Abraham sat back in his chair. "Well, sir, rest here a moment, and tell me a story."

Berachiah loosened his coat and stretched out his feet. "My favorite tales are animal fables, the old-fashioned stories that point to a moral or a proverb. Now, let me see . . . perhaps I will tell you about the lion with bad breath":

"Once upon a time–and a long, long time ago it was–there was a lion who became sick. His mane got patchy and thin and mottled.

His brown fur turned gray with splotches of bare skin. He was so weak that he had not eaten for many days, and now his digestion was upset. His stomach felt stale, his teeth were spotted and brown, and his breath smelled absolutely terrible.

"Slowly and tiredly, the lion paced through the sandy plains and the rocky places near his cave at the edge of a forest. Suddenly, he came upon a donkey.

"The donkey jumped back. The lion roared weakly; he felt awful. 'Listen, you pitiful creature,' he said hoarsely to the donkey. 'Does my breath smell bad?'

"What should the donkey say? Did he dare to tell the truth? He shook and he shivered. 'Well?' roared the lion, coughing.

" 'All right–yes. I am afraid that it does,' answered the donkey.

" 'What?!' said the lion. 'How dare you insult me, the king of the beasts.' And with a swipe of his massive paw, the lion killed the donkey. The exertion was almost too much for the lion. He lay down and rested. He did not have the energy to eat the donkey. Eventually, however, the lion got up again and slowly he went on his way. He padded through dense thorn thickets and low bushes and tall grasses. Soon, he met a small bear.

"The lion was in a foul, foul mood. 'Aha!' he roared. 'And what are you doing, walking in my path?'

"The bear shivered. 'I am sorry–I will move away from here immediately.'

"The lion coughed. He took a deep breath. 'Just a moment,' he said. 'Tell me the truth, bear: does my breath smell bad?'

"The bear looked nervously at the lion. He hesitated. He looked around. Then he said, 'Well, to tell you the truth, Your Majesty, I did detect a whiff of strange odor–but I am certain that it was the wind. Your breath is sweeter than honey.'

" 'What?!' roared the lion. 'How dare you lie to me, the king of beasts.' And with a swing of his heavy paw, the lion killed the bear, and this time the lion managed to eat some of the animal.

"The lion lay down. He rested for many hours, and he began to feel a bit better. He stood. He shook himself. Then he started to walk along again. He walked at the edge of the forest, following the tall grass and the reeds that grew beside a stream. The day was ending–it was turning cool. A fox darted out to the stream.

"The lion gave a deep moaning roar five times. The fox jumped, and he began to shiver and to shake. 'Listen, fox,' said the lion, 'smell my breath.' The lion stared at the fox, he opened his mouth, and he roared again five times directly at the fox. 'Now tell me–does my breath smell all right?' he asked.

"The fox thought a moment. What did he dare say? He shivered and he shook. He was trembling all over. Was he ill? Was he catching a cold? Quickly he said, 'I would be most happy to oblige, Your Honor. However, I cannot smell at all because I have a cold.'

"A cold? The lion was just beginning to feel better from his own illness. The lion stepped back–and the fox turned, and quick as the wind, he ran off, far, far away.

"So, Rabbi," Berachiah had said to old Achselrad, "when all answers are wrong, then no answer is right." And old Rabbi Achselrad nodded and nodded, and he stroked his tangled beard. . . .

What? Yes, yes, Rabbi–I am about to continue. I was just thinking quietly here, in the warm Narbonne glow of the stove. Now, where was I? Oh yes, my grandmother told me that old Rabbi Abraham had written once to ha-Nakdan; this was a few years after the two men met in Cologne. Achselrad had written to ask the famous storyteller again about foxes and fables and also about the old and sunny Rabbi Meir of Palestine, and this is ha-Nakdan's reply, a letter which came in a packet early one weekday morning in the late cool spring:

"To my holy colleague,
Abraham, the son of Alexander–

"I thank you for your letter, which I received last week. It is good to hear news of the thoughtful scholarship that flourishes under your direction in the Jewish communities of the rich valley of the River Rhine. I know that the good Lord God (blessed be He) has shined down His warm smile, His loving kindness, and His benevolent radiance upon you and all your colleagues and upon the many eager young children in your yeshivas, amen.

"Yes, Rabbi, you are right in calling me a 'fabulist,' although I write other more 'scholarly' things and I also translate academic works.

When I was younger, I felt uncomfortable saying it–but the truth is: I am simply a storyteller. And of all the stories, I like fables best. Fables are rather specialized and modest stories. They are not complex or intricate or multilayered; instead, they are direct and simple and they take place in the immediate world around us. Fables illustrate particular moral rules. And they use animals as the main characters–but these creatures are really just humans in disguise.

"You have asked where my fables come from. The answer is: they come from *everywhere.* You see, Rabbi, by tradition and by training, I am only a poor copyist. Fortunately, the world is filled with stories to copy. I listen, and I simply write them down. I began as a copyist of academic treatises, helping out my father. Soon I also produced some translations. However, when I sat at a blank piece of paper, I always felt equally blank. I never could create new things. Instead, I have always looked around and written what I saw or heard or what I read elsewhere.

"The rest of my family works in the rarefied realms of scholarly Hebrew studies. I, however, am a common daydreamer. I cannot help myself–somehow it is built into me. Once I became immersed in fables, I could not find my way out again. To me, stories are irresistible. Fortunately, I have never been far from their reach, for they have always been everywhere around me. Why, what else is ordinary conversation but stories, stories, and more stories? Anecdotes are the currency of our common speech, Rabbi; in everyone's mouth, both young and old, a story sits in wait. So I listen, and they tell.

"As I have said: I am a poor inventor. If I have any skill at all, then it is simply the ability to put into Hebrew–into clean, clear, modern Hebrew–the old tales of others. By now, I have written down more than one hundred Fox Fables. None of them is truly original. But originality is not the issue with fables–fables are reflections of our everyday lives, built with materials just sufficiently exotic to give them a certain strange freshness.

"Of course we fabulists all follow old Aesop, who lived on the Greek island of Samos in the days of the Prophet Isaiah. Next came the great Rabbi Meir, eight hundred years later in Palestine. Rabbi Meir was a pupil of Rabbi Akiva (may both their names be forever blessed). After his days with Akiva, Meir studied with Elisha ben Abuyah. Rabbi Elisha was born before the destruction of the Temple, he lived through many difficult eras, and finally he became a Sadducee – that is, Elisha studied non-Jewish traditions in order to understand the cultures around him.

"In contrast, Meir was a traditionalist. He could not bring himself to bend any of the old Jewish rules. So Meir remained a Pharisee, a traditional Jewish separatist. In fact, he became a great Pharisee teacher. He refounded the Palestinian schools at Ushu, just southeast of Tyre. And, as you know, Rabbi, the *Aggadah* is filled with tales of his skill as a teacher of ethics.

"Old Meir was a brilliant scholar. He knew the Greek and Latin literatures, and he had absorbed the Mediterranean tradition of teaching through fables. But as a Pharisee, Meir could not introduce the classical stories in their non-Jewish form. Therefore, he reworked and remolded the tales and he set them in our ancient Hebrew tradition. The Talmud records that he collected three hundred fables – but I have only been able to find about thirty of his fables anywhere in the Talmud and the Midrash.

"Eventually, Meir had a disagreement with the Patriarch, bitter words followed, and Meir left Palestine a few years before his death. Meir died somewhere in Asia Minor. When word of his death filtered back to the great centers of Jewish learning, it was said in the synagogues: 'And now, with the death of Rabbi Meir, great fable writers have ceased to exist in the world.'

"The writers' *bodies* may have ceased to exist, Rabbi, but their fables have not disappeared: they still live on today. You asked about fables of reversal, stories where the beneficent Lord God (blessed be He) saves the good man by putting the wicked man in his place. Here is a fable that I have heard repeated many times. Although it has traveled far since those olden days, initially it was set on its Hebrew course by the great Rabbi Meir, he of the most blessed memory.

"Once upon a time, begins the tale, there was a fox, a small, reddish, white-footed fox. This fox was clever but good-hearted and it meant no harm to others. One day, the little fox was padding through the brush, not paying close attention to where it was heading, when it ran into a wolf. Wolves usually travel in packs, but this wolf was alone, and it was hungry. The fox stopped. This wolf was an animal killer; the other creatures knew him and they avoided him at all cost.

"The fox looked around, but there was no escape. The wolf crouched down. He growled. He tensed his muscles. What could the fox do? Quickly he said to the wolf, 'Ah, my friend, you look hungry. If you want to enjoy a good meal, a very special dinner, then take my advice. Today is Friday. There is a Jew just down the road. He is preparing a tremendous feast for the Sabbath; he is setting out bread and meat and fish and cakes. Offer to help him, and he will reward you with all the food you can possibly eat.'

"Well, the wolf *was* quite hungry. He listened to the fox, and he thought that this seemed to be sound advice. Why bother to run and fight for his food? If the Jew has already collected a table full of delicacies, that would be much easier – besides, if the Jew refused, then the wolf could simply steal whatever he wanted and run away. So the wolf bounded down the path, he turned into the courtyard of the Jew, and he began to speak. However, no sooner had the wolf appeared, then a host of men rushed at him and beat him with sticks, so that he was lucky to escape with his life.

"Bruised and cut and black-and-blue, the wolf was furious. He ran off in search of the fox, and very soon the wolf located him. The fox was in his burrow, a hole that he had taken over from an old badger. The wolf sniffed and growled; then he began to dig. 'I will tear that fox from limb to limb,' thought the wolf. 'I will eat every single rib and bone.' The fox cowered in a far corner of the hole. His long ears lay back. His tail was between his legs. As the wolf came nearer and nearer, the fox said in a shaky voice, 'My friend, do not carry on so. Calm yourself.'

" 'I am no friend of yours!' roared the wolf.

" 'Oh, yes,' said the fox, 'we *are* friends. The problem here is your father.'

" 'What?!' cried the wolf. 'What has my father to do with this?!'

" 'Listen,' said the fox, 'I forgot to tell you that one time a Jew asked your father to help him prepare for the Sabbath. In return, the Jew invited your father to the feast afterward. But your father was impatient. He ate everything in sight. He completely devoured all the delicious food, and he did not leave the Jew even one little chicken bone.'

" 'I never knew this,' said the wolf.

" 'Ah, undoubtedly your father was ashamed to confess to you,' said the fox. 'In any case, now you can understand why the Jew beat you.'

"The wolf was still digging, but he had slowed a bit. Quickly the fox continued: 'Because we *are* friends, I feel sorry for you. Therefore I will share a secret: I will show you a special and amazing treat. We will *both* be able to dine well. Follow me.'

"The fox leaped out of the hole and the wolf followed closely. In a short time, they reached a water well. The fox waved its long bushy tail. At the top of the well, two buckets were suspended on either end of a single rope; when one bucket went down, the other came up as a counterweight. The fox climbed into one bucket, and it slid down, down, down to the very bottom of the well.

"After a few minutes, the wolf called down, 'What are you doing down there?'

"The fox called out from the depths of the well, 'What do you think I am doing? I am eating, of course. This is simply amazing! You have never seen anything like this. There are meats and cakes. There are roots, roast rabbits, and rutabagas. There are cooked hens. There are crabs and whelks–and, my friend, there is a cheese as big and as round and as yellow as the moon!'

"It was getting dark. The wolf peered down. Sure enough, he saw the moon, reflected in the water below. 'Just a moment–let me have some of those things, too,' called the wolf. 'Remember–*I* am the one who was hungry. I am the one who needs a meal.'

" 'Wait your turn–there is plenty of food, and I am starving. I need to eat my fill.'

" 'If you do not come up immediately, fox, then I will eat you too!' said the wolf.

" 'All right, all right,' said the fox. 'Get into the other bucket. You are heavier than I am, so you will slide down here and you can take my place.'

"The wolf climbed into the other bucket, and he slid down quickly into the depths of the well. At the same time, the bucket with the fox came up. The fox reached the surface. He jumped out and he chewed through the rope, which fell down, down, down to the bottom of the well with a splash.

" 'Say–it is dark down here,' called the wolf. 'Where is the food? All I can feel is water. . . . And what are you doing? Let me up immediately!'

"The fox looked down. The evening was darkening. He could not see the gray wolf in the darkness, but the fox could hear his heavy breathing. The fox was quiet a moment. Then he said, 'My friend, are you a biblical scholar? If you are not, then let me remind you of a certain proverb':

Kind deeds, both generous and brave,
  Protect the righteous-spirited,
But selfish rogues will be enslaved–
  By their own fierce greed they'll be misled.
Yes, the pious man is saved
  From disasters he would dread,
While wicked men who misbehave
  Drown in those selfsame griefs instead.

"And then the fox ran far, far away.

"Your humble friend and colleague,
Berachiah, the son of Rabbi Natronai"

Good evening, Rabbi. Are you having difficulty sleeping again? Put your feet up on the side bench here. I will open the stove door and push the coals back; there is nothing like that white glow to wash away the cares of a hard day. The oven is warm and tranquil and calming and soothing, here in the back room of the yeshiva. But, Rabbi–outside these walls, the vast, tangled, deep-shadowed world can look very, very different. . . .

Well, I am thinking of a time when I saw something frightening. In some ways, it was like the glow of this very oven, but it was neither warm nor tranquil nor soothing. I saw a glow, I shivered and I shook, and then I ran.

I was a boy–perhaps I was ten or eleven years old. It was the evening. Night was just over the hill. I was walking alone on an old road, past the fields beyond our village. Shadows were deep and grim; the trees were old. I walked fast. I felt tense and uneasy. Around the bend was a thicket of brush and bramble, there was dead wood, there were dried weeds. As I came near, the air darkened. No one was about. A small animal scrambled in the leaves. And then there was a glow. It was just like the white glow of this oven, but it was not warm and calm and happy. No, Rabbi–it was cold and alien and forbidding. It was somewhere beyond the trees. I saw it for only a moment, and then I ran. I ran and ran and I did not dare to look behind me until I reached my home, shivering and shaking and cold and ill.

What had I seen? What spirits of the night? I do not know, and I do not want to think about it too deeply. It may have been the same spirits that have lurked along roadsides for generations. It may have been those spirits that have plagued travelers since time immemorial. These are strange nighttime roadside spirits – but are they the spirits of dead people, or are they evil demons?

Perhaps they are only the stern enforcers of the Law and the protectors of sacred Jewish objects. . . . What do I mean? Well, I am thinking of a story that my grandmother told me; it was about nighttime spirits and a Gentile traveler of long ago, in the medieval years when Achselrad was the Chief Rabbi of Cologne. Achselrad (that is, Rabbi Abraham ben Alexander) was my grandmother's favorite rabbi – he was a mystical scholar from those dim old days when demons were more common than they are now. That was a time when even sneezing could upset the demons, and when an angry demon might turn you into a carrot on the slightest provocation. In those demon-filled days, Rabbi Achselrad was responsible for protecting the Jews in all the surrounding Rhine regions, including such small communities as Bruhl, Deutz, Kalk, Kierberg, Mulheim, Rondorf, Sechtem, and Siegburg, and he was also the Chief Rabbi for the larger towns such as Bonn and Duren.

One year, a new synagogue was built in the town of Duren. Jews throughout the Rhine region heard the news and celebrated. The Jewish community of Bonn had an extra set of Scrolls of the Holy Scriptures, and they decided to donate it as a present to the Duren community. What a wonderful community *mitzvah!* In Duren, the congregation thanked the Lord, they thanked Bonn, and they chose a pillar of the community, a good and pious man named Avidan ben Machir ha-Levi, to arrange for the transfer. Avidan traveled to Bonn to bring home the Scrolls – however, he ran into a strange and completely unexpected problem and he was forced to journey north to Cologne to consult with the famed Rabbi Achselrad.

When Avidan arrived in the Jewish Quarter of Cologne, he located the synagogue building, and he stepped in the front door. He went through the anteroom. He walked into the main prayer hall, which was filled with wooden benches. Avidan admired the twelve stained-glass windows with their colored lions and snakes. He looked up fondly at the Holy Ark made of stone, and he walked to the door of the back study room. There, in the morning light, he found the Rabbi sleeping at his desk, for old Rabbi Abraham had worked all night on his mystical treatise the *Keter Shem Tov.* Along the sides of the room, the yeshiva scholars were sitting on the worn benches talking quietly among themselves.

White-haired Baruch ben Jacob looked at the stranger. "Yes, my friend?" he asked.

"Sirs," began the newcomer, "my name is Avidan ben Machir. I live in Duren. It is fine old Jewish community, and now we have built a beautiful new synagogue."

The old men of Cologne smiled: they had heard of the Duren synagogue.

"Now," continued Avidan, "we need a sanctified Torah. By the grace of the great Lord God Almighty, Bonn has given us a beautiful set of Scrolls of the Law–it is named 'Aharon.' "

The Cologne scholars were nodding their heads and stroking their beards.

Avidan shook his head. "You will not believe this," he said. "The day came for us to move the Scrolls. I was there to supervise. But did we dare to carry it on a Jewish wagon? Ah, if only God were willing! However, we knew better than even to try. We could not take the chance: Jews have been attacked recently on the road between Bonn and Duren, and we could not risk the most holy Scrolls. So we were forced to arrange for a Gentile carter to make the actual move."

The Cologne scholars frowned and they muttered among themselves.

"Yes," sighed Avidan, "it is a sad story. . . . But let me continue: We hired a wagon to bring the Scrolls to Duren. These parchments, the Aharon Scrolls, are a second set in Bonn. They are kept in the Holy stone Ark, next to the primary Scrolls for the Bonn synagogue. I had the honor of taking them down. I said a blessing, I pulled aside the curtain, and I began to lift the Scrolls. But I could not budge them. The Scrolls were as heavy as the heaviest iron rock. Why, gentlemen, the Aharon set of Scrolls weighed more than sixty times sixty boulders: ten men could not even make them wiggle the slightest bit!"

The sages were silent and stared intently at the Jew from Duren. Some of the old men shook their heads, some tapped their feet, some raised their eyebrows, others frowned. The scholars whispered among themselves. Finally, old Shimshon ha-Zaken said quietly, "Demons."

There was much nodding, muttering, stroking of beards, and shaking of heads. Then white-haired Baruch ben Jacob cleared his throat: "It is demons, Avidan. There is no doubt."

Avidan raised his eyebrows. Baruch continued: "Now, my friend, to expel demons from a place, you must go through a careful ritual. Here is what you do: First, mark off the edges of the haunted area with string."

"With string?" repeated Avidan.

"Yes," said a younger scholar, Elisah ben Samuel, "with string. Next, have ten men carry a copy of the Holy Scriptures around the border."

Avidan creased his forehead. "All right," he said slowly.

"These men must carry the Holy Scriptures," continued Joshua ben Eliezer, "*and* at the same time they must repeat the Priestly Benediction":

> May the Lord bless you and watch over you
> May the Lord make His face to shine upon you
> May the Lord be gracious and good to you
> May the Lord look down kindly on you
> And may He give you peace, amen.

The many scholars nodded, they stroked their beards, they murmured "amen."

"I see," said Avidan, tapping his finger on his chin.

But Lewe ben Anselm said, "This is only the beginning, Avidan. Next, the ten men must walk around the entire border again, and they must recite the anti-demonic psalm. You know that psalm, Avidan – it is the one that begins":

> You who enjoy God's protectiveness
> Resting in His Heavenly shade,
> Admit He is your strong fortress
> Your refuge and your barricade.

The Holy One will soon subdue
The fiercest gales that rainstorms bring
For He is continuously guarding you
In the shelter of His mighty wing.

"and that ends":

When he calls to Me, I will answer:
I will help him in his strife,
Then I will bring him lasting honor
And will give to him long life.

So a good and humble person–
He who trusts and follows Me–
Will enjoy My full salvation
Through a glorious Eternity.

Avidan nodded, but he asked, "Is this really necessary?"

"Is this necessary?" repeated Menahem ben Joel. "Why, it is more than necessary, my friend, it is *absolutely required.* And it is only *part* of what must be done. Next you must say the biblical passage:"

> Yet if their stubborn spirit is broken and they accept their punishment in full, then I will remember My covenant with Jacob and My covenant with Isaac–yes, and My old covenant with Abraham–and I will remember the land.

Menahem's colleague, Moyses ben Nathan, stroked his beard, and he said, "That, Avidan, was from the Book of Leviticus. You must now recite three passages from the Book of Isaiah, namely":

Never again shall you be Forsaken,
No more shall your land be Desolate.

"and":

God is Heaven's custodian–
He also made the earth and sun
He carved out every wondrous canyon
And He set all Life upon the run–
And when the Lord was finally done
God said aloud to everyone:
"I am the Lord, the God of Zion;
There is no other One."

"and":

> May the Lord grant you a blessing on your granaries and on all your farming and on your labors; may the Lord, your God, bless you in the land that He is giving to you, amen.

Avidan was looking very uncomfortable. But old Shimshon ha-Zaken nodded and coughed and said, "Then, Avidan, there is one final pronouncement. Stand still and say: 'With the consent of God, with the consent of the Torah, with the consent of all Israel, and with the consent of those in Heaven and on earth who guard all the Jews, may it be forbidden to any demon, male or female, in human form or animal or invisible, to invade this place from this time forth and for ever more, amen.' "

Then the Cologne scholars nodded and murmured and stroked their beards – and old Rabbi Abraham continued to doze.

"This is such a long and involved procedure," said Avidan doubtfully. He shook his head. Then he looked at Rabbi Abraham. "What do *you* think, Rabbi?" he asked.

The Rabbi opened his eyes. "What?" he asked. He looked up, and he blinked. "What do I think?" he asked. "Well, I think that one should always trust in the Almighty Lord God, blessed be He."

Avidan looked puzzled. "But, Rabbi, how shall we get the Scrolls of the Law to move?" he asked.

The Rabbi raised his eyebrows. "That is quite simple," he answered. "You tell them."

"I tell them?"

"Of course," replied the Rabbi. "You tell them – but you must speak with respect. You must say to the Scrolls: 'Good Scrolls, we are going to travel to – to' . . . Where is it that you are taking them?"

"To Duren," replied Avidan.

"Yes, of course, so tell the Scrolls: 'We are going to travel to the city of Duren,' " continued Rabbi Achselrad. " 'You will then be given a new and consecrated home.' . . . And, Avidan, you must address them by name. Do you know the name of your particular Scrolls?"

"They are called 'Aharon,' " said Avidan.

"Good," said the Rabbi. He tapped his chin. "Then, after you make your polite speech, tie this holy incantation on the top of the

Scrolls." And Rabbi Abraham reached into his desk. He removed a small parchment square and took out his pen. There was the light scritch-scratch of his pen as he set down the appropriate Hebrew inscription. Then he sat back and read and reread the incantation. The Rabbi nodded to himself, he rolled the parchment tightly, he tied it with seven tiny threads, and he handed the amulet to Avidan.

Avidan ben Machir felt better. He smiled, and he stood. Then, with a slight bow, he left the yeshiva and returned to Bonn. In Bonn, Avidan went straight to the synagogue and into the main prayer hall. The Scrolls of the Law stood in the Holy Ark, a stone closet whose wooden doors had carvings of vines and candlesticks and lions. A gold lamp burned constantly in front of the Ark. Inside the Ark, the Scrolls were wrapped in a white cloth stitched with silver braid along the edges and embroidered with purple lions. Dried rose leaves were spread on the floor of the cabinet.

After Avidan had opened the cabinet doors and had pulled aside the heavy curtain, he bowed and he addressed the Scrolls of the Law respectfully. He said, "O Scrolls of the Law–O blessed Aharon–Let me repeat the holy words from the Book of Numbers. When Moses moved the Ark of the Covenant of the Lord, he began each day by reciting":

Almighty Lord rise up anew,
  Protect us at Your side
And may our bitter enemies too
  Be scattered far and wide,
And as to those who scorn You–
  Dissolve them like an ebbing tide.

"So, Aharon, honored Scrolls of the Law, now we must move you from place to place, just as did Moses. Specifically, you are going from Bonn to Duren, in the holy and protected spirit of the great Lord God Almighty, blessed be He. You will then be given a new and consecrated home."

Avidan said this solemnly, standing before the Holy stone Ark. Next, he tied Rabbi Achselrad's amulet onto the top of the Scrolls, alongside the silver chain. Then he lifted the Scrolls. They were as light as a feather, as weightless as a spring leaf. The other men nodded and smiled and took the Scrolls from Avidan. They wrapped the Holy Scrolls inside a velvet cloth, they tied the velvet with a silk band, and they carried the whole bundle out to the horse cart, setting it carefully on a pillow in the back.

(Normally, of course, two adult Jews must accompany the Scrolls whenever they are moved. But Rabbi Abraham had ruled that the names of two adult Jews might instead be written on a parchment and tied next to the amulet: in this way, two Jews would still accompany the Holy Scriptures.)

"Listen," said Avidan to the carter, "take special care of this bundle. It is a sacred Jewish object. Let nothing rest on the package. Do not lie on it yourself–in fact, do not even lean against it."

"Yes, yes," said the carter.

"There is a copy of the Bible wrapped in the bundle," continued Avidan.

"Fine," said the carter.

The carter climbed up to his seat, and he started off on his journey. First, he stopped at the Bonn magistrate's office to pick up a package for the Duren city hall. In less than an hour, the wagon had been filled with other supplies and packages from Bonn, and the driver passed out of the town gates with his deliveries for the city of Duren.

Night descended. The wagon crossed the River Swist. Three evening stars were shining in the eastern sky. When it became too dark to continue, the driver stopped. He stepped down from his seat. He unloaded his pack, and he ate some dinner; then he lay down to sleep. It was a cool evening. The ground was wet and hard. The carter stretched out uncomfortably, then he stood and climbed back into the wagon and he pushed a number of packages aside. He was quite tired. He lay against the bundle that contained the Scrolls, and he fell fast asleep.

Now it was the deep dark hours of the night. Suddenly the driver was awakened. Something hit his shoulder. Something banged his head. His leg hurt. Was there a stab in his back? The carter jumped from the wagon. He peered back inside. There was blackness there and nothing more. He stepped backward. No one was about: there were no animals and there were no people. Could it be spirits? The carter listened–but all that he heard was an ancient silence, await and awash in the nighttide dark.

What could be the problem? Was it the Jewish package? The wagon driver had heard strange stories about the Jews. At night, he had been told, Jewish spirits gather in the synagogues. They wear ghostly prayer shawls, and they hold ghostly services. Once, a man fell asleep in a synagogue and awoke in the midst of these ghosts and was beaten until he ran out into the night. Could these same Jewish spirits be here on the road to Duren? The driver knocked on the side of the wagon to drive away the demons. He listened – he heard nothing – so he knocked again three times.

There were no sounds from the wagon. The wagon driver stood listening: he stood deep in a vast and tangled nighttide world. The wind was far away in the trees; everything seemed empty and alone and distant. Slowly, the carter climbed back into his wagon. Again he lay down. A sharp object hit his leg. The carter jumped from the wagon, shaking and shivering. Was this a demon? The driver could not understand. He looked carefully all about. Animals could sense demons – why was his horse so calm? The carter shook his head. Undoubtedly these ghosts came from that Jewish bundle; cautiously the driver reached into the wagon and pushed the wrapped Scrolls far to one side. Then he climbed back in and lay down on the other packages; he shivered once or twice, but soon he fell asleep again.

The wagon driver slept peacefully throughout the night. He awoke refreshed the next morning. He peeked out of the wagon. The wagon itself was gray and ordinary and harmless. The trees, the grass, the dirt – all seemed quite normal. The road was rutted and empty; the sky was far and blue. The driver stood cautiously. He reached into his pack and got out some bread and cheese. The bread was chewy. The cheese was crumbly and strong. And now the carter felt revived; in fact, he felt very fine and young and strong. So he shrugged his shoulders and took a deep breath. He stretched his back. Finally, the carter climbed onto the front seat, he tapped his horse on the flank, and he continued on his way.

Late in the day, the driver reached Duren. He stopped at the city hall and unloaded packages. He went down another street and stopped again. Eventually he made his way into the Jewish Quarter where he delivered the Scrolls of the Law to the new synagogue. The men of Duren took the bundle. They unwrapped it, and, with prayers and blessings, they set it in its honored place in the Holy stone Ark.

The Scrolls called "Aharon" served the Jewish community of Duren for many generations. When finally the parchment was so worn and the ink was so chipped that it could no longer be repaired, the "Aharon" was buried in the Duren cemetery in a clay container and pious Jews always requested to be buried nearby. And as for the wagon driver? He shook his head when he remembered that night, but he never mentioned his strange experience to anyone, and my grandmother only learned of this story at night in a far-off, long-ago, nighttide medieval dream.

Good evening—I was just resting my eyes. Feel free to join me here by the stove. An old man can doze forever by a warm stove; I suppose that is because I have been especially restful during these later years of mine. . . .

What is that, Rabbi? Well, I mean simply that the good Lord God follows the lead of each man. I have been calm and restful—so God gives me sleep. Were I active and energetic, then of course He would keep me awake for all hours of the night in order to give me the chance to play out whatever it was that I was itching to do. We have free will; we control our own lives. Is that not what you preach, Rabbi? Certainly Maimonides said, "A man has control over all his actions. He himself determines whether he does right or wrong: in neither case is he controlled by fate or by the detailed plans of God."

Of course when He turns His mind to it, the Omniscient One *knows* all. The Talmud says that "everything is foreseen by God." But the Talmud goes on to add that "nonetheless, full freedom of choice is given to man." God can see all, but He need not necessarily intervene. *You* choose your own path, Rabbi, and then the great Lord God Almighty gives you the opportunity to persevere, to follow out that path.

Yes, each man chooses the nature of his own life. And as to the responsibility for good or for evil? That rests solely on one's own shoulders. Moreover, because the whole of the human race descends from the same one ancestor, no one can plead that his wicked behavior is the fault of his parent: we all have an equal heritage and we all have an equal heritage to be good, should we so desire. . . .

What is that, Rabbi? Sleepiness? Of course this is relevant to my sleepiness. I do not think that I have it muddled at all . . . Well, just listen a moment–the reasoning is quite straightforward. Now, I begin with Psalm 18:

To the faithful man
You are ever-present,
With the blameless man
You are loyal and constant–

But with the savage man
You are curt and callous,
With the vengeful man
You are harsh and pitiless.

You raise the humble man
To a place of trust
But bring the haughty man
Down to earth's dry dust.

Each man shall be allotted his chosen course of life, says the psalmist. And for me it is very simple: I have chosen a quiet and sleepy life.

And to top it all off, the first verse of the same psalm points out how we can all sleep safe and sound and secure under God's protective right arm:

I enjoy God's protectiveness
Resting in His Heavenly shade
I love the Lord–my true fortress
My refuge and my barricade.

From this, then, I learn that my chosen life-style of rest and sleep is holy–so you can see that my reasoning is quite clear-cut.

Do not forget, you have often pointed out that we set the tone for our own lives, Rabbi. To the generous, the Lord is generous. To the miserly–well, the Omniscient Lord God holds back His beneficence from them. Nonetheless, we can always change our ways. For example, my grandmother once told me about Nachum, the old miser of Cologne, a man who finally changed his course and for whom the Lord changed *His* course also:

This took place a long, long time ago, in medieval Cologne, where, on the western outskirts of the city, lived a rich man named Nachum ben Aryeh ha-Kohen. Nachum had businesses and lands and gold, and he had chests full of silver pots and plates with detailed engravings and inlaid precious stones. And where did he get all his wealth? Nachum was a moneylender: he was a banker and a broker, and once he got his hands on a coin he would do everything in his power to keep it in his storehouses forever.

Nachum was rich–also he was stingy. He never gave a thing to the poor. He helped no one with money or food or clothes. He even avoided the synagogue except on holidays so that no one could ask casually for a donation. To put money in the poor box felt like a waste. If a man was poor, thought Nachum, then he had already proved that he was incapable of holding on to money; the poor are poor because they are spendthrifts and lazy.

To Nachum, holding a polished gold coin in his hands was soothing and secure. Whenever he had to give away even a single coin, his life felt empty and his stomach got hollow. Nachum could not share: he cared far too deeply for the things that he owned, and he felt that his belongings were ruined if other people handled them. Nachum loaned nothing. He bought few things, and in general he avoided contact with other people. The townsfolk nicknamed him "Nachum the Miser."

Nachum was tightfisted. Nonetheless, he performed one community service. Nachum was a *mohel:* he circumcised newborn Jewish boys and consecrated them into the faith of Yahweh. Nachum once said: "I must do *something* to be a good Jew, and circumcision is the prime initiation ceremony for Judaism." Circumcision comes on the eighth day after birth, when the little baby also formally receives his name. Some scholars say that circumcision originated with the Egyptians and that Joshua introduced the custom to the Jews at Gilgal, where he "rolled away the reproach of the Egyptians" by circumcising the Israelites. However, Nachum believed the more literal biblical history that sets the beginning of the custom back at the original covenant of God with the Patriarch Abraham – in the Book of Genesis, God says to Abraham: "This is how you shall keep My covenant between Myself and you and your descendants after you; circumcise yourselves, every male among you." Although he was an unsocial character in all other respects, Nachum surprised others and himself by performing circumcisions – and listen to this: he never charged a penny for the service.

Nachum ben Aryeh often sat in his bean garden. One morning as he was sitting in the garden and thinking of nothing in particular, a stranger walked in and said, "Good morning sir, my wife has had a little son. I would like you to consecrate him."

Nachum the Miser looked up and said, "Well, this is my duty. Wait a moment, and I will follow you home. Tell me – where do you live?"

"Unfortunately, I live quite far away," said the stranger. "But I will drive fast. I have good horses and a light wagon. And in the end, I will reward you for your troubles. You can have, if you wish, a large chest of gold – in fact, I will give you ten gold coins in advance."

At the mention of gold, Nachum's eyes lit up. Nachum never charged for his services, but he did not mind accepting presents. The stranger took ten gold coins from a purse. Nachum held them in his hands. The coins felt smooth and warm and powerful. Nachum smiled and went into his house. He took a bunch of keys from a hook in the hallway. In a storeroom, Nachum looked over the securely locked chests that held his treasure, he added the ten gold coins to one of the chests, he replaced the keys, then he bolted the door and the gate and he followed the stranger into the street.

The waiting wagon had a cushion on the front bench, and the horses were fine and strong animals. The stranger headed east. At first, he drove at a slow unhurried pace. Nachum the Miser knew the countryside well. "Hmm, I did not know that there were any Jewish folk living out this way," he thought to himself. Soon the stranger whipped his horses and they tore along at a great speed. They flew by fields and woods and mountains and valleys. They drove all day, until a mist fell and the night began to descend.

They had driven all day, and Nachum had not heard one single bird or insect; he had not heard a tree rustle or a brook splash. Still they continued, on and on and on into the night, and when the moon rose at last, Nachum looked fearfully around him. And then–but how could this be? The mist had risen, and it seemed as if the horses cast no shadows in the bright moonlight! The wagon sped on at a breath-taking speed. They neighed and they snorted and pounded the road. The journey was an endless flight with the wind.

Finally, Nachum built up his courage. In a shaky voice he asked the driver, "Where are you taking me?"

"Oh, do not worry–we will soon be at my home." As the stranger spoke, the dawn broke and the sun shone on a little golden-green hamlet. It was a village in a valley, in a vast meadow between two wooded hills, and all was wet and green and peaceful.

The road wound gently up to a thatched house. The wagon stopped, the men got down, and immediately they were surrounded by strangers who greeted them and led off the horses. *"Sholom aleikhem"* said voices high and low, rich and dry. The stranger was walking ahead into the house. Nachum followed. The hallway was dim and cold; inside it seemed more like a cave than a house. The walls were stone. The rooms were caverns with high, dark, stone ceilings, but they were filled with finely carved wooden tables, chairs, and shelves. The floors had thick red carpets. Tapestries hung on the walls. Candles were lit in every corner. Dim lightly ringing echoes came from every-where at once.

Nachum stood silently. He was weak and dizzy from his ride. Everything seemed distant–the walls and the ceilings were far, far away. Candlelight sparkled from far edges of tabletops and silver dishes. Doors had carved ivory handles. Chests had bands of iron and inlaid gems. Even the nails in the wood glittered–were they silver or even gold?

His host was talking: "I must go and see to my guests. Feel free to walk around, Nachum Aryeh."

Hearing his full name scared Nachum. Was this an evil omen? Nachum watched his host disappear around a dark corner. He looked around. Sculptures were set in niches in the walls. These niches were like little rooms containing carved animals and tiny human figures. There were miniature tables and trees. Nachum put out his hand. The little figures were as smooth as a gemstone and as cold as ice. It was like a dream. Nachum wandered from room to room. Everything was mysterious. Curious paintings were everywhere. All manner of carved objects and strange wall hangings filled the corners. At last, Nachum stepped into a room with a young woman in a bed and a child beside her in a crib. The crib was made of silver and the blankets were edged with gold.

As soon as she saw Nachum, the woman called him over to her bedside.

"Ah, thank the good Lord God – I am happy to see you here," she said quietly. "You will be doing a wonderful deed for me by circumcising this tiny boy."

Nachum was frightened, and he remained silent.

"I know you are afraid," continued the woman. "As you suspect, you are now among demons. My husband is a demon. The other men living here are evil spirits too. And all the wonderful things that you see here? They are only illusions: they are as unreal as mist, and they would dissolve if they were ever removed from this house."

The young woman sighed. After a moment, she said, "I am a human being like you. I am trapped here forever – but you will be able to return home."

Nachum's mouth was dry and his arms were weak.

The young woman looked up at him. "You must think that you are lost," said the woman. "Well, you are not – you must simply avoid certain things."

"Quickly, tell me what they are," said Nachum.

"These are the rules," said the woman. "Do not taste any food or drink while you are here. Then, do not accept any presents, regardless of how trifling they seem."

Nachum nodded: he had heard these rules before when dealing with creatures of the Otherworld. The young mother smiled and patted Nachum on the hand. Nachum left the room, wandering through the dark passageways until he found his way back to the main room where his host had left him.

Soon the demon host returned, talking and joking with his friends. It was the day before the circumcision, and together the demon and Nachum prepared the room. They put a chair–an ornate wooden chair with a silk cushion–at the wall on the west side of the room; this was for the Prophet Elijah, the Messenger of the Covenant, who comes along with the child and is present at every circumcision. Nachum put a copy of the Holy Scriptures on the chair and covered it with a plain silk handkerchief. Would the Prophet Elijah actually come to this unholy place? Nachum was uncertain, but the demon seemed to have no doubts.

"Come with me, and meet my son," said the demon. Once again, Nachum the Miser entered the room of the mother and child. Weakly, Nachum intoned prayers and incantations to guard the child against evil spirits and ghosts who populated the shadows, waiting to harm newborn children. "How can I be saying these things in a den of demons?" thought Nachum–but he continued through the entire ritual because he was too afraid to stop.

Next, a vast rich meal was laid out in the dining room. The demons ate and drank and talked and laughed. Nachum sat uncomfortably. "I am unwell and not hungry," he said whenever someone passed food to him. Candles made the room seem bright and shiny, but the soul of Nachum the Miser was dim and miserable. He barely heard what anyone said. The room seemed cloudy; gloomy shapes swirled around and around in his mind.

Was it hours and hours that they sat and ate? To Nachum, it seemed days. Later he lay in a bed that smelled of gentle meadow perfume, a bed of the softest, coolest silk, but Nachum could not fall asleep. He lay awake, shaky and silent. He heard strange sounds, he saw black shapes, he felt cold vapors.

Then came the morning, the eighth day after the child's birth. Nachum dressed shakily. The demon host led the miser back to the main room, and the child was brought in a small white cart. The other demons crowded around. Wine and raisins and a cup of oil were put on the polished table. Nachum lit two candles. Nachum's chest was tight. His hand shook, his throat was dry, his legs were weak, and his heart beat too fast and too loudly. The air was thick and heavy, like cotton in his throat. In a strangled voice, Nachum sang the service as best he could, but as the congregation of demons chanted with him, the strange wail of their voices made him shiver and shake and it chilled his poor old Jewish blood.

The prayers were over. Quickly Nachum ben Aryeh ha-Kohen performed the circumcision. "Amen," said the father. Everyone cheered and began to eat pieces of honey cake and golden bread. "It is a personal day of fasting for me," said Nachum weakly when anyone looked at him. The demons raised their eyebrows and shrugged their dark and hairy shoulders. Presents appeared: gold and silver balls and toys, small dolls, embroidered blankets, and baked goods in strange shapes laid out on carved bone dishes.

Someone took the little baby back to his mother, and the crowd moved into the dining room. A cock was killed and roasted. Why, these demons were celebrating a holy rite! How could this be? Would God accept this mixture of the sacred and the profane? Or would Nachum suddenly be struck dead? Nachum shook his head – he did not understand how all of this could be happening.

Eventually, the demon father came over to Nachum. "You have not been eating, my friend," he said. Nachum mumbled, "It is a personal fast day." So the demon host said, "Fine, we will eat together later, after sunset, when your fast day is over." Now the miser's heart sank completely. "I am doomed," he thought. "They will keep me here forever – they may even kill me." He sat and shivered and shook.

Hour by hour the day dragged on, and then the black night fell. Nachum sat miserably in a corner, watching the endless eating and talking and laughing. It seemed a nightmare. Again the demon host brought Nachum to the main table. "I am not feeling well," said Nachum hoarsely. The demon shrugged and turned his attention to his friends. Nachum sat in a stupor.

Suddenly Nachum's host arose and motioned Nachum to follow him down some damp steps. "Oh no! This is definitely my last hour on earth," thought the miser as he followed his host through a dark and gloomy passageway. The demon opened a heavy wooden door. But instead of ending up in a dungeon, the Miser found himself surrounded by beautiful treasures. There were wooden dishes and cups, candlesticks and key holders and silver spice boxes. Gold coins were heaped in a chest on a table. Ivory carvings filled another box on the floor. Fine silks were piled on a chair.

"You have done me a great service," said the demon. "I know you do not charge a fee, but as a present I want you to accept a token of my appreciation. Choose whatever you like from among all these things."

The miser knew that these treasures were only mirages; also he knew the dangers of accepting any gift, no matter how small or worthless. To eat or drink in the mystical dark Otherworld or to take even the tiniest item would bind him there forever: he would never escape and return home alive. Every child in medieval Europe knew this. Nachum rubbed his fingers along his shirt, and he shook his head.

"Ah, if only I could take a jewel or two–just one small diamond. If only I dared to touch them," he said to himself. He could almost feel his hands reaching out toward the glittering, shining, wondrous objects, but he did not actually move. After what felt like hours of silence, he finally said out loud, "Thank you–but as you know, I accept no fees. I am wealthy. I have all the silver and gems that I want at home. Thank you just the same."

The demon raised his eyebrows but said nothing and only led the miser into the next room. This room was small and cramped and the rock walls were lined with hooks, and on the hooks were bunches of keys of all sizes and shapes. "Perhaps," said the demon, "you would like to take a set of keys home with you. Look here at this one, for example."

Nachum stared. Then he reached out. Those were his keys! They were the keys to his locked chests of gold and jewels and money: they were the keys to his storerooms.

"Those are my keys!" cried the Miser. "How did you get them?"

"The keys were given to me, my friend, when you gave them up," said the demon in a cold voice. "Yes, you gave them up when you never helped the poor, the needy, or the sick. Do you think that things in the world are yours to *own?* Well, they are not! Things are merely on loan to you. And if *you* do not have the strength to pass them on to others, then I will gladly give them away for you."

The demon held the keys beyond Nachum's reach. Then he slowly put them back on the hook, and he pushed Nachum out of the room.

Nachum ben Aryeh was shaking and shivering. His eyes did not focus well: everything seemed blurred. Nachum's head ached. His arms felt like leaden stones. "I wonder if I am dying," he thought miserably.

Vaguely, Nachum heard the demon say, "It is time for you to leave." Somehow Nachum found himself at the outer door. A wagon appeared. Nachum was in a fog, a cloud, a stupor. Was he riding in a wagon, or was he dreaming? It seemed as if the wagon ran and ran silently through the dark night. Out of the green woodland valley they sped, across the plain, and back toward the human towns and villages. Clouds flew by. Mists cleared. The wagon stopped at the miser's door, and he got down. No sooner did his feet touch the ground than the horses and the driver vanished from sight and a cold chill wind blew through the black night sky.

Nachum ben Aryeh ha-Kohen stepped into his front door. His keys were on the hook where he had left them. But were these really his keys? Shakily, he took them down and opened his treasure chests and his strongboxes. Everything seemed in order. Nachum looked behind his locked doors. The ten gold coins initially given him by the stranger were gone–otherwise, all Nachum's original valuables remained safe and secure and untouched.

But Nachum the Miser did not feel safe and secure and untouched. He went to his bedroom; he sat on his bed. He sat there all night and then through the next morning. In the afternoon, he went to the synagogue, but he felt dull and heavy and old and he did not respond when others talked to him. Was he praying? He himself did not even know. At night, he managed to walk home. He fell into his bed, and he slept the dreamless sleep of the dead.

The next morning was bright. "What a terrible dream I have been having," thought Nachum. He was ravenous, and he ate a large breakfast. He put two gold coins into his pocket and he went to the synagogue. After the service, he dropped the coins into the poor box. Now Nachum felt strong and young and fine. He went home. Then he walked about in his vegetable garden, talking to himself.

Nachum looked at his bean plants. "I am not too old," he thought. "I still have the freedom of choice." And then, although there was no one to hear, he said aloud, "I think I will give a special donation to the Benevolent Society."

Nachum went to the rabbi, who listened silently and with open eyes. The rabbi called in the shammas. The shammas too raised his eyebrows–but he gladly accepted the money. And soon it was apparent that old Nachum had become a new man. He distributed clothes and food and valuables to the destitute. He gave money to the poor box in the synagogue and to the Benevolent Society. Needy people blessed his name. People no longer thought of Nachum as a miser; in fact, the community elected him *Parnas* of the congregation during the next year.

Nachum himself continued to live modestly, but now he found ways to help others, not only with his money but also with his time and his advice. Each Tuesday afternoon, he sat in the synagogue and counseled young Jews on business matters. Each month, he paid an allowance to three families that had taken in orphans. Often, he gave dowries for poor girls. When he heard of someone who was ill or suffering from financial difficulties, he paid their taxes. In his old age, he gave his business free and clear to two of his longtime employees. Then, after he retired, Nachum divided each of his days into two parts: half he spent in his garden, and half he spent in the yeshiva, as one of the respected old scholars. Eventually, Nachum ben Aryeh ha-Kohen died quietly and contentedly, and when he was buried, a long train of men slowly followed his coffin to its eternal rest, amen.

Rabbi, I was just talking about you to Reb Marcus. I told him you are our Daniel. The hero Daniel could explain riddles. He could unbind spells, he could solve problems, he could untie knots. And it is the same with you. Of course it has always been the same with great rabbis: holy men are blessed untiers.

. . . Ah, Rabbi–do not be so modest. . . .

Yes, yes–sit down. I am always happy to talk. A story? You are always asking for stories–it is fortunate that my grandmother told me so many. Let me see . . . well, speaking of Daniel, there is the old story that Rabbi Petahiah told about Daniel. . . .

Exactly, my friend–that was Petahiah ben Jacob, the world traveler. Old Rabbi Petahiah toured the entire world, far from Germany–but let me begin in Germany, in Cologne, with the young Rabbi Asher ben Yehiel. When he was the leading Jewish scholar in Cologne, Rabbi Asher spent most of his time writing and reading. Asher studied the Torah and the Talmud in the little back room of the yeshiva, where for centuries the Cologne rabbis had worked and thought and argued with themselves, and above this study room was a loft for storage. One sunny morning, Rabbi Asher felt too lazy to work seriously or to think deeply or to argue passionately. Instead, he was rooting around among the old manuscripts, when he found a letter from Rabbi Petahiah ben Jacob of Regensburg to one of Asher's predecessors, Rabbi Abraham ben Alexander, the mystic Achselrad of Cologne.

"*My dear Rabbi Abraham*–

"I have just met a fine young man, a Jew from Strassburg. He has agreed to carry this letter to Rabbi Eliezer ben Joshua, also of Strassburg, who I am certain will then arrange to transport it to you. I write to wish you and your family well, to convey my fondest greetings to all the Jews of your blessed community in Cologne, and to praise the good Lord God (blessed be He) and His Almighty Name for ever and ever, amen.

"I will not trouble you with the details of my many wagon rides and my subsequent sea voyages. Suffice it to say that safely they brought me here to the Oriental regions, regions that are so near to the great Holy Land where someday the Messiah shall return and deliver us and resurrect all souls and rebuild the Temple on Zion, amen. I write now in order to record for you some details of the lands and the peoples that I have seen in these old and foreign realms. The bright and glorious hand of God is visible everywhere, if only we look–praise the Lord Yahweh-Elohim.

"As you might imagine, my old friend, I have had many, many adventures in arriving here. I hope–if the good Lord is willing–to relate these events to you in person. For now, let me just say that after touring the Holy Lands of Palestine, I turned northeast, and eventually I found myself in the ancient city of Palmyra. Once upon a time Palmyra was a great and wondrous center of the old world, but now it is a collection of the poorest Arab hovels.

"Palmyra is known among the Arabs as Tadmor. It is a week's journey northeast of Damascus and five days' journey from the River Euphrates. Here, in the Syrian desert–in the dry lands rising far above sea level–is an oasis. It is an ancient rest stop for caravans, and the great trade routes all cross here. Once, the city had strong walls, but now they are broken. There was a famous palace called the 'Temple of the Sun,' but recently a terrible earthquake knocked down many of Palmyra's old buildings; all that remains of the temple are a few ruined columns, and its courtyard is now an open market.

"The marketplaces are quiet and poor. At one time, however, Palmyra had rich traders and merchants. There was an aristocracy. The city had shops for silks, jewels, perfumes, and fine clothes. Pearls, incense, and carpets were traded. Treasures were collected, stored, stolen, and hidden. There were even Palmyran armies.

"Many people still live in the town. There are two or three wealthy estates, with well-maintained courtyards and gardens and fountains. In the eastern sector, two thousand Jews live within the city walls. But these Hebrews know little of the ways of European Jews–Palmyra has no contact with Europe and it does all of its business through the Arab world.

"Jews are Jews, however, and I have been welcomed warmly. Everyone wants to talk with me and to hear of my travels and especially to learn about Germany. In return, I am flooded with local stories and anecdotes. And, Abraham, how many tales have I heard about lions! Why is this? Undoubtedly, it is because lions populate the grasslands and jungles not far from here, and once you meet a lion, you do not forget it. Lions are sleepy-eyed and powerful. Their muscles ripple at every step, and their paws are like tree trunks. Lions fill the Holy Scriptures–most notably, of course, there is the famous story of Daniel. Recently I have heard a strange variant of that tale–let me write it down for you:

"In the vicinity of ancient Babylon, there once lived a terrifying and mighty beast. It was a large and ancient lizard, almost a dragon, and the local Babylonians feared it and worshiped it as a god. In those olden days there was a brave Babylonian general named Belshazzar; Belshazzar was a prince, the son of the last Semitic king of Babylon, whose name was Nabonidus.

"Besides being a warrior and a nobleman, Belshazzar was also a priest of the local Babylonian religion. Belshazzar heard that a certain Jew–our very own Daniel–was telling people that the dragon was only a fierce animal and that it was not a god. Belshazzar called Daniel to the royal court. 'Listen here,' said the general, 'you may have your own religion, but you cannot go around speaking poorly of ours. This dragon is more than a wondrous monster: it is one of our gods. And clearly this is a living beast–therefore, it is a living god. Now, I expect you to change your attitude and to acknowledge this fact. It would also be a good plan for you to show this god some respect and to pray to it for forgiveness and protection, my friend.'

"Daniel frowned. 'Your Honor,' he said, 'I am a Jew. I was born a Jew and I will die a Jew. I pray only to the one Lord, the ancient God of my fathers. He is our eternal protector. *He* is the only living God, mighty and awe-inspiring, omnipotent and timeless.'

"Belshazzar sighed. 'Listen, Mr. Jew,' said the prince, 'if you do not think that this lizard is a deity, then obviously you imagine that you can kill it.'

" 'Certainly,' said Daniel. He thought a moment, and then he said, 'And, Your Highness, I can slay it without holding a lance or a sword or a knife.'

" 'Very well,' said Belshazzar, 'do your best.'

"Daniel nodded and bowed, and he went home. In his kitchen, Daniel cooked a mixture of tar and fat and flax and hair, and he flavored it with lamb's meat. Then he made some iron hatchets with many sharp points, and he rolled the hatchets inside a thick lump of his sticky mix. The whole lump was smooth on the outside and deadly on the inside. Daniel took this weapon to the dragon's cave, and he set it down at the opening. Then he made strange mewing noises in order to entice the giant lizard to come out and eat the weapon.

"Soon the dragon lizard emerged. It looked like a huge serpent. It had a long, twisting, scaly body. It had four legs and two wings. It had a fearsome head with red eyes and two huge fangs and a forked tongue that whipped in and out continually. The creature smelled the lamb's meat, it roared and opened its mouth, and it swallowed the lump whole. Then it began to crawl toward Daniel. The fat and tar dissolved in the dragon's stomach. The claws on the hatchet were as sharp as the finest knives; they began to dig into the animal's stomach, and soon the dragon ripped itself apart as it crawled along the ground. With a massive groan, the terrible animal closed its eyes and it died a fearsome death.

"Daniel grabbed the beast by a wing, and he tugged and pulled and dragged it back to the prince. 'Well, sir,' said Daniel, 'here is your god.'

"A number of other priests were standing in the court when Daniel entered. They were angry. 'Black magic,' said one. 'Evil trickery,' said another. 'Sorcery and demons,' said a third. The priests went directly to King Nabonidus and demanded that the Jew be put to death.

"Nabonidus shrugged his shoulders. 'We have enough trouble,' he thought, 'without having to contend with Jewish sorcerers.' 'Take the Jew to the lions' pit,' he declared. So Daniel was put in chains. He was led to the king's huge lions' pit, where seven hungry lions paced back and forth and back and forth. Usually, the keepers fed the lions two cows and two sheep each day. When Daniel was thrown into the pit, he went in alone – there was no other food that day.

"Ah, but our ancient God is great – the Lord is good. And so here is what happened:

"At the same time, in the far-off land of Palestine, the Prophet Habakkuk (who was a native of the city of Shunem in northern Israel) was busy doing the Lord's work, which consisted of spreading his motto: 'The righteous man shall live and prosper to the extent of his faithfulness to the Law of the Lord.' It was evening. Habakkuk boiled some pottage to feed the local reapers, the poor migrant farm workers. Habakkuk put the pottage and some bread in his sack, and then he walked out to the fields to feed the men and women who were working late that evening. Just then, an angel of the Lord appeared. He stood in front of Habakkuk the prophet, saying, 'Go, Habakkuk, and carry this pottage to the town of Babylon. Give it to Daniel, who is stuck in the king's lions' pit.'

"Habakkuk stepped back. He raised his eyebrows. Then he answered, 'My lord, I have never seen the town of Babylon. I am afraid that I know nothing of lions or lions' pits, and I do not know a man named Daniel.'

"The angel of the Lord shook his head. He reached over and he picked up the prophet by the nape of the neck, just as a cat carries her kitten. Together they flew off in the wink of an eye to the city of Babylon on the east bank of the River Euphrates. Habakkuk saw the vast city walls. He saw the wondrous stone palace originally built by the king Nebuchadrezzar. A smooth road led down from the palace in a gentle circle, and at the edge of the road was a hole in the ground surrounded by an iron fence – this was the king's lions' pit. The angel of the Lord set the Prophet Habakkuk, with his satchel of food, inside the iron fence in the town of Babylon, far, far from Habakkuk's home in the Holy Land of Palestine.

"And when he had recovered his breath and when his heart had stopped beating at twice its normal rate, the Prophet Habakkuk took a deep breath, he swallowed twice, and he called down, 'Daniel – Daniel, are you in there? Take this food which our God has sent for you.'

"Daniel looked up. 'What? Who are you? What is happening?' he asked.

"Habakkuk handed down the food, but he said nothing more. Daniel stretched out his arm. He reached for the pottage, which was in two watertight skins. He took hold of the loaves of bread. And Daniel said, 'Hallelujah, to our one great God!' He ate the bread and he threw the pottage to the lions. Then he prayed, and he said, 'O Lord our God, You have remembered me. You have not forsaken all those who follow and who love You – hallelujah and amen, Ancient One.'

"Then Daniel lay down, and he slept a peaceful sleep. And so it came to pass that each day the angel of the Lord brought the Prophet Habakkuk to feed Daniel and the lions, and each day Daniel lived safely. After seven long days and seven long nights, the king sent his son Belshazzar to check on the lions. Belshazzar looked down. There was Daniel, sitting calmly on a rock in the lions' den. The prince was shocked. He called the keepers. 'Why have you protected this Jew?' he asked. But they answered, 'We have done nothing, Your Highness. We have not even fed the lions.'

"Daniel called up to Belshazzar. 'It is true, prince,' he said, 'my God has protected me.'

"Daniel climbed up to the edge of the fence, and the guardsmen and the lionkeepers helped him to climb over the top. 'Your Honor,' said Daniel to Belshazzar, 'the Jewish God cares for His flock of followers.'

"Belshazzar took Daniel back to his father. Old Nabonidus looked at Daniel and raised his eyebrows. 'This Jewish sorcery is quite powerful,' thought the king. 'It can cause trouble.' 'Well,' he said aloud, 'clearly this Jew is not destined to die now. You are free to go.' And Daniel walked safely out from the court of Nabonidus and back into the city of Babylon, where the ancient Lord Almighty continued to protect him, amen.

"That is the local story, Abraham – and I will end my letter now. Palmyra is filled with new friends, but at night I think of you, my old friend. Undoubtedly you are sitting quietly in the bright, warm, magic light of our ancient protective Lord God, the same God Who watched us and protected us in Cologne just as He does here in Palmyra. Do you remember when we too fought dragons and lions once upon a time? It was summers and summers gone by, in magical hot afternoons on the banks of the River Rhine. Now it seems to me like a Night Tale from long ago. Did it really happen? I remember two small boys in a very big world. There were tall scratchy grasses and a blue bowl of a sky far, far overhead. Great and awesome beasts stalked somewhere just out of sight. Perhaps they were lions and dragons. But of course the good Lord God smiled down and protected us–besides, we were brave and strong, as only little boys will ever be again. So amen, my brave old friend–hallelujah and a warm, warm amen.

"Your childhood friend,
Petahiah, the son of Jacob"

Hello, Rabbi, I will be with you in a moment–I cannot leave until every tablecloth is folded, otherwise the day has not ended properly. . . . There, now I am finished at last and can sit next to you by the stove. Tomorrow night begins the Sabbath again, praise the great Lord God, amen.

To me, the Sabbath always means mystical poetry. My grandmother said that it was Rabbi Abraham Achselrad who first introduced mystical poetry during the synagogue service for certain Sabbaths in the springtime. On the Sabbath *Zakhor,* before *Purim,* and on the Sabbath *Parah,* just thereafter, Rabbi Abraham had his congregants read the poetry of Eleazar Kalir from his *Shivata.* Achselrad also loved the poetry of Meir ben Isaac of Worms and the poetry of Rabbah ben Nahmani of Pumbedita in old Babylonia. Do you know any of the Rabbah's hymns? One that I remember is his little verse for the Sabbath:

The old lane, the spring lane
A warm light like golden grain
White rain, bright rain
Sabbath morn in Heav'n again.

I wonder if old Rabbi Abraham ever heard that little rhyme? I am certain he would have liked it. Although he was very pious, he was a mystic, and he was also a romantic. In his younger years, Abraham had had many wild adventures, traveling far and wide. Once, he visited King Ferdinand II of Castile, the king of Leon.

. . . I have mentioned this before? Did I tell you that King Ferdinand was a simple man with no political talents? His reign of thirty years was unremarkable, although there was constant petty fighting until he beheaded some unruly local nobles. When he died at age sixty-one, Ferdinand II was thought of as a good knight and as a stalwart soldier. But I cannot help wondering: Did he die happy? As my grandmother once told me: "The truly happy man, the man with God's warm blessing, is he who ends a full life contented with himself." . . .

What is that? Abraham ben Alexander? As I said, my grandmother reported that he had spent one Sabbath in the royal court at Leon, in northern Spain. There, surrounded by the courtiers, he dissolved an attendant page boy: he made the young man disappear by dispersing him into thin air after dinner.

. . . No, no, I am not inventing this – my grandmother said this is exactly what she had heard.

And this same strange Rabbi Abraham was a prolific writer too. Unfortunately, his most famous Kabbalistic tome, the *Keter Shem Tov* – a book of mystic lore – has never been published; it still lies in the Cologne yeshiva as forgotten crumbling papers above the rabbi's study room. Old Abraham Achselrad was always writing in this manuscript – although I do not know whether he continually wrote new things or whether he merely polished and rewrote the old. In any case, my grandmother said that it was in the dim early hours of the morning, while he was working on the *Keter Shem Tov,* that Rabbi Abraham looked up, and in the yellow light of the candle he saw a holy sight.

At that time, Abraham ben Alexander was an old man. He had written many books. He had thought deeply for long hours. He had seen strange and wondrous sights. But his favorite memories were still of early days; they were springtime days when he and Petahiah had been young yeshiva students. Long ago, the two boys had played in the fields outside the city walls. In warm weather, they had lain on the dusty banks of the wide River Rhine with rains falling gently all around. And as old Abraham Achselrad thought back and remembered those fine times, he smiled. He felt a cool wind. He saw a springtime light. Was it like this long ago, on a warm afternoon, when the rains fell like mist on his face? The candle flickered lightly, and Rabbi Abraham ben Alexander thought that there, in the doorway of the old yeshiva of Cologne on the River Rhine, stood a stooped and ancient man with a misty dusty beard.

"Hello?" said the Rabbi.

The figure remained silent in the doorway. Rabbi Abraham blinked and winked and rubbed his eyes. The specter wavered dimly. Was it the candlelight? Were Achselrad's old eyes playing tricks?

Achselrad was an old man. He sat with an old man's slouch, and he waited with an old man's patience, watching with old man's eyes. So, time passed quietly until, eventually, the specter in the doorway smiled and it spoke, and when the figure talked, it talked in a quiet ancient voice.

"Greetings, good Rabbi. My name is Rabbah bar Nahmani."

A little breeze skittered through the corner of the old study room.

Abraham Achselrad nodded. He tapped his chin and stroked his beard. Rabbah bar Nahmani had been a great Babylonian teacher at the beginning of the fourth century. The Rabbah had been charismatic. He had been larger than life. For twenty-two years he headed the Jewish Academy at Pumbeditha. And what an arguer he was! Waving his hands in the air and talking at an incredible rate, he tied together obscure points, he cleanly and neatly summarized the most complex of ideas. He could flip a statement on its head and its side and with a slice of his tongue he would cut it in half. He would listen for a moment and then he would unearth deeply hidden contradictions (which he could dissolve away like a mist), and this won him the title "uprooter of mountains."

The Rabbah radiated energy, logic, and clarity. When scholars followed the holy words as the Rabbah recited them, the edges of the letters actually became more crisp. The words were large and bold and thick. The lines were clean and smooth and even. The ink became pungent. Each page of text stood like a solid rock.

Rabbah bar Nahmani spoke well and he spoke forcefully – he said what he thought. He said his mind clearly and loudly, and he was always irritating the local officials. One day, the Rabbah denounced the government's school tax, and he persuaded all his twelve hundred students to refuse to pay. A royal bailiff was sent out with orders to seize him–but the Rabbah was forewarned and he fled during the night. Rabbah bar Nahmani trimmed his beard and wore old clothes. He wandered through the outlying countryside. Unfortunately, he was no outdoorsman, and soon he died of exposure in the jungles. When his body was discovered by searchers from the academy, they brought it back to Pumbedita and seven days of mourning followed. The royal Queen Mother heard the news, and she felt so badly that she herself paid the school's tax money and in this way the Jewish community was once again financially safe.

Rabbi Abraham had heard this and many, many other stories about the Rabbah. Old Achselrad looked at the spirit, he raised his eyebrows, and he asked, "You are the Babylonian 'uprooter'?"

The Rabbah smiled. "Ah, good Rabbi, that is what some people have called me. When I was in my middle years, I roared out at sloppy thoughts. It seemed to the young men around me that I could uproot all weak and careless statements. I had no patience for those glib bits of speech that pedantics throw about. I could not tolerate the half sentences that roll off the tongue and that slip into the ear but that dissolve like swirls of midges when you try to close in on them for a closer look."

The spirit of Rabbah bar Nahmani nodded to himself. Then he continued: "That was in Babylonia, long, long ago. Apparently, Babylonia has become a rather vague region nowadays. In our day, Babylonia was the whole district between the two great rivers of western Asia, the River Tigris and the River Euphrates. Northern Babylonia is mountainous, while southern Babylonia is flat and marshy. Each region was like a different country and each vied to be supreme. In the north were the cities of Akkad, Babylon, Borsippa, Kish, Kutha, and Sippara; in the south were Erech, Eridu, Gishban, Larsa, and Ur. The Jewish kingdom in Babylonia was centered in the north, at Nehardea and Pumbedita, and after the destruction of Pumbedita at the end of the sixth century, the academy moved to the city of Perisabora."

The Rabbah stopped talking. The ancient spirit seemed to fade. Perhaps that was all it had to say. Rabbi Abraham waited. Soft noises slipped in from outside the yeshiva. Were they the wind? Were they ancient voices? Old Achselrad could not tell. After a time, Rabbi Abraham said, "And what about *you,* Rabbah?"

"Me?" asked the spirit. It shone and glowed in the doorway, and then it repeated: "Me? Well, Rabbi Abraham, let me see. . . . Originally, I came from Mamala, a little town in the old Galilee region west of the River Jordan. I had three brothers, Chananya, Kailil, and Ushaya, and we were all as poor as grasshoppers. My brothers were cobblers, but try as I might, I could never keep my mind on shoemaking. As far back as I can remember, it was *words* for me–the words of the scholars in my village were magic and golden, and they completely captured my mind. I was always making up stories and arguing with myself. I simply could not concentrate on any manual task. I was an utter failure at handwork, and this upset my brothers. Finally, I gave up all pretense: I was no craftsman and I was no tradesman. I packed a sack, and I journeyed to Nehardea, the central city of Jewish culture in Babylonia. And along the way, I begged and I borrowed, and I arrived thin and very, very hungry.

"But what did I find? Not long before, Nehardea had been a warm and dusty city of old Hebrew scholarship–however, now the town was destroyed. Instead, Pumbedita had become the new center of Judaism. So I went to Pumbedita. There, my teacher was Rabbi Judah ben Ezekiel, a wise and kind man; his Academy of Jewish Learning was known throughout the world. After Rabbi Judah died, his position was offered to me. But I had barely grown a beard. I was too young–even I knew it–and I declined the job. Instead, I became the principal of the local preparatory school, with my friend Joseph ben Chiya as my assistant.

"The famed Mar Huna–an old and very wealthy man–became head of the academy. When Mar Huna died a decade later, I finally agreed to take over his job. At that time the academy had more than a thousand students. Like my predecessors, I lectured on law: both legal and religious. But I also talked about every other aspect of Judaism, even about the smallest things of everyday life, such as our clothes and food and our fleeting thoughts. I took to beginning my lectures like this: I would stand quietly a moment and look around, then I would choose some distracted young man.

" 'Tell me,' I demanded loudly. 'What are you thinking?'

"And no matter what he said, whether it was about Torah, *tallit,* or toenails, I would find a way to say: 'Very well–here is how a Jew should view this subject . . .' Then I would document my stand with an appropriate verse from the Holy Scriptures, always beginning my recitation with: 'This is because the Great Law has commanded such views in the holy Book of *such and such . . .*'

"Frankly, Rabbi, I had a gift–God gave me a vast and well-organized memory. Related passages from throughout the Bible and relevant sayings of the sages would flash to my mind instantly. And when I spoke, I was in a trance. I saw nothing and no one in the room. I was enveloped in a holy fog. I could talk on and on for hours. I felt glorious in those days: the *Shekhinah* of the Lord smiled down radiantly upon me. I like to think that I set a high standard for scholarship and that it then continued for hundreds of years."

The old Babylonian spirit nodded and smiled.

"Of course," continued Rabbah bar Nahmani, "in my day, we already had large and masterful footsteps to guide us. We owed our style and our inspiration to that great scholar, Mar Samuel of Nehardea. He had been Rabbi Judah's teacher, so I was his intellectual grandchild. It was Mar Samuel who set out the format of legal analysis that has now become codified in the *Mishnah.*

"You may not know this, Rabbi, but Mar Samuel was as interested in medicines and herbs and in the stars as he was in religion. He invented a wondrous healing eye salve. And he was forever drawing up calendars and charts and complex interconnected lists of natural elements.

"Within the realm of Judaic scholarship, Mar Samuel's special strength was civil law. In those days, the talmudic tracts were mainly oral. We learned all the arguments by heart. We repeated them aloud. We chanted and chanted until the singsong rhythms rolled back and forth and up and down, and we passed these chants to our students in the same way. Even today, I can still recite hours of the great Samuel's thoughts. For example, it was Rabbi Samuel who made it possible for devout Jews to live under alien political laws. Samuel based his interpretation on the Book of Jeremiah, where, in a letter to the elders among the Jewish exiles, the Prophet Jeremiah had written":

> Support and uphold any city to which you have been carried off, and pray to the Lord for the welfare of your new hometown. Remember: your protection, safety, and succor depend on the success and the peace of the land in which you presently reside.

" 'The law of the local government is law,' said Mar Samuel. And this has become the talmudic injunction: 'The law of the State is the law.' Ever since Mar Samuel's day, it has been a religious duty for Jews to obey the laws of the country in which they are settled, and now the law of the state is as binding as any Jewish civil law."

The Rabbah held up his right hand. "Nonetheless," he continued loudly, "the legally correct behavior is not always the ethically correct behavior."

The Rabbah stood tall in the doorway, lecturing to his students. "Here," he said, "we must always look first to God's Law. Begin by trusting the God-given guidance emanating from your own soul, then study the Torah, and finally consult your elders.

"Civil governments change. Legal systems come and go. It was only a few years before my time that the great city of Nehardea was laid to waste, ruined in a battle when Odenathus, the Palmyran adventurer came and destroyed that fine old city. Then the Jewish community moved to Pumbedita, and suddenly Pumbedita was the focus of the intellectual life of the children of Israel. The state had shifted–but God's Law remained an eternal unwavering rock, amen."

And the mystic Rabbi of Cologne nodded, although his eyes were closed. Abraham ben Alexander was a student again, long ago, in a yeshiva far away. His mind drifted, and the worn wooden benches turned to old smooth logs and summer days faded together again. And suddenly he heard the gentle ancient voice of old Rabbah bar Nahmani continuing:

". . . eternal Sabbath Queen," the spirit was saying. "In our day, we also celebrated the mystical Sabbath in verse. There were strong God-revering hymns–and there were also small homey poems, such as":

On the holy Sabbath night
Your tired eyes are closing tight
Under blankets cool and light
As a gentle wind-borne flight
Carries the nighttide symphonies–
  Of cracking in the oakbed knees
  Of cricking in the whiffle-trees
  While floating on the high starbreeze.

You dream of ancient springtime ways
From your magic childhood days
With glowing morning sunlight rays
On loafs and rounds, a golden glaze
The soft bread, warm and full whole-grain
  In steaming piles, raisin, plain –
  And then you wake to dawn's refrain,
  Brightly baked and fresh again.

A fine, warm, Sabbath-morning poem, it came fresh-baked to Cologne from that dusty Holy Land of far, far away. And Rabbah bar Nahmani was continuing: "I am surprised that I still remember that old poem."

Old Achselrad opened his eyes. The spirit of the Rabbah shimmered and shined in the doorway. Rabbi Abraham rocked calmly in his chair.

"Ah, Rabbi," said the spirit, "I find that even old men can remember some things very, very well."

And old Rabbi Abraham nodded, remembering back; but he said nothing at all.

"And," said Rabbah, "do you know, my friend, what now I remember suddenly? I remember one day long ago when I was talking to my little daughter.

"Yes, Rabbi Abraham, I had a daughter, named Emera, a beautiful little sandy-haired child. I remember once – before she had turned into a girl and when she was still just a bright little child who sparkled and talked and jimped and jumped every single second and who could never ever sit still – I remember that she asked me: 'What is Heaven?' "

The spirit of the Rabbah smiled. "What is heaven?" . . . I smiled then, as I smile now. "Heaven is a wonderful place, my little child," I said. "God lives there, far up in the sky. You will go there when you die. Your friends and your family will live there someday too. And the clouds float by and angels sing and everything is calm and peaceful and happy all the time.

" 'Emera opened wide her bright, bright eyes. 'It is in the sky?' she asked. 'But how could He just stay up there without falling down?'

" 'Do you mean God?'

" 'Yes.'

" 'Well, my little girl, God sits on His Great Throne of Glory.

And the angels fly around Him, and they are singing all the time,' I said.

" 'Will we fly there too?'

" 'Oh yes,' I answered.

" 'I will take you there when you die,' she said.

" 'Thank you,' I said.

"After a moment of silence, she asked, 'But how will I get you there, Father? I can't lift you: you're too heavy.'

" 'I will not need my body then,' I answered, 'just my soul–the special holy thing that is inside of me. My soul will fly up to Heaven. And a soul is lighter than a bird, and, little girl, it is prettier than the prettiest cloud.'

" 'Good,' said Emera, 'and I will fly up with you too. And we will hold hands along the way, so that you will not be afraid.' "

Good evening – come sit here by the stove. The night fire will soothe you. That warm glow radiates into every corner of the room, and it flows into every corner of us too. As Psalm 36 says, it shines high into the skies:

> Your love radiates throughout the skies,
> Your Truths light mountaintops above
> With joys beyond a brilliant sunrise.
>
> O Lord, Who shelters living things,
> How bright and warm Your lasting love –
> We're safe beneath Your strong broad wings.

The warmth of the Lord radiates into every corner of the world – likewise, His omniscient judgments fill the universe, so no one escapes. The righteous are rewarded, and the wicked are punished. Of course everyone is given the opportunity to do right, to act kindly, to live thoughtfully and charitably, to be humble, modest, and God-fearing. But in the end we are all judged on the choices that we have made. . . .

What is that, Rabbi? *We* ourselves actually made the judgments?

Yes, I suppose that is true–as the Talmud says: "All the judgments of the Holy One, blessed be He, follow only in kind; they are on the basis of measure for measure." We earn our own rewards. Look at the scriptural examples: Joseph buried his father in the land of Canaan, therefore Joseph himself was buried in Canaan. Abraham gave water to his holy visitors at Mamre, and later the Lord gave springwater to the parched Jews in the Sinai near Kadesh. Abraham gave bread to his visitors, and then God repaid the wandering children of Israel with manna. Also, Abraham accompanied the ministering angels from his tents toward the city of Sodom, therefore the all-present Holy One accompanied Abraham's descendants in the wilderness for forty years.

Yes, God follows our lead. The judgments of the Lord match our lives–and such judgments are for *all* men, not only the Jews. This is common knowledge. Even in ancient Egypt it was said that every dead man faces a divine trial before he is admitted to the Great Hereafter. In the Egyptian vision, God sits in the vast Judgment Hall of Heliopolis. He is the ruler and the judge of the dead, and He is helped by forty-two assessors. The Judgment Hall is a great echoing stone court. In the center is a balance. All our deeds, say the Egyptians, are carved permanently in our hearts–both our sins and our charities are engraved ineradicably. Therefore, the heart of the dead man is set on the right pan, and divine Truth is set on the left. Behind the balance stands the Egyptian god Thoth, who intones the measurement, which is then inscribed forever in the Book of the Dead.

These final judgments come *after* death. In life, nothing is final–one can always change. But men are impatient. We reach out for the ungraspable. We want to know everything in advance. Can we see the Judgment Balance from here? Can we catch a glimpse of the final decision in the making? We search for omens and signs. We study dreams and portents. In the Middle Ages, court trials included a holy ordeal, a divination to test the Almighty Lord's wishes and will. What did the eternal balance hold at the moment? To test the divine judgment, a defendant might be required to plunge his arm into boiling water or to carry a piece of hot iron or to walk barefoot over a sharpened plowshare. The righteous are always preserved in the end–so, would not the Lord protect an innocent man along the way?

Medieval ecclesiastical courts set forth holy ordeals, and often old Abraham ben Alexander had to intervene in order to protect his congregation. Rabbi Abraham knew that in the end the Lord *would* preserve the innocent. However, the exact details of His mysterious operations could be rather convoluted. Sometimes there were temporary disappointments and even setbacks. Fortunately, with a bit of help, seemingly miraculous ends could follow from dismal beginnings. For example, there was the time that the Lord God Almighty inspired old Achselrad to eat a piece of paper in order to save a poor Jew. . . . You have not heard about this? Well, I will tell you the story exactly as I heard it from my grandmother:

As you know, Abraham ben Alexander, Achselrad of Cologne, is the author of that mystical treatise called the *Keter Shem Tov.* It is a wondrous and magical Kabbalistic book, but unfortunately it was never published. In any case, it was one summer morning, in the month of *Tammuz,* while he was writing this very book, that Rabbi Abraham looked up; there, in the light of the candle, he saw Isaac ben Anselm ha-Kohen standing in the doorway, pale and shaken. "Rabbi," said Isaac weakly, "I need your help. I am about to be arrested for robbery."

Now, Rabbi, let me tell you what actually had happened:

We begin with Oskar Hiller, a rough and homely man. And who exactly was this Oskar Hiller? Well, Oskar Hiller was a tanner in medieval Cologne.

Tanning is a tough and dirty profession. Oskar's skins came from the neighboring slaughterhouse. Oskar dragged the skins into his yard. He cleaned them and he soaked them in lime. He stretched them and scraped them, he washed and squeezed them, he soaked them in vinegar, and he washed them again. Next, he put them in the tanning solution, made from oak and birch, and he soaked them for two weeks. Finally, Oskar dried the skins and sold them to leather finishers. All this work, Oskar did completely by himself: he bought the skins, he made the solutions, he worked the leather, and he sold the tanned skins from a dirty, smelly shack behind the Cologne *Kuttelhofe,* the main slaughterhouse near the River Rhine. Oskar's leathers were rough and irregular, and Oskar was like his leathers.

One evening, Oskar was sitting by himself in a local tavern. At a nearby table was a Jew, Isaac ben Anselm. Isaac was a middleman – he bought and sold finished leather goods. "I can always tell if the leather came originally from Oskar Hiller," Isaac was saying. "Oskar's leather is splotchy, bumpy, and pitted, just like Oskar. The finishers call him Oskar 'the Splotcher' Hiller."

A companion laughed. "Yes–Oskar *is* a bit of a splotcher all around," he said. "He looks splotchy, and he makes a splotch of his life."

What did that mean? Well, I am not certain, Rabbi–but at that hour and in that company and with the smell of meat and wine and hot breads rolling about, it seemed like a clever thing to say.

A wave of anger rushed through Oskar. "I try my best," he muttered. "Let *them* make leather–it is not as easy as they think. Who are they to say these things? That Conrad is a fumbler himself. Albert is stupid. And as for the Jew, Isaac–why, he is thin and weak, but he thinks that he should be a king; and he cannot be trusted–he would as soon steal from you as look at you."

Oskar muttered and he grumbled, but somehow the name "Splotcher" took hold. It was as if Isaac had let loose a cricket in the town. From then on, "Oskar the Splotcher" chirped in the inns, in the stores, and in the streets. No matter what the subject, sooner or later, "the Splotcher" came up. Was there a stain on the table? Someone would say, "Ah, the Splotcher was here." If the sky looked patchy with clouds, you might hear: "I see that the Splotcher was at work on the weather today." People joked and called out and laughed, and everyone had a "splotch" story to tell. Oskar hated walking through the streets–he hated hearing the talk and seeing people point and laugh. Soon, he thought only of revenge.

It was a few months later, and it was nighttime. Oskar was sitting on a wooden beam jutting out of the edge of a house. He was muttering to himself and looking at nothing in particular. Down the street two young men jumped from the shadows. They pushed an old man who was passing by, they stole his purse, and then they ran away.

At first, Oskar did not react. It had all happened so fast; it was over in the wink of an eye. The old man was stunned also–he did not see who had done this to him, but he started to shout. Suddenly Isaac ben Anselm turned a corner. And what was this? A group of guards had been checking the nearest gate and now they too were walking down the street from the other direction. The guards heard the shouts. They walked faster. As they passed Oskar, he said without thinking, "It was that man. That Jew Isaac did it!"

Isaac saw the guards moving toward him. He saw hands pointing. He heard the old man shouting. What should he do? The city guard ran toward him. Isaac ben Anselm began to tremble, and then he ran and ran and ran. Back went Isaac toward the Jewish Quarter, and he did not stop until he came to the synagogue and the reassuring figure of old Rabbi Abraham ben Alexander.

Rabbi Abraham listened to Isaac's story. The mystical old man nodded. He closed his eyes. After a moment, he opened his eyes again. "Isaac," said the Rabbi, "there is a well-known Hebrew proverb: 'Even the whole world cannot overcome a man with a divided beard.' "

"What does that mean, Rabbi?" asked Isaac.

"It means that a thoughtful man, a careful and judicious man, strokes his beard before he acts," answered Rabbi Abraham, running his fingers through his beard. "This man parts the hairs and he neatens the skeins as he ponders and plans. In the end, he will prevail."

"Is that relevant to my problem, Rabbi?" asked Isaac.

"We will see what we will see, Isaac," said the Rabbi. Old Achselrad tapped his chin. "Sleep here this evening," he said. "Together, we will go to court tomorrow morning."

Isaac lay down by the stove in the back room, but he could not sleep. The next morning after prayers, Isaac stood in the doorway of the little back room, waiting for the Rabbi to finish his writing. Eventually, Rabbi Abraham put down his pen and tapped his chin. Then he stood, and he put on his hat and his coat. Without glancing backward, he left the small study room of the yeshiva and he walked through the main prayer hall, which was filled with wooden benches. The Rabbi passed the twelve stained-glass windows with their colored lions and snakes. He went by the Holy stone Ark. He stepped out of the main door, and he strode off to the ecclesiastical courthouse, with Isaac ben Anselm hurrying behind.

Rabbi Abraham walked in the front door, and Isaac followed. The two men entered the courtroom where the Archbishop himself was presiding – this was Archbishop Adolph of Cologne, a noble and honorable prelate. The Rabbi stood in the back of the courtroom. The Archbishop looked up from his writing. He knew Rabbi Abraham.

"Rabbi," said the Archbishop sadly, "one of your Jews has robbed an old man. We have an accuser who witnessed the entire crime. I see that you have brought the culprit, and I appreciate this, but I am afraid, Rabbi, that the criminal, Mr. Isaac Anselm, must be imprisoned."

Isaac saw Oskar sitting at the edge of the room, and Isaac's heart sank. Still, Isaac said, "I am not guilty, Your Honor."

"Yes he is!" answered the tanner immediately.

The Archbishop said nothing. An assistant magistrate stood and said, "Your Honor, it is one man's word against another. We must let the good Lord decide."

The court official looked up at the ceiling for a moment, then he continued: "I suggest that we leave the judgment of this matter to God. Let there be a drawing of lots. We can follow the usual procedure." He turned to lecture the court. "I will put two pieces of paper in the ordeal box," he said. "On one piece of paper, I will write the word 'guilty'; on the other, I will write 'not guilty.' The Jew can draw a piece of paper from the box."

The official was facing Rabbi Abraham. He raised his eyebrows, he smiled, and he bowed. "This is a holy court," he said. "It is a religious court. So let us rather have the *Rabbi* choose the paper. Then it will certainly be a holy judgment. God will decide whether Mr. Anselm is guilty."

The Archbishop nodded. "Very well," he said.

The assistant magistrate was a friend of Oskar Hiller. He took two pieces of parchment from his desk. He sat down. He took out his pen and carefully he inscribed the words – but he wrote the same word, "guilty," on both pieces of paper. Then he folded the papers immediately, and he put them into the box.

"Now," said the official, again raising his eyes toward the ceiling, "let us look to Heaven for divine judgment."

The official set the box on a table in front of the Rabbi. Rabbi Achselrad looked at Oskar, he looked at Isaac, and he looked at the Archbishop. The Rabbi stroked his beard, parting and neatening the long white hairs. Rabbi Abraham closed his eyes a moment; then he asked, "Have you a Bible here, good Archbishop?"

"Of course," replied the Archbishop, and he instructed one of the court officers to pass a leather volume to Rabbi Achselrad.

"Now, let us read from the Book of Isaiah," said the Rabbi.

"I respect your religious views, Rabbi," said Archbishop Adolph, "but is this really necessary now?"

Rabbi Achselrad was holding the Bible. Suddenly his eyes opened wide. Then they closed tightly. He became weak; he sat on a nearby chair. His body trembled. After a moment, the Rabbi gently set down the Bible.

The Archbishop began to stand. "Are you all right, Rabbi?" he asked.

Rabbi Abraham opened his eyes. He looked toward the ceiling. "I have just had a vision, Your Honor," he said. "I have seen the great hill of the holy Lord of Hosts, towering high into the clouds of Heaven, amen."

There was a moment of silence. Old Abraham Achselrad continued: "And now I have seen also that the Book of Isaiah of the Holy Scriptures is quite important. If you will be so good as to hand me that Holy Book again, then I will read a bit of the appropriate verses":

On this hill, the Lord sets out
A fine rich meal for the devout
With fruit wines, with dark rich stout
And honeycakes and cream and trout.

Then our holy Lord will swallow
The shrouding veil of grief and woe,
The cloaking fog, Death's bleak hollow
Shroud–to lead where none dares follow.

And God will dry the bitter tears
From sad faces, wiping fears
From all young children,
A comfort through their growing years.

Oskar looked at the assistant magistrate. The two men felt shivers in their backs.

But Archbishop Adolph was watching the Rabbi intently. "It is beautiful verse," said the Archbishop. When Rabbi Abraham remained silent, the Archbishop added, "And certainly that is a noble and holy sentiment, Rabbi."

Gently, Rabbi Abraham closed the Bible. He rubbed his hands along its cover. "You are a noted cleric, Archbishop Adolph. What would you say that this verse means?" asked the Rabbi.

"Clearly it means that salvation will come and then true believers will be delivered–as was actually the case with the coming of our Lord Jesus Christ."

"Well, Your Honor, I would say that this verse has another special meaning–one that is relevant here and now," said the Rabbi.

"You would?" asked the Archbishop. "Then pray tell, Rabbi Achselrad: What do *you* read into this verse?"

"I would say, Archbishop, that God will swallow evil and will let goodness and truth prevail."

The Archbishop frowned. "Exactly what are you saying, Mr. Alexander?" he asked.

"I am saying this, Archbishop: I have had a vision. I have seen that this man Isaac is innocent. And I shall prove it to you."

"Well, what do you propose?" asked Archbishop Adolph.

"I propose," said Rabbi Abraham, "to draw lots, exactly as your assistant magistrate has suggested. Then we shall put our faith in the Lord."

Archbishop Adolph creased his forehead, and he looked at the Rabbi. "This has been a long and convoluted route to a very simple end," he said angrily.

"Perhaps," said Rabbi Achselrad, "but also it has been a *holy* route."

The Archbishop just shook his head and pointed to the box containing the two pieces of paper. The Rabbi reached into the box. He took out one piece of parchment. He read the paper and he said a blessing. Suddenly he put the parchment into his mouth and, to the astonishment of the entire courtroom, he chewed up the paper and swallowed it.

The Archbishop looked sternly at the Rabbi. "What did the paper say?" he asked.

"It said 'not guilty,' " said the Rabbi.

Worriedly, Oskar looked at his friend, the court official. "Just a moment," said the assistant magistrate to the Rabbi, "how can we believe you?"

Old Abraham Achselrad reached into the box. He took out the

other piece of paper. He handed it to the Archbishop, who said: "The word on this paper is: 'guilty.' Obviously, the other paper must have been 'not guilty.' "

The Archbishop stared at the Rabbi. After a moment of silence, Archbishop Adolph said quietly, "We must recall the last verses of Psalm 11":

The Lord is alone
Forever omnipotent
On His golden throne
The seat of judgment.

With stern impartiality
God tries all souls–
He weighs men fairly
On the Judgment Poles.

"The Lord has weighed Isaac Anselm on the Judgment Poles. Mr. Anselm has been found *not* guilty. Now he is free to go."

What? Yes, Rabbi, that is the whole story; there is no more.

Ah, good evening again, Rabbi. Yes, I know – it is always hard to sleep when there is a full moon. Just put your feet up on the side bench and I will open the stove door. Let me push the coals back. There is nothing like that white glow: it washes away the cares of a hard day.

I know that it *has* been a hard day and also a long evening for you. But later tonight you will finally fall asleep and dream of wondrous things. In your dreams, you will be young again, running through a gentle, magical world. There, the leaves of the trees are such strong greens that they take your breath away. The air is thick and cool and fresh. The wind is just about to lift you up and let you fly through the branches and into the clouds and over the mountains and through the wispy, wondrous heavens beyond.

And just around the corner will be your childhood loves, and you will walk hand in hand with them again. The dirt will be crumbly and warm under your toes. The sun will be gentle. Rays of light will glow through the trees like the purest golden arms of the wondrous Lord God, and you will be curled like a tiny little baby again, rolled in your mother's warm womb, sighing gently, comfortable forever, asleep, afloat, and alone, amen.

Ah, Rabbi, all the most golden God-given times of your life will be mixed and tangled together, and they will roll gently through your sleep. Then you will awake refreshed and happy tomorrow morning. A little shiver will run through your back. The sun will be streaming in your window. The day will dawn as bright and cool and warm and glorious as ever it has for you or me or for anyone before or since – well, anyone but young Keren, whose mornings would never ever be like that. But as for her dreams, Rabbi – well, who knows? I hope that she dreamt wondrous dreams.

. . . Young Keren? Well, I suppose I can tell you her story, but I must take a deep breath and settle in here quietly. And still I hesitate, Rabbi; I would not like for you to lose your happy sleep. . . .

Very well, Rabbi. Now where can I begin? Do I start with Keren or with her father or with a poem? I suppose that first comes the poem:

Do not leave the synagogue
Before the *Amidah* is read:
Remain standing in the holy hall
While the prayers are being said –
For to cut your benedictions short
And to hurry off instead
Will give your children endless grief
And may speed your own deathbed.

You can hold off early Death
With prayer, humble and dignified
By standing in the prayer hall
And chanting with a pious pride;
For when Dumah, death's black angel
Stands breathing cold outside
He will wait patiently until
Your full prayers are satisfied.

And when last you leave, full hale and whole
And restored by the *Amidah* prayer
Fear not if Dumah takes your soul,
For Heaven will then await you there.

My grandmother told me this poem to introduce the story of Keren, the daughter of Shua and Miluta ben Jesse. Had Miluta ben Jesse ha-Levi left the synagogue early during the *Amidah* prayer? Or was he being punished for some other sin? I do not remember exactly what was the cause, but in any case, Miluta had a sad, misshapen little baby daughter.

The baby had been born too early. The birth was long and slow, and then the baby was tiny–she could fit in the palm of one hand. She was wrinkled and blue; she looked like a strange, naked little animal. She did not breathe well, and she coughed and she squeaked. This was their only child, and Miluta and Shua named the baby Keren.

They wrapped the baby warmly. It rarely opened its eyes. Shua held up the little baby's arms, but Keren did not react. Most of the time, Keren kept her head to one side. She stretched out in a long, uncomfortable curl. Her tiny feet shivered. Shua talked to her and stroked her little round stomach, but Keren hardly moved and Keren hardly ate–instead, she slept and slept and slept, all day and all night. And her parents were very silent.

Keren grew slowly. She was always small. Her arms jerked. Her legs seemed stiff. Sometimes, her whole body shook uncontrollably. She could not roll over by herself. Even when she was three years old, Keren could not sit up without having someone hold her–and then, all the while, Keren would not hold still but she rolled and twitched and bobbed from side to side. The years passed slowly; they went hour by hour and day by day.

Ah, Rabbi, this is a very sad story. Let me sit here quietly a moment . . . All right; now I can continue:

The child's parents raised her as best they could. The mother, Shua, was always quiet. She smiled little. She had stringy hair, her cheeks looked hollow, her eyelids were dark and sunken–I am sure that you can picture her. The father, Miluta ben Jesse ha-Levi, was thin and shaky and grim. And, sadly, there was very little money. Miluta collected discarded pieces of wood, he trimmed the splintered edges, he smoothed the ends, and he resold them. Shua took in other children and cared for them during the days. All the while, Keren remained as dependent as a baby. She could barely do anything like a normal child. She could not even drink properly. A neighbor suggested feeding her by pouring milk and gruel through a hollow tube. Keren coughed and cried, but somehow the milk went down. Keren made strange sounds, but she did not talk. She jerked at loud noises. Sometimes her eyes opened wide for no apparent reason. Her muscles stayed tight and tense. She always seemed to be bent into strange positions.

The local herbal healer advised borage tea. Borage? No, I do not think you can find it around here nowadays. My grandmother often referred to it, but now it has fallen out of fashion. Originally, it was a Mediterranean plant, strong and spindly, growing in any kind of soil. I saw it many years ago: the plant itself is rough and white and stiff and prickly, and its leaves are deep green. I tell you this, because if you *can* get ahold of some leaves and flowers – especially leaves that are still green – it makes a special and wondrous tea. It has a light cucumber taste. It makes the eyes sparkle and the blood quicken, and it gives strength and then a sudden flood of well-being. Borage comforts the heart, Rabbi – it purges melancholy, it quiets the shaky tensions. There is even the little rhyme:

I, Borage
Bring courage.

In any case, the Jewish herbalist prescribed borage tea mixed with a touch of wine and sugar for Keren. "This is an ancient tonic," said the herbalist to Shua, patting her hand. "If anything will work, it is borage." It cost Shua all of the dowry money that she had brought to her marriage, but she fed a cup of the herbalist's borage tea to Keren two times each day. Was there any change? The family watched for one week and then for two; soon seven weeks came and seven weeks went; the dowry money was gone, but neither Shua nor Miluta could see any difference in Keren.

Early on, Old Abraham Achselrad had offered a healing amulet. Miluta looked at Shua – Shua shook her head no. "We had best trust in the direct healing powers of the Lord," she said quietly. "Besides, undoubtedly we have sinned and now we are paying for our misdeeds." Amulets ask for special intervention. Who were Miluta or Shua or even Keren, for that matter, to deserve privileged treatment? "We are just poor, common, ordinary Jews," said Miluta. "What have we ever done that was outstanding or special or heroic? God certainly knows what He is doing; it is immodest and irreverent to challenge Him in any way."

Rabbi Abraham looked at Shua and he looked at Miluta, but he himself said nothing. After the couple left the yeshiva, Achselrad took out a piece of kosher parchment and he made a special amulet; he wrote a holy incantation. Rabbi Abraham wrote Keren's name, and in small Hebrew letters, he wrote seven times:

May God our Great Protector then
Grant sleep and peace and calm
To all His weak young children
And hold them gently in His palm,
Amen.

Then, when he remembered and in the quiet hours of the night, the old Rabbi would pat the amulet and say a small extra prayer for Keren and for Shua and Miluta.

Years passed, and Keren grew, but she got no better. She had to be carried from place to place; she wore a diaper. The family talked to her, and at times they could even pretend that she was normal. They patted her and stroked her. But she was not normal. Keren was always bent, she made groaning sounds – perhaps she hurt – no one knew.

Keren lived on and on for seven long, slow years. And then one day she caught a bad cold. It went to her throat and then to her chest, and although it was the summer and the weather was warm, Keren shivered and shook and quickly worsened and died. When Rabbi Abraham heard, he sighed; "Whom God loves best dies young," thought old Achselrad.

The Burial Society came, and with their help the family dressed Keren in a fine white robe. Miluta set his *tallit* in the bottom of the small coffin. The ladies from the Burial Society gently folded Keren's body into the position of an unborn child, a normal little womb-wrapped baby, so that someday she might roll and roll smoothly into the Holy Land beyond the grave. They put her hands at her sides, and they sprinkled spices over her pale white body. Then they put a plain white linen cap on her head.

The Rabbi performed the burial rites. Before the Rabbi said the last prayer at the cemetery, Shua asked to open the coffin once more. Old Rabbi Abraham looked off across the park. Sunweed and jonquil dotted the horizon: blues and yellows and pinks were scattered afar.

An open coffin was not allowed. The Rabbi looked up at the sky. It was white. There were wisps of floating clouds. "Certainly," said Rabbi Abraham to Shua.

The mother, Shua, looked down and held Keren's hand. Old Rabbi Achselrad looked down too at the eyer-sleeping child. She was so calm. She was resting. There were no wrinkles on her forehead; her eyes were closed; finally, her muscles were relaxed. No loud sounds jarred her. No bright lights startled her. She was curled smoothly like a round little baby again, rolled and wrapped in her mother's warm womb, sighing gently, comfortable forever–asleep, afloat, and alone.

Good evening. I see there is no sleep for the weary. If you are cold, then sit here on the bench; I will stoke up the oven. When we get old, we get cold more easily. Your blood cools in old age – but this evens your temperament. Also, you become farsighted: you can finally see the horizons. Everything takes on a broad scope; small things seem less important. Even our proud accomplishments no longer seem so crucial or so monumental. Looking back on life, we old men say, "Ah, that was good," but we rarely say, "That was the *best.*" Now we are satisfied with things that gently keep us warm. We do not need the extremes – we do not need to freeze or to boil.

And, Rabbi, how nice it is to have a little smile in your old age! Perhaps a bird hopping on the ground tickles us for some inexplicable reason. Or a baby suddenly looks up at you, cross-eyed but serious. And is that a light pat on the back from a friend? Or, you may simply smooth the hair of your grandchild. These things are more than enough for old men, and certainly they were enough for old Janni. Janni? That is what his mother called him – you would know him as Jannai, the Hebrew poet. He lived in Palestine in the Dark Ages, but I am told that once he somehow drifted to Cologne and visited old Abraham Achselrad. Yes, yes – I know that they lived more than two hundred years apart, but time cannot separate holy souls. You will see your parents again someday, will you not? Of course you will – so let me tell you about Jannai's visit:

Once upon a time, on a summer day in medieval Cologne, a thin old traveler slipped into the back room of the Cologne yeshiva, where Rabbi Abraham ben Alexander was working. In those days, all manner of pious pilgrims came through Germany each week from the Holy Land. Wanderers appeared at all times of the day and night in the old wooden yeshiva. These strangers walked in, weary and wide-eyed, brimming with wonder tales from distant lands and from far-off shores. So it is not surprising that travelers came from distant times as well. On this medieval summer day, a wayfaring spirit floated in through the synagogue. It was the spirit of an old man; it stood barefoot and wavering in the doorway of the back room, where it found Rabbi Abraham writing in his tome of mystical Kabbalistic lore.

Rabbi Abraham felt the presence, and he looked up. The stranger smiled. "Hello, Rabbi," said the dim and dusty spirit. "May I come in?"

"Certainly," said the Rabbi.

"My name is Jannai," said the stranger.

Rabbi Abraham nodded, and he stroked his beard. The Rabbi knew of Jannai. Once Jannai had been a poet, a Hebrew bard in the Holy Land two centuries before. Had he now appeared again, barefoot at the door of the back room of the old yeshiva in Cologne? Rabbi Abraham stared a moment, and then he set down his pen. "Please come in, Mar Jannai. Perhaps you would like to sit down and rest," said the Rabbi.

"Thank you very much," said Jannai. He slipped lightly into the room, a pile of prayer books seemed to move of its own accord, and the spirit settled on the floor, leaning against one of the worn benches. Rabbi Abraham smiled at Jannai. Jannai smiled back.

"Are you just passing through Cologne?" asked the Rabbi. "Or do you plan to stay for a while?"

"Well, Rabbi, I am wandering these northern Rhinelands, looking to see how my distant brethren live," said Jannai. "May I rest here for a bit?"

"Certainly," said Rabbi Abraham.

The spirit continued to smile. After a moment, the Rabbi said, "Tell me a little about yourself, my holy friend."

The Rabbi sat back. Jannai stretched his bare feet in front of him. "I am a Jew from Palestine, Rabbi. I was a writer."

Rabbi Abraham nodded. Jannai wavered, although there was no breeze, and then he too nodded. "Yes, Rabbi, I was a writer," said the spirit. "Actually, I was a poet. In those days . . ."

But Jannai's voice seemed to drift away. Was he still speaking? Then the voice got louder, and Rabbi Abraham heard: ". . . the Jewish inhabitants of the Mohammedan countries soon adopted the Arabic language. Arabic is closely related to Hebrew: many of the roots and forms of words are similar.

"Now, during those centuries after the fall of the Jewish nation–those five or six hundred years before my time–we Jews seemed to have lost some of the grace of Hebrew. When I grew up, the speech was sloppy and rough. In everyday talk, Hebrew was mixed with Chaldee and Greek. This was no material out of which to form beautiful literature.

"Ah, but the Arabs, Rabbi–the Arabs were different. They loved their language. They revelled in its poetry. They sang the sounds. The written words curled in beautiful lines, and the Arabs worked to keep spoken Arabic pure and accurate and beautiful too. So when we Jews began to speak the Arabic of our neighbors, we were touched by the joy of their speech. It was wondrous. Could we not do the same in Hebrew? We wanted lush Hebrew poetry and wild and wondrous Hebrew tales.

"And there were practical reasons for Jews to pay more attention to Hebrew: we were self-conscious. Our Arabic neighbors were well educated and eloquent. A Jew needed to quote the Torah in order to make his case in a marketplace discussion. Exactly where in the Bible is it said that on the mountain of Zion the Lord of Hosts shall one day prepare a banquet of rich fare for all His faithful people? What is the required restitution for a man who kills another's cattle in anger? How does one go about building a holy altar, such as the one on Mount Ebal where Joshua conducted a reading of the Law? When mixing with the Arabs and when arguing with the Mohammedans, we Jews felt obligated to know the Holy Scriptures in detail. And, Rabbi, it would not hurt to be able to quote a *lyric* form of Scripture in order to balance the lyric form of the Koran."

Rabbi Abraham nodded. The spirit of Jannai continued: "That is the time in which I grew up. It was a time when Jews felt we needed a Hebrew language that was ornate and literate and filled with poetry.

"As I said, Rabbi, I lived in Palestine when the Mohammedans ruled the area. We Jews lived in pockets in the large cities. We were small groups, and our neighbors saw us as foreigners and transients. Jerusalem itself was a Mohammedan stronghold, and it was in my day that the great Mohammedan shrine, the *Kubbet es-Sakrah,* the Dome of the Rock, was built.

"Still we Jews had complete religious freedom. And all around me young Jews were setting down religious ideas in verse. We had a huge and ancient Hebrew vocabulary, but it had never really been used in polished meter: it had never been turned to poetry. In the beginning, we followed the style of the Arabs. But while the Arabic bards sang of swords and battles and chivalry, of wild loves and implacable enemies and vast treasures, we Jews tried to capture God and His Laws, and the saddened among us told of the dissolution of the ancient Jewish nation. In this way, suddenly, Rabbi, there were reams of Hebrew poetry."

"Excuse me, Mar Jannai," said Rabbi Abraham, "but whatever happened to those books of poetry?"

Jannai looked at the Rabbi for a moment. "Books?" asked the spirit.

"Did you not say 'reams of poetry'?" asked Abraham Achselrad.

Jannai smiled. "Oh, that was just an expression. There were few books, if any," he said. "You, my German friend, live in a culture of books, but we were a culture of the spoken word. People memorized their poems and recited them by heart. It is much better to carry a poem in your heart than in your hand, my dear Rabbi."

Old Abraham Achselrad stroked his beard and nodded.

"In those days," continued Jannai, "we had more leisure time. The original holy service from the ancient days was short, and its prayers were simple. Even the addition of Psalms did not fill the available time for worship.

"Those were leisurely years, Rabbi. Our synagogues were fine places in which to pass the warm and easy mornings and evenings. And of course on the Great Holidays, such as *Rosh Hashanah* and *Yom*

Kippur, the congregation remained in the synagogue from dawn to dusk. So the rabbis were always wondering: How can we fill out the services? What should we do to extend the devotions? The answer was *poetry.* Rabbis could add liturgical hymns and other holy verses. Our first great liturgical poet was Jose bar Jose Haiathom. Rabbi Jose used Hebrew words and biblical themes, and–just like the original Hebrew Psalms–his verses had repetition, repetition, repetition rather than rhyme.

"Old Rabbi Jose's poetry was fairly simple. But we were surrounded by the rich, complex verse of the Arabs, and we Jews could never remain satisfied in the face of such an astounding luxuriance of language. Thick, colorful, lush words tempted us–but most especially, Rabbi, there was rhyme. Rhyme was magic. It tingled in the ear and it rolled on the tongue. It was irresistible."

Here Jannai paused; he was quiet for quite some time. Old Achselrad waited patiently. Eventually, the spirit said, "I think, good Rabbi, that I may have been the first Hebrew poet to introduce full rhyme into the synagogue. Soon afterward, many poets followed; for instance, the well-known Kaliri–that is, Eleazar ben Kalir–was a student of mine.

"Undoubtedly there were other rhyming poets working somewhere in the region, but I cannot recall them now. I remember only the fever that took hold of me when I began to compose. I was carried away by a holy muse. I set down prayers for all the special Sabbaths. And I always wrote in parables–it was the aggadic form, the anecdotes and stories I had absorbed in my youth.

"I loved the *Aggadahs,* the narratives of the rabbinic teachings. I must confess that I could never completely separate the *Aggadahs*–the narratives–from the *Halakhah*–the technical rules. Certainly both spring from the same soil, and both share the same roots and aim at the same goals. In principle, however, I suppose that you could distinguish them this way: the *Halakhah* are the bedrocks, the regulations and the laws, while the *Aggadahs* are indirect guides and opinions. Still the *Aggadahs* are equally important. The Talmud reminds us: 'Is it your desire to know Him, He Who brought the world into being? Then be certain to learn the *Aggadahs;* from them, you will come to know the Holy One, blessed be He, and therefore you will be able to stay close to His ways.'

"*Aggadahs* start with the words of the Holy Scriptures, but *Aggadahs* play with these words. I do not mean that they take the holy words lightly. It is just that *Aggadahs* are sagas and legends, tales, poems, and allegories; they are ethical reflections and historical reminiscences. As one old sage has said, 'The *Aggadah* hangs its gorgeous tapestries on the eternal golden nails of the Bible.' The *Aggadah* are gardens with 'flowery mazes, exotic colors, and bewildering fragrances, all sheltered within the courtyard of the holy Temple.' "

Jannai smiled at Rabbi Abraham. "Listen to me, Rabbi–I am beginning to sound like a lecturer, and you are being quite patient and polite. I am really no scholar. It is simply this: the *Aggadahs* suited my own particular temperament. I looked at myself and said: Janni (that is what my mother called me), Janni, can you write a bit of *Aggadah,* some little verses that other people could enjoy? Well, Rabbi, I could and I did. I sat down and wrote little aggadic stories as poems–and these were for the general populace, not for a small circle of intellectual elite. I suppose that no one recites these verses any longer. Here are two simple poems that I remember":

How can that gaunt old beggar man
Be destined for an Eden's Garden,
The sunny glorious restful land,
The Lord's celestial skyblue Heaven?

Why, when people cry throughout the land,
When they grieve and they are sad,
This poor man simply pats their hand,
He smiles at them; then they feel glad.

"And":

A wicked and a good man
Once died upon a Sabbath late,
And their eternal life began
As they stood at Heaven's gate.

"The good man," so the Lord decreed–
"In Gehinnom, shall he spend one day
For a single evil wicked deed
He committed in his earthly stay."

Then God looked at the wicked one:
"You get an hour in Paradise
For one good deed that you have done
On earth with selfless sacrifice."

The wicked shrugged and then he said:
"Give my hour to the other instead,
So he shall never have the dread
Of Gehinnom's torments upon his head."

"For this," the Almighty Lord decrees,
"You'll *both* enjoy the gentle breeze
Forever, under cedar trees
In My land of eternal ease."

"That is fine aggadic poetry," said Rabbi Abraham.

"Thank you," said Jannai. "To me, they sound rather simple now. Actually, most of my poetry never saw the light of day – although some was used in the synagogue and a bit of it was printed in manuscript form.

"You know, Rabbi, at one time I had hoped to be the best of poets. I worked day and night. But also I waited: I polished and rewrote; I put things off and did not let others hear most of the poems. In fact, I protracted my work until most of those whom I wished to please had sunk into the grave. Success and miscarriage became empty sounds, and in the end I dismissed my work with a sort of frigid tranquility, having little to fear or hope from either censure or from praise."

"Have you then disowned these wonderful poems?" asked the Rabbi.

"Oh, no," said the poet, "it is only that their reward has changed: I have taken them in again, and now I am happy with them in a way that is small and close and personal. Now I love them like my children. I love these little verses just because they are my own – fine and bright and full of my own modest life and my own best efforts.

"You see, Rabbi, once, when I was young and strong and proud and a dreamer, I wanted to write the best poetry ever written. And when I wrote, I felt that it *was* the best. But since then, Rabbi Abraham,

I have read much other fine poetry. There are greater poets than I, my friend. So how do I reconcile this – I who once wanted to be the greatest poet who ever lived?

"I will tell you the truth. It is like this: the world is a full place; it is varied and complex, and many, many wonderful people have written poetry here. More importantly, though, many wonderful people have lived their lives as best they can here, and this is the great truth that finally I have understood. Now, looking back two centuries, I can say this: I myself am happy with what I have done. When I think of my poems – that is, when I can actually remember them – I take them in my hands and I feel like those early times in my mother's lap."

Jannai sat back and smiled. "My mother sang me songs, and she would give me the lightest, most gentle mother's pat. 'Janni,' she said, 'you are my golden little boy.' And then she gave me just a teeny tiny caress of the cheek too. That was more joy than I would ever need – and now with my poems I feel this same way, and I am as happy as I can be."

Good evening.

Are you having difficulty sleeping again? Put your feet up on the side bench here and I will open the stove door. Let me push these coals back: the white glow will wash away all the worries of your hard day.

Yes, Rabbi, I too find staring at the oven mesmerizing. It is mesmerizing, and it is restful.

Nowadays I get tired staring at most things. Jumbles of letters and lists of words can make me feel as if I have climbed ten flights of stairs. But here in front of the stove the blanketing glow washes over my eyes; it whites out my vision completely, and I relax. I wonder why I tire when reading. Perhaps all those words are becoming too deep and too difficult for a simple old man. Perhaps old age is finally wearing me out.

Ah, well–it makes little difference, for I no longer have the energy to try and understand the deep mysterious matters of this world. I suppose that all Kabbalists must have been young. They were so energetic. The Kabbalists were always discovering new charms and magical incantations from the hidden numbers in the Holy Scriptures. They never tired of their mystical studies. Day and night, they dug into the secret symbols behind the holy words, and then they used these symbols and charms in their amulets, the *kameya,* which were adorned with magic squares and secret symbols and planetary names and with the names of angels and demons and holy places.

For instance, there was the *kameya* of lead. It was the amulet of the planet Saturn, ruled by the angel Agiel and countered by the demon Zazel. The numerical version of the amulet was:

4	9	2
3	5	7
8	1	6

When added in any way, horizontally, vertically, or diagonally, these numbers total 15. Of course, before the Christian era, we Jews had no numerical symbols: we just used letters. The letter version of the amulet was:

dalet	*tet*	*bet*
gimel	*heh*	*zayin*
het	*alef*	*vav*

And the magic sum – 15 – is the value of the two Hebrew letters *yod* and *heh,* which is the shortened form of the holy tetragrammaton *yod heh vav heh.* Here, the total of all three columns of figures is 45, which is the sum of the expanded tetragrammaton *yod vav dalet-heh alef-vav alef vav-heh alef.* This is a wondrous, intricate, magical design. Obviously it could work out so perfectly only because it has been intended that way by the great and glorious Lord God Himself, amen, amen.

Such magic squares were the heart of the *kameyas,* but the Kabbalists used other mystical symbols too. The planet Saturn had the symbol:

Saturn's angel Agiel had his own special symbol:

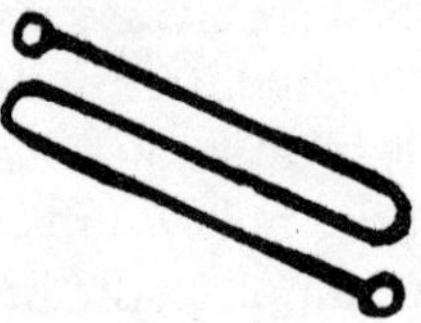

–while the corresponding demon, Zazel, had the symbol:

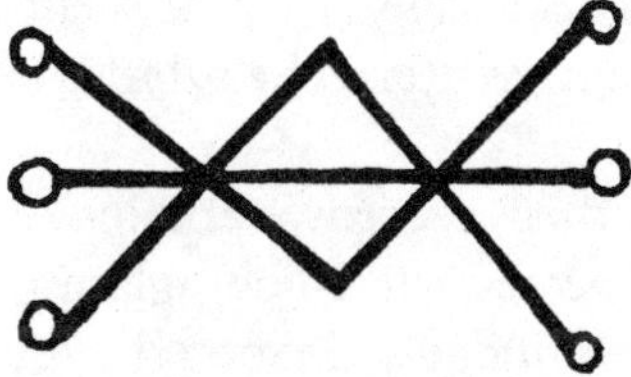

Numerology and symbolism became almost a separate language for the Kabbalists. The Kabbalists changed the shapes of the Hebrew letters and then they invented *new* letters, so eventually there was a special Kabbalistic Hebrew alphabet, with secret pronunciations and with hieroglyphic-like symbols.

By the Middle Ages, the Kabbalah was a great and mystical religion; it was a culture all its own, with its own language and its own philosophy. . . . What? Well certainly Kabbalism was Judaism, but it was Judaism that emphasized the absolute complexity of the world. Our world is so complex, said the Kabbalists, that it is *incondensable.* None of its Truths can be written in simple, clear statements with only one layer of meaning. Instead, the holy words were endlessly deep. At some level, a connection could be found for even the most disparate ideas. Therefore, we are only limited in our understandings by the time and the energy that we devote to studying the infinite depths of God's great Truths.

I wonder if old Jehuda ben Saul was a Kabbalist. (Rabbi Jehuda? He was two rabbis before you.) Jehuda was a scholar who always saw untold complex depths in what, to others, seemed to be the simplest of biblical passages. Ah, the great Jehuda ben Saul is a warning to us all, Rabbi: scriptural analysis is fraught with difficulties. A biblical passage is a complex thing. A scriptural verse is not what it appears at first. Even the scholar must work at it and work at it–and in the end he can never be certain that he has grasped a full understanding. Therefore, a scholar must always remain modest. As the Hebrew proverb reminds us: "Whisper your virtues in a low voice, but proclaim your faults aloud."

In any case, I remember hearing Old Rabbi Jehuda proclaiming the faults of his students quite loudly during a lecture: "What?! Why do you ask me that?" he shouted, pounding his reading desk, the synagogue *almemar.* "That is such an insignificant matter! You children are like the man who spent all his time trying to decide whether fish dream." He shook his head sadly; then he went on to tell them; "Now here is a really important matter: The word is '*Sh*ibboleth,' not '*S*ibboleth'!"

The boys raised their eyebrows and looked at one another.

"Shibboleth!" repeated the Rabbi, glaring down at his charges, "from the holy Book of Judges, Chapter Twelve."

Rabbi Jehuda stared at the boys, the boys looked at the floor, and there was silence; so the Rabbi said, "You do know, of course, what is a shibboleth?"

After a moment of silence, one of the bright young men, Moshe ben Samuel, said, "Yes, Rabbi, 'shibboleth' means ear of corn."

Rabbi Jehuda looked at Moshe for a moment; then he nodded. "True," said the Rabbi. "And do you also know that knaves and fools invent catchwords and shibboleths to keep honest men from coming to an honest understanding?"

Again, the Rabbi stared down at his charges. The boys looked puzzled. "Need I say more?" asked Rabbi Jehuda.

The yeshiva students hesitated. After a moment, young Moshe ben Samuel said, "Perhaps, good Rabbi, you would say just a bit more."

Rabbi Jehuda stepped back. He raised his eyebrows. "You want more, Moshe? Then I shall give you more. 'Shibboleth' comes from the old Hebrew word 'shabal.' "

The Rabbi cleared his throat; the students settled in for a lecture. "Listen, my untutored boys," continued Jehuda, " 'shabal' means to grow, to increase, to flow–so 'shibboleth' not only means ear of corn, it also means stream, or even floodwater.

"Now, this word 'shibboleth' was used as a test by Jephthah, the Gileadite, a general and one of the warrior Judges of old Israel. You see, boys, the enemy Ephraimites grew up with a different dialect from the native Gileadites: Ephraimites could not pronounce *sh,* and they said '*s*ibboleth' instead of '*sh*ibboleth.' Therefore, Jephthah's men used the word 'shibboleth' as a test for disguised Ephraimites at the fords of the River Jordan. Any man who was identified as an Ephraimite by his pronunciation was seized and killed–hallelujah and amen."

"Amen," murmured the students.

The Rabbi struck his fist on his desk. "So, here it is, young men!" he shouted. "This is the first evidence in the Great and Holy Scriptures that, after the tower of Babel, mankind had different local dialects. Why, even *Hebrew* was pronounced differently between neighbors!"

Rabbi Jehuda surveyed his charges. No one spoke. After a moment, the old man continued: "Undoubtedly, Hebrew was the original speech of mankind, the language from which all others were descended. Of course how could it be otherwise? The Holy Scripture itself is written in Hebrew."

There was a long silence. The Rabbi was tapping his fingers on his desk and staring at the boys. Was he waiting for a question? Finally, young Moshe ben Samuel asked, "Tell me, Rabbi – what does the word 'Hebrew' mean?"

Rabbi Jehuda ben Saul stood absolutely still for many minutes. "All right, young man, I will tell you. It is quite simple. 'Hebrew' comes from the word 'ibhri,' and 'ibhri' comes from the word 'abhar.' So, 'Hebrew' comes from 'abhar,' meaning to pass across."

"To pass across?" repeated Moshe.

"Exactly," said the Rabbi. " 'Hebrew' means to pass across the farther bank."

Moshe looked puzzled. Rabbi Jehuda said, "Young man, think a moment. Abraham, our first father, was initially named Abram, from *ha-ibhri,* 'the other-sider' – that is, 'the man who passed to the other side' across the River Jordan. You see, Moshe, Abraham was a crosser and a traveler; he was a wanderer, seeking a new land and a new God. So, Abraham was the first Hebrew."

The Rabbi looked at his fingers. He looked at the ceiling. Then he sighed. "That," he said quietly, "is what some men say. And yet others say something else entirely." He voice drifted away; he seemed lost in his thoughts. The old man's eyelids drooped. He put his head in his hands, and he closed his eyes. The yeshiva students waited politely for a few minutes. A thick silence lay on the walls, on the floor, on the benches. The Rabbi had fallen asleep.

Yes, old Jehuda ben Saul had fallen asleep; he was exhausted from his struggles with the holy words. Scriptural analysis is more complex than it might appear to the novice. Words hide more than they reveal. No one knew this better than the medieval scholar Abraham ben Alexander, the mystic Achselrad of Cologne. Achselrad was always looking deep into matters, peering below the surfaces in his strange, mystical way. Rabbi Abraham saw the handwork of the Divine One at every turn: he saw the incontestably incomprehensible interventions of the good Lord God (blessed be He) in everything, and he knew the endless unfathomable depths of holy letters and of holy writings.

Rabbi Abraham had studied with Rabbi Eliazar, the mystic of Worms. He had learned the Kabbalistic alphabet, which was used for writing holy amulets. The script of the Kabbalists was strange and it was powerful. It was wondrous and it was magic, and one time it saved a small Jewish school in the northern outlying village of Wevelinghoven.

The story of the mystical Kabbalistic script and the village of Wevelinghoven was told to me by my grandmother long ago. Would you like to hear it? Good. Then I will tell it to you.

Once upon a time, said my grandmother to me, there lived in medieval Germany a man named Sallu ben Meshulam. Sallu was the local scholar and schoolteacher in the village of Wevelinghoven, a small town on the River Erft. Wevelinghoven would be only about one day's journey northwest of Cologne, except that vast marshes lay directly between the two cities. A traveler from Cologne had to go north out of his way, either along the River Rhine or the River Erft; so in those olden times a trip between Cologne and Wevelinghoven always took at least two days.

Wevelinghoven was a small rural community, but it had a number of Jews, and the Jews had their own school. What did this Jewish school, this *heder,* look like? It was all one room, a rickety little peasant house with a thatched roof. The house tilted to the left. It had one window–or was it two?–actually, Rabbi, I am not certain, because there were *two* holes in the side wall, both of which were stuffed with pillows in the cold weather. On Sabbaths and on holidays, its dirt floor was sprinkled with sand. In the corner was a stove, and above the stove was a shelf on which Sallu slept. Sallu's children slept piled together in a bundle on a cot next to the oven on the right, while Sallu's wife slept on a cot next to the oven on the left. During the day, the cots were covered with blankets, and when Sallu's wife was baking, the blankets were overlaid with sheets of noodles or rows of biscuits on clean white cloths.

Behind the oven was a chicken coop where hens were raised.

One wall had a cupboard with a breadbox and cups and little pots. On top of the cupboard was a sieve, a broom, a grater, and wooden spoons. By the front door was a wooden water tub that leaked and a towel that was always wet. In the middle of the room was a long table, two long benches, and one old wooden chair. And when the room was full with students, everyone shouted, and the hens were always clucking behind the stove.

The *heder* was very noisy, and one summer day into this din walked the main church beadle from the Dom, the great cathedral of Cologne. The beadle walked in, and he was knocked backward by a wave of yelling. The beadle stepped out again. The church was so quiet–why were these Jews so noisy? The beadle took a deep breath. He was the church messenger and constable. He had been sent by the head priest on orders from the Archbishop Philip von Heinsberg to close down the local Jewish schools in all the surrounding communities.

Evening was coming on. The beadle took another deep breath, he stepped in the door, he marched up to Sallu, the schoolteacher, and he stated the decree. "What is that?" said Sallu, startled. "I said," shouted the beadle, "the Archbishop, Philip von Heinsberg, his holiness of Cologne, has ordered that this school be closed." The children quieted down. Sallu's wife stopped cooking. The hens stopped clucking.

"I will return in a week to check on you," warned the beadle.

Sallu was very worried. He sent the students home. He sat at the table. What should he do now? The trouble came from Cologne–perhaps the solution would come from Cologne also. Sallu told his wife to cancel the school session for the next few days. He packed his satchel and he traveled down the River Erft to the River Rhine and then up the River Rhine to the town of Cologne. In Cologne, Sallu found the Juden Viertels, and there, deep in the old Jewish Quarter, he quickly located Judengasse Street. Sallu went down the alleyway to the synagogue. He stepped in the front door; he walked through the anteroom, past the twelve stained-glass windows in the main prayer hall, and in through the door of the back study room. There, the Rabbi was bent over a book.

"Rabbi," he began, "we are in great trouble in the village of Wevelinghoven. I am Sallu ben Meshulam; I am the teacher at our little *heder*. Just yesterday . . ."

Old Abraham Achselrad sat back in his chair. He listened patiently to the whole outpouring. When Sallu had finished his story, the Rabbi closed his eyes. Soon, his breathing became slow and regular and he seemed to have nodded off to sleep. After a few minutes, Sallu said quietly, "Rabbi? Excuse me, Rabbi. . . ."

Rabbi Abraham opened his eyes. "Young man – do not be afraid. You can return home now. I will give you an amulet, a letter, and some instructions. Have faith, my friend; the Lord will provide."

From his desk, the Rabbi took out a small silver box covered with mystical inscriptions and numbers on both sides. Next, the Rabbi took a clean piece of kosher parchment from a drawer. He tapped his chin a moment and then he wrote three lines of mystical Kabbalistic script. Carefully, he folded the letter in half and he sealed it with a drop of wax. "Now, Sallu," he said, "let me teach you three incantations and their use. You must follow my instructions exactly. Then trust in the good Lord God (blessed be He) – He will save your school."

Sallu listened, and carefully he repeated the instructions. He took the amulet, and he took the letter. Then he thanked the Rabbi. And Sallu ben Meshulam returned home to Wevelinghoven.

The next week the beadle appeared again. The little *heder* was filled with students. It overflowed with people. It was even noisier than it had been the week before. In marched the beadle. "I see that you are still conducting classes," he shouted to Sallu. "I am afraid that I will have to report this to the priest, who will, of course, inform the Archbishop."

"We cannot talk above the noise in here," said Sallu to the beadle. "Come into the yard."

Sallu led the way. Out the front door they marched. They walked around the building and off beyond the town – where, behind the *heder,* the lands rolled away into the edges of the great gray marsh. Sallu stood back. He faced the beadle. He took the amulet from his pocket, he waved it in the air, and he repeated the first incantation that he had learned from Rabbi Achselrad. From the Book of Exodus, Sallu chanted:

You blasted them with windy spells,
The sea turned into bottomless caves,
They sank down through the murky dells
Like stones from old forgotten graves
Under the tumbling roaring swells
Beneath the endless wind-lashed waves.

Suddenly the beadle sank to his ankles in the wet and marshy earth.

The beadle could not move his feet. He became worried. "I am warning you," he said. "This is no way to treat an official of the Church. The priest will report this to Archbishop Philip, and he will send his troops!"

The schoolteacher only nodded. Then he waved the amulet, and he chanted the second incantation, again from the Book of Exodus:

> The watery abyss has covered them
> And they sank into the depths.

At this, the beadle sank to his knees in the mud. Black thick ooze coated his hands. He could move only his head. He was very frightened, and he said weakly, "The Archbishop will send his army. They will destroy your schoolhouse and maybe even your entire village."

But Sallu waved the amulet for a third time, and he recited the last incantation, from the Book of Jeremiah:

> All Babylon shall drown
> Never to rise to power again
> After the mighty Lord sends down
> Disasters from on high in Heaven.

The earth trembled. Beneath his feet, the beadle felt rocks cracking, and the deep ground fell away. The beadle sank farther and farther. Soon he was up to his chin in the mud. He could not move at all. He could barely talk. The beadle could smell the old mud, the rotting wood, and the plants of centuries gone by; he was wrapped in the deep, dank, ancient smell of old, old oceans. "All right, all right!" he called out. "Just let me free, and I will stop bothering you and I will cause you no more problems."

The schoolteacher hesitated. Then, following Rabbi Abraham's instructions, he said, "You must do more than not bother me. You must also deliver a message. Here is a note from Pope Urban III to the Archbishop Philip von Heinsberg." Sallu took out the letter that the Rabbi had given to him. "Will you take it to the Archbishop?"

"Yes, yes – certainly!" said the beadle.

But Sallu ben Meshulam had more to say: "The message reports that the Pope specifically wishes that this village be protected," he continued. "Do you *promise* to deliver the note?"

"My God, I have already promised," said the beadle. "What more do you want? Yes–I swear that I will deliver the message!"

So the schoolteacher nodded, and he waved the amulet and he recited from the Book of Isaiah:

The Lord, your God, He smiled
And took you by the hand,
Saying: "Fear not, My holy child–
For by your side I shall always stand."

Thus said He–God of field and hill
God of mountain and sea, the Lord of Israel.

Sallu ran back to the schoolhouse, and then it began to rain. Big drops came down. The water fell faster and faster, until there was a downpour. A sudden summer shower arose, with curtains of water that hid the surrounding countryside. The rain came down in sheets and torrents. The beadle found that he could wiggle his right hand. His right arm was free; then his left became unstuck. Soon the rain had washed away all the mud and the muck and the plants and the ooze. The beadle dragged himself from the marsh. He stood there, sore and wet and muddy. The rain stopped. Ragged black clouds raced across the sky. The beadle took the note that Sallu handed to him–a note that the Rabbi had actually written–and he went back to the city of Cologne, feeling miserable, wet, and cold.

The beadle could not read, but he took the parchment note to the Archbishop as he had promised. The beadle walked north up Bechergasse Street to the great Catholic Cathedral–the Dom–in which the three famed kings of Cologne are buried. (Those kings–Kaspar, Melchior, and Balthazar–were the three wise men who came from the East to see the infant Jesus.) The Archbishop was in a small library at the side of the building.

Archbishop Philip sat back at his desk and he opened the note. The Rabbi had written it in mystical Kabbalistic Hebrew, and when it was turned upside down the letters looked remarkably like Latin. At the top, the mystical symbols looked like words, while at the bottom, they appeared to be the Pope's official seal.

Philip von Heinsberg stared, but he could not read the note. He squinted and he blinked. The words were tantalizingly familiar, but he could not figure out what they said. Was he getting old? Were his eyes finally failing him? But how could he, the Archbishop of Cologne, not read Latin – and the Latin in a note from the Pope no less? Archbishop Philip nodded and he said, "Hmm."

Minutes passed. The Archbishop turned the paper around and around. He held it up to the light. He frowned, he nodded, he said "Hmm" many times. Finally he said to the beadle, "Yes, yes – I see. Now tell me, my friend, exactly what did the schoolteacher tell you that the Pope wanted?"

"Apparently," answered the beadle, "the Pope has decided to spare that particular Jewish school." He stopped, he looked at the Archbishop, and then he asked: "Is this not what the letter reports?"

Again the Archbishop looked at the mystical Kabbalistic script. "Yes," he sighed, "I suppose that *is* what it says." And so the rickety Jewish *heder* of Wevelinghoven was saved – although by now it has long since disappeared.

Good evening, Rabbi. . . . No, I was just resting my eyes. Please, join me here by the stove; it will work its white magic on the two of us. . . . What? Yes, I suppose that I misspoke – I know that Jews have no white magic, just as we have no black magic. "White" and "black" are about the *purpose* of magic: they are about the goals of the magician. We Jews are more interested in the *means* of the magic. Wondrous magical things do happen for Jews: apparitions and holy noises drift in at night, prayer books move in the stillness of the synagogue, demons are turned into piles of dust. But to us *how* these things come about is all-important. If these wonders are not brought about by Divine inspiration then they are a sacrilege, no matter what their purpose.

Angels and good spirits can be used in holy magic. But demons, dybbuks, devils, and idols must forever be kept at four arms' lengths, as the Book of Leviticus commands:

> Do not resort to ghosts, evil spirits, or demons. Do not make yourselves unclean by seeking them out or by associating with them in any way: they are not among My sphere of holy children – and I am the Lord.

It is never permissible to ask an idol to perform a good deed or even a selfless humane act. As the Most Holy One says in the Book of Genesis:

> If you are honorable and upright
>   then you will be blessed evermore.
> But for others, Sin is a demon-wight
>   that is crouching at your door.
> Yes, the idol Sin waits quiet out of sight
>   hoping to slyly tempt and lure:
> It will even promise you the sun at night–
>   ah, but then it will master you for sure.

False gods and graven images are simply unacceptable; it does not matter what they offer or promise or do–as poor Elisha found out. . . .

What is that, Rabbi? Well, I suppose that the story of Elisha is not well known nowadays. I heard it from my grandmother, many years ago, and she took as her authority the mystical Abraham Achselrad. Old Rabbi Abraham often had dealings with demons while he did his best to keep them away from his congregants. Sometimes the old Rabbi succeeded. Sometimes he did not. For example, there was the time when a simple man named Elisha ben Alexis was entrapped by a cunning demon:

Elisha ben Alexis ha-Kohen lived in medieval Cologne. Strange things had happened to Elisha recently, therefore he went to see the mystic Achselrad. It was a springtime night. Rabbi Achselrad was studying in the back room of the yeshiva. Elisha walked quickly through the main prayer hall, which was filled with wooden benches. He passed the twelve stained-glass windows with their colored lions and snakes, he looked up at the Holy stone Ark, and he walked to the door of the back study room. It was late, but the weather was mild, the windows were open, and the Rabbi was bent over a book.

"Rabbi Abraham?"

The Rabbi looked up in the candlelight. "Yes?"

"Rabbi, my name is Elisha ben Alexis. I have a question."

"Please ask it," said the Rabbi.

Elisha sat down. "I was wondering, Rabbi: can one give charity if the money comes from questionable sources?"

Rabbi Abraham raised his eyebrows and he set down his book. "I think that you had best tell me the whole story, Reb Elisha," he said.

Elisha sat quietly for a moment; then he told his story to Rabbi Abraham. Elisha looked down at his shoes as he talked, and the Rabbi said not a word.

It all began, reported Elisha, when he had been digging up the ground in order to enlarge his garden. He chopped away tree roots and he pulled up rocks; then he struck a strange hard object. Elisha tugged and pulled, and finally he got the thing out of the ground. He brushed it off. Why, it was an old marble statue! It was a fat little man, a short, round man with small eyes and small ears, who sat silently with his hands folded over his round, round belly.

Elisha set the statue on a rock. He walked around and looked at it from all sides. Perhaps this was worth some money, he thought. Suddenly the statue spoke. "Please clean me," it said. Elisha jumped back. Was he imagining things? No one else was around. The statue had not moved. Elisha frowned. Then the statue said, "Good sir, I have been underground for a great many years. I would like to feel neat and clean again." Elisha stood stock-still, staring. "Are you hard of hearing?" asked the statue. After a moment, Elisha said, "No." "Good," said the statue. "Then would you mind wiping some of the dirt off me?"

Elisha took a rag and, very hesitantly, he wiped the statue. The statue said no more. Elisha stood waiting. Nothing happened. Elisha shook his head and went back into his house.

Elisha lived alone. The next day, he looked out at his garden. The statue was exactly where he had left it. The garden appeared unchanged. The day was cool and gray, and Elisha set to work again. As he dug, Elisha looked at the statue frequently. Nothing unusual happened, and Elisha began to feel more comfortable. Eventually he took a rest and he stepped closer to the statue. There was a gold coin on its head. Why had Elisha not noticed this before? He looked around. The garden was empty. Voices could be heard from far away, but nearby there was only the gentle sound of the wind. Curiouser and curiouser, thought Elisha, and he took the coin into the house.

A few days later, Elisha was again working in his garden. He heard a cough, and he looked up. No one was around. Then the statue said, "My good friend, I need your help. Now, now–do not be afraid. I mean you no harm. In fact, I gave you that gold coin to thank you for cleaning me the other day. I myself cannot move: I am merely an old statue left by people who have long since gone from this part of the world. Another statue like me has fallen over in a yard behind Unter Taschenmacher Street. It is covered with dirt and weeds. Once, this poor statue was a friend of mine, and I hate to think of it lying there with its face in the mud. Would you be so kind as to go and set it upright?"

Elisha stood silently. This was a strange request. Perhaps it was even unholy. Certainly it was dangerous. Jews were not welcome outside the Juden Viertels. How could Elisha just wander into a Gentile's yard on Unter Taschenmacher Street and fiddle with this unknown man's statue? Leaves blew through the bushes at Elisha's side and dry grasses rustled. Elisha ben Alexis ha-Kohen shivered.

"I know that this is outside of your neighborhood," said the statue, "but it is really a modest request."

Still Elisha did not move. "Listen here, good Elisha," continued the statue, "there is no reason to be afraid. If you go tomorrow night when there is no moon, then you will be quite safe."

Elisha was worried and confused. Extraordinary things seemed to be happening, and they were carrying him along before he had time to think; the world was rushing by. Elisha looked around him. The sky was above his head; the ground was beneath his feet. The trees and the houses seemed the same as always. Then the voice from the statue said, "I ask this as a favor, my friend, but there are also ten gold coins under the statue. They are for whoever sets the Taschenmacher statue upright. Why should you let someone else claim the money, when you could obviously use it?"

Ten gold coins–why that was a fortune! "All right," said Elisha, and the statue gave him detailed instructions.

The next night, Elisha wore black clothes and a dark cap. He waited until late at night; then he walked down Judengasse Street, staying in the darkest shadows. As his statue had said, there was no moon and no one was out and about. At the edge of the Jewish Quarter, going north across Klein Budengasse Street, Judengasse Street changed its name to Unter Taschenmacher Street. Elisha felt shaky and weak. He crept up Unter Taschenmacher Street. There were strange noises at the corners of the walls and fences. These were not the voices of people. Were they perhaps demons? Elisha shivered. Soon he found the yard; it seemed to be a great distance from the safety of the Juden Viertels.

The gate to the yard was ajar. Elisha stopped. He took a deep breath. Why was this terrible adventure not over? If only he were leaving and heading back to safety. Elisha forced his feet to walk forward. He tripped over a small mound of dirt. There were piles of leaves and sticks. Then, in the back, Elisha saw the statue. It was the robed figure of a woman. At first when Elisha tried to lift it, it would not move. Elisha took a deep breath, and with a grunt he managed to set the statue upright. He saw a cloth purse underneath. Elisha picked up the purse and he walked as fast as he dared out of the yard.

Elisha was afraid to look back. Quickly he walked down the street. He was certain that he was being followed. Was someone about to stop him and hit him? Would he be robbed or arrested? He felt even weaker than before, but somehow he kept walking, walking, walking. The welcoming gates at the edge of the Juden Viertels loomed ahead; then he was through the gates and he ran and ran back to the safety of his home. Elisha closed the door behind him and lay on his bed, breathing heavily, hot and damp and shaky. Sometime later Elisha fell asleep in a bundle of clothes and blankets, and then it was the morning. Elisha opened the cloth purse and he found ten gold coins. Later he took them to the synagogue and put them all in the poor box.

For a few days, Elisha avoided the statue in his garden. One morning, the weather was fine. Birds called from the bushes. Light breezes blew the leaves. A gentle warm sky smiled down, and Elisha ventured over to the far edge of his yard. He could not resist looking at the statue. There it sat in the morning sun, round and gray and weather-worn. And what was this? Something glittered on the statue's head. It was a gold coin. No, it was a neat stack of five gold coins! Elisha looked around him. The yard was empty. Slowly he walked to the statue, and he took the money. Elisha stood still. Nothing happened. There were no noises. He turned to go, but then he heard a quiet voice say: "Give the money to a charity, my friend–to a Jewish charity."

The next morning, after the prayer service, Elisha put the five gold coins in the poor box. Then, each day, he checked for money, and each day there were five gold coins on top of the statue. "Keep one coin, and give four to charity," said the statue one morning. And Elisha did. Each morning after prayers, he put four gold coins into the poor box. Other men heard the coins drop in, they looked at one another, and they marveled at Elisha's unstinting benevolence. Still, Elisha felt increasingly uneasy. He thought about consulting Rabbi Achselrad, but he hesitated. This was a strange and magical business, perhaps a demon was involved, and Elisha thought that he might be doing something very wrong.

Elisha continued to feel worse and worse. He had trouble sleeping and eating and concentrating on his work. He had nightmares and bleak daydreams. So eventually Elisha built up his courage. He went to the synagogue at a quiet time, when the back study room was empty, and now he was talking with old Rabbi Abraham.

Here Elisha paused a moment in his story. He looked up at Rabbi Abraham. "Is this too strange, Rabbi?" he asked.

"It is strange," said Abraham ben Alexander quietly. "But who is to say what is *too* strange? Only the good Lord God (blessed be He) is the true Arbiter of strangeness."

Rabbi Abraham's voice seemed to fade away. Elisha looked at the Rabbi. The Rabbi had closed his eyes. His chin had sunk to his chest, and he was breathing heavily and slowly. Reb Elisha was not certain what to do. Finally he said gently, "Rabbi?"

Old Achselrad opened his eyes. He looked up at the ceiling. He said something very quietly. Elisha bent toward the Rabbi. "What did you say, Rabbi?"

Silently, the Rabbi looked at Elisha. Rabbi Abraham ben Alexander stared at Elisha as if he were trying to see inside the man, and then the Rabbi said, "Elisha, my friend, in the holy Book of Deuteronomy, we are told":

> You shall not make for yourself any idol or other carved image; moreover, to no visible shape in the heavens above or on the earth below or in the waters under the earth shall you bow down or worship.

Elisha waited for more advice, but old Achselrad had closed his eyes again and he seemed to have fallen into a deep sleep. Eventually,

Elisha ben Alexis stood up and slipped quietly out of the Cologne yeshiva.

Elisha remained very, very worried. He did not know what to do. Should he avoid the garden altogether? He stopped collecting the coins. One day, Elisha was hurrying through the front of the garden when he heard a voice. It was the statue speaking, and it said, "Good Elisha, you look worn and weary. And you have forgotten to take the charity coins."

"I have been busy," said Elisha.

"Well, my friend, just come over and collect these coins; they are for the poor and the needy," said the statue. Elisha walked to the statue and picked up a large pile of coins that had spilled at the statue's feet.

Elisha was walking away, when he heard the voice of the statue again. "Oh, by the way, my friend," it said, "I do not mean to bother you. But I wonder if you would help me out in a small way. As you know, I cannot move on my own. It is dark these nights, as the year wanes. It would be a great help if you would light a lamp in front of me. I must confess I am like a child, and I see fearsome shapes in the shadows late at night. A light will be comforting: it will keep me company and let me sleep more easily."

Was this an innocent request? The garden began to have the feeling of a shrine. The statue was acting like an idol. Elisha had a sudden vision of a small firelit room, a niche, a tiny cavern in a great wall. It was dark and dim and damp. Many candles stood in circles at the foot of the little catacomb and echoes sounded far in the distance. Elisha shook himself–and once again he saw his garden, and the unreal feeling passed.

Elisha said nothing. He went straight to the synagogue, and he put all the money in the poor box, keeping none for himself. He said the *Shema* three times. When finally he went home, he stayed in the front of his house, far from the back garden. Still, something seemed to pull his thoughts to the statue. Its request was so simple. And the statue seemed genuinely concerned for others: it had wanted to help a fellow statue, and it gave alms to the poor and the helpless in the community.

Elisha walked outside. He looked at the statue from a distance. It was small and round and gray. It was like a weak little child that could do nothing on its own. That night, Elisha came out after dark. He lit one candle in front of the statue. Should he say a prayer? Perhaps this would make the candle more holy. Elisha could not remember the exact words for the lighting of candles. He began: "Blessed are You Who has commanded us to light the nighttime candles." But as he said these words a wind arose and blew out the flame. Elisha shivered. He looked around. Silently, he relit the candle; then he went back into his house.

Money continued to appear each morning. Elisha gave much to the community charities and the daily poor box, but still there was extra. Soon, Elisha was rich enough to stop working entirely. He did not need to grow anything in his garden because he could afford to buy all the vegetables that he could possibly eat. Elisha dressed well, and he ate good food. He got less exercise and he began to get fat. Over the years, his hair thinned, his skin whitened, and his ears shrank. Elisha got rounder and shorter. His *tallit* no longer fit around him, and his *tefillin* would not stay in place – they were always wrapped awkwardly, and they slid and slipped and became hopelessly entangled.

Elisha was not comfortable in the synagogue. He felt itchy and restless and crowded whenever he was there; he felt at odds with the holy aura. Demons pushed and shoved him from all sides. Whispering voices made it difficult for him to concentrate on the service. One year, it was *Rosh Hashanah.* Elisha was praying, and eventually there came the verse in the *Alenu* prayer that goes:

> It is our duty, it is our task, to praise the Lord of all, to tell of the greatness of the Creator of the universe. He has charged us to keep His Word alive, unlike the other nations who worship and bow down before idols and other vanities. We are different: we bend our knee and bow down and give thanks only before the supreme King of kings, the most Holy One, the Lord God Almighty, blessed be He.

Suddenly, a dark mist seemed to surround Elisha. The other worshipers were frightened. They fell silent. They looked at Elisha in horror, and he hurried out of the synagogue.

Now Elisha was shunned by the Jewish community. People were afraid to talk to him. He began to frequent the Gentile streets and markets and inns. He continued to grow smaller and rounder and he became almost unrecognizable by his old friends. Some people said that his face had changed so much that you could not be certain that

Elisha was in fact the same man. Perhaps a demon had taken over his body. Or maybe the original Elisha had simply gone away and another man had come to live in his place. Could he be retrieved? Could the original Elisha ben Alexis ha-Kohen be found and restored again? Or was it too late? People shook their heads. Even old Rabbi Achselrad did not seem to know the answer.

What is that, Rabbi? No, my grandmother knew no more, except that as he aged, Elisha ben Alexis became a fat little man who spent most of his life sitting in his garden, and, as he sat, he folded his hands over his round, round belly.

Ah, Rabbi, I am glad to see you here alone. I want to apologize for my outburst during the service this evening. It was just that Reb Anton was muttering during the prayers again. He actually said, "snakes"!

What? "Shakes"? Well, it *sounded* like "snakes," and one must be careful what one says in the synagogue. A casual comment is a serious matter. One cannot simply say "snakes" and think nothing of it. Snakes are carriers of much power, and not only through their venom: they are also the agents of all manner of powerful magics, both good and bad. For example, if you dream of a snakebite, it is a good sign–it means that sudden prosperity is in your future. And then the old rabbis could open any lock by smearing the right foot of a male raven with the fat of a snake and stroking the lock with it. You have never heard of this? Undoubtedly it was before your time. Besides, you are a rabbi who shies away from such mystical matters. But I can tell you, Rabbi: you should definitely pay more attention to snakes.

Snakes live everywhere. . . . Yes, yes, I know they are rare around here, but that is in their usual snaky form. Snakes, I will have you know, come in many guises. For instance, beware of heavily cloaked strangers: huge serpents can appear at your doorstep bundled like men. (Of course, you can always tell a snake from a true man, because serpents are deathly afraid of thunder; that is why they live in caves.) In any case, speaking of serpents and caves, I am reminded of the story that my grandmother told me about snakes and old Petahiah. Apparently, this story first reached Europe in a letter from Rabbi Petahiah of Regensburg to Rabbi Abraham ben Alexander, the mystic Achselrad of Cologne.

"*My dear Rabbi Abraham–*

"I have just met a fine young man, a Jew from Leipzig; he has agreed to carry this letter to the Chief Rabbi there, Rabbi Nathan, who I am certain will then arrange to transport it to you. I write to wish you and your family well. Also let me convey my fondest greetings to all the Jews of your blessed community in Cologne, and as always I praise the good Lord God (blessed be He) and His Almighty Name for ever and ever, amen.

"I will not trouble you with the details of my wagon rides and my subsequent sea voyages. Suffice it to say that safely they brought me here to the Oriental regions, regions that are so near to the great Holy Land where someday the Messiah shall return and deliver us and resurrect all souls and rebuild the Temple on Zion, amen. I write now in order to record for you some details of the lands and the peoples that I have seen in these old and foreign realms. The bright and glorious hand of the good Lord God (blessed be He) is visible everywhere, if only we look–praise the Lord Yahweh-Elohim.

"At present, I am in the city of Jebeil. As you might imagine, my old friend, I have had many, many adventures in arriving here. While touring the Holy Land of Palestine, I turned east from Jerusalem and went to the town of Jericho. (The natives now call it er-Riha.) Outside the city, I saw a vast camp, a city of nomads. From a distance, they looked like flecks of pepper scattered atop a sea of salt, for the black goat-hair tents seemed mere dots on the white sandy desert. Nearing, I could see several women sitting cross-legged before an enormous bowl in which they were preparing greens for the next meal, and hordes of children were crowded around the women, the tents, and the camels.

"I am told that Jericho means 'fragrant city of the moon god.' It lies in a valley of the River Jordan, north of the Dead Sea. There is a great spring here, and Jericho is an oasis city. The spring is the famed one that was blessed and purified by the Prophet Elisha; Jews call it Elisha's Spring, but the Arabs call it *Ain es-Sultan,* the Sultan's Spring. Jericho was the first Canaanite city to be attacked and conquered by the Israelites, and since those biblical times it has been overrun again and again. The city has always been prized because it is one of the most fertile places in all of Palestine. Fruit grows freely all around: palm trees are everywhere. Nonetheless, today's Jericho is a poor village. The ruins and mounds (especially near the spring) remind one of more magnificent days. There is an old tower in the center of the town, and there are some poorly maintained aqueducts, and the surrounding mountains hold monasteries, tombs, and holy caves.

"Caves, my good friend Abraham, are quite sacred and mystical here. Spirits inhabit the caves. And then too, men have always taken refuge in these caves. When Lot left Zoar, he lived in a cave with his two daughters. When the five kings of Canaan fled Joshua, they took to the local caves. David hid from Saul in the caves of Palestine. Moreover, caves are the most honored burial places in the Holy Land; there is, of course, the famed cave of Machpelah where Sarah and the Patriarchs are buried. It is no wonder that the old stories in these regions often take place in caves; for example, recently I heard this story about a serpent and a cave:

"Once upon a time, there was a poor orphan named Benjamin. At a young age, he was taken in by a large family of cousins. His aunt and uncle were quiet and poor, and they were always tired. Benjamin was a good boy: he did what he was asked, he never complained, and he followed his cousins wherever they went.

"The family barely had enough food, and Benjamin often dreamt of fancy meals – of honey and cakes and hot meats – but one night, a strange old man appeared in his dream. The man had a long white robe and a tangled beard. He looked like a rabbi, but he was no one that Benjamin knew. The old man held out a gemstone, a diamond with a tiny candle sparkling inside. The man said nothing, but Benjamin heard him talking, nonetheless. How could this be? Ah, Abraham, anything is possible in a dream, and so the boy was not surprised.

"The old man's voice said, 'Benjamin, here is a diamond. Take it and sell it. With the money, you will develop a good business, and then you will become rich. You will build a magnificent house. You will wed happily. You will have shops and farms. You will eat fine foods and drink rich wines. And, you will soon have a daughter as beautiful as a gemstone. Raise her well and guard her carefully, because one day you will have to exchange her for the diamond. But, if all goes well, you will never lose her.'

"This was a puzzling speech. How could Benjamin give up his daughter and yet not lose her? The old man faded away, and Benjamin awoke and he remembered his dream. However, it was still the dark hours of the night, and the boy fell back asleep and whatever dreams he had thereafter are not recorded.

"In the morning, Benjamin awoke. He had a strange feeling. His arms tingled. His stomach felt light. It was still early, and he put on his coat. He walked outside and looked around. It was a sunny morning with the clouds high and white and the sky blue and light. The grass was a misty sea. But no one else was about. Was the world empty of all mankind? How could this be? It felt so bright and so warm.

"Benjamin walked out into the field. It was a bright morning and Benjamin found that the shining dew was still on every buttercup. The boy bent down. Why, what was this? The glistening dew was not water–it was a diamond! This was just as in his dream. Benjamin picked up the gem, he turned it around and around in his hand, and he stood for many minutes, looking at the glittering crystal.

"Benjamin walked to the marketplace. How could he sell this fancy gem? People would think that he had stolen it. He wandered about with the diamond in his pocket. Then he remembered a friend of his, a boy named Adel. Adel's father dealt in jewelry. Benjamin went to their shop and he called Adel out into the back alley. Adel's eyes went wide as saucers when he saw the diamond. Yes, he would get his father to buy the stone, he said, and he ran with the gem into the shop.

"This was a magnificent gem, and Adel's father wanted the diamond badly. He gave Adel much less money than the stone actually was worth, but to Benjamin it was a fortune in gold coins. So Benjamin thanked Adel, he pocketed the money, and he walked around the marketplace.

"Benjamin was quiet and small. Softly and timidly, he bought and sold a number of goods. By the end of the day, he had doubled his money. Then, day after day, he wandered about the markets, buying and selling trinkets and clothes and knives and small fancy utensils. He bought jewelry and he sold jewelry. He bought and sold spices. Soon he was walking from town to town. And in a few months, he was carrying on a vigorous trading business.

"Years passed – seven years came and seven years went – and the youth became a very rich merchant. He was the husband of a fine wife. He was the father of a beautiful daughter named Hodiah. Hodiah was pretty and talented. She was an especially good seamstress and was known throughout the region for her fancy embroidery. Benjamin smiled proudly at the endless compliments he got for Hodiah.

"Everything was going very well for Benjamin. Then one day, when Benjamin was returning home from a business trip, a huge serpent suddenly slipped out of the forest. Benjamin began to run, but he became weak; his legs ached, and he could barely move. He shook and shivered and trembled. The serpent glided around the rocks. It slid past the trees. It slithered nearer and nearer. And then there was a voice. Did it come from the serpent, or did it come from the air? Benjamin could not tell, but he heard: 'Once, you were given a diamond, Benjamin. Now you must give it back.'

" 'But I sold the diamond long ago,' said Benjamin weakly.

" 'Your daughter is your diamond. You must give her up in marriage,' said the voice.

" 'Yes, yes, I will,' said the merchant, and the serpent vanished and there was only the wind and the dust and the brush blowing along the edge of the road.

"Benjamin was weak and shaky. He looked around at the empty road. What was this all about? he wondered. He remembered that the great Book of Genesis says: 'The serpent was more subtle and more crafty than any other wild creature that the Lord God had made.'

" 'Something terrible is about to happen,' thought Benjamin – but what was it?

"Benjamin hurried home. He looked gray and tired. He sat in the kitchen. His heart beat quickly. Benjamin's wife was worried. 'Have you come back with a disease?' she asked.

" 'No,' said the merchant, 'I have fallen into a strange dream. Somehow we shall be forced to marry our daughter, and I fear that the circumstances will be very sad.'

"This strange pronouncement came to Benjamin's wife out of the blue. Whatever was her husband talking about? She opened her eyes wide, she tilted her head, and she looked at her husband. He seemed to be quite serious.

"Benjamin's daughter, Hodiah, was listening too. 'Father,' she said cheerfully, 'do not be such a worrier. I myself have not the slightest idea to whom I could possibly be engaged. However, if I am destined to be married, then the good Lord knows all about it, so I am certain that it will be a happy marriage.'

"Benjamin only shook his head sadly.

" 'Listen, Father,' said Hodiah, 'our lives are really quite fine. You have always been a good and loving father, you have been a rock and even a saint. You should have confidence in yourself–and in me, too. God will ensure that things will work out well in the end.'

"Benjamin was worried, but he did not know what to say, so he patted his daughter on the hand.

"Weeks passed. Months went by. Two years came and two years went. Life seemed normal. Benjamin's wife and daughter forgot about that one strange day, but Benjamin still lived with a hidden fear. Then one night, there was a knock at the front door. Benjamin opened the door, and looming large in the doorway was a heavily cloaked man. Benjamin stepped back. The cloak slid to the ground, and Benjamin saw that the man was really a serpent, the same snake that had come after poor Benjamin on that terrifying day years ago. The serpent had black, shining eyes. Its glinting scales were rimmed in gold. It opened its mouth and two sharp teeth like long curved needles shone in the candlelight that came from inside the house. 'I am here,' hissed the snake, 'to marry your daughter.'

"Benjamin's knees weakened, and he leaned against the wall. Hodiah was standing behind her father. Her eyes went wide. Then she said, 'I cannot marry without an engagement ring.'

"The snake hissed and flicked out its pointed tongue, and a black ring fell at her feet. Hodiah picked it up. She looked at her father, and then she put the ring on her finger. 'Very well,' she said bravely, 'we will be married.'

"Benjamin stood stunned. But Hodiah stepped out the door, and she and the snake disappeared into the night. It was only moments later when they returned. 'I am now married, father,' said Hodiah. Benjamin shook his head, and he had tears in his eyes.

"The snake glided into the house and into Hodiah's room. 'Bring me a cup of milk,' he said. Hodiah got a cup of milk. She went into her room with the snake and closed the door. The snake drank the milk, he shook himself from his head to his tail, and his snakeskin slid off smoothly. The serpent had shed his skin, and now a fine young man stood before Hodiah.

"Hodiah's eyes were wide, and she said, 'I knew that there was magic afoot here.'

"The young man said to her, 'My dear, there is a long and difficult tale behind all this. If you want to live happily with me, do not ask any questions and do not tell anyone, even your parents, what you have seen. Every morning, I must leave you–but I will return at nightfall.'

"Ah, Rabbi Abraham, this young man was strong and handsome and dark-haired. He talked with a deep, quiet voice. He was sincere and kind, and he knew all manner of fascinating stories. You can well imagine that the daughter fell in love with him immediately. Hodiah was enchanted. She felt like she was in a dream. How could anything more wonderful happen to her?

"In the morning, Hodiah awoke and found that the serpent was no longer there. At first she was in a panic. Then she remembered that there was some kind of terrible curse on her beloved husband and that he would have to be gone during the days. Meanwhile Hodiah's parents had not slept a wink the whole night. When she came out of the bedroom alone, they asked her endless questions. However, all that Hodiah said was, 'Everything is all right. My husband must be gone during the days. We will see him again tonight.' What was this? thought the parents. What in the world was going on? But the poor parents could get no further information from their daughter.

"The serpent arrived nightly. Each evening, the girl gave him a cup of milk. Then the snake drank the milk, he shook off his skin, and once again he became a handsome young man. The couple was quite happy together, but the parents were confused and upset. Then, of course, the neighbors noticed that a terrible creature spent the evenings in the house of Benjamin the merchant. People talked and raised their eyebrows, and when Benjamin's wife was in the marketplace everyone pointed and shook their heads.

"Nights came and nights went. Benjamin became angry. 'You say that you are a good daughter,' he said to Hodiah, 'but is this how we raised you? You are living with a snake. You refuse to explain anything to your own parents. The neighbors ridicule us. Your mother and I are worried sick. You should be ashamed. No, you should be more than ashamed–you should be mortified. You are married to a snake!'

" 'How can you be so cruel, Father?' said Hodiah. 'You do not trust me. After all these years, have I ever done anything to make you doubt me? My husband is no snake. He is a man. Each evening, he drinks a cup of milk and he slides out of his skin. He is actually the kindest and most handsome young man that I have ever met, and I am proud of him!' And Hodiah ran back into her room. Ah, but now she had blurted out the secret. When the snake appeared that evening, he did not drink the milk. Instead, he said sadly, 'My good wife Hodiah, you have broken your promise. You have told my secret. Now I must leave you. Good-bye.' And he slipped from the house and into the black of the night.

"Poor Hodiah did not even have time to apologize. In the wink of an eye, the serpent had vanished. Hodiah sat silently on her bed. After a long while, she looked around her room. She found that one of her blue embroidered handkerchiefs was missing. Had her snake-husband taken it? Hodiah sat up all night. She remained in her room all the next day, and she refused to answer her parents' questions. She ate a bit of bread and soup that night, and she cried herself to sleep.

"Days passed, and slowly Hodiah fell into a routine. Each morning, she washed and came out of her room, she ate some bread for breakfast, and she sat quietly and sewed or looked out the window all day; then she had some bread for dinner and she went to bed. She did not have the energy to speak to anyone, and she only nodded or shook her head in response to questions.

"Now, Abraham, we turn for a moment to the next-door neighbors, another Jewish family with a small daughter. One day, this girl was playing outside with her doll. A dog passed by, it grabbed the doll, and it scampered off. The child followed the dog. The dog jumped and ran off beyond the edge of the town, and the child trailed behind.

"Suddenly a squirrel leaped out of the bushes. The dog stopped and barked and growled. It ran after the squirrel, and it dropped the doll. The little girl reached the spot where the dog had been, but the doll was nowhere around. The child looked under bushes, in the leaves, behind logs. Beside a small heap of rocks, she found a large burrow, a rabbit hole or a fox hole. 'Perhaps,' she thought, 'my doll has fallen down this hole.'

"The girl crawled into the tiny dirt cave. The hole went straight on like a tunnel for some way; then it dipped suddenly down, so suddenly, that the girl had not a moment to think about stopping before she found herself falling down. She landed on a heap of sticks and dry leaves. And there was her doll! The girl was not hurt; she jumped to her feet. The hollow burrow was dark and scratchy, but the child felt warm and fearless. She looked around, she frowned for a moment, and then she saw that the tunnel widened ahead. There was a light and an opening. Out climbed the child, and her eyes grew wide as she stood in a lovely garden looking at a magnificent stone house.

"Was she near her own home? Had she come out into the world through a back entrance to the rabbit hole? The child was hungry. Slowly and cautiously she walked over to the mansion. No one was around. She peeked in the door. The first room she saw had a table filled with fine food. She stepped in the doorway. Everything was silent. The child walked up to the table and she ate some of the cakes; they were warm, and they tasted wonderful. But what was this? Suddenly she heard voices outside. She hurried into a corner and hid behind a huge pottery jar.

"Into the room slid ten huge black snakes. They glided to the table and curled up on the ten oak chairs. The snakes sipped milk from ten porcelain cups and suddenly all ten snakes shook themselves and slipped from their skins, and then there were ten handsome young men sitting at the table.

"The ten young men threw their skins out a window. They bowed their heads, and they said a quiet prayer":

> We pray, O Lord, Who gave us breath,
> Send us a maid who's bold and brave;
> Have her face the serpent's death
> Down here in the night's dark cave–
> And have her burn our skins as well
> To save us from this evil spell,
> Amen.

"After this strange prayer, the young men ate and drank and talked and even laughed. Then they walked into the next room, where they fell asleep on ten downy featherbeds. The hidden little girl saw one of the men take out a handkerchief from his pocket and kiss it and sigh sadly. Why, this was a handkerchief that the child recognized! It was one of the delicate blue cloths embroidered by her neighbor, Hodiah.

"But now the child herself was very, very tired, and soon she fell asleep. In the morning when she awoke, all the serpents had vanished. The girl peeked out from her hiding place. Everything was silent. She stood and stretched and smoothed her dress. She was hungry. She ate some bread that she found on the table. Then, timidly and looking carefully around at every step, she left the stone mansion.

"The girl found her way back to the tunnel, and from the tunnel she hurried home. All the time, she looked behind her, and every strange noise made her heart beat faster. At home, her mother hugged and hugged her. Where had she been? The girl was too shy to tell the details. 'I was lost and I slept in a little cave in the woods,' she said.

"When finally she escaped from her mother's hugs and questions, the little girl went to the neighboring merchant's house to speak to Hodiah. The child told how she had found a cave, and she told about the blue embroidered handkerchief. Hodiah gasped–then she hugged the little girl. And together they went off immediately to the underground house. When they reached the cave, Hodiah managed to squeeze through the tunnel. And the two girls–one a child and one a young woman–entered the palace holding hands, and together they hid behind the large stone pot in the dining room.

"Again the serpents slid into the room that evening. They drank the milk, they shed their skins, they said a prayer, and they ate honey and cakes and hot meats; then they talked and laughed. Hodiah recognized her husband. Did she dare rush out and hug him? She was afraid that once again she would ruin everything. Then she remembered the prayer. The snakes had thrown their skins out the window. Perhaps if she burned the skins, then everything would be all right.

"After the young men had gone to bed, Hodiah crept out of the house. Underneath the window, the snakeskins lay in a heap, black and shining in the moonlight. She threw a match onto the pile. The skins flared up in flames. They crackled and they burst, and they ripped and burned and evaporated in a hot wavering wind. The young men ran out of the house. They were wide-eyed and open-mouthed. Then they cheered, and Hodiah's husband came over and hugged and squeezed her until she was practically sore.

"The ten men and Hodiah trooped into the dining room. The little girl was still peeking out from behind the stone jar. Hodiah reached down, took her hand, and sat the child at the table. All the young men were talking at once, but this is the story that Hodiah's husband eventually told to her:

" 'My dear, we are ten brothers. Our father was a famous rabbi. One sad day, our mother died, and soon father remarried. Our stepmother is a sorceress, a witch named Lamia. She had one son of her own; he was the youngest of all us children, so he would inherit the least, and of course he would never succeed my father in the rabbinate.

" 'When my father died, Lamia consulted with her strange and wicked relatives. Together, they devised an evil incantation and turned us all into snakes. Then, when we disappeared as young men, the entire inheritance went to Lamia's son and he became the rabbi. Eventually we discovered that our only hope–the only cure–was to have a young woman come and burn our shed skins. Actually, my father learned of this in the Afterworld, and he appeared to *your* father in a dream, trying to unchain us from our terrible fate. By the Lord's good grace, my father's plan worked, and you have now saved us. The spell is broken at last!'

"No one slept that night. The next morning, all the brothers and Hodiah and the small girl crawled out of the cave and returned above ground. When Benjamin opened his door the whole company walked in, talking and laughing and congratulating one another. Benjamin stood back. His eyes opened wide. It was as if an entire fair had come to town and had marched right into his home.

"Then the whole story was told once and it was told twice, and after three hearings, a wonderful wedding was arranged that same day. The ceremony took place in the local Wedding House, and people came from near and from far. There were special feasts for seven days. The local Jews were all impressed with Hodiah's husband: his learning, his calm, self-confident speech, and his measured judgments gave them a sense of security and respect. Soon he was invited to be the town's rabbi. The young couple lived modestly, they gave charity freely, and they became a model for all the families in the congregation.

"Now Benjamin was happy and finally at peace. He never again dreamt of the old man – but sometimes he still dreamt of fancy meals of honey and cakes and hot meats. Then, when he awoke, he would put on his robe and go into the kitchen and make a fine and delicious breakfast. And would he eat it alone and all by himself? Certainly not – he shared it with his two young grandchildren, the loves of his old age, Hodiah's boy and girl.

"Well, Abraham, that is a cave story as told to me just yesterday evening. It is a happy story, in spite of the fact that it is also about serpents of whom, once upon a time, the Almighty One had said to the first serpent, 'I will make an enmity between you and the woman, between your brood and hers.' Ah, Abraham, even in the childhood of our world, things were so complex and intertwined and unpredictable that onetime prohibitions have been turned on their heads and evil can sometimes lead to good. I suppose that is God's way with all things. Our world is rich with entanglements. It is filled with brambles and vines. It has unimagined twists and turns. Therefore we are forever immersed in its heady complexities, and we are absolutely overwhelmed every single time that we step out the door. Who can say what will happen next? And then after it has happened, who can really explain it? Only the Omnipotent One Who watches over every sparrow knows all the reasons – and although He smiles and smiles with His wondrous sunshine radiance, still He says little aloud.

"Your childhood friend,
Petahiah, the son of Jacob"

Hello, Rabbi. I will be with you in a moment. I cannot leave until every tablecloth is folded, otherwise the day has not ended properly.

Well, I am finished at last – now I can sit next to you by the stove. At the end of the week the stove is especially warm and magical. Look into the open oven door and you can see the end of this world and the beginning of the next, with light white angels slipping and sliding among the clouds in that eternal glowing summer sky of the Great Hereafter. It is the end of this world, and soon we shall sleep peacefully forever in the next great world, amen.

Ah, yes, I understand, Rabbi. Somehow I am not sleepy yet, either. Everyone says that old people are always falling asleep, but I sleep less now that I am old. It is the nature of old men to go into their last days awake and open-eyed. When you get old, Rabbi, you will find that you have more time – but if you are like me, you will just muse away the hours and not get much accomplished. I sit and remember and review and dream, and the hours speed quietly by.

It is like my grandmother, who quietly reminisced to herself for hours and hours on end. When she talked to me it seemed as if she were taking up in the middle of a story. Sometimes she talked to herself and sometimes she talked aloud, but it was a story that she was telling herself continuously.

In fact, that is exactly how she described her favorite old rabbi, Abraham ben Alexander, the mystic Achselrad of Cologne. He was a continuous storyteller. He lived to be seventy years of fine old age, and all that time he was writing or talking or having visions, and his life seemed to be one long continuous story, with adventure upon adventure upon adventure.

Rabbi Abraham's adventures, real or imagined, found their way into his books, for this strange Rabbi was a prolific writer. Unfortunately, his most famous Kabbalistic tome, the *Keter Shem Tov*–a book of mystic lore–has never been published; today it lies in the Cologne yeshiva as forgotten crumbling papers above the rabbi's study room. Old Achselrad worked on this book night and day, year in and year out. My grandmother told me that it was early one summer morning in the year 4947, while writing this very manuscript, that Rabbi Abraham looked up, and in the yellow light of the morning he saw a young congregant named Daniel ben Martel standing in the doorway.

Daniel had a letter, a sealed package for Rabbi Abraham ben Alexander, Achselrad of Cologne, the Chief Rabbi of the Rhine region in Germany. And where was it from, this parchment letter? Daniel's father Martel was a wine exporter, and yesterday a Jewish merchant coming north from Provence and heading to Antwerp had delivered a number of packages to Martel. Among them was a letter from the city of Toledo in Spain. On the outside, it was addressed to many important European leaders, including Pope Clement III, Emperor Frederick, King Alphonso of Portugal, King Henry of Germany, King Richard of England, King Philip Augustus of France, King William of Sicily, Duke Henry of Saxony, Archbishop Philip von Heinsberg, and Rabbi Abraham ben Alexander of Cologne.

Rabbi Abraham looked at the envelope. He raised his eyebrows, he thanked Daniel, and after the boy had left, old Abraham Achselrad opened the letter.

"*To the Leaders of the World*–

"This is the year A.D. 1185. We Sages and Astrologers of the great city of Toledo have collected together, and we now pen this letter to recognize an imminent disaster and to save the World as best we can from the impending Doom and Destruction. We hereby notify Pope Clement III and other leading men of note and import. Sirs, be forewarned: the World will be destroyed in two years, in September of the year A.D. 1187. All signs are unmistakable. The stars and the planets speak like trumpets.

"And what will happen in those fateful days? There will be vast winds and awesome storms; there will be drought and famine, pestilence and earthquake and death. People must be advised to forsake their houses: even the most well-built mansions and castles will fall. Righteous citizens should seek the safety of mountains and caverns. We warn you: Go to holy Christian places. Find havens in far mountain retreats. And especially those who live in the low-lying World must protect themselves against the storms of sand that will enshroud the seacoasts of the East.

"The terrible time will arrive suddenly. One moment the sun will be shining, birds will be singing, and light breezes will be blowing. Then a thick darkness will descend. All sound will cease. Vague waves of light and shade will roll over the land. The sky will turn red, and all the Earth will be tinged with blood.

"The darkness will thicken like a blanket; it will be like a suffocating woolen cloth. All towns close to the shore will be covered with sand and dust and ash. A poisonous wind will arise everywhere. Lightning will flash. In the midst of the wind, a Voice of Thunder will be heard, which will destroy the hearts of all those who listen. As the most holy words in the Book of Zechariah warn":

> The angry Lord is cloud-borne,
> Like lightnings shoot his arrows,
> And a blast upon His celestial horn
> Roars forth the fierce tornadoes.

"Next, there will be a tremendous tide. It will be a wall of water higher than ten houses, and it will come roaring in from the endless seas. Everything that is in its path will be swept away. The shores and the low-lying areas will be washed clean through all the plains and to the very bases of the mountains. All plants, food, and animals will be gone. Drinking water will be spoiled with the salt of the sea. Cows and horses and corn and wheat will be washed away, as in the days of the original Great and Fearsome Flood when: 'Lightning bolts flew fast and thick, thunder poured with the whirling rains, the life-giving earth split and flooded. Ocean's deep streams crossed the tops of the seas and rushed the trembling lands. And the great islands cracked in two and sank beneath the many oceans, never again to see the dawn.'

"For our own city, the destruction will be terrible. Here in Toledo, the greatest of all southern cities, the River Tagus will fill its precipitous gorge; it will flood the Castillian plateau, as far as the mountains. Our city will become a besieged island. Buildings will be leveled. Only the magnificent cathedral will withstand the deluge. Food will be swept away by the raging river and the torrential rains, and animals will perish. People will be driven to despair by the devastating winds and weathers. And this terrible scene will be repeated over and over throughout the World of man.

"Great leaders of the World–do you doubt the truth of this inevitability? Each year in the past when a certain conjunction of planets and stars has occurred, there has been a disaster. In the year 436 B.C., a great famine struck at Rome and thousands of starving people threw themselves into the River Tiber. In the year A.D. 42, Egypt was overwhelmed by a terrible famine; then the wicked Egyptians suffered again, this time for seven long years beginning in the year A.D. 1064. The wild East Indies, beyond Asia, has been hit by famines in each of the star-crossed years A.D. 650, 941, 1022, and 1148. Then, of course, there were famines in Europe in the year A.D. 879 and most recently in the year 1162. For every single one of these disasters, astrological signs portended an inevitable terrible event.

"But now the greatest doom yet is about to fall upon us. The astrological indications are unmistakable. There will be a calamitous conjunction of all the planets in the sign of Libra, the Scales, and in the tail of Scorpio, the Dragon, at the end of the month of September. It will be at the time of the full moon. To add to the catastrophe, the sun will also enter into the same conjunction. In fact, this is when the equinox, as symbolized by the Balance–that is, the Scales–will be held between the claws of the Scorpion, which is the symbol of darkness. Such a rare occurrence can only be brought about through the Foreknowledge and the Will of God Himself; undoubtedly, He wishes to set forth an awesome Sign of the Changes to which all mutable things are subjected under His Omnipotent Hand, amen.

"But, you may ask, how can we be *certain* of this impending storm of Death and Destruction? It is through the ancient science of Astrology. Astrology has long shown that the sun, the moon, the stars, and the planets control the fates of men; these heavenly bodies rule all affairs, now and in every age before and hereafter.

"The wise Babylonians first instituted inspectors of the heavens, who watched and recorded the movements of the celestial bodies. They found that the five planets, Jupiter, Mars, Mercury, Saturn, and Venus, interact in potent ways with the movements of the sun and the moon. The overlaps of the planets' lines of movement and also the halos around them set off cosmic vibrations that radiate down and guide everything on the Earth below.

"By now we have millennia of records. We know for certain that the most dramatic and dire phenomena follow Eclipses of the sun, which come at regular intervals and which are driven by the tides of the universe. The ebb and the flow of the cosmic tides produce great Eclipses every generation–every eighteen years–in order to remind each succeeding generation of men of the inestimable Power of God and His eternal heavens.

"Thus, the present worldwide disaster will be foreshadowed by an Eclipse: immediately before the terrible conjunction of the planets, there will be an Eclipse of the sun, obscuring it entirely. Then the moon in the opposition will also be totally Eclipsed. The sun will become fiery red, distorted, and angry. From out of its black disk will come Holy Rays, like the halo of a saint, and the sun will seethe under the glory of the halo. This will signify approaching bloodshed in the neighborhood of a great river in the East and similarly for a great river in the West.

"The planet Mars rules the house of the Scorpion, and the Great Disaster will be under the influence of Mars, which incites violence and which undoes the benign influence of the other planets. The stones of Mars are red stones: they are rubies, haematites, jaspers, and bloodstones. The sky will turn red, red rocks will arise from the earth, blood will flow through the rivers, and plants, trees, and animals wili bleed uncontrollably. Savage fires will roar through the countryside–as the Bible tells us":

Fire will chew your cedars' skin
And every pine will howl in pain–
Alas, the lofty trees have fallen:
The mighty woods are now aflame.

"The day of Mars is Tuesday; therefore, a Tuesday will be the day of the worst destruction. Sickness will abound. Skin will turn yellow. All tongues will become dry and parched. Maliciousness and jealousy will seize reasonable men, who will rush about in a frenzy of madness. As the Book of Zechariah prophesies in the Bible: 'On that day, a great panic, sent by the Lord, shall fall upon them.' Doubt and ignorance will seize Jews and Mohammedans alike until they forsake their synagogues and their mosques; their sects will be utterly destroyed by the will of God. High and secure Christian retreats will offer the only refuge for the World: there is eternal safety in our Lord Jesus Christ, amen.

"It is declared and prophesied in the Book of Judges: 'The stars fought from heaven.' Know you, therefore, to leave the lowlands as soon as you see the Eclipse; for then, most surely, the heavenly battle shall have begun. Retreat to the sacred Christian shrines–go to monasteries in the mountains–and pray and be holy, for God is Great and God is Good. We depend on Him for all things both Great and Terrible. By His hand must all be cursed and blessed, and in the end, it is He who shall give our final rest.

"Magister Johannes Davidis Hispalensis
Of the Basilica de Santa Leocadia
In the city of Toledo"

The letter was dated in the Christian year 1185 (that is, the Hebrew year 4945), so it had been two years in the traveling north. By then the great Day of Doom had passed: it had come and gone on an earlier Sabbath, the *Shabbat Shuvah* in *Tishri* of the year 4947.

Rabbi Achselrad set the letter down on his desk. He looked around at the worn wooden benches and at the piles of prayer books. He looked at the little stove in the corner. The Rabbi stood up. He walked over and put the letter into the stove, where it burned quietly, there in the back study room. A gentle summer wind blew through the Jewish Quarter of old Cologne. It rushed and it whispered. It carried hints of light-white angels among the summer clouds of the Great Hereafter. The wind was a spring-summer wind, and it ruffled the children's hair as they ran and played in the Juden Viertels along the River Rhine, and it rushed on through the town and out past the cemetery and down along the hillsides, and again it was once upon a time on an eternal summer day, long, long ago in the medieval town of Cologne.

ood evening, Rabbi. Of course – sit down here by the stove.

No, I was not thinking of anything in particular. Well, actually I was remembering my father. You know, it is strange – I am not really certain what he was like, this father of mine. I recall many things about him in great detail. There are many pictures in my mind in which he is frozen in the midst of some action or another. He is about to talk. He is climbing a step. He has just laughed. But at the same time the thing that ties it all together, the spirit that turns these frozen vignettes into a person, is not really him. Instead, my father is a feeling, a feeling of *mine.* There is something else – something beyond the person himself – that makes these images and memories into my father. It is some personal idea that I have. How can I say it? There is a certain Fatherness.

Fatherness? Well, it is big and stern and hard, and at the same time it is warm and protective and loving. Yes, it does sound like God, Who is exactly all these things at once. But can any real person ever be like that? For us mortals, Fatherness is a dream; it is a myth, an ideal. It is too Godlike for a person to try and live up to the standard set by the sages: "Be swift as a leopard, light as an eagle, fleet as a hart, and strong as a lion, and do the will of our great Father Who is in Heaven."

Undoubtedly, my real father was only a simple man, but now I remember the mythic father better than the real man. Ah, well . . . in any case, this spirit of Fatherness in its pure form–this special deep-seated, all-encompassing protective figure–must certainly be God Himself. The Lord is our one primal Father; as the Talmud says:

> Beloved are all Israel: they are called the children of the All-present Holy One, for the book of Deuteronomy says–"You are the children of the Lord Your God."

Yes, the Lord is an ancient wondrous Father, and He wants what all fathers want: our love forever. "All the miracles, wonders, and mighty acts which I perform for you," said He, "were not done with the goal of receiving a reward. For whatever could you give to Me? Instead, you should simply honor Me like the dutiful children that you are. You should simply revere Me, love Me, and call Me your Father."

How many times did I hear that quotation from my grandmother, Rabbi. God wants no reward. What? Rabbi, you are such a dialectician! You always turn everything upside down. Yes, yes–I admit to what you say. God *does* ask for a reward: the finest of rewards *is* having your children "laugh aloud and hop and skip as we walk free, and smile as they look up at me." So I concede your point: the Almighty Lord God *does* receive a reward after all.

And with so many children, God must be very well rewarded and very, very happy. I certainly hope that is the case. You rabbis are fortunate like Him too, because you have hordes of children. Not only is each of you a father to his own children, you are a father to a whole community. All of us look to you for support, and, by the grace of God, you listen to our complaints, you pat us on the head, and you give us counsel, advice, and strength. And sometimes, Rabbi, we laugh aloud and we walk free, and always we look up to you.

Now, now, Rabbi, do not be so modest. No matter how much of a scholar you are, you are always a father too. It was certainly that way with another famous old rabbi, Rabbi Abraham ben Alexander. He was a great father. Why, even his name was "father": Abraham means "father of a multitude." Of course, at the same time "Father Abraham" was also a serious scholar. Night and day you could find him working on a set of Kabbalistic tomes of mystical knowledge, the most famous of which was the *Keter Shem Tov.* In fact, it was one afternoon while writing this very book that the Rabbi heard a noise and looked up. One of the Rabbi's congregants, Simeon ben Aram, was standing sadly in the doorway. And why was he there? And why was he sad? And what had this to do with spice boxes? Well, said my grandmother, the basic problem was that Simeon needed a father. Let me tell you Simeon's story:

Once upon a time, said my grandmother, Simeon ben Aram had been a man of great riches. He had lived in a mansion in the wealthy parish of St. Brigit within the medieval city of Cologne. Simeon had uncounted numbers of gold coins. He had silver pots and pans and plates and cups. He had carved boxes and statues; he even had ornamental musical instruments. His businesses were so numerous that his managers were always surprising him with details that he had forgotten. He had ten servants. His wife and his children dressed like royalty. All seemed well as far as the eye could see.

Ah, but no one knows beforehand how the wheel of fortune will turn. As my grandmother would say, "The good Lord God, blessed be He, whirls and twirls our little earth in His holy palm." And so it happened that, in an important business deal involving spice boxes, God whirled and twirled the earth, and Simeon ben Aram ha-Kohen suddenly lost a tremendous amount of money.

Now, you may ask, what did one business deal actually mean to Simeon? Did it really represent a serious problem? Well, I will tell you: the loss was painful, but it was also a signal. It was biblical, Rabbi–Simeon's life was exactly like that passage late in the Book of Genesis:

> Then Pharaoh said to Joseph, "In my dream, I was standing on the bank of the Nile. Then there came up from the river seven cows, fat and sleek, and they grazed on the reeds. After them, seven other cows came up–these were poor, gaunt, and lean; in fact, I have never seen such thin weak creatures in all Egypt. But these lean cows devoured the first cows, the fat ones. The fat cows were swallowed up, but no one could have guessed that they were in the bellies of the others, which looked just as thin as before."

> And Joseph nodded and said to Pharaoh, "God has allowed you to see what He is going to do in the future. First there are to be seven years of great plenty throughout the land. After them will come seven years of famine–and in those days, all the years of plenty in Egypt will be forgotten, as famine ruins the entire country."

Just as in the Bible, Simeon ben Aram began with seven prosperous fat years. Everything went beyond his expectations. If he bought and stored oats, then the next season a poor crop followed and this made his stockpile twice as valuable. If he sold his wine stores, then the next season wine was plentiful and he had protected his money. Demand always ran high for his imported gems and silks and cut glass. His managers and workmen were surprisingly honest. His family remained healthy. The sun shone every morning.

But then followed seven long lean years. It began with the loss of a shipload of ornate spice boxes: Simeon had borrowed money to buy the fancy carved boxes, and after the loss he was left with neither the boxes nor the money for his creditors. Next, rain and storms destroyed the oat crops on his two farms. Theft and fire emptied storage buildings in Bonn. Investments seemed to evaporate everywhere. Workers left him. His son developed a strange weakness in his stomach. And Simeon's creditors had no pity for him: they took away his palatial mansion in the parish of St. Brigit and also his rental properties in the parish of St. Mary ad Gradus.

The district of St. Mary ad Gradus was home to wealthy Gentiles. There were a few Jewish houses in the district, and these Jews were taxed heavily and were subjected to unannounced special fees. At one time, Simeon had owned two houses in the parish of St. Mary ad Gradus. Now, the special taxes and fees and the loss of his businesses had overwhelmed him. His houses were gone, and he had exhausted all his savings and his other resources. Each morning when he awoke the sky seemed gray, and Simeon said to himself, "What disaster will today bring?" Soon, nothing whatsoever remained of his great wealth. Simeon moved into a small cottage in the Juden Viertels, where he lived with an unmarried cousin, Markus ben Elisha. Markus was a shopkeeper who sold kosher meat, and Simeon became his assistant.

Simeon ben Aram ha-Kohen was discouraged. He was worn out by unrelenting misfortune. But the good Lord God had sewn Simeon together with tough fibers. In time, Simeon adjusted himself to his new position. He managed to earn enough money to support his family. Still, he said, "How can I have fallen so low? Was it really *me* who lived in a king's mansion and who had five other houses? Were there times when my meals were carried to my bedroom by bowing Gentile servants? Did I really eat honey every day and wear silk and velvet?" Simeon shook his head in disbelief.

Several more years passed, and the mysterious wheel of fortune turned once again. A fire broke out in the store and everything was destroyed. With no store, his cousin Markus could sell no meat, and he decided to move back to his hometown of Dusseldorf. Markus sold his cottage, so Simeon moved in with a neighbor and paid his rent by tending the neighbor's garden. To earn a living, Simeon managed to barter for a horse and a wagon and he became a carter, carrying all manner of goods, packages, and people.

Poor Simeon. To feed his horse and his family, he ate less himself. He worked in the garden late at night and early in the morning so that he had the full day to haul things around the city in his wagon. No longer did he reminisce about his mansion and his wealth and his servants. Instead, he said to himself, "Ah, how I wish I had those wonderful days in the meat shop. Then I could relax and talk all afternoon. In those days, there was plenty of food for my family. We had our own bedroom. The cottage was warm in the winter. I got enough sleep at night. I did not have to worry about a horse that seems always to be getting sick." Simeon sighed, and tiredly, he continued on his way through the dark and winding streets of old Cologne.

Again time passed. Seven weeks came, and seven weeks went. The Great Festivals rolled around, but nothing seemed to improve for Simeon. In the yeshiva, too, things went on much as before. Old Abraham Achselrad thought and he prayed and he read. He conducted services, and he married couples. He judged cases. He argued points of Law. But most often he wrote in his Kabbalistic tomes of mystical knowledge. And through it all, Abraham ben Alexander remained a father to his congregation. People came to him to complain and to be comforted; they wanted advice and reassurance and a pat on the back. The Jews of Cologne believed that the Rabbi was larger than life and that he would protect them always.

Old Achselrad did his best. The Rabbi knew that sometimes his best was only to listen–and listen he did, often and always. For example, one afternoon while writing his *Keter Shem Tov,* the Rabbi heard a noise and he looked up. There standing in the doorway was Simeon ben Aram ha-Kohen. Simeon was sad and upset.

Rabbi Abraham looked up and he raised his eyebrows. Simeon stepped into the room and immediately began to talk. "Let me tell you, Rabbi," he said, "misfortune has struck again." Simeon sat down heavily on a worn bench by the door. "Once, I had a two-wheeled wooden cart. It was topless, but it was roomy. And even if there was no top, at least I had a hat and a cloak to keep off the weather. And then what good was a cart without a horse? So of course I had a horse too."

Simeon sighed. The yeshiva students had finished their lesson in the study hall. Two young boys stood in the doorway to listen. Simeon was quiet a moment, lost in thought; then he continued: "Now what do I have? The axle to the cart is broken beyond repair, and of course I have no money to replace it. Meanwhile, my horse was not eating well. Suddenly it sickened and died. And with no money, how could I ever buy a new horse? I had nothing to sell and nothing to trade. So I had no choice. A carter was for someone else; I gave up the business.

"And now what am I? I will tell you what I am–I am a porter. It is just me and my two arms. I walk about, bent under heavy loads. I carry everything on my own shoulders. And do I earn enough even for bread? No, I do not."

The Rabbi nodded and listened silently. Lewe ben Anselm, one of the sages on a bench near Simeon, also nodded sympathetically. Simeon shook his head. He looked at Lewe and said, "Reb Lewe, I was well off when I was a carter. I owned a horse and a wagon. I carried passengers and merchandise to the markets. I carted luggage and vegetables and clothes–I carried anything and everything. On some days, I had planks and barrels and stone; other days, there were baskets of melons and potatoes. I cannot even remember all the different things that I hauled in my day. With a wagon you can carry anything–and you can carry more than one thing at once, piles and piles of goods. True, I was paid a pittance, but I got by, thank the good Lord God (blessed be He). But now look at me. I have to carry everything on my own poor shoulders!"

Another old man, Moyses ben Nathan, shook his head: "What

terrible luck you have. I remember when you had a mansion. You lived the life of luxury. We used to have an expression for a wealthy man. We said, 'Ah, he is a Simeon!' Why, you must have had ten houses! And you owned boats and farms and carriages. You had servants and gold. I can hardly believe that you are the same man, Simeon."

Simeon stood up and paced around the room. "Do not talk to me of such nonsense," said Simeon. "Mansions, houses, servants, gold? I have forgotten all those fantasy-land things. I would be happy to have a cottage and a horse and a cart. Just imagine having your own garden! Or how about a room that is warm and toasty in the winter – and then having the time to sit calmly in that room and to eat a bit of extra bread. Now *that* is luxury!"

The boys in the doorway were listening wide-eyed. The smallest one was about seven years old; his pants were patched and frayed and his jacket was too large. Finally, he could not resist, and he said to Simeon, "I wish that I had a horse and a cart too. But I do not even have a father to buy one for me."

Simeon raised his eyebrows and he looked at the boy. The boy continued: "Do you still have your father?"

"No," said Simeon, "he is long gone, young man."

"Oh, then I guess you are like me," said the boy sadly.

They were both quiet for a moment. Then the boy said, "Would you buy a horse and a cart for your children?"

"Yes, I would if I could," answered Simeon ben Aram ha-Kohen.

"Then they are lucky," said the boy.

Ah, good evening again, Rabbi. It is always hard to sleep when there is a bright half-moon, so sit down, put your feet up on the side bench here, and I will open the stove door.

It is no wonder you are feeling restless. The moon pulls and tugs on all our worldly affairs: as it grows stronger, the waxing moon encourages growth here on earth; but as it weakens, the waning moon radiates vapors that shrink, shrivel, and dissolve things and that cause decay. Rabbi Eliazer ben Judah, the mystic of Worms, studied the phases of the moon. The brain, he wrote, contracts as the moon shrinks; this causes mental problems. And Rabbi Eliazer also discovered that as the moon diminishes wet cloth rots faster, old wood crumbles more quickly, and grain and fruit decay almost overnight.

In contrast, as the moon enlarges, the world grows stronger. The best marriages begin during a waxing moon. School should begin on the day of the new moon. And do you plan to start a new business? Then open your shop on the day of the new moon. Also, I have been told that it is a good plan to make the transition from weakness to strength–from waning moon to waxing moon–by fasting, so all Kabbalists fasted on the eve of the new moon. But now, Rabbi, as the moon is once again waning, we are entering a very dangerous period.

Be careful: it is in this last quarter that disasters occur. In fact, it was in the last quarter of the month that Hillel ben Lewe met his accident.

You do not know about Hillel? Then let me tell you what I learned from my grandmother:

Once upon a time, said my grandmother to me, there lived in Cologne on the River Rhine a pious scholar named Abraham ben Alexander, Achselrad of Cologne. In Rabbi Abraham's congregation was an old man named Hillel ben Jacob. Hillel had a young friend, a rather wild young man, named Hillel ben Lewe.

The two Hillels were fast friends, although they were very different. The old man, Hillel ben Jacob, was slow, cautious, and reflective; the young man, Hillel ben Lewe, was impetuous, active, and headstrong. Nonetheless, they got along famously and somehow they blended together well. Hillel ben Jacob and Hillel ben Lewe spent long hours with each other. They talked, and they listened to each other. People were always surprised to see them walking side by side in the street. The townsfolk shook their heads. Who knew why such opposites became friends? Perhaps it was because they both had the same first name.

Hillel ben Jacob was a gardener; he grew beans and cabbage, and most especially he grew peas. Hillel ben Jacob told his young friend all about peas. "They are an ancient type of vegetable," he said. "The Egyptians grew them, and peas have always liked ancient peoples, such as the Jews." The younger Hillel listened and nodded. Old Hillel continued: "Peas are just like gulls: they like cool weather and sandy soil and they like to fly high." And what did old Hillel mean by this? He meant that the pea vines climb high and so they grow best on fences.

Old Hillel showed young Hillel how to plant the peas every two weeks, beginning before Passover and continuing for the next month. Then, when the pea pods appeared – usually beginning in the summer month of *Sivan* – there would be seeds ripening continually and Hillel could pick new peas each morning, day after day. Late in the summer, toward the end of the month of *Av,* he began planting a second crop, and these pea pods grew until the damp and frosty weather set in after *Sukkot.*

Hillel ben Lewe came and worked with the old man in the garden.

"In general," said the old gardener, "peas are a sociable lot, so plant them close together.

"But," he warned, "peas do not like some of the other vegetables: they do not get on well with onions or leeks or garlic. On the other hand, they enjoy the company of carrots, radishes, and beans. I plant my peas near the beans."

The two men put up low fencing for the peas to climb. They dragged in barrels of water during hot and dry spells. ("Although," said Hillel ben Jacob, "peas are not good swimmers–it is important that their soil is loose and airy and dry.") Old Hillel taught the younger man to spread wood ashes on the soil, to "sweeten" it for the peas, and he reminded Hillel ben Lewe that keeping the vines well-picked encouraged new pods to grow. At the end of each season, the two men split the harvests: they ate fresh peas right from the vine, they dried sacks of pea pods for themselves, and they sold both fresh and dried peas in the market.

Hillel ben Jacob and Hillel ben Lewe worked together, and they relaxed together. Over the months and the years, they influenced each other, although they would never admit it. At first, old Hillel had been very quiet; now he said what was on his mind almost without thinking. At first, young Hillel had talked nonstop; now he listened quietly for hours. One day, the young man surprised the old gardener. "I have composed a poem," he said. Old Hillel raised his eyebrows. "So–recite it to me," said the old man. And Hillel ben Lewe said:

In worn torn shoes
Came two old Jews
To the River's edge,
To the black rock views.

Against skyblue
How fine to view
One bent old man
Standing, smile askew.

"Is that about our walk last week?" asked old Hillel.

"Exactly," said young Hillel.

"Was that really the way that I looked?" smiled the old man.

"Well, that is what I remember," said the young man.

It was summer. The moon had passed its midphase, and it began to wane. The nights became darker. The demons felt bold, and they hissed and laughed and plotted. One evening, young Hillel ben Lewe was at the inn playing *Goose,* and old Hillel ben Jacob was watching quietly in the background. A wicked demon was hiding in the shadows.

What is that, Rabbi? You do not know the game *Goose?* I suppose rabbis do not get to play games much nowadays. *Goose* is an old French game; originally it came from the Greeks, and it was very popular in the Middle Ages. There is a board with a drawing of a twisting scroll laid out as a path of sixty-three spaces. This path is called the *Jardin de l'Oie* (the Goose Garden). On every ninth space is a picture of a goose, and on other spaces are drawings of inns and bridges and labyrinths and courthouses; on a few spaces there is the symbol of a death's head.

The players sit around the edges of the board. They throw the dice and move their markers. If you land on a symbol, then you follow the rules. For example, at an inn you must stay overnight (that is, you wait an extra turn), or if you come to a death's head then you must begin again at space number one. Before each move, you put a penny on the table, and the first person to reach space number sixty-three collects all the money.

Hillel ben Lewe was sitting at the *Goose* board with two other men. Young Hillel was quite a drinker, and the bartender had kept Hillel's glass filled with hard beer. During the first game of *Goose,* Hillel was happy, calm, and confident. The liquor made him warm. He talked fast. He spoke great thoughts. During the second game, the room grew hazier. Was there a soft humming, even when no one was talking? Things seemed light and misty. Young Hillel felt unsteady, and if he did not concentrate, he saw twins of his cup and the board and the man across from him. Young Hillel talked loudly and said only half his sentences. Well, well–was it his move again? Three spaces–but what was this? Had he counted four spaces already? "You are cheating!" shouted the man across from Hillel. "Give me back my money!"

"What?" said Hillel. "Just play the game. Don't complain."

"I said to give me my money!" said the man.

"I will not!" said Hillel, pushing the other man's hand aside.

The man shoved Hillel. Hillel fell back in his chair. Another man came over. Hillel swung his fist at both men. The first man grabbed his money, the second man hit Hillel on the head with a wooden stool, and Hillel fell over onto the floor–and the wicked demons hissed and laughed in the corner. Old Hillel ben Jacob rushed over. He looked at his young friend. There was no outward cut. The young man was breathing. Had Hillel simply fainted? Was it the liquor and the late hour? Old Hillel helped his friend to stand, but young Hillel remained weak and groggy, and Hillel ben Jacob walked with young Hillel to the old man's house.

Usually after a night of drinking at the inn, Hillel ben Lewe would awake feverish and exhausted, sick and giddy. His ears would ring, his heart would pound, and his head would ache terribly. But now young Hillel did not seem to be able to wake fully. He shook his head, but he remained dizzy. His headache got worse and worse. Old Hillel put young Hillel to bed. "My neck is very stiff," complained the young man. "And I am incredibly thirsty."

Old Hillel gave his young friend a drink of water. He put a warm towel on the young man's neck. Then he sat back. What should he do? Perhaps he still had some Miriam's water. That would certainly help.

What is that, Rabbi? You do not know about Miriam's water? Sometimes I wonder how you can be so wise and still know so little. In any case, I will tell you. The Miriam in Miriam's water is the biblical prophetess, Aaron's sister. As you recall, Miriam died and was buried in the district of Kadesh during the forty years of wandering. Kadesh was a bone-dry place, and there Moses and Aaron performed a miracle: they struck a solid rock at a spot known as Meribah and pure spring-water gushed out. Today, waters from Miriam's spring at Meribah flow through all the rivers of the world at the end of each Sabbath. And these waters have remarkable healing powers. It is worth collecting some Sabbath water in a clean vessel–while remaining absolutely silent–and then saving it, because any ill person who drinks the Miriam's water will be cured.

As I was saying, old Hillel found some Miriam's water in a covered pot on a shelf. "Here, drink this," he said to his young friend.

Young Hillel looked blankly at the old man. Did the young man not recognize him? To young Hillel, the world seemed to move ever so slowly; eventually, however, he sipped the water, he coughed, and then he became sleepy and confused.

Now old Hillel was even more worried. He tried to remember remedies that his grandmother had used. He thought of the old adage: "Every cure is the opposite of the ailment." Cold cures fevers, and heat cures chills, he thought. But what would cure a head injury? Perhaps something soft–so old Hillel gently wrapped young Hillel's head in a blanket and set him sleeping on a feather pillow. The young man moaned. He said strange things. He moved his body very, very slowly. When old Hillel spoke to him, young Hillel rarely answered.

Old Hillel remembered that the Talmud teaches: "If one is suffering from faintness, then eat honey and other sweet things because they restore light to the eyes." It was morning now and Hillel went next door and borrowed some honey from his neighbor. He spread it on a piece of bread; then he shook young Hillel. "Wake up, my friend," said the old man. At first, the younger man looked confused. "Eat this," said old Hillel. Young Hillel looked at him blankly. The old man put a piece of the bread against the young man's mouth. Young Hillel took one bite and then two. Eventually he ate the entire piece of bread and honey. Then he lay down. Was he asleep? An hour later, he moved his arms, but now he was only half-awake and half-asleep.

Days passed. Young Hillel remained dizzy and confused. He could barely be roused. But, every once in a while and for just a few minutes, he would talk normally. One evening he actually sat up. "My friend," he said weakly, "we must be getting to the garden. In this dry weather, the peas need water." Old Hillel said quickly, "Yes, yes, Hillel, just as soon as you are better. Now lie down again and rest. Try to build up your strength." The young man smiled and lay back down. He closed his eyes and dozed off. Was he better? Young Hillel moaned, and for two days, he did not answer when the old man talked to him. The great Rabbi Eliazer of Worms had warned that when the moon wanes, the brain shrinks and wrinkles. "Young Hillel has hit his head," thought old Hillel sadly. "The moon is waning, and now his brain must be shriveling."

Old Hillel ben Jacob sat by the bedside of young Hillel ben Lewe. The old gardener feared the worst. Night after night, old Hillel sat silently at his friend's side. Night after night, the moon diminished. Night after night, young Hillel worsened. And one night it was coal-black outside in the late, late dead hours. Hillel ben Jacob's old eyes were very tired; his old body was very heavy. The house was thick with dusty silence. Then Hillel ben Jacob began to shiver, and he thought that he heard a voice chanting faintly:

Late one darkling summer night
A bleak fog of mist and light
Slipped downward in its cold damp flight
Creeping over the far gravesite –
It settled thickly, dank, alight
As a grim gray nighttide tombstone blight,
An old gray shroud, a cold cold fright
Of death upon a darkling night.

Hillel ben Jacob looked up. In the doorway stood a dark figure. The figure turned – it turned, and Hillel ben Jacob saw that it was Dumah, the Angel of Death, standing covered from head to foot with unwinking eyes. Dumah held a bloody sword, and his breathing was like the sound of dry leaves rustling and rustling in the blank autumn wind.

Dumah, the Angel of Death, turned slowly. He turned slowly and silently and smoothly and darkly. Was he speaking? Old Hillel thought that he heard the holy words of Psalm 102:

Lord, long ago You built
A foundation for the world –
All the dirt and rocks and silt
Were the handiwork that You unfurled –
But someday these things all shall wilt
Like flowers, a crumbling dissolving chord
While You will still endure, O God our wondrous Lord.

Like our daily clothes
The woods and hills, the whole springtide
Will someday decompose
And will be cast aside,
As yesterday's fading rose
They'll fall apart and blow away
And vanish in a windy day.

But You are otherwise,
Unchanging, solid, constant:
Your years eternities comprise
With no end to them triumphant–
And, Lord, our children will give rise
To other children, then to more
Who renew again the Truths of Your most holy, holy splendor.

And Dumah stood with his unwinking eyes and his drawn and bloody sword–and he stood and he stood and he stood.

Finally, old Hillel said, "You have come for my friend."

And Dumah, the black Angel of Death, nodded, but he did not speak.

Yes, Rabbi, Dumah nodded, and he did not speak. And old Hillel looked down at his dying friend. Time did not pass. The stars stopped in their courses through the heavens. Everything was still. There was no wind or creaking of the walls or the floors or the doors. The light did not change. Old Hillel sat. And dark Dumah stood.

Hillel looked up at the black angel. "Can you take me instead?" asked the old man quietly.

Who knows why Dumah nodded yes. Was it because both men had the same first names? Did Dumah feel sorry for the young Hillel? Or was it truly the time for old Hillel ben Jacob to die? My grandmother did not know, and I do not know either.

In any case, Dumah, the black Angel of Death, nodded again, but he did not speak. Hillel ben Jacob smiled, and he closed his eyes. He thought of his pea gardens. He remembered the words from the Book of Ecclesiastes: "I undertook great works, I did: I built myself houses and planted vineyards. Yes, I made myself gardens and parks, and I planted all kinds of flowers and vegetables and fruit trees in them. And then I made myself pools of water to irrigate the groves of green growing plants." And swift as an eagle, Dumah reached over. He slipped the silver soul from the white-haired head of old Hillel the gardener. Dumah, the Angel of Death, pulled the light and holy soul from Hillel ben Jacob ha-Levi, and together they sped off to Heaven, beyond the ends of the dark summer sky. And as the black angel passed through the nighttime celestial vault, the soul glinted and shone in the wondrous Heavenly starlight of the eternity of forever, which rolled out through the cosmic tides and far beyond the great green Garden of Eden. And the next day Hillel ben Lewe awoke, fully recovered.

Good evening, Rabbi. Although it is late, I see that there is no sleep for the weary. Perhaps you will feel sleepy later. As they say: "If not now, then soon, and if not soon, then later." So wait patiently, my friend: sleep will come eventually. With me it is like this: When I can, I sleep, and when I cannot sleep, then I think. Apparently, the good Lord God has decreed that tonight is the time for reflection.

What am *I* thinking about? Well, let me see . . . I suppose I was thinking of my family. My wife (may she forever receive God's great blessings, amen) has been gone for many years now. Then there was little Erinna-anne; she was my tiny daughter who died well before you came here. Yes, Rabbi, it is sad to miss these people now. But at least they were with me for a time, and in a way they are still here, even today. I remember those people and the many times we had together. I have not had an exciting life, but it was full, and I am content. Of course, excitement can be a curse–those people with the wildest and most action-packed lives miss out on the endless little things of family, friends, and home. I think a good case in point is Eldad.

Why, Rabbi, how could you not know about Eldad ben Mahli ha-Dani?

Well, then, let me tell you about him:

At the end of the ninth century, a strange man appeared among the Jews of northern Africa. His name was Eldad ben Mahli. Eldad was dressed exotically, he spoke old Hebrew mixed with Arabic, and he told a tantalizing story. Eldad introduced himself as a member of the Tribe of Dan; he said that descendants of Dan had remained together after Saragon had displaced them from northern Palestine fifty generations ago. Eldad reported that descendants of the other ten northern tribes of Israel had also held to the faith and were now living in small pockets of Judaism dispersed throughout Asia and Africa.

"My people remained isolated," said Eldad. However, a great wanderlust had come upon Eldad himself, and after uncountable adventures he found his way into North Africa. From North Africa, he traveled to Babylonia. Many Babylonian Jews were skeptical of Eldad's story, but Yom-Tov Kahana ben Jacob, the Gaon of the city of Sura, interviewed Eldad for two days and declared with wonderment, "This man truly is a Jew from the Lost Tribes."

Then Eldad continued his journeys. Eventually he found his way to the Rhinelands, where he met Rabbi Amram, the Chief Rabbi of Cologne at the end of the Dark Ages. It was a summer afternoon. Wheeling birds could be heard far overhead, the wide-open windows let in the cries of tanglepickers, turnstones, and windhovers. The light was changing, blending warmly the blues and yellows and pinks of God's distant summer skies.

Rabbi Amram was writing in the small back study room. Something caught his attention. Was it a noise or a change in the light? The Rabbi looked up, and in the doorway stood an elderly weather-worn stranger.

"Hello," said the Rabbi.

"My greetings to you, Rabbi," returned the traveler. "May I come in?"

"Certainly," said Rabbi Amram, and he cleared a place on one of the benches along the wall.

"I am Eldad the son of Mahli of the Tribe of Dan," said the stranger, and old Amram opened wide his eyes.

What? Yes, yes, Rabbi, I am about to continue. I was just thinking quietly in the glow of the stove. Now, where was I? Oh yes,

Eldad came into the rabbi's small study room in the Cologne yeshiva, and he set his satchel on the floor.

"My name, good Rabbi, is Eldad," repeated the stranger. "I am Eldad ben Mahli ha-Dani. I come from far, far away, beyond the Rivers of Cush. I have been traveling for many years."

Eldad looked around. "Here I am in Cologne," he said, "but it may as well be Bonn or Vienna or Antwerp. The European cities all seem the same to me, and now I cannot get myself in the habit of staying in one place. If I sleep for a night on one floor, then it seems that I must find another floor for the next night."

Eldad sighed. He patted his trousers, smoothing them a bit as he slouched on the bench; then he stretched out his long, thin legs.

"Well," said old Amram, "you are certainly welcome to stay here tonight." The Rabbi began to search for an old blanket that he kept behind the prayer books and benches in his back study. "You speak with an accent that I cannot place. Are you a Jew?" he asked as he rooted around.

"Yes," answered Eldad. "As I said, I am from the ancient Tribe of Dan, one of what you would call the 'Ten Lost Tribes.' Of course we are not really lost: we have an independent nation south of Egypt, and nearby are Jewish nations descended from the Tribes of Asher, Gad, and Naphtali."

Rabbi Amram stopped rooting among the prayer books. He stared at the traveler. Eldad was looking at his shoes, and he continued: "Most of my countrymen are content to remain at home, although on rare occasions a few have journeyed off, never to return. Apparently, they do not usually reach these European Jewish centers, because my arrival has surprised people. In fact, my stories are hardly believed.

"I find, good Rabbi, that I have now become a professional traveler, an amateur historian, and even a philologist. Recently I was in Spain, but before that I came through Mesopotamia, Egypt, and Kairouan. It has been five years, or perhaps almost six, since I left home."

The Rabbi raised his eyebrows, and he sat down again at his desk. "This is quite a strange introduction, my friend," said old Amram. "Please make yourself comfortable on the bench. Perhaps you will take a meal with me later. Now, however, I would like to hear your whole story." Eldad stretched his legs again. He nodded, and this, then, was the narrative of Eldad Mahli, who was born in regions now lost to the Jews.

"Basically," began Eldad, "I am a Jew from the Land of the Lost Tribes. As you know, fifty generations ago, many Jewish Tribes were separated from the ancient centers of Israel. In the Holy Scriptures – in the Second Book of Kings – it is said":

> The king of Assyria invaded the whole country of Israel and, reaching Samaria, he besieged it for three long hard years. Then finally he captured Samaria and he deported its people to Assyria and settled them in Halah and on the Habor (the river of Gozan) and in the cities of Media.

Rabbi Amram nodded.

"Sargon was the king of Assyria," continued Eldad. "He was the successor to Shalmaneser. Sargon captured the city of Samaria and deported more than twenty-seven thousand Jews from the Northern Kingdom of Israel. The Bible reports that the Jews were sent north to Assyria and beyond to Media. Undoubtedly many Jews remained in Assyria. However, a number of men from the Tribes of Asher, Dan, Gad, and Naphtali soon made their way back down south, and quietly they established independent nations in Africa beyond Egypt. My countrymen all descend from the Tribe of Dan. In my travels, I have finally put together a picture of the locations and the customs of the scattered remnants of the other Tribes. If you would like, I can tell you a bit of what I learned."

"Please do," said Rabbi Amram.

"Very well, Rabbi," said Eldad. "Let me begin by saying that few of my countrymen trade with Mediterraneans or Europeans. On the other hand, *I* had long thought to myself: 'Eldad, the young people around you always have a taste for the unusual. Perhaps you can make some money by importing exotica. Undoubtedly there are strange foods and clothes and artworks to be bought cheaply abroad.' One day, I met a man, a Jew from the neighboring Tribe of Asher, who had the same idea. We decided to become partners and to set out on a buying expedition. We sold all our belongings, we borrowed as much money as we could, and we headed out beyond our comfortable borders for the great unknown northern world."

Eldad stopped. "Might I have a drink of water, Rabbi?" he asked. The Rabbi pointed to a bucket and dipper. Eldad took a sip and smiled. Then he continued: "My companion was named Karassa. He had already been to Egypt once, and he led us safely through that land and then to the vast Mediterranean Sea beyond. We boarded a small ship to tour the ports of Africa and Asia, with the plan of buying whatever struck our fancy along the way. We had been out on the water only two days when the Almighty Lord God blew up a vast and thunderous storm."

Eldad opened wide his eyes and began to recite:

Suddenly a squall struck screaming from the west–
A tremendous hurricane with thunderous clouds abreast.
Both forestays and the mast were knocked toppling aft
Lengthwise along the ship, cracking it in half.

Cabin planks ripped out, the rudder tore away;
Oars were blown across the deck and out into the bay.
Then the storm let fly another bolt of wild and awesome thunder;
The ship reeked of sulphur and all the men went under.

The ship bucked and split; men were flung into the sea
And though they bobbed around the wreck, drenched in its lee,
They soon sank like sodden earth and lay within the depths,
Their families never more to hear their evening homeward steps,
For the Lord had turned His radiant face from the sad catastrophe.

"Yes, Rabbi," continued Eldad, "most of the men were drowned. However, the good Lord God (blessed be He) was merciful to us two Jews. Karassa and I each found a waterlogged plank. We clung side by side, floating up and down on the waves in the gray morning light. The sun beat down with an awful heat; we were parched with thirst. Miraculously, we were washed toward land late in the day. We still had the strength to swim, and soon we were lying on the beach praying and resting in the sun, praise the great Lord God, amen, amen."

"Amen," said Rabbi Amram.

"Did we lie there for hours? It seemed like forever. We dozed and when we awoke, four brown men had surrounded us. They were tall and wore only cloth belts. They carried long sharpened sticks. From the sound of their words, I thought that they may have called themselves 'Romaranus,' but I could be mistaken. The men pushed us to our feet and prodded us along, and we were marched back to their village. Karassa was thick and fat. He was killed and eaten immediately. In those days I was even thinner than I am now. My captors put me in a locked hut and tied me to a post. Then they brought me food, hoping, I suppose, to fatten me up also; however, I ate nothing and drank only water and I said the *Shema* every time I felt hungry, which was perhaps sixty times a day and twelve times each night.

"I stayed in that hut for at least a week, when the good Lord God (blessed be He) suddenly worked another miracle. Into the village came an army, a band of light-skinned men. They spoke a form of Arabic, and when I identified myself, they took me along with them when they left. I was terribly weak: I could hardly walk, but I forced myself to move although I was at the point of tears and I groaned with every step. After days of torment, we reached a city called Azin.

"In Azin, I recovered; then I worked as a slave for a wealthy man. I was treated fairly well. I ate two large meals each day. I had charge of the bookkeeping for his business, which was trading in all manner of fancy wines and liquors–and never a barrel, cask, or bottle left the city without my approval, Rabbi, I will tell you that. Anyway, one day an out-of-town merchant met me to arrange for a shipment of palm wine. The merchant spoke Arabic, Persian, and Hebrew. We started talking in Arabic, but soon we switched to Hebrew, and he told me that he himself was a Jew of the Tribe of Issachar. When he heard my tale, he bought me outright, for thirty-two pieces of gold. Then he returned with me to his country, where I was received warmly and was free to do as I pleased.

"I learned that, after the Great Deportation by Saragon, the men of Issachar remained where they had been transplanted and never ventured south. Now they live along a mountainous seacoast, under the distant rule of Persian kings, and, by paying high taxes to Persia, the Jews of Issachar remain quite independent. In their tightly knit community, they adhere entirely to Jewish Law; frequently, they quoted to me the verse from the Book of Joshua":

> If you hope to prosper, then you must never forget the Law of Moses. Keep these commandments before you day and night; repeat them often, and observe them always.

"During all my stay there, the only serious arguments I ever saw were over interpretations of the Holy Scriptures. These Jews do not believe in warfare, and they have few weapons. Most men are merchants. (And there is no thievery or unscrupulous business practice among them.) In addition, a few Jews have large herds of cattle and camels. All in all, it is a fine and holy country, amen."

"Amen," said Rabbi Amram.

"To the east of the descendants of Issachar," continued Eldad, "live the children of Zebulun. This Tribe is mainly wanderers, nomads of the mountains of Paran. Their towns are cities of tents made of skins, and as the seasons change the towns disappear, only to pop up elsewhere, as if swept up one night by the great Hand of the Almighty Lord God and planted suddenly in some new spot at the dawning of a new morning.

"This region holds many pockets of the ancient Jewish Tribes. The Reubenites live to the north. They are city dwellers, and they have formal Jewish schools where Hebrew is taught; in fact, it was there that I first saw the full Mishnah and Talmud, documents unknown in my home country. Just to the south, the remnants of the Tribe of Simeon still live in Babylonia in small enclaves away from the large cities. Also, Jews in some of the remote Babylonian towns identify themselves as descendants of the Tribe of Manasseh–a tribe that split into two major divisions in the far olden days.

"Six of the twelve tribes journeyed south after the Assyrian destruction of Northern Israel. Two of them, the Tribe of Ephraim and a clan from the Tribe of Manasseh, settled in the Nejd region of Arabia. These Jews are warriors and nomads, with fierce brave horses. They live in the high oases that are surrounded by good pastures. A few of these Jews are farmers, growing dates, wheat, and barley, but most raise cattle and trade in horses. The villages in that area are made of sun-dried bricks, and the tents are made of skins."

Here, Eldad stopped and held up his hands. "Let me see, Rabbi," he said. "Have I reviewed all ten of the Lost Tribes?" He began to count on his fingers: "There was Issachar, Zebulun, Reuben, Simeon, and

Manasseh–these remained north of Palestine. Ephraim and a clan from Manasseh settled south in Arabia. Asher, Gad, and Naphtali went farther south and into Africa–this makes nine–and of course my Tribe of Dan makes ten."

Eldad nodded to himself. Rabbi Amram was listening carefully. "What can you tell me about the history of the Tribe of Dan?" he asked.

Eldad thought for a moment. "Well, Rabbi," he began, "it is like this. At first, the Danites were sent to the city of Gozan, which is in Assyria north of the River Euphrates. The local people were not happy to have a horde of southern strangers. They would not sell us food or clothes. We could not find houses. So the elders among us decided we should slip away and set up our own state somewhere to the south. We needed a resting place–but we were unsure as to where to go.

"We left as a group at night. We moved south, past Damascus, skirting the old kingdom of Dan. We stayed to the east of Mount Hermon. We went through Bashan and Ammon and Moab. We passed quietly through Edom, and we made our way across the Sea into Egypt. As we traveled in Africa, we followed the southern border of inhabited regions, and finally we came to the Land of Cush, which you call Aethiopia. There we settled. It is a good and fertile region, and now we have built fields and vineyards, gardens and parks. The countryside has streams and springs and underground waters. We grow wheat and barley; our farms have vines, figs, and pomegranates, and there are honey, olives, and cream for all. Even the stones are good to us, for there are iron and gold and copper in the hills.

"With the fine and bountiful richness of the land, we prospered. What more could we want? We have rarely felt the need to venture out into the difficult cruel world beyond. I am one of the few Danites so plagued with the wanderlust that he would come as far as the cold northern regions of Europe.

"And now that I am here, Rabbi, sometimes I wonder if I shall ever return."

Then suddenly Eldad was finished speaking, and he sat quietly.

Rabbi Amram said, "That is a remarkable story, my friend." Both men were quiet: the Rabbi and the wanderer sat together without speaking for many minutes. Eventually, Rabbi Amram set out some bread and some wine. The late afternoon shadows were lengthening.

"Do you have a place to stay for the evening?" asked the Rabbi. "Yes, I do, thank you, Rabbi," answered Eldad ben Mahli. Eldad smiled. He picked up his satchel, he turned, and he walked out of the wooden yeshiva in the Juden Viertels of medieval Cologne.

I do not know where he might have stayed that night. Was it even in Cologne? He had been traveling constantly for so many weeks and months and years that he did not know how to stop. Eldad was a man without a country; he was a man without a family or a people. He wandered up and down the Rhine Valley and throughout western Europe, and eventually he found his way to Cordova.

But by then something in Eldad seemed to have changed. He sat in the door of the old Cordova synagogue. He watched the wheeling birds overhead – the tanglepickers, the turnstones, and the windhovers. The light sky turned dark, and then the dark sky turned light. The changing clouds slipped south and east, toward the Holy Land. Eldad ben Mahli ha-Dani sat, and he watched. He watched the birds and the clouds and the winds and the seasons. He thought about the Holy Land, and one day when no one else was about, he died quietly, sitting there in the doorway of the old clay synagogue in Cordova.

Good evening, Rabbi. Sit, put your feet up on the side bench, and I will open the stove door. Let me push the coals back. There is nothing like the white glow of the oven to wash away the cares of a hard day. Yes, those coals look like pieces of gold to me too. They glow like the sun or like the yellow gold of the angel Nakiel, who, as you know, is also the angel of diamonds and agates.

Gold and diamonds, emeralds, agates, and rubies–these are potent gems, but you and I shall probably never own them. Of course, there are powerful stones that are more common. For instance, there are the many different *yahalom* stones. You can find them in any river, and they will ward off demons. I was telling Reb Moishe about *yahaloms* just the other day: he had never heard of them. Imagine, Rabbi–a Jew who knows nothing of *yahaloms*! People pay much less attention to stones nowadays. That is definitely a loss: the world is weaker and less magical without stone powers.

Stones are filled with ancient strengths. Even the common stones have hidden powers, but the gems are specially blessed. Once, long, long ago, the great Lord God Almighty invested all gems with magical powers. In medieval times everyone knew this. Everyone wanted gemstones–and we Jews were the gem merchants of Europe. Jews traveled the world over, by sea and by land. They visited Asia and China and the wild Eastern realms. And Jews traded in everything exotic–furs, gold, pearls, silks, silver, skins, spices, wools, and especially gemstones. Even rabbis and famous scholars–writers such as Berachiah ben Natronai ha-Nakdan–studied precious stones. And in those days all the histories of gems, all the academic descriptions of precious stones, began with the famous passage from the Hebrew Holy Scriptures. You know the one, Rabbi: it describes the sacred outfit of the Jewish high priests:

> Make the chest-plate of the priests with four rows of three precious stones. The first row should have sard, topaz, and carbuncle; the second row should have turquoise, lapis lazuli, and emerald; the third row should have jacinth, agate, and amethyst; and the fourth row should have beryl, onyx, and jasper. And each of these stones shall correspond to one of the twelve sons of Israel, to each of the twelve tribes by name.

Yes, gems have mystical powers.

What are the unique powers of each of these twelve sacred stones? Well, I will tell you.

First, there is sard, the orange chalcedony, the *odem* stone. Sard is the stone of Reuben. It prevents miscarriages and increases fertility. This is quite a potent stone because it counteracts poison, it wards off plagues, it dissolves grief, it keeps you modest, and it diverts your mind from evil thoughts.

Second, there is topaz, the yellow crystal, the *pitdah* stone. This is the stone of Simeon. Topaz will chill the body, but surprisingly it also encourages warm emotions such as love and romance and faithfulness.

Third is carbuncle, the red garnet, the *bareket* stone. It is the stone of Levi, making one wise and farsighted, openhearted and young.

Fourth is turquoise, the sky-blue gem, the *nofech* stone. Turquoise is the stone of Judah; it brings money, business success, strength, and victory in battle.

Fifth, there is lapis lazuli, the rich blue sapphire, the *sapir* stone. It is the stone of Issachar and is the physician's favorite, curing all diseases, especially poor sight.

Sixth, there is emerald, the green jewel called *perla,* the premier *yahalom* stone. This is the stone of Zebulun. Emeralds bring success in trade, they help your sleep, they subdue serpents, they calm your friends, and they preserve peace.

Seventh is jacinth, the orange hyacinth gemstone, the *leshem* stone. Jacinth is the stone of Dan, and it has one magical property – it is the stone of pure strong love.

Eighth is agate, the banded yellow chalcedony, the *shebo* stone. Agate is the stone of Naphtali. Use it for balance: it prevents stumbling and falling, even in high and difficult places. It can also make a person invisible, and it turns the weapons of your enemies against themselves.

Ninth, there is amethyst, the violet-blue crystal called *cristalo,* the *ahlamah* stone. Amethyst is the stone of Gad. It strengthens the heart, it gives courage, sincerity, honor, and faithfulness, it prevents drunkenness, and it wards off demons.

Tenth, there is beryl, the blue-green gem, the *tarshish* stone. Beryl is the stone of Asher; it soothes a troubled spirit and it aids digestion.

Eleventh is onyx, the many-layered chalcedony, the *shaoham* stone. Onyx is the stone of Joseph; it is a stone of elegance and grace, and it makes your speech smooth and gentle to hear.

Twelfth is jasper, the green chalcedony, the *yashfeh* stone. Jasper is the stone of Benjamin. It is a calming stone – it holds back harsh words, it eases the temper, and it restrains the blood.

These twelve gems are agents in God's earthly army. They are protective guardians. The great Lord God (blessed be He) has sprinkled them in the hillsides throughout the earth, and they wait quietly to help mankind. Few people seem to realize it, but the holy gems work today just as they have worked before, over the long, long ages past in our dusty, stone-filled world. There are endless stories of the protective powers of precious stones. For instance, there was the time that a cat's eye gem, an agate, helped a Jew from medieval Paris. . . . Certainly, my friend. I will be happy to tell you that tale:

I suppose I should begin when Louis the Seventh was king of France. King Louis protected Jews. The king encouraged trade, and all manner of Jewish businesses soon filled Paris and the surrounding communities. However, in the year 4935, Louis's son, Philip the

Second, succeeded his father. Philip Augustus became king when he was only a boy of fifteen, and young King Philip soon drove the Jews from France.

You see, to avoid war, Philip's father, King Louis, had given up his outlying lands. Now the French empire was a long narrow strip hemmed in by the Angevin Empire (ruled by King Henry the Second of England) on the west and by the kingdom of Arles on the south and east. Why not continue to expand our realms? thought the other rulers. Philip's uncles and the neighboring barons attacked the new young king from the north. King Philip found himself in constant battles. Money for troops and supplies ran low. Philip raised taxes three times. He instituted import, export, and travel fees. Then, one night, a demon whispered in the ear of Philip Augustus. Encouraged by a religious hermit of Vincennes, the young king had all the Parisian Jews seized for ransom while they were praying in their synagogues. The king also canceled all the Christian debts to Jews; then he taxed the Christians twenty percent on the forgiven debt.

This was the replay of an old, old problem. In Europe, Jews had never been safe from the whims of the local monarchs: Jews were not full citizens of any European country, and they had no home country to which to return. The French Jews had no choice. They paid their ransoms with money, property, merchandise, valuables, and even clothes. They gave up fields, vineyards, barns, wagons, horses, hens, and wine presses. The Talmudical College of Paris closed. With no homes, no goods, and empty synagogues, Jews left France for Spain, for Germany, and for Italy.

One of the exiles had been a wealthy dealer in precious stones and jewels. This was Jedahiah ben Mendel ha-Levi. In those difficult times, Jewish property was searched and all valuables were confiscated, but before he left Paris, Jedahiah managed to hide one box of jewels, which he secretly gave to his good friend Clement Stolle, a Christian neighbor. "Someday," said Jedahiah, "a new king will take power. Perhaps I will return and claim my treasure." Clement sadly shook his head. He took the box. It was oak with iron bands. Inside were gold brooches, gold rings, pendants, sapphires, unmounted gemstones, and a great quantity of coins. The gemstones included two large agates, one of which was a beautiful cat's eye agate. Agates are known for courage, boldness, and warding off thunder, lightning, and evil. Would they protect this treasure from the demons abroad in the world? Only time would tell.

Clement Stolle had known Jedahiah since the two were small boys. He promised to guard the box. The two men shook hands late one night, and Jedahiah left the city for safer havens. Jedahiah wandered out, and years and years passed–and eventually the two men grew older and grayer.

Ah, Rabbi, but the world does not stand still. As my grandmother said, "The good Lord God, blessed be He, whirls and twirls our little earth in His holy palm." Many years later, King Philip Augustus suddenly invited the Jews to return. The French business community had deteriorated. Tax collections were meager. King Philip wanted to revive his economy. He wanted to build monuments throughout Paris. The king planned colleges and a new palace, to be called the "Louvre." He was reorganizing the marketplaces. He was constructing new walls and fortifications along the right side of the River Seine. He was paving the city streets. King Philip had great, grand plans, and he needed a bustling city with money and goods flowing like a rushing river. "Let us bring back the Jews," said the king. When Jedahiah heard the news, he raised his eyebrows in wonder. He had grown up in Paris–it was his childhood home–so Jedahiah ben Mendel ha-Levi was among the many Jews who returned to France.

Jedahiah came back. He found that no one stopped him. No one questioned him. No one searched his belongings. No one bothered him because he was a Jew. There were small storefronts available to rent or to buy. Perhaps he could set up his old import-export business. Perhaps he would become a Parisian gem merchant again. Jedahiah felt hopeful. He went to the house of Clement Stolle. A young woman answered the door. No, she said, she knew no Clement. There was no one named Stolle living there. However, an old neighbor remembered Clement. Yes, reported the neighbor, Clement had lived there, but he had become ill and poor and it was rumored that he had gone to live with distant relatives somewhere in the Rhine regions. Was it Bonn? Or perhaps he had gone to Cologne. The neighbor was uncertain.

"Ah, well," thought Jedahiah, "I guess I will have to begin again from scratch. If Clement became poor and sick, undoubtedly he was forced to sell my valuables." Jedahiah walked for many hours that afternoon. He tried to keep his mind on Paris and on his new life and on a realistic future, but he could not help thinking of the treasure that he had left behind. The gems were special; some were irreplaceable. Could they still be with Clement? Is such a thing possible after all these years?

Jedahiah closed his eyes. He remembered his old friend. He pictured Clement standing in his doorway, young and strong and handsome and smiling. "I have no family," thought Jedahiah. "Clement was my closest friend. Even if we have no money, perhaps we can start a business together. It would be better than working alone. I remember many fine times that we shared when the world was younger and when everything was possible." Jedahiah opened his eyes. He smiled. He would go off to Germany and find his old friend Clement Stolle.

It was a summer afternoon, and after days of travel Jedahiah had come to the Juden Viertels of Cologne. He was far from home. He needed a place to stay. He wanted some companionship and advice. He was directed to the synagogue at the end of an alley along Judengasse Street. The air was warm, the alleyway was dusty, and suddenly Jedahiah felt in no hurry. He stopped. He looked at the weeds. The lambsfoot growing along the edge of the building were fuzzy, as they always were in the long thick days of summer. Jedahiah sighed. After a moment, he took another deep breath and he winked and he blinked and he stepped in the front door of the yeshiva. Jedahiah walked into the empty main prayer hall, and he made his way back to the study room where he had heard voices. There, he found the Rabbi bent over a book; a number of old scholars were talking on the benches.

Jedahiah introduced himself. "Gentlemen," he continued, "if you will give me a moment, I need your advice."

Jedahiah ben Mendel sat down on one of the benches. He told his whole story from beginning to end. The old sages listened attentively. "I searched in Bonn," he concluded, "but Clement was not there. I have been told that a Clement Stolle lives here in Cologne." Jedahiah hesitated a moment. "But, sirs, something is holding me back. Now that I am so close to finding my old friend, I wonder: should I bother him? It has been many, many years. He has grown older, and I am certain that he has changed. Should I continue to search him out? What if he lost my gems? What if he was forced to sell them? Undoubtedly he has seen hard times. How can I dare to embarrass him? And then, perhaps, he, a Gentile, would no longer wish to be friends with me, a Jew." Jedahiah looked down at his hands and he sighed.

The sages sitting on the benches looked at one another and they looked at the Rabbi. Rabbi Abraham was sitting quietly, watching Jedahiah. After a moment, white-haired Baruch ben Jacob said, "When a child enters the fold of Judaism, eight days after he is born, three things are wished for his life: good deeds, marriage, and an understanding of the Torah."

The jeweler looked puzzled. Hurriedly, a younger man, Elisah ben Samuel, said, "What Reb Baruch is pointing out is that doing good deeds – righteous holy acts – is part of God's covenant. Your old Gentile neighbor was a fine, God-fearing person. Undoubtedly he too, in his own way, has tried his best to fulfill this most ancient covenant. Undoubtedly you will find that he has done good deeds and that he will be proud of them."

"Amen, Elisah," said Joshua ben Eliezer. "So here is our counsel, Reb Jedahiah: go and search for this man. Find what has happened to him. Thank him for his help. Do not judge him. And then you too will have fulfilled your covenant."

The sages nodded. They stroked their beards. They murmured among themselves. One of the other scholars, Lewe ben Anselm, said, "Exactly. By all means, find this Mr. Stolle, Jedahiah, and renew your friendship. This is the highest gift that you two can exchange."

Again, the many scholars nodded and murmured among themselves. Some of the men stroked their beards; others tapped their chins. Jedahiah, the jeweler, nodded too, and he waited politely. There was silence; then Menahem ben Joel looked at his neighbors and said cautiously, "Remember the Book of Ecclesiastes":

> And again I saw emptiness under the sun: there was a lonely man, working hard without a friend. And this is the greatest emptiness, this toiling alone. Two are incomparably better than one – together, two men can always find some success in their work, because, even if one falls, the other can help his companion up again.

The sages smiled. Moyses ben Nathan felt brave, so he added, "That is well said, good Menahem. And I should like to point out that the Talmud reminds us that a man should *always* have a friend. With a friend you can study. With a friend, you can eat and you can relax, and also you have someone to whom you can tell your secrets."

Now the old sages looked at Shimshon ha-Zaken. Reb Shimshon was tugging at his beard. He coughed, then he said, "Gentlemen, I would contribute this: Jedahiah still has doubts. This bespeaks *demons.* I fear that the original demon is still at work muddying the waters. Listen to the evil ones no longer, Jedahiah! Have faith in the Lord–hallelujah and amen."

"Amen," said Baruch, and the other scholars said "amen."

Now the old men became silent and they looked at Rabbi Abraham. Abraham ben Alexander, the mystic Achselrad of Cologne, was quiet a moment; then he said, "All that you say, my good colleagues, is quite true. It is true and right and holy. You should not abandon your search, Jedahiah. However, I believe, along with Reb Shimshon, that some evil demon continues to plague you. Therefore I will give you a holy parchment for your protection."

And the Rabbi took from his desk a square piece of new kosher deerskin. On it he wrote:

> May the most holy Lord God protect Jedahiah the son of Mendel the Levite; as the psalmist sang:
>
> If I lift up my eyes to the tall hill
> Will I find any guidance on high?
> Salvation comes only through God's will–
> *He* made the hills and the sky.
>
> The Guard of Israel never sleeps
> The good Lord defends your soul–
> No foes will strike from the nighttime deeps,
> No evil crawl from the midnight hole.
>
> God protects against all evil things,
> Guarding from ill winds and blight–
> He shelters you with mighty wings
> Through the darkness of the blackest night.

Rabbi Abraham rolled the charm into a tight scroll, he tied it with seven knots of a fine white thread, and he handed the amulet to

Jedahiah. "Wear this on your left arm at all times," instructed the Rabbi.

Jedahiah ben Mendel ha-Levi took the amulet. He stood, and with a slight bow, he said, "Good Rabbi and scholars, thank you for your counsel."

Again, Jedahiah bowed; then he left the old yeshiva building. It was early afternoon. The day was still sunny. Jedahiah walked down Judengasse Street. He looked along the edges of the buildings: lambs-foot weeds were everywhere. Why had he never noticed them before? Jedahiah talked quietly to himself as he walked down the street and out of the Jewish Quarter. Judengasse Street became Unter Taschenmacher Street at the edge of the Juden Viertels, and here Jedahiah began to ask people about Clement. One man directed him to the next. Six times men were questioned, and six times Jedahiah received helpful directions. Soon a chain of seven men had been queried–and yes, the last man knew a Clement Stolle.

"Hohestrasse Steet," said the man. "At the far end of Hohestrasse street there is an alley and two shacks. Clement lives in the shack on the left."

Jedahiah hurried down the street. He found the alley and he found the shack. He knocked on the door. There was no answer. But wait–there was a shuffling noise. A latch was unlocked, slowly the door was opened, and there stood Clement Stolle. He was thin and gray. He walked with a cane, a gnarled crabstick crutch. His beard was stubbly. Jedahiah looked at the old man and he looked at the room beyond. There was only a bed, a bench, and a table, and inside it was dark and it was cool.

Clement's eyes opened wide. At first, he said nothing at all. His cane slipped from his grasp. The two men stooped to pick it up at the same time. Clement smiled. Jedahiah smiled. And then they stood and hugged. Hello, hello–what can I say? What are you doing here? Is it really you? How have you been? Come in and sit down.

It was not long before Clement said, "Just a moment, old friend." He shuffled over to his bed, he pulled out a sack from underneath the mattress, and he handed it to Jedahiah.

"What is this?" asked the Jew, but he knew already.

"Here is your treasure," said the Gentile, patting the sack. "I have guarded it well."

"But how could you have done a thing like that?" asked Jedahiah, opening the bag. "Obviously you have suffered. This is too much to expect even from a friend."

"How could I use something that did not belong to me?" answered Clement. "I think, in fact, that these valuables kept me going. When times were difficult, I always said, 'Ah, Clement, at least you have guarded old Jed's gems.' As long as I had the jewels, I knew that I was doing a heroic thing–no one could ever ask more of me. But, my friend, I am happy to see you. I am tired of being heroic; now I would like only to rest a bit."

Jedahiah looked closely at the treasure. Yes, he could remember each piece. Every single thing was still there. But what was this? One of the agates, the fine gold and green cat's eye, had faded. How could a gem fade? Gems were harder than iron, stronger than steel, fiercer than a lion. Their colors were dyed within them for all eternity. The colors are the gems' divine powers. Was it possible that this stone had used up its power?

Jedahiah had heard that gemstones could fight evil. Once upon a time, the great Lord God Almighty had stored holy magic within this cat's eye stone. It was once upon a time, long, long ago, when all things great and small were established forever, in the first days of Creation. The Omnipotent One had created a world of vast tangled complexity. This incondensably complex world would occupy God with endless matters of importance forever into the future; therefore, in the beginning, He also created guardians. The omniscient Lord God made gemstones to protect His children far and wide throughout the generations. Quietly, these tiny beacons of holiness worked for His children in constant and unimagined ways. Had the good Lord God known every single thing even at the beginning of time? Had He seen that this very stone would fight with demons five thousand years later in the cold northern climes of Europe? Jedahiah held up the cat's eye. He looked at the dull stone. He smiled, and he felt very warm and happy.

Clement watched as Jedahiah was lost in his thoughts. Jedahiah shook his head a moment; then he stood and hugged his old friend again. "You are more than a friend," he said. "You are like my own brother." Then Jedahiah ben Mendel ha-Levi gave all the valuables to Clement Stolle. "I cannot take all of these," said Clement, pushing them back. "Very well," answered Jedahiah, "give me the cat's eye."

Clement handed the agate to Jedahiah, and the two men smiled once more.

Clement and Jedahiah returned to Paris. Within the month, they set up a jewelry importing business together. They sold gemstones and fancy jewelry to both Jews and Gentiles, and their business was a great success. Jedahiah and Clement remained fast friends to the ends of their long and happy lives. In the end, when they were both bent and old and gray, they sat together on cold winter nights on low benches before the stove. Jedahiah would hold his worn cat's eye agate in one hand and he would push the coals back with a stick in the other hand; then a white glow flowed from the oven and it washed away all the cares of their long, hard lives. As they stared into the coals the two men saw golden glowing gems, and they were blessed by the angel Nakiel, who protected them forever and ever, long into the deep medieval night.

What is that, Rabbi? No, no, I was just resting my eyes. Please feel free to join me here by the stove. (I think you will be too warm on that bench: try the one nearer to the wall.) An old man like me can doze forever by a warm stove; I suppose that is because I no longer fear demons.

During the night you are particularly susceptible to demonic attack: your soul leaves your body when you dream, and your guard is let down ("when the tenant leaves town, then there is no one to look after the house"). For this reason a fear of demons can keep you awake, especially when you are young. But, now that I am old, evil spirits are just hollow winds to me and I am sleepy all the time.

In fact, I hardly think of demons any longer. Of course it is not only my old age–it is also the city life. We live in a bustling town. We are surrounded by tools and buildings and machines, so we rarely pay attention to the many spirits hiding in the shadows around us. However, it is different in the countryside. Farmers have time to think. They keep an eye on the nooks and the crannies and the underbrush, and they are always finding demons, dybbuks, and evil spirits. Plants attract demons, you know–plants are often haunted by evil spirits. Plant demons can take the form of a child, a man or a woman, or an animal, such as a fox. Such demons lurk in the dank valleys in outlying areas, and they blight the lives of farm families.

What is that? Certainly I can give you an example. I remember the sad story of a grain demon that roamed the Rhinelands long ago. This happened in the Middle Ages. In those days, the towns were still isolated pockets in the endless woodland countryside, and, once upon a time in those mysterious demon-filled countrysides, there lived a poor farmer named Maleachi ben Aram ha-Kohen.

Maleachi farmed on the rocky soil near the western road outside of Cologne, and he barely eked out a living. He worked long, tiring hours, turning the soil, removing sticks and rocks, and planting, watering, weeding, and hoeing. At the end of the summer and into the fall, he harvested whatever plants had managed to grow. Daily he chased away the insects and the animals which enjoyed his plants more than he did. Maleachi worked in all weathers, and one grim and cloudy day when Maleachi was working in the vegetable garden near his house, a little fox crawled out from among the bushes.

The farmer made a halfhearted swipe at the animal with his hoe. The fox did not move. Then, in a small dry voice, the fox said, "I am starving. Feed me." Maleachi was startled. He stepped back. He took in a quick breath, and he raised his eyebrows.

For a moment, there was only the sound of the wind. But again the fox said, "I need food. I am very hungry." The farmer became frightened. His heart began to beat quickly. What should he do? Clearly something supernatural was at work. Maleachi did not dare to anger the spirits, so he returned to his farmhouse, he took some bread from the pantry, and he brought it outside for the fox. The farmer tossed the bread on the ground in front of the animal. The fox did not look up. It bent its head, and in one swift gulp it swallowed the bread. "More," said the fox.

The farmer looked around. Were other spirits watching? He went back into the house. He brought out the entire loaf of bread and tore it into pieces and spread it on the ground in front of the fox. The fox ate the whole loaf. Again it said, "More." Soon poor Maleachi had given the animal most of the extra food from the storage room.

"I am still hungry," said the fox. The animal had a strange and frightening look in its eye. Maleachi shuddered. He returned to the house. There was nothing in the pantry cupboard, so he brought out a cheese from the kitchen. The fox ate that immediately. By now Maleachi felt cold; he shivered and trembled. Suddenly the fox looked around. It bounded away into the bushes. It became a slippery rustling sound in the fields far beyond. Then it was gone without a trace, leaving behind a cool, damp, fear-filled feeling like a foggy cloud covering the worried farmer.

Maleachi was shaking. However there was nothing to do but to continue his work. Weakly, he picked up his hoe and he returned to his garden. Maleachi shook his head; he looked forward to sleeping that night and to forgetting the whole unsettling experience. That evening, Maleachi told the story to his wife, Blume. "What will we do now?" she asked. "We have no bread or cheese. We have only a few dried vegetables in the storage shed."

"I could not help myself, Blume. There was something very frightening about that animal," said the husband. "It was some sort of evil spirit–it was a grain demon. But with no more extra food here perhaps it will go and bother other people."

The next morning, Maleachi awoke to low gray skies. He was tense and uncomfortable. He stepped outside and looked around. He could not see under all the plants; he could not see inside all the bushes. Was the evil animal around someplace? Maleachi picked up his hoe. He stood by the pea plants. Suddenly the fox appeared at the side of his house. Maleachi stopped hoeing. His stomach felt tight. The fox sat silent and motionless.

Just then Maleachi's wife came out of the door. She saw the fox. It turned its head toward her and said, "I am very hungry. You must feed me." The animal was small and thin; its legs were like plant stalks. Blume felt sorry for it. She went into the kitchen and brought out the last of their stored meat, which the fox gobbled up immediately. "More," it said. The fox's voice was low and raspy, and it made Blume shiver. She went back into the kitchen and returned with a bowl of pottage. The fox lapped up the cold cereal; then it turned as if frightened, and it bounded away into the bushes. Soon the fox had become a slippery rustling sound in the fields far beyond, and then it was gone without a trace, leaving behind a cool, damp, fear-filled feeling like a cloud or a fog enshrouding the worried woman.

Maleachi stood watching silently. He looked at his wife and she looked at him. Neither said a word. After a moment, Blume went into the house and sat in the kitchen, and it was many, many minutes before she began to feel comfortable again.

The couple filled the rest of their day with normal chores. They did not mention the fox, and they went to bed early. The next day, the fox was not seen, but an ill wind hung along the hillsides. Then on the following morning, the fox stood waiting outside their farmhouse when Maleachi and Blume awoke.

There was no extra food at all. Did the fox know this? It said nothing; it only sat by the front door. The farmer and his wife walked in and out through the back door. They tried not to look at the animal, which sat and sat like a silent Egyptian statue. All that day and for the following days, too, the fox sat motionless and silent. A stifling curse seemed to have descended on the farm. The land and the house were gray and dim. Furniture and clothes felt dirty. The farmer and his wife were weighted down by a heavy cloud. The plants became wrinkled; then they withered–and slowly but steadily all the crops began to die.

Maleachi ben Aram had two fields beyond his vegetable garden: one was for oats and one was for barley. Usually at the beginning of the hot month of *Av,* when the oats had begun to seed, Maleachi took off the husks and sold the oat kernels for porridge and for *matzohs.* Soon after, when the barley had begun to seed, Maleachi ground off the husks and sold the barley pearls for stews, for malt, and for flour. In years gone by, both grains grew rapidly. In the best of times, oat spikelets fanned out from stalks that were more than a meter high, and the barley looked like golden wheat.

This year, however, the fields were patchy and mottled and they looked like trash heaps. No grain grew. The plants were stunted and weak. Small black dust covered the leaves. Red dots coated the stems. Then grasshoppers and flies began to chew the stunted plants. Quickly Maleachi planted beans, but animals ate them at night. The remainder of the vegetable garden had wilted also: everything was failing everywhere.

Maleachi tried the most well known remedy: he cut a large onion into quarters, he boiled it for an hour, and then he added seven garlic cloves, each cut in half. The mixture cooled in the sun for a half hour;

then Maleachi sprinkled the onion water over all the plants. Was it working? Maleachi watched hopefully for the next few days. Insects and worms stayed away, but the plants remained as sickly as ever.

A gray mist hung on the horizon every morning. To Blume, the skies seemed fuzzy and dank, the clouds were low and thick. Her food tasted bland; even the water was wan and weak. Evilness covered the land, and it was beyond their meager powers to push it away. "Go ask a rabbi," said Blume to her husband. "Get some holy counsel."

Maleachi was tired. His arms were heavy; his spirit was worn. Maleachi nodded his head, but he did nothing.

The next day, Blume said again, "Please, Maleachi, talk with someone. I am sick and very worried." So, that afternoon, Maleachi went into Cologne and consulted with Rabbi Achselrad, the Chief Rabbi for all the Rhine region.

Rabbi Abraham closed his eyes and listened intently. When Maleachi had finished talking, the Rabbi remained silent. His head nodded. He began to breathe deeply and regularly. Had he fallen asleep? After a few minutes, Maleachi said quietly, "Rabbi, are you awake?"

"Yes, yes," said Rabbi Achselrad. He opened his eyes and stroked his beard. "I fear, Maleachi, that a demon is at work here."

"Yes, it is certainly a demon," said Maleachi.

"You know, my friend," said the Rabbi, "demons are everywhere: they surround us. I think it was the Babylonians who first realized that all the petty annoyances of life–headaches, sudden falls, quarrels, stubbed toes, broken utensils–result from the mischief of demons. Each part of the body wrestles constantly with its own particular demon. The Egyptians discovered that demons (which they call *jinn*) swarm so thickly that you must even ask their permission before pouring water on the ground. Otherwise, you might accidentally drench a demon, and this would make it so angry that it will immediately turn you into a locust."

Maleachi shook his head worriedly.

"Therefore," continued the Rabbi, "I advise a protective amulet."

Again the Rabbi stroked his beard; then he began to prepare a protective charm. He took a small parchment square from inside his desk and he wrote a short prayer, asking the beneficent Lord God Almighty for rain, warm weather, and lush plant growth. Rabbi Achselrad invoked Mathariel and Ridyah, the angels of rain, and Kutiel and Luel, the angels of groundwater. He requested fine harvests under the radiant glowing *Shekhinah* of the great Lord Yahweh-Elohim. He sealed the charm with the names of the four rivers of the Garden of Eden–Pishon, Gihon, Perath, and Hiddekel. Then old Rabbi Achselrad tied the parchment into a tight scroll and he handed it to the farmer. Maleachi thanked the Rabbi, and he returned home happily.

However, things continued to worsen. The turnips that Maleachi had planted one by one at the beginning of the cold month of *Nisan*–the turnips that he had planted in a well-sheltered sunny side of the springtime garden–these turnips now had wilted leaves and thin, spindly roots. Their green tops were brown. Their stems were sickly white. In fact, the vegetable plants could not be told apart from weeds.

Maleachi complained to his neighbors. In the village, sitting on a bench beside a worn stone cross, an old Gentile said to Maleachi, "Listen, my friend, this is a grain demon. There is no choice but to kill it. Yes, yes, I know that is a harsh task, but there is an added benefit in the end: if the blood and the bones of the grain demon are spread on the young plants, then the harvest will be full and lush. The death of a grain demon actually brings good fortune to your farm."

The old villager lowered his voice and he looked around. "I know this for a fact," he said quietly. "A witch confessed this to me on her deathbed."

Maleachi listened and nodded. Later, he reported to his wife. Blume could not believe what she was hearing. "Maleachi, how could you hurt any animal–even this fox! And if this *is* a demon in disguise, then there will be a revenge: you will be killed and our house and our farm will be destroyed. Do not do anything foolish."

Maleachi felt ill. He wanted this problem to end. He wanted the fox to go away. He wanted to forget everything. But he said, "All right, wife, we will wait a little longer." And the couple continued their discouraging life.

It may be hard to imagine, Rabbi, but in fact matters degenerated further. Drought came. Strange new plant sicknesses turned the leaves black and powdery. Giant grasshoppers swarmed in and ate even the bark from the trees. Animals trampled the gardens at night. Nothing edible grew. All the vines and stalks were stunted and twisted and brown, and their leaves were pale and thin. And often the farmer thought that he saw the fox far off in the fields. "Does this animal have a burrow nearby?" wondered Maleachi. "Does it live in the grass at the edge of the woods? Maybe I can find its home and scare it off. Perhaps I can even kill it." But again Blume persuaded her husband to consult with Rabbi Achselrad.

"Very well, I might as well talk to the Rabbi," said Maleachi to Blume. "Clearly there is nothing useful I can do here." So the farmer returned to Cologne. He went into the Juden Viertels and he walked down Judengasse Street. He turned into the alley leading to the old yeshiva building. Maleachi stepped in the front door, he went through the anteroom, and he walked into the main prayer hall filled with wooden benches. Maleachi passed the twelve stained-glass windows with their colored lions and snakes, he looked up at the Holy Ark made of stone, and he walked to the door of the back study room. The Cologne synagogue seemed so very far from the countryside. Was God so distant from Maleachi's farm?

It was late afternoon, and Rabbi Abraham was bent over a book. The Rabbi looked up. Maleachi sat tiredly on the worn bench. In a low voice, he reviewed the entire situation – the fox, the farm, the failures. The Rabbi shook his head sadly. He closed his eyes; then he opened his eyes. "Let me write you a more powerful charm," he said.

Old Rabbi Achselrad tapped his chin and he frowned. He pushed aside his books, looking among the piles of papers on his desk. He frowned again; then he reached into a drawer and he pulled out a clean piece of white parchment made from the skin of a kosher calf. The Rabbi picked up his pen. On one side of the paper he wrote the *Shema,* followed by seven mystical words. On the other side, he wrote:

> Mighty is Yahweh-Elohim, Who blesses Israel with food and drink. May the Almighty Lord save Maleachi, the son of Aram the *Kohan,* and his good wife Blume from all manner of evil spirits and demons. May the gentle rains come in season, may the warm winds blow apace, and may the Grace of Yahweh-Elohim shine on all of Maleachi's lands.
>
> May this come to pass in the Name of the great Lord God and in the names of the angels Aniel, Gabriel, Hasdiel, Kabshiel, Metatron, Michael, Rahab, Raphael, Ridyah, Sandalfon, Shamriel, and Uriel – Yah, Yah, Yah, Yah, Yah, Yah, Yah, Yah, Eheyh, Ahah, Ahah, Ahah, Ahah, Yehu, Yehu, Yehu, Yehu, Yehu, Yehu, Yehu, Yehu, Yehu. Amen, eternally hallelujah – thus shall be Your will, *selah* and amen.

The Rabbi wrote this in Hebrew, in his small, neat script. Then he rolled the parchment into a tight scroll. The parchment had tiny dark veins like the back of a human hand. Rabbi Abraham rubbed the edge of the paper. Then he tied the scroll with seven white threads and in each thread he put seven neat knots. The Rabbi tapped the amulet on his desk. He handed the scroll to Maleachi. Maleachi thanked the Rabbi, and he turned to leave.

"Just a moment, Maleachi," said Rabbi Abraham. "There is serious evil afoot here."

Maleachi nodded; this was not news to him.

"Maleachi," continued the Rabbi, "I warn you: Be patient. Be very, very patient. Do not do anything rash. Pray and wait and trust in the Lord."

Again Maleachi nodded. The Rabbi stared at the farmer, and Maleachi lowered his eyes. "Thank you, Rabbi," he said wearily; then Maleachi left Cologne.

Maleachi tried to feel hopeful, but in his heart of hearts he was quite discouraged. Were the plants improving? Maleachi could see no change. What would happen in the fall? How would the couple live through the winter? It all seemed so hopeless. The farmer and his wife were always tired and hot; frequently, they went to bed hungry. The fox sat on the hillside every evening, and the farmer had nightmares, night after night after night. In one dream, he was trying to climb a tall and wondrous hill. He knew, in some mysterious way, that the name of this hill was ha-Har ha-Meushar, "The Happy Mountain." In the dream, Maleachi walked slowly. Everything was confused and tangled. He could not find the right path. Then Maleachi saw a young animal – a goat with pointed ears and a long bushy tail – and suddenly he found that he had killed the goat. Now his feet stopped moving altogether. His legs were caught in the brush and the branches. He felt slow and heavy and tired, as if he were stuck in mud or in thick, thick water. He looked up and he saw ha-Har ha-Meushar squat and afar. Then Maleachi awoke, and he felt weak and even more tired than when he had gone to bed.

Finally one evening Maleachi could not fall asleep at all. He tossed and he turned. He was hot and tired and angry and he was very, very discouraged. As was the custom with farms, Maleachi's house faced the south. His bedroom was in the back; his window looked north toward his fields and up a slope. In the light of the bright moon, Maleachi could see the shape of the fox sitting like a trim, silent Egyptian statue in the north fields above his house.

It was the middle of the night. Maleachi got up. He got out of his bed and he dressed. The fox sat quietly by the far edge of the ruined garden. In the nighttime blackness, Maleachi could not see the reddish hints in the fox's coat. In the dark, dark hours, Maleachi could not see the long bushy tail draped on the ground. All Maleachi saw were two evil gleaming eyes and a pointed black nose. The eyes were unblinking; the nose pointed at the farmer's heart. Maleachi gritted his teeth, he lifted his axe, and he killed the fox. Then he sprinkled its blood on the plants, and he spread its broken bones in the fields beyond.

The next morning, Maleachi felt empty. His head and neck ached. He was tired. He avoided the gardens. He did not eat. Was he feeling worse than usual? Perhaps he was – but then again, perhaps he was not. Days passed: seven days came and seven days went. A gentle rain fell for two days. The plants turned green. New shoots appeared; the old stalks were strengthened. Peas and beans and turnips began to grow. Sun followed rain, and rain followed sun.

For a while, Maleachi was elated. He smiled and he hummed. In contrast, Blume felt detached and sad and quiet. Something unholy was in the air. Then Maleachi too began to feel uneasy again. The couple found their plants growing, but the world was still gray. Their nights remained sleepless. It was not that strange noises kept them awake – no winds or bumpings or voices arose in the dark late hours – instead, all was blank and dull and thick and empty.

"I am frightened," said Blume to Maleachi. The farmer was frightened too. Blume suggested that Maleachi return to Cologne to see the Rabbi. But what exactly would he ask of Rabbi Abraham? The crops were improving. The weather was good. How could he say that he was frightened when things appeared to be going well, when the sun shone in the mornings, when the rains came apace, and when there were no clear fears or threats?

Maleachi could not confess that he had killed the fox. He could barely think about it himself. He could not tell his wife – and he would never dare to tell the Rabbi. But Blume continued to say: "Please, husband, go into Cologne. I am sure that there is a prayer to say or something else that we can do to make us feel better. We are not right with God. I just know it."

Finally, Maleachi agreed. He took his horse and his wagon and he rode into the city. He wandered up various streets looking for the Juden Viertels. Had they changed the streets recently? What were these buildings doing here? Suddenly he found himself far over by the northern gate, the Eigelstein Gate. And what was this? The entire area was deserted. How strange for the middle of the afternoon. Maleachi turned and headed south. He passed the ancient church of Saint Gereon, which was dedicated to the early Christian martyrs–the Theban Legion–some of whom were buried in the crypt inside. The church building looked stark and cold and forbidding, and Maleachi hurried by.

Maleachi looked up one street and down the next. Where was Judengasse Street? All the passersby seemed sullen and fierce and angry, and he feared asking directions. "Is this Cologne?" he finally called out. The nearest man stepped back and scowled and then hurried on. *Was* this Cologne? wondered Maleachi. He was lost. Eventually, his horse found the city gate. Maleachi passed beneath the bell tower, and again he found himself on the road home. Maleachi shrugged and continued on. "Did you see the Rabbi?" asked Blume later. "No," said Maleachi sadly, "let's not talk about it."

That afternoon, Rabbi Abraham needed to stretch his legs. At the moment no one was about at the old yeshiva. Abraham Achselrad stood up. He walked through the main prayer hall, and he looked out the front door. The Rabbi looked up into the sky from the synagogue courtyard and he saw a dark halo around the sun. The Rabbi looked down the alleyway. It was deserted. Where were all the people? The Rabbi stood still for a moment. He noticed a clump of dried weeds near the wall of the yeshiva. Suddenly Maleachi came to mind–Maleachi, the farmer with the dried crops, the ravaged wilted plants, and the ancient grain demon. Rabbi Abraham ben Alexander felt very sad. He shook his head; then he turned and walked slowly back into the synagogue building. Old Achselrad knew that Maleachi ben Aram would never return to the Cologne yeshiva again.

Rabbi, it is good to see you here this evening. When you walk into the room, the world seems brighter.

What is that? Yes, certainly the world will be brightest when the Messiah walks in. Someday *Mashiah,* the anointed one, will arrive; he will come to "brighten and perfect the world through the establishment of the kingship of the Almighty, amen." It is possible that the Messiah could arrive any day now, but I fear that his coming is probably a long, long way off, although I pray for it daily. As it is said in the Book of Micah:

> Other people give their prayer
>   To many little gods of yore
> But *we* will ever pray before
>   The Lord, our God, Whom we adore
> Daily now and for ever more.

So we pray and still we wait, surrounded by a world of other old gods, "little gods of yore." That is why it is so comforting to see you, my friend: you come *now,* you are *our* connection with God, you bring a holy presence here today.

Ah, when will the Messiah come? Will we ever see him on this earth? Strong and holy men certainly have tried their best to hurry his coming. Do you know the story of Rabbi Aleydis ben Samuel, who tried to hurry the Messiah? It happened long ago, and news of it reached Europe through a letter of the famed traveler Petahiah ben Jacob of Regensburg.

Petahiah's travels were at the end of the twelfth century, in the days of Achselrad, well before Asher ben Yehiel was the Chief Rabbi of Cologne. And why do I introduce Rabbi Asher? Well, it is simply that when he was the leading scholar in Cologne, Asher spent most of his time writing and reading in the back room of the yeshiva; this room was where Cologne rabbis had always passed endless hours working and thinking and arguing with themselves. Above the back study room was a loft for storage. One day when he was rooting around among the manuscripts in the loft, Rabbi Asher found a letter from Rabbi Petahiah of Regensburg to Rabbi Abraham ben Alexander, Achselrad of Cologne, and this is what it said:

"*My dear Rabbi Abraham*–

"I have just met a fine young man, a Jewish merchant from Strassburg; he has agreed to carry this letter to my old colleage, Rabbi Solomon ben Meyer, who I am certain will then arrange to transport it to you. I write to wish you and your family well, to convey my fondest greetings to all the Jews of your blessed community in Cologne, and to praise the good Lord God (blessed be He) and His Almighty Name for ever and ever, amen.

"As I have written before, wagon rides, sea voyages, and endless walks fill my head with a tangle of fantastic pictures. But through it all, the Lord has protected me, safely bringing me here to the Oriental regions, regions that are so near to the great Holy Land where someday the Messiah shall return and deliver us and resurrect all souls and rebuild the Temple on Zion, amen. I write now in order to record for you some details of the lands and the peoples that I have seen in these old and foreign realms. The bright and glorious hand of the Lord is visible everywhere, my friend, if only we look–praise the Lord Yahweh-Elohim.

"Yes, I have had many, many adventures in arriving here. I hope–with the good Lord willing–to relate more of these events to you in person. For now, let me just say that before my great tour of the Holy Land of Palestine, I passed through the country called Little Tartary. Little Tartary is sixteen days' journey in width, through flat plains with no mountains at all. Beyond this region extends a sea–which I am told is actually an inlet of the ocean–called the Gulf of Perekop. Across the choppy waters is the famed Land of the Khazars, and in Khazar I continued my journey for a week and a day.

"Even to Regensburg the occasional Oriental traveler brought reports of a kingdom in Asia ruled by a Jewish king. Perhaps you have heard such tales in Cologne also. I am convinced that the stories refer to the land of the Khazars. The Khazars are a strong people–they are *physically* strong: they resemble solid oak barrels. Originally, they came from farther east, and they take their name from a Turkish word, *Kusa,* which names a tribe of Huns. The capital of this country is Amil near the mouth of the River Volga. You may not believe this, good Abraham, but the Khazars are Jews. Yes, my friend, a form of Judaism is the religion of this far Asian country. The Khazar kings claim to be descended directly from Meshech the son of Japheth. I have been told that a century ago one of these kings, King Aleidis, wrote a long letter to the famous Abu-Yussuf Chasdai ben Isaac ibn Shaprut of Cordova. In it, King Aleidis described his land and his people, their religion, and their history.

"Aleidis explained that Meshech had a son named Togarma, and then Togarma had ten sons: Agijoe, Balgad, Bisal, Cusar, Ouvar, Sanar, Savir, Tirus, Ugin, and Zarna. The Jews of the land of the Khazars are all descendants of the tribe of Cusar, originally great warriors who conquered lands as far away as the River Danube near Constantinople. In fact, some say that the name Khazar is actually derived not from the Turkish word *Kusa* but rather from the Jewish name Cusar. But after all these years, who is to know? Only the good Lord God remembers this fact, and He has not yet told the answer to man.

"In any case, the Khazars are a very ancient people. They have lived always in the borderland between Europe and Asia, contending with the Russians to the north, the Mongolians to the East, the Persians to the south, and the Europeans to the west. Now, however, their greatness is in decline. The Khazars live scattered throughout the whole of the wild steppe country; they are as numerous as the sands of the sea, and Khazar farms and herding regions dot all the open countrysides.

"The king of the Khazars has three royal cities, side by side, on the banks of a river. During the winter, he remains at home with his queen, the princes, the various officers, and a host of attendants. But in the month of *Nisan,* the entire royal company leaves the city to go out into the fields and gardens: each branch of the royal family has a hereditary estate, and springtime calls them out onto their own particular homelands. The king himself begins the year by journeying around the entire kingdom, starting at the River Arsan, and he travels for months, resting, hunting, and fishing as he goes.

"During my stay, the king was in the farthest corner of the kingdom, and I was welcomed by the rabbi of a small local community. The customs here are at once familiar and different. The words and actions have, to me, an almost a dreamlike air. Many local rituals revolve around the coming of the Messiah, and as soon as I arrived I was told about happenings, events, and phenomena that portend his final reappearance. For instance, here is one story that I heard in great detail:

"Once upon a time, there lived a famous, pious, and mystical Khazar Rabbi named Aleydis ben Samuel. He was a powerful spiritual leader. He had broad shoulders and bushy eyebrows; he had a booming voice and an unrelenting will. He was a pillar of strength to all the community. Every day he said to himself, 'How can I make things better for the Jews?' He looked about him. He saw many pious men who sought God, who loved truth, who were charitable and honest and good. 'It is time for a new kingdom of peace,' thought Rabbi Aleydis. 'It is time to force the coming of the Messiah.'

"But how could this be done? The Rabbi studied and prayed and thought. He kept this question in his mind at all times, even as he taught his students. Among the Rabbi's disciples were five especially devout young men, pure in heart and in intention. They were wide-eyed young mystics, Kabbalists who had delved deeply into the secret truths of the *Zohar.* Night and day, they sat with Rabbi Aleydis, poring over their sacred studies. They counted letters in the Holy Scriptures. They communed with angels. They knew the names of the gods of Egypt, Babylonia, and Assyria.

"Rabbi Aleydis taught these five young men all the hidden wisdom of this world and the next. Together they sat sadly, lamenting the exile of God's *Shekhinah* and feeling the sorrows of the Jewish people in their dispersion. The Rabbi read aloud and he lectured. He pointed out how the existence of evil is actually compatible with the infinite goodness of God. There is an unbridgeable gulf between God and man, he said. The most wondrous and inscrutable Intelligence has produced creations that seem mysterious and that we can study forever and ever without end. In fact, there can never be simple understandings and complete explanations, said Rabbi Aleydis.

"One day, the Rabbi came to a firm decision. 'My students,' he said, 'it is our sacred duty to drive all evil from the world. This will speed the coming of *Mashiah,* the Messiah, the anointed one. Finally we will have our holy king, the hostile enemies will be defeated, all the dispersed shall return triumphantly to the land of Israel, the righteous, humble, and meek shall inherit the earth, the dead shall be resurrected, and the Day of Judgment shall arrive. Then the Holy *Shekhinah* will return from its long, long exile, amen.'

" 'Amen,' repeated all the young men fervently.

"One of the students said, 'But how should we begin, Rabbi?'

"And Rabbi Aleydis answered, 'We will begin by praying and fasting–then we will capture Samael and the other evil demons.'

"The young men looked at one another. Could five boys and one man actually do this? The Rabbi looked so strong and confident. The students felt a surge of energy, they took heart, and they followed the Rabbi's lead. The young men and the Rabbi began to pray and to fast. They put on white cloaks. They renounced every worldly interest. They purified their bodies and their thoughts. They became thin and holy, and then they started on their quest.

"Their early adventures were indescribable. They wandered far and wide. They suffered. They prayed. They walked great distances, and they endured long silences. One day, they met the angel Sandalfon on a cloudy windswept plain. The young men could not look upon his magnificence. Rabbi Aleydis looked away too but said, 'O great angel, I could no longer face the suffering of my people in exile. I could no longer watch as our enemies trampled us underfoot in the dust. Therefore, we have come to drive away the demons, the demons who whisper evil thoughts into the hearts of the weak and who dim the holy flame of our faith. Great angel, I wish to return the *Shekhinah* to its ancient luster of those days when it radiated down on the Great Temple in Jerusalem. It is time, Sandalfon, for the Messiah to return to the earth.'

"Sandalfon smiled, and the sun came out from behind the clouds. 'May God be with you,' he said. 'The angels in Heaven agree. Yes, the Messiah should come; he should bring the final Redemption for the Jewish people.' Sandalfon shook his head. 'But I am afraid that you are taking on an impossible task. Samael and the other evil demons have vast and untold powers. Even we, the angels, cannot overcome him. Only if God Himself stands by you will you succeed.'

"Sandalfon sighed. 'But you cannot expect God to support you unless He believes that the right time has come for the return of the Messiah.'

" 'I am certain that the time is now,' said the Rabbi.

" 'We will see what we will see,' answered the angel. Sandalfon thought a moment, then he said, 'I myself cannot help you. Perhaps, however, you might consult with my older brother, the angel Metatron.'

" 'And how will I find him?' asked Rabbi Aleydis.

" 'You must fast and pray and purify yourselves. When you no longer notice the cold and the hunger, then wash seven times in a mountain lake. After that find a cave, eat only spices, and recite the Ineffable Name formed by seventy-two holy letters.' And Sandalfon disappeared in a whirlwind.

"Angels are everywhere–and so, unfortunately, are demons. The mighty Samael heard Rabbi Aleydis, and he shook in anger. 'The angels are toying with me,' thought Samael. 'How dare they encourage a mortal on such a hopeless quest? The Messiah can never appear when there are still so many weak and sinful men among the Jews. Aleydis is a fool, but he is also stubborn. I will have to watch him carefully.'

"Meanwhile, Aleydis ben Samuel and his five disciples left the windy plain in the valley. They climbed high into the mountains. There they found a cave, and they made it their home. They prayed. They fasted. They bathed in the lake. Slowly, the tentacles of this sinful world dissolved. The Rabbi and the five young men floated through their days. They slipped gently through the nights. A crystalline purity lit the skies, and eventually one day the angel Metatron appeared.

"His face was like the sharp sunshine. His voice was like a roaring waterfall. 'Why are you here?' he called out. The words echoed in the rocks.

" 'Great angel,' began the Rabbi. 'I have no selfish intentions: I do not come for myself. I want to lead the Messiah, *Mashiah* the anointed one, back into the world of men. I want to end the exile and the suffering of the Jewish people. Can you tell me how to vanquish Samael and his evil horde of demons?'

"The sky was blindingly white. The angel Metatron frowned and said, 'You are but a man. Your efforts will be useless in the end. It is not only that Samael is powerful. Now is not the time for *Mashiah*. The Messiah will come only when God wills. Give up your dream, old man. Return home.'

"Rabbi Aleydis said, 'Metatron – wondrous angel – I cannot turn back. What is a life worth if it is not lived to the limits? I must do this deed or give up my life in the process.'

"Metatron shook his head sadly. 'You will fail,' he said. 'Nonetheless, I cannot do less than my best also.' Therefore, the great angel quietly told the Rabbi seven mystical formulas. In addition, he set an amulet, a silver metal plate, upon a rock at Rabbi Aleydis's feet. On one side was engraved the Ineffable Name; on the other side were written the numbers:

6	32	3	34	35	1
7	11	27	28	8	30
24	14	16	15	23	19
13	20	22	21	17	18
25	29	10	9	26	12
36	5	33	4	2	31

which add up to 111 in any direction, even diagonally.

" 'Now Rabbi,' warned Metatron, 'you are tough and you are persistent. It is possible that you will capture Samael temporarily. You may even see the Golden Gates of Paradise, looking as if they were at the end of a far open lane. But do not be fooled. Under no circumstances can you let down your guard with Samael. Do not take any pity on him. Do not give him food. Do not even give him spices to smell. Otherwise, he will strengthen and escape, and all your efforts, your supreme and superhuman work, will have been wasted.'

"Metatron shook his head again, then he disappeared in a whirlwind. When the angel had gone, the Rabbi picked up the shining amulet. It was both cold and warm at the same time. Rabbi Aleydis ben Samuel and his five disciples climbed farther, to the top of Mount Sheir. The weather had turned grim and cold and snowy. Wild dogs barked and lunged at them. Were these actually demons sent by Samael? The Rabbi pronounced two incantations, he waved his amulet, and the pack of animals fell back, growling and snapping.

"Now the men saw snowcapped mountains that jutted up to Heaven itself. The air was thin. The sky was the darkest blue. Each step was a terrible weighty chore. Their feet felt like lead. Rabbi Aleydis recited the mystical formulas, the *zirufim* that the angel Metatron had taught him. Then a bit of strength returned, and the six pilgrims climbed on and on and on.

"As they rounded a rock cliff, a river of icy water rushed across their path. The waves were as tall as a man, and they knocked huge chunks of ice and rock from along the banks and threw them down the mountainside. The Rabbi stepped back. 'In the name of Rahab, the princely angel of the Seas, be calm!' said Rabbi Aleydis, and he held up the amulet and recited the biblical verse from the Book of Exodus to quiet a raging torrent:

With an angry blast from Zion
The raging seas stood tall:
The ocean formed a canyon,
Each wave a towering wall.

Then the waves subsided, the river flowed more slowly, and the men crossed safely over the rocks.

"Next, they came to an iron wall, cold and black and rough. Behind it stood the evil angel Samael himself, towering in wait. It was Samael who had possessed Saul in biblical times. It was Samael who had stirred up the conflict between Abimelech and the Shechemites. Samael had been the lying spirit in the mouth of the prophets, as Yahweh's messenger enticed Ahab to his doom. Samael had been the adversary of Joshua, in the prophecy of Zechariah. And Samael had tempted David, as the Holy Scripture reports in the First Book of Chronicles: 'Now Satan, setting himself against Israel, incited David to count the people.'

"Rabbi Aleydis knew of Samael's evil power. But the Rabbi would not turn back. He took his walking stick and with the mention of God's Ineffable Name, he struck the iron wall. A crack appeared, and then there were two. Suddenly the wall split apart and the Rabbi and his followers stepped through. Dogs barked and lunged. Rocks crashed nearby. Thunder rumbled. The five young men cowered, but the Rabbi took the holy amulet and he held it up. He waved the silver plate, which gleamed and glinted in the sun, and he called out mystical *zirufim.* Ice fell, winds roared, and it rained a cold slashing rain. A large dog lay weak and panting at the Rabbi's feet; this was Samael himself. Quickly the Rabbi tied the dog's feet with ropes, and the evil angel was caught at last.

"Immediately, the dog transformed itself into a human shape with wings and claws and fiery eyes. It was the angel Samael in his most terrifying appearance. But the evil angel remained bound and he could not move. Samael seemed weak and sad, although his eyes were deep and black and evil.

" 'You have won, Rabbi,' he said. 'I waited for you. Then I unleashed my powers, but the Name of God was too much for me.'

"Rabbi Aleydis stood back and said nothing.

" 'I have been here for many days,' said Samael, 'ever since I heard that you were coming. I waited, Rabbi–and now I have lost.'

"Samael looked down at the ground. 'Yes, I have been here many long days and many long nights. I am tired, and I ask you, holy sir, for a last bit of kindness. I know that you cannot release me. Instead, just give me something to eat–anything small, for I am famished and weak.'

"Rabbi Aleydis recalled the warning given by Metatron. 'I am afraid that I cannot do that,' he said quietly to Samael. And the Rabbi turned away.

"The Rabbi's five followers were energized. They felt that all of Heaven was within their reach. The Messiah would be free to descend with them to earth. Now it was only a matter of time. Even Rabbi Aleydis was impatient. He called to his disciples, 'Hurry, my friends; we are near our goal. Soon the Golden Gates of Heaven will open wide for us. Paradise will overflow. The holy Messiah will come forth; he himself will welcome us, barefoot and with sword in hand – hallelujah and amen!'

"All this time, Samael was saying in a quiet, sad voice: 'Please, young men, give me just a little water and a crust of bread; for now I am dying.'

"But Rabbi Aleydis was hurrying away. He rushed on toward a golden glow just past the far mountaintop. The Rabbi saw the Golden Gates of Paradise, looking as if they were at the end of a far open lane. He ran toward Heaven, and the disciples ran after him. But then the last young man looked back. He looked back and he saw tears in Samael's eyes. He heard the wicked angel say, 'At least say a prayer for me. At least do me the kindness of offering up a few words to the Lord. And if you are to leave me to die, then drop a bit of spice on my robe and my beard so that in my last moments, I can once again feel the scent of the great *Gan Eden,* from which I have been banished forever.'

"The last young man stopped. Samael seemed small and weak and pitiful. Samael closed his eyes. Had he stopped breathing? And had he suffered in the end? The boy watched and stared, and slowly, very slowly, he walked back. He bowed his head and said a silent prayer. Then he took a bit of spice from his pouch and lightly sprinkled it on the robe and the beard of the evil angel Samael.

"Immediately tongues of searing flame shot from Samael's nostrils. His muscles bulged. His eyes flew open. He tore his bonds. He let out a terrifying shrieking wail. Hosts of hissing demons swept in on a hurricane of winds. Packs of howling dogs rushed from behind every rock. The Rabbi and his disciples fell back and disappeared down vast cavernous cracks and crevices in the ice, and the mountainsides slid and tumbled and piled into the snowy canyons on all sides, roaring and crashing and finally dissolving into a vast curtain of powdery mist.

"And far, far off in Heaven, far beyond these small cold mountains, in the Great Court of Final Judgment, the Almighty Lord God looked down. He looked down, and He creased His forehead. He shook His radiant head. 'Men – even well-meaning, heroic men – cannot change foreordained events,' said He.

" 'No human has the power to end the exile. I alone, the Almighty Lord God, will redeem the children of Israel. I alone will determine when the right time shall come,' said the Lord.

" 'When will the anointed one appear as king?' He continued. 'When will the enemies be annihilated? When will the dispersed return to the land of Israel? When will the righteous, the humble, and the meek rule supreme? And when will come the resurrection of the dead and the last Day of Judgment?'

"Again God shook His head. 'That time,' He said, 'is in My hands and in My hands alone.'

"Sadly the Messiah put on his sandals, for he knew that he would not soon be walking barefoot back into the warm and dusty world of mortal man. And the great God Almighty raised His right arm. He looked at the Messiah. He looked at the endless host of angels, now as silent as the clouds. " 'Who,' He roared, 'will raise up *Mashiah* the anointed one from the East? Who will drive kings before Him, scattering them with His sword like dust and with His bow like chaff before the wind? And Who has summoned the generations from the beginning? It is I, the Lord.

" 'I am the first,' said God, 'and, to the last of all men, I am He.'

"Yes, good Abraham, He is the first and He is the last, amen. And at last I must end my letter. But I am calm and at peace because the Lord watches us closely, and I know that He will not hold back the Messiah forever. The warmth of these Holy Lands gives hope to my soul. To us mortals, it seems a long way from the golden, dusty Holy Lands to the cold Rhinelands of home. But to holy spirits, the distance is only the breadth of a finger: the sunny dazzle of these regions radiates north instantly, swept by the holy spirits. And one day, *Mashiah* the anointed one will finally begin his walk here. Then *he* will radiate like a warm sunshine breeze through the Jewish communities everywhere. He will draw the holy southern warmth behind him, and in an instant, in the glorious days of our Resurrection, the world will suddenly be adazzle with the Lord's radiance. God's *Shekhinah* will be swept north and *Mashiah* the Messiah will lead us back with golden footprints to our ancient warm and Holy Land again. Hallelujah and amen, good Abraham – I wish you a most golden hallelujah and a warm, radiant, and holy amen.

"Your childhood friend,
Petahiah, the son of Jacob"

Hello, Rabbi. I will be with you in a moment. If every tablecloth is not folded, then the day has not ended properly.

There, now I am finished at last and I can sit next to you by the stove. Tomorrow night begins the holy Sabbath again, gently raining down music and joy upon our peaceful resting faces–praise the great Lord God, amen.

Ah, the gentle Sabbath; it is a day forever being filled with holy music. Do you know the Sabbath poem by Gedaliah ben Moyses? It goes:

> The birch woods heard the glorious song
> The light trees joined the singing throng
> As the old man with his dogs and deer
> Danced and sang and his harp rang clear,
> He jumped and hopped and the pine needles here
> Skittered at his feet, music tickled his ear,
> Flowers whispered and waved, and branches of trees
> (Especially young birches, white ladies knees
> Skirted in bramble and sandy wildpeas
> Wafting wood smells and dancing in the breeze)
> Swept the sky with cloudlets windblown

White winds sang, angels peeked unknown
From behind the clouds where God's music shone
And gleamed in the dream, in the city of Cologne
In a light Sabbath dream in an old Jewish town
On the wide River Rhine with the gray-green stone.

Such a mystical Sabbath picture! Gedaliah wrote it to describe the famous dream of old Abraham Achselrad, my grandmother's favorite medieval rabbi.

Why, yes, Rabbi–I will gladly tell you the story:

It was a fine summer afternoon, said my grandmother to me, on the day before the Sabbath. The men were sitting talking idly in the rabbi's little study room. It was a warm, gentle, restful afternoon. The windows were open, a light breeze blew in, and it felt to the old men like holy spirits and Sabbath angels were washing through the worn wooden yeshiva. No one was speaking. Suddenly out of the silence, one of the scholars, old Shimshon ha-Zaken, said, "Gentlemen, 'the Torah guards; therefore, guard the Torah.' I never forget that we are protected by the Holy Scriptures and that, at the same time, our chief task as Jews is to protect the Torah in return."

Why did old Shimshon say this? No one knew. But the other sages nodded, and Lewe ben Anselm said, "Amen, Reb Shimshon. As the Talmud tells us: 'Just as the world could not exist without *ruach,* so it is impossible for the world to exist without Israel.' "

Again the men nodded and they murmured, "Amen."

Then old Reb Joshua said, "Well, Lewe, I presume by *ruach* you mean the 'winds' and not the 'spirits.' "

"That I do," answered Reb Lewe.

"Then I agree," said Joshua. "These atmospheric *ruach* wash and dry the world: they keep it clean and comfortable and moist. Three winds–south, east, and west–blow every day. And the great north wind is a companion to them all."

A younger scholar, Elisah ben Samuel, said, "Yes, Reb Joshua, the Omnipotent One adds the north wind to control the extremes of the other three winds."

"Exactly," said Joshua. "The north wind is neither too hot nor too cold. It tempers the others. It makes them more gentle and more helpful, and, in this way, they become easier for the creatures of the world to enjoy."

Then white-bearded Baruch ben Jacob said, "Ah, Joshua, even with the restraining influence of the north wind, the east wind still stirs up the whole world like a demon."

There was a rustling among the prayer books as a little wind skittered through the room. Joshua ben Eliezer nodded. "The east wind can be uncontrolled and wilsome at times," he said. "Why, my friends, the east wind makes the firmament black like a tough young goat."

Lewe ben Anselm stroked his beard and said, "But the north wind is closest to God's great Heaven. The north wind sings through the skies. It makes the firmament pure like gold."

"Ah, yes, Reb Lewe," said Menahem ben Joel. "The north wind clears the sky of clouds. But then without clouds we have no rain, and a drought may follow."

Then Moyses ben Nathan said, "The good Lord God (blessed be He) provides. And I must say that His scheme is ingenious: as soon as the north wind whisks away the clouds, the south wind follows and brings rain and showers, and this makes the plants grow anew."

The scholars smiled and nodded and muttered among themselves. Old Shimshon ha-Zaken coughed. He rubbed his cheek, he stroked his beard, and he said, "Let us straighten out these matters, gentlemen. Now, the north wind is beneficial in summer and it is harmful in winter. But the south wind is harmful in summer and it is helpful in the winter. This is simple enough.

"The west wind always bodes ill–storms or dry spells or other weatherly problems come from the west. And as to the great east wind, the wind from the sunrise dawn of the world, the glorious high and fresh east wind? This wind is always a blessing. It is the *east* wind that carries the music of the heavens on high. The east wind comes from the celestial regions, where the harps of the angels play pure music and joy, amen, amen. Is this not true, Rabbi?"

The scholars stroked their beards and tapped their chins. They looked to the Rabbi–but the Rabbi was asleep. Old Rabbi Abraham had been writing all night in his book on mystic Kabbalistic lore, the manuscript entitled *Keter Shem Tov*. Rabbi Abraham was breathing heavily and his eyes were closed, so after a while Elisah asked loudly, "And what do *you* think, good Rabbi?"

Achselrad blinked and winked. He yawned; his eyes closed again. He did not see the seven scholars and he did not hear the conversation in the little wooden back room in old Cologne. Instead, the Rabbi was having a dream, an afternoon dream. It was a mystical musical dream, and he was far, far away. Steadfast old Abraham was talking to himself: "Now, old man," he thought, "it is time to enjoy life and to play a bit. Music is a good thing in these country fields, on the confined trails, and in the pleasant shady places."

What was this? The old Jewish Rabbi, so unmusical in his waking life, was a fine musician in his dreams. He had owned a lovely harp. But now it was gone. The Rabbi looked around him. He looked up, and he looked down–then a little sparrow chirped and reported that the harp had drowned. So old Achselrad sadly set out to brush the sea, to sweep the billows. First he swept the water lilies into piles. Then he swept the rushes into heaps. Rabbi Abraham raked up bits of sedge and seaweed. However, he did not get his harp: the instrument had vanished.

Steadfast old Abraham returned to the shore. Suddenly he heard a sad noise; a birch tree was weeping. The Rabbi looked carefully. Why, it was just a small tree, almost a shrub. But it was also a hardy tree. It had round thin branches and small toothed leaves, and the birch bark was white and thin and soft as paper. And now the handsome young tree, this curly grained tree, was crying out. Old Rabbi Abraham asked, "My lovely young woman, what are you weeping about? My light and leafy sapling, why are you crying? No one is hurting you. No one is taking you to war. Are your children perhaps in danger?"

A rustling went through her branches and the tree answered, "Old man, I am crying because I am sad. I am timid and helpless. I suffer a hundred troubles. I have a thousand defects. Here in a world where I would like to be happy and to give happiness, I am alone and lonely. I am beset by thoughtless and cruel neighbors.

"What can *I* do that is special? Nothing, really–I can only stand here weeping quietly until someday I am knocked over by a wild wind. And meanwhile I am at the mercy of all the evil forces. It is not just heavy winds and storms. In the summer, the herdsmen wander about with their knives. They carry axes. They slash my fine dress with their swords. This summer, all manner of loud and thoughtless men walked here in the forest, beating the wild woods, sharpening their axes on my branches.

"So, that is why I am weeping, old man. I am unlucky; I am defenseless. I stand and wait as the demons surround me all summer, and then by the fall I am worn-out with worry. Grief changes my looks. My face turns pale. My leaves dry and wrinkle. And as to the cold winds? They are agony! The frost cracks my branches and the wind demons strip me of leaves. Then suddenly a gust carries off the last of my warming leafy furs–I am exposed and I freeze in the grip of the harsh weather. Is there no other way? I am tired of this cruel life. Can I not turn somehow to eternal joy and good?"

Old Rabbi Achselrad looked at the tree. It was graceful and slender and gray. It looked delicate and strong at the same time. Its leaves were a bright, clear green. The Rabbi said, "You really are a lovely tree, my light young woman. Stop crying. I have a solution, my leafy sapling. The good Lord God (blessed be He) will turn your crying into the musical sound of happiness." And the Rabbi prayed to the great Lord God, blessed be He, for a song of everlasting joy and goodness and happiness to come from this small birch.

"Now close your sad eyes," said the Rabbi. And then old Rabbi Abraham set about to make an instrument, a new harp, right there in the wilderness, on the tip of a misty headland. He built a fine new harp. He carved the ornaments from bits of wood drifted up onto the beach of a foggy island. The Rabbi worked hard and patiently. Soon the instrument was finished: a lovely harp had been created. To sing, the harp needed thirty strings, thirty pure tones made from sheep catgut. The post and the top were carved oak. But where did the back of the harp come from? What was used for the triangle back? And from where came the hollow soundboard that gently rang and sang, that chimed the notes of the strings? It was a wood more durable than any other, impermeable to water and tough and dark and handsomely grained; it was a wood that polished to a fine shine. It was birch wood, and it came from the sad tree that now could sing happily and joyously forever.

The harp was ready to play. But did the Rabbi dare to make music, even here, far from a synagogue? After the destruction of the Temple, the great rabbis had declared a time of mourning. Instrumental music was banned. But could one deny music forever? How long could Jews remain in mourning for the destruction of the Great Temple of Solomon? If it is seven days of mourning for a man, then should it be perhaps seven centuries of mourning for the House of God? Well, it was now long past that, thought Old Rabbi Abraham ben Alexander, the mystic Achselrad of Cologne.

Music is holy. It is like a strong wind, and it lifts the soul higher than can words alone. As the Second Book of Chronicles recalls, King Hezekiah – the most faithful of the kings, who gave more attention to the Temple and its service than any other king since Solomon himself and who restored the full service within the Great Temple – this Jewish king "posted the Levites in the House of the Lord with cymbals, lutes, and harps, and they stood ready with the instruments of David, and the priests waited with trumpets. And as the service began, the song to the Lord began too, with the trumpets, led by the instruments of David, king of Israel, and the singers sang and the trumpeters sounded. And Heaven rang with a chorus of joyous music."

So now the Rabbi closed his eyes. He sat along the river on a gray-green stone, and he chanted a short and holy prayer.

May the Lord bless this harp
  May He watch over it
May the Lord shine His face
  Smiling down on it
May the Lord then be gracious
  And good and kind to it
May the Lord look happily
  On this fine wooden harp
And may He give it peace and joy
  And wondrous heavenly song.

Then, in his dream, the Rabbi rested on the stone, on a wooden pine bench, on a smooth iron seat. He opened his chest of musical notes. He unlocked his song box. He set the harp across his knees. Then the spirit of the tree was released into the world and the song seemed to sing all by itself. Before the Great Mourning, in the glorious days of the Great Temple, woodwinds and strings had filled the holy services, and now Rabbi Abraham heard them all singing again in a holy, ringing, joyous woodland chorus.

The Rabbi closed his eyes and he played his harp. The great mountains around him sounded out like organs. The crags and cliffs rang and echoed. The stumps on the heaths jumped. Sticks shook and cracked. Rocks on the shores bounced and clinked. The pines in the hills made a joyous noise. The Almighty Master Himself was infusing all with glorious music. A thousand birds were chattering in the trees and in the skies and on the old man's hat and shoulders.

Yes, my friend, when the woods heard the glorious instrument, then all the trees and plants and animals were happy and they joined the chorus. The old man of the wilderness with his dogs and deer and rabbits danced with both feet as he played, and when he skipped and hopped about, the pine needles and leaves skittered and scattered at his feet to the sound of the music. The flowers sang and waved. The branches of all the trees–especially the groves of birch which grew where the soil is thin among the brambles, the heather, and the tall, tall grasses and which danced in the wind and which wafted a resinous deepwood smell over all–these branches waved and shivered and blew and seemed to rush along to everywhere at once. And the white clouds frollicked all around, all around. The breezes sang. God's magnificent wispy beard blew in the skies, and the tiniest angels peeked out from behind the clouds to see what joy had happened somewhere in a wondrous dream, an afternoon dream, in a mystical musical Sabbath dream, in the far-off city of old Cologne. Ah, yes, Rabbi–it was a dream that blew into the old Jewish Quarter with the ancient winds that rushed across the gray-green stones of the dark medieval River Rhine, once upon a time, a long, long time ago.

Well, good evening, Rabbi. I was just thinking about your reminder at yesterday's Sabbath service: soon it will be *Rosh Hodesh,* the first day of the month.

No, it is not really the new moon that I was thinking of. I was thinking about mothers.

I was remembering the first psalm that we always read for *Rosh Hodesh,* Psalm 113:

Sing the praises of our Lord:
Let His holy Name ring out
Through the skies, send the word
From the golden sunrise flame
To fiery sunsets – chime a chord:
Chime forth God's great holy Name!

Above all nations, afar, windblown
His glory unfurls the morning sky –
Ashine among the clouds alone.
Who is like the Lord Almighty,
Sitting on His high-backed throne
And guiding all humanity?

He raises poor men from the ashes,
Rescues beggars from the pigpen;
He sits the weak beside the princes
And settles women with their children
In happy homes of warm embraces,
Mothers in His great rich garden.

Sometimes, Rabbi, I forget that *Rosh Hodesh* is a Mother's Day, too.

Of course *Rosh Hodesh* welcomes the new moon, and the holiday has an ancient, almost pagan, feel to it. At one time, work was suspended on each *Rosh Hodesh.* Sacrifices were offered in the Temple. The *shofar* was blown. Everyone crowded around special meals. But where do the mothers fit in?

Yes, that sounds right to me also – it must be the new moon: after *Rosh Hodesh,* the moon begins to reemerge from its total blackness. Perhaps rebirth makes us think again of mothers. Mothers affirm life; they are renewers and they are all-embracing. They surround you with warm, loving arms. They give you enwrapping hugs. Mothers are the deep, rich earth with her forests and seas and mountains. No child should ever be deprived of a mother. That is why old Achselrad smiled at Pora's riddle. You do not know the story of Pora's riddle? Well then, Rabbi, let me tell it to you:

Once upon a time, in medieval Germany of the twelfth century, there lived a pious scholar named Meir ben Ahaz. Meir married very late. His wife, Pora, was young and good-hearted, but she had been a poor orphan. In his old age, Meir fathered a single child. Soon afterward, he died, leaving his young wife penniless. Pora had no skills and no relatives. She begged and she borrowed. She sold rags and wood, she cleaned stables, and she barely made enough money to support one person. Pora lived with her baby in a shack behind the bakery, where she was given discarded bread. She was always exhausted from walking about, carrying her baby and looking for food or work. Her hair was matted and stringy; she was never clean. Moreover, the townsfolk thought that, loving as she might be, Pora was none too intelligent and they feared for the baby's health and safety and, of course, for its future education.

It seemed to onlookers as if the child was often hungry. Certainly it was not washed frequently. It looked weak and thin. Was it, in fact, ill? Would it even survive to adulthood? And if so, would it ever have a proper Jewish upbringing? People talked and talked, and they shook their heads.

One day, a wealthy young couple from Bonn came to the *Parnas* of the Cologne congregation. "We have tried for twelve long years to have children," they said. "But the good Lord God has withheld a baby. Is there an orphan who needs adopting here in Cologne? Is there some small child who needs a loving family, a family that can provide him with the best clothes and schooling?" The *Parnas* met with other community leaders. For months, everyone had been worried about Pora's child. The community decided that for the safety of the little infant it should grow up in the care of a real family, and now the Bonn couple offered the perfect opportunity.

The local civil law – the German law – followed in the old Roman traditions. Any child could be legally adopted by another family with the consent of his natural parents. After adoption, the child gave up his ties and inheritance rights from the original family and he acquired full ties and inheritance rights from his new family. In Cologne, the Jewish law was similar to the German law: adopted children were full members of their new families when the adoption was sanctioned by a formal court decision. Therefore, the Cologne community convened a *Bet Din* to rule formally on the fate of Pora's child.

The *Bet Din* met on a Thursday, court day in the Juden Viertels of medieval Cologne. It was a warm summer afternoon on the *Rosh Hodesh* of the month of *Av,* long, long ago. Rabbi Abraham ben Alexander and the two other judges sat on a bench by the Holy stone Ark in the main prayer hall. After the other cases had been heard and decided, the Rabbi stood at the *almemar,* the synagogue's main reading desk. He looked around him and said, "At this time, we shall hear the case of Pora, the widow of Meir ben Ahaz."

The precenter stood. He nodded to the rabbis. He had, he explained, been asked by the *Parnas* and other members of the community to describe the unfortunate situation.

"This young woman," began the precenter, "is very poor. She has no regular job. Sometimes she cleans for Gentile women before holidays. Sometimes she helps out at the stalls in the Heu Markt: she cleans up after the horses, and she collects fallen grain from the carts. Sometimes she just sells wood and cloth scraps that she salvages from garbage heaps. Because of her jobs (or, more often, her lack of them) she cannot help being dirty and poorly dressed. No one knows how she manages to provide food for her child, whom she carries in a sling on her back. And, gentlemen, this woman lives in a broken shack behind the bakery."

The precenter looked at Pora. "Recently, the well-known family of Lemhule ben Schoenemannus of Bonn offered to welcome this baby into their home. Imagine," he said to Pora, "what a fine life *you* would have had if such outstanding parents had taken you in. Now–and I mean this in all kindness–I think that it would be best for your child to grow up with the many advantages offered by the couple from Bonn. These people have money and family. They will ensure that your baby will be healthy and well educated."

The precenter turned to the judges. "Today, this little child is quite poor. It is wrapped in old cloths instead of dressed in clothes. It is dirty and hungry. And what does the child have to look forward to when it reaches school age? Education is the responsibility of parents. A father and a mother must train their children for a life membership in the community of Israel. Children are secure links in the chain of Jewish continuity; as the Book of Deuteronomy commands us: 'Teach these things to your sons and to your sons' sons also.' "

Now the precenter paused. He stepped toward the three judges. "Religious heritage comes from our elders," he said. "It must be transmitted strong and clear and unchanged to the generations that are still unborn. Who will do this for the widow's young child? She herself cannot. Therefore, let us assure that this poor young child has the opportunity to grow up strong and fine and healthy. Let us give him a warm home where he will be well cared for, where he will be guaranteed a fine education. Then he too will become a well-forged link in the chain of Jewish tradition."

Pora, the widow of Meir ben Ahaz, sat silent and sad.

The judges also sat in silence. They listened to the presentation with no comment. No one else offered an opinion. There were no loud voices, there were no soft voices; in fact, there were no other voices at all. Everything was calm and orderly. So, as no more was being said, two of the judges stood, and they turned toward the small back room of the yeshiva where they would have their private conference, where they would say a brief prayer, and where they would reach a final decision.

Then Rabbi Abraham coughed. He coughed, and he frowned. He stroked his beard; he tapped his chin. "Mistletoe," he said.

"Mistletoe?" repeated old Baruch ben Jacob.

The two other judges stood looking at the Rabbi.

"Yes, yes–mistletoe," said the Rabbi, still frowning. "You gentlemen know the mistletoe plant: it is a vine, it has yellow flowers, it has white berries."

The many scholars sitting on the benches raised their eyebrows; they stroked their beards and tapped their chins. The two other judges looked at each other. Mistletoe? Rabbi Achselrad was a strange and mystical man, and although he was quite holy, he often said strange and mystical things. The old men remained silent, waiting.

After a moment, the Rabbi continued. "Mistletoe, gentlemen, is a plant of *twos.* The main stem forks into two smaller stems, and then each branch forks–even the little berries appear in twos." Rabbi Abraham nodded his head. "And that," he said, "is like this situation here. There are forks–there are alternative stories, my friends. I wonder, now, what is the other side to this story that we have heard?"

The two other judges sat down again on their bench.

The Rabbi raised his eyebrows, and he looked at Pora. Pora looked down at her feet. She said nothing at first; then, slowly, she stood. She said, "Rabbi Abraham . . ."

The old Rabbi stroked his beard. "Yes?" he said.

"May I say something?" asked the widow.

"Certainly, my good woman," he answered.

Pora hesitated. "Well," she began softly, "well . . . let me put a question to the sages, if I might."

The seven sages of Cologne sat on two wooden benches beside the judges. They stroked their beards and looked at one another. Rabbi Achselrad raised his eyebrows; then he nodded.

The woman looked at the Rabbi. She talked quietly. "I remember something that my late husband once told me, Rabbi Abraham. In the Book of Judges, Samson says":

> Let me pose for you a riddle. If you can guess the answer, then I will give you presents of linen and clothing. But if you fail, then you must give me what *I* want.

"So, Rabbi, I would like to do the same."

The Rabbi tapped his chin. This young poor unkempt woman seemed to know the Holy Scriptures. Rabbi Abraham closed his eyes. Then he opened his eyes and he said, "All right, young woman."

The woman faced the seven bearded men. "If you please, sirs – answer me this," said Pora. "What is the lightest thing in the whole world, what is the sweetest, and what is the hardest?"

The old men were silent. Then they began to murmur among themselves.

Finally, old Baruch ben Jacob said, "There are many light things in the world." He began to count on his fingers: "There are eyelashes, dust, sunbeams, and wind. But I would say that the best answer is a feather."

Young Elisah ben Samuel said, "Ah, Baruch, I agree that there *are* many light things in God's great world, but undoubtedly a cloud is the lightest. The clouds float over everything and even up to Heaven, where (as the holy Book of the Prophet Nahum says): 'the clouds are the gentle dust at the feet of the Lord,' amen."

"Amen," repeated Baruch.

The other sages nodded, and Joshua ben Eliezer continued: "That is very well said, my friends. And as for the sweetest thing? This is the simplest of the questions. Obviously, the answer is sugar."

But Lewe ben Anselm said, "Sugar is an acceptable answer, Reb Joshua, but we are looking for the *best* answer. This means a biblical answer. Obviously, the young woman is thinking of honey, because in the Book of Judges (in the very section that she quoted to us earlier) the answer to one of Samson's riddles is: 'What could be sweeter than honey?' "

And all the men smiled and nodded and they stroked their beards and murmured among themselves.

Next, Menahem ben Joel said, "Now, stone is the hardest of all things, and –"

"Just a moment, Menahem," said Moyses ben Nathan. "You are forgetting that iron is harder than stone."

"Well, iron is harder than many types of stone," answered Menahem. "However, some stones – especially certain gemstones – are harder even than iron. And iron bends, but stone can be completely unforgiving. In the Holy Scriptures, for instance, the Prophet Zechariah reported that the Almighty Lord God described the worst of the unforgiving and compassionless populace as having 'hearts as adamant as stone.' "

"Yes, yes–this is very good," repeated old Shimshon ha-Zaken, "clouds and honey and stone are all fine answers."

The old sages nodded and stroked their beards; they looked at the young woman, who sat listening politely and silently. Rabbi Abraham also looked at the woman. He smiled, but he said nothing. Then Pora, the widow, said, "Those certainly are fine answers."

Again, the old sages nodded. "But," continued the woman, "they are wrong."

What?! The old men stopped stroking their beards. How could someone doubt the sages of Cologne? How could a poor and untutored woman, an orphan with no scholarly training, a cleaning woman who could not even speak Hebrew, criticize or question seven bearded old Jews? Does not the holy Book of Leviticus command us: "You shall stand and respect the elderly; you shall give honor to gray hairs, defer to the aged, and revere your God"?

Old Shimshon ha-Zaken looked at his colleagues, he coughed, and he said, "Do you have better answers, my good woman?"

"Yes I do," said Pora.

"And what might they be?" asked white-haired Baruch.

Pora stood. "The lightest thing in all the world," she began, "is an only child in its mother's arms. And the sweetest thing? Why, certainly it is the sound of that little child laughing in its mother's ears."

Pora smiled and she looked down at her feet. After a moment, she said quietly, "And, gentlemen, as to the hardest thing in all the world . . ."

For a moment she stopped talking. Then they could barely hear her when she said, "The very hardest thing of all is for a mother to see her only child, a little baby whom she held every day and every night, whom she nursed, and with whom she smiled and laughed and cried, being taken from her forever."

The prayer hall remained silent. The old sages looked at the ceiling or the fringes on their *tallit.* The Rabbi nodded and nodded and stroked his beard, and the precenter sat down on a bench. The three judges looked at one another; then Rabbi Abraham said, "I think that the Cologne community can support one more child." So the community took up a collection, and the child remained with his mother Pora, the young untutored widow of Meir ben Ahaz of Cologne.

It was a warm *Av* afternoon, Rabbi, and as people walked out of the old yeshiva building they felt an embracing breeze. In the great wide world outside, the gardens were breathing calmly in the late day; the squash and the rutabaga and the pea plants were sighing and relaxing in the summer arms of a light and easy afternoon. It was *Rosh Hodesh* once again. Gentle summer breezes blew. Tonight or tomorrow, the first slivery crescent of the moon would be seen again, renewed in the sky, and the world would be reborn for yet another month in the unending recurrent cycle of God's great motherhood of eternity.

Ah, good evening again, Rabbi. I know how hard it is to sleep during the night of a new moon. It is a strange night, a night when all bright things in the nighttime sky have come to an end. Well, put your feet up on the side bench here, my friend, and I will open the stove door. Let me push this coal back. There is nothing like the glow of the oven: it washes away even the darkest of nights.

What is that? Another story from me? All I know are the old-fashioned Night Tales, the grandmother fables: old men tell old tales, Rabbi. But if it is an old tale that you want, then I will tell you one about an old man, a pious old man named Rabbi Jacob, who lived in the medieval Jewish community of Cologne.

Let me see – where shall I begin? Perhaps I will start at the end:

One day, after a short illness, Rabbi Jacob died, and no one in the community knew a thing about his family. Long before, he had been a childhood acquaintance of Rabbi Achselrad, the Chief Rabbi of the Cologne region, but somehow Achselrad too seemed to know little about the old man. If you asked him, old Achselrad would get a strange, faraway look in his eye. One time he said, "It is true that in my youth we spent some weeks of a summer together – but this is all quite vague in my mind. It happened too long ago, so how can I remember everything, every little detail? And even then, at the very time, I did not get the story exactly straight." Yes, this was a strange answer. But it was all that he said. And who dared to question the Chief Rabbi any further?

So all that was known was that once, when he was young, Jacob came from a family of holy officials living in the region of Nuremberg in Bavaria. Jacob was a walker and a wanderer. He liked nothing better than to hike east and south, past the town of Heilsbronn and into the forests surrounding the River Altmuhl. Young Jacob was always wandering about in such scenic spots as the Dragon Pond and the Cloud Cave and the Rising Mist Dells. In that area, pines spread like vast armies throughout the canyons and gorges and they filled the valleys, and everywhere there were distant prospects of wet and wild woodlands without end.

Jacob walked and walked, amidst the firs, the pines, and the larches of the Bavarian countryside. Once, on a moonlit night, he met young Abraham ben Alexander – in those days, a student on a private pilgrimage. The two young men formed one of those intense night-and-day friendships that happen at times when one is young and living life open-eyed, strong, and close to the edge of the world.

Jacob was four years older than Abraham. The two young men composed poems for each other. They declared an undying bond of friendship. Their words seemed eternal and forever. Their thoughts were as deep as the sea. They talked of all things under the sun, and for the first time they understood why rocks are so cold, why mint leaves are so pungent, and how it is that the sky could be endlessly deep. They walked and they argued. They hiked among the meadows and the weird gorges of the River Altmuhl, and they discovered truths about every single thing in the world. The cities behind them were only vague dreams – they were phantasms and mists – and the two young men had little to say about themselves or their families or their homes or the careworn things of their past. It seemed a lifetime compressed into days, but it lasted only a few weeks, when finally Abraham ben Alexander had to leave to report back to his yeshiva. Then the realities of their lives took them in separate directions.

Later, when Abraham was an old man and when Jacob was a very old man, Rabbi Jacob appeared in Cologne. He would come daily to the synagogue of Rabbi Achselrad and sit quietly and pray. The two men hardly talked: they nodded and smiled, but they had little to say to each other. In fact, what more *could* they say? Once upon a time they had said everything, and since those days the world had fogged and faded and become distant and muddled and much, much more complex.

By now, old Rabbi Jacob had been in Cologne for six or seven years. He was becoming forgetful. He could never remember the young men's names. Was this Isaac or Issachar or perhaps even Hiyyah? Old Jacob squinted at a familiar face. Is that black-bearded boy a Joshua, or is he a Josiah? Rabbi Jacob shook his head: it was a mystery to him. After the *Shema* in the morning service, Rabbi Jacob found himself forgetting the verse from Psalm 104:

> You made countless complex things
> Using Your wisdom faultlessly–
> Your creatures fill the earth's broad wings
> With wild and wondrous intricacy.

"What is that psalm again?" he would whisper to his neighbor, forgetting that this extra talk is strictly forbidden during the service. And afterward he would embarrass the men by asking repeatedly: "What is that psalm after the *Shema?*"

Why was old Rabbi Jacob becoming forgetful? White-haired Baruch ben Jacob said to Menahem ben Joel, "Perhaps old Jacob has eaten something that was already chewed by a mouse or a cat."

The younger scholar, Elisah ben Samuel, nodded and said, "Or inadvertently he may have eaten a chicken heart."

"Or some olives," added Baruch.

"Undoubtedly," offered Joshua ben Eliezer, "old Rabbi Jacob drank water in which someone had washed."

Lewe ben Anselm rubbed his finger along the worn edge of his *tallit,* which he always wore in the yeshiva, and he said, "The Talmud also warns us that you become forgetful if you place one foot over the other while washing them."

Menahem looked at his colleagues. *"Pillows,"* he said solemnly. "Beware of using your clothes as a pillow. That is very, very bad for the mind."

"Any number of mistakes could affect your memory," said Moyses ben Nathan. "If you walk between two women, you are in danger. Or if you read the inscription on a tombstone out loud, your mind will be affected. Likewise, if you wipe your hands on your clothes, if you put on two shirts by mistake, if you sew your clothes while you are wearing them–in all these cases, your memory will deteriorate or even disappear."

The sages stroked their beards and nodded and tapped their feet. Old Shimshon ha-Zaken coughed and said, "Gentlemen, I cannot dispute your authority, but I think that the most likely cause is fingernails. If you cut your nails one after another in the order of the fingers then you will always have a problem with your memory. People forget this, they cut their nails improperly, their memory worsens, and then, of course, they get into trouble because they forget it again. Why, you have probably forgotten it yourselves!"

Shimshon coughed again, then he continued: "So, I will remind you: cut your left nails first, in the order 4, 2, 5, 3, and 1; then cut your right nails, in the order 2, 4, 1, 3, and 5. I taught this to my children with the rhyme" [Shimshon touched his fingers as he recited]:

Begin with the left hand:
Finger four first and
Last is the thumb–
Then on the right hand
Finger two first and
End with littlest one.

The old scholars muttered and they stroked their beards.

After a moment, Reb Baruch walked into the main prayer hall and sat down next to Rabbi Jacob. "You are becoming forgetful, my friend," began Baruch. Rabbi Jacob nodded. "Listen," said Baruch, "I have some advice: Be certain to eat bread baked on coals; also eat soft-boiled eggs without salt." Rabbi Jacob nodded again.

Reb Menahem had come in and was standing nearby, listening. "In addition," said Menahem, "chew a splinter of wood in your free time. And whenever you have the chance, repeat the name of the angel Poteh, the guardian of memory." Again Rabbi Jacob nodded.

Elisah ben Samuel walked over. "Gentlemen," he began, "it is clear that Rabbi Jacob needs a very strong antidote.

"Rabbi Jacob, you had best try the most powerful remedy, and it is this: Eat hazelnuts for nine days. Begin with six nuts, and add six more each day. Next, eat pepper seeds for nine days. Start with one seed and double the number every day until you are eating two hundred and fifty-six pepper seeds on the ninth day. Count them out carefully: if you make even a single mistake, then the remedy will not work."

Old Jacob nodded, but Elisah was not yet finished. "Now, Rabbi Jacob," he continued, "there are some words that I want you to remember. Each time you are about to eat the seeds, stop and recite the following verse from Psalm 119":

> From Your Laws I never waver,
> Your paths are constantly in my sight;
> I recite Your words forever–
> Your holy Laws give deep delight.

Again Rabbi Jacob nodded two or three times.

"Wait a moment," said Elisah, "there is still more. And I hope that you are paying close attention: Grind cloves, dates, galingale root, ginger, long peppers, and muscat grape nuts in equal quantities. I will repeat that: cloves, dates, galingale root, ginger, peppers, and grape nuts. Beat them into a paste with olive oil, and eat a little before breakfast each morning. Now, my friend, all this takes eighteen days. Be certain to follow the *whole* routine."

Rabbi Jacob nodded once and he nodded twice. The other men patted him on the shoulder, and they all wished him well.

Days passed. Seven days came and seven days went; then seven more days came around. Rabbi Jacob did not improve. Sometimes he forgot what he was saying. At other times he stopped in midsentence. He would raise his eyebrows; then he would just turn and walk away. Once he said, "Can you Torah or pass?" He would come to the synagogue late in the mornings, or on some days he did not appear at all. He did not wear his socks or his hat. One day, Reb Moyses found that old Rabbi Jacob was pushing the cover sideways on the prayer book. Had he forgotten how to open a book?

Rabbi Abraham asked one of the well-known Cologne Jewish physicians what to do. *"Diet,"* said the doctor. "Be sure that this old man has plenty of liver and meat, and also milk, kidneys, and fish." This was expensive fare, but Rabbi Abraham managed to get some fish and chicken livers for a meal for old Rabbi Jacob on some Sabbath evenings.

Then one day, Rabbi Jacob said to Rabbi Abraham, "Why are you always trying to make me do what you want? Do you want to keep me locked in a closet?" Old Achselrad opened wide his eyes and he did not know what to answer.

One of the wealthy women of the congregation loaned Rabbi Jacob a necklace with both a carnelian and a sapphire. Carnelians are the magic stones of the month of *Tammuz:* they cure depression and pessimism and they strengthen the mind. Sapphires are the magic stones of the month of *Elul:* they cure madness, and they too strengthen the mind. Rabbi Jacob wore the healing necklace for a week, but it had no effect.

Abraham Achselrad sighed and returned the necklace. Then he sat down at his desk. Perhaps, he thought, an amulet would help. He took out a square of kosher deerskin. The piece of parchment had a rough dark spot in one corner; Rabbi Abraham rubbed the spot with his finger until it felt smooth. Then he uncapped his bottle of sacred ink mixed with incense, and, after saying a silent prayer, he wrote the *Shema* on one side of the parchment. When the ink had dried, he turned over the parchment and he wrote:

> May Your favor, O Yahweh-Elohim, be with Mar Jacob as it was with the Patriarch Joseph, the righteous man–as it is written: "And the good Lord God (blessed be He) was with Joseph and covered him with grace and made him obtain favor in the sight of all those who saw him."
>
> Heal and protect Rabbi Jacob, in the names of the four archangels, Gabriel, Michael, Raphael, and Uriel, who direct the four heavens, and also in the names of the twenty-one angels–Baradiel, Barkiel, Ben Nez, Galgaliel, Kochbiel, Lailahel, Mathariel, Ofaniel, Rahab, Rahmiel, Rashael, Rehatiel, Ridyah, Ruchiel, Safael, Samael, Sawael, Shalgiel, Shamshiel, Sikiel, and Yorkami–who are princes over all the various powers of nature.

As Psalm 104 says:

> O holy Lord, our Divinity,
> You are great and wise and bright
> Clothed in Your holy majesty
> And wrapped in robes of light.
>
> You formed the whole world's retinue
> Its people, beasts, and trees
> And all of life looks up to You
> For water, food and warmth and ease,
>
> And when Your holy breath blows in
> Life heals its aches and pains
> As new strength slips into the skin
> Of creatures great and small again.

Rabbi Abraham rolled the incantation into a tight scroll and he tied it with a thin red healing thread, making seven neat knots and quietly saying the seven mystical Names of God.

The Rabbi tried to feel hopeful. He tapped the parchment scroll absently on his desk. He looked at the shafts of dusty motes in the late afternoon sun by the window. He stroked his beard. He shook his head, and he sat and sat. Slowly his mind drifted, and he thought about nothing in particular.

Finally, he took a deep breath and he stood and walked into the main prayer room. He said, "Rabbi Jacob, let me tie this amulet on your arm. It may help you to get along better."

The old man looked startled. He stood up as if to run away, but he could only walk in short, shuffling, hesitant steps. He walked backward; he hurried, and he looked so terrified that Rabbi Abraham only stood and watched and did not dare to follow.

A few days passed, then seven days came and seven days went. Soon, Rabbi Jacob did not get out of bed. The men of the congregation took turns sitting quietly, praying at the bedside. Old Rabbi Jacob hardly ate at all, and then he caught a cold. Late one summer afternoon, Rabbi Abraham felt a blank muffled dullness roll through the main prayer hall of the synagogue. The old wooden building was empty and silent; a dog whined outside somewhere far, far away.

The Rabbi got up from his desk and he walked to the door. He peered into the darkening hall. He bowed his head. He knew that Dumah, the black Angel of Death, had come and gone. And soon the bedside watcher returned from Rabbi Jacob's house The old man had died.

The Rabbi called for the Burial Society, who arranged for the funeral and the burial. Rabbi Abraham did not know anything about old Rabbi Jacob's family, and no one else knew, either, so the headstone on the grave read simply:

Rabbi Jacob, an old man, died 21 *Elul* 4916
Now he rests at the feet of the good Lord God
In the Garden of Eden
Amen

Rabbi Jacob's headstone was a flat rectangular rock with a grooved border. Old Rabbi Abraham rubbed his hand along the writing and read the inscription to himself two times. Then he turned, and, without looking back, he walked home into the Jewish Quarter: he returned to his small Jewish family in the medieval city of Cologne. And later, whenever there was a direct wind and an unclouded moon, a tear came to his eye as old Achselrad recalled his early green days in the spring of a long-ago year. Achselrad remembered the firs and the pines and the tracks of the old mountains–and memories overflowed. With their once-ago scents and smells and with their original gleams and glints and glows, the old-time thoughts poured out like a rich, rich, old Jewish wine.

Rabbi, it is late for you to be here; I was just about to close everything for the night.

Ah, yes, I too find the oven soothing. Sit here on the bench and I will stoke up the coals again.

There, that is better. So, here we are together once more. The two of us have sat many nights in this little room, my friend; it is small and protected and comforting. At times like these, it is hard to remember that there actually are other parts to our lives. There are markets and homes and streets. There are bright mornings and active days filled with people and eating and work and outdoor winds and weathers. But at the moment all of that feels like an ancient distant story: it is like an epic from some far-off time, no different from the old medieval days of the *Song of Roland* or of *Njal's Saga* or of the many romances of good King Arthur.

Did all those heroic and magical things ever really happen? The great storytellers did not recount the facts in the way that we find in a newspaper. No – the epic storytellers closed their eyes and wove their tales. They piled together the feelings and the impressions of the events. They retold and reworked little human scraps of history into a beautiful tapestry, into a quilt of myth and Night Tale.

And, Rabbi, once upon a time the world was *filled* with storytellers. There were speakers, singers, and poets. There were rhyming costermongers and streetside buskers; there were troubadours, jongleurs, and bards. Little anecdotes and high adventure were wound together continually into poetic dramas. Large epics rolled forward on waves of bravery and loyalty and ruthlessness. Even short stories and modest verses became tales of larger-than-life people.

In medieval days, the storytellers and songsters traveled throughout Europe from town to town, from fair to fair, and from castle to castle. They composed verse that told wondrous human tales, especially of the courts of southern France. The troubadours' poems were sung with a lute, and the singers lived as wanderers, as transients in the local courts. They moved from place to place when their welcome wore thin, but some local nobleman or another was always willing to take them in because the gentry wanted to be poets themselves.

In those days, troubadours sang of chivalry and knighthood. The life of a knight was romantic and idealistic. To be a king, you had to be born a prince, but anyone could become a knight simply by acting nobly and by doing valorous deeds. Knights were heroic Christian soldiers. They formed a society held together by unwritten high ideals. The knight protected the weak. He defended the helpless. He fought infidels. He served a chosen lord. Knights were generous: they gave their money and their time to the needy. And a knight was faithful to his lady, ready to defend her at all costs.

Everywhere and at all times, the knight was the champion of right over wrong and justice over injustice, oppression, and selfishness. These were old biblical ideals to which Jews could aspire. However, the medieval knight was first and foremost a Christian. Therefore, there were no Jewish knights. Nonetheless, there were Jewish troubadours and court poets. One of these was Susskind of Trimberg. You do not know the name? Well, Susskind lived in the days of Rabbi Achselrad, and I will tell you about him:

As you know, Rabbi, Abraham ben Alexander was the Chief Rabbi of Cologne in the last half of the twelfth century. At that time, all manner of wanderers filtered through the Jewish communities of Rhineland Germany. These travelers came wide-eyed and worn and filled with wonder tales and with reports of ever-new potential Messiahs. Occasionally, the pilgrims were singers: sometimes they were transients from minstrel troops, and sometimes they were itinerant *hazans*.

One mild summer afternoon, in the month of *Av*, Rabbi Abraham was working in the small back study room when he heard a beautiful new voice singing in the main prayer hall. Rabbi Abraham was a mystic scholar, and now the Rabbi suddenly had a mystical feeling. He lifted his head. He looked toward the door. He heard a wonderful chant: Susskind of Trimberg had wandered into the synagogue and was singing a holy psalm of prayer.

Susskind's voice was light. His words were a misty rain shower–and he was singing in German! Medieval Germany could be a stark, unwelcoming place for Jews. Yet somehow this hostile land had given birth to a Jewish poet who could sing in the German language and who could rhyme and knit words together in the local vernacular. And on that afternoon, old Abraham Achselrad lifted his head in the back study room in the old Cologne yeshiva. He raised his eyebrows. He opened wide his eyes. He listened to the fine singing that floated back to him from the main prayer hall. And he felt a happy, joyous, mystical shiver.

It was a warm, lazy day in medieval Cologne. Abraham listened for many minutes. Then he stood, and he walked to the doorway. Sitting on a wooden bench before the Holy stone Ark and in the golden light of the afternoon sun filtering through the twelve stained-glass windows with their colored lions and snakes was a man in a dark coat. The man had his eyes closed, and he was singing a hymn. Rabbi Abraham waited. The singer stopped. He opened his eyes. "Hello, Rabbi," he said, smiling at Abraham Achselrad.

"Hello," said Rabbi Abraham. "Welcome to our synagogue."

"Thank you," said the man.

"Would you like to join me in the study room? I can offer you some bread and wine."

"That is very kind of you, Rabbi," said the stranger. "Let me introduce myself. I am Susskind. I am a poet–a modest troubadour, a keeper of the spirit of chivalry, and, until recently, a resident of the small town of Trimberg."

"Well, Reb Susskind," said Rabbi Abraham, "it is a pleasure to have a man of poetry and music visit us here."

Warmly, the two men shook hands, and they went into the back study room. They talked and talked for many hours, and after the evening prayers Susskind and Rabbi Abraham continued their conversation late into the cool night.

Susskind had come from the east, and he reported the news. A terrible fire had raged in Halle. Rumors of battles abounded in the region of Erfurt. The Archbishop of Cologne would soon be returning from a meeting with the Pope. Was the Count of Munster preparing for war? Susskind and the Rabbi talked on and on, discussing the political events in the surrounding countryside. The hour grew very late, the night deepened, and, eventually, Susskind's talk turned to poetry.

"I have been a minstrel, a messenger, a wanderer," he began. "Recently, I lived in the castle of the lord of Trimberg. The castle is stone, an old stone building called Bodenlaube, and it stands on the ridge of a vine-covered hill. The estate is just behind the small town of Trimberg on the River Saale in western Franconia. Have you ever seen the area? No? Well, in that region the River Saale rolls quietly through hills, on and on and down toward the quiet valley of Saalberg.

"What a calm and delicious place to live! On fine days, the castle and the trees and the sky are reflected in the black river. The woods are green and brown. The fields are endless. In that Eden, I lived as court troubadour. I had my own room in the castle. I ate with noble knights and beautiful ladies. I passed the afternoons at games and hunts. Every night I sang for them and for their guests; I played my lute and I would lightly tap my foot on a hollow wood. I had no money, but I had a roof and food and good company, and I was free to create songs. I am, Rabbi, a romantic–in the style of Walter von der Vogelweide and Wolfram of Eschenbach. You do not know of these poets? It is no matter; they are not at all religious. In any case, in Trimberg I was a poet of romantic knighthood and leisure and the noble life.

"At the castle, I sang about the courtly traditions of chivalry. My songs told of pure women and athletic hunting and ancient battles. I sang in German, the language of the countryside. In epic poems I described the awesomeness of death and dissolution, those eternal truths which make a mockery of temporary setbacks and of poverty. My heroes were knights who were fine men because they acted nobly at all times. Knights never gave in to outside forces – in this way they were completely free:

> The mind of the heroic knight
> Teems with noble thoughts all night
> Leading to daytime acts of might
>   that glide through steel alone,
>   that split the thickest stone,
>   that cut cruelty to the bone.

And I felt, Rabbi, that I, too, had found free thought – free and powerful thought that could glide through steel and stone and cruelty."

Susskind stopped a moment and took a deep breath. Then he continued: "But one day Count Wilhelm, the nobleman, whose bread I ate, whose children and wife and friends I had entertained, whose nights I had filled with laughter and with tears and with all the other transporting joys of song and poetry – this same count dismissed me with a cruel statement. 'No Jew ever can be truly noble,' he said. 'In fact, you are simply parasites, living off the hard work of others.' "

Susskind shook his head. "Some demon must have whispered and hissed in the count's ear. My days as a troubadour were suddenly cut short":

> Song's Muse lulled me, bade me play –
> I was her golden Hebrew songster –
> Then suddenly I find today
> She cares for me no longer
> And I must end my poet's career –
> Ah, I sing before the lords in vain;
> So now no more a balladeer,
> I roam, a bitter quiet man
> A silent songless Jew again.

"Yes, Rabbi, I was dismissed in the wink of an eye. It was over and done in an instant. I was stunned. I could not speak. The nobleman, Count Wilhelm of Trimberg, left the room. A servant entered. I was to pack my satchel, he said, and be gone by sunset. At first, I could not move a muscle; all the blood was drained from my body. I was filled with the heaviest of stone. Did hours pass? I cannot recall. Eventually, I shook myself; then slowly I gathered my things. My arms were heavy and my legs were thick and tired, but I forced myself to walk. And no one stood in my way, Rabbi, and not one single person stood at the door to see me out.

"First, I tried the estate next door, a vast country manor with four barns and many tenant farmers. But the neighboring lord was equally cold. What was happening? Had I committed a mortal sin? Did everyone in the world know? I slept in a barn that night. Then the next morning I set off. I wandered back to the west–west toward the Rhinelands.

"Trimberg sits along the edge of the River Saale in Franconia. I walked the woodland heights, continuing upriver through the hills. I passed through many big cities–Nuremberg, Wurzburg, and Frankfurt–but now it all seems vague and blurred and dreamlike. Long ago, I had had some training as a physician, and I earned a little money with medical advice and a little money by singing. I begged, I took charity, and I slept on synagogue floors. The Jewish communities treated me kindly, but the German folk ignored me. I am afraid that even with the best of intentions, Rabbi, we Jews can never be successful poets in Germany."

Susskind sighed. "Ah, but once a poet, always a poet," he said. "You can never revert to some other life, Rabbi; you can never do anything else with all your heart. So I keep at it. I talk aloud to myself. I sing when I walk. And I have even managed to write down a few of my latest poems. Let me show you–"

Susskind pulled a parchment from his pack. "Here is a recent song":

Thick trees of rainy rilly hills
Green leaves as dripping misty hoods
In gray pine wildwood water-wills,
My wet and wondrous rain-washed woods.

But I left my rockstone castle crag
And rain-soaked larchwood hills behind,
I walked out with my wanderbag
From rich green song-filled woodlandkind.

And now my happiest refrains
At eventide or over wines
Still shiver with the olden rains
And woods and roots and tangled vines–

These light and quiet evening poems
Of human days, of younger dreams
In rain-wrapped woodland misty homes
Sing sweet, but then are gone it seems. . . .

"What is that, Rabbi Abraham? The *back* of this parchment? Well, this is the epilogue. I am writing a whole collection of poems, and this is the postscript to my manuscript. Listen":

In my small poems
The ink's uneven,
And as I read
I find my flowers
Are confused
As to the season–
Berries grow
Amidst the rocks.

But don't complain
Of crooked verse
Of mismatched lines,
Unfinished strokes:
I've grown old
And finally see
Our Path to Heaven
Is quite bumpy
Just the way
It is.

Good evening, Rabbi. You are having difficulty sleeping again? Well just put your feet up on the side bench here. Let me open the stove door and push the coals back; their white glow will wash away the cares of your hard day.

I heard your final prayers tonight. There is no use denying it – you are overworked. Even an old shammas like me can tell. I kept one eye on you when I was cleaning the dishes, and I saw that you were watching the door, hoping Reb Elbaum would leave early. But then Reb Anton stayed late to discuss Psalm 51, the verses:

> Within me build a happy heart
> Give me a calm new soul to start
> Then let Your radiance inspirit me
> To breathe new life as I grow free.
>
> Awaken fresh joys in all I find,
> And grant me, Lord, a thoughtful mind
> So to sinners I can explain
> How to return to You again.

Keep me ever from all harm
Protected by Your mighty arm
And I will praise with psalm and song
Your revivals for my whole life long.

"I have sinned," says the psalmist. "So may God wash away history, and let me begin again, just as a newly born child." That is why this psalm is used in conversion ceremonies. Converts are considered to be newborn children. They are circumcised and given new Hebrew names and educated in Jewish Law from the beginning. Then God accepts them as His children, welcoming them with open arms, with protection, with love, and with all the joys of Heaven, amen.

And the good Lord God also accepts those who return to the fold, who reconvert; this happened with Anschel ben Menahem, a pious man from Opladen, a small town that is a few hours' walk north of Cologne. When Jews leave their faith it is because they have been driven out by demons – so, when they escape from the clutches of the evil spirits, the converts invariably return. Anschel ben Menahem ha-Levi left Judaism in order to protect his community from a demon. Do you know the story? No? Then let me tell you exactly what my grandmother told me:

At the end of the twelfth century, Abraham ben Alexander was the Chief Rabbi of Cologne. In those days, the rabbinate of Cologne was the spiritual head of all the nearby Jewish congregations, notably those in Deutz, Kalk, and Mulheim. Rabbi Abraham was also responsible for the outlying communities of Bensberg, Berg, Gladbach, and Immekeppel to the east, for Bruhl, Rondorf, Sechtem, Sieburg, and Wahn to the south, for Bedburg, Bergheim, Horren, Kastor, and Kerpen to the west, and for Hitdorf, Neukirchen, Ohligs, Stommeln, and Opladen to the north. This last town – the city of Opladen – is a small dyeing and cloth-making community on the River Wupper in the hills northeast of Cologne.

In those days there lived in the town of Opladen a learned and pious man named Anschel. Anschel was a cloth merchant. One year on the eve of *Rosh Hashanah* Anschel felt very strange, and that night he dreamt of his dead father, Menahem ha-Levi. "I love you forever, Anschel, my son, my golden little boy," said the old man sadly, "but I am afraid that you must convert."

Anschel awoke in a sweat. What a terrible nightmare! The next night was quiet. But Anschel remained worried. He put on sackcloth. He fasted for two days. He said prayers from morning until night. Now he felt better. By the time that *Yom Kippur* arrived, Anschel's nightmare had faded. But on the eve of *Yom Kippur,* Anschel again dreamt of his dead father.

"My son – my golden little boy," said Menahem, "you must convert." "How can I do such a thing?" said Anschel in his dream. " 'How?' you ask," said the spirit. "Well, it is simple: go to the priest and declare your allegiance to Christianity. The priest will arrange the rituals." "No, father," said Anschel, "it is not really *how,* it is *why.*" "Ah, *why,* my son," said the spirit, "*why* is another matter." "But can you tell me why?" asked Anschel. "We spirits can hear the plans for the future in the Great Celestial Court," said old Menahem. "I suppose that it is breaking no sacred confidences to tell you that the son of a local Gentile official will be killed. Jews will be arrested. By converting, you can save them." "But father, how –" began Anschel. Menahem interrupted: " 'How' again? I am afraid that I can say no more . . ." and the spirit disappeared and the dream ended. Anschel awoke upset and in a sweat.

Again Anschel put on sackcloth. This time he fasted for three days. He said prayers from morning until night. But Anschel felt no better – he was weak and he was worried. The nightmare remained vividly before him; so Anschel ben Menahem ha-Levi went to Cologne to see Rabbi Abraham ben Alexander, the mystic Achselrad, for counsel.

Early one Friday morning, Anschel packed a satchel and he traveled south. It was late in the afternoon when he reached the old synagogue behind Judengasse Street. There, Anschel found the Rabbi reading a book in the small back study room; a number of scholars were seated on benches along the wall, talking quietly among themselves.

The Cologne sages greeted the merchant from Opladen. Why had he come? they asked. It is a sad tale, he answered. The old men nodded and murmured sympathetically. Anschel sat down on an empty bench and the old sages listened to his story. Conversion?! Why, he must be misinterpreting his dream. White-bearded Baruch ben Jacob shook his head, saying, "It was not your father who spoke to you in this dream, it was a demon."

The other men nodded solemnly. Then a younger scholar, Elisah ben Samuel, said, "Yes. Remember, good Anschel, the number of demons in the world is enormous. It is overwhelming. In fact, it is unimaginable. The whole atmosphere is a crowd of demons, thick as dust, numerous as the motes in a sunbeam, uncountable as the drops of rain in a storm."

And Elisah's neighbor, Joshua ben Eliezer, said, "We are in constant peril: demons can attack at any time. This is especially true at night, when a mysterious dimness settles over all and when our souls are lulled by sleep from their normal watchfulness."

"How true, good Joshua," continued Lewe ben Anselm. "Remember, Anschel, after your nighttime studies (during which time the holy words are protecting you), you must wrap yourself tightly in your blankets. Do not leave even the slightest little crevice for a demonic hand to reach in and snatch your soul."

Anschel looked around the room. The sages were nodding seriously. They muttered. They stroked their beards. Rabbi Abraham sat quietly with his eyes closed; his breathing was slow and heavy. Was he asleep? And if so, was he dreaming? After a moment, Menahem ben Joel said, "Undoubtedly, Anschel, these dreams occurred on a Wednesday or a Saturday night. On these two nights, hordes of particularly devastating spirits are let loose in the world."

But the traveler from Opladen said, "No, my friends–actually, I had these dreams on two *holy* nights: the eve of *Rosh Hashanah* and the eve of *Yom Kippur.* And you will recall that this year these nights were a Tuesday and a Thursday."

The scholars were silent for a moment; then Moyses ben Nathan said, "Well, any night can be trouble, Anschel. For instance, you cannot leave food or drink out overnight at *any* time, or it will be invaded by evil spirits. And certainly you would not dare to go outside alone on any night–at any time before the bright and protective *ki tov* dawn–even during a major holiday."

The sages nodded and nodded and said many "amens," and finally old Shimshon ha-Zaken coughed and in a hoarse voice he said, "In any case, we are certain that this must have been a demon, for what Jewish father could ever ask his son to give up Judaism?"

Anschel listened uncertainly. No one said anything further. The old men all seemed to be waiting for a word from Rabbi Achselrad.

After a moment, Anschel ben Menahem said, "And what do *you* think, Rabbi?"

Abraham Achselrad opened his eyes, and he looked at Anschel. He blinked – then he stared at the man from Opladen for many, many minutes.

"I think," said the Rabbi quietly, "that you must convert, Reb Anschel."

There was a quiet gasp from the sages, but no one said a word. "I was afraid you would say that," said Anschel. He looked down at his feet. "Actually, Rabbi, I knew that would be the answer."

Rabbi Abraham looked very sad. Slowly Anschel stood and walked from the synagogue, and he returned to his home community – and Anschel converted to Christianity. Anschel went to the priest in the church of Opladen. "I wish to become a Christian," he said. The priest opened wide his eyes; then he patted Anschel on the back. "Return tomorrow," said the priest. "If you still feel the same way, then we will proceed."

The next day, Anschel returned. He was washed, to free his soul from its many un-Christian stains. He was anointed with oil and balsam in order to consecrate his soul anew. A white cloth was laid on his head. His body was sealed with the sign of the cross to protect his soul, and he stood so that the shadow of the priest's hands fell upon him to illuminate his soul with the Holy Spirit. He drank a sip of wine and ate a bit of wafer to fill his soul with God, and he sipped a cup of milk and honey for a sweet new life. Then Hans Opladen, as he was now named, stepped from the church as a Christian.

In the Jewish community of Opladen there was disbelief. People shook their heads. Tears came to their eyes. How could Anschel do such a thing? The congregation wept and fasted. Men tore a corner of their shirts. The next week, Anschel ben Menahem ha-Levi was excommunicated formally and fully. And it was not *niddah,* the mild penalty of separation. No, Anschel ben Menahem ha-Levi was put in *herem.* He was completely excluded from the temple, from the yeshiva, and from all association with the faithful. It was a sad, sad time indeed.

Seven weeks came, and seven weeks went. Hans Opladen's cloth business prospered, as wealthy Christians now frequented his store. Soon a year had passed. Then five days after the eve of *Rosh Hashanah,* the holy New Year, a young Gentile boy was killed: he was Johann, the son of Ernst Berg, a local official, the warden of the cloth-makers' Guild, and an advisor to Bernhard, the Count of Munster, who ruled much of the Westphalian countryside.

An evil demon had been hard at work. Not only had it driven the murderer to his deed, the demon had also whispered, "It was the Jews." With this rumor abroad, two Jews were arrested and imprisoned. The Opladen Jewish community was beside itself. They petitioned the local magistrate, but Ernst Berg said grimly, "I am a religious man. In the Bible, in the Book of Deuteronomy, it says–"

> The rest of the people will hear of this and be afraid, and never again will such an evil thing be done among you. We must show no pity: there must be eye for eye, tooth for tooth, hand for hand, foot for foot, and life for life.

And the representatives of the Opladen Jewish community were dismissed and were ordered to make no more statements or petitions about the case.

When Hans Opladen heard the news, he immediately traveled south to consult with Rabbi Abraham. The two men met for many hours in the small back study room. Old Abraham Achselrad gave Hans an amulet and detailed instructions; then the once and former Jew returned to his hometown of Opladen.

The city officials of Opladen would not hear a Jew's appeal. Jews were not even allowed in the main city building, and the accused Jews had to hire Gentiles to represent them in court. But Hans Opladen was no longer a Jew. Moreover, Hans was now a member of the cloth-makers' Guild; so he went to visit Ernst Berg.

"I am Hans Opladen," he began.

"Yes, yes–I know who you are," said the warden.

"Your Honor," said Hans, "I have important evidence regarding the sad circumstances of your son's death."

"Then you must present them to the court, when the Archbishop convenes it next week," said Berg.

"I cannot do that," replied Hans.

"You cannot? And why is that?"

"The evidence can only be seen in the cemetery," said Hans.

Berg was silent a moment. A chill wind had crept into the room;

it swept into the corners and curled along the edges of the floor. Ernst Berg shivered and frowned, and he looked intently at Hans. "Are you certain?" he asked.

"Yes, sir," said Hans.

Again Berg was silent. "Exactly what do you propose, Mr. Opladen?"

"I know that this is an unusual request, but I would like you to meet me in the *Leichenhauser* of the cemetery tomorrow afternoon," said Hans. "Also we will need your closest advisors and at least two of your guardsmen."

Ernst Berg tapped his chin. "Very well," he answered slowly. "However, I warn you that you had better not be wasting my time."

"I will not," answered the converted Jew. Hans Opladen left the room and he left the building. Hans walked out into the street. The afternoon had slipped by; the day had worn on. Evening was blanketing the town, and now began *Yom Kippur* for the Jews of Opladen.

Was Hans still a Jew? Hans had been born a Jew and in his heart he remained a Jew, and on this Day of Atonement he fasted. He said quiet prayers at night. He slept in a black robe with a rip along the edge. When he awoke the next morning, he continued his prayers. Then in the afternoon, he went to the Christian cemetery.

When in Cologne, Hans had been given a sacred amulet by Rabbi Abraham. Now Hans held tightly to the amulet as he met Ernst Berg, his two guards, and a small retinue of advisors in the cemetery. In Opladen, the Christian cemetery was beside the church, and it had a *Leichenhauser* at the side gate. (The *Leichenhauser* was a stone house with five rooms, each with a stone bier. Before they were buried, bodies were checked for signs of life each day for five days by the church beadle. Evil spirits slowly filtered from the bodies, and after five days the bodies were finally pure and they could then be buried.)

Quietly, the men entered the chamber of Berg's dead son. Spirits watched from the shadows. Ancient forces lurked in the walls and under the floors. Hans sat on a stone bench. He closed his eyes. He began to sway; he shook strangely. Ernst Berg watched intently. Hans opened his eyes, and he opened his hands. The small silver amulet shone and gleamed. But where was the light coming from? The air was cold and silent. Then Hans stood and put the amulet on the hand of Johann, the dead boy. There was a deep, ancient silence. A dark cloud passed across the sky. Chill winds crept into the graveyard from somewhere beyond the fences; an evening pall had slipped into the *Leichenhauser* from the hills of the nighttide deep.

For a moment, nothing happened. Then suddenly a small hazy shape wavered along the wall. The shape expanded. It became a dark aura. It rose up, and it appeared to be Johann himself, larger than life and sad and young and grim.

Silently, the spirit shape raised a wavering arm, and the arm pointed directly at the man standing next to Ernst Berg. The man shouted, "No, no–stop! It was not me: it was the Jews!" But the dead child pointed and it pointed, and it seemed to grow larger and to fill the room, in the silence of a dark and cold autumn day. There was a pressure in the air. It was irresistible. It inflated the wavering spirit, which grew larger and larger and which pointed and pointed and pointed. The guilty man jumped back. "Stop!" he yelled. "Please stop! O Lord, have pity on me. All right, I admit it! I struck him and killed him, but it was a mistake!"

The wavering arm continued to point. The outstretched hand seemed to reach for the man. The true murderer sat on a stone bench along the wall, and he looked away and he shook and wept.

Then suddenly the shape was gone. The wall was blank. The room was empty. Everyone felt stunned and broken and silent.

At first no one moved. Eventually, Ernst Berg, the warden, said sadly to the guilty man, "It was you, Franz?" Franz only looked away. Then Berg motioned to the two guards. They stood beside the guilty man. "Well," said the warden, as he turned to Hans, "so–the Jews are not at fault after all." Ernst Berg shook his head. Sadly and silently he walked from the *Leichenhauser* and the cemetery and he returned to his home, where he closed the door and he sat and wept alone.

So the true murderer was arrested, the Jews went free, and Hans Opladen came back to his congregation. Hans was allowed to reconvert; in fact, he was welcomed back into the fold with open arms and with hugs from all. Then, like a newly born child, he was renamed–and he chose the name Anschel ben Menahem ha-Levi. And much, much later, when Anschel died, he sat alongside his father Menahem in the Great Hereafter, and the father patted his son and smiled and said, "I love you forever, Anschel, my son, my golden little boy."

What is that, Rabbi? No, no, I was just resting my eyes. Please feel free to join me here by the stove. Actually, an old man like me can doze forever by a warm stove: dozing keeps away the child-ache.

Child-ache? Well, my grandmother called it child-ache. I am not certain whether it means wanting to have children around and underfoot or wanting to be a child again. Actually they may be the same thing. It is all tied in with remembering. Do you remember when you were very, very young? I mean two or three years old. I remember one day–it was in a springtime that was rainlit and green-gray with cloud-covered skies. I was standing outside, a child all alone and small on a vast path near my home. The trees' leaves were dark and round like green pebbles; the bark had a silver sheen that was finely etched with lines of brown. The grasses were wet, the path stretched down along the housefronts forever, and, as far as I could see, the lane had no ending. A large oak tree stood along the misty lane, alive and watching me. No one else was all around, and, thoughtful and remotely, massive old brown houses peered from deep within their dark front porches. They loomed in rows, akin to a giant woody orchard of temples old and wise, solemn but not forbidding, each mysterious and warm inside.

Yes, Rabbi, that is the very first picture I recall, and I remember it with an ache, a child-ache. None of us is immune, and no amulet is powerful enough to counteract it. Certainly nothing protected Maacah–nothing would allow Maacah, the wife of Nashon, to rest until she had children. Maacah? Well, she lived in the far-distant days of the mystic Achselrad. She was married to Nashon ben Azaraiah ha-Kohen, and the couple lived in the village of Gangelt, two full days' journey west of Cologne.

Nashon and his wife, Maacah, had been married for ten years, but they had no children. Nashon accepted his fate–who was he to question the ways of the good Lord God, blessed be He? However, Maacah saw things differently. What is the value of life, she asked, if it is without its greatest treasure of all, a child?

Maacah worried and worried, and she could hardly sleep. Perhaps the problem was her diet. First, she tried eating only fruits; then she ate only meats. She fasted and she prayed. She went from doctor to doctor and from specialist to specialist. Still no children appeared. She turned to herbal healers, skew-eyed hermits, and mystical heretics. "A child is a blessing," she told them, "and each child is his own special blessing. But, my life is empty of these blessings." The healers, hermits, and heretics were sympathetic; they offered herbs, prayers, and charms–but nothing helped.

One day, Maacah heard that Rabbi Achselrad was not only a famous scholar, he was also a great miracle worker. Gangelt was a long, uncomfortable journey from Cologne, but Maacah set off alone to see the Rabbi. It was summer. The air was warm and heavy, and the traveling was slow and tiresome and wearing.

The childless woman reached Cologne uneventfully. She got directions to the Juden Viertels, and there she located the alleyway that led from Judengasse Street to the synagogue building. It was early on a weekday afternoon, and she found Rabbi Abraham sitting by himself in the back study room. He received her politely, and she poured out her soul to him. Maacah wept and she pleaded. She stood and she waved her arms. "Rabbi," she said in a loud and trembling voice, "bless me so that I may have a son or a daughter; otherwise, my life will not be worth living. Although the sun seems to keep away my pain during the days, at night I cannot sleep because of the great ache that I feel, especially in the late dark hours."

The Rabbi listened to the woman. He nodded. He tapped his chin. He stroked his beard. Then he said to her, "I have never been to Gangelt. It would help me if I could picture the town. Perhaps you would describe your village for me."

"Of course, of course," said the woman. Maacah told the Rabbi how the town itself had a small market with only three buildings. She described the local river and the fields and the hillsides. She listed the important citizens and the members of their families and their successful and failed children. There was no formal synagogue, said Maacah, and the Jewish men got together to pray in the small *heder,* the one-room schoolhouse run by Reb Joshua. Then Maacah told her entire life story, from her childhood through her marriage. Finally, she described her house and her yard and her goats and her chickens and her garden.

Rabbi Abraham listened patiently. Sometimes he opened his eyes wider, sometimes he squinted and blinked, sometimes he frowned. Often he tapped a finger on his desk. When Maacah had stopped talking and when the Rabbi had finally heard her entire answer, he nodded and said, "Now, let me think."

Rabbi Abraham closed his eyes. He took a deep breath. He settled back in his chair. His breathing became slow and quiet. Was he asleep? After a few minutes, he opened his eyes again. He looked around strangely; then he said, "My good woman, I have had a vision. In your village lives an unusual man. I think that he sits by a well. Do you know him?"

"Certainly," replied Maacah, "he is called the "mad water-drawer." He lives by himself in a tumbledown hut."

"Ah, yes, exactly," said the Rabbi. "Now, my good woman, this man is really a demon."

Maacah's eyes widened. "Yes," continued old Achselrad, "I am afraid that he is a demon in human form."

"Oh, Lord in Heaven, protect us," said the woman, shivering. "This is what we always suspected."

"Well, *he* is the cause of your problems," said the Rabbi. "Now, Maacah, go home. Ask this man to bless you. It is the demon's fault that you are childless, and only he has the power to reverse the evil."

"But what if he refuses?" asked Maacah.

The Rabbi looked up at the ceiling. He stroked his beard. Finally he said, "Listen, young woman, here is what you do." Maacah bent forward to hear, but instead of saying anything, old Achselrad muttered and nodded to himself. Was he talking to someone else? Was he hearing voices? Was he conversing with angels and demons? Maacah sat back. She smoothed her dress. She looked around.

Meanwhile, the Rabbi had reached into his drawer. He took out a clean piece of kosher parchment. He closed his eyes and said a silent prayer. Then in his small, neat handwriting he wrote the *Shema* on one side of the paper. Old Rabbi Abraham wrote in sacred ink, ink that had been mixed with incense. When the ink had dried, he turned the parchment over and he wrote:

> In the name of Yahweh-Elohim, the Lord God of Israel, we shall do and we shall prosper and we shall be fruitful.
>
> May Akriel, the angel of barrenness, and Armisael, the angel of the womb, grant to Maacah and her husband Nashon, the son of Azaraiah, children of health and light. Maacah and Nashon have held fast to the Law of the Lord, and as it is said in the Book of Deuteronomy: "Then shall the Lord love you, bless you, and cause you to increase. He will bless the fruit of your body and the fruit of your land."
>
> Now we beseech the holy Lord God (blessed be He) by the power of His greatness and in the names of the seventy great angels of the God of Israel–especially: Sanvi, Sansanvi, and Semangelaf–and under the prayers of all the righteous people and by the powers of all the signs and symbols and holy words written and inscribed herein, to restrain and to repel all demons, dybbuks, devils, and *lilin*–both male and female–and to protect Maacah, her husband, and her future children (by His good grace) and to guard them all like the apples of His eye and to preserve them in their goings out and in their comings in, from now until forevermore.
>
> Amen, *selah,* amen–Yahweh-Adonai, amen.

The Rabbi drew a circle around this inscription. Outside the circle, at the four corners of the parchment, the Rabbi wrote the names of the four rivers of Paradise–Pishon, Gihon, Perath, and Hiddekel. When the Rabbi finished writing in his neat and tiny script, he rolled the parchment into a tight scroll and he tied it with a cotton thread. The Rabbi tied and untied the thread – he knotted and unknotted it seven times – then he handed the charm to the woman.

"Now," said Rabbi Abraham, "sneak up on the man when he is dozing by the well. Then quickly tie this onto his shirt. Wake him, and take hold of his sleeve. And do not let go, no matter what he says or does, until he blesses you. And when finally he gives you his blessing, be certain that he swears on the name of Yahweh."

Maacah, the childless woman, thanked the Rabbi and headed home. She crossed the River Erft and then the River Roer, and after two long days she reached the little town of Gangelt. Early the following morning, Maacah went out to look for the mad water-drawer. Each day, this strange man would sit by the well and for a penny he would draw two or three bucketsful for any passerby. Maacah saw him from a distance, and she watched and she waited. Finally, late in the day, his head began to nod. Then the woman did not hesitate for even a single moment. She ran to him. She tied the parchment amulet on his shirt, and she held his sleeve. The demon water-drawer awoke with a start.

"What is this?" he cried.

"Please, sir," said Maacah, "bless me so that I may have a child."

"I will do nothing of the sort," he said, coughing angrily. "And let go of my sleeve or I will hit you."

The woman held tightly. "Please, you simply *have* to bless me!"

"I am just a water-drawer. But now I am getting angry. Not only will I hit you, I will also go to your husband. You have attacked me for no reason, and I will tell him. In fact, I will tell everyone what they undoubtedly suspect of all you evil Jews – that you beat children and steal chickens, that you go out at night into the countryside, and that you say your prayers backwards. I will even spoil your food and poison your water. Now let me go!"

A great child-ache welled up in Maacah, and she held fast. "I will not let you go until you have blessed me," she said. And she began to cry.

"What have I ever done to you?" asked the demon. "Let me go!"

"Never. I would rather die first," said Maacah. She tightened her lips and she tightened her grip.

"Ah, evil woman, I wish that you *would* die!" yelled the demon. The demon threatened and he coughed and he hissed and he spat, but he could not actually harm Maacah because of the amulet and because he was caught in her grasp. Finally, the demon said, "All right, all right–I will bless you. You shall have a child. In fact, you will have two children. Now let go!"

"Do you swear to that on the name of Yahweh?" asked the woman, still holding the demon's sleeve.

"Yes, yes–I swear on the name of Yahweh that you shall have two children," cried the demon.

"And will they be healthy and happy children, and will they live long and quiet lives?"

"Yes, yes–they will be long-lived and healthy! Now let me go, and take that terrible parchment from my shirt," said the mad water-drawer. "It is burning my skin!"

So Maacah let go of his sleeve, and she removed the amulet. The demon stood up and he hobbled off, rubbing his arm, and the next day the water-drawer was seen no more in the town. The water-drawer had disappeared, and no one knew where he went. In a week, his tumbledown shack was blown apart by a storm. It was the talk of the whole village of Gangelt, and no one understood why or how it had happened.

After this, Maacah tied the amulet to her bedroom door. And then the Lord remembered Maacah, and He gave her children. Exactly one year after she had received the blessing of the madman demon–in the summer of the next year–Maacah and her husband, Nashon, had two little baby boys. The twins were wrinkled and pink and healthy as potatoes, and they were strong and very special. Maacah tickled them and she held them, and the child-ache was a thing of the past. The house was suddenly warm and glowing, and life was full and intense–and much, much later, in the new child-ache of her old, old age, Maacah was still as happy as happy could be.

Rabbi, it is good to see you at this late hour. Come and sit down. Actually, I knew you would be coming along. The oven coals flared up, and, as they say, "When the flame leaps high, a guest is nigh."

Oh, yes, Rabbi, there definitely *is* something to these visions of the future. Howling dogs foreshadow a death. Sneezes warn of disaster. And itches are especially revealing. My grandmother told me that if your foot itches then you will be traveling soon, if your ears itch you will hear news, and if your eyelids itch you will see something new. Itchy eyebrows mean that old friends will return. If your forehead itches then other people are looking for you, if your palm itches you will find money, if your nose itches you will be angry soon, and if your tongue itches you will speak of wise things. The good Lord God (blessed be He) tells your future through your body.

Nowadays we forget how to see the future. However, in medieval times people used all sorts of divinations. For instance: on Monday evenings after sunset you could go into a field and locate a yellow mallow plant. You would face east, toward Jerusalem, and dig a hole. Bow, circle the spot one time, then bow again. Now you ask about the future, saying:

If my hopes and ventures
Will end in a success
Then, my golden flower,
Stay in your open dress–
But if I'm doomed to failure
Then hide your yellowness.

To learn the future, return the next morning and check to see whether the flower is open or closed.

Religious rites can also predict the future. Many people set a lighted candle in a safe place during the Ten Days of Penitence between *Rosh Hashanah* and *Yom Kippur.* If your light blows out, then you will not live through the year. But if the candle burns down all the way to the end, then you have at least one more year of life. As you know, Rabbi, your fate is decided on *Yom Kippur.* However, the decision is inscribed finally and irrevocably in God's Celestial Book of Records on the night of *Hoshana Rabbah,* the seventh day of the Feast of Tabernacles. On the night of *Hoshana Rabbah,* you can go out and look for your shadow in the moonlight, and if you find that your shadow has a head, then you still have another year to live, praise God.

And do you know why a halo around your shadow means that you are about to die? What? Why *of course* these are real and useful signs. Just be patient and let me explain. You see, each day when the good Lord God (blessed be He) has finished His signing of heavenly proclamations, He wipes a bit of the glowing ink from His pen onto the hair of a worthy man. God looks down and chooses someone whom He is about to take back unto Himself, and, with His pen, the Lord gives him a shining nimbus, a halo. This is how Moses himself came to have beams of light emanating from his head.

But this is old, old lore–even my grandmother had difficulty remembering it all. I am afraid it is too powerful and mystical for me: divination is for the clever and the wise and the especially holy. I myself prefer to look into the past, not into the future. For me, remembering the days gone by and imagining myself walking and talking with those who are now gone to the Great Hereafter–that is all I need. Fortunately, memory takes no magic or divination.

We have many special windows into the past. We can always look backwards through the writings of our ancestors. We hear our parents and our grandparents speak again in their ethical Wills, the anecdotal testaments that they wrote down once long ago for their children and for their children's children. As you know, every father is bound by the good Lord God to leave a set of moral rules for his children's guidance. Sometimes these are just a few lines, two or three helpful thoughts. Other times, they are long documents, such as the statement of Jared ben Sasson ha-Levi, a good and common man of old medieval Germany.

Jared ben Sasson ha-Levi was a common man from the medieval city of Coblenz. One summer, when Jared reached the age of fifty-five, his brother-in-law, Moyses, said to him, "Jared, if you should die (may the good Lord God, blessed be He, let you live another twenty-one years, amen), where can I find your Will?"

"My Will?"

"Yes, yes," said Moyses, "your Will."

"I do not have a Will," said Jared.

"What?! You have not written a Will?"

Jared shook his head. "I own no property. You know that I am a middleman, so I do not have a large stock of merchandise," he said. "My children will simply divide my few possessions when I die."

Moyses frowned. "Listen, old man, you owe your children more than that. You owe them some advice."

"I *do* give them advice – and usually, Moyses, it is more than they care to hear," said Jared.

"Jared, Jared," said Moyses, "do you remember nothing? Were you not listening last week when the Rabbi reminded us of the passage in the Book of Genesis?"

> For I have known him and I have taken care of him, and I have charged him to instruct and to command his children and his children's children and all his household after him. Let his descendants conform to My commandments, let them keep the way of the Lord, and let them do what is right, what is just, what is true, and what is holy. Then, I shall give to him and to his children and to his children's children all the joy and the happiness that I have promised.

"This means that you have an obligation, Jared, to instruct and to command your children. You must write down the rules for their lives.

After I heard the Rabbi, I sat down and wrote out my whole life philosophy. It is your duty to your children. So I advise you, brother-in-law: sit down immediately and write out a Will."

"Moyses, what do I know about life philosophies? This sounds like the job for a scholar or for a practiced writer. At the very least it is a task for a rabbi," said Jared.

"Then go to a rabbi, Jared. But do not put this off any longer," said Moyses. "You are not getting any younger as we stand here and talk."

Moyses shook his head and left. Jared sat down and thought. He thought all day, and he decided that Moyses was right. The next morning he said to his wife, "My dear, I must go to Cologne for a few days." Then he kissed his children, and he set off north for Cologne in order to ask the great Rabbi Abraham to help him write his last Will and Testament. As you know, Rabbi Abraham was a famous writer. He wrote the *Keter Shem Tov,* and he was recognized throughout Germany as a deep and wise Jewish thinker. Therefore, when Jared ben Sasson ha-Levi decided to have a Will written, he thought immediately of Rabbi Abraham Achselrad.

Jared traveled north along the River Rhine, passing through Andernach, Remagen, Konigswinter, and Bonn, and on the second day he reached Cologne. There he found the Jewish Quarter, and he went to the old synagogue. Jared walked through the main prayer hall filled with wooden benches. The twelve stained-glass windows with their colored lions and snakes filtered the late afternoon sun in long, warm shafts. Jared passed the Holy Ark made of stone, and he walked to the door of the back study room. In the little back room, Rabbi Abraham ben Alexander was bent over a book, reading and thinking.

Jared waited patiently.

After a few minutes, the Rabbi looked up. "May I help you?" he asked.

Jared said, "Are you Rabbi Abraham ben Alexander, the writer?"

"I am."

"Rabbi, my name is Jared ben Sasson ha-Levi. I live in Coblenz. My brother-in-law has reminded me that it is my duty to leave a Will for my children."

Rabbi Abraham nodded. Jared continued. "This is a rather frightening task, Rabbi. Can you help me to write a good Will?"

The Rabbi looked at the books and the papers on his desk, then he said, "Give me a few minutes to finish what I am doing, Reb Jared."

After about ten minutes, the Rabbi said, "Now I am ready to write for you. Let me take out a new sheet of paper."

The Rabbi got ready to write. Jared took a worn parchment from his pocket, and he handed it to the Rabbi.

"What is this?" asked Rabbi Abraham.

"Well, Rabbi, it is a blessing that I have always liked. My father passed it down to me. Do you think that it would be proper to start the Will with this poem?"

The Rabbi read words aloud:

Our Father high in Heaven
Please smile on us again–
On me and on my children.

Father on white cloudlets
Shine with golden sunsets
Enwrap us like warm blankets.

Ancient Parent wise
Fill the vast blue skies
Over the family that I prize.

Then please also watch anew
My children's children too
Whom I shall never get to view.

Old Achselrad nodded. "This sounds fine to me," he said. "Shall I write it first?"

"Yes, please," said Jared.

Rabbi Abraham copied the poem. After a moment, the Rabbi said, "All right, Jared–continue."

"Good. Now, please address the document:

"To my children, and to their children–

"This, then is my Will and my Testament to my children. These are the things that my sons and my daughters shall do and consider at my request after my death, amen.

"My sons and my daughters, listen carefully, learn from my life, and follow my suggestions. My warnings and my cautions will help you through difficult times: they will make your life happier in the end.

"Let me begin by reminding you that I was your parent. Does this seem an obvious statement? It is something to face out loud now that I am gone. I comforted you and raised you. I told you what was right and what was wrong. I fed you and clothed you. I made certain that you had an education. To you, this may seem selfless. Actually, it was selfish, because I hope that you will continue in yourselves that which is me.

"Before, you relied on me. Now you must become independent. *You* must be the parents when your own parents are gone. I know that you did not think that death would ever divide us. Of course you had unpleasant times, but you did not really know the lonely trials of daily life. You did not know how it is to face things when there is no parent in the background, when there is no father as the final protector. Who will be as gentle and caring and tender to you as I have been? Who will take my place now that I am gone? The truth is that there is none but me; a parent cannot ever be replaced. However, perhaps now you yourselves have embodied sufficient parts of me to have some of that *fatherness* live on in your souls, comforting you a bit in spirit although my clayey body is gone forever.

"This would be a bleak statement, were we not a religious people. To the nonbeliever, the universe is empty and comfortless after his parents die. Fortunately, we have the immortal Lord God (blessed be He). As the Talmud says: 'In the image of God made He man. Beloved are all Israel, for they were called *children* of the All-present. And it was with a special love that God called them His children – you are children of the Lord your God.' Yes, my children, God is our original Father. He is eternal. He persists. He will always be there to comfort you, as He has comforted me, amen."

Jared paused. "Please put an empty line in here, Rabbi, to let my children take a breath as they read."

"Certainly," said Rabbi Abraham.

Then Jared continued:

"Now, my children, I am fifty-five years of age, and today I sit down to remind you of some things that I have learned. First: be faithful forever. By faithful, I mean humbly follow the Law of the Lord. The Torah has much of the Law written within it. But could all the Truths of God be condensed into five holy books? Can all the world be summarized in a few written words? Of course it cannot. The whole Law is to be found in one place and in one place only: it is in your hearts. So begin by looking faithfully within yourselves and reading therein God's holy Truths.

"Some of these Truths you can read already, with no training. But we must also grow and learn in order to understand fully the language of our soul. This growth and learning comes from the study of the Torah, where so many of the sacred Truths are crystallized and written quite clearly. Moreover, young people, the world is a noisy place: confusing winds and cross-currents make up our daily weathers. When you listen to your heart with your softest and tiniest ears, you may not always know if you are hearing the holy words from within or the strange noises from without. Here, the Torah will guide you, my children. So, after looking within yourselves, next you must study–and study daily."

Jared stopped reciting. "Yes, Reb Jared?" prompted Rabbi Achselrad.

"I was trying to think, Rabbi," said Jared slowly. "I like the holy proverbs. Do you know a proverb that I might insert here?"

Rabbi Abraham tapped his chin. "Well, how about–"

Listen, My student,
  Take My teachings as guide,
Know My commandments,
  Study Law at My side
And the years of your life
  Shall be far multiplied
As the lights in the heavens
  Thick with stars far and wide.

Jared smiled. "Ah, that is fine. Please write that down."

After a moment, the Rabbi said, "Very well, my friend, continue."

"So, my children, read the Holy Scriptures–and also I advise you to write. I regret that I am not a good writer. To express your thoughts with pen and ink leads to the best understanding. Remember how the famed scholar Samuel ha-Nagid has said, 'O pen of mine, speak for me and tell of kindness and insight and thoughtfulness!' So too I tell you: 'Write, O my children. The written word opens your eyes; it teaches you your hidden thoughts.'

"Pass writing on to your children, and when you teach them, emphasize steadiness and persistence. There is an old saying: 'It will be enough for a child to learn only one single letter a year, so long as he learns it well.' Then too, when you or your children write, read all your works a second and even a third time, for no man can avoid slips. Do not hurry. Write to the best and highest standards that you can. As our sages have said, 'Who is it that removes his clothes and exposes his nakedness everywhere? It is he who hurriedly writes a document filled with mistakes.' "

"Just a moment," said Rabbi Abraham. "Let me finish writing this down . . . All right, Reb Jared, please continue."

"My children, be thoughtful, true, and elegant in what you say and in what you write. I advise that you keep even your handwriting beautiful. The form of the words will shape their content. And, as with all things that you do in life, be critical of what you have written. Improvement is always possible. Never stop learning and growing. You are good children; you are fine people. I know that you have wise and understanding hearts. Therefore, all that is needed is to do your best with humility and to listen to the guidance of the Lord.

"Now, my dears, in all my years, I have learned a few things. Let me offer a few practical suggestions to you. Try, children, to live lives of peace. Do not contend with others. Do not meddle or . . ."

"Rabbi, can you suggest an appropriate proverb here?"

Rabbi Abraham put down his pen. He stroked his beard and said, "How about–"

Avoid by all means
  Battles not your own,
For if you intervene
  In arguments unknown
It's like standing in-between
  A mad dog and its bone.

Jared smiled. "Ah, that is exactly what I wanted," he said. Rabbi Achselrad wrote down the proverb; then he nodded to Jared.

"Do not meddle, and do not enter into disputes with people who will not listen, not even on matters of the Torah. Do not badger people. Remember the holy saying":

Carrying stone is tiresome
And sand is a dead weight,
But listening to an endless drum
Is worse than either fate.

"Remain open and honest. Do not work deviously, even if you are convinced you are right and even if you hope for a good and holy result in the end. It is better to have behaved with honor than to have won a victory by deceit. And although you must never lie, sometimes it is best to keep your ideas quietly to yourself.

"Also–do not separate yourselves from your people: remain involved in your congregation. Within the community itself, try to follow the wishes of the majority and listen carefully to others. (But do not trust the words of the young as much as the counsels of the old.)

"In business, be cautious. There is an old saying: 'One can blow up a dream to be bigger than the night.' Do not let wild hopes blind you to the modest realities of life–do not be a bird that sees the grain but not the net. Remember what the sage of blessed memory said in the Book of Proverbs":

A simple man accepts trustingly
Every word he hears,
But a clever man must actually see
To believe his own ears.

A wise man proceeds cautiously,
Scorning smooth soft words;
A foolish man goes heedlessly,
Rushing blindly forwards.

Jared smiled at the Rabbi. Rabbi Abraham nodded and continued writing.

"We fill our days with many small matters, and these are also important. Dress well and keep your household neat. You feel and think and behave as you look, and you must feel and think and behave to the highest and finest of standards.

"Avoid exotic foods and drinks. Do not eat anything in excess, especially sweets and spicy dishes. All in moderation is the best way. Be moderate in your possessions, too. The joys of a happy heart and a warm home are unmatched by those objects, such as jewelry and gold, which can never be taken into the soul or carried beyond the grave. The righteous and the honest shall inherit a fortune, but the greedy and the wicked shall inherit nothing–so say the proverbs.

"This moderation should extend into all parts of your life. For example, avoid travel for travel's sake. Do not risk your life by taking to the open road. Instead, stay quietly at home; as the old saying goes: 'There is no greater honor than to stay at home.' Build a safe, happy life in your own home, among your own family. Of course, do not lock yourselves within four walls: do not shun the good Lord God's great natural world. One of our finest blessings is the land, the soil, and all the plants, so even in the city, attend to your gardens."

Here Jared paused. "Rabbi," he said, "I would like another holy proverb at this point."

Rabbi Abraham frowned for a moment. "Well, Reb Jared, how about this?"

> Work out-of-doors before you rest;
>   Garden neatly, with wondrous plants.
> Found, at first, a plentiful harvest–
>   *Then* begin your household dance.

"Perfect," smiled Jared. "To continue: And, my golden children, may . . ."

"Just a moment," said the Rabbi. He finished writing the proverb. "All right, Jared, go on."

"And, my golden wonderful children, may your faces shine upon others. Do extra things for other people. Be helpful and kind. Smile and say a friendly word to someone every day. Lift a heavy load for an old man; carry a shopping sack for an old lady. Tell a child that he is good and beautiful. Each selfless, helpful deed puts out a root, and in the end you will be 'like a tree with innumerable deep toes. So that even if all the winds in the world come in a rush and blow with all their might, they cannot stir you from your place, and your leaves shall always be green, even in years of drought, and fruit shall grow continuously among your branches.'

"I can only repeat the advice of the sages: Tend the weak and the poor and the sick. Give advice when asked. Counsel the troubled. Lend a hand to the fallen. Help the destitute and the needy. Then, my lovely children, the Great Lord God Almighty will help you too, for we are all poor and needy in His sight. Give money, food, clothes, and help to others; in other words, be a good Jew, for Jews have always shared with those poorer than themselves."

Again Jared stopped. "Rabbi, would you help out here with a passage from the Holy Scriptures?" he asked.

The Rabbi nodded. He tapped his chin and stroked his beard, and then he repeated aloud as he wrote:

> As the great Lord Almighty told Moses for all the people Israel – When you reap the harvest of your land, do not collect the crops all the way to the very edges of your field. In addition, do not gather all the loose and fallen ears of your crop, and do not completely strip your vineyard or collect the fallen grapes. You shall leave these extra bits for the poor and the alien.

"Thank you, Rabbi," said Jared, and he continued:

"Each synagogue has a poor box, a *kupta;* be certain to put a few coins in it every day. Give a bit of money at marriages and at funerals and on all holidays. There will always be poor people. Moreover, the wheel of fortune turns in unpredictable ways. At any time you too may become needy. And if not? Well, what do we need with money in the end? Shrouds are made without pockets.

"Wealth is fleeting, but families persist beyond the grave. Devote yourselves to your children, as I have to mine. Teach your children as best you can. Bring them into the light of the Torah – make it a rule in your homes to read the Scriptures together. Be tender, be loving, be the parent that you have imagined God to be; it will make *you* happier even than your children. As the proverbs say":

The blessings of the holy Lord
Bring to us our best reward,
Our soul's most treasured grace.

God stores his wonders quite close by–
They're in your heart in rich supply
And in your child's embrace.

"Yes, I thank you, my children, for God's blessings *are* in your embraces, amen. Care patiently for your own children in sickness, and give them many little pleasant joys during their days of health. Then you are certain to die happy, as I am sure that I shall."

Jared ben Sasson stopped for a moment. The Rabbi looked up at him. Jared's eyes were half-closed; his brow was creased. He seemed to be talking to himself. The Rabbi waited patiently. Eventually, Jared continued aloud:

"And I ask, my children, that you reread this, my Testament, at least once each year of your lives; then share these words with your children also, when they grow old enough to understand. Try to fulfill my requests and you will, with the grace of the good Lord God Almighty, prosper to the ends of your days.

"Of course, I write these words knowing full well that none of us is perfect: our memories fail, our resolves weaken, and we act hastily, carelessly, and selfishly. You will make mistakes, my children. I am certain that you have made mistakes in the past, but at the moment I have forgotten them–and so shall the Almighty Lord. Has my long-gone father forgotten my sins? I am certain he has, for when we meet our parents in the Great Hereafter we are always their perfect young and innocent children once again and forever, amen."

There was silence. "Is that all, Reb Jared?" asked Rabbi Abraham.

"Yes–I think that is all," said Jared.

"How about instructions for your funeral?"

"Should that be included?" asked Jared.

"Yes," said the Rabbi. "I think that a word about your burial would be appropriate here."

"Very well, Rabbi.

"As to my burial, I ask you all – my sons, my daughters, my wife, and my friends – please give me a quiet and small funeral. Do not use a fancy coffin: I would like a plain wooden box. When I die, clean my old body and dress me afresh, as if it were a bright Sabbath morning. Be sure to put a prayer book in my hands before you quietly close the coffin top forever.

"Now, children, at a distance of thirty cubits from the grave, set down my coffin. Put it on the ground, and drag me the final distance to the grave by a rope attached to the front of the coffin box. Every four cubits, stand and rest a moment, and do this seven times. In this way I will find a final atonement for all my many sins, amen.

"Finally, put me in the ground at the right hand of my father. Yes, set me in the rich black earth beside my old father. And, good children, if the space be a little narrow between graves (as I seem to remember that it is), then I am sure my father loves me well enough to slide over and to make room for me by his side.

"Then, my loves, do not forget me, and I will never forget you. And if the great and wondrous Lord God is pleased to someday bring you back to me – as I know that He shall, with all my heart – then I will ever take you in my arms as my perfect young and innocent children once again. And we shall all walk home in Heaven together:

I pray, Lord of pedestrians
You'll grant warm winds at Your command
As my children hold my hands
And walk me to the Promised Land;
Give us blue skies with white clouds
Let my children laugh aloud
Make them hop as we walk free –
Have them smile and look up at me.

"Your loving father
Jared, son of Sasson the Levite"

Then Rabbi Abraham ben Alexander read the entire Will back to Reb Jared. Jared listened happily with his eyes closed. Afterward, Jared signed the Will, he thanked the Rabbi, he put three gold coins into the poor box, and he returned to Coblenz.

Jared ben Sasson ha-Levi was a modest man, a common man, and a quiet man. He did not worry about the future. He faced each day anew. Jared set his Will on the bookshelf next to his prayer books. There the document sat for twenty-one years until Jared finally died, on the first day of *Rosh Hashanah.* The next day Jared was buried beside his father's grave, on the righthand side. After the funeral Moyses took down the Will and read it aloud to Jared's children, and they were both happy and sad at the same time. And in later years they read and reread it to their children – young bright-eyed boys and girls whom Jared had never seen.

Hello, Rabbi, I will be with you in a moment. If every tablecloth is not folded, then the day has not ended properly.

There, now I can sit next to you by the stove. It is late, but I am not sleepy either. I am old, awake, and, I must confess, happy.

I am happy simply sitting here, musing lazily. Thoughts drift in and out of my mind. Little phrases roll round and round in my head: "Katal, katalta, katalti; kittal, kittalta, kittalti–pokat, pokadeti, pikat–pik–pik–pik–" Then, floating at the edges of my vision when I am completely relaxed, I see bits of Heaven, with its towering clouds and clear streams and sheep. Yes, yes, Rabbi. Heaven has sheep in the meadows far, far away, and it has blue flowers–chicory, I think–dotting the hillsides. Ah, my friend, these are magical musings, and they are as good as the best of magical dreams.

You know, when I was young, I used to pray for magical dreams: it was the only way that I could ever hope to fly. Before I went to bed, I would recite the dream psalms seven times. I still know them by heart, Psalm 23 and Psalm 42.

Why is Psalm 42 a dream psalm? Well, I am not exactly certain myself–perhaps it relates to a dream of the mystical Rabbi Achselrad.

I will tell you about old Achselrad's dream, but first let me begin with the psalm. As you remember, the middle verses of Psalm 42 are:

> Patiently I wait for You,
> When I think of You, I am awed;
> I praise You ever again and anew
> As my Deliverer, my one true God.
>
> When the waves washed over me,
> I still had faith and prayed to You–
> And though from Hermon's lofty peak
> From springs of the River Jordan too
> From the hill of Mount Mizar
> And from the wild ocean's vastest deep
> The rapids rushed spectacular,
> Waters tumbling with a wilding sweep–
> Yet still You heard my humble prayer
> And saved me from Death's briny heap.

These verses tell of overwhelming oceans, with waves as tall as a synagogue and with winds that charge like falling mountains. The psalm sings of seas with cold ocean sprays that smack the decks of shivering ships.

The great Lord God has created awesome forces in the seas, Rabbi–and it was the fierce Northern Seas that suddenly came to the mind of old Abraham Achselrad, one summer afternoon long, long ago. Rabbi Achselrad had been working on his mystical treatise, the *Keter Shem Tov.* He was tired and he was musing. He closed his eyes. Was he hoping for a wondrous magical dream? Rabbi Achselrad thought of Psalm 42. The grandeur of the seas rose around him in a wave, and then the Rabbi suddenly found himself dreaming of his old friend, a boy named Shallum ben Mannus ha-Kohen.

The Rabbi had known Shallum when they were both young. Shallum ben Mannus was wild and adventurous. He had big deep eyes and thick black eyebrows. He always waved his arms. He knew ancient Night Tales about dark and mysterious caves. He had seen dybbuks and treasures. He had touched the horse of a knight.

When the boys gathered to listen to him, Shallum warned that the woodlands were crowded with armies of bandits. Evil princes ruled the countrysides; farmers shuttered their houses as soon as the evening curfews were rung. Only synagogues were safe, said Shallum–and then only when two candles were burning. Christian churches were haunted after midnight, and Christian graveyards were overrun by ghosts who shone faintly when the moon was hidden.

Shallum had dared to wander alone after midnight. He had found that the nightside lands were grim and hollow and dense with demons. Glowing rocks lined paths leading to bosky dells. Plants that looked small and timid by day waved with thick black tendrils at night, as if they were overgrown evil grapevines reaching out for you in the moonlight.

Shallum had seen all these things himself, and he talked of them constantly. Deep-eyed young Shallum knew the strange colors of the night. He told incredible stories every time you saw him. His life was overflowing with wild events and people and animals. But young Abraham ben Alexander had wondered: Could there really be so much time in one day? How could Shallum manage to see so many new wonderments in those few hours between meetings? Did he compress a whole lifetime into a few thick, rich, tangled years? Ah, perhaps that was it. Perhaps Shallum lived faster than other boys; perhaps he was actually eighty by the time that he was eighteen. Yes, Shallum may already have lived a full life, because one day in a wink and a flash, he was gone.

One day Shallum just disappeared. He was gone, and no one knew where he went. No one ever heard from him again. Had he already finished his life, which he had lived so very fast, or had he instead found adventure? Was he studying in a famous yeshiva? Had he gone off to new and wild countries and become rich? Did he command great ships? Did he hunt wild animals? Was he an advisor to kings? It was a great mystery–and the mystery was never solved. So every once in a while, the Rabbi thought again of Shallum, and on this very afternoon, years and years later, young Shallum came to mind as the Rabbi was remembering Psalm 42 in a dream one strange and tired summer afternoon.

Rabbi Achselrad had mused, his mind drifted, and suddenly he was asleep. Why, *here* was Shallum–young and active and deep-eyed! And the Rabbi was young too, and once again he was following his childhood friend. Apparently, the two of them had decided to travel, because they were taking a ship, with coils of long, cold, salty ropes and slick damp decks and with bitter winds in the sails. Day after day and night after night they sailed; on and on, they slid over the waves. They traveled far into the North Sea. The heavens shone with an Ice Sky, white and rose and orange and lit by a white rainbow that glowed as cold as a halo of snow. And the oceans were chunky and filled with large rumbling floating islands of ice, which crashed and gnashed and smashed one another in sea-filled thunder.

There was land in the distance, and off the western shores, the currents swept north with a crash and a roar: backwash and whirling undertides rushed the seas down around to the north. Steering was impossible. Gales blew from the east. Tempests roared from the south. Ship after ship was wrecked on the ice. The ship of Shallum and Rabbi Abraham crashed into waves of floating snow. Finally they stuck fast and could not move at all, at all–they could not move at all.

The two Jews of Cologne were alone, but they were surrounded by other ships caught in the frozen seas. The Rabbi and Shallum put planks between the ships. The two men did not dare to stand in the wild winds; instead they crawled across, clinging to the wood as cold as iron. The ghost ship alongside creaked and groaned. Its sails were ripped to long, thin shreds–the winds had slashed and slashed, and the sails were torn to strips. Ice coated the deck with a pebbled glaze. And the sailors were gone. They were dead, and their names were written on the walls. Who had written those names? And were they written in brown ink, or were they scratched in blood?

The Rabbi began to make a list of the lost people, while Shallum gathered all their belongings. He took the piles of clothes and jewelry and books and ornate utensils and knives and he put these in the hold of one small ship. The Rabbi crawled across the plank, he climbed down onto the ice, and he walked back to the shore. He looked up the beach. He looked down the beach. It was bleak and empty as far as the eye could see. Rabbi Abraham bent down and filled his pockets with pebbles; then he returned to the boats.

Shallum stood and read aloud the list of the dead. For each name, Rabbi Achselrad dropped a pebble into the small ship. The list went on and on. Finally it ended, and the Rabbi recited, from the First Book of Samuel: "If any man has set out to pursue you and if he takes your life, then the Lord your God will wrap your life up with all its treasures and

He will put it with His own treasure, for ever and eternity, amen." Then the two men wrapped the lives of the dead with all their treasures for ever and eternity, and they sealed the hold and they tugged and they pulled and they freed the small boat and they pushed it off, and quickly it was swept far out to sea, in the cold, cold Northern Sea. Shallum and Abraham stood in the wind, and they watched until long after the little ship had drifted out of sight.

Then the two men wandered on. They crossed from ship to ship. They went into empty cabins and cold black holds. They searched the decks; they looked under bundles of frozen canvas sails and ropes. Eventually, they became separated. The dead ships were scattered through the snow, and now the Rabbi found himself near the shore. Shallum was gone. The Rabbi called out, but his voice disappeared in the wind. He stepped down onto the snow, and he walked to the beach. He looked behind him. No one was around. The world was empty: Shallum was gone.

Rabbi Achselrad walked inland. The rocks became boulders. Forests appeared, dark and dim and damp and cold. Rabbi Achselrad walked for thirty days and thirty nights, and he ate seeds and roots and old crumbling nuts. And one day, he came out into a field and the field led to a plain, and there across the frozen white land was a castle surrounded by a high wall.

The Rabbi walked to the front gate, and he stood outside looking in. The castle was far beyond the wall. In the distance, a man came out of the castle. He was young and dressed all in white; he wore a *tallit* and a linen cap. Was it Shallum? No, he was even younger than Shallum: he was a boy, a student. Ah, he was a long-dead pupil of the Rabbi – he was Isaac ben Safir. The boy stood at a distance, and he did not speak. A north wind and a south wind swept around Isaac, who was now only a misty figure. Was Isaac dissolving in the wind? The Rabbi stared and he blinked. The north wind was cold. The south wind was warm – it had scents and light warm hints of spring. The south wind rushed and pushed aside the cold chill of the north. Tiny voices sang in the south wind; they rolled along with the smell of fresh baked bread and gentle wine and smooth, soft satin pillows and with the tiny caresses of his children's hair.

Could this be Paradise, the Great Hereafter? Perhaps it was, but Rabbi Abraham was still alive: the gates were shut, the walls were high, and the Rabbi could not enter. Abraham stood and felt the breeze, and all too soon the scene slipped away. A great distance widened between him and Isaac. The north winds blew harder; they were cold and dark, and the skies became gray, and soon Rabbi Achselrad found that he himself was walking away from the wall and away from the castle and away from the springtime breeze.

Old Rabbi Achselrad walked and he walked; then he came to a mountain. The mountain was small and near and at the same time it was large and far, and in the side of the mountain was a cave covered by a shimmering gray curtain. Behind the curtain was a voice–it was the voice of Shallum ben Mannus, and it called out: "Abraham . . . Abraham . . ." Then it chanted:

Towering cracked rocks
Ice black shales
Craggy stone blocks
In dark night vales–
The old men are gone
Beards curled in vines
Walking before dawn
With deep hooded eyes
Waving oak staves
Chanting low tones
From cold dark caves
Below cellar stones
Stirring north squalls
Through bleak gray skies
Past deep mountain walls
Far from God's eyes.

It was a strange poem–a poem as strange as only wild young Shallum could chant. The Rabbi wanted to reach Shallum. But was this really a curtain in the mountainside? Or was it a heavy rain shower, wet and gray and silver and shimmering? The Rabbi pushed it aside; he lifted the curtain, and he saw that he was standing in front of the cave of the night storm winds. The winds were thick and wild and chill. They whipped out of the opening that the Rabbi had made in the curtain. They blew, and they uprooted trees and they drove the waters over the shore and they broke the ships at sea with a vast and mighty crash.

All the world was swept along. Mountains and clouds rolled and fell and tumbled. The oceans churned. The waves smashed and splattered. Ships were splintered and scattered. Forests shivered, leaves whipped through the brush, branches cracked and fell. Then the bones of old men were blown into a pile; they were caught in a twirling whirlwind and blown far, far away, to a place where timid little angels collected them for graves in some other after-land, a place where men could lie forever under warm skies with gentle rains and mild, mild winds and light-fingered clouds, amen.

The Rabbi held to the edge of the curtain with all his might, but he himself was blown and lifted like a leaf or a feather. He was swept high into the air. His beard rolled and waved and it flapped in the breeze. His long robes curled and tossed and sighed. And tumbling and rolling through the clouds he found himself falling back to Cologne, windswept, windled, worn, and alone in his small back room. And as to Shallum? Why, Shallum was only a vague and misty Northlands memory. Old Rabbi Achselrad lifted his head from the papers on his desk. He found that his hair was rumpled and his shirt was damp and cool, and even on that late summer afternoon it seemed as if a cold damp rush of wind had blown into the old yeshiva from somewhere far, far, far to the North.

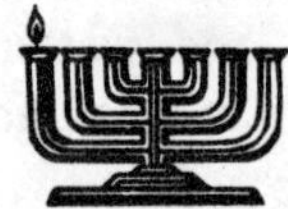

Good evening, Rabbi. Of course, sit here by the stove. The night fire helps me to become sleepy also. You and I probably do not have enough activity during the days to tire our muscles fully. What? Yes, it is true that you stand all day, but do you dance? No, I am not joking with you. Jews are dancers. Why, in the Middle Ages, dancing was the most popular Jewish athletics. Medieval Jews jumped and bounded, they kicked their heels, they leaped and two-stepped and hopped in a circle. The men danced wildly. But they danced apart from the women, who were more restrained: women danced in a line or a circle and followed a leader who had a little pair of cymbals and who invented steps as she went along.

It is a *commandment* to dance; Psalm 149 says:

> Praise the glorious Lord.
>
> Sing to the Lord a fine new song
> Sing His praise to the faithful crowd
> Let all rejoice in their Creator strong
> And send hosannas to the highest cloud.

The needy will laugh with joy aloud
The poor can praise His Name in dance
The weak will sing Him psalms of joy–
For God rains down luxuriance.

And if this is not clear enough, the next psalm says:

Praise the Lord and harmonize:

Praise God with uplifted eyes
Praise Him from the golden sunrise
Praise Him under Heaven's blue skies.

Praise God for His mighty hand-works
Praise Him for His endless wonders
Praise Him for His glorious creatures.

Praise God as the lute and harp sing
Praise Him with the trumpet blaring
Praise Him with bright bells and dancing–

Praise the Lord and harmonize.

No one can resist the commandment to dance, Rabbi. God has built it into our souls. When you dance, you tickle every single place throughout your body. You feel the wind rush and the sea flow and the earth roll. You fly and fall, and every move is fearless and controlled and as joyous as the best of dreams. It is no wonder Jews dance on any happy occasion, not only at weddings and on *Purim*.

At the same time, of course, there must be some decorum, and medieval rabbis, like old Abraham Achselrad, were quite firm: "Men and women shall neither rejoice together nor mourn together" was a common saying in those days. (Even young children did not play in mixed groups: boys played with boys, and girls played with girls.) Of course the restrictions on dance did not apply to husbands and wives, as Isaiah and Gitel certainly understood. Who were Isaiah and Gitel? Well, I will tell you about them–but let me begin backwards, because the first that I heard of Gitel was when she was already a widow:

It was a cool day, an autumn day. Rabbi Abraham was writing his massive tome the *Keter Shem Tov.* He heard a noise and looked up, and he saw one of his congregants standing in the doorway. It was Gitel, a widow, who had once been the wife of Isaiah ben Alexis ha-Kohen.

Gitel was in tears. "Come in," said the Rabbi. Gitel took one step into the room. She wiped her eyes with her hands. Her daughter was being married. Yes, of course the Rabbi knew: he would be marrying the young couple. Well, anyway, Gitel was very poor. She had managed to get free use of the Community House, the "Wedding House," for the meal after the ceremony. Relatives had agreed to contribute food: chicken, honey, noodles, and cakes had all been promised. The daughter was loaned a dress from an aunt. Another aunt was giving the white *sargenes* to cover her clothes, and the bride was using Gitel's old wedding veil. Gitel was worried about all the meals for the succeeding seven days–but most of all Gitel was upset about the decorations. To raise money, she had sold everything fancy that she had. She did not even have candlesticks to place on the main table. How could there be a wedding with no candlesticks? But everyone had given so much. How could she ask for anything more? And now with a completely bare table, with the room in pitiful darkness, would anyone feel up to singing and clapping and dancing? Certainly Gitel would not–she would be humiliated in front of her friends and relatives and new in-laws.

The Rabbi nodded sympathetically. "Now, now," he said, "things will work out." "No," said Gitel, "it is simply terrible." And she began to cry again. Rabbi Abraham patted her on the shoulder. He looked around the room. He gave her a linen towel to dry her eyes. "I will be right back," he said.

Old Achselrad walked into the main prayer hall. At the side of the Holy stone Ark, there was a seven-holdered gold candelabrum, and on either side of the candelabrum were two individual silver candlesticks. The Rabbi picked up the candlesticks, he carried them back into the study room, and he handed them to Gitel.

"Where did these come from?" asked the widow.

"They are gifts of God," said the Rabbi, "as is everything in this world, amen."

And what could Gitel say but "amen" and "thank you"? The

Rabbi smiled, and the widow left the synagogue. Then, before Rabbi Abraham knew it, it was evening. Friday dusk settled on the town. The first three points of starlight glinted in the graying skies. Night had come, and the shammas–Chayim ben Meir–went to look for the candles. But what was this? The two beautiful silver candlesticks were gone!

Chayim hurried into the little back study. "Rabbi, the candlesticks have been stolen!" said the shammas. He stood in the doorway. His heart beat quickly. There was a sinking feeling in his stomach.

The Rabbi looked up. "Be calm, my good Chayim," he said. "This is not a bad event, it is good. No one stole the candlesticks. They have left of their own accord. They have gone quietly and early, to light our way into the World to Come: they have wandered off into the Great Hereafter."

And the Rabbi smiled and Chayim bowed his head. He started to ask something more, but the Rabbi's faraway look swept the words from Chayim's head. And what was Rabbi Abraham thinking of? It was the old widow Gitel. Gitel was a fine woman. She had always tried her best. Her husband had been Isaiah ben Alexis ha-Kohen. He was many years older than Gitel, and now he was dead. Isaiah had been a bookbinder. It was a family craft, a special apprenticed skill, and Isaiah was good at it. He never had much money, but he and his wife managed somehow. Every Thursday, Isaiah gave Gitel enough money to buy the Sabbath staples, *hallah,* fish, meat, wine, and wax candles. On Friday morning, Isaiah piously closed his shop at ten o'clock, and then he went to the synagogue.

The Sabbath was very important to the couple. Each week they would look forward to it. Sunday they remembered the Sabbath of the previous day. Monday and Tuesday were workdays. Wednesday was when they planned for the shopping. Thursday was the shopping day itself. On Friday, Gitel prepared the house and the meal, and Isaiah went to the synagogue, where he sang the Song of Songs and prayed all day until the very end of the evening services. Then Isaiah returned home, and the Sabbath began. Isaiah and Gitel rested and prayed. They wore their best clothes; they ate and they drank and they relaxed. Isaiah returned to the synagogue on the Sabbath day itself, he studied the Law, and he felt at peace and very glad. This remained their custom until finally Isaiah began to get old and weak.

Isaiah no longer had the energy to work as he did before. In fact, binding one book might take him four days or even a week. He could hardly earn any money at all. When Thursday arrived, Gitel could no longer afford to make all her traditional Sabbath purchases – for most weeks there was only *hallah* and a little wine. Still, at ten o'clock on Friday morning, Isaiah always closed his shop, and he walked slowly and shakily to the House of Study to begin his Sabbath prayers.

It was the late autumn of his life, and one Thursday morning Isaiah found that he did not have even a single coin to give to his wife. He could not beg for money. Never in his life had Isaiah accepted charity, and he would not begin now. Isaiah was sad; it seemed that the Almighty beneficent Lord was busy elsewhere that particular week. Isaiah sighed and he shook his head. He said a few quiet words to himself, and he accepted that this was just the way it must be, amen.

"Listen, Gitel," said Isaiah, "there is an old saying: 'When the sun rises, then the fever will disappear.' There will always be a new day, and the new dawn will bring hope and healing and health."

It was Friday morning. Before he left home, Isaiah told his wife, "I plan to come home tonight later than usual from the synagogue." Isaiah ben Alexis ha-Kohen made up his mind to fast through the Sabbath. "If I cannot eat," he thought, "it will be easier if I come home late; I will take the opportunity to purify my thoughts and my soul." But how about Gitel? "Oh, I will fast too," she said quickly. Isaiah shook his head, and he left home with a tear in the corner of his eye.

Gitel went around the house, cleaning for the Sabbath. She had no meal to prepare, so she wiped and she washed every single thing, the edges of the windows, the chairs, under the stove. Then, in a back cupboard, she found a jacket in the woodbox. "Well, well," she thought, "I had forgotten all about this old coat." The jacket was dusty, but once it had been a fine embroidered coat with silver buttons overlaid with gold. She took it out of the box and she washed it. "Really, it is quite handsome," she thought. "How long it has been since Isaiah has worn it!" Gitel looked closely at the buttons. They had metal loops of silver, each with a disk of gold as big as your thumbnail. "Isaiah is an old man – he will never wear this again," thought Gitel. Then she thought: "I can sell this jacket; then we will have a bit of Sabbath money after all."

It was the last day of September, and in the Gentile quarters this was the feast day of Saint Jerome (who had first translated the Bible into Latin for the Roman Catholic Church seven hundred years earlier). The marketplaces were full of milling people. Booths sold food and clothes and utensils. People laughed and drank and roamed about. Gitel found a loud merchant who paid her three gold coins for the jacket; then Gitel hurried back to the Jewish Quarter. She bought candles, *hallah,* wine, fish, and meat, and, fine woman that she was, she put the remaining money into the synagogue poor box. Gitel hurried home to prepare the dinner.

It was quite late when Isaiah finally shuffled home from the synagogue. The weather was cool. He held his coat tightly about him. But what was this? Candles were burning in his house. Isaiah ben Alexis thought sadly, "Ah, my poor wife could not keep from telling her troubles to the neighbors. Now we are the objects of pity and charity." He shook his head.

In came old Isaiah, walking out of the cold. Everything was warm and Sabbath bright. The table was sparkling and filled with food. There was wine for the benediction, and there were *hallah* and meat and cakes. The large saltcellar was in its place of honor in the center of the table. Isaiah looked about him. He patted his wife's hand. It was the Sabbath.

Gitel saw that Isaiah was sad. After the wine blessing, Gitel said, "Listen, husband–now do not interrupt me–I did not have to beg for money, and I certainly did not steal. Do you remember how you once had an old embroidered jacket, the one with the silver and gold buttons? Well, I found it after you left for the synagogue this morning. I washed it and I sold it. I hope you do not mind. Undoubtedly God decided to give us a good Sabbath after all."

Isaiah felt a shiver and a tingle. He felt warm and cool at once, and he was very happy. There was even a tear in his eye. "I do not know what to say," he sighed, and he sat back in his chair.

Gitel smiled. Then Isaiah smiled too and he stood up and smoothed out his white *tallit,* which he always wore for the Sabbath meal. Isaiah looked down at his embroidered *tallit;* gently he rubbed his fingers along the tiny white and blue stitches that his mother had put on the edges, long, long ago. And Isaiah thought of the old embroidered jacket–he could still picture it clearly. He remembered the section of the Second Book of Samuel where it says: "David, wearing his embroidered priest's jacket, danced without restraint before the Lord."

Isaiah felt happy, and for a moment he felt young again. He wanted to jump and to leap. He took his wife by the hand and they began to dance. Then, although they were alone, Gitel felt shy. "Sit down, Isaiah," she said, laughing. Isaiah ben Alexis smiled and patted her hand. After they had finished the soup, Isaiah stood and bowed and took Gitel by the hand. They danced and danced, and after the sweet *tzimmes,* the dessert, they danced for yet a third time.

And when the old man danced, Rabbi, then I am sure that all the angels in Heaven danced too, jumping and swooping and lightly rolling on the celestial breezes and getting caught in the wispy tangles of the beard of the great Lord God Almighty. And He Himself smiled His silvery radiant nighttime smile, and all the clouds and hills and rivers, all the asphodels, bellwind, and sunweed, all the plants and animals and trees smiled back–even those who were already fast asleep–they smiled deep in their own warm, peaceful, Sabbath sleep.

Good evening. Yes, Rabbi, I know how hard it is to sleep on the night of a bright half-moon. Put your feet up on the side bench. I will open the stove door and push the coals back; the white glow will wash away all the cares from your hard day.

No, I have nothing to offer you to drink, my old friend and cross-patch. Oh, I am just teasing. Did you ever hear the old rhyme:

Cross-patch, draw the latch,
Sit by the fire and spin;
Take a cup and drink it up–
Then call your neighbors in.

What? No, I guess it just slipped into my mind. Those childhood chants are rooted very deeply; perhaps you remember:

Oats, peas, beans, and barley grow;
Oats, peas, beans, and barley grow–
Not you nor I nor anyone know
How oats, peas, beans, and barley grow.

Here the farmer sows his seed
And there he stands to take his ease;
He stamps his foot and claps his hands
And turns around to view his lands.

These childhood rhymes are always rolling around in my head, even more nowadays than before. Who knows when or where or how I first heard them? Was it from my grandmother or my parents or from other children? In any case it was a long, long time ago; it was when the world was large and magical and young and when the autumn scents could fill you up and roll you over and float you away. It was a time when the breezes were golden and cool and warm all at once and when the colors of the flowers and the sky were the same and when the fall grasses were as tall as your waist. Ah, well. . . .

What? A story from me? Rabbi, all I know are the children's tales, the grandmother fables. You need something new and fresh to keep your mind keen. Otherwise you will become an old man like me, and you will find yourself constantly musing and dozing and nodding off in front of the stove.

An old man?! What do you mean you are already an old man? Do you really think that sixty years is old? Why, you are still a child. When you reach eighty, *then* you will be old. You doubt that you will live to see eighty years? If so, Rabbi, then you will never grow old. All right, all right. I know no special stories, but those children's rhymes remind me of gardens, and gardens make me think of Moisin, a gardener in old Cologne.

You see, once upon a time, just to the west of Cologne on the dark River Rhine, there lived an old man, a farmer, a lover of wildflowers, and an amateur scholar named Moisin ben Joshua ha-Levi. In his spare time, Moisin wrote poetry. For example, he wrote:

In childhood what a rich dessert
Were the last warm days of fall–
Some fields were bare, just empty dirt,
Others were left natural.

Wheat was cut, and summer leaves
Were scattered by the plougher
With old dried stalks, broken sheaves,
And a melon's orange flower.

Cantaloupe, pepper, pumpkin
Roundly lay in bumpy rows
With long striped squashes drinking in
The earth's fall juice before the snows.

And tall yellow sunflowers,
A thousand golden moons
Proudly standing, waving towers
In autumn's sunbright noons.

An endless world abuzz, it shimmers
With ants and bees and trees
With gold green grasshoppers
And with butterflies and chicories.

Windblown bees in the asphodels,
Mice skittering through the grassy maze–
And all the good dry field smells
Tingling like the brightest days.

Rolling fields and endless hills,
The sky a forever dome–
Ah, people are just small frills
In such a rich thick spacious home:

Only our Almighty God,
Glory pouring through the skies,
Is vast enough and wide and broad
To match this wondrous world in size.

Now, Rabbi, tell me the truth: is this not the most beautiful of poems?

In any case, my friend, as befalls us all, this wonderful literary gardening farmer died one day, one cool, clear, autumn day. Two days earlier, he had sat down next to his wife. The old farmer was holy and pious and somewhat visionary. He sat with his eyes closed for many minutes, quietly holding his wife's hand. Then he said to her, "Sherah, I am going to die, my dear."

Sherah opened wide her eyes and she began to say something, but Moisin interrupted: "Now, now, my good wife, listen a moment. I have seen in a dream that I will die very soon. It will be a quiet, calm death, and I have no fear.

"Something else was revealed to me: my body will remain perfectly preserved, even long after my death, if only you wrap me in my prayer shawl and sprinkle it with spices. So here are your instructions, my dear: Please put me in the loft. Then leave the door closed. But you may consult me on any important matters and I will always answer you as best I can."

Such a strange speech! As you might imagine, Sherah sat stock-still in her chair. She was in shock. She looked at her hands; she did not dare to look at Moisin. "I cannot believe this," she said finally. "Please tell me that you are not really dying."

"I am afraid that it is true."

Tears were in Sherah's eyes. "But we are still young, Moisin."

"We are not so young, my love," he said. "But listen, dear, you know how we used to have spring columbines in the garden?"

"Yes."

"They were white and blue and delicate and happy. I loved those flowers."

Sherah said nothing.

"And what happened to them?" continued Moisin. "We did not watch them closely. After a few years, they simply slipped away: the columbines left the garden quietly when we were not looking. . . ." Moisin paused. "That happens to life. It just slips quietly away when you are not looking."

Then, two days later, Moisin ben Joshua died peacefully in his sleep, and his soul slipped quietly away when no one was looking. Sherah passed seven long and sad days of private mourning. She tore a hem on her black dress. She wore no shoes, she ate and drank little, she sat in the dark, and she said nothing.

No one came to join the mourning, for no one knew that Moisin had died. Sherah and Moisin lived far in the country. No neighbors visited, Sherah had no friends, and she was all alone. Sherah followed her husband's instructions: at week's end, she carefully carried her husband's body to the loft, where she wrapped him in his beautiful white *tallit* with the embroidered trim; then she sprinkled spices on his old body, and she left him on a cot.

Sherah knew that one month was the longest time allowed for

mourning, and after three more weeks she finally left her house. Her supplies had dwindled. She walked all morning until she reached the market, she shopped quietly, and in response to questions, she said, "Oh, Moisin had to go away on family business. I do not know all the details."

Sherah's house was in a small valley between two tall hills. She never saw her neighbors. The road ran behind some trees by her house, passersby were rare, and she was alone all the time. Now Sherah farmed and gardened by herself. She hardly spoke when she came to town to shop. When people asked about her husband, Sherah would say only: "Yes, Moisin is still away." Sherah lived in silence and she had all the time in the world to think and to daydream. Had she done the right thing? What would God say? Sherah did not know. There was no one to ask, and she stayed away from the loft.

One day, the rains came and did not let up. The chickens were soaked and bedraggled and unhappy. All the crops seemed drowned. Silently, Sherah watched the water wash away young plants. After the steady downpour ended and the weather turned cloudy and damp and gray, she did not know what to do. Should she try and replant the tangled green masses? Should she reseed the garden? Should she just give up for the year?

In despair, Sherah went up to the loft. She listened at the closed door. There was absolute silence. Timidly, she said, "Moisin. Moisin, can you hear me?"

There was no answer.

"Moisin," she repeated softly, "what should I do now? How can I save the garden?"

The wind blew outside. After a moment, a dry whisper slipped under the door. "Sherah, my love," it said, "dig new ruts and drain the water from the garden. Prop up the remaining plants as best you can. Then sprinkle all of next year's seed in the bare patches."

Then there was silence. After a few moments, Sherah went back downstairs. She followed the directions, and the garden prospered. Now that she had begun, Sherah took to consulting her departed husband more often. She asked farming questions. She asked financial questions. She told him stories when she was lonely. Most often there was just a silence, but sometimes she heard the quiet dry whisper: Moisin was listening and he was keeping his promise.

This went on for many years. One day, a distant cousin of Moisin came to Sherah. "May I stay the night?" he asked. "Certainly," said Sherah. "And where is Moisin today?" he asked. "Moisin has gone on a long journey," said Sherah, "perhaps as far as the Holy Lands." The cousin raised his eyebrows. Moisin had never been a traveler. He had always loved gardening and farming. Moisin had been a man tied to his land and his plants. Sherah shrugged her shoulders. "All men change," she said. "Suddenly the wanderlust came over Moisin." The relative said nothing, but when he returned to Cologne he told the curious story of Moisin's abrupt change of character.

Eventually, word reached Rabbi Abraham. Old Achselrad had known Moisin. Moisin ben Joshua was a man of the land. Moisin was a man who was never happier than during the harvesting festivals of *Shavuot* and *Sukkot.* Moisin was a man who often would quote God's instructions to the dispersed Jews (from the Book of Jeremiah): "Your exile will be long. Therefore, build houses and live in them, and then, farm: plant gardens, and harvest and eat the produce." Old Achselrad, too, found it strange that this devoted gardener should suddenly up and leave his farm.

Then one day, old Rabbi Abraham was sitting at his desk. He had been trying to write in his book of mystic lore, the *Keter Shem Tov.* But the Rabbi's pen did not want to form the letters, and his mind kept rolling around and around, repeating little childhood rhymes of old Hebrew words. At first, he hardly noticed when a slight breeze slipped into the back room and riffled the pages in the Holy Scriptures which lay open before him. The Rabbi looked down. There, he saw the verses of God's covenant with the Patriarch Abraham, from those first ancient years when he was still named Abram. On the evening of that distant day–at the time of the Book of Genesis–the Almighty Lord had said:

> And you, good Abram, shall join your fathers in peace and shall be buried on your own land in a good old age, and, later, the fourth generation of your descendants shall return here and shall farm in peace.

Suddenly Rabbi Achselrad seemed to see a woman. He blinked and he winked, and he stared and stared. Was it Sherah, the widow of the old farmer Moisin ben Joshua? The Rabbi shook his head gently and the vision passed, but he knew that he must send for the widow Sherah – and so he did.

In three days' time, Sherah, the widow of Moisin ben Joshua ha-Levi, came timidly into the synagogue of Cologne. Rabbi Abraham looked at the woman. Then he said quietly, "There is something you must tell." Sherah looked down. She tapped her foot. She cleared her throat. Rabbi Abraham waited patiently. But Sherah said nothing – her mouth was dry; she felt weak.

"Come, come, my good woman," said the Rabbi. "It is time to speak. Remember: God knows everything already."

Sherah nodded and rubbed her hands. Still she could say nothing. The Rabbi sat quietly. One minute passed; then two minutes came, and two minutes went. Eventually, Sherah began to talk, hoarsely and slowly, and soon she finished, loudly and quickly, and when she was done, she had told the Rabbi the whole story from its very beginning to its very end.

Quietly, the Rabbi said, "I am afraid that this is not the Jewish way, Sherah. We must bury your husband."

"Can we at least bury him on the land that he loved so much?" asked Sherah.

"That we certainly can," said old Achselrad.

Together, the Rabbi and the woman went back to the farm, and they got the body in order to bury it. They washed and dried the old man in lukewarm salt water, poured lightly through a sheet. Sherah combed old Moisin's hair one last time. And Abraham Achselrad said (from the Book of Ezekiel):

> I, the Lord your God, will gather you from every land and bring you back to your own soil. I will sprinkle clean water over you, and you shall be forever cleansed from all taints and ills and sins, amen.

Then Sherah and the Rabbi dressed the body in Sabbath robes and covered it again with spices. They put Moisin in a coffin of unplaned wood, laying the old body on his prayer shawl. Gently, they folded his limbs into the position of an unborn child so that someday he might roll smoothly into the Holy Land beyond the grave. A small pebble was put under Moisin's chin, a tiny rock from his beloved garden.

As they worked, Sherah thought, "How curious – the body seems to cast no shadow"–but the sky was cloudy and the day was gray, and Sherah could not be certain. Finally, Sherah and the Rabbi closed the coffin. Later that afternoon, the shammas arrived to help. The Rabbi, the shammas, and Sherah carried the coffin out to the garden and they buried old Moisin at the edge of his land, under a set of fine old oak trees. Rabbi Abraham bowed his head and he repeated from the Book of Jeremiah: "May his soul become like a watered garden, and may he never want again, amen."

Sherah went to visit her husband's grave at least once a week, but she never heard Moisin's voice again. In the spring, wildflowers grew over the grave and wild columbines appeared. Bushes and berries flourished there, and birds and animals came–and in that spot there was a garden, just as we might remember from our childhood days, where the green grass grew all around, all around, where the green grass grew all around.

"Undoubtedly you can recognize it even today," said my grandmother, who told me this story. She looked off, somewhere far, far away. "Are the oak trees still there behind the house?" she asked herself quietly. She stopped, she looked at me, then she smiled and said, "I do not know about the trees or the grave marker, my golden little boy. I only know that as you walk by that spot suddenly there is the scent of a day when you were young and wild and green and when the world was a bold, bold place, bigger than big and wider than wide and more wonderful than your little bursting self could ever hope to imagine outside a farmland summertime dream."

Good evening, Rabbi. No sleep for the weary? Well, if you are cold, then sit down here on the bench and I will stoke up the oven. Yes, yes, I will be happy to tell you a story, although really I think we only talk to ourselves. I suppose I will tell *myself* a story and, of course, you are most welcome to listen in.

What is that? I am an old man, my friend, so I have told you the simple truth: we talk only to ourselves; we hardly hear what others actually say. In fact, we live entirely in our own worlds. But this is good–it is what the Almighty Lord God intended, amen.

On occasion, I have heard other people say the same thing, but more often everyone pretends otherwise. We pretend, even to ourselves, that we are listening closely to others or that we are being listened to. Each of our lives is difficult, and I suspect that we do not listen to others because our souls are not strong enough to take on the burdens of other people along with our own burdens. Of course, the sages remind us that we are stronger on the Sabbath. We receive an extra soul on the Sabbath. Perhaps we also listen to others more empathetically on the Sabbath. What do you think, Rabbi?

The old sages were speaking figuratively? They were being symbolic? I do not think so, my friend. I have actually felt this extra soul. There is no question that I am revived each Friday night, when a second soul arrives on loan for the restful holy Sabbath. Do *you* not feel invigorated during the Sabbath? And then are you not weak when the Sabbath departs, whisking away with her the additional soul? Why else do we need to take a whiff of the spice box–the *Besamim Buchse*–at the *Havdalah* ceremony? The three stars appear in the night sky. Loath to say farewell to the wonderful Sabbath, the *hazan* stretches out the first words of the evening prayer: *Vehu rahum.* But the second soul already has slipped away into the night. So in the *Havdalah* ceremony that follows we each take a sniff from the spice box–this bolsters our remaining spirit and it helps to sustain us through the trials of the next week.

My grandmother told me that it was Ephraim the Old of Regensburg who first instituted the spice-box ceremony. In those days, spices were rare. They were expensive and coveted, and they were stored in very fancy containers. Usually the spice boxes were shaped like miniature castles, with turrets and battlements and towers because, of course, God Himself is a Tower of Strength and Deliverance. As it is said in the Second Book of Samuel:

> The Lord is my great champion,
>   My fortress and my stronghold,
> The ancient All-protective One
>   Who came down to us from days of old–
> Yes, God is my shield and garrison,
>   He is my mountain tower bold.

In any case, it was Ephraim of Regensburg who made spices a formal part of the Sabbath ceremony. Ephraim the Old lived during the Middle Ages, in the days of Rabbi Achselrad. Rabbi Ephraim rarely left his hometown, but he wrote much and corresponded continually. My grandmother reported to me about one of his letters to Rabbi Abraham ben Alexander, Achselrad of Cologne.

Once upon a time, said my grandmother to me, in the town of Cologne on the Rhine, there lived a pious and mystic rabbi named Abraham ben Alexander. (What? Please be patient, Rabbi. I am just setting the stage for the story of Rabbi Ephraim.) It was late on a cool autumn night in the month of *Tishri.* The wind blew a few drops of rain against the walls outside. Rabbi Abraham paced up and down in the main prayer hall. He walked barefoot. He was deep in thought. And why was the old Rabbi walking, and why was he thinking? He had had a vision. Old Achselrad had seen the form of a stranger, thin and bearded, old and frail, but strong of will. Rabbi Abraham did not know what to make of this sight. He stroked his beard, and he paced back and forth and back and forth.

After a few moments, a boy appeared in the doorway. Rabbi Abraham looked up. "Rabbi," said the young man, "I have a letter for you. It is from Regensburg."

Rabbi Abraham took the packet. Was it from his old friend Petahiah ben Jacob? No – it was from Rabbi Ephraim, that is, Ephraim ben Isaac. Rabbi Abraham opened wide his eyes. He had never met Ephraim the Old, and he had never corresponded with him. Rabbi Abraham did not even know that Rabbi Ephraim was still alive, but he certainly knew of the famed Rabbi by reputation.

You see, in those years there resided and taught in Regensburg a scholar named Ephraim ben Isaac, known as Ephraim the Old and also called Ephraim the Great. He had spent his early days in France, but after studying in Regensburg he remained there, and gradually he established himself as the respected but crotchety old man of the Regensburg Jewish community.

Let me tell you a bit about the Regensburg of those days. Regensburg was one of the centers of Judaism in northern Europe. Regensburg is in Bavaria, and Bavaria had had Jewish enclaves for centuries. Jews farmed large tracts of land there, and Jewish merchants of Regensburg were middlemen in the trade between the eastern and the western countries of the civilized world.

Regensburg itself is on the right bank of the River Danube. In the Middle Ages, it was the residential city of Bavarian kings and princes and dukes. Initially, it was a Celtic settlement named Radespona; in Latin, this became Ratisbon. In the Dark Ages, Ratisbon was a Christian center: St. Emmeran founded an abbey there in the seventh century, St. Boniface established a bishopric in Ratisbon during the next century, and the famed Old Cathedral of Regensburg was built in the eighth century.

Regensburg's Jews were organizers. There was nothing they

enjoyed more than being in constant motion, buying and selling, moving and juggling, balancing and pushing and pulling. They exported knives, swords, saddles, textiles, wines, and wooden utensils. And as for imports? In Regensburg it was mainly spices, silks, and fancy textiles. In the twelfth century the Jews of Regensburg finally were granted formal trade rights (the privilege to import and export "goods of every kind in the old manner, especially gold, silver, and other metals") by Emperor Frederick I. Also, there was Jewish banking. What better to do with money than to have it earn more money for you? Certainly you could not eat it. So, money went from the Jewish community to Gentile businessmen and noblemen, to local Guilds, and as loans to the clergy near and far. Why, in the year 4867 (the Christian year 1107), the Jews of Regensburg even loaned five hundred silver marks to the Archbishop of Prague.

The Juden Viertels of Regensburg was protected physically: it was tucked away in a secluded quarter of the city. Legally, the Jews were independent, and the Jewish Court decisions were accepted by the other city courts. The Regensburg Jews were responsible for defending their corner of the city (the West Gate) and they set up their own local guard. Jews also decided how to divide their tax burden. However, the Jews of Regensburg, like most European Jews, did not own the land on which they lived. Jews were always secondary citizens, residing everywhere at the pleasure of kings, dukes, and other Gentile landowners.

It was here, deep in the Juden Viertels of Regensburg, on the western edge of the city, that Ephraim the Old lived and worked and eventually died. By the time of Abraham Achselrad, Ephraim was already the author of a set of *Tosafot,* commentaries on several talmudical treatises; in addition, he had written poetry and hymns (four *Zulat,* a *Meorah,* an *Ahavah,* and eighteen *Selihot*). Old Rabbi Ephraim had strong opinions, and he said them loudly. Some considered him to be arrogant and ornery. He criticized everyone who opposed his own ideas—and his views often differed from orthodoxy. For example, he permitted the synagogue to be decorated with paintings of animals (in opposition to the decision by a respected rabbi from Mainz). And Rabbi Ephraim made the startling declaration that Jews could hunt with hounds and with falcons, as long as no animals were mistreated.

Once he had settled in Regensburg, Rabbi Ephraim never left. He never traveled. However his fame spread–and this was as much for spices as for anything else. It was Rabbi Ephraim who introduced the spice box–the *Besamim Buchse*–for the *Havdalah* prayers. Rabbi Ephraim proclaimed: "The *Havdalah* closes the restful Sabbath. At that time, a Jew must be revived and reinvigorated in order to work through the hectic week ahead; his own natural soul must be strengthened by spices at the end of the Sabbath." And so it came to pass ever after.

This was the Regensburg rabbi who wrote to Abraham ben Alexander of Cologne–and, on that summer evening long ago, Rabbi Abraham stood and wondered at the curious letter in his hand.

"My esteemed colleague,
Abraham, the son of Alexander,
Of the city of Cologne–

"I send you my fondest greetings from our congregation here in Regensburg. We are a quiet town, and often we look to the great centers of Jewish learning, cities such as Cologne, for inspiration. I write to you because I hear strange rumors from Cologne. Out of respect, I have taken the time to set down a few words–thoughts of mine, which I hope that you will not take amiss.

"Let me begin straightaway. I understand, good Rabbi, that you give out amulets rather freely. I know that these items are prized by the uninformed, but I must say that I discourage their use here. I tell my congregants: 'If someone offers you an amulet, if someone tells you that it will help in curing disease, in acquiring favors, or in becoming rich, then do not accept it and do not believe them. Instead, place your trust wholly and directly in the great Lord God, blessed be He, amen.'

"And why is this? Why avoid amulets? Amulets, invocations, and enchantments only serve to provoke demons. In fact, these artificial and man-made contrivances are idols themselves. They hold no wisdom. They shorten one's life. They are contrary to God. Consider this: Amulets aspire to invoke angels. Now, good Abraham, you know that the names of angels are not mentioned in the Holy Scriptures. This is to prevent men from attempting to influence the holy Host. God does not wish us to write charms filled with all manner of angels' names. Whoever deals in such witchcraft will meet with inevitable disaster. Even verbally, one should not invoke an angel by name.

(Likewise, I remind my congregants not to fall into such heathen practices as speaking rhymes when starting a journey or when praying for a cure.) No, my friend, pray directly to the good Lord God, blessed be He: it is He Who will guard you from evil, amen.

"As you well know, Rabbi Abraham, God will always see you through any difficulty. He will watch over you. He will guide you. When necessary, He will even communicate with you directly through dreams: nowadays the voice of God does not come from a burning bush–it comes in the still hours of the night, for God is the Master of Dreams. You may have heard a recent instance of the Almighty Omniscient One's shepherding here in Regensburg. One day, after much study and deliberation, it seemed to me appropriate to rule that the sturgeon is a *kosher* fish. Ah, good Abraham, we mortals can delude ourselves. Fortunately, the all-seeing Lord keeps us on the straight and narrow path of His truths. In a dream that very night, the good Lord God (blessed be He) made it clear to me that I had made a mistake. The sturgeon is *not* kosher. The next day I humbly announced my error to the congregation, and I published a formal statement to that effect. So–trust in God's direct Word, not in amulets.

"Well, enough about amulets. I am certain that this is only a temporary backsliding in the ever-forward march of the righteous Jews of Cologne. The second matter I would mention is *candles.* Yes, my friend, I am writing about candles. Presently, it is the morning, so it is an appropriate time to tell you my thoughts about morning candles in the synagogue. Recently I have heard that you suggested it is unnecessary to light candles on bright mornings. Is it possible that you have said one might omit lighting them in the synagogue even on holy days? I am certain your words must have been twisted by the time that they traveled all the way to Regensburg.

"Candlelight during the day is not a case of 'carrying water to the river'–the synagogue candles are neither superfluous nor useless. In a practical sense, candles add to the indoor light even during the day. More importantly, however, candles increase both the joy and the solemnity of all occasions. Light banishes evil from dark places, and *extra* light banishes extra evil, the long grim edges and the wisps and tendrils of demons which lurk forever in corners and in shadows.

"Candles are an ancient gift of God: Moses built the gold candelabrum for the Holy Tabernacle. Solomon set ten golden candlesticks in his Great Temple, and after the Babylonian captivity, the golden candlestick was again placed in the Temple. In the Great Temple, candles and lamps were lit well before the beginning of the night; this glorified the holy sanctuary. And then, of course, there are the lights of *Hanukah*–these have always been lit before the evening falls.

"To those who continue to question me, I compare these two passages of the Holy Scriptures. First, there is the last verse from Psalm 97":

> A glittering harvest of white holy light
> Will come to those who act aright–
> So, you who are good Israelites
> Rejoice in the Lord, our God of might,
> Praise His Name through the holy night
> And keep forever His paths in sight.

"Second, there is this passage from the Book of Jeremiah":

> Because you have not listened to My words, I will silence all sounds of joy and gladness, all voices of mirth, the voices of the bridegroom and the bride, and the sound of the handmill and the millstones, and I will darken the day and I will quench the light of every lamp.

"Clearly, Rabbi, light is for joy and sacred celebration, whereas darkness is for punishment.

"In any case, my friend, I do not mean to go on and on at long lengths about this matter. Although I must speak my mind, I do so only out of affection for my brother Jews. I wish you health and peace. I hope for long and glorious days for you, your learning, your house, and all your followers. May the great and beneficent Lord God bless you all, amen.

"And now, Rabbi Abraham, I close my letter to you by asking an unusual favor: Please do not reply to me. Perhaps this will seem a strange request, so I will tell you exactly why I have asked it. I am an old man–rather thin and frail–and currently I live mostly in my revery. Except on the wondrous invigorating Sabbath, it is just me and my one worn old soul to cope with the long days and the many trials of my life here in Regensburg. But now I sit back, my friend. I imagine you in your holy study reading this letter. You are calm and strong and at ease. You smile and nod as you read. Times are difficult here, and I would like with all my heart to imagine them better elsewhere. If I do not hear from you, Rabbi Abraham, then I can picture you always as I wish–and I will know as sure as the sun will rise tomorrow that somewhere there always is a fine, bright, and wondrous dawn.

"With deep respect,
Ephraim, the son of Isaac,
Of the city of Regensburg"

Good evening, Rabbi. Are you having difficulty sleeping? Put your feet up on the side bench; I will open the stove door. Let me push the coals back so that the white glow can wash away all the cares of your hard day.

I heard your final prayers tonight, and there is no use denying it—you are overworked. Even an old shammas like me can tell. How long have you been a rabbi? More than thirty years? That is many tiring days and many long nights. Now you are finally in the Era of Understanding in your life, the time when you "calmly meet your old age," as the famous talmudic chronology of Judah, the son of Tema, would say. Each era—each phase of life—has its natural activities, its own joys, and its special comforts. And of course each phase has its own unique problems.

What? Yes, I have heard that also: some say that a man's life is divided into four phases—

Twenty years a-growing
Twenty years in blossom
Twenty years a-stooping
And twenty years declining.

But I do not think that is the Jewish way. We hardly see the stooping and the declining in those last graying years. Instead, Jews see the calming, the reflecting, the looking inward, backward, and Heavenward.

And I can tell you this, Rabbi: in our later golden years, there are no more dramas to play out. Little things such as leaves and children and a light meal and a spring breeze become the true substances of life. That crack over there, for instance–yes, the one at the edge of the door. It is something to admire, at least to an old man like me. No, I am quite serious, my friend. The crack is shaped like a mountain with a stream running down and with glens and gorges–now, now, Rabbi, do not laugh. I love to look at that crack. I muse and float off toward some distant cool land where . . . well, enough of my rambling; I am just talking aimlessly, drifting along with no real story in mind.

What? All right, Rabbi, it is true. I confess that I am never *completely* storyless. But that is not my doing: it is by the good graces of my grandmother (may God grant her every wish in the Great Hereafter, amen). In the late phases of her long life, she filled my head with endless tales. Once she even told me a tale about life's phases. It was the story of Shneior ben Meyer ha-Levi, a pious man who lived in those long-ago days of medieval Germany when Jews were bright sparks in the dark, dark ages of Europe.

Shneior, said my grandmother, began his life as a very poor man, and although he ended his life happy, he was still poor. "It is my one regret that I am not wealthy," he said in his old age to a friend. Now this was a great surprise–Shneior had never seemed to want fancy things. Shneior's friend opened wide his eyes, he raised his eyebrows, and he said, "Shneior, I never imagined that you wanted lots of money."

"Listen, Joseph," answered Shneior, "if I had enough money, then I would have a large crown made for my wife. It would be gold and silver; it would have rubies and diamonds. Of course, she would probably not wear it. But there is nothing I could ever do to repay her sufficiently for her support."

Well, Rabbi, this, then, is their story, but it is not very dramatic.

It begins with a young woman, Timna, the daughter of Kalba ben Urshraga, who was one of the richest men in town. It begins also with our Shneior. Shneior's father was long dead, and Shneior made a meager living as a ragpicker. Who knows how Timna met Shneior? And who can say how they began to talk with each other? Only the good Lord God recalls the answer now, and He is smiling silently. Nonetheless, we *can* say that somehow the rich girl fell in love with the young ragpicker, and on his promise to study and become a scholar if ever he had the opportunity, they secretly became engaged.

"What?!" shouted Kalba when he discovered the engagement. "You are throwing away your life! I absolutely forbid it!"

Timna would not listen. She was young and in love. It is in youth that our dreams glow most brightly, and it is in youth that we have the strength to live those dreams. Although the Holy Scripture reminds us: "You shall stand and respect the elderly, give honor to gray hairs, defer to the aged, and revere your God," this is not a statement for children. What child can temper his glowing dreams? What child can ignore the brilliant crisp colors of his magical childhood world? In fact, this is why the Almighty Lord God put children and puppies on this earth in the first place: it is to remind us of the vivid, magical, larger-than-life edges of the world. So eventually Kalba's warnings and his threats and his dismal prophecies only drove his daughter from their home. Timna and Shneior were quietly married, and Timna moved into the small hovel where Shneior lived with his mother.

Shneior and Timna were happy, but they had very little food and money. The neighbors tried to help. They brought Timna their sewing and mending and cleaning rather than take it elsewhere, and Timna worked hard. She took in washing. She ran errands. She watched children and she delivered messages, and never once did she complain. Shneior's mother was small and old and frail, and she could contribute nothing to the household. The threesome never had enough money, and years slipped by in poverty. Shneior got older and older. His cheeks wrinkled, his hands became calloused, and white hairs were sprinkled through his beard. Shneior never had the time or the extra energy to become the scholar he had dreamt of when he was young.

One day, Timna said, "Shneior, life is moving along. Will we ever do all that we had dreamt? We cannot put things off forever, or they will have to be completed in the Great Hereafter. Why not spend some time studying now?"

"Ah, Timna," said Shneior sadly, "I would like to study. But how can I do that? Both of our heads will turn completely gray before I ever become a scholar. I am forty years old, and I am just learning to read Hebrew. I will never make any real progress."

"You are still young," said Timna.

"I am old," said Shneior. "In fact, now I am *too* old."

"No, my dear, you are not old," answered his wife. "The Talmud says that an old man is someone who has learned things, someone who has studied. Even *I* know this from the Talmud: 'Who truly deserves to be called "the Old"–that is, *ha-Zaken?* Only he who has studied and acquired the Torah.' "

Timna put on a coat. "Listen, husband," she said, "come with me." And she led him out of the house and into the town square, where they stopped beside a water well. The edge of the well was built of a large stone with a deep, smooth groove, and the well rope slid through this groove as people lifted the bucket up and down. The groove was green with tiny flecks of sparkling white, and the groove fit the rope perfectly. Timna slid her finger up and down the rock. It was as hard as polished metal, and it was cool and even. "Look at the hole in this rock," said Timna. "Can you imagine the strength of the person who drilled it?"

"No," said Shneior, "I have never met him. He must have lived here before my time."

"Do not be foolish, Shneior," said his wife. "The hole is caused by the rope. As it slides down into the well, it cuts the stone. I do not know how many years it took, but given enough time, the rope has sculpted the stone."

"Of course, of course. I see your point," said Shneior. "If such a soft material can cut stone, then the words of God's Law–which are as hard as the hardest iron–will certainly make a lasting imprint on my heart, if given sufficient time."

"Exactly," said Timna. "If you take the time, then you are certain to learn."

The couple returned home, and Shneior vowed to spend half of each day studying. So, every day Shneior got up early and went to the yeshiva. He prayed and afterwards he listened to the men talking. Then he went out and gathered rags. Shneior brought the rags home to his wife and mother, who cleaned them and repaired them for sale, and who also sewed them into clothing for themselves. Shneior even burned old rags as fuel in the winter because he could not afford wood.

(This made so much smoke that the neighbors complained. But Shneior said, "If you think that the smoke is bad in *your* house, then you should see ours. But, as the Book of Proverbs says: 'Even bitter food tastes sweet to a man who has had nothing to eat.' Besides, I cannot do any better and also study.")

In the late afternoons, Shneior would return to the yeshiva. He listened to the scholars arguing and lecturing. He tried his hand at reading and discussing. He did not mind when the others laughed or criticized. In the winter as he walked home late at night, he sometimes stood outside in the cold and looked at the snow piled frozen on the rooftops. And even in the bitter weather with the flakes swirling around him, he would feel the great words of the sages falling like a blizzard from Heaven, and he would smile and feel overwhelmed; then he would shiver with joy and not with coldness at all.

Shneior continued both to study and to deal in rags. In the spring, in the first week of March, there was the Cologne Spring Fair, at the time of *Purim,* and Shneior would sell the best of the rags that he had collected all winter. In the autumn, in the last week of August, there was the Cologne Autumn Fair, a few weeks before *Rosh Hashanah,* where Shneior would sell the best of the rags that he had collected in the summer. Both Shneior and Timna took pride in the rags that he sold. Timna would stitch a hem around each rag, and Shneior's rags were clean and tidy and one might even say that they were festive.

During the week Shneior studied in the morning and in the evening. He studied *and* he worked, for he knew that the Talmud declares: "It is both good and important to combine Torah study with a practical occupation. A fully occupied mind, heart, and hand have no place for sin. Moreover, without practical work the Torah may remove a man *too* much from the world and thus lead to arrogance and sins."

For twelve long years Shneior attended the study group in his congregation. Shneior ben Meyer was now fifty-two years old, and finally he felt that he might be called a scholar. He could read and write with the best of the men of Cologne. Although he was twenty or thirty years older than the young scholars in the yeshiva, he had earned a special respect, for does not the Talmud instruct us:

> Some men try to learn from the young–to whom are these men like? They are like those who eat unripe grapes; they are like those who drink

> wine directly from the fermenting vat. But other men learn from the elderly–to whom are *these* men like? Ah, they are like those who eat ripe grapes; they are like those who drink wine that has been aged properly and that is now deep, rich-tasting, and mellow.

"I started late," said Shneior at times, "but now I have caught up with the others."

Timna loved to hear Shneior talk about religion and philosophy. "All things can be seen through the crystal of the Torah," he said to her once, "and I have gained a fuller view of the world. My days are filled to the brim. I do not have many material goods–but I would not have the time to use them if I had. I wish, however, that you, my good wife, were better provided for." Then Timna smiled and patted his hand. "I am perfectly happy," she said.

Life rolled on. The days passed. The seasons came and the seasons went. Shneior's life evolved gently, rolling on from phase to phase. One day he said to Timna, "You know, my dear, each age, each phase in life, has its special role. Now I find that I am ready to counsel." Timna looked up at him and she raised her eyebrows, so Shneior quoted the famous talmudic chronology of Judah, the son of Tema:

> At five years old, you read a Scriptural page.
> At ten years old, you begin to study *Mishnah.*
> In three more years, the Commandments you engage.
> At fifteen years, you wrestle with the Talmud.
>
> At eighteen years, you marry to start a lineage.
> At twenty years old, you earn a full wage.
> In ten more years, you see beyond the average.
> At forty years comes the strength of middle age.
>
> At fifty years, you give *others* tutelage.
> At sixty years, you calmly meet your old age.
> In ten more years, you're now a white-haired sage.
> At eighty years, you comprehend your heritage.
>
> Then ninety years and you rest gently in the last stage
> Until one hundred comes, a distant sunset day
> When quietly you remember, as you disengage,
> All of life's rich phases rolling on away.

Yes, Rabbi, life has its many natural phases. The contented man learns to do those tasks and to enjoy those joys that fit most comfortably into each particular phase. Shneior lived within his natural phases–his life's comfortable niches, which changed with time–and he grew old smoothly and gently. Shneior was happy and content with his natural roles, and the world about him followed his lead. The people and the events and the places were all content also; in fact, they rose respectfully in the presence of his gray hairs, giving him a quiet honor and deference as he aged.

Shneior ben Meyer ha-Levi never earned much money. But his wife, Timna, was content, and she grew old smoothly and gently and happily also. One day Shneior realized that he was *ha-Zaken:* he was an old man. Often old Shneior sat in the sun smiling and musing and dreaming–as the Book of the Prophet Joel says: "Your sons and your daughters shall prophesy, but your old men shall dream dreams." So Shneior and Timna dreamt dreams. They dreamt and they lived in peace and blessed contentment until the very end of their long and happy lives, and one day in the cool autumn month of *Heshvan,* they quietly died together, at the natural time in their lives.

What is that, Rabbi? No, I was just resting my eyes. Please, join me here by the stove. An old man like me can doze on and on and on beside a warm stove. I suppose that is because I love to season my food with garlic.

What do I mean? Well, garlic heats the body so you can sleep better on cold nights. Of course, garlic is also a great remedy for many other things. It cures stomach troubles. The Talmud says that garlic makes your hair glossy and your face shine. And do you know the remedy for a toothache? Take a plant of garlic that has only one head, rub it with oil and salt, put it on your thumbnail (on the side where the tooth hurts), and surround it with a rim of dough. This works for earaches too.

It is no wonder that we Jews have always loved garlic. In the Bible, the wandering Israelites fondly remembered how in Egypt they had had "fish for the asking, cucumbers and watermelons, leeks and onions and garlic." Ah, yes – the sparkling golden garlic! What, Rabbi? Well, that is true – garlic cloves are usually pale and straw colored, but sometimes they can be gold. No, no, I mean *real* gold. You have never heard of gold garlic? I know of this firsthand. Let me tell you a special story of gold garlic, a story that I heard from my grandmother. It is about Haggith, the midwife who was beset by a cat demon:

Once upon a time, said my grandmother to me, in the old medieval days of Germany, there lived a devout woman named Haggith. Haggith was the widow of Elishama ben Aaron, and she was a midwife. Haggith lived in Waldbrol, east of Cologne, with her son, his wife, and their child. The family was quite poor. Although midwives were highly respected and Haggith was the only midwife in the town of Waldbrol, she earned very little money. The Jews in Waldbrol all lived in poverty. Usually the new mothers could not pay her – but Haggith worked because she loved newborn babies and because otherwise the mothers would have no one to turn to. Of course everyone appreciated Haggith. When they could, neighbors gave her extra food and old clothes and sometimes a few coins. Haggith always said, "I am certain that in the end I will be rewarded sufficiently and that I will go straight to Heaven – and when I die I will leave my children and their children with fine golden memories, amen."

One day Haggith sat outside her house, embroidering. She was tired; the night before, she had helped to deliver a bright little baby after a long day of labor. Haggith closed her eyes; her head nodded. Suddenly she heard a scritch and a scratch. She looked down. A beautiful cat was creeping along the edge of the house. The cat stretched and sniffed. It seemed to be looking for food. Was this a wildcat? Haggith knew that wildcats are ferocious and untamable. They fight fiercely; they eat other animals, such as rabbits, mice, and birds. Then too, wildcats love mountains and forests where masses of rocks and cliffs poke through the trees and where deep crevices offer protected homes. Wildcats have long, thin tails and broad gray patches. But this cat seemed happy around people and yards and houses, and this cat had a short, bushy tail and a light brown fur coat. Perhaps it was a mousing cat from a granary or a barn – maybe it was even a family cat.

The cat rubbed against Haggith's legs. It purred. It rolled on its back; it batted a leaf with its paw. "This poor cat must belong to a family," thought Haggith. "Now it is lost. Undoubtedly it is hungry." Haggith knew the passage from Deuteronomy where God says: "I will provide pasture in the fields for your cattle, and then you shall eat your fill." This means that a Jew must always feed his animals before he himself can have a meal. So the midwife smiled at the cat and said, "My friend, let us find you something to eat immediately."

Haggith went into the house. She brought out some cheese, which she crumbled and tossed on the ground. The cat ran over and began to eat the cheese. But what was this? As Haggith bent down to pat the cat, she noticed that the animal was fat and pregnant. "Well, well," said Haggith, "if you were a person, I could be your midwife." Haggith smiled at the thought – but, Rabbi, as my grandmother used to say, "Who can tell the future in a thing like this?"

Haggith played with the cat. Later it disappeared. Days passed, and the cat did not return. Seven days came and seven days went; then one dark autumn night, Haggith was awakened from her sleep by the sound of running steps. There was a rap at the door. Haggith's son and daughter-in-law were fast asleep. Perhaps some woman was in labor. Haggith got up hurriedly. She dressed and she opened the door.

It was a black night. A man, a stranger, stood there tired and sweating. "Grandmother," he said politely, "would you come with me? My wife is about to give birth and there is no one to help."

"Of course," said Haggith, and she put on a coat. Then she stepped outside and closed the door behind her.

Haggith could barely keep up with the man as he strode on, hurrying down the main street. Waldbrol is a small town. Soon they had passed the last house and were crossing an open field. The wind was cold. Haggith wrapped her arms around her chest. Shadows and clouds tore across the black sky, fraying and dissolving at the edges. No humans lived out here. Was it possible that the man was really a demon? Haggith shook and trembled all over.

"May the good Lord save me," Haggith said to herself, but she did not utter a sound aloud. Haggith could not stop shivering. She was afraid that she would stumble and fall. She felt weak. Would her feet fail her altogether? The wind rose again. It blew her hair and it whipped her coat, and Haggith squinted to keep the dirt and the leaves from her eyes.

After a time, the walkers reached an arch, a rocky bridge, with each stone ten meters high. Everything was dark and gray and cold and – why, it was not a bridge, it was the entrance to a cave! On walked the man, deep into the cave, and he said, "Grandmother, please come in. Here is my home." Weakly and shakily the midwife followed.

Before this, Haggith was scared–now she was petrified. Her arms were tight. Her legs were weak. She was hot and cold at once. Everything seemed dark and dim, and Haggith could not bring herself to look around her. She followed the stranger down a long passage. Small stones fell from the walls. Water dripped from above. Shapes moved in the shadows. Reremice and blanktees fluttered just beyond her vision. On and on they walked, and echoes followed; then suddenly they stepped into a vast and cavernous room. Crowds of demons laughed and hissed. The creatures were hairy and ugly: some looked like people, and some looked like cats.

Now the stranger turned to her. He stared at Haggith, and then he said, "My wife is in here," and he pointed to a small cave to their right. Haggith was pale. She stepped into the room. And what did she see? There in a gentle light from two candles, lay the cat, the same cat who had visited her just one week ago! Then, curiouser and curiouser, this cat opened its mouth and said, "Listen, my friend, I am sorry that you are so frightened. But you did volunteer to be my midwife, and now I need your help."

Haggith was trembling, and the cat said, "Please stay calm. No one will hurt you. My only advice is that you should not eat anything while you are here and that you should accept no gifts–otherwise, you will have to remain forever. However, I know that you will be careful and brave, and in the end you will have a fine golden reward for your grandchildren."

Haggith sat down. She took a deep breath. Eventually her heart beat more slowly and her hands stopped shaking. "Very well," she said to the cat. Haggith sat by the cat and talked to her. She told the cat how to breathe and how to relax. Hours passed. The demon father came in to the room many times with dishes of food and cups of drink. Each time, Haggith refused politely. Then the time arrived and a tiny male cat demon was born. Again the father came into the room. He saw the newborn baby. His eyes opened wide. He smiled and he cheered, and the entire company of demons heard and they cheered in the next room. The noise echoed in the vast cavern. It rolled throughout the halls, and it even reached to the celestial skies where the angels stopped their singing for a moment, wondering at the strange noise from the dark medieval German countryside far, far below.

The newborn's father was the chief of the demons. He turned to the midwife. "This is wonderful–just wonderful! Whatever you want, you can have. Ask for anything: gold, money, silks, gems."

The cat mother quietly shook her head no, and the midwife said, "No, thank you very much. I want nothing. The price for a good deed is the deed itself."

"That is impossible!" said the chief demon angrily. "You must take something. We do not accept charity. We pay for what we receive."

"*Now* what can I do?" thought the poor old woman. If she accepted a gift within the Otherworld of the demons, then she would be bartering for her soul. Quickly Haggith rolled sixty times sixty ideas about in her mind. Then she remembered that some garlics were hanging outside the cave. She could take these *after* having left the cave. Perhaps then she would be safe. So Haggith said to the chief demon, "That is very kind of you. I could use some garlics. May I have a bunch of the garlics that are hanging outside the door of your cave?" And the midwife saw the cat gently nodding her head yes.

The demon raised his eyebrows, but he said, "Certainly."

"And, good sir," added the woman, "I really am quite tired. May I leave now?"

The demon bowed, and he escorted her from the little side room. The midwife and the demon walked through the vast cavern, down the long dank tunnel, and out the entrance to the cave. There at the door hung bunches of dried garlics. The chief demon reached up. With a snick of his knife he cut down the largest garlic and handed it to the midwife. "Thank you," she said. "My blessings to you," he answered.

Then the demon led Haggith back to the edge of the town and he turned and disappeared, striding as quickly as the wind. Slowly, Haggith walked down the main street, and she returned home. She was tired. She felt empty. It was the silent dark hours of the morning, just before the dawn. Haggith reached into her coat and took out the garlic. "What a strange reward," she thought. She dropped the garlic at the edge of the house, she touched the *mezuzah* on the doorpost, she kissed her fingers, and she stepped into the cold, dark hallway. Haggith walked back to her room, and without taking off her coat, she sank into her bed, where she slept the deep sleep of the peaceful dead for many, many hours.

The next morning, her grandchild woke Haggith up. "Where did we get so much gold, Grandmother?" asked the little girl.

"Whatever are you talking about?" said Haggith, as her granddaughter pulled her toward the front door. There, the two of them stood with wide eyes. They looked down at gleaming yellow crescent-shaped stones; the garlic cloves had all turned to pure gold. Then the child was picking them up and rolling them around in her hand and chattering away, and Haggith just stood and watched in wonder.

After that, Haggith, the widow of Elishama ben Aaron ha-Kohen, remained in Waldbrol, where she lived a long and quiet life. She gave the golden garlics to her children and to her children's children. After many years, Haggith died quietly, and the children of her great-great-grandchildren are now scattered all over the world. Some even live in the Holy Land, and until this very day each of us keeps a piece of the golden garlic.

Garlics symbolize the happy, rich meals of days of ease and luxury – as the wandering Israelites wistfully recalled: "Ah, in the olden days, we had fish for the asking, and we had cucumbers and watermelons, leeks and onions and garlic." Our golden garlic cloves are a reward and a reminder of my great-great-great-grandmother, Haggith the midwife. What is that, Rabbi? Yes, you heard me correctly. My grandmother passed on to me a golden clove of garlic – for that was *my* great-great-great-grandmother Haggith who once upon a time on a medieval autumn night left a golden gift to her great-grandchildren's children, unknown to her then, but loved dearly all the same.

Rabbi, I am glad to see you here alone. I want to apologize for my outburst during the service this evening. It was just that Reb Anton said he felt tongue-tied during the prayers. Imagine inviting disaster during a holy moment of prayer! Why, in the olden days, in the strict and pious days of our fathers, Reb Anton would have been ordered to leave and never to return.

What? Well, I am talking about *tyings*–bindings, tyings, and entanglements of all manner. You do not know what I mean? Rabbi, Rabbi–do you not tell the mother to loosen the bride's hair before her marriage? Do you not remind the groom to untie all the knots on his clothing? Does the Burial Society not check for any knots or ties on a shroud? And you know the child's rhyme:

Evil spirit, my own slave
Sitting on the rotting grave
Walling off the weak and sick
From all touch of healing magic,
Go and tie a silken knot
And bind the ugly witch up taut.

Are her cruel lips firmly tied?
Then also knot her tongue inside
And go and sew her wicked throat–
Then wrap her in an overcoat
And never let her wriggle free
Until the good Lord blesses me.

These are childish superstitions? *Of course* they are superstitions, Rabbi, but as my grandmother said many times, "Superstitions may be silly, but you should never take them lightly."

Do not fool with bindings and tyings or with any other magics. Ah, would that Berachiah ben Samuel had only followed that advice! Yes, yes, Rabbi, it is another story told to me by my grandmother (may her memory be forever blessed). Actually, it is one of the strange tales recorded by Rabbi Petahiah and then rediscovered by Rabbi Asher while he still lived in Germany. Rabbi Asher–the famed Asher ben Yehiel, who later emigrated to Spain–worked and studied in the little back room of the Cologne yeshiva. Above this study room was a loft for storage. One day, late in the cold autumn month of *Heshvan* when he was rooting around among the manuscripts in the loft, Asher found a letter from Rabbi Petahiah of Regensburg to Rabbi Abraham ben Alexander, Achselrad of Cologne.

"*My dear Rabbi Abraham*–

"I have just met a fine man, a young Jew from Zurich. He has agreed to carry this letter to my colleague, Rabbi David of Basel, who I am certain will then arrange to transport it to you. I write, old friend, to wish you and your family well, to convey my fondest greetings to all the Jews of your blessed community in Cologne, and to praise the good Lord God (blessed be He) and His Almighty Name for ever and ever, amen.

"I will not trouble you with the details of my many wagon rides and my subsequent sea voyages. Suffice it to say that safely they brought me here to the Oriental regions, regions that are so near to the great Holy Land where someday the Messiah shall return and deliver us and resurrect all souls and rebuild the Temple on Zion, amen. I write now in order to record for you some details of the lands and the peoples that I have seen in these old and foreign realms. The bright and glorious hand of God is visible everywhere, if only we look–praise the Lord Yahweh-Elohim.

"Yes, my old friend, I have had many, many adventures in arriving here. I hope–with the good Lord willing–to relate more of these events to you in person. Now I am in Baghdad, and I have come down through the country of Armenia. Armenia is east and south of the Black Sea and it is south of the Caucasus Mountains–the Mountains of Ararat. These mountains are breathtaking. Great wooded gorges cut through the rock, and each gorge empties a river into Armenia; these rivers are the upper waters of such ancient streams as the River Euphrates, the River Tigris, the River Aras, and the River Churuk. Armenia also has wide open plateaus, which are empty, cheerless places. But, Abraham, the huge valleys make up for this bleakness–the valleys are tangled, rugged, wild, and grand.

"Most Armenian villages are on gentle slopes in the valleys. Each house is built into a hill; the back is a cave and the front is made of stone and wood and thatch. Ruins of old stone buildings are everywhere, as if one house is simply abandoned when it wears out and a new one is built next-door. The people are farmers and herders. They live on cereals and fruits and fish (huge trout), and they also have mules and horses. I found the Armenians quiet and distant, and I did not stay there but pushed on southward until I reached the great city of Baghdad.

"The Jewish community of this region is under the direction of the Exilarch of Baghdad. You may have heard of the previous Exilarch, Daniel ben Solomon (may his name ever be a blessing for all the Jewish people, amen). Mar Daniel has just died, and Samuel bar Ali ha-Levi has assumed all religious and judicial power. Rabbi Samuel is, in brief, a Jewish prince. The Exilarch of Baghdad rules the Asiatic congregations from Damascus to India and from the Caspian Sea to Arabia. He personally appoints all the rabbis, judges, and other civil and synagogue officials–and he has the power to reverse any of the others' decisions. The king of Persia sets the national Jewish taxes, which he collects from the Exilarch. However, the Exilarch decides how much extra to tax the Jews, how to divide the tax burden, and how to spend the moneys. In addition, the Exilarch of Baghdad is the head of the local Jewish college.

"Undoubtedly, you will be hearing about Samuel bar Ali ha-Levi;

therefore I will send back to you and to my European colleagues some information about the man. Mar Samuel behaves like a king. He is regal and proud and ambitious, and he traces his family directly to the Prophet Samuel. Mar Samuel has a winter home and a summer home, and both have large gardens and both are staffed by servants. He even has his own contingent of guardsmen who enforce the punishments of the Jewish courts. The title that Mar Samuel prefers is 'Gaon Samuel.' In formal documents, he signs himself as successor to the famed Babylonian Gaon Saadia Sherira from two centuries ago, and Mar Samuel says that his goal is to build the Baghdad school to be the supreme institute of Jewish learning anywhere in the world.

"Let me describe Mar Samuel in action. The main room in his yeshiva is like a royal court. Samuel sits at a table with nine other judges, each of whom has a special area of expertise, but for every lecture or for every case, Mar Samuel himself has the final word. In his black robe and red cap, he sits quietly, usually with his eyes closed: sometimes, he seems a motionless statue for hours. Then the other judges' presentation ends. Mar Samuel opens his eyes, and in dry tones he says a few words, such as: 'So it is in the Book of Genesis' or 'So also said the Gaon Saadia' or 'In the *Sayings of the Fathers* we learn: . . .' or 'Thus, he shall be fined' or 'He is banned from further commerce' or 'He is now excommunicated.' All nod – and then comes the echo; for every single word of Mar Samuel is repeated aloud by the head *Amora.*

"It is strange to see such royal behavior in a Jewish religious leader. Ah, well, Abraham, in other letters I will tell you more about my experiences here and about the city of Baghdad and about my many excursions to neighboring towns. I have been warmly received throughout the region, and now I am overflowing with adventures. You know my passion for unusual tales, and I would like to tell you a story that I heard just yesterday about the Messiah and a poor Jew named Berachiah ben Samuel who lived on the outskirts of Baghdad. Berachiah, so I was told, had not a single coin to his name. Nevertheless, he sat night and day studying the Torah with a pure heart, as the good Lord God (blessed be He) has bidden.

"One Friday morning, Berachiah's wife discovered that once again they had no money. How was she to buy *hallah,* fish, meat, wine, or candles for the Sabbath? 'I suppose,' she said to Berachiah, 'that you are going directly to the synagogue. You have no regard for your family! Can you not try to earn a bit of money for once? Get us a few coins so that the children and I will not starve. At least go to the marketplace; borrow money, or beg if you must. Do not be proud—accept leftovers from the stallkeepers. But bring us home *something* so that we can celebrate the Sabbath properly!'

"Berachiah nodded and he shuffled out the door. Lost in gloomy thoughts, the poor man made his way to the marketplace.

" 'How does she expect me to come home with anything when I have no money? Instead of studying the Torah, now I have to worry about money!' Berachiah shook his head. He walked along, muttering and grumbling to himself, and he almost bumped into a stranger who stood back and said, 'Well, well—*sholom aleikhem!*'

" '*Aleikhem sholom,*' answered Berachiah automatically. He stopped and looked up and he saw an old man with a long, gray beard. For some reason, Berachiah could not make out the details of the man's face. Was the sun too bright? Was there a strange shadow? Was Berachiah getting old himself and were his eyes now becoming cloudy?

"The old man smiled at Berachiah. 'You look puzzled,' he said. 'Also, I could not help noticing that you are a bit distracted today. Is something bothering you?'

" 'Oh, it is the usual,' answered Berachiah. 'There is not enough time in this life to study *and* to earn a living. I really could use more money for the family, but I cannot seem to concentrate on practical matters.'

" 'I understand, my friend,' said the stranger. 'I too find it difficult to concentrate on such practical worldly things. I can appreciate your putting the study of Torah above all else. I do not have much to offer you except a kind word and a supportive pat on the back.' The man frowned for a moment, then he said, 'However, come to think of it—here, let me share something with you.' The old man pulled a worn cloth sack from a deep pocket of his robe. 'This is a marvelous bag. And I will give it to you as a present.'

"Berachiah took the sack. He held it up and turned it around. He raised his eyebrows. The sack was brown and stained and worn, and it had an old white cord that tied together the opening. 'I cannot even sell this dirty sack as a rag,' he thought. He stood still and he looked at the old man.

"The old man smiled and waited patiently. Finally, Berachiah said, 'Well, it is very kind of you, but I think we have a sack just like this one at home.'

" 'Oh, I doubt it,' said the stranger. 'You see, this sack will swallow anyone. All you need to do is to call out: "Little sack, little sack–swallow this man!" And, believe me, it will do exactly as you say. Then be certain to tie the top of the sack and recite this charm' ":

Bind him with an iron chain
Tie him with a band of brass
And never let him loose again
Til Judgment Day has come to pass.

"Berachiah raised his eyebrows. 'Ah,' he thought, 'I am talking to a madman.' However, out loud he said, 'Well, I will remember this. Thank you again for the gift.' And then Berachiah continued walking to the marketplace, dragging the old sack behind him.

"As you might imagine, Abraham, the stranger was quite serious. In fact, the stranger was actually the Messiah–*Mashiah,* the anointed one–who had come down to earth early to see how matters stood for the Jews. But Berachiah ben Samuel did not recognize *Mashiah.* Berachiah was still trying to think of ways to get some holiday food. When he reached the markets, Berachiah found a sympathetic stallkeeper and he was given some day-old *hallah.* 'Bless you,' said Berachiah. He put the bread into the old sack and he headed home. He gave the bread to his wife, who sadly shook her head, he put the sack under his bed, and he went to the synagogue to pray.

"However, from that day on, the wheel of fortune turned for Berachiah. Was it the doing of the Messiah or was it the inexplicable wandering ways of the world? I do not know, Rabbi, but in any case things somehow began to go very well indeed for Berachiah. He inherited money from an uncle. His son set up a cloth business with the money and it was a tremendous success. Berachiah's studies brought him a permanent position in the yeshiva, and the community even paid him a small salary. His children grew happily. His wife stopped complaining. Sorrows shunned his doorstep and the sun shone brightly each morning.

"Ah, but like many men who grow rich, Berachiah ben Samuel

forgot that all wealth is just a temporary loan from the good Lord God (blessed be He). Did Berachiah give to charity? No, I am afraid he did not. Did he take the time to teach children? No, he did not do this either. Did he support poor families in the neighborhood? Well, Rabbi, Berachiah did none of these things. He even neglected his daily study sessions on Wednesdays in order to have an extra afternoon in the marketplace.

"So one day the Almighty Lord God shook His head. 'Enough is enough!' He said. Lightning flashed, thunder roared, and the Most Holy One sent Dumah down to take the life of Berachiah ben Samuel. Berachiah felt very weak that morning, and he stayed late in his bed. Then suddenly Dumah, the Angel of Death, was at the head of the bed, standing silently like a cold black rock and covered from head to foot with unwinking eyes. Dumah held a drawn and bloody sword and his breathing was like the sound of dry leaves rustling and rustling in the blank autumn wind. The black angel looked down and said, 'Berachiah, son of Samuel, your final hour has come.'

" 'Please go away. I cannot die yet!' cried the old man. 'Leave me in peace!'

"But the Angel of Death would not leave Berachiah. Dumah stood there and he raised his sword, the cold, cold Sword of Death. The sword moved smoothly through the air with a ringing sound, and the dying man saw that he could resist no longer. Then he remembered his sack. Berachiah reached under the bed, he snatched up his sack, and with his last weak breath he said, 'Little sack, little sack–swallow the Angel of Death!' And immediately, Dumah, the black Angel of Death, disappeared into the little sack. Then Berachiah tied the top of the sack and in a shaky voice he recited:

Bind him with an iron chain
Tie him with a band of brass
And never let him loose again
Til Judgment Day has come to pass.

And Dumah did not come out and the old man did not die.

"In the meantime, on the Golden Throne of Glory, the Celestial Judge sat waiting impatiently for the Angel of Death to arrive with the soul of Berachiah. Where was Dumah? The brow of the Great and

Holy One clouded over. Anger creased His forehead. Thunder rumbled at His shoulders. The skies darkened. 'Gabriel! Michael!' called the Lord. 'Go down and see to events on the earth. What has delayed the death of Berachiah ben Samuel?' Then the Almighty Lord God raised His right arm. 'Go,' He repeated, 'and find out what is keeping the Angel of Death.'

"The two archangels sped down from the white, cloud-lined, celestial court. They flew from Heaven, and when they came to Berachiah's house in Baghdad, the archangel Michael went into the room first and asked, 'Where is the Angel of Death?'

"Berachiah looked at the angel. He was afraid, and he did not answer. Again and again, Michael asked him the question. When he saw that he could not hold off the angel, Berachiah picked up his sack and cried, 'Little sack, little sack–swallow the angel Michael!'

"Suddenly Michael disappeared into the sack. Berachiah tied the top of the sack and he recited the incantation, and the great archangel Michael did not come out and the old man did not die. 'This is amazing,' thought Berachiah nervously. 'What will happen next?'

"Now Gabriel stepped into the room. Angrily he said, 'How can you do this, old man? Have you no respect for the holy Host?' But Berachiah picked up his sack once again, saying, 'Little sack, little sack–swallow up this angel too!' Of course Gabriel also disappeared into the small magic bag. Again Berachiah tied the top of the sack and he recited the binding incantation. Berachiah looked at the old cloth bag. He shook his head. 'I do not know where all these angels are going, but I know that this cannot end well,' he thought.

"At that moment, yet another angel of the Lord was passing by. He heard the commotion of the archangels and he opened wide his bright, bright eyes. This little angel listened well with his softest and tiniest ears; then he flew up directly to Heaven. 'O Lord my God,' said the angel, 'there is an old man in the city of Baghdad who is disappearing the host of archangels!'

"*Mashiah* the Messiah was standing beside the Golden Throne of Glory. He heard the angel's report, and he remembered how he had given the magic sack to a poor man he had met in Baghdad once long ago. 'Lord,' said the Messiah to God, 'this strange situation is my fault. Let me go down. I will find this man and fix what I have set wrong.'

"The great Lord God Almighty frowned but said nothing, so

Mashiah, the anointed one, descended again to earth. Again the Messiah assumed the shape of an old man, and he went in search of Berachiah ben Samuel. Soon the anointed one found Berachiah's house. He walked into the bedroom and said, 'Listen here, Berachiah – what is the meaning of your shameful conduct? Explain yourself!'

" 'You too?!' cried Berachiah angrily, not recognizing the Messiah. 'How many more of you holy envoys will come down here and browbeat a poor old man?'

" 'Why – do you not recognize me?' began the Messiah. 'I am –' But before the Messiah could finish what he had begun to say, Berachiah picked up the magic sack and cried, 'Little sack, little sack! Swallow this one too!' And *Mashiah,* the anointed one, also disappeared into the little sack. Quickly Berachiah tied the top of the sack and recited:

Bind him with an iron chain
Tie him with a band of brass
And never let him loose again
Til Judgment Day has come to pass.

And the Messiah did not come out. Berachiah jumped from his bed. 'This is no place for me to stay,' he thought. He and his wife immediately packed their belongings and moved to another city, and no one ever knew where they ended up.

"When he left Baghdad, Berachiah took the sack with him. The magic sack was like the mouth of a cave that led into a strange and tangled region, and it took endless years for the angels and the Messiah to find their way back out. The magic sack is still somewhere on this large and dusty earth. Perhaps it is crumpled in a old loft in the ancient warm lands. Or perhaps a wandering Jew has taken it to the cold northern regions where it lies underneath torn prayer books in some forgotten attic. Anything is possible, and I myself do not know where it is. I only know that because the sack is somewhere on the earth, the Messiah still hesitates to return.

"So, Abraham, that is the story exactly as I heard it. These bindings and tyings are tricky matters, my old friend. We are counseled always to take care – for, once things are tied together and intertwined, they are very, very hard to disentangle. But I am not worried about entanglements. Entanglements are life. We live hugged and enwrapped, forever bundled and tangled. Plants entangle: vines and roots twine about one another, grabbing onto other plants and rocks and sticks and earth. Animals entangle, babies cling forever to their mothers. And as for us people? Why, we become entangled when we grow up together, as you and I did, in those lazy, dusty summer days when all the springtime world was young. And, my old and young Abraham, never untied from us shall those days be until the sun grows cold and the moon dims forever, and by then, of course, we will be warmly wrapped in God's great and glorious vine-filled Garden of Eden, entangled together once again, amen.

"Your childhood friend,
Petahiah, the son of Jacob"

Hello, Rabbi. I will be with you in a moment. My day has not ended properly until every tablecloth is folded.

There, now I can sit next to you by the stove.

I am not sleepy either, but sometimes staring at the stove helps: everything fades into a bright white fog. After taking my eyes from the glow of the fire, the fog is everywhere; the edges of the world melt away, fading and disappearing. It is like that day when old Abraham Achselrad found that the words he was reading disappeared and melted away.

You see, once upon a time, old Achselrad was sitting at his desk. He was tired. He had been staring at his candle. Perhaps some little demon was playing a trick, for as the Rabbi squinted and stared and rubbed his eyes and tried his best to concentrate, he could not read the letters of the Kabbalah, late that autumn afternoon. The black lines and the curls and dots went in and out of focus – they became entangled and woven together with no rhyme or reason.

Old Abraham Achselrad was tired. The Kabbalistic letters slipped into pairs. They wound together. They faded away. Achselrad's mind wandered. He found himself trying to tap his fingers and his feet at the same time. He rubbed a toe along the hole in his sock. Absently, he repeated over and over to himself, "katal, katalta, katalti; kittal, kittalta, kittalti–pokat, pokadeti, pikat–pik–pik–pik–" Then he heard a noise. Was it a voice, a small voice, coming from the main study hall?

The Rabbi got up. He stepped around his desk. He walked past a pile of prayer books and out into the cool main prayer hall, which was lit by the late-afternoon autumn sun, a sun that filtered in golden shafts through twelve stained-glass windows filled with colored lions and snakes.

The Rabbi stopped and he looked. A little boy sat among the prayer benches, talking to himself. The boy was about six years old; he was dirty and thin. His feet did not reach the floor, and he was swinging them back and forth.

"Hello," said the Rabbi.

"Hello," said the boy.

"What is your name?"

"David."

"Who are you talking to?"

"I am talking to Pushtak and Nemosha," answered David.

"And who are they?" asked the Rabbi.

"They are my dragons–but you can't see them."

"Oh," said Achselrad. He looked at David. David looked at his knees and at the benches and the ceiling, and he swung his feet back and forth.

"Would you like some bread?" asked the Rabbi.

"Yes," said David.

The Rabbi went into the back room and brought out some bread. David chewed the middle carefully and he left the crust.

As he ate, David patted his leg and he tapped his foot on the bench. The Rabbi sat across from him on another bench. "What is your whole name, David?" asked Rabbi Abraham.

"It's just David. I am David ben Menachem."

A light wind blew outside, somewhere far away.

"Tell me about your dragons," said the Rabbi.

"They are invisible. They live on the roof."

"What are they doing here?" asked Rabbi Abraham.

"I keep them in my pocket."

"They must be very little," said the Rabbi.

"Oh no, they are very big," said David. "They cover the whole roof at night. And they are strong and they guard me from demons."

"How can they fit in your pocket?" asked the Rabbi.

"I shrink them when I take them with me."

Rabbi Achselrad nodded and smoothed out his robe. "What do they look like?" he asked.

"They look like dragons," said the boy.

"And what is that like?" asked the old man.

David looked up at the ceiling, then he said, "Well, Pushtak is all green with little Pushtak things that stick out of him from his bottom to his head. And he has a big nose."

"Does the other dragon look like Pushtak?"

"Of course," said the boy. He wiggled his feet a moment. "But," he continued, "Pushtak is the father, and Nemosha is the mother. And Nemosha is white with white claws and white on her bottom. They both have flowers sticking out of them to make them more beautiful."

"Do they have any children?"

"Yes, but they are all eggs still."

"Why were you talking to them just now?"

"Pushtak wanted to sit over by the cupboard there."

"The cupboard?" asked the Rabbi. He looked around. "Do you mean that stone box with the lions and the vines carved on it?"

"Yes."

"That is called the Ark. Inside, there are the holy Scrolls of God's Law," said Rabbi Achselrad.

"I knew that it was important," said David, "so I told Pushtak not to sit over there. Dragons are not allowed to sit on the Ark."

"You are probably right," said old Abraham ben Alexander.

The Rabbi sat looking far away. The little boy was swinging his feet. After a few minutes, the boy said, "I first met them when I was a baby, when I was two years old. They were littler, and now I grew up to be bigger and bigger."

David looked at the Rabbi. "Why does everything start out little and then get big?" he asked.

Rabbi Achselrad shrugged his shoulders. "I do not know the reason, my little friend," he said. "It is just the way that the good Lord God made the world work."

"Oh," said the boy. "Well, Pushtak and Nemosha grow bigger every day." Then he added, "They are invisible, you know."

"I know," said the Rabbi. "I cannot see them."

"Only *I* can see them," said the boy.

The Rabbi nodded. "Where are they now?"

"They are sitting reading quietly." The boy sat quietly too. Then he continued: "They taught me how to see them. I turned out to be their mother. Most of the time, in the days, they stay in the house with my grandmother, who is sick. They are afraid of other people."

"What are they afraid of?" asked Rabbi Abraham.

"They are afraid of grown-ups," said David, "but they always protect me, even though I am their mother."

The boy ate some more of the bread.

"What do Pushtak and Nemosha eat?" asked the Rabbi.

"They eat oats. And they like bread and sugar too. They can eat anything because they have such big throats. They can swallow anything. They can eat a table if they want."

Old Achselrad nodded. "Do they talk?" he asked.

"They just sing, but *you* don't know how to understand them," said David. "Even I have to listen to them carefully."

David looked at his shoe, and then he continued: "And when they go out to play, they never go without me, because if they do they will get distracted and follow someone else home and get lost. At night, they have this big, long bed. There is a little bed for the baby to lie next to the mother–and the father is on the other side. They all sleep in my room, and even their bed is invisible. (In the morning, I have to take it away so that nobody will trip over it.) At night I say, 'Is everyone asleep?' and if there is no answer then I know that they are all sleeping."

Rabbi Achselrad stroked his beard. David and the Rabbi sat silently. The late-afternoon sun filtered through the stained-glass windows, rolling around the dust shafts, gently and lightly patting the two Jews on the back. Then the little boy was talking again. "Are you a rabbi?" he asked.

"Yes," said Abraham ben Alexander.

"You are old," said the boy.

"Yes, I am," said the Rabbi.

"I will get old someday too," said the little boy. "When I grow up,

Pushtak and Nemosha will still be little. When I grow up, they will be five and I will be a grandmother. Pushtak likes me as his mother – I am the only mother that he knows. But when I am a grandmother, then they will still be only five-years-old, and then when I die, they will still be little and they won't be able to take care of themselves. They will be scared without me, and they won't be able to do things. So, you see, that's my problem."

"Maybe they will grow up with you?"

"No, they are too little – they can't grow up."

"Perhaps you could give them to your children," said the Rabbi.

David thought for a moment. "Yes," he said, "they will need them to take care of them."

Again the two Jews – the old Rabbi and the little boy – sat quietly. The Rabbi stroked his beard. The boy swung his feet.

"I think we had better leave soon," said David.

"Yes, your parents are probably wondering about you," said Achselrad.

"No, my grandmother is sick. She told me to go play, and I came here."

"Is she your only parent?" asked the Rabbi.

"Well, Pushtak and Nemosha are my parents too," said the boy.

Good evening, Rabbi. Of course–sit here by the stove; the late-night fire helps me to become sleepy also. You and I are not blessed like old Reb Elbaum. Once again I saw him nod off during the last prayers this evening, swaying piously even while asleep. He must have inherited some magic from the mystic Achselrad.

It appears that you and I also could use a dose of Achselrad tonight. My grandmother said that Achselrad could put men into a sleep trance by waving a gold coin before their eyes. Ah, old Rabbi Abraham Achselrad, he was always conjuring visions in the synagogue. I doubt whether he would be tolerated nowadays, but he was also a scholar, and he claimed that his visions came from the most devout and pious study.

Rabbi Abraham could even call up the spirits of the dead. In those days many rabbis claimed that it was very difficult for the dead to speak, so one should never use incantations to force them to talk. Rabbi Achselrad felt differently. The deceased, wrote old Achselrad, may be questioned during the first twelve months after death (during which time the body remains intact in the grave). (Of course talking with a corpse directly is unholy, so you must speak only to the immortal spirit.)

As you know, Rabbi, holy men can call the dead by name with secret pronouncements, and the ghost will rise feetfirst from the grave; at this point clouds slip across the sun and a cool breeze rolls in. Other people may see the shadows, feel the wind, and hear strange sounds, but only the holy mystic can have a full conversation with the dead. Talking with spirits can be a dangerous business, and Rabbi Abraham invoked the dead only in dire circumstances, such as on the day he saved poor Shemaiah ben Adiel ha-Kohen with a holy conjured vision in the Archbishop's Court.

This was in the early winter, in the month of *Ḣeshvan,* in medieval Cologne. As you know, Abraham Achselrad worked night and day on a set of Kabbalistic tomes of mystical knowledge; the most famous of these was the *Keter Shem Tov.* (Unfortunately, this book was never published, and now it exists only as a secret manuscript hidden in the loft of the ancient Cologne yeshiva.) One cold evening, while he was writing this very book, Rabbi Abraham looked up, and in the waning light of the day he saw a crowd of his congregants huddled fearfully in the doorway. "Please," called one of them, "come quickly and help rescue Shemaiah ben Adiel. He has been charged with murder!"

Now, this is what had actually happened:

In the town of Cologne lived a Christian named Eberhard Brisch. Eberhard had never learned to read or to write, but because his father was a friend of the Archbishop, Eberhard had become the beadle of the St. Laurence parish. Eberhard spent each afternoon at the inn; he drank, he gambled, and he told stories with five or six other men who made their living as hunters and trappers. Usually, he told the innkeeper to keep an account of his bill. Every month Eberhard would get paid, and then he would give one gold coin to the innkeeper as credit against the ever-increasing tab. Eberhard continued to promise to settle his account, but it grew larger and larger. Eventually, the innkeeper – a Jew named Shemaiah ben Adiel ha-Kohen – got tired of losing money. "Pay your full account," he told Eberhard, "or you will have to drink somewhere else."

Eberhard was angry. How could a Jew talk this way to an official of the Church? The other men at the table muttered and grumbled too. This Jew was getting too high and highly – "We will fix him," they said. The men all walked out of the inn together and they began to plot and to plan.

Shemaiah ben Adiel was happy to see them go. Each day they would each buy a single beer and sit at the best table by the fire for hours. They were loud and grim and rough, and sometimes women were afraid to come in and buy Shemaiah's bread.

What, Rabbi? Yes, I *did* say bread. You see, Shemiah ben Adiel loved baking, and he himself made the best oatcakes and sourdough bread in all of Cologne. In fact, housewives came from outlying areas to buy Shemaiah's honeyed oatcakes.

Baking was only one of Shemaiah's hobbies. Shemaiah was an energetic man, and he dabbled in all manner of businesses, including buying and selling and even financing. People of every size, shape, and color came through his inn, and Shemaiah acted as a middleman in goods of questionable origin. One thing he sold was beavers. Beaver meat tastes like pork, and beaver glands contain the strange healing substance called *castoreum*–but, most of all, everyone wanted beaver pelts. Beaver is the finest of furs–thick and brown on the outside and gray and silky underneath. Beaver pelts are strong and soft, and they were used for collars and cuffs and trims and for lining cool-weather clothes. But beavers were not common in the Rhinelands, and anyone who trapped a beaver was supposed to pay a special tax to the local noblemen.

One night, one of Eberhard's friends, a trapper, came to the back door of the inn. He knocked, and the cook opened the door. "Is the innkeeper around?" asked the trapper. Shemaiah ben Adiel came into the back room. The trapper had a large wet sack. "Listen," he whispered to Shemaiah, "I have two huge beavers here. I will sell them to you for two gold coins each." Shemaiah frowned. "I will give you two gold coins for the whole bag," he said. The trapper hesitated. "All right," said the trapper finally, "it is a deal."

Shemaiah dragged the bag over to a corner to open it. "No, no," said the trapper, "someone might see us–your cook just walked by again. Listen, my friend, I trust you to pay me tomorrow. I want to get out of here before anyone catches us. Check the bag when things are safe." Then the trapper slipped out the door and disappeared into the night.

Shemaiah shrugged his shoulders. He pushed the damp sack against the wall under a table. He tugged at the rope to get the bag far out of sight. The wet rope dug into his hands. "This is incredibly heavy," he thought. "Beavers weigh less than a child, but this sack feels as heavy as a man. I may have gotten a good bargain," thought Shemaiah. It was late. Shemaiah was tired; he closed the back room and headed for bed. But scarcely had he fallen asleep, when he heard another knocking, a loud banging, at the back door.

Shemaiah put on his clothes. Again he went out to the back room and he unlocked the door. Eberhard Brisch pushed his way into the room with two guards. "Move back," said Eberhard to the innkeeper. The men searched the room. They found the bag and they ripped it opened. Inside was the waterlogged corpse of a man: it was the body of a Gentile baker who had been missing for a week from the St. Laurence parish!

The guardsmen tied Shemaiah's hands with rope. He was dragged to a wagon and brought into the main section of town. There he was jailed, to be tried the next day in the Archbishop's Court on charges of murder. The next morning, word passed quickly through the surrounding parishes. People wanted to see the trial, they wanted revenge, and they came in crowds from the St. Laurence and the St. Albans parishes. The local men and boys were angry. "This Jew has killed one of our men," someone shouted. "Put him to death!" Was a riot in the making? Terrified Jews rushed into the synagogue, where Rabbi Abraham Achselrad was writing in the back room.

Rabbi Abraham listened to the confused and fearful reports. He stroked his beard. His forehead creased. He rubbed his chin. Then he stood, and he put on his hat and his coat. The Rabbi left the small back study room of the yeshiva. He walked through the main prayer hall with its many wooden benches. He passed the twelve stained-glass windows with their colored lions and snakes. He went by the Holy Ark made of stone, he stepped out the front door, and he strode off to the courthouse.

The Archbishop was already in court. This was Archbishop Adolph of Cologne, a noble and honorable prelate. Archbishop Adolph knew the Rabbi. "Rabbi," said the Archbishop sadly, "I am afraid that one of your Jews has committed murder. We have accusers, and we have the body. I have no choice, Rabbi – Mr. Shemaiah Adiel must be hanged."

Rabbi Abraham looked sad. "I see," he said quietly. He looked around the courtroom. In the front was sitting Eberhard Brisch. Rabbi Abraham frowned. "Sir," he said to the beadle, "have you nothing to contribute to these proceedings? Did you have no role at all?"

Eberhard Brisch looked at the Archbishop. "Your Honor, you know that I am an upstanding member of the Christian community. The Rabbi is trying to confuse matters. Will you let these Jews drag good Christian citizens through the mud? Get on with your sentencing."

The Archbishop looked at the Rabbi. The Rabbi continued to stare at Brisch. But the beadle set his mouth tightly and he said, "We found the body in the Jew's room. Clearly he is guilty."

There was silence in the courtroom. Rabbi Abraham closed his eyes for a moment; then he asked, "Have you a Bible here, good Archbishop?"

"Of course," replied the Archbishop, and he motioned for one of the officers to pass a leather volume to Rabbi Achselrad.

"Let us read from the First Book of Samuel," said the Rabbi.

Archbishop Adolph held up his hand. "Just a moment, Rabbi. I respect your religious views, but is this really relevant now?"

Abraham Achselrad was holding the Holy Scriptures. The old worn book shined in the courtroom candlelight. Suddenly the Rabbi's eyes opened wide, and then they closed tightly. Rabbi Achselrad became weak; he sat on a nearby chair, he took a deep breath. Then he gently set down the Bible.

"Are you all right, Rabbi?" asked the Archbishop.

"I have just had a vision," said Rabbi Abraham. "I have seen the Heavens and the Great Throne of Glory."

There was silence for a moment. "Yes, Archbishop, I have seen the Heavens. I have seen the firmament of the good Lord God (blessed be He) – He Who sees all and Who demands justice for all, especially for His children, the Jews. In addition, I have seen that the First Book of Samuel is quite important here," said old Achselrad. "And if you will be so good as to hand me the Holy Book again, then I will read a bit of those verses." And the Rabbi read aloud:

> Then Saul put on different clothes and went in disguise, accompanied by two of his men. He came to a strange old woman at En-dor and he said, "Old woman, tell me my fortunes by consulting the dead–call up the man I name to you." But the woman hesitated; so Saul swore for her this oath: "As the blessed Lord God lives, no harm shall come to you for this." Then the woman did as Saul had asked, and soon they saw a ghostly form coming up from the earth. It looked like an old man, and it came up from Sheol wrapped in a worn gray cloak.

The Rabbi bowed his head and he closed his eyes, so the Archbishop said, "Well, yes, of course, Rabbi, that is a most serious and holy passage."

"It certainly is," said the Rabbi. "Now, my good Archbishop, you are a noted cleric. What would you say that this verse means?"

The Archbishop thought for a moment. "Let me see . . . this is where Saul defies all the accepted religious practices and he consults directly with the dead."

"Yes, Archbishop–so it is. But this also means something to us today," said the Rabbi.

"Oh? And what else would you read into this verse, Rabbi?" asked the Catholic cleric.

"Saul has gone to the witch of En-dor. Poor Saul had lost the counsel of the Prophet Samuel, the last great Judge of Israel. Saul feels weak and confused. He seeks Samuel's wise advice once again, and we see that the good Lord God (blessed be He)–He who is the Guardian of all Israel–allows the living to reach out even into the spirit world for counsel, plucking forth a man long dead and gone," said the Rabbi.

The Archbishop looked at his councilors, he looked at the Rabbi, and he pursed his lips. "Can you be a little more specific?" asked the Archbishop. "Exactly what are you saying, Mr. Alexander?"

"I am saying this, Archbishop: I have had a vision. Just as Saul's interview with the spirit of Samuel tells the honest truth about his world, so *our* interview with the spirits can give the honest truth about *our* world. And the truth is this: a man who presently stands unaccused is in fact the murderer in this very case. Archbishop, I propose that the spirit world should reveal this truth."

Then one of the officers laughed. "Has the Bible really told you all this, old man?" he asked.

"Yes, it has," said the Rabbi. "My good Archbishop, what are you going to do? An angry mob has collected. Will you allow innocent people to be hurt or to be killed, when you know well enough that the accused Jew is not guilty?"

The Archbishop frowned. "At the moment, Rabbi," he said, "I know no such thing; in fact, I have been told exactly the opposite."

The Rabbi shook his head sadly. "Slander is a powerful weapon, Archbishop," said Rabbi Abraham. "As the scriptural Proverb says":

> Do not defame your neighbor
> Without proof or full support:
> Do not misrepresent him before
> A judge or in a public court.

The Rabbi nodded to himself. "Now, in this case, another man, a Christian, has committed slander. In fact, he is the guilty party," said Rabbi Abraham. "And I can prove this to you."

Eberhard Brisch turned pale. His heart raced; his throat became dry. However, the Archbishop was not watching the beadle. Instead, Archbishop Adolph tilted his head and he looked intently at old Achselrad. After a brief silence, the Catholic cleric said to the Rabbi, "If you can prove what you say, then no harm will befall any of you Jews." And he gave orders that the people in the court and the people in the street should all remain quiet.

Rabbi Abraham nodded again, and he said, "Thank you, good Archbishop. First, let me ask that you lock the court, so that no one will be able to escape."

Eberhard Brisch looked around him. He felt very weak, and his heart pounded. The Archbishop instructed his officers to stand by the doors.

Rabbi Abraham Achselrad sat down. He closed his eyes. He began to sway. He shook strangely. The members of the court raised their eyebrows and looked at one another. Then the pious old Jew opened his eyes again and he took a small piece of white kosher parchment from his pocket. The Rabbi covered the top of his head with a handkerchief, and he wrote a charm with holy names on the paper. The Archbishop could see that the charm began with a quotation from the Book of Exodus: "For I am Yahweh, your Restorer–I, the Lord God, am your Healer . . ." but Archbishop Adolph could not make out the remainder of the words.

When the Rabbi finished writing in his neat and tiny script, he rolled the parchment into a tight scroll and he tied it with a cotton thread. The Rabbi tied and untied the thread–he knotted and unknotted it seven times–then he placed the charm on a table next to a large, gray, blank wall. There was silence, and the court darkened as each candle flame contracted to a small white dot.

For a moment, nothing happened. Then suddenly a hazy shape wavered along the wall. The shape expanded. It became a dark aura. It rose up, and it took the form of the beaver trapper, larger than life and sad and grim. Silently, the shape raised a wavering arm, and the arm pointed directly at the beadle, Eberhard Brisch.

Then a muffled voice said, "I found a dead body. It was in the water. I brought it to Eberhard, the beadle, for burial."

Brisch jumped up shouting, "No, no–stop! That is a lie!"

But the voice continued: "And Eberhard said to me, 'There will be plenty of time for a proper burial. Meanwhile, this body will serve another purpose. You know that the Jews are a hardened, bloodthirsty race. They crucified our Lord Jesus Christ, and even today they seek Christian blood for their Passover. They use Christian blood when they bake their Passover cakes, and they do this as a sign of their triumph over our Lord. All Jewish bakers use Christian blood. For example, there is that damned Jewish baker Shemaiah. You can do a holy Christian deed by smuggling this body into the baker's inn. The Lord will thank you.' "

Eberhard shook his head violently, but the wavering arm continued to point. The dark figure of the trapper pointed and it pointed, and it seemed to grow larger and to fill the room in the silence of an afternoon darkening to evening. There was a pressure in the air. It was irresistible. It inflated the wavering spirit, which grew larger and larger and which pointed and pointed and pointed. Finally the beadle yelled, "Stop! Lord have pity on me. All right, I admit it! But for all we know the man *was* killed by a Jew. It is possible!"

Suddenly the shape was gone. The wall was blank. The room seemed empty. The candle flames burned white and round, and every single person was worn and weary; everyone felt stunned and broken and silent.

No one moved. Eberhard Brisch sat back in his chair and he looked at the floor. Eventually, the Archbishop frowned and he motioned to the guards, who went and stood beside the beadle. "Well," said the Archbishop, as he turned to the Rabbi, "what do you suggest here, Mr. Alexander?"

Rabbi Abraham shook his head sadly. "Just as if they were hens, evil deeds eventually come home to roost," he said. "Was this poor man killed by design or by accident? Did the trapper, in fact, kill him? We will never find out for certain–only the Almighty Lord God knows. Perhaps the trapper is now dead; certainly his spirit is already a wanderer, and I cannot help but wonder whether it bears the curse of Cain":

> As the Lord said: "Now you are accursed and banished from the ground which has opened its mouth wide to receive your brother's blood, which you have shed. You shall be a vagrant and a wanderer on the earth."

"In any case, Your Honor, it appears that Shemaiah ben Adiel can be released."

The Archbishop nodded, then he said: "The testimony of the trapper's spirit shows that Mr. Brisch, the beadle, is guilty of slander at the very least. This is a religious court, and two passages from the Book of Exodus are often cited for slander":

> In the full strength of Your triumph, You cast the rebels down: You let loose Your fury and it consumed them like chaff

"and"

> You, O Lord, stretched out Your right hand, and the earth engulfed them.

The Archbishop tapped his chin and looked thoughtfully at the beadle. Old Achselrad waited a moment, and then he said: "Your Honor, I would interpret these verses to mean that the Lord Himself will give the appropriate punishment, both to the trapper and to Mr. Brisch."

The Archbishop raised his eyebrows. He looked at his councilors, he looked at Shemaiah, and he looked at Eberhard Brisch. Then Archbishop Adolph nodded two times, and formally he dismissed the case.

Shemaiah ben Adiel was set free, and the trapper was not seen again in Cologne. Eberhard Brisch remained the beadle of St. Laurence. Unfortunately, he continued to hate the Jews, and he is the subject of other sad tales.

Shemaiah, however, felt as if the sun had begun to shine on him again after the grayest of gray days. He sat down and he composed a poem, praising God and Rabbi Abraham and recounting the entire story of his deliverance. Later that month, Shemaiah gave a huge feast, where he read the poem, and this became a yearly event. Each year on the day of his court release, Shemaiah closed his inn to all but Jews. The inn served meat and wine and Shemaiah's special hot sourdough bread with honey. Everyone had a large free meal. The poorest Jews of Cologne were set at the head table, and Shemaiah ben Adiel ha-Kohen smiled and smiled as he waited on them himself.

Ah, good evening again, Rabbi. It is always hard to sleep on the night of the full moon. Do I see you shivering? Perhaps the spirits of the dead are out and about tonight. Just put your feet up on the side bench here and I will open the stove door. Let me push the coals back. There is nothing like that white glow, washing away all the cares of a hard day and keeping the demons at a safe distance.

This little back room with its warm oven and smooth benches and cool floors is like a holy, peaceful children's world. It is a very safe and protected place. Here, there are no people telling you what to do; no one makes you feel that you are insignificant and unimportant. Out in the rooms beyond–out in the streets and offices and shops of the great, wide, overwhelming world–pushy men and angry women elbow you aside. But here there is no one but you and me in a blanket of childhood calm.

True, my friend, this is a snug nighttime world, a children's world of bedclothes and blankets. It is that same imagined world that we always try to recreate around us, night and day, even to the very ends of our lives–and it is a world that we are always purging of the sharp and broken edges that are thrust in at all angles by outsiders. The little child's world is so simple. It is a place where things work out neatly and cleanly; it is a world of commonplace magic. You know, Rabbi, this brings to mind my little daughter, Erinna-ann. When she was perhaps five or six years old, she told me a story about protecting her older brother. I have to smile now, because she did not even have an older brother. But she talked to us about the problem very seriously. "The other boys are bothering him," she reported. "First," she said, "I told the boys to be nice, and next I told the boys' mothers that they were being mean." These things did not work, so finally (she said) she was forced to use her magic and she *made* the boys act nice.

Ah, if the world only worked that way! But it is late at night, so let me confess something: the world really *does* have magic hidden underneath. At least I hope it does. Many times, as events unfold in my life, I try not to look too closely or listen too critically. I just sit waiting for strange and wonderful things to scurry and bustle out from beneath the piles of papers and prayer books and shawls in the corner. Frequently I lean back here in this little room, musing and dozing and nodding off in front of the stove, as magic swirls all around me.

Of course, I know that even with magic you cannot always protect your older brother or your parent or even your child. What? No, I am not rambling; I am thinking of a very specific incident. It happened long ago in medieval Germany along the wide River Rhine. In those days, there lived a pious and somewhat mystical scholar named Abraham ben Alexander, Achselrad of Cologne. Rabbi Abraham had a yeshiva, and one of its faithful members was a man named Hanina ben Jethro ha-Levi. At the time of this story, Hanina was already an old man. Hanina had married a young woman, and he had a daughter, Rebecca, and a son, Kenan. One day, in his old age, Hanina shivered uncontrollably–just as you did earlier this evening–and this shiver was the beginning of Hanina's sad story.

What is the problem with shivering? Well, I used to think that shivering was caused simply by the cold. But that is not the reason at all. You shiver when the spirits of the dead are about. Hanina ben Jethro knew this, and one day he suddenly found himself shivering and shaking and trembling, and, I am sorry to say, this may have cost him the life of his son.

You see, Hanina ben Jethro angered easily. Often, he said bitter things quickly, without thinking. One evening when he went to the synagogue, Hanina found a stranger sitting in *his* seat in the main prayer hall. Hanina suddenly shivered and shook and he became afraid. And then he was angry at himself for being afraid, and he thought, "Is this stranger really a man? Probably this is a demon. Maybe it is some dead spirit haunting the Holy House of Study, and, worse yet, this demon is tainting my very own seat!" It may have been that Hanina was cold or even ill, but in any case he could not stop shivering. Then, instead of leaving or consulting the Rabbi or just holding his tongue a moment and thinking quietly, Hanina tightened his muscles and he said to the man, "Here now! Get up! Move somewhere else. You have no business sitting in a seat that belongs to another man."

The stranger was poor and ill and rather weak-minded. He looked up dumbly. Hanina hurried over and pushed the man off the bench. The stranger stood up. He was bewildered. As if in a daze, he walked to the anteroom. Then he sat by the door and he actually began to cry. The sound rose to Heaven. And, as with all the cries of the helpless, it slipped into the right ear of the Great and Almighty Lord God sitting on His Golden Throne of Glory.

God turned His head toward the sound. He raised His mighty eyebrows. Angels stopped playing. There was a sudden silence in Heaven. The Great Lord Almighty heard the crying, and He creased His brow; then He sent his messenger Dumah, the black Angel of Death, down to earth. "Take Kenan, the son of Hanina ben Jethro, the Levite of Cologne," commanded the Almighty One. And just at that moment, a cloud passed across the sky in Cologne and Hanina felt a chill in his back, and he continued to shiver and shiver and shiver.

In an instant, Dumah, the Angel of Death, arrived in Cologne. Suddenly he was standing at the side of Hanina ben Jethro. Dumah stood without saying a word. He was covered from head to foot with unwinking eyes. He held a drawn and bloody sword. His breathing was like the sound of dry leaves rustling and rustling in the blank autumn wind.

Hanina recognized the angel. The old man shivered uncontrollably and he said, "Why have you come here? Has the time arrived already for me to die? Am I now to leave this world of troubles and trials?"

The Angel of Death stood with his unwinking eyes and his drawn bloody sword, and in the oldest and dustiest voice of all he replied, "No, Hanina, God has sent me to take away the life of your son, Kenan."

Hanina grew very, very pale. He stepped backwards; his whole body shook. "But Kenan is still so young," he said. "Why ever would you take him now?"

"Kenan's time has come," answered the holy Angel of Death, "and you have actually hurried his death."

"Me?!" cried Hanina. "But what did I do?"

And Dumah answered in dry, deep, rustling tones, "Today, son of Jethro, you spoke cruelly to a poor and weak-minded man. You pushed him. And you did all this in the synagogue, the holy house of God. There was no call for this. You have acted thoughtlessly before – and this was the final time."

Hanina's heart pounded. He was weak and dizzy; he leaned back against the wall. "If I am guilty, O Angel, then so be it. But why punish my son?"

"It is the word of the Lord."

"Then, good Angel, let us have a reprieve," pleaded Hanina. "I beg of you – let me have more time. Let me have one month. Perhaps I can arrange something for my son."

"I do not know what you can do," said the Angel.

"I do not know myself," said Hanina slowly. "I do not know. . . . I only know that I must have some more time. Listen, good angel, I have made only one serious mistake during my life. For the sake of all the good that I have done, I beg you: grant me a month's reprieve."

The Angel of Death was silent for many minutes. Only the dusty sound of his breathing could be heard like a chill autumn wind in the leaves before winter. Hanina trembled. Finally, Dumah spoke, "Very well, Hanina, son of Jethro, I grant you thirty days." Then Dumah, the black Angel of Death, disappeared from Cologne and returned to Heaven. God said nothing, but He was angered fourfold with Dumah, His messenger, the cold black Angel of Death.

Meanwhile, Hanina paced and paced. He turned over all possible ideas. There must be something he could do. In his mind he reviewed all that he knew about Death. Finally he decided on a plan. He went to his business partner. "I am selling," said Hanina.

The other man was eating. He put down his bread, and he sat back in his chair. "You are selling, Hanina? You are selling what?"

"Everything," said Hanina. His partner looked at him in silence and then he shrugged.

So Hanina sold as much of his goods as he could. Then he divided all his money and his property into three portions. One-third he kept for himself and his family, one-third he gave to the poor and to the needy, and the final third he gave to his son, Kenan, to give to the poor and to the needy, for it is said in the Book of Proverbs:

Wealth is a light commodity
  On Judgment Day,
But goodness, alms, and charity
  Shall heavily weigh.

Generous acts and virtue,
  Kind words with each breath–
These will all protect you
  From a sad and early death.

So all the goods and wagons and clothes and jewels and books were sold. The money was collected, and then it was dispersed. Was God watching? Was His resolve softening? Seven days came and seven days went, and soon twenty-nine days had passed–but Hanina had thought of nothing more to do. It was now the dark, dead hours of the night. Hanina could not sleep. He lay in his bed and he stared out his doorway. Was there a dim light in the hall, or were his eyes just remembering the bright light of day? Hanina ben Jethro ha-Levi pulled on his clothes and he stepped out into the hallway. There was silence throughout the house.

Yes, the house was thick with old silence. A dog whined outside, somewhere far, far away. Hanina peered into the dark hall. There by the steps stood a dark figure. The figure turned. It turned, and Hanina's heart sank. He saw that it was Dumah, the Angel of Death, and this black angel stood covered from head to foot with unwinking eyes and held a drawn and bloody sword, and his breathing was like the sound of dry leaves rustling and rustling in the blank autumn wind.

Dumah, the Angel of Death, turned slowly. He turned slowly and silently, smoothly and darkly. Was he speaking? Hanina thought that he heard the holy words from the Book of Genesis, where

Abraham and his son Isaac go off alone together for the sacrifice to the Lord:

> Isaac said to Abraham, "Father . . ." And Abraham answered, "What is it, my son?" Isaac said, "We have the fire and the wood and the knife, but where is the young animal for the sacrifice?" Then Abraham was quiet a moment and finally he answered sadly, "God will provide Himself with a young animal for a sacrifice, my son." And the two of them went on together in silence, and soon they came to the place of which God had spoken.

Yes, Rabbi, the Angel of Death had returned to Hanina's house. Dumah stood and said quietly and clearly, "Hanina–Hanina, son of Jethro–now has come the time for the death of your son, Kenan."

"No! Please go away!" said Hanina.

The sounds woke the family. Hanina's wife and son and daughter came into the hall and they all stood white and terrified, with eyes as wide as smooth round saucers.

Dumah stood at the head of the steps, silent and unmoving, as large and as steady and as cold as a black night rock. Then Dumah the Angel of Death took a deep and dusty breath. Magically he filled out and clothed himself in the four fearsome garments of cruelty, anger, wrath, and severity. He was as tall and as dark as a huge bare tree on the blackest of winter nights. He was a wraith, a warrior, a battle tower. He unsheathed his sword, he pointed at Kenan, at Kenan's small neck, and he began to swing his cold, cold sword slowly and inexorably toward the boy.

Hanina jumped. He stepped in front of the sword. "Please, kill me instead!" he cried.

"All right," said Dumah. His dusty, ancient, bell-like tones rolled on: "Yes, I will kill you, but you must hold still, and you must look me unflinchingly in the eye."

Hanina shook and he shivered, and as Dumah began slowly to swing his cold Sword of Death, Hanina tried to remain strong and steady, but he could not. Hanina blinked and he trembled, and his shoulder jerked by itself. Dumah stopped his swing in midair. He said, "You are too afraid. I cannot kill you." And again he turned and began to swing the cold, cold sword at the small boy's neck.

Now Hanina's wife jumped in front of the sword. "Please – stop. Kill me instead!" she cried.

"Very well, I will kill you," said the Angel of Death in his deep and dusty bell-like tones. "But you must stand firm and tall and look me in the eye."

Dumah, the black Angel of Death, was covered with unwinking eyes. He was a terrifying sight, clothed with the four garments of cruelty, anger, wrath, and severity. From around him, like a vaporous blanket, came blackness deeper than a starless night. There was a deep, hollow ringing in his voice. Hanina's wife tried to stand tall, but at the last moment she looked away and she shivered and shook as Dumah began to swing his cold, cold Sword of Death. So the Angel stopped his swing. The sword hung motionless in the middle of the air. Dumah said, "You, also, are too afraid. I cannot kill you." And once again he turned and began to swing his sword at the boy's neck.

Now Hanina's young daughter, Rebecca, who was younger than her brother – Hanina's only son – hopped and ran, and she jumped in front of the sword. "Please, kill me instead!" she cried.

The Angel of Death stopped his sword in midair, where it hung shining in no light at all. "Very well," said Dumah to the small girl, "I will kill you. Stand firm and tall and look me in the eye."

The young girl stood firm and she stood tall. Little Rebecca stood in her white nightdress, unmoving, as Dumah's cold bleak arm began to swing the heavy Sword of Death. A deep, muffled, ringing tone rode like a wave through the room. The girl watched and she waited. The sword slid through the air: it swung in a slow, even, inexorable arc through the air.

"Stop!" yelled the son. And Dumah, the Angel of Death, stopped. The sword hung ringing in midair. Angels looked down from Heaven. A stunning silence filled the depths of space and time.

"Please, Angel. Kill me," said Kenan quietly.

The black angel had the patience of eternity. "Very well," he said. "Stand tall and stand firm, and do not move." Again the black angel pulled the sword back, back, back. Again he took a mighty swing. Kenan stood tall, and he stood firm; he stood unmoving and unflinching. And as the sword approached the boy, young Kenan looked the Angel of Death straight in the face and at the last moment he said only, "Rebecca," and he smiled the smile of life and he looked Dumah straight in the face. And the sword swung smoothly on and on and it slid through the air and the angels looked away, and with a ringing sound in all of Heaven and earth, Kenan ben Hanina ben Jethro ha-Levi died. Then in the twinkling of an eye, Dumah pulled the soul from young Kenan's head and whisked it off beyond the moon and the stars and into the far blue celestial eternity of forever, into the endless tides of the night of God's cosmic forever, amen.

Good evening, Rabbi. Yes, it *is* a good evening. In fact, it is a poetic evening, an evening when gentle words come comfortably to the tongue, all of their own accord. It is an evening when the Almighty Poet lets us endlessly float rolling, ringing phrases into the air. Tonight we can talk back and forth as smoothly as angels drinking fine wines and playing happily in the celestial breezes that slip and slide in and out of God's great, white, wispy, cloudlike beard.

I do not know why I feel this way, Rabbi. Perhaps it is because you mentioned Abraham ibn Ezra–Rabbi ben Ezra–this afternoon. I picture him with a long, wispy, cloudlike beard, sitting beside a white brick wall somewhere in Spain. It is a bright morning, a barefoot morning. He is very old, and he looks back in his old age. Ben Ezra looks back with a wide patient vision over his life as a wanderer, and he smiles. This backward view looks good to him: it looks good all the way from his young years when he could not stop moving and talking and writing to the recent times when he has been sitting and thinking and watching and reminiscing.

I suppose that most people remember ben Ezra for those restless young years. They picture an ever-traveling scholar–articulate, thoughtful, poetic, inspiring–a compelling man who shaped the

Jewish thought and culture of medieval European days. Of course, most of his writings are the works of this young wanderer: they are collections of notes rather than completed essays. But as for me–I always think of him first as a poet, a poet of his later years.

To me, ben Ezra was first and foremost a poet. Do you know his poetic version of the Book of Isaiah? I remember especially the verses where the good Lord God, promising us the new Jerusalem, says:

Now daylight comes from more than sun
Another nightlight outshines the moon,
It is God, your everlasting beacon–
The Lord's glory brings an eternal noon.

Fear not that the sun sets each evening,
Do not worry when the moon hides at night,
The bleak skies of your sad cold mourning
Have changed to a dawn that is golden and bright.

Righteous and happy shall be all your sons
Forever at peace in your rich green lands–
There, *you* are the truly blessed ones,
The glorious works of God's own hands.

And you few shall become far more–
You, little nation, shall grow strong–
With the Lord you will march to the future
Singing happy psalms as you walk along.

This is new to you? Well, I have a rather good memory. My grandmother first recited it to me many, many years ago; it was when she told me about Rabbi ben Ezra. Here is what I remember:

Abraham ben Meir ibn Ezra was born in the city of Toledo at the end of the eleventh century. In those days Toledo was war ravaged and impoverished; farmers kept most of their produce for their own families, the taxes were high, and the little food and oil and clothes that were available sold at very high prices. Finally ben Ezra left Spain. He was already a rabbi, a linguist, and a recognized Jewish scholar. He had memorized great portions of the Arabic works of his Jewish compatriots, who were still little known outside Spain. Abraham ben Ezra traveled and traveled, and he carried the cultural treasures of the Spanish Jews into far-distant communities.

Ben Ezra wandered through North Africa and Egypt. Then he went to Italy, where he lived in Lucca, Mantua, Rome, and Verona. After Italy, ben Ezra taught in southern France, in Narbonne and Beziers, and in northern France in Dreux. Next, he traveled to London and then back to southern France. Ben Ezra talked easily, and he captivated listeners everywhere. Gentle, light, and witty thoughts slipped from his tongue. The phrases rolled and floated into the air, seemingly without thought, as smoothly as angels drinking fine wines and playing happily in the celestial breezes.

When he settled for a time in some place, ben Ezra would also write essays. His writing was spare and clear and direct, and it was widely read. He wrote on Hebrew philology, he wrote biblical commentaries, and he translated short works from Arabic into Hebrew. Abraham ben Ezra wrote two famous volumes called the *Moznayim* (the *Scales* or the *Balance*) and the *Zahot (Correctness)*. These were the first expositions of Hebrew grammar written in Hebrew. Ben Ezra wrote about everything that he saw and heard and felt–philosophy, mathematics, astronomy, and geography–and one of his textbooks on algebra was even translated into Latin. In his later years, ben Ezra wrote Hebrew poems.

Ah, Rabbi, how could one man know so much? My grandmother said that ben Ezra just opened wide his bright, bright eyes and listened well with his softest and tiniest ears and then all things seemed crystal clear to him. He saw across the countryside; he saw through the past and into the future. Ben Ezra lived at a time of mystical days, a time when the world was both young and old and when it was larger than a person and full of mysterious corners. It was the end of the Dark Ages, just before old Rabbi Achselrad assumed the rabbinate of Cologne, and in those days and at that time, Abraham ben Meir ibn Ezra was the archetypic wandering Jew. But even then, ben Ezra occasionally remained in one place. For instance, he lived for four or five years in the grand old city of Rome.

At the end of the Dark Ages, Jews lived freely and comfortably in southern Italy. When ben Ezra arrived in Italy, he found that he loved the climate and the people. First he lived in Lucca; then he lived in

Mantua, in Rome, and, more northerly, in Verona. In each community, ben Ezra was welcomed warmly–but he never received much more than his daily needs. ("Try as I might to become wealthy," he once joked, "the stars oppose me. If I were to take up shroud-making, then men would stop dying. Or if I made candles, the sun would never set.") He was a poor but holy messenger, a carrier, an interpreter, a purveyor: as he traveled, ben Ezra spread the Spanish Jews' view of the Holy Scriptures, a detailed, complex, and methodical exposition of the Bible that covered everything from spelling and punctuation to literary and historical allusions.

Ben Ezra loved Italy. To him, the Italian air seemed always warm and invigorating. In Rome he walked daily along the River Tiber, crossing and recrossing the bridges, feeling the ancient nobleness of mankind in the walls, the temples, and the churches. At that time, Rome felt young, bubbling with the strength and confidence of its new independence. A Milanese monk, Arnold of Bescia, gave animated speeches. "Be bold," he said. "Rule your own destiny." The Romans became courageous. They elected a local senate, composed of common people: the senators were merchants, shopkeepers, and farmers. The power of the bishop was reduced. Democratic regulations, rules, and reforms were argued back and forth, and many were tried out. However, each restriction on the Pope or on the German emperor that passed the Roman senate brought an angry reaction from those sovereigns, small battles flared continually, and these conflicts occupied the Romans for the next twenty years.

At the same time, the city was at peace with its Jews, and ben Ezra remained in Rome for a number of years. He taught and lectured and wrote, and through him, the city of Rome set a standard for the whole Italian Jewish community. Ben Ezra linked the Jews of Italy to the Jewish scholarship of Spain and North Africa. In addition, ben Ezra became a tie between the Jewish community of Italy and Italian scholars, because he was fluent in Latin. Italians, you see (as distinct from much of the rest of medieval Europe), still wrote exclusively in Latin, not in the local Italian language.

Even in Italy, though, ben Ezra wrote his major works in Hebrew–these were his *Moznayim,* his *Zahot,* and his commentaries on the Pentateuch and on the five books of the *Megillot.* In his commentaries, ben Ezra carefully dissected the most complex biblical passages.

"Stick close to the original," he advocated, pointing out that over the years many Gaonim had introduced extraneous material. "Learn from the oral traditions," he advised, arguing that the Karaites constrained themselves by not accepting the additional information that we have inherited through careful word-of-mouth teaching. Then he also warned: "Do not be seduced by the fantastic or the obscure." Simple biblical stories, said ben Ezra, may mean exactly what they say.

Ben Ezra had a famous student, Solomon ben Abraham Parchon, initially from the town of Calatayud in central Spain. Solomon followed ben Ezra through Italy, and finally Solomon settled in the university town of Salerno. There, he taught Hebrew and biblical commentaries in a methodical, almost scientific, style; also, Rabbi Solomon compiled a widely used Hebrew dictionary. The Italian Jews were proud of Rabbi ben Ezra and Rabbi Solomon Parchon, but somehow no great Italian Jewish scholars seemed to arise in their wake. Although it was a time when Hebrew literature bloomed elsewhere, there are no great Jewish works from the native Italians of that era.

Perhaps old ben Ezra was simply too unique a figure to copy. He was certainly a man of contrasts. On the one hand, he cut through to the essence of things. He was quick-witted and clear-sighted. Long and tangled arguments became short and simple for him. He could take a word and define it precisely, and then he could hold it up to the light and redefine it even *more* precisely. His convictions were energetic, he flung his arms when he talked, and, once he had begun, he was unstoppable.

On the other hand, ben Ezra loved mysticism. He talked about clouds of piety and vapors of faith and personal inexpressible surges of joy and rapture. He loved a pervasive ineffable God, into whose hands he happily resigned his lot. Ben Ezra believed in astrology. In the mornings when he swayed and prayed, he actually felt the tug of the stars, the planets, the moon, and the sun, influences that no man could possibly avoid. Old ben Ezra was at once a sharp critic and logical analyst of the letter of the Law and a mystic and religious astrologer. One could enjoy this wild, warm, articulate man – but who could ever copy him?

When ben Ezra left an area, stories immediately grew up about him, answering the myriad mysterious questions about his personal life. What was ben Ezra's true family history? Some said that ben Ezra had married when he was young and that he had a son named Isaac. But where was his wife, and who were his wife's family? What had happened to his children? No one knew the answers for certain.

One often-repeated story tied ben Ezra to the family of the famous poet Jehuda ben Samuel ha-Levi. When ha-Levi's daughter had grown into a woman, her mother was continually reminding the poet to find a suitable husband for their only child. One day, ha-Levi was wrestling with a *Purim* poem when his wife said, "We will be dead and gone before our daughter is married, Jehuda." The poet was tired. He looked up and said, "All right, all right–the very next unmarried man who comes to our door will become my son-in-law." His wife raised her eyebrows, but she said nothing.

The next day, a poor wayfarer came to the local yeshiva where Jehuda had gone to write in peace. The stranger was friendly but dusty. He had a torn satchel. His shoes were tied with rope, and clearly he was hungry and tired. "Come home and stay with me for a few days," offered ha-Levi. The young man accepted gladly. As the two men entered the poet's house, Jehuda's wife took in a deep breath. Was this vagabond to be her future son-in-law?

After dinner, the poet sat at the table, staring at a paper. He was still working on the *Purim* song, and he was nearly finished. But the last verse seemed weak and dull. It lacked the special uplift of the Lord. It had no color; it had no spirit. It was just a simple general statement and not a direct insight or better yet a true immediate feeling. But ha-Levi could not find the right thoughts, the fit words, in his chest of verse. Old worn phrases rolled around over and over in his mind. Nothing rang clear and clean and fresh and true. Had God's great *Shekhinah* dimmed for a moment? Was holy inspiration failing him? In frustration, ha-Levi pushed the paper and the pen aside, and he walked off to bed.

The stranger had sat silent for hours in a corner. Ah, Rabbi, what was on his mind? The candle still burned at the table. The young traveler stood up. He walked over to the table and read the poem. He read it once, he read it twice, he read it three times; then he sat down and he finished the verses himself.

It was late when the stranger fell asleep, and it was late when he awoke. Meanwhile, Jehuda ha-Levi awoke early the next morning. He came into the kitchen. The stranger was asleep on a blanket by the stove. Jehuda sat down in order to study the poem in the early dawn light. Perhaps in the holy *ki tov* dawn the words would come more easily. But what was this? Had an angel been there during the night? Jehuda read the words and he opened wide his eyes. The poem was finished. The last words were good and right and beautiful and holy. Jehuda looked down at the stranger. Just then ha-Levi's wife came into the room.

Jehuda showed her the poem and said quietly, "Not many men in the world could write with such clarity and swiftness. Could it be that this is really an angel? He calls himself Abraham ben Ezra. He looks like a mortal. In any case, it would be a wondrous gift to have him as a son-in-law."

Did ben Ezra marry ha-Levi's daughter? I do not know. I know only that he wandered and traveled for many, many years afterward and that he turned to his own poetry only when he had become an old man. Even in his sixties, he was still writing texts on mathematics, astronomy, and astrology as he finished his stay in Lucca, Italy. And, ever the wanderer, ben Ezra then left Italy for southern France in the year 4916, at the age of sixty-six.

The next four years in southern France were a quiet time for the old traveler. At the age of seventy golden years, ben Ezra went from France to London. There he wrote a book on the philosophy of religion and he also wrote a defense of the Sabbath, "The Sabbath Epistle." Back in southern France again, ben Ezra revised his commentary on the Pentateuch and he composed yet another book on grammar (the *Safah Berurah*). The old man wrote with his usual freshness, simplicity, confidence, and clarity–and now his works began to contain more poetry.

Eventually, in the great circuit of life, ben Ezra returned to Spain. One day, when he was seventy-eight years of age, he found himself in Calahorra, a city of northern Spain, in the province of Logrono. Calahorra sits on the slope of a hill along the left bank of the River Cadaco. It was the first day of the month of *Adar* of the year 4927. Old ben Ezra awoke in the early hours of the morning. He was staying with a young Jewish scholar. The family was asleep and ben Ezra stepped into the cool, dusty yard. The sky was blue and deep as an ocean. Two clouds were tiny mountain islands far to the east toward

Jerusalem. As ben Ezra watched, the clouds dissolved–and then the sky was an endless blue from far to wide.

Abraham ben Meir ibn Ezra was going home: tomorrow he was going south to Toledo. Old ben Ezra leaned on a stone wall, looking down at the town of Calahorra. The city's skeleton was Roman architecture, with columns and aqueducts and temples and amphitheaters. People were filling the markets; they dragged grain and oil and flax, they pushed barrels of wine and olives down from carts. A white cathedral stood beyond the market. It shone in the early sun. And over the cathedral, all the way from the south to the west, not a cloud could be seen, not a bird was flying, not a single thing marred the pure endless blue of God's glorious heavenly plain. It was a bright morning, a light morning. It was a barefoot celestial heavenly morning, and old Abraham ben Meir ibn Ezra stood that morning in his warm bare feet. He felt happy and dizzy. He sat down, he breathed quietly, and he closed his eyes–and there old ben Ezra finally breathed his last and then ben Ezra died.

Good evening, Rabbi. If you are having difficulty sleeping then put your feet up on the bench and I will open the stove door. Let me push this coal back – soon the white glow will begin to wash away all the cares of your hard day.

I tried to ease your life a bit this evening. I know how you hate to reprimand anyone, so I took it on myself to speak to Reb Mandel.

Yes, it was about his excessive talking. It is an old rule: no one should interrupt the prayers by a single extra word. As it is said: "When you are praying, then do not answer even if a king greets you."

Rules and rules and more rules – we are surround by them, but where are the constables to enforce the rules? We have no constables: there is just one old man – me. The shammas must remind everyone of the rules. And my head is swimming, because the Holy Scripture is simply *filled* with detailed rules. Hidden in the great and holy words are rules that I never would have recognized. Who could guess that it is unholy and even disastrous to begin cutting your fingernails with your third finger? What? Well, Rabbi Jehuda ben Saul was quite clear about this matter. He was a master at uncovering cryptic regulations, strictures, and deep meanings woven in mysterious ways among the sacred words. I remember one day, for instance, when I walked in as he was lecturing his students:

"What?! Why do you ask me that?" he shouted. He pounded his reading desk, the synagogue *almemar.* "You children are like the man who worried whether fleas have belly buttons." Rabbi Jehuda shook his head sadly. Then he continued: "Now *here* is a really important matter: we must respect the hard worker!"

The Rabbi stared down at his young charges. "Respect the hard worker!" he said. Then he continued more quietly: "And how do we know this? I will tell you how. It is from Deuteronomy, Chapter 25: 'You shall not muzzle an ox while it is treading the corn.' "

Old Rabbi Jehuda nodded his head. "And here is another very serious point," he said. "A father should never strike his grown up son."

He paused for a moment. "And how do we know *this?* Leviticus, my friends – Leviticus, Chapter 19: 'You shall not put an obstruction or a stumbling block in the way of the blind.' "

Again the Rabbi stared at the boys. The boys looked at the floor, and there was silence, so the Rabbi said, "Need I say more?"

The yeshiva students looked at their feet, but after a moment, young Moshe ben Samuel said, "Well, Rabbi, perhaps you could say just a bit more."

Rabbi Jehuda stepped back. He raised his eyebrows. "I should say more? Do you need me to spell it out for you, Moshe? Clearly, young man, a son cannot see his father as a real person. A son will always think of his father as a saint. A father is larger than life. He is all-knowing; he is omnipotent. That is why we call the Lord our Heavenly Father."

Moshe looked puzzled. The Rabbi struck his fist on the reading desk. "Moshe, Moshe – think! A son is blind to his father. Now, the *young* son needs correction and he may be punished. But the *grown* son is already set in his ways, he feels like a self-sufficient adult; to the adult, physical punishment is an attack, not a correction, and a physical reprimand from his father cannot be understood, accepted, or defended against.

"I am afraid, Moshe, that when you grow up, you will find that any physical punishment is a hurt and only a hurt. The grown son is blind to the real meaning of any punishment. Among adults, words are the only acceptable currency of change. A physical insult is battle: it is warfare. A grown man's father can correct him with reason, with words, and with argument–but physical punishment is merely a cruel stumbling block in the path of a blind man."

Rabbi Jehuda surveyed the boys. Then he closed his eyes and stood completely still. Time hung immobile in the air. To the boys, old Jehuda looked like a statue–perhaps he had died and was frozen forever at his desk. Suddenly the old man moved again. He took a deep breath, he opened his eyes wide, and he said, "And now for the most important point yet–"

Once again he stared down at the students: "*The Sabbath regulations may be broken to protect a life.* Yes, boys, I know that this may amaze you, but life itself comes above Sabbath ritual. And how do we know this? How indeed! The Holy Scripture says it loud and clear. In the Book of Exodus, Chapter Thirty, the Almighty Lord God (blessed be He) said to Moses, 'You shall keep the Sabbath, because it is a holy day for you.' "

The old Rabbi looked up toward Heaven. "I repeat, young men: 'it is a holy day for *you.*' The Most Holy One said that the Sabbath is holy for *men,* not for Him."

The Rabbi looked down at the boys again. "The Sabbath is not an absolute immutable tribute to the Lord. It is not a required sacrament that transcends entirely our mortal existence. The Sabbath has been given to *us* as mortals. The Sabbath is not ethereal–it is physical.

"And," continued the Rabbi, "the Sabbath has been delivered into our living mortal world. The Sabbath is a part of our weekly existence–and it must be balanced against all the many, many complexities of this real and tangled bodily existence of ours."

There was silence. Then Moshe said, "But good Rabbi, in the very next line the Holy Scripture says: 'If anyone profanes the Sabbath, then he must be put to death.' In fact, it goes on to say: 'The seventh day is a Sabbath of sacred rest, holy to the Lord. Whoever does work on the Sabbath day must be put to death.' "

Rabbi Jehuda looked down at young Moshe. "Of course, the holy text goes on to say this," said the Rabbi, "for that was the Word of the Lord, amen."

In the ensuing silence, a few students murmured "amen." Rabbi

Jehuda closed his eyes. Was this the end of the lesson? The students looked at one another, but then the Rabbi was talking again.

"Moshe," said the Rabbi, "the holy passage certainly says *whoever does work on the Sabbath must be put to death,* but I see that you misunderstand the word 'work.' "

The Rabbi opened his eyes widely and he said loudly, "What is work?"

He pounded his desk. "Work, my young men, is not simply activity."

The Rabbi shook his head and he frowned. "Work is not all possible movements and actions. On the Sabbath we can think and talk and walk; we eat and drink and laugh. We even study. On the Sabbath, a pious Jew does not fall into a senseless, inactive, blank dull stupor."

Again old Jehuda pounded his reading desk. "A Jew prays," he said. "A Jew eats. A Jew studies. Yes, my boys–he prays, he eats, he studies, he rests, and he worships. A Jew does those things that maintain his sacred soul in the appropriate condition to meditate on the Word of the Lord. And are these things work?"

The Rabbi raised his eyebrows. "Certainly not! The things that a Jew does on the Sabbath may be difficult, but they are things that have to do with pure religious life. Work, on the other hand, is for the physical and secular life. But the Sabbath day is a rest from the secular affairs of existence.

"Now," continued the Rabbi, "God has woven a tangled world. What is work at one time, may not be work at another time. In fact, it can actually be a religious task at certain times. And how can we distinguish these two times? Well, frankly there is no one general rule, except: When in doubt, consult a rabbi."

Rabbi Jehuda nodded. "Let me give you an example," he continued. "It is a religious duty to maintain your soul in an appropriate condition for worship. Always be prepared to pray. And, of course, the soul's house is the body, so life is a minimal necessity for a man to worship God. We learn in Psalm 88:

> Lord, why work wonders for dead men?
> Can departed spirits sustain You again?
> Only live men can your memories save–
> New children preserve You beyond the grave.

"You see, the worship performed by the living is not the same as the worship performed by departed spirits: they are completely different tributes to God. Life is a religious obligation – therefore, in the extreme and unusual circumstances of preserving life, one may do what would otherwise seem profane on the Sabbath. For example, it is not work to save a life on the Sabbath."

Tiredly, the Rabbi closed his eyes. "Blessed be the Almighty Lord God," he said quietly. There was silence. The Rabbi opened his eyes. He tapped his chin. He stroked his beard. "I suppose," he said, "that this is quite a bit for you young men to absorb. Yes, it is much to learn and much to remember – but, of course, you do have time."

The Rabbi nodded his head. "Hallelujah and praise the Lord!" he said, looking intently at the yeshiva students. "You have plenty of time, for it is only the year 4893."

Rabbi Jehuda tapped his fingers on the reading desk. The young men looked at one another. "It is the year four thousand eight hundred and ninety-three," said the Rabbi. "It is not even the year five thousand yet, and the world is to last for a full *six* thousand years. Think of it, young men – you still have a thousand years until the Final Day of Destruction. And how do I know this? I will tell you how –"

He began to count with his fingers. "There are six thousand years in the life of the world for six reasons:

"First, the great name *Yahweh* contains six letters.

"Second, the Hebrew letter *m* occurs six times in the holy Book of Genesis.

"Third, God created the world in six days.

"Fourth, the patriarch Enoch, who was taken to Heaven without dying, was the sixth generation from Adam. (That is, Enoch came after Seth, Enos, Cainan, Mahaleleel, and Jared.)

"Fifth, Leah gave to Jacob six sons, founders of six of the twelve tribes – Reuben, Simeon, Levi, Judah, Issachar, and Zebulun.

"And sixth, the glory of the Lord rested like a cloud on Mount Sinai for six days before He called down to Moses out of the cloud.

"Moreover," concluded the Rabbi, "the number six itself contains three pairs of holy twos – thus, we know that":

> The first two thousand years were for God's Law of nature,
> The next two thousand years were for His written Law,
> And the last two thousand years are for His Law of Grace.

The Rabbi nodded and closed his eyes. "Two thousand years are for His Law of Grace," he repeated–and old Rabbi Jehuda seemed already to be resting somewhere far, far away, lost in the last two thousand years of the Lord's World of Grace, amen.

Ah, the great Jehuda ben Saul, he is a warning to us all, Rabbi: there are always more rules and regulations and meanings hidden in the holy words and waiting patiently to be discovered. The Holy Scripture gives us a never-ending task. You rabbis uncover the sacred rules, and then we shammases enforce them. Of course, *I* merely remind the members of the congregation–for what power and authority do I really have? But, in the medieval days, the shammas was the Jewish constable. He was the overseer of the synagogue, he was the executor of the sentences of the Jewish court (he even gave the physical punishments), he was the town crier and messenger, and he was an appointment calendar and an alarm clock.

In the larger medieval towns, there were other law-enforcement officials: there were street police and watchmen, and there were gatekeepers who locked the gates at the edges of the Jewish Quarters each night and then unlocked them in the mornings. The street police and the constables were appointed by the city, and they were never Jews. Well, Rabbi, I must amend that statement: once upon a time there *was* a Jewish town constable.

You see, once upon a time in medieval Germany in the countryside of Westphalia, there lived a young man named Jechiel ben Martel ha-Levi. At first, Jechiel was a young cowherd, but later he became a constable. How could a Jew be a constable in the Gentile countryside? That is a good question, Rabbi, and I will do my best to give you a good answer:

In the end, Jechiel lived in Hohscheid, but I will begin at the beginning, in Bonn. Originally, Jechiel came from the vicinity of Bonn, where his father had been a farmer. Jechiel's father, Martel ben Nashon, had married a woman from Cologne, the sister of Kenan ben Simon. Soon after the children were born, their father died. It was a tragedy. Their uncle Kenan came, and after the funeral, he took the family north. Relatives from both sides of the family contributed some money, and Uncle Kenan managed to settle Jechiel's family in the country south of Remscheid, where they worked a small farm.

Bonn was, of course, a large and commercial city. After the family moved north to the Remscheid plateau, they lived in the midst of a farming community. Although Remscheid had some metal works, trade was of secondary importance, the local market was small, and a man's wealth was measured by the size of his herd of cattle. Jechiel's family were the only Jews. They farmed vegetables, and they had no cattle. The widow held everything together as best she could, but the family was very poor, so the children were hired out to watch the cattle herds of the neighbors.

Each herd was tended by five or six children. The Gentile boys made Jechiel chase the strays and keep them out of the woods. Jechiel was small and weak and Jewish, and he was pushed and taunted and hit. "Walk the cows at an even pace!" they told Jechiel. First they would say, "Walk faster!" then they would say, "Walk slower!" Other times, they threw garlics and cabbages and turnip greens into the herd. "Keep those smelly leaves away from the cows!" they ordered, and Jechiel had to collect the garlics and the greens before the cows ate them and tainted the milk. Jechiel always walked with his head down, and he hardly talked to anyone.

One day, some calves at the edge of the herd wandered into the brambles and then into the woods beyond. Jechiel followed. He was feeling tired; he did not want to have to pull the animals back. Perhaps he would be lucky and the calves would return on their own. Jechiel walked slowly after the animals. The calves walked deeper and deeper into the woods. Then there was a clearing, and Jechiel stepped out onto the edge of another field, a wildflower pasture. The sun was shining, the day was very hot, and the meadow on the hillside felt steamy.

Two young children were lying in the grass. Were they sleeping? Jechiel walked over to them. The children seemed feverish. Jechiel pulled them into the shade. He went back into the woods, he took off his shirt and soaked it in the stream, and he brought it back to the field. He wiped the faces of the children, and soon they began to recover. Jechiel did not know what to do next, so he took his stick, he went over to the calves, and he prodded them back into the woods. Then the cowherd and the animals slowly made their way back to their home pasture on the other side of the woods.

Meanwhile, the mother of the children had been collecting herbs and roots in a basket, and she had walked over a ridge and out of sight. When she returned, she found her two little children sitting happily in the shade.

"That cowherd fixed us," they reported. "The sun was burning. We were sick. Then this man came with some cows and he put us in the shade and he washed us. We were weak before and could not move. Now we are feeling much better."

"What cowherd is that?" asked the mother.

"The one who was driving the cattle," they answered.

The mother took her children home. "Stay here," she told them. Then she went in search of the cowherd. She walked up the hill. The pasture was empty. The woman went through the woods to the second field, and there she found Jechiel sitting quietly at the edge of the field, watching his animals. "Come back with me," she said. "You have helped my children. Let me give you a meal and some better clothes."

"Thank you," said Jechiel, "but I cannot leave these animals."

The mother took a flask of milk from pockets deep within her blouse. "It is a hot day; take a drink," she said. Jechiel took the flask. It was a pottery jar with a fat belly and a small neck. He took one small sip. The milk was delicious, warm and yellow and sweet and gentle.

The woman pointed to a large boulder. It weighed five hundred or a thousand kilograms–in fact, who knows how heavy it actually was? "Go pick up that stone and throw it," she said.

Jechiel opened wide his eyes. He looked at the woman. She smiled at him. He shrugged and walked over to the rock. He could roll the boulder, but he could not lift it. Then the woman said, "Well, young man, try some more milk."

Jechiel was used to doing what other people told him. He came back to the woman and took a second drink. The milk was fine, lightly golden, and rich; it was refreshing and invigorating. He went to the boulder. Why, what was this? He could almost lift it off the ground. He strained, but still he could not pick it up.

He looked at the woman. She stood there smiling but saying nothing. Jechiel raised his eyebrows; then he took a third long drink of milk. He stood for a moment looking at the woman. She nodded and said, "A prayer would be helpful too, young man."

Jechiel closed his eyes. Silently he recited the *Shema* three times. Then he picked up the boulder and he threw it like a light pebble as far as the woods.

"Very good," said the woman. "You do not have to be afraid any longer. You are strong, both inside and out."

Jechiel stood silently. He looked at the woods; then he looked down at the ground. The woman continued: "Now, young man, I know that you have had a difficult time–and in part it is because you are a Jew. But those days of trouble are past; now you may go wherever you want. Here is my advice: do not remain a herder any longer. You will have other business. Remember you have done fine good deeds, *mitzvahs.* God is looking out for you. You are now strong–also be brave and good and true and righteous. That is sufficient for success."

Then the mother turned and left, and Jechiel stood there, looking after her uncertainly. The day was warm. His hands were damp. The grasses itched his legs. Jechiel watched, and after a while he could no longer see the woman. Insects and birds and wind made distant noises. Had he imagined the whole adventure? To Jechiel, it all seemed unreal.

Jechiel shook his head and he returned to the other cowherds. "Where have *you* been?" they asked. "It is time to round up the strays. And you missed the meal, so we ate your bread." One of the other boys pushed Jechiel toward the center of the herd. Jechiel fell against a cow. "Watch out, clumsy!" said the boy. Jechiel stepped toward the boy and picked him up like a shirt or a shoe and threw him to the ground. "Hey!" called another boy, but Jechiel knocked him down too. The other boys stepped back. What was going on here? How could this small, weak Jew suddenly be so strong? They called him names, but they kept their distance.

The next day, Jechiel told his mother that he was not returning to the cattle herd. "I will work the farm with you," he said. His mother opened her eyes wide, but she said nothing. The woman looked out at her land; then she shrugged her shoulders and nodded, and Jechiel set to work.

In one morning, Jechiel cleared the entire back field of boulders and huge logs, pulling stumps from the ground with his bare hands. His mother stood watching in amazement. Jechiel worked all day from sunup to sundown and in that one day he doubled the size of their garden. Then Jechiel worked in the fields every single day, rain or shine. The small farm flourished and Jechiel himself began to grow also. His muscles filled out. He was as big as a giant. He had arms like tree limbs. Jechiel farmed with his bare hands, and peas and rye and barley and melons grew as thick and strong as their farmer. The little farm family had few clothes and no valuables, but Jechiel and his mother and his brothers ate well and they were content.

Ten peaceful years passed, and eventually Jechiel's favorite knife became badly chipped. One day Jechiel went to the small nearby town of Hohscheid in order trade some food for a new knife. In town, Jechiel looked around quietly and talked a bit with the other men. The afternoon wore on. Suddenly a man ran in, calling, "It is the von Heinsberg army!" The shopkeepers, the helpers, and the customers jumped up, they left the shops, and they began to run and hide.

Jechiel looked around. "Wait a moment," he said. "What is going on here? What are you afraid of? What is about to happen?"

Another man said, "Get up! Go off and hide. You may be big, but you are no match for a whole gang of men. The army of the Archbishop, Philip von Heinsberg of Cologne, is coming. No one can stop them. They will go from shop to shop and take whatever they want. But if we stay out of their way, at least they will leave eventually."

Jechiel frowned and he said, "Well, I am not moving."

"Do not be a fool," said the other man. "They will hurt you or even kill you."

Jechiel shook his head. He remained in his seat, he closed his eyes, and silently he recited the *Shema* three times.

The shopkeeper and the men looked at Jechiel for a moment; then they all fled.

After everyone had left, the town was very quiet. The wind blew and soon it turned into the sound of men. Horses arrived, and the riders stopped–the army had moved in.

Von Heinsberg's men went from one store to the next. They pushed chairs and tables aside. They took dishes and cups and knives. They sat and ate bread and drank beer. They put dried beans and smoked meat in sacks. They piled clothes, utensils, and horse supplies in their satchels. Finally they saw Jechiel.

One of the soldiers pushed Jechiel's feet. "Move aside, peasant! Say, give me that cup you are holding!"

Jechiel gave up his cup. "And," said the soldier, "give me your coat and boots and wallet too."

"Will you pay for them?" asked Jechiel.

The soldier raised his eyebrows. "Of course," he said.

Jechiel gave his coat and his boots and his wallet to the man. "Well, big as he looks, this man is certainly scared," said the soldier, laughing with his companions. Two of the men opened Jechiel's wallet, but they found no money, only the knucklebones of sheep (which, as you know, Rabbi, are used to play the game *dibstones*).

"What is this?" said one soldier. "No money? Come along, then!"

"Where are we going?" asked Jechiel.

"You will see," said the soldier.

"I am afraid I cannot go with you. Also, I expect you to pay for everything you have stolen," said Jechiel.

The soldiers turned and laughed. One of them kicked Jechiel in the leg–and finally Jechiel got angry. His stomach tightened. For a moment he heard a roar inside his head and the world looked like a blur. He felt a rush of energy, a wave of strength, well up within him. He picked up the nearest soldier and threw him into the street. Then Jechiel followed. He swung out. He punched another man. He knocked over two horses. He kicked out and broke a man's leg. He was a wild man, roaring and swinging and pushing and throwing. The remaining soldiers grabbed their things and rode out of town.

Jechiel calmed down. He found his coat and his wallet and his boots. He took a deep breath. He was sweating. He washed his face in a dipper of water by the side of a store. Now it was beginning to get dark; Jechiel looked around and started to put things back on the shelves in the stores. Soon the first three evening stars peeked out in the dark blue sky. Shopkeepers began to walk back into the village from their homes, where they had been barricaded. The townsmen looked around. Two soldiers were dead on the ground. An injured horse hobbled about. Five of von Heinsberg's men were lying by a ditch, groaning. The townsmen stared in disbelief. Whatever had happened here? Could this one man have done such damage to an entire army? One of the shopkeepers said to his friend, "What shall we do?"

The second man shook his head. "It looks as if we have found a protector. We should do everything we can to persuade him to stay."

Another man said, "At least we can take up a collection and reward him."

A fourth man went up to Jechiel. "My friend, this is incredible! What can we do to thank you?" he asked.

Jechiel felt tired. He sat on a step in front of the main dry-goods store. "Well," he replied slowly, "I am just a farmer. I am not sure what to say."

One of the other townsmen said, "Listen, you must move down into the village here. We could use someone like you."

"I do not know what I could do here," said Jechiel. "I am used to farming. I am good with animals, and I have a certain strength, but I am really a country person."

A great many townsmen had collected and were talking. "It is late," said a man to Jechiel, finally. "Come home with me. I will give you dinner and we can talk further."

Jechiel was worn out. He looked at the nighttime sky. "All right," he said. So Jechiel stayed in town that night. He slept in the house of one of the merchants, and he was treated like a royal guest. He was given ten gold coins, and when the merchant found that Jechiel had planned to buy a new knife, the man gave Jechiel a fancy dagger with an engraved bone handle.

The next morning, a group of townsmen appeared at the merchant's house. The army of von Heinsberg had been terrorizing the village of Hohscheid for months, but suddenly the people of Hohscheid felt strong and hopeful again. The morning was bright. The air was clean. Leaves were a brilliant green. Jechiel must stay. They would give him an official position. They would give him a house, and they would pay him a salary.

Jechiel was a Jew, but the townsmen felt that he was not like city Jews. Jechiel was simple and open and honest. The mayor talked with the town council, and the men quickly agreed: Jechiel should become the town constable. Jechiel raised his eyebrows. "What is a constable?" he asked.

The townsmen looked at one another. Finally the mayor said, "Well, let me see. You will be responsible for our city's horses and carts. Also Hohscheid is a town with rules and laws, and the constable must enforce them. You can live in the old house by the stable; there is a garden at the side. And, of course, we will give you a salary–how about a gold coin each month?" Jechiel thought about this offer; then he nodded. The men patted him on the back, they said encouraging words, and so Jechiel became the constable of Hohscheid. He was the only Jew in town–and, Rabbi, he may have been the only Jewish constable in all of medieval Germany.

Jechiel's older brothers had moved to Bonn and to Cologne years before. Jechiel returned home and he moved his mother into the town of Hohscheid. Jechiel was happy taking care of the town horses. He fixed the two town carts on the rare occasions when they broke. He was the law enforcement officer in the mayor's court during its Wednesday morning sessions. And every morning before breakfast and every evening after dinner, he walked up and down all four of the town's streets. At most other times, Jechiel worked in his garden. When any difficulties arose, a few serious words from Jechiel were sufficient to avert trouble, because no one dared to challenge him. Jechiel smiled often, and he was calm and modest and responsible, and in those years Hohscheid was also a calm, peaceful, smiling town.

Eventually, Jechiel ben Martel married and he had a family. Jechiel lived a long and happy life, he had many grandchildren, and, when he was far into his old age, he died contentedly. Then Jechiel was carried gently up to the good Lord God's glorious celestial city in the sky. Jechiel marveled at how the city of Heaven had only four streets, just like Hohscheid–but each street in Heaven was an endless starry road lined with asphodels and chicory and wisps of glorious white cloudlets that rolled peacefully on and on over the hills and out beyond forever.

No, Rabbi, I was just resting my eyes. Please, join me here by the oven. An old man like me can doze forever by a warm stove; I suppose that is because my harvesting days are finally finished.

What do I mean? Why, certainly you know the proverb:

> Idle hands lead to the poverty heap
>   While busy hands grow rich anew–
> At harvest time the lazy sleep
>   But prudent men reap the rewards they're due.

Napping is acceptable only for babies and for old men–neither of us has any harvesting to do. When my grandmother grew old, her harvesting ended also, and she always slept for a short time during the day; it was usually in the afternoon, and when the weather was nice she napped outside.

Grandmother would sit in the sun every day that it shone; on sunny mornings she knitted at the edge of her mother's grave. At other times she sat on the bench in the garden with her eyes closed. Did she think deep thoughts or was she just enjoying the drift of the world? As an old man now, I would guess that she probably floated along on the clouds of fond memories. Grandmother would nod off contentedly; she said that she slept so easily because she was "beyond cares, worries, ill winds, and demons," and she would remind me of the proverb:

My son, practice and sharpen your talents–
  Then hold fast to those skills;
They're a necklace of great accomplishments,
  Of wondrous wishes and wills.

With these you can walk without a fear
  You will stand tall without worry or care;
Your sight will then be piercing and clear
  And your sleep will be peaceful and fair.

Next to demons, cautioned my grandmother, cares and worries are the greatest cause of sleeplessness. Ah, but that was *not* the problem with poor sleepless Meremar ben Anselm. You do not know about Meremar? Then let me tell you:

Once upon a time, said my grandmother to me, in the congregation of Rabbi Abraham ben Alexander, Achselrad of Cologne, there was a devout young man named Meremar ben Anselm ha-Kohen. Suddenly it came to pass that Meremar could not sleep at night.

Every night poor Meremar tossed and turned in the dark, dark hours. Endless night sounds assaulted him: creaks and groans and bumps and scratches. Thoughts of what he had done and of what he had not done flashed into his mind. Worries and plans about the future rolled around and around and around in his head. Each morning he got out of bed exhausted. Sunny mornings were worse than rainy mornings: on a rainy day he felt he *should* be exhausted, but on wondrous bright, sunshiny days he and the world were definitely at odds. How could he always be so tired during the day and yet unable to sleep at night? It was a mystery.

Meremar tried all manner of remedies. He tried staying up all night in a chair. He tried sleeping on the floor. He would drink warm milk just before laying down, or he would fast the entire day. He stuffed cotton in his ears; he tied a cloth around his eyes. Nothing worked. Then one night, Meremar noticed that the wall opposite his bed had a dark shadow. It was long and thin. It was spidery along the edges. If Meramar got close, the shadow seemed to slip away. And there was never any sign of the shadow in the morning. "Curiouser and curiouser," he thought worriedly. Finally Meremar ben Anselm ha-Kohen went to consult with the community elders.

Meremar walked to the back room of the old Cologne yeshiva. He waited politely in the doorway until there was a quiet moment in the conversation. The sages were talking and stroking their beards. "Gentlemen–" began Meremar. The old men looked up. Then, still standing, Meremar told them his problem and he shook his head: "Perhaps," he concluded, "the good Lord God is telling me that I do not need to sleep."

But white-haired Baruch ben Jacob said, "Meremar, my good man, every creature must sleep."

A younger scholar, Elisah ben Samuel, nodded, adding: "All animals sleep."

"Even insects sleep, Meremar," said Joshua ben Eliezer.

Then Lewe ben Anselm said, "And it is not only animals. Plants close their flowers at night and sleep."

Meremar listened politely.

Menahem ben Joel stroked his beard and said, "If you cannot sleep, my friend, perhaps it is because you have pains."

Meremar shook his head.

"Well, perhaps you work too much or you have too much excitement or you do not eat properly," suggested Moyses ben Nathan.

"No," said Meremar, "I do not think those things can be the problem."

The sages muttered and stroked their beards and looked to old Shimshon ha-Zaken. Shimshon coughed; he cleared his throat and said, "Perhaps you have forgotten to say the *Shema* at night."

"Definitely not," said Meremar. "I am very careful with my prayers."

The old men sitting on the benches shook their heads. They stroked their beards. They tapped their chins. They muttered to themselves. Finally Meremar turned to the Rabbi. "What do *you* think, Rabbi Abraham?" he asked.

Rabbi Abraham was sitting back in his chair. His eyes were closed. At the sound of his name, he awoke with a start. "What do I think?" he asked. He looked around at the sages and he looked at Meremar. "Ah, good Meremar, I think we must all trust in the glorious Lord our God (blessed be He)." And the sages nodded and smiled, and they stroked their beards and they murmured "amen" and then again "amen."

Meremar thought about that sentiment for a moment. He nodded also; then he said, "But Rabbi, what about my sleeplessness?"

"Your sleeplessness?" asked the Rabbi. "Clearly, in order to advise about your sleep, Meremar, I must go and see your bedroom."

Rabbi Abraham put on his hat and his coat, and he walked out into the Jewish Quarter of medieval Cologne, an ancient city on the wide, dark River Rhine. It was the autumn. Light winds played through the streets. Were there the sounds of ships from warm ports far away? The Rabbi stood a moment. He bent his head, he opened his eyes, and he listened. On some gently-winded days, the Rabbi thought he could hear the sounds of the Mediterranean or even of the sun-tanned Holy Lands beyond. Old Achselrad often listened to the winds:

He would monitor the gentle breeze
Through ancient atmospheric seas
And map the clouds adagio
From far below.

"Now, this autumn wisp of wind right here
Peeking in the window mirror
To whisper, then to disappear–
Do you hear?

"Once it came from David's tongue,
Another fall–the world was young
When first he breathed the holy word
We've just heard."

Yes, Rabbi, old Achselrad listened, and he thought that he heard ancient holy words. You see, angels carry those words forever in the light breezes. Holy gentle winds continue blowing for eternity: they mix into our everyday weathers and flow always and everywhere throughout our vast, thick, incondensably complex world. And that is what the Rabbi heard as he stepped out the front door of the synagogue. Rabbi Abraham listened to the winds and he looked down the road. Then he smiled and nodded and began to walk toward Meremar's house.

When he reached the house, Rabbi Abraham went in the back door. He walked to the bedroom, and he saw that there was a vague spidery shadow on the wall. The old Rabbi stood silently. He listened to the winds, and soon a chill breeze seemed to come from the shadow, carrying the voices of two demons speaking to each other (may the good Lord God protect us from such evils).

As the Rabbi stood listening and wondering and shivering slightly, he heard one demon cough and hiss and say to the other demon, "Ah, you old and evil spirit, I see you are lurking about here even in the daytime."

"Yes, you strange and wicked creature," said the second demon. "I am enjoying our games. It is simply delicious to torment the poor Jew who lives here. I cannot wait until this evening to keep him from sleeping again."

"I must congratulate you," said the first demon in a rustling dry voice, "it was a brilliant idea to whisper to him: 'The *Shema* is enough.' Now he actually believes that it is sufficient to say one small *Shema* prayer at bedtime."

"Well, I must admit that it was a stroke of genius," answered the second demon, hissing and coughing and spitting and laughing. "And the great fun of it is that if anyone asks him, he will swear he is following all the right rules."

When Rabbi Abraham heard this, he had no doubts about the problem. It is said in the Talmud: "Although a man has already recited the *Shema* in the evening service of the synagogue, it is a religious duty to repeat it again at bedtime. Moreover, every man should add at least one other scriptural prayer – for example, the verse from Psalm 31:

> You ignore the idol worshiper
> And You redeemed me, God of virtue:
> I am grateful and now I'm holier –
> I put my fullest trust in You.

The Rabbi nodded to himself and he sat on the floor of the bedroom. He covered his head with a handkerchief. He took a square of kosher parchment from his pocket. On one side the Rabbi wrote the *Shema,* followed by seven mystical words; on the other side he inscribed the magical numbers:

11	24	7	20	3
4	12	25	8	16
17	5	13	21	9
10	19	1	14	22
23	6	19	2	15

which when added in any row or column or even diagonally always equal 65. Underneath these numbers he wrote:

> Mighty is Yahweh-Elohim of Israel, He Who brings restful sleep in its proper time. As it is said in the Holy Scriptures: "Jacob set out from Beersheba towards Harran, and he stopped for the night when the sun had set. Then, taking one of the stones there, he made it a pillow for his head, and he lay down to sleep a deep and holy sleep."
>
> Yahweh, our God, is Yahweh the *one* God. Amen, *selah,* amen–sixty times amen.

Rabbi Abraham Achselrad rolled the parchment into a tight scroll. He tied the paper with seven white threads, and in each thread he put seven neat knots. He strung the small parchment scroll on a slender white rope. The Rabbi stood. He held the scroll by the rope, he looked at it a moment, and then he turned and left the bedroom and went back to the yeshiva.

The old men were muttering among themselves. Meremar was sitting quietly and patiently. The Rabbi returned to his desk, and he looked at Meremar for a moment.

"Now, Meremar," said Rabbi Achselrad, "here are my instructions: Take this amulet. It is a sleep charm. Tie it to the post of your bed, the post that is nearest to Jerusalem. Touch it gently each night before you climb into bed. Then before you lie down say the *Shema.*"

"But Rabbi, I *do* say the *Shema* faithfully each night," said Meremar.

"And that is good and appropriate," said Achselrad, nodding.

"But, my good man, this one prayer is not enough. Actually, Meremar, the Talmud prescribes a large set of prayers and psalms, even for the busy man."

Meremar looked worried. His throat began to feel dry.

"However," continued the Rabbi, "the minimum requirement is at least one more humble statement following the *Shema.* I suggest the fourth verse from Psalm 31 – that is":

> You ignore the idol worshiper
> And You redeemed me, God of virtue:
> I am grateful and now I'm holier –
> I put my fullest trust in You.

Meremar repeated the verse two times.

"Then," said the Rabbi, "in addition to the prayers, follow this routine when you lie down in your bed –"

Rabbi Abraham sat back in his chair: "Stretch out and make yourself absolutely comfortable. Contemplate the Lord for a moment. Then tighten your body and relax it, one area at a time."

Meremar raised his eyebrows and he looked at the other sages. "Pay attention, Meremar," said the Rabbi. "Now, you should start with your feet; then tighten your legs, your hips, your stomach, and so on – all the way up to your jaw; following your jaw, tighten the muscles *inside* your throat and your stomach. Now relax completely. After you are entirely relaxed, then imagine that you are a wine vat.

"Now do not laugh, my friend: I am very serious. Imagine that you are a wine vat and imagine that the spout is on the bottom of your right toe. In your mind, open the spout and let the wine flow out. As the wine flows, it empties you completely. Finally, when you are just a light and empty shell, begin to recite the *alef-bet* backwards slowly, one letter with each breath: "*tav, shin, sin, resh,*" and so on. When you reach *alef,* keep breathing in the same even rhythm. Soon you will be asleep."

Old Rabbi Abraham made Meremar repeat these instructions two times. Then he had Meremar repeat the verse from Psalm 31 again. Finally, the Rabbi set his hands on Meremar's head and he recited from the Book of Numbers:

May the Lord bless you and watch over you
May the Lord make His face to shine upon you
May the Lord be gracious and good to you
May the Lord look down kindly on you
And may He give you peace, amen.

The Rabbi smiled, and Meremar ben Anselm smiled–and then Meremar ben Anselm ha-Kohen left the old yeshiva. Meremar went home. Carefully he tied the amulet onto his bedpost, and he immediately heard a strangled howl. There was a cough and a hiss and a raspy cry. Meremar felt a cool wind pass through the bedroom, but he saw nothing. He was afraid. Quickly he stepped from the room, sweating. Later, he ate his dinner, and at night, he followed the Rabbi's instructions–he said the *Shema,* he repeated the verse from Psalm 31, he contemplated the Lord, he relaxed, and he imagined himself to be an emptying wine vat–and even that first night he fell asleep, although it was not until late into the cold dark hours of the night.

Each day Meremar patted the amulet before he went to bed; then he followed the Rabbi's sleep routine. And each night, Meremar fell asleep earlier and earlier. Then one night, Meremar awoke in the deep dark hours. He looked in front of him and he realized that the wall opposite his bed was blank and smooth and even. The night air was light and cool and fresh. Meremar took a slow, deep breath. The shadow was gone. Meremar smiled, and he fell fast asleep once more.

Rabbi, would you like to share a hard-boiled egg with me? I always eat an egg at the end of the week, just before the Sabbath. Of course I never *begin* the week with an egg. Never eat eggs just after the Sabbath: eggs are associated with mourning, and who wants to start a new week with sad thoughts?

Eggs are magical things. Egg yolk will stop a cut from bleeding, and eggs can heal the spirit, too. When the powers of evil loom up inside of you, eat an egg with the name "Pipi" etched on it; soon you will become calm again. In fact, writing words on an egg is always a good plan. You can memorize biblical verses by writing them on the shell of a hard-boiled egg, and, when you eat the egg, the words will pass directly into your heart.

And for love? Well, I will tell you what they did in the olden days. First you must discover the identity of your true love, your future wife or husband, in a dream. So, secretly take some salt from one house, flour from a second house, and an egg from a third, knead them together, and eat the mixture at bedtime. Your true love will appear in a dream.

Second, in order to persuade that person to marry you, you must get them to look into a mirror made magic with an egg. And how do you get magic into a mirror? Begin with an egg that was laid by a black hen on a Thursday (the day that the Almighty Lord God, blessed be He, created birds). Bury the egg at a crossroads after sunset. Three days later, dig up the egg, sell it, and buy a small mirror. Finally, to infuse the mirror with the appropriate magic, you must bury it at the same crossroads and say: "May the good Lord God bless this mirror and give it the power of love in the names of the angels Aniel and Hagiel, the guardians of the planet Venus."

What is that, Rabbi? Superstitions? Perhaps they are – but as my grandmother said, "Superstitions may be silly, but that is no reason to ignore them." And grandmother certainly never ignored eggs: eggs connect us with the Otherworld, as old Rabbi Petahiah learned many times.

Exactly, Rabbi – I am speaking of Petahiah ben Jacob. He was the brother of Rabbi Isaac ben Jacob ha-Lavan (Yizchak the White, also known as Isaac "the Wise") of Prague, who wrote a profound commentary on several talmudic treatises. Petahiah himself wrote a book; it was called *Sivuv ha-Olam (Around the World),* and it described his travels through Poland, Russia, the land of the Khazars, Armenia, Media, Persia, Babylonia, and Palestine.

Rabbi Petahiah's adventures were at the end of the twelfth century. This was in the days of Abraham Achselrad, and it was well before Asher ben Yehiel was the Chief Rabbi of Cologne. Why do I mention Rabbi Asher? It is simply this: when he was the leading scholar in Cologne, Asher spent most of his time writing and reading. He studied the Torah and the Talmud and he always worked in the little back room of the yeshiva, where for centuries the Cologne rabbis had passed hours on end, working and thinking and arguing with themselves. Above the back study room was a loft for storage. One evening, when he was rooting around among the manuscripts in the loft, Rabbi Asher found a letter from Rabbi Petahiah of Regensburg to Rabbi Abraham ben Alexander, the mystic Achselrad of Cologne.

"My dear Rabbi Abraham –

"I have just met a fine young man, a Jew from Ulm; he has agreed to carry this letter to my friend Rabbi Joedelyn of Augsburg, and I am certain that the good Rabbi will then arrange to transport it to you. I write to wish you and your family well, to convey my fondest greetings to all the Jews of your blessed community in Cologne, and to praise the good Lord God (blessed be He) and His Almighty Name for ever and ever, amen.

"I will not trouble you with the details of my many wagon rides and my subsequent sea voyages. Suffice it to say that safely they brought me here to the Oriental regions, regions that are so near to the great Holy Land where someday the Messiah shall return and deliver us and resurrect all souls and rebuild the Temple on Zion, amen. I write now in order to record for you some details of the lands and the peoples that I have seen in these old and foreign realms. The bright and glorious hand of God is visible everywhere, if only we look–praise the Lord Yahweh-Elohim.

"I have had endless adventures in arriving here. I hope–with the good Lord willing–to relate these events to you in person. For now let me just say that after touring the Holy Land of Palestine, I turned north and eventually reached the city of Apamea in Syria. Apamea lies inland from the coast, on the River Orontes, north of Damascus and south of Antioch. Once, this was a golden city, a treasure city, a museum city for the Seleucid kings, with vast fortresses and palaces of bejeweled rooms. Gardens were beside every building. Countless stables of noble horses filled the city and ringed the playing fields and the arenas. Arcades were lined with trees. Even the saucemen wore embroidered cloaks.

"Apamea is ancient. It grew in the beautiful valley of the River Orontes in the days of Ezra the Scribe, and it was named by the first Seleucid King, Seleucus Nicator, after Apama, his wife. The city was a place of arts and culture and leisure for hundreds of years, through both the Greek and the Roman eras. Finally, in the seventh century, Apamea was overrun and largely ruined by the Persian king Chosroes. It was rebuilt by the Arabs, but recently a terrible earthquake toppled many of the buildings. The acropolis hill remains, with two old Greek temples, and there is still the original open-air marketplace.

"It was in the marketplace that I met a few Jews. One of these gentlemen invited me home, and I have stayed with him for two days and two nights. Yesterday evening, we heard a servant, an old sparsely bearded nomad wearing a knit cap, tell a very strange story. Now, good friend, I have often told you tales that I heard here on my travels, and many of these tales sounded familiar. Here is one, however, that is quite strange and new. It gives me the unreal feeling of dreams: it is like peering into another world–but at the same time it seems to be a world I can almost remember. What do you think?

"First the servant recited a short Arabic prayer; then he began to chant.

"Once upon a time, in the most ancient of the olden days, both Earth and Heaven were good friends; this was when they were actual beings, creatures created by the dear Lord God, the white-bearded Father of us all, amen. One day, Heaven came down from the celestial regions to visit Earth, his friend, and said, 'I am restless: I need some adventure–let us go out into the forest together and hunt for animals.'

" 'Fine,' said Earth. Together they walked into the forest with their bows and their arrows and with a big ax and a sack. They hiked all morning. They heard birds far away, but they saw no animals at all.

"Earth shook her head. 'The forest is strangely quiet and empty today,' she said. 'Perhaps we will find something in the fields.'

"The two ancient beings left the high-canopied woods and stepped out into the open lands. Again they walked and walked, and by evening time, when the first three stars were just beginning to peek out into the eastern sky, Heaven and Earth still had seen no animals, no creatures whatsoever.

" 'Well,' said Heaven, 'before we give up entirely, we should walk along the river.' So that is what they did. And there at the edge of the river, they found a mouse–one single mouse–a small, snuffling little creature, all alone. Earth reached down and caught the mouse and put it in a sack, and Heaven and Earth sat on a gray-green rock at the edge of the river to decide what to do next.

"Earth looked at the river. Then she looked at Heaven. Who would take the mouse? Both beings were tired. They felt that their day had been wasted. How could either one of them return home absolutely empty-handed? But the mouse was tiny: it was simply too small to divide. Heaven said, 'Listen, my friend, you may as well let me take this mouse home. It was my idea to come to the river–and in truth I am your senior, anyway.'

" 'Oh?' said Earth, 'and how do you figure that?'

"Heaven stood up. 'It is a matter of record, young woman. The

Holy Scripture begins: "In the beginning of Creation, God made Heaven and Earth." Obviously, the All-knowing One (blessed be He) made Heaven before He made Earth.'

" 'Well, age is meaningless,' replied Earth. 'Importance is determined by other things. You see, my old friend, the heavens and all the other creations were made for the benefit of the Earth.'

" 'I do not know by what reasoning you come to that conclusion,' said Heaven.

" 'It is quite simple,' said Earth. 'God put all the plants and the animals and the humans on the *earth*. Even the lights shining in the heavens were created "to give light on Earth," as the Book of Genesis clearly tells us.'

"Heaven stamped his foot. 'It is a sacrilege to twist the holy words that way!' he said.

" 'I only speak the truth,' answered Earth.

" 'Obviously, there is no reasoning with you,' said Heaven. 'Leave the sack here. We will consult with the Lord–He will decide.'

" 'Fine,' said Earth.

"Angrily, Heaven went home. But the great Lord God was far away at the time, preoccupied with other matters. Heaven sat and brooded and finally he decided to stop the rains. Heaven held back all the celestial waters and it did not rain. Not even one drop of dew fell from the mountaintops. Plants withered. The dirt dried to dust. Rivers ran low, sea rocks appeared, fish died, and even the bottom mud dried and cracked and flaked. Animals got thirstier and thirstier, and soon they too began to die. A wide and terrible famine swept through all the lands, and people had nothing to eat.

"This was in the far ancient days, at a time when Apamea was still a small village named Famia. At that time and in those days, a man named Alexandri ben Saul ha-Levi came back to his hometown, the village of Famia, after a long trip. Alexandri was a holy rabbi and a mystic. He walked alone into Famia. The streets were deserted. The gardens were brown and filled with dry stalks. The dust and dirt were like sand. The sunshine was a white sheen.

"Rabbi Alexandri was hungry and thirsty. His family was dry and worn. They could not stand; they greeted him softly and weakly. Alexandri was sad. He went to his little back study room. He opened his satchel, and he found that he still had one flask of water and one hard-boiled egg left from his travels. Alexandri closed the door. He put the water and the egg in a bowl. Quietly he said seven mystical *zirufim.* Next he said the blessing before a meal":

> Blessed be You, O Lord our God, King of the world – You Who feeds the whole world in Your goodness, with grace and kindness and mercy. As the psalmist sang:
>
> God gives food to all His creatures,
> And His love endures forever;
> He gives shelter to His children,
> And His love endures forever;
> So give thanks to the God of Heaven –
> For His love endures forever.
>
> And due to Your great love and goodness, we have not lacked food and we will not lack food forever. For the sake of Your great and Ineffable Name, please take care of all and do good to all and provide food for all Your humble creatures. As the psalmist sang:
>
> Each creature lifts its eyes to You
> And You give food when it is due –
> With open arms and a bountiful hand
> You give full meals to the hungry man.
>
> Blessed be You, O Lord our God, Who feeds us all, amen.

"Then Rabbi Alexandri repeated certain ancient incantations. As the Rabbi said these words, a tingling crept into his stomach. His mouth watered, and, before his eyes, wine overflowed the bowl and the egg divided into more eggs and into meat and bread and cakes. Rabbi Alexandri carried the food and the drink out into the main room. His children's eyes became wide. His wife's mouth opened without a sound. Then suddenly everyone was eating and laughing, and the Rabbi and his wife and his entire family had warm breads and light meats and fish and honey cakes galore. They ate and they talked. They relaxed and they laughed. And later they slept as well as they could ever remember.

"The next day, Alexandri invited his friends and relatives to his house. When they had all collected, the Rabbi emerged from his room with a meal such as had never been seen in the small village of Famia before. The people could not believe their eyes. A wonderful dinner followed. Everyone laughed and even cried and they sang and danced, and they all felt light and happy as could be. Then, Rabbi Alexandri provided food for the entire village each day. The townspeople swarmed to his house each morning. They crowded into his front room. They spilled out into the courtyard, and it was all that Alexandri could do to carry food continually out to the hungry masses from his little back room. Then, each evening, the Rabbi fell into his bed utterly exhausted.

"Needless to say, people from the surrounding countryside heard about the endless food, and they came in crowds to Famia. In addition, the townsfolk had sent for all their friends and relatives, and the friends and relatives told *their* friends and relatives. Everyone had suffered terribly from the drought and the famine. Finally they could eat and drink as much as they wanted. Rabbi Alexandri gave them meats and breads and milk and cheese. His tables had chicken and lamb and fish and cakes. Oranges, almonds, dates, and raisins filled the bowls. Wine poured from vast kegs.

"Newcomers were astonished–their eyes and mouths opened and did not close until all the feast was gone. The young danced. The old laughed and joked. Whenever the people needed more food or more drink, Rabbi Alexandri went into his room, he closed his door, and, with blessings and with holy incantations, he commanded the same original egg in the same original bowl of water to produce food–then all imaginable drinks and delicious edibles poured out and filled the little room from the floor to the ceiling and from wall to wall.

"And what did the Rabbi answer when people asked where the food came from? He said, 'I brought back a vast supply of food and drink from my travels, and I have them all stored in a hidden underground warehouse.' It was not a very believable story, but he kept his little room locked and everyone was too busy eating and drinking to discover the truth.

"People left later and later and they arrived earlier and earlier. The poor Rabbi slept less and less, and he became more and more tired. In the mornings before sunup, people sat on the doorstep and looked in the windows and they talked loudly and pounded on the door. Then if the Rabbi was slow in refilling the tables, there were complaints. 'I am hungry, and *she* has eaten twice!' 'This boy took my bread!' 'Where is the honey?' 'Where are the oatcakes?'

"The news of the endless supplies of food and drink was spreading from town to town. Every village in Syria heard of Famia and the wonder-working Rabbi Alexandri. One morning, when Alexandri ben Saul awoke from his all-too-brief sleep, it was hard for him to open the door of his house. People from the farthest towns and villages had come and were waiting there to eat. People filled the town like endless blades of grass in a field, and their number was much too large to count.

"Still, Rabbi Alexandri did his best. He repeated the seven *zirufim,* he said the blessing before a meal, he recited his incantations, and then food flowed. Out from the little room came the meat and the bread and the drink. The Rabbi rushed and he carried and he served. How could he stop when people who had not eaten for days or perhaps weeks now could eat and drink their fill? But the huge number of people trampled the town. The buildings were damaged. The Rabbi's doors were broken, his furniture was cracked, his rugs were torn, and soon the door to his little back room would not close properly.

"And of course poor Rabbi Alexandri himself became worn to a stalk, just like his dried garden plants. He was thin and tired; he felt cramped and itchy. He was a captive, hemmed in and besieged by work and by noise. Would it never be quiet? Would it never be cool and calm? Where were the far and distant breezes? Where were the gentle open spaces under God's endless skies, spread like blue plains above the mountains forever? Where were the windswept, peopleless, silent lands, hinting of hosts of light and of a myriad gentle angels? The Rabbi stopped for a moment. He looked up at the sky, and he sighed. Perhaps the town could just feed itself.

"Alexandri was exhausted. In desperation, he put the egg and the bowl out in the middle of the town square. The crowds surged forward. There was pushing and shoving, there was shouting, there was excitement and playing and wrestling–and then the egg and the bowl were both smashed. Alexandri ben Saul ran to the center of the crowd. He picked up the pieces. People were quiet. The Rabbi held up the bits of shell; they sparkled in the sun with three distinct layers: a beautiful blue like glazed porcelain, a burnished gold, and a white like the thinnest springtime cloud.

"The Rabbi tried to stick the pieces of shell together with wax, but they did not fit properly. He tried commanding the broken pieces to produce food and drink–Rabbi Alexandri tried once, he tried twice, he tried three times–but nothing worked. The people began to talk and to complain. They were hungry and impatient and angry. 'Hurry up,' shouted someone. 'My children are starving here,' said someone else. 'Why is no one doing anything?' asked another. 'This Rabbi is a fake,' yelled a voice.

"People complained and pushed. They walked about. They argued. And slowly–very slowly–the crowds thinned. Families went home. Everyone was hot and tired and hungry and discouraged. A few hangers-on sat by the Rabbi's house. The day dragged on and on. Now the streets were almost deserted. The gardens were brown and filled with dry stalks. The dust and dirt were like sand, and the sunshine was a white sheen. The night came and the night went, and the next morning only a few people gathered at the Rabbi's house. A man pounded on the door. 'I am afraid that there is no more food,' said Rabbi Alexandri. Eventually, the hopeful few went away.

"Soon no one came to the Rabbi's house. Even his friends felt that Rabbi Alexandri had let them down. When the Rabbi saw them on the street and when he waved and spoke and greeted them, they would not answer. Poor Alexandri ben Saul shook his head and looked down at the ground. Why did everyone expect that *he* would provide for them? Rabbi Alexandri was sad, and he was discouraged. He was not their king and protector. He was not God. The Rabbi shook his head again. He went back to his study room, and he sat for many hours. He read through his book of incantations. Was there anything else to try? Where was the great Lord God Almighty all this time? Was He attending to some other far-off business? Perhaps He had given up on His children.

"Thinking these gloomy thoughts, Rabbi Alexandri ben Saul stared absently at the wall and at the floor. Suddenly he saw a small mouse run by. 'Where is this mouse going?' wondered the Rabbi. He reached out and he caught the little animal. 'Maybe,' thought Alexandri, 'this creature is hurrying off to see the Lord.' Rabbi Alexandri held the mouse in his left hand. With his right hand he wrote on a piece of parchment":

To the great and glorious Lord our God–

Please, O Lord, remember Your children and give us sustenance again.

A humble and loving child,
Alexandri, the son of Saul the Levite,
from the city of Famia, in the country of Syria

"The Rabbi tied the parchment around the body of the mouse, which rushed and scurried and bustled away as soon as it was released. 'Godspeed, speed to God,' said Alexandri ben Saul ha-Levi.

"The mouse ran out of the house and down the street. At that moment, Heaven was looking down from atop the mountains. He saw the mouse. He smiled. 'Aha,' he thought, 'so Earth has finally relented.' Heaven scooped up the mouse and strode off among the clouds, and the rains that had been stored up for days and weeks and months broke through and fell upon the world at last. It rained for two days and two nights. And when the sun came up on the morning of the third day, Rabbi Alexandri ben Saul ha-Levi rose early and found the shining dew alight on every buttercup.

"And then, Abraham, everything was finally wet and normal again. Yes, this is a strange story, and it is an ancient story, my friend. It feels almost dusty. The desk at which I write is old and worn and dusty too. And now as I look at my hand, I see that even *it* is old and worn. Ah, we are aging, my friend, and sometimes I wonder whether I shall see you again in the cold Rhinelands of Europe. If not I will await you patiently, sitting beside Heaven, that ancient being who lives above Earth. There, you and I will surely meet, and we will sit side by side in the great green gardens of forever. Will we feast on old Rabbi Alexandri's meals–eggs and honey and sweet wines everlasting–as we rest peacefully in the warm and radiant smile of the Great Celestial Lord? Undoubtedly, we will. Then, Abraham, just as Rabbi Alexandri dreamt, we will look out across the peopleless blue plain of Heaven–I can almost see it now, stretching above the mountaintops and under the white-bearded Father of us all. Good-bye for now, Abraham—good-bye and a warm amen.

"Your childhood friend,
Petahiah, the son of Jacob"

Hello, Rabbi. I will be with you in a moment; every tablecloth must be folded, or the day has not ended properly. Ah, now I can sit next to you by the stove.

I cannot seem to take my eyes away from the coals. In them I can already see the Holy Land into which – the good Lord willing – I will roll someday like a smooth round bottle beyond the grave. But will the world remember me then? I wonder.

Someday I will be dead and gone. Will I have made the slightest dent in the world? Will somewhere there be a bit of a "shammas imprint" that lasts more than a few weeks after I have gone? Oh, I pretend I will leave something lasting, but who can ever say for sure? Perhaps some old letter of mine will survive. One day, my great-great-grandchild will be rummaging in the attic. And what is this? He finds a yellowing paper. Why, it is from his great-great-grandfather! The little boy sits down on a dusty box. He reads the letter, and he pictures me and my world. He might see a bit of today through my very own eyes, then long gone and far away. And for just an instant, his soul might feel the depths of time and space, eternal and endless, ancient and holy. You know, my friend, this was how old Rabbi

Achselrad must have felt when he came across the fragment of a manuscript from the unknown Gershom ben Meshullam.

I have never told you about that letter? I was only a boy when I heard about it. My grandmother often sat up late with me on cold dark evenings. We wrapped ourselves together in the comforter, and she told me stories from medieval days. One night, she told me how Rabbi Abraham Achselrad was, as usual, studying in the small back room of the Cologne yeshiva. Papers were piled in disarray on his desk. It was getting dark; the night candles were lit. Suddenly, a cool breeze, a light evening wind, arose like a gentle Sabbath angel. It blew open his copy of the Holy Scriptures to the Book of Psalms.

The Rabbi raised his eyebrows. Then he looked down at his desk, and he read these verses from Psalm 71:

You will ever fill
  The stanzas of my praise,
And though I am not agile
  With a poetic phrase,
Still I will begin a reverent tale
  Of Your creative days,
Trying for the full detail
  Of all Your handwork says.

From my earliest years
  Your world seemed a masterpiece
And I continue to marvel here
  At Your oaks and mice, Your doves and geese–
Yes, I still smile with youthful glee
  Though now I am old and gray–
And, Lord, please look down and comfort me
  To my final blue-skied day.

I will describe Your woodsy world
  For the future generations,
Singing of Your works unfurled
  And of Your great creations;
I will praise Your untold creatures
  To the highest Heaven–
The fish, the birds, the tall green firs–
  And all else You have ever done.

Somehow, these sacred verses seemed to glow in the yellow candlelight. "Curious," thought Rabbi Abraham, "I wonder what holy mysticism is afoot this evening?" Old Achselrad tapped his chin. Was there a noise at the door? The Rabbi looked up, but no one stood in the doorway.

The Rabbi shook his head. He looked afresh at his papers. His desk was too cluttered. He picked up a pile of papers. It was time to retire them to the loft above his back room, where, in the dim, dusty corners, rabbis and scholars had for centuries stored the products of their thinking and writing.

Slowly, Rabbi Achselrad climbed the ladder. He lit a candle in the little attic. He set his papers on a pile of prayer books. Where should he store things tonight? He looked around, pushing some torn prayer shawls aside. And what was this? Thin, spidery handwriting, black and neat, caught his eye. Achselrad sat down. He picked up the parchment, and he began to read. It was an old document, a short account of the economics of a small community near Cologne. It seemed to be a bookkeeping report to one of his predecessors, Rabbi Yehudi ben Solomon.

Underneath the report was another set of papers. Below the dry accounting there was the end of a brief manuscript–or was it perhaps a long letter? It was written in the same thin and slightly shaky hand. The first part was missing–the narrative picked up only at the end. The Rabbi opened wide his eyes, and this is what he read:

"And now I have yet another young grandson with me. He stays around the house to help me out because today there is little that works well in me except my tongue. We have neither cow nor horse, sheep nor lamb, cart nor wagon. But we do have a handful of turnips and a fire. And, of course, I have many a fine memory.

"I have been twenty-seven years hard at work learning this bit of Hebrew, ever since old Rabbi Samuel passed away. I have kept at it in my spare time, between chores and jobs. Recently I have had more writing time because things have been quiet and the times are thin. But in the past, something or other always seemed to come my way, one thing after another, a job or a windfall gift, to keep me from being hungry. I have always had faith that He that gave us teeth will also give us bread, and I have managed to survive. Through it all, I have persisted in my writing. How many times have I heard some neighbor say, 'There is no use in the countryside for Latin, and certainly there is none for Hebrew.' Ah, but now that I have written these memoirs, I can say that these men are wrong. If it were not for my daily scribbling, I would have been worrying constantly about the small and fleeting problems of life, and I would have had nothing to look forward to in the evenings.

"From the city, you might think that living in the country is a terrible difficulty. But life is not really very rugged for those who understand the ways of nature. Nature is rich and plentiful. Out here, deep inside the woods and the fields and the streams, the good Lord God (blessed be He) has seen to it that there are always extras – there is always something more around every corner. A countryman will see new things forever. It is like studying the Torah: there is always layer upon layer of new and wondrous things to uncover.

"Consider plants, for example. They are useful for eating, and they are also good for clothing, for decorations, and for medicines. My grandmother knew the healing herbs as well as the edible ones. She made me memorize the plants, their names, their virtues, and their dangers. In the fields and in the hills, she showed me how to live among the plants. She demonstrated the mixtures and powders and teas which, if they were not always good tasting, at least purged us faithfully of our ills. To me, even as a tiny boy, the plants became a living ocean in which I swam. The greenery of nature was like waves and seaweed and clouds, with ever-changing, new, and surprising entanglements. And every single leaf was different. Pick a dandelion leaf and you will see that its edges are absolutely special; they are its very own and they match no other ever seen under God's great sun, amen.

"And what were my green young days like? Well, I will tell you briefly. The grown-ups worked in the fields and vineyards, in the gardens and barnyards, and in the stables and houses. We children helped everywhere. I was the youngest and I became the tagalong herbalist, until my grandmother died when I was about nine years old. And, Rabbi, did the sun shine every day? It must have, for even three generations later, those days are brighter to me now than the candlelight at my right hand. I remember the bellwinds, chicory, gromwells, jipijapas, knotroots, rabbitweeds, sunworts, and tangleberries. I collected vegetables and seeds and nuts and dried fruits. And I cut herbs for our rabbits, as well as for the family. I gathered vine shoots and all manner of dried plant stems and canes, and I bundled them and brought them back to the house for kindling.

"Of course my jobs followed in the cycle of the seasons. At the end of the summer, I helped to bind and cart the wheat and the oats. Later, I gathered raisins at a neighbor's farm after grape harvests. And do not think that these chores were boring. Everything was big and bright and surprising. Even the horses, stomping in tireless circles, were big-eyed, warm, and magical creatures. After the winnowing of wheat, I watched the men tie straw into bales. We children would follow the wagons everywhere, and I remember especially how, at the mill, crushed wheat was slowly ground into flour. Then afterward there was nothing better than the new-baked bread.

"I do not think that memory deceives me when I say that we were rarely ever sick. Instead, it seems, at least now that I look back on it, that we children were always healthy and running through the fields. When I picture those days of rushing and running and jumping about, I remember gathering purple wildflowers and stringy plants. Always, there were tiny seeds and fruits on the ground. And we caught insects and even birds–jackdaws and tanglepickers–when we were quick and (as we used to say) 'snatchy' with our hands.

"Well, anyway, Rabbi, I once thought that there would be nothing to say in these memoirs. But, as you see, beginnings lead to middles and middles travel on and on of their own accord–and now I have slipped downhill toward the end. Along the way I have set down nothing but the truth. I had no need of invention, for I still have a good deal of memories left: it is amazing what a lot there is in an old man's head when he starts talking. All the same, I wrote only a bit of the whole; what I have written down are the things and the people that meant the most to me. I considered the whole course of my life, and special things and special people were the first to come back to life in my old-man's memory.

"I have brought other people besides myself into my story. How could I not? We live entangled with others. So I have told the complex, tangled stories of others as well as of myself. But if I had been timid and had not mentioned them, then the story would have been less true. Our world is a collection of tales about people–actually, our world is simply a crowd of people, all hoping and working and getting tired and in the end trying to rest at peace in the Sabbath of old age.

"My neighbors and I have been poor and simple people, living from hand to mouth. Still, I suppose that we would have been no better off as rich misers. We accepted the life that our wondrous Master, the good Lord God (blessed be He), made for us. We ploughed our fields with only the hope in God to carry us through the hard years.

"Every place has special features and strange people, and certainly we had characters of our own here. There was old Yashcke the crank, whose right side drooped and who started every sentence with a 'No.' There was Otmein, who had tiny eyes and never seemed to listen and whom, I must say, you always wanted to strike with a stick. Or Clarenda–now long dead–who looked black and evil and made everyone's stomach tighten whenever she walked by. And, Rabbi, these people are now all dead and gone and buried. Yes, we certainly had our strange ways and our failings–I no less than the others. But in the hardest of times, we did what we had to: we went on living as best we could.

"All of these people have been good people. Now that I am old, I can see that almost every one of them tried his best. You know, Rabbi, I remember them all fondly, and I wish that I could take them by the hand again. I would now be easier on some of them. To some, I should, I admit, like to apologize and perhaps even to give them a hug. They were all fine, fine people. Even in my young and tough and prideful days, I never truly disliked any of them, but I could have been kinder and more of a friend. I laughed when I should have been quiet, and I pushed when I should have turned away. And, then, I turned away when I should have said a kind word or given a pat on the shoulder. Ah, well, it is all done and past.

"Let me see, what else I can say? I look up now, and what do I see? My house has only two rooms. In fact, the whole village is small. It is a little pocket in a great and busy world, and again and again the winds roll along and blow over us, whisking the high-flying turnstones and windhovers across the sky. The storms are so violent that, when they blow up, you dare not put your head out any more than would a rabbit that crouches in his burrow when the rain and the thunder and the lightning are flying. I remember working in the fields at dawn when the weather was decent–but then on some days, by nightfall, the skies had blackened, the trees were bent, and we feared for our lives. The out-of-doors was our business, however. In this little place there was time only to live our lives and to weather the storms – nothing else could be done.

"Still, as I look back, I remember a good life. Sometimes there was extra money, sometimes there were fine stews and warm breads and cheap drink. There were laughing friends and high times; there were light hearts and nights with wondrous company. Ah, Rabbi, in those days, we would walk home together, easy and friendly, after laughing and stories, just like the children of one mother, secretly wanting to link arms and hold hands but too shy to dare. For me, that is gone now: the high heart and the fun are passing quiet from the world.

"But I see that I am rambling on, Rabbi, and now I should end. I have written all these details because I would like somewhere to have a memorial of it all, plain and simple as I now see that it was. One day, there will be no village here. The young people usually go, and they rarely return. God has given me the chance to preserve those days that I have seen with my own eyes, so when I am gone, other men will know what life was like in my time, in my place, and among the neighbors that lived with me. I want some record to live of our times, for I wonder if the likes of us will ever be again.

"I am old now. Many a thing has happened to me in the running of my days. Have I seen sacred wonders? Have I heard angels? Well, I guess that there *have* been small wonders and distant angels. If you live long enough, then you will see everything, and God has created a great world full of many, many little worlds. People have come into the village around me, and they have gone out again forever. Children upon children have popped up like little Brussels sprouts. Ah, Rabbi, I certainly am old. There are now only two older than me alive in all the surrounding countryside. The days are becoming cloudy, and I take it as a warning that death is not far off. Dumah, the black angel, will be bringing his cold sword to the head of my bed sometime soon.

"I am old, but I can remember long ago, Rabbi – even being at my mother's breast. She would carry me onto the hill in a basket she had for bringing back the roots and the wood chips. When the basket was full, she carried me home under her arm. Then I remember being a boy. One vision I have is like a painting. I am wearing a blue jacket, blue as a morning sky. I am frozen in the middle of running. There are tall scratchy grasses. The sky is cloudy. It is so cloudy that all above me is a pure white light everywhere; in fact, that is still what I imagine God's radiant *Shekhinah* to be like. And I also remember being a young man; I remember smiling and feeling strong enough to break trees. Those were many fine days, and now they seem to have happened in other, far-off lands.

"Since the first fire was kindled in this isolated region, I wonder if any other person has bothered to write about the simple life here. Well, far in the future this writing will tell our great-great grandchildren how we lived once upon a time, long, long ago. My mother used to go about carrying wood chips and turf. She did it so that I would have some time free from work in order to study in the local schoolhouse. Eventually I got a bit of Hebrew, and it has proved enough to set down my memories. I hope, through the many good graces of the Great Lord God Almighty, that she and my father see this memoir. Mother and Father, you can breathe easily again and feel happy. Rest, please, in the Blessed Kingdom of the Great Hereafter, where I shall see you soon. Then we will all walk together hand in hand. And I hope too that every reader of this little story will also meet me afterwards, walking gently in the golden hills of the Land of Eternal Peace, amen.

"Written down
in the evenings of
Tammuz, Av, and Elul in the year 4897
by Gershom
the son of Meshulam"

Rabbi Abraham finished reading. He looked away from the old letter, and he rested quietly, with the paper lying in his lap. Then old Achselrad stood, he blew out the candle, and he took the parchment down from the loft and put it on his desk. He would copy it into his *Keter Shem Tov*. My grandmother said that later the Rabbi put the original parchment fragment back in the loft above the old yeshiva in Cologne. And is it still there? Frankly, Rabbi, I myself do not know.

Good evening, Rabbi. Good evening and *Sholom aleikhem.*

Why of course, sit down here. The night fire helps me to become sleepy also. Clearly you and I are not blessed like old Reb Elbaum, who nodded off during the last prayers this evening. He has learned to sway piously even while asleep; undoubtedly he acquired some magic from the mystic Achselrad.

In those days, much magic was abroad in the world. It was not only the angels and the hidden saints–the *Lamed Vav Tzaddikim*–and the holy prophets like Elijah who could induce sleep and make rocks move and tickle an old man into dancing a happy Sabbath dance. Mystic rabbis had these magical powers too. Even the average Jew could work a bit of magic and have a taste of Heaven's joys right here on earth: in those days, it took only a friendly *"Sholom aleikhem."* But many a Jew missed out on the experience, especially with the Prophet Elijah.

You do not know about Elijah and the missed *Sholom aleikhem?* I first heard of it from my grandmother when she told me the tale of Menachem ben Anschel ha-Kohen, a pious Jew who lived in medieval Germany at the time of Rabbi Abraham ben Alexander, the mystic Achselrad of Cologne:

Did this happen in the early spring, or was it in the late winter? At the moment, I forget. In any case, I do know that old Rabbi Abraham was dozing one day, in the back room of the Cologne yeshiva. It was warm in the study room, and he had stayed awake all night, writing in his tome of mystic Kabbalistic lore. Before he fell asleep, Rabbi Abraham had been muttering to himself, "*Sholom aleikhem, Sholom aleikhem . . .*" and this set the other men in the room to talking.

White-haired Baruch ben Jacob was saying, "You gentlemen all know the wonder-working rabbi, Rabbi Anschel ha-Kohen of Coblenz."

The other scholars nodded.

" '*Sholom aleikhem!*' he called out one night," continued Baruch.

Lewe ben Anselm looked puzzled, but a younger scholar, Elisah ben Samuel, said, "Ah, Reb Baruch, undoubtedly you are speaking of the time when Rabbi Anschel took five of his disciples on a long journey."

"Exactly," said Baruch. "You see, it was very late at night when the travelers came to an inn in a small town near Hersfeld. One of the young men knocked at the door, and the Rabbi called out to the innkeeper, '*Sholom aleikhem!*' "

"Amen," said Moyses ben Nathan. The other men nodded. Baruch nodded silently also. As Baruch seemed content with what he had said so far, Elisah continued the story: "As I recall, Baruch, the innkeeper refused to get out of bed because it was a cold night."

Baruch looked around at his colleagues; then he said, "Yes – so the Rabbi became angry. 'You impious man!' he called out. 'I said, *Sholom aleikhem!*' Still there was no response from inside the darkened inn."

The many sages muttered. They stroked their beards. They shook their heads.

Baruch shook his head also. After a few minutes of silence, Elisah prompted Baruch: "And then what did the Rabbi do?"

"Why, he did what any angry rabbi would do in those circumstances," said Baruch. "He declared, 'Ah, wicked fellow, I hereby decree that your inn shall burn down tomorrow!'

"Now the innkeeper became worried. Could the Rabbi actually do this? The innkeeper got out of bed, and he opened the door. In trooped the angry Rabbi and his five angry students."

Two of the old Cologne sages, Joshua ben Eliezer and Lewe ben

Anselm, said "amen" at the same time. Another sage, Menahem ben Joel, nodded silently.

Baruch sighed and stroked his beard and he said, "To be safe, the innkeeper immediately brought out a honey cake and he offered the travelers some sweet wine to go with it. This made the Rabbi feel better. In fact, after a few cups of wine, the Rabbi raised his hands, he bowed his head, and he intoned, 'I now decree that your house shall *not* burn down tomorrow.' "

Old Shimshon ha-Zaken coughed.

Baruch looked at Shimshon severely. "And then, my friends," said Baruch, "a holy miracle occurred. Just as the Rabbi had declared, the inn remained whole and safe and secure the next day. Now, I know that these wonders are not common, but the five students of Rabbi Anschel have each attested solemnly to this very fact."

"Ah, praise the Lord," sighed Menahem ben Joel.

"Amen," said the other scholars.

"And," said Baruch, "I remind you that it was all because of a *Sholom aleikhem.*"

The old men on the benches seemed a bit unclear as to what Baruch meant, but they did not have time to ask him. A light breeze whisked through the back room, and at the words *Sholom aleikhem,* Rabbi Abraham suddenly awoke with a start.

The Rabbi sat up and looked around as if he did not recognize the other scholars. He winked and he blinked, and for a moment he seemed to see a white, bright, and radiant light. Perhaps old Achselrad had just had a vision–certainly he had just had a dream. As you know, Abraham Achselrad had been a pupil of Eliazer, the mystic of Worms, and the aging Achselrad was somewhat of a mystic and wonder-worker himself. And now Rabbi Abraham had had a dream: he had dreamt of a congregant named Menachem and also of the Prophet Elijah. And who exactly was this Menachem? Well, I will tell you:

Once upon a time there was a man, a pious man, a holy man, named Menachem ben Anschel ha-Kohen. Menachem was the son of the very same wonder-working rabbi of Coblenz (may a blessing be on both of their names, amen) of whom the Cologne sages had just been talking. By now, Menachem was an adult, a scholar in his own right, and he was a member of Rabbi Achselrad's congregation in Cologne.

But Menachem had grown up in the city of Coblenz, where his father had been a famous mystic and a holy, wonder-working rabbi.

When Menachem was a boy in Coblenz, his father was always discussing his favorite prophet, Elijah. "Elijah," said Rabbi Anschel, "brings the presence of our great God, our Heavenly Father, down to us here on earth. Elijah is a friend to the Jews. He is an intermediary. He is a wandering spirit. Elijah is like an angel, and he can intervene for us with the Almighty Lord God."

Menachem leaned forward on his little bench. Rabbi Anschel waved his arms as he continued: "The Prophet Elijah can call upon God directly. Once, my son–as you no doubt recall–Elijah was challenged. He was laughed at. He was scorned. 'Is there really a God of the Israelites?' called out the doubters. 'Do you have a King of kings?' asked the heathens. 'Or is He only a Servant of servants?' 'Will this God show His powers and work miracles?' asked the disbelievers. Elijah stood tall and he stood firm. 'Ah, my friends, before kings and before common people, God will show His presence,' he declared."

Young Menachem nodded. He pictured Elijah with a long white beard and with a flowing white prayer shawl. He imagined the prophet standing taller than the tallest man. Elijah had strong arms and carried a stout wooden staff. And his voice! Why, Elijah talked just in the way that thunder rumbles and that great bells toll!

"So," continued Rabbi Anschel, "at Mount Carmel, Elijah built an altar of stone. Then he placed a sacrificial animal on the altar. Next, Elijah poured water over the sacrifice and the altar. Just imagine this, my son! How would he light the wet sacrifice? How would he make a burnt offering? 'Upon my life, this sacrifice shall burn!' he vowed. 'God shall work His wonders. And you who are caught hesitating between God and the idols must then choose. And those of you who are the faithful–take you the Lord!' Amen, amen."

"Amen," whispered Menachem.

"Then Elijah bowed down," said the Rabbi, "and he prayed. All was silent. Nothing happened. People shifted and fidgeted; they began to whisper. Suddenly the sky darkened, thunder boomed, and the fire of the Lord fell upon the earth. It split the wood, it lit the altar in a flash, and it consumed the burnt offering and the wood and the stones and it sizzled the water into steam, and the people fell back in fear and awe, amen, amen, amen!"

The Rabbi took a deep breath, he lowered his head, and for a moment he said no more. Menachem was wide-eyed, and he too took a deep, deep breath.

"And, my son, Elijah remains Israel's guardian," continued Rabbi Anschel after a time. "The great prophet never died. Instead, he was flown to Heaven in a fiery chariot. Today he is often abroad on the earth, wandering about in different guises. As you know, we wait for him at Passover, leaving a fifth cup of wine, a cup of Elijah, on the seder table. And Elijah does come, my son. Sometimes he looks like an old traveler; sometimes he is invisible. But one day, he will return in his original strong form. This will be at the End of Time, when terrible cataclysmic struggles arise. Then the Prophet Elijah will appear. He will unite the peoples and announce the arrival of the Messiah, of God's eternal kingdom, and of everlasting Peace. As it is said in the Book of Malachi":

I, the Lord, say:
"Elijah will reign
On Judgment Day–
He will come again
And then will tether
Fathers with children
And bring together
All long lost kin."

Rabbi Anschel nodded to himself, and he said, "Elijah's name means 'Yahweh is God.' Nowadays we think of him as a gentle protector, a household spirit. But in fact, he is the strongest, the grandest, and the sternest of the Hebrew prophets. In the Holy Scriptures, he appears suddenly, stark and powerful. Elijah the Tishbite, of Tishbe in Gilead, comes out of nowhere, saying, 'I swear by the life of the Lord the God of Israel, whose servant I am, that there shall be drought–neither dew nor rain will fall in these coming years–unless I give the word.' Ah, Menachem, *there* was a prophet as tall and as strong as an oak."

The Rabbi fell silent. Menachem could see the oaken prophet, towering and terrible in the evening light, standing like a handsome warrior on a mountain against a gray-white sky.

"And now," said his father, "long after those ancient biblical days, Elijah remains the protective spirit of Jewish people and their households and of wayfaring Jewish scholars everywhere. Elijah wanders and watches. He crosses the earth, visiting all the dispersed Jews. Elijah slips into our homes, especially at Passover and at important ceremonies such as circumcisions. Sometimes we can see him, but usually only fleetingly, and usually he looks like a bent, dusty traveler. But, my son, just greet him with a friendly *Sholom aleikhem* and you will feel his holy glow, you will hear his gentle, deep voice, and you will see a bit of Paradise and the eternal kingdom to come, amen."

Menachem was enrapt. He could hardly move. Elijah is God's wandering messenger on earth. Elijah is the Jew's guardian spirit. Elijah foreshadows the coming of the Messiah! Menachem could wait no longer. He simply had to see the Prophet Elijah. "How can I see him tonight?" he asked his father.

Rabbi Anschel patted his son on the shoulder. "Be patient, young man. If you study the Torah, if you read every word, then soon you will find the prophet–or he will find you."

Menachem immediately went to his room and began to read. Each night he carefully repeated the holy verses aloud, word after word, sentence after sentence, and verse after verse. He pored over the sacred books late into the night. At any unusual sound, Menachem would look up hopefully–but no one came. Where was the prophet?

After a week, Menachem went to his father. "I have done what you told me to do, but Elijah has failed to appear," said the boy.

"Ah, my good and hardworking son, do not be so impatient. When you deserve to see him, then he will come." Rabbi Anschel smiled, but Menachem just sighed.

Rabbi Anschel had a small yeshiva in Coblenz, and Menachem often stayed late with his father. One night, as Menachem sat at the desk in his father's house of study, a poor wanderer came in. He was hot and dirty. His clothes were gray and torn. Patches were sewn over his jacket and pants, and these patches were laid at all angles, one on top of the other. His shoes were held together with rope. And as to the man himself? He was short and he leaned to the left. His nails were cracked. He had a large, bent nose. His beard was uneven, both thick and thin at the same time. Dried leaves were caught in the back of his hair. On his shoulder, there was a heavy pack filled with old bones and rags and broken pots, and he and all his things were covered in dust and grime.

The man began to put his pack down. Crumbling leaves slipped out; dirt fell onto the floor. Menachem put up his hand. "Hold on a moment, sir. This is a holy place. Please set your things down out in the yard–and then dust yourself off too."

"I am very tired," said the wayfarer weakly in a high voice. "Let me rest here awhile. Then I will go out and look for another place to sleep."

"That is not a good plan," Menachem told him. "You cannot rest here. You are getting this building dirty. My father, the rabbi, does not like tramps to come and settle themselves here and get mud all over the place."

The stranger stood a moment. He tilted his head and stared at young Menachem. Menachem's throat felt dry. Would this old man continue to torment him? Finally, the stranger said, "May the good Lord God help you to serve Him in all sincerity, young man."

The wanderer spoke in a quiet voice: "May He lead all your doings and all your words to His name. May your peace and the peace of the elders and the scholars and the wayfarers and your friends and relatives and all your family be great. May our God bless them one and all, amen."

Menachem coughed and said hoarsely, "Amen," but he added nothing more.

The stranger sighed. He lifted his pack to his shoulders, he turned, and he went away. And for a moment, the doorway was lit by a white, bright, and holy light. But had you looked out in the street, then you would have seen only an empty road and you would have heard only the wind and creaking boards and far, far away the faint bark of a dog. And back in the yeshiva building? Inside, there was an empty distant silence too.

Later, Menachem's father came into the room.

"Well," asked Rabbi Anschel, with a smile, "have you seen the Prophet Elijah?"

"No, not yet," answered his son sadly.

"What? Was no one here this evening?" continued the father.

"Yes," said Menachem. "A poor wayfarer came in just before. He was dirty, so I suggested that he clean himself before he returned."

"But did you greet him?" asked the Rabbi hurriedly. "Did you welcome him? What did you say? Did you bid him *Sholom aleikhem?*"

"No, I did not. He was dirty and gruff, and I sent him away," Menachem answered.

"Why did you do that?" asked his father. "Did you not recognize the Prophet Elijah? Now I am afraid it is too late." And Menachem just opened wide his eyes, and he was sad and stunned and silent.

Many years later, he said, "I was but a child. I could not believe how empty and lost I felt. Was the world so distant and lonely? The walls seemed dark, the floors were hard and cold, the ceiling was tall and far away. I sat and sat for many hours. The yeshiva darkened, and the candles burned low and gray." Menachem sighed. "*Sholom aleikhem*–what a simple thing it is to say. It is a warm greeting; it is an easy greeting. But sometimes it is hard to remember."

"Sometimes it is hard to remember . . ." like the dream that old Rabbi Abraham dreamt once upon a time in medieval Cologne. Had Elijah himself, guardian angel of all wanderers, waifs, and wayfarers, actually come to Coblenz? Rabbi Abraham ben Alexander, Achselrad of Cologne, seemed to waken for a moment. He sat up. He winked and he blinked, and he said something very quietly. Was it *Sholom aleikhem?* The scholars on the benches were not quite sure. Old Abraham Achselrad yawned a large and holy yawn and he put his head back down on his desk. The Rabbi immediately fell asleep, and again he dreamt his holy dream with its white, bright, and radiant light–and the many sages saw him sigh and smile. Then a gentle wind passed through the back study room on the late afternoon of that spring or winter day; it was like a Passover eve wind, and it whispered the *sholom aleikhems* of angels and old prophets and it welcomed all and sundry, near and far, to the Juden Viertels in medieval Cologne of a long, long time ago.

Ah, good evening again, Rabbi. It is the night of the bright half-moon and I know it is hard to sleep. Put your feet on the side bench here while I open the stove door. Let me push these coals back. There is nothing like the white glow of the stove to wash away the cares of a hard day.

I heard your final benediction tonight, Rabbi. Clearly you are overworked; even a shammas like me can tell. I kept one eye on you as I cleaned the dishes, and I saw that you were watching the door, hoping that Reb Elbaum would leave early. But then Reb Anton stayed to discuss the famous passage from the Book of Numbers:

> Then the great Lord God Almighty opened Balaam's eyes to the hidden mysteries of the world – and Balaam saw the angel of the Lord standing before him in the road with his sword drawn. Balaam bowed his head and he said, "I have done wrong. I did not know that you stood here in the road confronting me. But now, if my journey displeases you, then I am ready to turn back."

Balaam was a Gentile prophet. He was the seer who was sent by Balak the Moabite king to curse Israel but who, instead, blessed Israel in the end. Balaam was in some ways like Jonah: he was a prophet who wanted to go where he was not sent. And like Seligmannus, Balaam met Dumah, the black Angel of Death, in the road one day and bowed his head and turned aside. What? No, Seligmannus was not a prophet. He was an ordinary Jew; he was a merchant from old Cologne.

Certainly, I will tell you his story. I will tell it just as I heard it once long ago from my grandmother:

Once upon a time, said my grandmother to me, in the medieval Cologne of old Rabbi Abraham ben Alexander, there lived a pious man named Seligmannus ben Jehudah ha-Levi. Seligmannus was a merchant, a wanderer, and a salesman; he dealt in fine dyed silks, as had his father and his grandfather before him, amen.

What? Of course there is more, Rabbi. I only closed my eyes for a moment–can an old man not take a little rest? Now you have interrupted my thoughts. Let me see, where was I? Ah, yes–as my grandmother said, "There is a new question to every answer." Did you ever hear her say that? You never knew her? That is too bad; you missed a fine woman. Anyway, I first heard about the endlessness of unanswerable questions from my grandmother, may her soul visit happily with the souls of her parents forever. What is that? Seligmannus? Just be patient, Rabbi:

Once upon a time, said my grandmother to me, in the early days of the Jewish communities in Germany–at the time of Rabbi Abraham ben Alexander–there lived in Cologne on the River Rhine a pious scholar named Seligmannus ben Jehudah ha-Levi. He was a merchant who dealt in dyed silk. . . . Rabbi, Rabbi–please be patient and ask me no questions. Remember, there are no answers. This is just a story.

As I was saying, Seligmannus bought and sold dyed silk. Dyeing is an art that is older than old. In biblical days, cloth was soaked in fruit juices and in boiled flowers or leaves or barks or roots. In more recent times, earths and muds were added, especially the white alumina earths and the red iron earths. These made the stains more permanent. Persia, India, and China perfected the cloth dyes, and travelers brought the Eastern recipes to Phoenicia and to Egypt. But then for some reason the art of dyeing disappeared in much of Europe during the Dark Ages.

A few pockets of cloth artisans persisted, however, especially in Sicily, where silk production was a Jewish monopoly. In fact, throughout the Middle East, Jews were the main dyers and manufacturers of silk. In Syria, for instance, most Jews were dyers, and two famous medieval travelers, Rabbi Petahiah in the twelfth century and Rabbi Nachmanides in the thirteenth century, reported that the only permanent Jewish residents of Jerusalem were dyers. Through the Jews, dyed silks were exported to Italy and to Southern France, and, from there, local merchants distributed them all over Europe.

One of these local European merchants, Seligmannus ben Jehudah, made his home in Cologne. One winter day, Seligmannus was traveling, returning to Cologne from Antwerp. The afternoon was ending, evening was beginning, and Seligmannus stopped at an inn in the countryside east of Erkelenz. Originally the inn had been built for Christian pilgrims; now, however, it was owned by a Jew who took in all manner of passing travelers.

The innkeeper was an old and cranky man. He himself needed to make a short trip to Kaster for supplies. But he did not want to go alone and he did not want to go with some unknown companion; the innkeeper knew well the kind of problems that travel could bring. Carefully he studied each traveler going east. The innkeeper preferred a young man who was easy-going. He hoped for a Jew, but one who would pay his own expenses. Also, he wanted an experienced traveler. Then Seligmannus appeared. Seligmannus was experienced, and he seemed trustworthy and likable. He was a Jew and he was going to Kaster, and, yes, he would be happy to have a companion. So, after a brief talk, Seligmannus agreed to travel together with the innkeeper, and the innkeeper and the merchant set out walking east early the next morning.

It was cold. The travelers kept their hands clenched in their pockets and their arms tight against their chests. Their breath was white; their beards were frosty. To take their minds off the cold, the two men began to talk. After a while, the talk turned to saving money and to giving money away.

"I always like to remember something I once heard a rabbi say," said Seligmannus. "Charity is a family gift."

"It is a *family* gift?" repeated the innkeeper.

"Yes," said Seligmannus, "charity is goodwill toward the community and its members – and to a Jew, the community is your family."

"Listen, my friend, I have a wife and four children. I have enough difficulty satisfying *that* family," complained the innkeeper.

"Well, I understand," said Seligmannus, "but I think that we should relieve the suffering of others if it is at all possible." The innkeeper frowned. Both men stamped the snow from their boots, and they walked on and on.

After a few moments of silence, the innkeeper said, "I have heard these fine-sounding statements many times. Such things *sound* good. But are they realistic, my friend? How can you help others to feel better if you are not feeling good yourself? And how can you possibly begin to help others when your own family is suffering? No – it is clear that first you must provide for yourself and next for your own family – only *then* can you consider other people."

"Perhaps," said Seligmannus, "but I remember a rabbi telling me that the entire world is founded on three things: on studying the Torah, on worshipping God, and on giving charity to others."

"Well, I could go along with that," said the innkeeper, "if only you were to add that charity begins at home."

The two talked back and forth in this way, until they met a blind man. The man was standing, shivering, at the side of the road, and his eyes were open but he could not see. There were no houses nearby. Was he hoping for a ride in a wagon? Was he lost? Was he just waiting for fate to find him? Seligmannus stopped. "Hello?" said the merchant.

"Hello," said the blind man. "You sound like a well-to-do gentleman. And I hear another man beside you. Can you kind men spare a little charity?"

The silk merchant opened his canvas sack; the canvas felt like wood in the frigid air. "Here – this is a special piece of fine cloth. It is Italian silk," said Seligmannus, and he gave the blind man a roll of beautiful silk. "Ah, thank you sixty times over!" said the beggar.

Standing there, the innkeeper shivered. He stamped his feet, he hugged himself, and then he began to walk on. Seligmannus followed. "What a waste," said the innkeeper. "You gave some very fancy silk to a blind man."

Seligmannus ben Jehudah shrugged his shoulders. "Even the blind can feel beauty," he said.

The road was rutted and the two men walked slowly. Already their toes hurt. They did not feel like talking. Soon, they came to a little hamlet. Two old wooden houses stood at the edge of the road with a well between them. There were some trees behind the well. Sitting on a broken wooden bench at the side of the well was a cripple. Apparently, he was the water-drawer, but everything was now frozen solid.

"Alms for the poor?" asked the lame water-drawer.

"Certainly," said the merchant. Seligmannus reached into his purse and took out two gold coins, as cold as ice, for the man.

"Bless you," said the cripple, and he turned to the innkeeper expectantly. However, the innkeeper looked aside. "It is freezing: we have to hurry on our way," he said to Seligmannus, and then the innkeeper continued walking along the road.

The air was icy. It stung the nose and it cut the throat. Stiffly, the two men walked on and on. Eventually they met a young beggar who looked perfectly healthy. He stood at a crossroads. He was wearing a scarf tied around his head to protect his ears from the wind. "Alms for the departed Jews," he said.

And why did he mention departed Jews? Well, I will tell you. In those days there were three classes of people who died in the Gentile world. First, there were good Christians who received holy rites – these were buried in proper cemeteries. Second, there were Christians who had not received the holy rites – they were buried like non-Christians at the feet of wooden crosses at certain country crossroads. Third, there were criminals and suicides – these were buried at night on the opposite side of the road with a stake through their bodies. Generally, when Christians buried Jews, they buried them with the second class of people at the crossroads. And there, at a crossroads beside a large, rough wooden cross, stood the young man shivering in the winter winds and begging for alms.

Seligmannus nodded. He stopped and looked about him. All was silent and cold. He rubbed his beard. Then he opened his purse and he gave a gold coin and a dyed silk scarf to the young man. The innkeeper was frozen, and he was in a hurry. He turned to Seligmannus. "How," he asked, "can this healthy young man dare to beg? He is perfectly capable of working. Now, Seligmannus, it is much too cold for us to stop here and talk. Let us get on with our journey before we become frozen solid and need to be buried by the road too."

The innkeeper walked ahead. Seligmannus followed and caught up with him. They walked in cold silence, and the day wore on. The sky began to darken. Distant rumblings floated toward them, and suddenly there was thunder. Yes, Rabbi, it was thunder in winter. And there was lightning too, with the great God Almighty roaring and flinging forth His stunning bolts of jagged white light. The lightning flashed from the clouds to the tips of the hills; as it says in the Book of Job:

> They listened to the thunder of God's great voice;
> They heard the rumbling of His low angry roar–
> Through Heaven's deep vault the echoes rejoiced
> As He roared and growled and let thunder soar.
>
> Flashes of His lightning streaked bright white,
> Stretching to the ends of the sky's black night–
> Then thunder again, sending sharp sudden fright
> And breaking the clouds with His incomparable might.

The voice of His majesty roared, and the skies became darker and darker. Heavy snows fell. The snow came down in sheets; it hid the distant countryside under shimmering gray-white curtains. And suddenly there stood a tall, dark figure, covered from head to foot with unwinking eyes. The figure held a drawn and bloody sword, and its breathing was like the sound of dry leaves rustling and rustling in the blank autumn wind.

Both men stopped. There was no mistaking the presence of death. This was Dumah, the Angel of Death, and he stood silent and grim and dark. The snow fell around them, hiding the world. But the black, black Angel of Death stood untouched by the storm.

Seligmannus looked at the innkeeper, who stood staring and staring at Dumah. The world seemed isolated, empty, afar. Were they atop a hill? Ever after, Seligmannus would remember one frozen picture: he would see the innkeeper standing there against the black sky with eyes as big as wagon wheels.

Dumah, the black Angel of Death, turned to Seligmannus. "Step back, son of Jehudah," said the Angel. "Step back, and stand aside."

Seligmannus did not move. "Step aside," said Dumah, "or you will be killed too."

Seligmannus was afraid. He was afraid, and he was alone. He bowed his head; he stepped aside and back. And then, with a slow, even swing of the cold, hard Sword of Death, Dumah killed the innkeeper and took his soul and together they flew off to the farthest reaches of the gray winter sky.

Now the snow fell more lightly. Seligmannus stood shaking. He did not know whether he had done the right thing. The innkeeper had been his companion. In that short time, he may even have become a friend. *Were* they actually friends? Seligmannus did not know the answer. But had he been able to answer this question, then still more troubling questions arose—for every answer there appeared a new question, a difficult question, a troubling question. Should Seligmannus have stepped back? If he had not, then Dumah surely would have taken *his* life. Should Seligmannus have risked his own life? Was there anything that Seligmannus could have done to protect the life of the innkeeper? Seligmannus was not certain. Endless unanswerable questions tumbled through his mind. Seligmannus felt alone and empty; his throat was dry, and his stomach tightened.

Seligmannus looked around him. The countryside remained grim and frozen; nothing seemed alive but the dark trees whose hard black branches frowned and curved away from him. The snows swirled in the wind. The ground was bleak and black and broken.

So, Seligmannus trudged on. Tiredly and slowly, he returned to Cologne. He felt worn and he felt weary, and the feeling never left him: from that day on, he was a much more silent man. Seligmannus ben Jehudah ha-Levi often thought about his walk from Erkelenz to Kaster, and he often shook his head. But he never told this tale. In fact, my grandmother learned of it only in a dream; for it has remained one of the many Jewish secrets that live forever like misty dim spirits in the corners of the old town of Cologne, a medieval city on the edge of the dark, wide River Rhine, the ancient River Rhine.

Good evening, Rabbi. No sleep for the weary? Well, sit down. Perhaps you are cold–I will stoke up the oven. The bright glow and the warmth of the oven are like the bright glow and the warmth of the Gates of Paradise. Of course the Golden Gates of Heaven are guarded by a beautiful angel, whereas the gates of this stove are tended by an ugly old shammas. In fact, that is the way to tell the real *Gan Eden* from an impostor, as ibn Alfachar knew. What do I mean? I was thinking of the story of ibn Alfachar and the ugly Moroccan gardener. You do not know that story? Then sit back and I will tell it to you:

We must go back to those medieval days when the Jews of Spain were the artisans of Judaic culture. Jews lived throughout the Spanish peninsula (except in the southern region of Andalusia, which held to a rigidly orthodox Mohammedanism), and the Toledo congregation was probably the most distinguished. The town of Toledo was filled with magnificent synagogues. The Jews of Toledo were wealthy and learned, and they included scholars, skilled craftsmen, and even warriors.

The local Spanish king, Alphonso the Noble, believed that a

strong society was a diverse society, and he appointed many Jews to high positions. One of Alphonso's favorites was Abraham ibn Alfachar. Ibn Alfachar was a scholar and a politician. He was proficient in Arabic and Hebrew and he wrote essays and poetry. Daringly, King Alphonso sent Abraham ibn Alfachar as an ambassador to the court of Morocco. At that time, Morocco was ruled by a very conservative Mohammedan, the Prince of the Faithful, Abu Jacob Yussuf Almostansir. Prince Almostansir did not allow Jews to live in his kingdom; nonetheless, practical politics forced him to receive ibn Alfachar respectfully.

Ibn Alfachar was greeted politely. He was shown to a quiet, well-furnished room. Then he was given a tour of the prince's private gardens, known throughout North Africa as a botanical showplace. The gardens were vast and lush and overwhelming. The flowers and the shrubbery were colorful and aromatic. There were *arar* trees, cork trees, and citrus trees, both lemons and limes. And as for other fruits? Ibn Alfachar saw apricots, chestnuts, melons, mulberries, plums, and walnuts; he found almonds, dates, figs, pomegranates, and quinces, and of course grapes and olives. The garden's flowers were blue, yellow, and red–iris, marigold, and poppy–with other shades of blues from morning glories and from borage.

It seemed like the great *Gan Eden,* thick and green and wild and splashed with color. And like the *Gan Eden,* Prince Almostansir's garden was overseen by a fearsome creature: but in Morocco the head gardener was a huge, misshapen man, as strikingly ugly as the gardens were beautiful. Later over dinner, Prince Almostansir asked ibn Alfachar how he liked the gardens. The Jew answered, "I would have thought that this was Paradise, but then I noticed your head gardener. He is not the most beautiful of characters, Your Highness. I know that, for Mohammedans, the gardens of the Great Hereafter are guarded by the handsome angel *Redvan*–however, the gateway to hell is tended by the ugly demon *Malek.* Is that perhaps what we see here?"

The Prince shook his head: "*Redvan* is temporarily elsewhere. We chose an ugly gatekeeper just for you, my friend. You see, we wanted to be certain that you could have a tour. This is a *Mohammedan* Paradise, and the great Mohammedan angel *Redvan* would not have admitted an infidel Jew."

It is interesting, Rabbi, that you do not even recall the name of Abraham ibn Alfachar: he was so influential in his time. In Spain, his cousin Jehuda ibn Alfachar–also forgotten today–was even more well known in Jewish circles. Jehuda became entangled in one of the endless disputes over the doctrines of Maimonides. You know, of course, the great medieval translator and author David Kimchi. Yes, exactly, he wrote a set of biblical commentaries that are quite well known in the Christian world. Well, Jehuda ibn Alfachar caused immense difficulties for Kimchi, and here is the story:

Let me see–I suppose I should begin with a letter. This was a letter that came to Rabbi Abraham ben Alexander, Achselrad of Cologne, on one cold winter afternoon in the month of *Tevet.* The letter was from David Kimchi–already famous as a translator, commentator, and Judaic scholar–and it arrived on a bright afternoon when the tiny white sun had a keen bite to it.

In those medieval days, the Jews always spoke in the local language of their land. Writing, however, was different. In Europe, Hebrew remained the literary language of the Jews, but in Mohammedan lands Jews wrote in Arabic instead. Therefore, many fine Jewish books were originally Arabic and needed translation into Hebrew before they could be read in Europe. Provence in southern France bridged the Mohammedan world and Europe, and two families of translators and scholars grew and developed alongside each other in Provence. One family was the ibn Tibbons and the other family was the Kimchis. My story is about the Kimchi family–that is, Joseph Kimchi and his two sons, Moses and David.

The Kimchis had come to Narbonne from Spain. Joseph ben Isaac Kimchi grew up in Seville, in the years when the strictly orthodox Mohammedan Almohades moved into southern Spain from Northern Africa. The Almohades did not permit Jewish or Christian worship, and eventually Kimchi moved his family to the Jewish community of Provence in southern France.

The Jews of that time were not satisfied with just one translation of important works. Joseph Kimchi knew both Arabic and Latin; therefore, the local Jewish patron, Rabbi Meshullam ben Jacob of Lunel, encouraged him to retranslate such famous books as Bahya's *Hovot ha-Levavot (Duties of the Heart).* Kimchi also translated into Hebrew a set of Arabic studies on the history and structure of the Hebrew language. Besides translations, Kimchi wrote his own books on grammar and language, including the *Sefer ha-Galui,* the *Book of Demonstration,* and the *Sefer Zikkaron,* the *Book of Remembrance,* in which he methodically classified verbs by their internal stems. In addition, he wrote commentaries on the Book of Proverbs, the Book of Job, and the Song of Solomon. (Now, just be patient, Rabbi. I am coming to David, and Jehuda ibn Alfachar will be along shortly thereafter.)

So now for David. He was the youngest and the most famous Kimchi. One might even say that David Kimchi taught the Hebrew language to the Jews and the Christians of Europe. His great work is the *Sefer Mikhlol,* the *Book of Completeness.* This has two parts: first, there is a grammar, called simply *Mikhlol;* second, there is a dictionary or lexicon, called *Sefer ha-Shorashim,* the *Book of Roots.* In addition, David Kimchi wrote commentaries on various parts of the Bible, notably on the Book of Genesis, the two Books of Chronicles, the Book of Psalms, and the Books of the Prophets. These are models of clean, clear, easy-to-read analyses, and in spite of their anti-Christian remarks, they have been widely used by Christian theologians, and they shaped the authorized English version of the Bible.

This, then, was David Kimchi, the author of the letter to Rabbi Achselrad. Kimchi's winter letter answered an earlier one from the Rabbi.

"My dear friend and holy colleague,
Abraham, the son of Alexander–

"I have long heard of the thoughtful scholarship that flourishes under your direction in the Jewish communities of the rich Rhine valley. I know that the good Lord God (blessed be He) has shined down His warm smile, His loving kindness, and His full *Shekhinah* on you, on all your colleagues, and on the many children in your yeshivas. May He continue to bring you joy, success, and happiness forever, amen.

"In your letter, you asked me about translations. It is a subject I think of day and night: it is a vocation at which I pass my most enjoyable hours. I suppose, therefore, that I could take a moment to sit back and reflect about it in general.

"Let me begin by confessing that I like to write: I like putting words down on paper, neatly, cleanly, and smoothly. But it is not composing things from thin air that is the most fun. Actually, I find invention a tiring task. Instead, I would rather take the words and the ideas of others and craft them into a form that is pleasing to my own ear and to my own eye. I like to mold words into sentences that hold those thoughts I imagine were intended by the original author. In this way, for a time, I become another person and I look through his eyes and I hear with his ears.

"At first glance, translation might seem to be a very special, even peculiar, form of writing, quite different from original prose. Original prose comes directly from our senses. We have five senses and we have discovered that all our sensory experiences can be funneled through the written word. In fact, one might say that writing is a transformation. In original prose, writing is the transformation of direct sensory experiences into a set of symbols. For example, I might see and feel a sunset; then, when I write a paragraph, I transform my sensations into the symbols of a narrative Hebrew description.

"Now, Rabbi Abraham, is this 'prose transformation' different from what one calls 'translation'? I think not–fundamentally they are the same. Translation is transformation too: in translation, one set of symbols (for example, Arabic symbols) is transformed into another set of symbols (for example, Hebrew symbols). In addition, however, we must never forget the *translator.* Just as with prose transformations, translation transformations always have an underlying active *person.* In translation, a person transforms his direct experience when reading one set of symbols into another set of symbols. However, as always with writing, the essential process is the transformation of direct sensory experiences into symbols. Therefore, I would suggest that translation is just a variant of the general human process of transformation that we call writing.

"Translation is writing, just like reporting or story writing or even poetry writing. All are transformations of a person's direct sensory experiences into certain standard symbols. As I have said, *transformation* is one way to look at writing.

"However, there are many other ways to examine this thing called writing. We can hold it up to the light and turn it in all manner of angles. Here, Rabbi Abraham, I will hold up writing for you–look at it in *this* particular light. What do you see? Why, it appears that some writing seems to be almost universal, while other writing is not.

"And what do I mean by universal? Universal writing is narratives, poetry, descriptions, and stories that are common to a great many people. Of course it is true that all people are different: every face and voice is special and individual and unique. However, at the same time, we are, in many ways, much the same. Universality is about the *sameness* of people. If one hundred men see a sunset, then a universal narrative is one that would cause ninety-nine of them to nod their heads simultaneously and say, 'Yes, yes – certainly we would call this a description of a sunset.' Agreement like this means that all these men have had direct sensory experiences that fit well with the words, the written symbolism, of this particular description. The description would be almost universal.

"Now, Rabbi, such a universality is a hope of most translators. Translators attempt to be straightforward and honest and true to the original – in other words, most translators hope to be universal. If one hundred Arabic-Hebrew speakers were to read the original Arabic document, then a good translation would undoubtedly be one where ninety-nine of the speakers would nod their heads in acceptance as they read the Hebrew rendition. The good translation would be a nearly universal translation.

"All right, Rabbi, now let us once again hold up this crystal called writing. Look at how it reflects the light *this* time. Why, there is yet another type of writing, one that can contrast markedly with the universal: this is idiosyncratic writing. Here, the primary goal is to capture one individual's peculiar world. Many poems and literary works fall at this end of the spectrum of writing.

"Idiosyncratic writing aspires to different values than universal writing. What does it matter if only one man in a hundred sees a sunset as a 'black blood rock'? Is this not a striking, albeit unique, vision? Humans are a complex lot – we like all manner of things. There are times when we like universality, and there are other times when we enjoy the experience of looking through the idiosyncratic eyes of another individual human, different as that experience might be from our own.

"Translation is not usually on this end of the spectrum: translation is a form of writing that commonly aspires to be universal and not idiosyncratic. Translation is usually judged with a value system that is related to universality and not to idiosyncrasy.

"The facts are that universality is a hallmark of the most useful translations. Still, recognizing this general constraint, I must add a tempering comment, a word to the individual translator himself. When you work, forget universality, my friends: translators should operate with value systems closer to idiosyncrasy. They should leave the value judgments of universality to some other profession, such as the literary critics. Remember: he who blindly copies word for word loses all the animating human cohesive spirit of the original. You can never completely cast the person out of the process. Each translation is always a view through a particular person's eyes, and that person cannot help – in fact, he *should* not help – but bring his own idiosyncrasies to bear on the world.

"Therefore, Rabbi Abraham, I say to each translator: immerse yourself in the work at hand, and write as you yourself see it most clearly. If your perspective resonates with many others in the world, then your translation will happen to have the nature of a universal work, and it will be called a good translation. On the other hand, if you have a strange vision, then your work will be idiosyncratic and it may even be considered a poor translation. This is not something that one can control. The fundamental ideal is simply to write well, that is, to put forth a vision that is fully true to your own self. This is the best that one can do.

"I fear that few translators satisfy this canon. Writers are often tempted to bend, to twist, and to temper their own peculiar vision. They listen to others too closely. They try to bridge two professions, the artist and the art critic. They attempt to guess at the viewpoints and the visions of their diverse readers. Such actions may produce a work that is universal by consensus, but they produce a broad and shallow work lacking internal coherence and consistency. These translators stitch together a weak patchwork, and they lose the poetry of writing.

"I mention poetry, because my own view, Rabbi, is that *poetry* is the highest form of literature. Good poetry is the epitome of an individual, idiosyncratic vision. Poetry cannot be translated in the sense of direct word-for-word transfer. Instead, a poem must be entirely recreated in the new language – and good poetry certainly cannot be written by consensus. Thus, poetry is the prime example of why the best translations must be personal, individual, and idiosyncratic efforts.

"A poem is not the intellectual exercise of a committee. A poem comes straight from the soul of one man. All translators should aspire to write poetry straight from their souls. In some cases, one's poem (that is, one's particular translation) will happen to be on the universal end of the spectrum; therefore, it will be enjoyed by many other men. In other cases, one's poem will be on the individual end of the spectrum; here, the poem will resonate with fewer men.

"But so be it, Rabbi. A truly poetic translator can only shrug his shoulders at this fact. We do our best when we write our books; we cast them out and let the world use our works as they will. In the real world there is no way around this way of writing, for our readers are a heterogeneous collection of individuals. The readers are not homogeneous, they are not identical ants, and certainly all readers need not be like ourselves. Those 'purists' who deride and criticize the poetic translator who lets his own special idiosyncratic soul loose in his works are thin and stultifying men indeed. Such critical purists are parchment figures who have so enwrapped their God-given individualities, their own unique personal richnesses, and their special gifts of divinity in swaddling clothes that only the weakest glimmer of God's complex radiant *Shekhinah* can ever shine through to warm the world around them—at least, Rabbi Abraham, that is *my* particular idiosyncratic view.

"Your humble friend and colleague,
David Kimchi, the son of Moses"

What is that, Rabbi? Jehuda ibn Alfachar? Yes, yes, I am coming to him.

Now, you can see from the letter that although Kimchi was a translator, he could not translate without putting himself directly into the writing. David Kimchi openly put his views into his translations, and this caused him trouble, because his views were sympathetic to those of Maimonides.

At the time of the troubles with ibn Alfachar, David Kimchi was already an old man, quite famous both as a grammarian and as an analyst of the Holy Scriptures. Nonetheless, Kimchi was actually excommunicated by the rabbis of northern France. Why was this? It was because the traditionalists in France were worried that Maimonides and his advocates, scholars such as Kimchi, were destroying Judaism. How, asked the traditionalists, could a Jew deny the holy magic of the Bible? How could a Jew say that the throne chariot of God was only a *vision* of Ezekiel? How could a pious Jew maintain that today's talmudical controversies would have no significance in the messianic period? The traditionalists angrily shook their heads: they could not go along with such irreligious heresy.

But Kimchi said: was not the Talmud written by men? Did these men not live in some particular time and in some particular land? Did they not see only certain trees and houses and hills? Were they not fallible and shortsighted, as we all are? How could the human-founded Talmud have any pretension to perpetual authority?

Old and weak though he was, David Kimchi decided to travel to Spain. Kimchi hoped to lecture and to argue in person in support of the followers of Maimonides, and he wanted to stand against Solomon ben Abraham who proposed, for example, that the Talmud was a literal truth. However, when Kimchi arrived at Avila, he became so ill that he had to abandon his journey. There in Avila, Kimchi wrote from his sickbed: in a trembling hand, he set down his arguments in a long letter to Jehuda ben Joseph ibn Alfachar, the chief representative of the influential Toledo congregation.

Kimchi asked ibn Alfachar to take a position that did not divide the French and Spanish Jewish communities over these intellectual issues. We must build a common foundation that is based on the old Judaic traditions, said Kimchi. Unfortunately, Kimchi had approached the wrong man; Jehuda ibn Alfachar had made up his mind against the intellectualists and the followers of Maimonides. Ibn Alfachar had concluded that Maimonides' system would subvert Judaism.

Ibn Alfachar was a thoughtful man. He was convinced that, if pushed to their limits, the views of Maimonides would take all the unknowable elements from the Jewish faith. If man could know and understand all, then what need would there be for God? The entire basis of religion would be destroyed. At first, ibn Alfachar decided that rather than perpetuate the debate, he would simply follow the example of the French rabbis and ignore Kimchi. If Kimchi chose to deny the essence of God, then he had stepped outside the pale of Judaism. Later, however, ibn Alfachar changed his plan, but when he wrote to Kimchi, the letter was arrogant, curt, and dismissive. This letter was made public. It was read in synagogues throughout Europe, and the followers of Maimonides, who had hoped and prayed for the support of the great men of Toledo, felt that they had been struck in the heart.

David Kimchi himself felt very badly; he was discouraged and saddened. He had intended only to speak for what he honestly felt was true and right and sacred. But ibn Alfachar was the younger generation. He was handsome, articulate, and vigorous. He talked with authority. He nodded with sureness. He waved his arms with strength. People of the time, especially young Jews, felt that ibn Alfachar was the victor in this duel of ideas. Perhaps he was – certainly David Kimchi died feeling defeated. But, Rabbi, the years went on and on. Decades passed; seventy years came, and seventy years went. David Kimchi's commentaries endured – in fact, they were among the very first books to be printed on presses, at the end of the fifteenth century. It was through David Kimchi's book of grammar that successive generations of Jewish and Christian scholars learned Hebrew; it was from David Kimchi's commentaries that the authorized Jewish and Christian Bibles were built. And as to Jehuda ibn Alfachar – who now even remembers his name?

Good evening, Rabbi. Come in and enjoy the stove. The warmth of the night oven is like God's sunshine smile, reminding us that the Almighty Lord God (blessed be He) will protect us always from harm. Sitting here is like basking in His sheltering arms, as the psalmist sang:

The Lord is my shepherd
My life is secured–
As I rest in green pastures
Beside the cool waters
He speaks to my soul
And toward His pure goal
He leads–through my youth
I have followed His Truth.
Yes, I am safe from all harm:
With His staff and right arm
He guards my least breath
Through vales dark as Death,
And with honey and veal
God sets a rich meal
And His wine overflows

To wash away foes;
By Him I'm soft held
As love unparalleled
Streams down like warm rays
Through endless sun-days.

When I close my eyes, Rabbi, I can hear my grandmother reciting this psalm to me, just as she did when I went to bed as a little child. She would pull the covers up to my chin, she would pat me gently on my back, and she would tell me one of her many, many stories. This particular psalm reminds me of a nighttime adventure from those dim, old mystical days in medieval Germany, days when the Lord was the shepherd and the protector of the Jews:

Once upon a time, said my grandmother to me, in the village of Haspe in Westphalia, west of Dusseldorf and north of Cologne, there lived a pious Jew named Aram ben Moshe ha-Levi. Haspe is in the valley of the River Ennepe, where the River Hasper joins it, running through rich, black farmland. Aram was a tenant farmer. He worked his small farm and he also managed a large estate for a wealthy Gentile landowner who lived in the neighboring town of Hagen. Hagen was a commercial center, with metal works and limestone and alabaster quarries and, of course, with shops and storehouses and bakeries.

Aram was a plain man with very little learning. But Aram was pious; he believed in the wonders of the Almighty Lord God, and he tried to do good deeds each day. Aram's father Moshe had farmed the same land. The Gentile landowner, a friendly old man, liked both Moshe and Aram, and they all lived on good terms with one another. The peasants of the countryside also respected Aram. He was honest and polite. He could be counted on to help raise a barn, to rescue a cow, or to lend a hand during a storm at harvesttime. In fact, the neighbors entrusted Aram with many of their affairs. When he went on business to the larger town of Hagen, which was often, Aram carried money for his neighbors and he made purchases for them.

One day, a young nobleman, Count Heribert Schach, arrived in the village of Haspe. Heribert was titled, but he had little money. His inheritance was small, but he dressed in fancy clothes, he ate expensive food, and he gave many presents to wealthy friends. Now he was feeling the pressures of creditors. "Perhaps," he thought, "I can appropriate a local business such as a successful farm. I will tax the workers and also have some extra money from a share of the produce. It will be a painless life." Looking about, he found the large estate that was managed by Aram. "Aha," thought Heribert, "I will just displace this heathen and have one of my own men take over. It will be an easy matter to get rid of a Jew. How can a Jew refuse the orders of a Christian nobleman?"

So, Heribert went to the landowner in Hagen. "Good sir," began Heribert, "I have come to help you out. I have had much experience managing my father's many estates. I find you have a farm in Haspe that is run by a Jew. Frankly, you need a devout Christian to take over. You need someone whom the Christian peasants will follow. I have decided to settle in the area, and I happen to have the time to take charge of your farm for you. I can move in and set up immediately."

The old landowner raised his eyebrows. "Well, that is kind of you to offer," said the old man. "However, there is really no reason to change things now. Aram, the Jew, took over from his father. These men have always paid their rent on time. They know their business, and they are well liked. The farm is profitable and the local people have no complaints. And then a Jew is a person too. How can I suddenly leave him without the means to support his family?"

The landowner paused and looked intently at the young count. Heribert was lighthearted and light tongued. He switched subjects quickly. He tapped his toe and said yes immediately. He dressed like a dandy from the city, not like a country gentleman. In fact, he looked weak willed and irresponsible. The old man shook his head. "No," he said, "thank you for your offer of assistance, count, but I had best stick with the Jew. He is honest and he does his job; I cannot ask for anything more."

"All right," said Heribert quietly. He turned and left, but he did not give up. He went to Aram directly. "Times are changing, my friend," said Heribert to the farmer. "Jews are no longer welcome in these parts."

Heribert stepped closer and lowered his voice: "I come from the city, sir, and I can see the inevitable future. You will be driven back to your homeland. I am sorry to have to tell you this, but soon other men will be treating you rather poorly. Already whispers are abroad. It would be good for you and your family to move now. You can get your belongings together at your leisure and in peace. You can establish yourselves in some large city where there are Hebrews of your own kind. Certainly it will be more difficult if you wait until the locals get angry at you and hurry you out. They may even destroy your things in order to encourage you along."

Aram stood with his hands on his hips. He listened and did not move. Then without a word, he turned and went back to his work.

The young count followed the farmer. "I will set the peasants against you," he said. "I am afraid that I may be forced to bring in the local troops. There are laws about Jews holding property, you know. I am sure you have violated any number of regulations. So I warn you, you are in for trouble!" Aram was silent as he continued working on a fence.

Heribert felt his neck muscles tightening. "Perhaps," he thought, "I had best speak to the village priest. The Church will support me. We can forbid the peasants from having any dealings with Aram."

"I will be back!" he shouted at Aram.

That afternoon Aram was in town, and he told everyone he met about the count's threats. The people were angry. Who was this count suddenly to come into Haspe and to try to run everyone's life? Heribert Schach was an unknown, a foreigner, an arrogant young dandy. The local people frowned and told Aram they would not listen to the count's rantings.

Later, Heribert walked through the town. He stopped at stores. He sat and drank at the inn. He complained. He berated Aram. He accused the Jew of stealing money during his shopping trips. He said that Aram paid no taxes. Heribert claimed that Aram practiced witchcraft and was descended from the original killers of Christ. "We must rid the town of this evil menace," said Heribert. "I will take over his farm–then things will get back to a normal, honest, Christian footing."

The townspeople were polite–after all, this was a count–however, they also were distant and noncommittal, and Heribert became frustrated. Heribert Schach felt like a little boy being humored by his uncles, and he got angrier and angrier. The next day, the count met quietly with a group of young men from Haspe. Perhaps for some cash they would waylay Aram when he returned that evening from a shopping trip in Hagen. The youths looked at one another, money changed hands, and the count smiled.

Meanwhile, Aram finished his business in Hagen. He got into his cart. Dusk was descending as he began the trip home. Hagen lies amid well-wooded hills in a valley where the River Ennepe meets the River Volme. The weather was cool; already the woodlands cast long, lonely shadows. Soon it was, as they say, between a dog and a wolf – it was neither twilight nor dark. The sky was overcast, and it rained steadily. By the time that Aram reached the forest, night had descended, and he allowed his horse free rein, for he could not see even one step ahead of him.

Aram was wet and uncomfortable, but a new and strange uneasiness fell on him. What could be the problem? There was something more than bad weather afoot. Aram felt that he must recite a psalm:

> God is our refuge, our strength, our aid,
> A divine help through all adversity
> Therefore we will remain unafraid
> Though the very earth shakes violently
> And the mountains are suddenly unmade
> And swept into the depthless sea.

Aram repeated this psalm over and over again. The forest continued to stretch, ominous and black, all around him. But what was this? The horse seemed to have lost its way. Were they now wandering about aimlessly?

Aram ben Moshe's uneasiness grew. He recited the protective verse from the Book of Exodus:

> Terror and dread fell upon them
> And through the might of Your right arm
> They all stopped, stone-still
> While Your people passed safe from harm
> Through the danger – by Your will
> Amen.

Aram's head ached; his hands shook. Was he getting sick? Why was everything so unfamiliar? Nothing like this had ever happened to him before. He felt weak and his heart pounded. Was he about to die, lost here in the woods? Times without number, his horses had crossed the entire length of the forest automatically, almost blindfolded. How could both he and his horse be lost?

Hours passed. At last dawn broke weakly, and finally Aram saw where he was. He had wandered past Haspe. Why, now he was almost to the village of Gevelsberg! Quickly, Aram turned around, he found the road back to his farm, and soon he reached his home–hungry, tired, and weak–but safe.

But, Rabbi, they who hope to tangle others in their sleeves find that they themselves are ensleeved in the end. The young count had waited impatiently at the Haspe inn for the return of the peasant boys. The town's curfew hour had come and gone–the night bell was rung, and home fires were extinguished. Soon it was nine o'clock, and then it was ten o'clock. Hour after hour dragged by, but there was no sign of the count's gang of townsmen.

Midnight arrived. Still Heribert had not heard from his hired ruffians. The young nobleman began to worry. What could have gone wrong? Had the thugs simply taken the money and gone to another inn? Were they laughing at his expense? Had they told other people? Had they betrayed him in some other way? These thoughts infuriated Heribert. He took his own horse and wagon and he went into the woods between Haspe and Hagen. Heribert was not thinking clearly, and I do not know whether he was looking for the Jew or whether he hoped to encourage the band of peasants. Perhaps he even planned to attack Aram directly.

A thick darkness, like that which fell on Egypt under Pharaoh, lay all about him. The young nobleman did not know the area well, and now he became lost. Suddenly he felt a rain of blows. He was pulled from his wagon. Dark figures leaped on him. They gave poor Heribert no time to cry out. They tore his clothes; they beat him with fists and sticks. Yes, it was as the old Hebrew proverb reminds us: "The ax cuts wood in the forest from which its handle came"–ill will bounces back onto its source. In the pitch-black darkness, the young count managed to crawl away; he hid in some thick brush. When the gang could not find the man they had been beating, they finally left the woods.

Later that day, Aram went into the town of Haspe. Everyone was talking about the count. He had appeared early that morning at the town inn. His clothes were torn; he was bleeding and beaten. He claimed to have been waylaid by robbers. Two of the young toughs from the town had been there at the inn. The count avoided looking at them, but they stared at him and soon they passed the word: Heribert Schach had been caught in his own trap. It was as the scriptural proverb reminds us:

> Kind deeds, both generous and brave,
> Protect the righteous-spirited,
> But selfish rogues are soon enslaved—
> By their own greed they are misled.
> Yes, the pious man is saved
> From disasters he would dread,
> While wicked men who misbehave
> Drown in those selfsame griefs instead.

Friends told friends; passersby heard and told their families. At street corners, in the marketplace, and behind closed doors, everyone learned that young Count Heribert had paid a gang to attack Aram but that the count had fallen prey instead. People talked and pointed and laughed. The count stayed in town for another day, but he felt the looks and he heard the laughs and the jeers—and the next evening he packed his satchel and, without paying his bill, he suddenly left the region and never returned again.

And as for Aram? Returning from Haspe, Aram had been protected: the Lord had been his shepherd through the valley of the shadow of death. Now Aram could rest in the green pastures, beside the cool waters. So Aram thanked God, and he returned to his farming. Patiently, honestly, and devoutly, Aram worked from morning to evening. Aram felt blessed, for the Lord softly held his family. God's unparalleled love streamed down like warm rays through endless sun-days, and Aram's family prospered and it grew. Over the years, the family of Aram ben Moshe continued to be respected by their neighbors, and Aram's sons inherited his job after him. The descendants of Aram ben Moshe were the only Jews in the region, but his children and his children's children lived faithfully and happily ever after in the sunshine of the great Lord God, amen.

At this point in my grandmother's story I was falling asleep. Undoubtedly, my grandmother pulled the covers up around my ears and patted me again on my shoulder. But all I remember is a warm and wonderful glow – much like the oven here tonight, Rabbi – and soon I was rocking softly and gently in the arms of the great Lord God for yet another wondrous dreamy night of deep childhood sleep.

Good evening, Rabbi. I was just resting my eyes. Please, join me here by the stove. An old man like me can doze forever by a warm stove; I suppose it is because I am too old to need wealth.

How does sleepiness relate to money? Well, my grandmother used to tell me that the lazy man becomes poor. Let me see if I can remember exactly what she said . . . I think she would quote the proverb:

A little extra sleep – a little slumber too –
  A little folding of the hands in daytime rest,
And poverty will creep in and sneak up on you
  Like thieving cruel bands of evil demon guests. . . .

What? No, no – do not get up on my account, Rabbi. I was just resting my eyes a moment. I was resting and musing. Well, to tell you the truth, Rabbi, I was thinking of demons – three demons, to be exact. It seems that in the olden days demons often collected in threes. For example, there was the time that three demons tormented an earnest young Jew named Naftali. In those days, in the dim old days of Rabbi Abraham ben Alexander, the mystic Achselrad of Cologne, myriads of demons lurked in the medieval shadows of the Rhinelands: when you heard a noise or saw a shadow, it was more likely to be a demon than the wind or a bird. And if you met a stranger on the road, then beware–he could as easily be a demon as a person.

But Naftali was not thinking of demons–at least not at the outset. You see, Naftali ben Avigdor ha-Kohen was a young Jew living on the western outskirts of medieval Cologne. On a neighboring farm lived a Gentile named Rainald. Rainald was tall and strong and loud; people were afraid of him, and he usually got his way. One day, the two men were walking to Cologne together. As they walked, they talked, and Rainald said, "You are a good man. It is too bad you are a Jew. Christianity has displaced your old religion. Why not join the modern world, my friend, and convert?"

"Ah, Rainald, you have things backwards," said Naftali. "Judaism is older than Christianity. It has stood the test of time. As it is said in the Holy Scriptures: 'What other nation is so great as to have statutes and judgments that equal the righteousness and the truth of this Law?' "

Then Rainald said, "Oh, I admit that Judaism is a good beginning, a foundation. However, the times change. It is *you* who is backwards–you Jews are still looking backwards. You blindly await the coming of the Messiah. But He has already come and gone. We are now saved. If you would only open your eyes, you could share in the joys of the present rather than hope wistfully for some magical future. And I would add that as a Christian you would find life much easier in our Christian world. Face reality, Naftali: Judaism is a relic of the past."

"Listen, my friend, I am a Jew because I am a Jew," said Naftali ben Avigdor. "It is the way I was born, and it is the way I will die. And, Rainald, it is a comforting thing to be. The only problem with it is the pressures from you Christians. In fact, ours is a much happier religion. You have such bleak rules and dour, critical, intolerant views of the world. I think that secretly most Christians would rather be Jews."

"What?! That is nonsense," replied Rainald. "Anyone who is given a free choice would pick Christianity over Judaism. I would be happy to wager money on this."

Naftali nodded and he said, "You seem very confident . . . so, we will put it to a test." Rainald and Naftali agreed to bet one gold coin each. They would ask three strangers which religion was the best: if the strangers picked Judaism, then Naftali would get both coins; if the strangers picked Christianity, then Rainald would get the money.

Three demons had been sitting, quiet as the clouds, on Rainald's shoulder. They could barely contain themselves. Now they hopped down. The first demon flew around the corner of the road and took on the form of an old man. As the two walkers approached, they saw the old man. Rainald looked at Naftali; then he said, "Hello, grandfather. How are you today?"

"I am well," said the old-man demon.

"Let me ask you something," continued Rainald. "If you had to choose–if you had complete freedom–which religion would you follow, Christianity or Judaism?"

The old man frowned and he looked at the young men. "Is this some kind of trick?" he asked.

"No, no," said Rainald, "we were just wondering what a thoughtful person such as yourself would say."

The old-man demon tapped his chin, he looked at his hands, he glanced up at the sky, and then he answered, "Well, I think that there can be no doubt at all: Christianity is best."

Rainald raised his eyebrows and looked at Naftali; then he nodded politely to the old man, and the walkers continued on. The old man turned back into an invisible demon, and he joined the other demons on Rainald's shoulders. The three demons laughed and coughed and hissed, and Naftali looked around, wondering at the strange sounds in the wind.

Soon there was another bend in the road. The second demon flew off around the corner. He stepped onto the edge of the road and took the form of a young man. When the walkers got near, Rainald said politely, "Good morning, my friend. May I ask you a question?"

"Of course," said the young-man demon.

"You look like a wise man," said Rainald. "If you could choose any religion and not fear the practical consequences, which would you pick, Christianity or Judaism?"

The young-man demon smiled and he said, "I thought for a moment that you might ask me something difficult, like why is there air? or how far is up? or what is the shape of thunder? But yours is a simple question, and the answer is clear: Christianity."

Rainald gave a polite bow. He looked at Naftali and again he raised his eyebrows. Then silently the two men continued walking toward Cologne.

When they were out of sight, the second demon twirled about, he became his ugly hairy self, and he hopped and skipped and flew off to land invisibly on Rainald's shoulder. The three demons grinned and hissed. In a moment the road took another curve. Now it was the turn of the third demon. Off he flew among the trees, and he came out just beyond the curve, where he turned into a weak old woman.

Rainald and Naftali stopped near the old-woman demon. "Greetings, grandmother," said Rainald.

"Greetings to you," she replied.

"You have seen much in your time," began Rainald. "I was wondering: do you think that Christianity is a better religion than Judaism?"

The old-woman demon tapped her walking stick, and she thought for a moment. She looked at her hands, she glanced up at the sky, and then she answered, "Yes, boys, I am quite certain that Christianity is the best religion." At this point in their journey, the road ran along the edge of the west wall of the city, and the old woman said "Good day." She turned, and she walked into the West Gate of the city of Cologne.

When she was out of sight, the old woman turned back into a demon. Then the demon flew up over the wall to join the others. Rainald and Naftali had stayed by the road. "Well," said Rainald, "I warned you. Unfortunately you now owe me some money . . ." and here one of the demons whispered in Rainald's ear ". . . in fact, you owe me three gold coins."

Naftali raised his eyebrows. "It is true that these people each chose Christianity, but we had wagered only one gold coin."

"Well, *I* meant one gold coin for each person that we asked," said Rainald.

"I only have three gold coins with me," said Naftali. "I cannot give them all to you."

"I am sorry to hear that," replied Rainald. "You are always telling me how righteous and honorable you Jews are. But I see that is only wild talk and windy bluster."

Naftali looked down at the ground. "Very well," he said slowly. He took out his purse and gave all his money to Rainald. The Gentile said, "Naftali, I would think very seriously about converting, if I were you." Then Rainald marched off into the city.

Poor Naftali stood silently for a moment. Then he walked into Cologne. After a while, he found himself in the Juden Viertels and he wandered down Judengasse Street. Naftali came to the alleyway leading to the synagogue. Slowly he walked down the lane, and he stepped in the front door of the yeshiva. He went through the anteroom and the main prayer hall. He passed the twelve stained-glass windows and the Holy Ark made of stone. He walked to the door of the back study room. Seven old sages were sitting on the benches. The Rabbi was bent over a book. An ancient holy aura, an old and sacred feeling, was in the room, among the prayer books and the wooden benches and the many white embroidered prayer shawls.

Naftali took a deep breath, he surveyed the men on the benches, and he said, "Good afternoon, gentlemen."

The sages raised their eyebrows. They stroked their beards. They tapped their chins. They nodded to Naftali, who sat down on an empty bench. There was silence. Naftali took another deep breath. Finally, he said, "Judaism is a good religion, is it not?"

The sages looked at one another in surprise. At first they were very quiet. Again they raised their eyebrows. Again they stroked their beards. Again they tapped their chins. After many minutes, white-bearded Baruch ben Jacob said quietly, "It is an *old* religion, Naftali."

"Amen," murmured the other scholars. A younger sage, Elisah ben Samuel, nodded and said, "It was the first religion to acknowledge God."

"Exactly, Elisah," said Joshua ben Eliezer.

Lewe ben Anselm looked at Joshua and then at Naftali. "Amen, Reb Joshua," said Lewe. "The Talmud reminds us that it is we Jews who have taken on the responsibility of the Torah. Therefore, our chief privilege, our main duty, and our ultimate challenge is to preserve and to study the inspired Writings, based on the Holy Scriptures, amen."

"Amen," said Baruch.

"Yes, yes," said Naftali, "I understand all this, gentlemen. I only broach the subject because three people I met today have told me that Christianity is clearly the better religion."

Menahem ben Joel raised his eyebrows. "I presume that these were three Gentiles," he said.

"Well, yes, I think so," answered Naftali ben Avigdor uncertainly.

"Then of course they would champion Christianity," responded Menahem. "But a Jew knows differently–hallelujah and amen."

"Hallelujah!" said Moyses ben Nathan.

And old Shimshon ha-Zaken coughed and said, "Naftali, you cannot believe what you hear in the streets. Why, for all you know, you may well have been talking to demons!"

The other sages nodded and they stroked their beards fiercely.

Naftali nodded too, but he said, "Undoubtedly. Still, it is upsetting to hear such talk."

The old scholars looked at one another and only shook their heads.

Meanwhile, Rabbi Abraham had been very quiet. His eyes were closed. Was he sleeping? Often he worked late at night on his Kabbalistic treatise, the *Keter Shem Tov,* and by the afternoon of the next day the Rabbi's thoughts seemed adrift in deep and holy matters. As the old men talked back and forth, the Rabbi awoke with a start. Naftali saw Rabbi Abraham lift his head. "What do *you* think, Rabbi?" asked Naftali.

Old Achselrad blinked his eyes. He looked around him for a moment. He blinked his eyes again, he tapped his chin, and then he said, "Young man, we must always trust in the good Lord God (blessed be He)."

"Amen," said Baruch.

The Rabbi nodded, he smiled, he stroked his beard.

"But, Rabbi," continued Naftali, "what do you think of demons?"

"Demons?" asked the Rabbi, frowning. "They surround us, young man. They are an ever-present danger. To protect yourself against demons, you need an amulet."

The Rabbi reached into his desk and he removed a small, square amulet, a silver box containing a holy parchment. On the front of the box there were the magical numbers:

4	14	15	1
9	7	6	12
5	11	10	8
16	2	3	13

which when added in any row or column or even diagonally always equal 34. On the back of the amulet were inscribed two lines from the Holy Scriptures:

For I am *Yahweh,* your Healer

and

I am that is Who I am.

Inside the box was a small parchment scroll on which was written in Hebrew:

Mighty is Yahweh, our Protector–
And by all these holy signs
May the bearer be spared forever
From wicked winds and ill designs.

May he be protected always
(And protect his family bright)
From evil spirits of the days
And terrors of the deepest night.

May no demons cruel and grim
Get their grasping claws on him,
May God guard his every limb
And keep his light from growing dim–

Amen, *selah,* amen.

The Rabbi gave the amulet to Naftali. "Hold this in your right hand, young man. If you must have dealings with demons, then approach them quietly. Be soft in your movements. You will see them, but they will not be able to see you. Then listen carefully to what they are saying. You will know what to do next."

Naftali ben Avigdor raised his eyebrows. Rabbi Abraham was studying a manuscript on his desk. "But Rabbi," said Naftali, "does this mean that I will be dealing with demons soon?"

"Most certainly," answered old Achselrad. "And remember the wall."

"The wall?" repeated Naftali.

Again the Rabbi was looking down at his manuscript. When Naftali saw that the Rabbi seemed to have nothing more to say, Naftali said gently, "Rabbi, you said something about a wall . . ."

Rabbi Abraham looked up. "What is that?" he asked.

"You said 'the wall,' " said Naftali.

"Yes, yes," said the Rabbi, "most definitely a wall."

Naftali looked at the old sages. They shrugged their shoulders and stroked their beards. The Rabbi was writing busily in his manuscript. Naftali sat patiently. Finally he stood, he bowed to the seven old men, and he left the yeshiva. Clutching his amulet, Naftali walked down Judengasse Street and through the city of Cologne until he reached the West Gate. There he saw the three demons sitting on the city wall; they were ugly and hairy, shimmering and wavering, and laughing and hissing and coughing in the wild east wind.

Quietly, Naftali came near, and with his amulet he was completely invisible to the evil spirits. He heard the first demon say, "Ah, we have done a fine, fine deed today. I am certain that the angels are as angry as could be." Then the demon laughed until he shook. After he caught his breath again, he said, "And when you said, 'What is the shape of thunder?' I nearly burst. It was a brilliant stroke!"

"Yes, I was rather proud of that, myself," said the second demon, and the third demon slapped him on the back and both fell over, laughing and hissing.

After a while the second demon stopped laughing. "As I always say," he continued, "what good is a day if you have not tormented a Jew? These Jews think they are so superior. They are always setting themselves up as examples of 'good' people and 'God-fearing' folk. I say they should fear demons a bit more."

"Exactly," said the third demon. He coughed and hissed and he said, "Well, that Jew will think twice before bragging about his religion–especially when it costs him money."

The three demons laughed and hissed and coughed and jumped. Then the first demon said, "Of course, this is not the only evil deed that I did today."

"There is more? Ah, how delicious. Tell us," said the second.

The first demon swung his feet as he sat on the wall. "Early this morning, I was in the little town of Mittel Sauerenbach – you know the one."

"Yes."

"Well, the daughter of a wealthy Jew has been in labor for three grim days there. I held up the birth for yet another day. And if the people only knew how, they could have given her the easiest and smoothest birth at any time," he said.

"Oh?" asked the third demon. "And how is that?"

"It is quite simple. *Roots.* Just feed the woman roots from the rye grain stored in a neighbor's rye shed. You have only to make a root paste from moldy rye, and you can set the final birth in motion immediately," answered the first demon. "That is an old demon recipe; it is quite unknown to the Jews."

"Ah, that is very fine indeed," said the third demon. "Those Jews will continue to suffer until they finally grow wise enough to listen to demons." The demon hopped up and down. He laughed and he hissed. Then he coughed until he seemed about to choke.

When the third demon had finally quieted down a bit, the second demon said, "A demon's work is never done. I too have been hard at work today. This morning I was not far from you. I was in the little village of Denklingen."

"That is a pretty little town," said the first demon. "It has two wells sitting side by side in the center of the town. The water from those wells heals weakness and fevers."

"Exactly," said the second, "and I used an old demon spell that I learned from my grandmother to dry up the wells."

"Ah, that is quite evil," said the third.

"Thank you," replied the second. "Of course there is also a simple remedy for this spell. All the townsfolk need do is sacrifice a black goat in the Hebrew tradition, then the water will return immediately."

"But of course they will not think of this," laughed the first demon.

"Certainly not," said the second.

Naftali listened carefully and quietly.

Finally the third demon said, "Ah, my foul and evil friends, I spent the morning in the city today."

"You were here in Cologne?" asked the second demon.

"Yes, yes, it was early this morning. Of course, with all the local demons here, it takes a bit of creativity to think of some new evil. But I managed." The third demon chuckled. "I slipped into the main synagogue. As you know, it is a very holy place: we demons cannot remain there too long, and I had to work fast. I looked around. The room was deserted. I hid the bottle of Sabbath wine; now it is behind the prayer books in the loft of the study room. No one will think to look there, and the Jews will not be able to say the evening *Kiddush* benediction to welcome the Sabbath this Friday."

As the demons were congratulating one another, Naftali slipped quietly away. What should he do with this information? He would right these wrongs himself.

First, Naftali walked to Mittel Saurenbach. The poor daughter of Reb Joshua was suffering in a very difficult labor. She was getting weaker and weaker. Each day she was fed some mother's milk. Each day she breathed the vapor of frankincense burned in a new clay bowl. Each day she inhaled the smoke of burning felt. But nothing worked. A red carnelian necklace did not ease the pain. She was sad and weak and afraid. On instructions from the local rabbi, she forced herself to stare for hours at the Scroll of the Law that had been placed in her room under a white shroud.

Naftali ben Avigdor arrived at night. He was not allowed in the daughter's room, so he went into the garden shed of the neighbor. The shed was filled with grain stalks drying and destined to be made into black bread. The rye straws were set in bundles along one wall; in a corner there were roots of the rye plants. Naftali ground the roots into a paste with wine and water. "Make the young woman swallow this medicine," said Naftali to the midwife. The midwife looked at Reb Joshua. "Yes, try anything," said the father. So the midwife gave the mixture to the daughter. At first, nothing happened, but then within a half hour the baby was suddenly born, smoothly and easily. Reb Joshua was so happy that he gave Naftali ten gold coins and a horse and a wagon.

The next morning, Naftali rode to the village of Denklingen. It was a cloudy, gray day. People stood around the dry wells. Two men were climbing into one of them to try and scrape the walls at the bottom. Naftali found the town mayor. "Listen, sir," said the Jew, "you must sacrifice a black goat. Then the water will return."

The mayor looked at his assistant. He raised his eyebrows, and he said to Naftali, "I do not believe in superstitions. Actually the solution is straightforward. You see, there must be something blocking the stream at the bottom of the wells. After a few days of scraping we will have it cleared out."

Naftali hesitated, then he said, "I know this sounds strange. So I will buy the goat myself, and I will sacrifice it."

The townsmen looked at one another. "It cannot hurt," said one man as he shrugged his shoulders.

"If it works," said the mayor, "we will pay you back. In fact, if it works we will even give you a reward."

"Fine," said Naftali.

Naftali took his ten gold coins and he bought two goats from a local farmer. One goat was black and one was white. He brought the goats to the town square and he tied them to a tree next to the wells. That afternoon, people began to collect and watch. Naftali bowed his head. Silently he prayed for absolution for the town from any sins. Then Naftali cut the rope to the white goat, and it scampered away to the east. A young boy ran after it. "No," called Naftali, "let it go." The boy came back, and the goat disappeared, never to be seen again.

Next, Naftali and two men lifted the black goat. They held it in the air, and the men walked the goat three times around Naftali's head. The animal baahed and bleated. Naftali recited two biblical passages; then he said, "This goat is our substitute. This goat is our surrogate. This goat is our atonement." The black goat was swiftly killed and it was roasted on a fire between the wells. Everyone had a taste, and the day took on a festive air.

Suddenly the sun came out from behind a cloud. And what was this? Water began to seep into the bottom of the well. The water seeped, then it flowed, and at last it gushed. People cheered. The mayor patted Naftali on the back, and true to his word, he gave Naftali back his ten gold coins and then ten more as a reward. The townsfolk invited Naftali to spend the night. Naftali thanked them, but he said that he had to return home, and he got into his wagon and rode from the town.

Naftali was tired, but he was feeling proud and happy, so he traveled all night. The next morning he found himself back at the gates of Cologne. Naftali stopped. He held his amulet tightly, but no demons were in sight. He looked around carefully, he shrugged his shoulders, and then he rode into the city and down the winding streets until he reached the Juden Viertels.

Naftali ben Avigdor returned to the old synagogue in Cologne. The shammas greeted him courteously. "May I see the Rabbi, please?" asked Naftali.

"Certainly," said Shammas Chayim. It was a Friday afternoon. Again the old scholars were in the small back room, talking quietly among themselves, and again the Rabbi was bent over a book.

"Excuse me, good Rabbi," said Naftali, "I have heard something about your missing wine flask."

Old Rabbi Achselrad looked up from his reading. He raised his eyebrows. He looked at the shammas. Chayim ben Meir frowned. He went into the main prayer hall and looked in the small cabinet beside the Holy stone Ark; then he hurried back into the rabbi's study.

"Yes, yes," said the shammas, "the Sabbath wine *is* missing!"

"Just a moment," said Naftali, nodding. "I know where it is."

The scholars looked at Naftali. "Well?" asked white-haired Baruch ben Jacob.

Naftali rubbed the amulet. "Now here is what happened. . . ." Then he reported the entire conversation of the three demons. At the end, Shammas Chayim climbed up into the loft. He pushed aside old manuscripts, torn prayer shawls, and disintegrating prayer books, and there behind a pile of crumbling books was the wine flask, far over in a corner. Chayim took the wine, and he climbed down the ladder.

"Be careful," said old Shimshon ha-Zaken, "this has been handled by a demon." He reached for the flask and inspected it carefully. All the old men stared at the bottle intently. Reb Shimshon handed the wine to the Rabbi. Abraham Achselrad held the bottle up. He looked at it from all angles. He set it next to his ear and he listened. He opened the top. He sniffed gently. He poured a drop on his finger and tasted it. Then the Rabbi said, "It is still fine and holy." Everyone nodded and smiled and relaxed.

Naftali felt very good indeed. He handed the amulet to the Rabbi. "Thank you, Rabbi," he said. "This amulet was a great help."

The Rabbi raised his eyebrows. "Did I not tell you that you would need this amulet again?" he asked.

Now Naftali raised his eyebrows. "No, Rabbi, you did not," he said.

"Well, you will," said the Rabbi, and he closed his eyes.

Naftali looked at the scholars. They were busy talking and looking at the wine flask. Naftali put the amulet back in his pocket. Quietly he stepped out of the back room and he put ten of his gold coins into the poor box. Then he left the synagogue. Naftali walked through the marketplaces; he walked up one street and down the next, and soon he had spent the remainder of his money on supplies to take home. He bought cloth, dried fruit, finished leather, flour, knives, and spices.

Naftali felt wonderful. He had spent all his money, but he was well stocked for the coming cold season, and he headed back home. As he was riding in his new wagon along the streets of Cologne, whom should Naftali meet but his neighbor Rainald. "Well, well," said the Gentile, "where have you been for the last few days? I thought you had no money. Did you steal this wagon?"

"I have had some good fortune," answered Naftali.

"I would guess you made your own fortune late one night, my friend," said Rainald. "Perhaps I had best ask the local officials if any wagons have been stolen recently."

"Now, now, Rainald. Why do you make such unfriendly remarks?" said Naftali. "You know me better than that. The truth is strange, but I will tell it to you." And Naftali told Rainald the entire story.

"So," said Rainald when Naftali was finished, "you can finally afford to pay off your full debt."

"What are you talking about?" asked Naftali.

"You owe me another gold coin. We agreed that you would pay for each person who declared Christianity the best religion. You paid for the three strangers, but you did not pay for *me*–I too am certain that Christianity is the best religion," said Rainald.

"Rainald, this is not the way I remember our agreement," said Naftali.

"Of course you would not want to remember the truth," said Rainald. "This is why it is said, 'A Jew sees whatever world he wants in the Bible.' "

"Listen, Rainald, even if I agreed with you, I could not pay: I have spent all my money."

"Well, my friend, you can always give me the silver amulet that you spoke of," said the Gentile. "I will accept that in payment."

Rainald looked threateningly at the Jew. "Very well," sighed Naftali, and he handed the silver amulet to Rainald.

"Thanks," said Rainald, and he walked off toward the West Gate. Rainald held on to the amulet; as he neared the edge of the city he heard laughing and coughing and hissing, and soon he could see the three demons sitting on the wall. The demons were hairy and ugly, and their arms and their legs were in constant jittery motion. Rainald walked right up to them. He could see them–ah, but somehow they could see him also. Rainald saw the demons staring at him angrily, but this did not bother him at all.

"All right, my hairy friends," said Rainald, "it is time to give some money to a Christian. If you can make a Jew wealthy, then the least you can do is to help out a true believer."

The three demons looked at one another.

"What are you talking about?" hissed the first demon.

"We would never help a Jew," said the second demon.

"We hate anyone who is a believer in *any* God," said the third demon, and then he added, "especially anyone who is a presumptuous, selfish lout."

Then the demons flew down onto Rainald like a thick black cloud. They pummeled him and beat him. They punched him and jumped on him, and they stole his money and left him battered, black-and-blue, and penniless. And when two men found him later and heard him mutter, "Demons," the men only shook their heads and walked away, for it is said in the Book of Proverbs:

Those who plot for selfish gain
  Get tangled in their evil chain,
But joy and comfort always rain
  On those who do good deeds again–
No grief or mischief ever stain
  Lives lived upon a righteous plane,
But greedy thoughtless men attain
  More suffering than old Abel's Cain.

Rabbi, I am glad to see you. I want to apologize for my outburst during the service this evening. Reb Anton was whispering during the prayers, and I distinctly heard him say: "Birds."

What? "Words"? No, no–clearly Reb Anton said "Birds." Now I know you are thinking, "What is the problem with birds?" Well, remember–Lilit takes the form of a bird, so birds should never be mentioned in the synagogue.

Yes, I am talking about the evil demon Lilit, the female spirit of the night. She is a wind spirit with glittering wings and long, disheveled, windswept hair. She flies about in the dark hours. She steals children (especially newborns) from their houses. Lilit was the first wife of Adam, but they had a bitter argument and she flew away. Adam asked God to find her, and the Almighty One sent three angels–Sanvi, Sansanvi, and Semangelaf–to bring her back. But Lilit refused to return.

The angels said, "If you do not come back, then one hundred of your children will die every day."

"Fine," answered Lilit, "and if you do not leave me alone, then I will weaken all human children until the eighth day of their lives.

Furthermore, if you take one hundred children of mine, then I shall take one hundred human children in return."

Lilit still roams the earth, Rabbi, and she causes immeasurable grief. Nowadays, to protect a woman as she delivers her baby, it is a good practice to draw a circle around her bed and also to inscribe on the door: "Admit Sanvi, Sansanvi, Semangelaf, Adam, and Eve–but bar Lilit." Also, keep the windows closed: Lilit takes the form of a bird, and she can fly in with any breeze.

So we must be wary of birds–they can be fearsome foes. What is that? No, "foe" is not too harsh a word. Remember the tale of Josiah and the Bird Wars? You do not know that story? It is an episode first recorded during the wanderings of Rabbi Petahiah, the world traveler.

Rabbi Petahiah's adventures took place in the days of Achselrad, well before Asher ben Yehiel was the Chief Rabbi of Cologne. And why do I mention Rabbi Asher? It is simply this: When he was the leading scholar in Cologne, Asher spent most of his time writing and reading in the little back room of the yeshiva. Here, the Cologne rabbis had worked and thought and argued with themselves for centuries. Above this study room was a loft for storage. One winter day, when the stove was too warm and when Rabbi Asher felt too lazy to work seriously, to think deeply, or to argue analytically, he was rooting around among the manuscripts in the loft. After a time, he found a letter from Rabbi Petahiah ben Jacob of Regensburg to one of Asher's predecessors, Rabbi Abraham ben Alexander, the mystic Achselrad of Cologne.

"My dear Rabbi Abraham–

"I have just met a fine young man, a Jew named Elisha ben Moyses from Weimar. Elisha has agreed to carry this letter to Rabbi Isaac of Erfurt who I am certain will then arrange to transport it to you. I write to wish you and your family well, to convey my fondest greetings to all the Jews of your blessed community in Cologne, and to praise the good Lord God (blessed be He) and His Almighty Name for ever and ever, amen.

"I will not trouble you with the details of my many wagon rides and my subsequent sea voyages. Suffice it to say that safely they brought me here to the Oriental regions, regions that are so near to the great Holy Land where someday the Messiah shall return and deliver us and resurrect all souls and rebuild the Temple on Zion, amen. I write now in order to record for you some details of the lands and the peoples that I have seen in these old and foreign realms. The bright and glorious hand of God is visible everywhere, if only we look–praise the Lord Yahweh-Elohim.

"As you might imagine, my old friend, I have had many, many adventures in arriving here. I hope–if the good Lord is willing–to relate these events to you in person. For now, let me just say that after leaving the land of Ararat, I traveled through the mountains as far as Nisbis and the City of Chosen Capha (which is also called the "Strength of the Great Rock" and the "Castle of the Rock") on the River Tigris. At Nisbis, there is a large congregation, numbering at least one thousand Jews, belonging to the synagogue of Rabbi Yehuda, the son of Bethera.

"From Nisbis, I went in three days to the city of New Nineveh. New Nineveh is in western Persia across the River Tigris from Old Nineveh. Old Nineveh was once, of course, the capital of the Assyrian empire. Old Nineveh is surrounded by rivers: the River Husur on the northwest, the River Gomal on the northeast, the River Zab on the southeast, and the River Tigris on the south and west. Once, dams controlled floods and guided the waters into special ditches and moats in the ancient city. Now, however, it takes great imagination to see this city as a teeming, canal-filled metropolis: Old Nineveh is but a set of huge mounds with crumbled ancient walls. True, you can still find the remains of the temple of Jonah (which is now an enormous mound called Nebi-Yunus), but it is a sacred place and cannot be explored by outsiders such as myself.

"In contrast, New Nineveh is an active city on the far side of the River Tigris. Not long ago, it was ruled by the Syrian Okailids–most recently, however, it has belonged to the Seljuks. In New Nineveh, as in Baghdad, aged ruins sit alongside ornate modern buildings. The streets are badly paved and very narrow. A small square in the marketplace is the only open area. The people seem to be living in another time. Even the dust is old. The language is some ancient tongue descended directly from Babel. And only a part of the city space within the walls is filled with buildings. Much of the town is occupied by cemeteries.

"The most notable structure in New Nineveh is the Great Mosque. The town's solid limestone walls are half in ruins, but today there are still five town gates: two on the west, two on the north, and one (a bridge gate) on the east. If you come through the east gate, you cross a stone bridge from an island. The gardens on the island grow vegetables, particularly watermelons, on rich soil that is overflowed by the River Tigris in the spring and in the summer. The main industry of New Nineveh is the manufacture of muslin cloth. Hides, cotton, and gum also fill the markets. Then, too, there are gall nuts gathered on the neighboring Kurdish mountain slopes and exported through New Nineveh for use by dyers; gall nut tea is used as medicine.

"Like much of this region, New Nineveh suffers extreme temperatures. In the summer it is unbearably hot; in the winter there is frost. People drink the water of the muddy River Tigris, and perhaps that is how I fell ill. To recover, I was advised to drink from the sulphur spring–the Hammam Ali–in the northeast corner of town, but I remained feverish and dizzy and weak, and after a few days, the physicians to Rabbi Simai–the local Chief Rabbi–said I would not live long. Travelers (especially Jews) who die here must leave half their property to the sultan. Therefore, a royal official was sent to my bedside to inventory my belongings. This angered me. Weakly, I persuaded Rabbi Simai to hire some guides for me and I ordered them to carry me across the River Tigris, where I might die in peace in the ruins of the old city.

"The River Tigris (which you would know as the River Hiddekel of the Holy Scriptures) is a great and ancient waterway here in Asia. It rolls down from lakes in Armenia and it empties into the Lower Sea, that is, the Gulf of Persia. In its upper regions, it runs through farm after farm, and marble, copper, and iron mines line the shores. Here, near Nineveh, the river is broad and shallow, and boats cannot have keels deep enough to keep them from being overturned by the waves. Instead, travel is by rafts called *kelleks;* these are made of woven reeds or of wood supported by inflated skins. It was a reed raft that took me across the river. In solitude, I passed a week of prayer and fasting, and through the grace of the Great Lord our God (blessed be He) I recovered fully, amen. I then returned to the New Nineveh side of the river, where Rabbi Simai greeted me warmly. Our first feast together was as delicious a meal as I can ever remember eating.

"Each country I see shows some new variant of mankind. People come in all shapes, colors, temperaments, and sizes. One day, I saw an incredibly small man walking through the marketplace here in New Nineveh. I stopped in my tracks. I stood still. I stared. Many times I had heard of small people, but I had never seen one so tiny or so perfectly formed. This little man was no taller than my waist! Miniature people, I have been told, were important members of the courts of the Egyptian pharaohs. A tiny, perfectly formed being was like a magical god, a coveted angel. The Egyptians even had recipes for dwarfing normal babies. Newborns were rubbed along the back with the grease of moles, bats, and dormice. Sometimes daisy roots and dwarf elder berries were mashed into a paste and fed as a cereal to the children – but whether any of these treatments actually worked, I have no idea.

"In any case, I stood in the marketplace of New Nineveh, enraptured. My guide said, 'Ah, that is one of the Pitikos.' Then he proceeded to tell me the most fascinating tale. Apparently, south of here, near Kushand Hairlahby, where there is a great lake with aromatic plants and trees, a group of miniature people lives. These are the Pitikos. They are dark skinned and curly haired. They are so small that they wear heavy shoes to prevent their being blown away by strong breezes. The Pitikos migrated from Africa, and *they* call themselves 'Akka.'

"The Pitikos herd miniature cattle and sheep and goats. Also, they hunt and they farm. The tiny people live together in a group of towns near vast river marshes filled with crocodiles. The rich, fishy marshes attract birds, which swarm nearby. All manner of water birds fill the swampy lands, but most especially there are cranes. These cranes are incredibly fierce, although most of the time they do not bother the other animals. However, once a year there is a terrible warfare between the birds and the Pitikos. Great congregations of cranes descend on the swamps as they fly south for the winter. This happens regularly, and the wise men among the Pitikos know the exact day each year when the battle is to take place. It is inevitable. Sadly the Pitikos take their families, their cattle, their flocks, and all their goods and hide them in caves under the ground. Then the men arm themselves with swords and lances, with bows and arrows, and with spears and clubs, and they prepare for a terrible fight.

"Now the sky darkens. Cranes blacken the air, as thousands of birds swarm in screaming flocks. Myriads and multitudes of winged demons roll down from the skies. Claws and beaks attack the miniature people. A dense cloud of raging, rattling birds peck and slash the men. Claws rip at arms and shoulders and faces. Attacking, swooping, calling, and rattling, the birds fly in flocks so dense that they block the sun and the sky. They roll down on the windy updrafts. They swoop through invisible valleys in the winds. Brave men cower, blood flows, and on both sides, many are slain before the sun sets. I have seen vases, good Abraham, with graphic pictures of the battles of the Pitikos and the birds, and it is a terrifying, awesome sight indeed. But the battle lasts for only a day. The next morning, the birds have withdrawn: a deadened peace reigns. The surviving Pitikos clean the area; then they bring their women and children and their cattle and sheep and goats from the hiding places.

"Here is a tale of the Pitikos that my guide told me. He said that he had heard this from a Hebrew. 'A Hebrew?!' I responded. 'Why, I myself am a Jew!'

" 'Well,' said my guide, 'let me tell you the exact story, so that you may preserve it and pass it on to your people.' "

"The story begins in Constantinople, where most Jews manufacture silk cloth. Not long ago, a big burly Jew named Josaiah ben Simon had left Constantinople on board a merchant ship; Josaiah was traveling as a representative of the local silk dyers. As a parting gift, his wife gave him a necklace of red coral, which, as you may know, Abraham, protects against lightning, whirlwind, shipwreck, and fire. (Red coral is also strung around the necks of children to preserve them from the falling sickness and to tighten their teeth.) Soon into the voyage, the coral turned pale yellow; then the necklace actually broke. A storm arose, the sails were torn, the ship struck rocks, and quickly it sank. However, with the help of the good Lord God (blessed be He), Josaiah swam and swam, and, exhausted, he reached the shore alone. He had landed at the edge of the country of the Pitikos.

"Josaiah pulled himself up on the rocks. He walked wearily along the shore. After some time, he heard voices and he walked toward the sound, where he was astonished to find a group of miniature people. Later, said my guide, Josaiah described them this way:

" 'All the people were less than waist high. Their hair was crisp and closely curled. Their noses were flat, and their arms were long. Some men were reddish-brown, but most were almost black. They wore bright beads and feather necklaces, bracelets, and arm bands. They lived in huts built of sticks. The Pitikos (or Akka, as they called themselves) preferred hunting and herding to farming. In fact, they were marvelous and daring hunters and skillful archers, darting in and out of the tall, tangled woodland vegetation with the greatest of ease.

" 'The Pitikos were also dedicated and affectionate family members. They even practiced circumcision, although they knew nothing of the Jewish religion. They were fond of music and they had numerous folk songs; they played stringed bows and they beat drums made of hollowed tree trunks covered with cattle skins. Most of all, they loved to dance. Sometimes an entire community danced together in a long line, twisting about like a huge rhythmic snake.'

"When Josaiah ben Simon appeared suddenly one day, the Pitikos welcomed him warmly. It was nearing the time of their terrible battle. Such a huge man would undoubtedly be a great warrior, they thought. 'You are just in time for the battle,' said one of the tiny bearded men. 'What battle?' asked Josaiah. The Pitikos looked at one another and then they sat down with Josaiah and explained to him about the endless annual warfare with the birds. They told of terrible attacks by clawed winged monsters. They told of fearful children and mothers and of courageous but sometimes futile attempts by the Pitikos men to defend the villages. Josaiah listened in amazement. Then he reassured them, and he promised to join in the fight against the cranes.

"The day of battle was fast approaching. A dazzling dawn arose, and Josaiah ben Simon ha-Levi went forth with the army of the Pitikos. But when he saw the sky darken and the endless waves of screaming birds, Josaiah's heart sank. There were swarms of broadbills, finches, shrikes, and sunbirds, storks, bulbuls, pigeons, and wrens, not to mention sparrows, jackdaws, herons, and hawks—and over and around and above them all, there were fierce flocks of angry cranes.

"Josaiah shrank back. He closed his eyes and repeated the *Shema* three times to himself; for good measure, he also recited these verses from Psalm 30":

Thank You, Lord,
For shielding me
From the bitter enemy
Who attacked with sword.

I called up from the precipice
With my final mortal breath:
"What use will be my sudden death
Deep in Sheol's bleak black abyss?

Can dead men ever praise or
Tell again Your wondrous story?
So, Lord, please come and rescue me
And be my holy savior."

"This gave Josaiah an infusion of courage. A wave of bravery washed over him. He rushed forward. He pushed, he slashed, he cut. He thrust and he parried, and he fought valiantly. In the end, he helped the tiny people to drive off their winged enemies.

"Many people were killed, but the birds suffered even greater casualties. Josaiah was a hero to the Pitikos. The next day he helped them rebuild their houses and stockades. But Josaiah had no taste for heroism or for warfare; he was homesick and in a hurry to leave. The Pitikos gave him a bag of gold. They escorted him to a far path which led eventually to an old road. The road passed through empty valleys and bare mountains, and after a time Josaiah found himself walking again among normal-sized people.

"Josaiah traveled through many strange lands. Then one day he saw Constantinople again, his home city, sitting on its hilly promontory at the western edge of Asia. Josaiah came to this ancient city from the west, and he entered the city through the three arches of the Golden Gate, the southernmost entrance in Constantinople's great western wall. Josaiah walked in through the Golden Gate, he walked past the markets, and he walked into the old Jewish Quarter. There, in the courtyard of the yeshiva, beside the little Jewish garden with its chicory, daisies, and asphodels, he met again his friends and his family. He told them what had happened to him. He showed them the gold. But few believed the details of his story.

"So, Abraham, that is the whole tale that my guide told to me. In spite of this story, I find it hard to think ill of the birds that I see here; in fact, I watch them fondly. Some peck about on the ground, and these remind me of hens, skinnier or longer or taller, but still hens at heart. And then there are the soaring fliers overhead, the tanglepickers, windhovers, and turnstones. They cry out above the warm sands here, just as they once did for you and me on golden afternoons in the far-off Rhineland skies. Ah, Abraham, these winged heralds are needles. Yes, they are needles weaving God's great cloth of magic, darting in and out, stitching among the fluffy white clouds which give us glimpses of Heaven remembered from our childhood. And now, my friend, these memories are little pocket pictures. We carry them ever after as reminders of the glorious celestial realms of Paradise, the Great Hereafter to which we all will fly away like birds in the last and eternal days to come. So hallelujah and amen, good Abraham; hallelujah and a winged celestial most heavenly amen.

"Your childhood friend,
Petahiah, the son of Jacob"

Hello, Rabbi. I will be with you in a moment. I cannot leave until every tablecloth is folded, otherwise the day has not ended properly. There, now I can sit next to you by the stove. The Sabbath has come again and we can all rest, praise the great Lord God, amen.

Sabbath is poetry. In fact, whenever I hear poems they bring Sabbath feelings and Sabbath smells, such as fresh bread and candles and all manner of other wide-eyed childhood rememberings. I love especially the ancient poems, the ones my grandmother would recite. Grandmother seemed to remember poems endlessly. Mostly, they were the poems discovered by her favorite medieval rabbi, old Achselrad of Cologne. Achselrad loved the mystical poetry of Eleazar Kalir, from his *Shivata,* and also the poems of Meir ben Isaac of Worms and of Dunash ben Labrat of Cordova. Do you know any of Dunash's poetic hymns? One that I remember is Dunash's little verse for the Sabbath:

Even on a winter night
The Sabbath slips in quiet and light
Warming houses, bright and blest
And bringing peace and gentle rest.

I wonder if old Rabbi Abraham ever read that poem. He would have liked it because, although he was very pious, he was also a mystic–and, to be honest, he was a romantic. In his younger years, Abraham tried many wild and romantic things and he traveled far and wide. Once, he visited King Ferdinand II of Leon. King Ferdinand's reign of thirty years was fairly unremarkable, although . . .

What is that, Rabbi? Certainly I have told you this before, for it is worth repeating twice. Old Abraham ben Alexander repeated many things in his life. He rewrote hymns and stories and poems in his famous Kabbalistic tome, the *Keter Shem Tov.* Ah, but the words were never exactly the same: Achselrad changed and the stories changed, as his life wound round and round and round. Yes, his life rolled round and round, and old Abraham never stopped writing, and my grandmother said that it was in the dark early hours of the morning, while he was writing and rewriting the *Keter Shem Tov,* that Rabbi Abraham looked up, and in the yellow light of the candle on his desk he saw a holy sight.

At that time, Abraham ben Alexander was seventy years old. In his later years, he had written many books, he had thought deeply for long hours, and he had seen strange and wondrous sights. Achselrad's favorite memories were of early days: they were springtime days when he and Petahiah had been young yeshiva students. Long ago, the two boys had played in the fields outside the city walls; they had lain on dusty banks of the wide River Rhine in warm weathers with rains falling gently all around.

Old Abraham Achselrad thought back, and he remembered those fine times. He smiled. He felt a cool wind. He saw a springtime light. Was it like this long ago, on a warm afternoon when the rains fell like mist on his face? It was winter outside, but already the old Rabbi felt the coming of spring. The candle flickered lightly, and Rabbi Abraham ben Alexander thought that there, in the doorway of the old yeshiva of Cologne on the wide medieval River Rhine, stood a stooped and ancient man with a misty, dusty beard.

"Hello?" said the Rabbi.

The figure smiled but remained silent in the doorway. Rabbi Abraham blinked and winked, and he rubbed his eyes. The specter wavered dimly. Was it the candlelight? Were Achselrad's old eyes playing tricks?

Achselrad was an old man. He sat with an old man's slouch, and he waited with an old man's patience, watching with old man's eyes.

And eventually the specter in the doorway moved and smiled and spoke, and when the figure talked, it talked in a quiet ancient voice.

"Greetings, good Rabbi. My name is Dunash – Dunash ben Labrat."

The wooden yeshiva had slipped back in time. Warm and dusty lands lay outside the doorway. A little breeze seemed to skitter through the corner of the study room, from far and away to the south.

Rabbi Abraham raised his eyebrows. Dunash ben Labrat! Why, Dunash was a legend. Old Dunash had been a grammarian and a poet. He belonged to the brilliant circle of Jews attracted to Cordova by the famed poet Hasdai. It was Dunash who had set off the Jewish "Golden Age" under the Moors in Andalusia. He had founded a school of scientific philology. He had written and taught Hebrew. And he had adapted the Arabian style of verse to Hebrew poetry, so that soon a new form of rhymed Hebrew poetry filled the synagogues of Spain.

Achselrad leaned back. A warm southern wind washed over him. Suddenly he opened his eyes. Had he been dreaming? Or had he been musing? There in the doorway was the shape of a man, and Abraham ben Alexander heard this spirit saying, ". . . and what is my city of Cordova like, Rabbi? Well, I will tell you: It is an old sunbaked city. It is on the southern slopes of Spain's Sierra de Cordova mountains, on the right bank of the River Guadalquivir. When you come upon it from a distance, you will see brick walls and narrow crooked streets. And everything gleams. All the buildings are whitewashed."

The spirit nodded. "I must confess that I grew up privileged," he said. "That was in the days of the great Jewish patron, Abu-Yussuf Chasdai ben Isaac ibn Shaprut. My father was the master of a vast estate outside the city. Our farm and those around us were grand lands, with vineyards and groves of olive trees; to a child they were filled with green corridors that marched on forever. We lived close enough to Cordova to see from our farm the glory of the city, the Mezquita. This is a mosque that was once the site of a Roman temple. It has a courtyard of shady palms and cypress trees and an endless labyrinth of pillars built of porphyry, jasper, and many-colored marbles and lined up in twenty-nine arched aisles. What a magical place for a child to wander!

"Ah, my Cordova – it had mosques and universities and libraries galore. And the beautiful city raised beautiful people: craftsmen, scholars, artists, and poets. There were Cordovan silversmiths (who came originally from Damascus) making fine silver filigree ornaments.

There were Cordovan leathermen (who were native born) engraving belts, jackets, pouches, and saddles. There were scientists and writers, too. But I could go on forever about our people."

The spirit of Dunash paused and wavered like a summer mist.

"To me, however," said Dunash, "Cordova was a land of poetry. In Cordova and all the Mohammedan kingdom around, a great poem was more wonderful, more praised, more celebrated than a victorious battle. Every nobleman, from the caliph down to the lowest provincial emir, was a patron. Everyone wanted writers and poets among his friends. Poets were appointed to high offices, poets were consulted on official matters, and poets were entrusted with the most important state affairs.

"There is no doubt, Rabbi, that my Cordova was the seat of civilization. In those days, Cordova was a verdant community of spiritual activity. It was a fragrant garden of joyous words as well as a center of serious study; we were surrounded by research, by excitement, and by clear thought. Both Christians and Jews were encouraged to be independent by our Mohammedan hosts. We learned the Arabic language, but we also studied our own languages in great depth–then we traded ideas and language back and forth."

The spirit became quiet. Was he finished talking? Or was he just stopping to remember those glorious days? Rabbi Achselrad waited patiently. After a time, the Rabbi said gently, "And, good Dunash, how about yourself? How did you come to write poetry?"

"What is that, Rabbi? My poetry? I was a student of the famed Hasdai. Now *he* was a poet. In my younger days, though, I was interested in language, in the hard analytical dissection of paragraphs and sentences and words. When I was still green, I came across the great new Hebrew dictionary written by Menachem ben Saruk of Tortosa. This dictionary was a wonderful tool, an advance in our scholarship. Reb Menachem traced systematically the ancient pure roots of words. Then, he separated out the additions–the suffixes, prefixes, and other edgings–that adorn and color the primal meanings. Menachem also listed the grammatical rules of Hebrew. With this archive in hand, old Menachem set about explaining the Holy Scriptures. It was a heroic effort, indeed. Today, my friend, I am an old man, and I can see this quite clearly.

"Menachem did a fine job. His writing was so natural that I could absorb his work unthinkingly in the same way that I breathed the air around me. I accepted Menachem's ideas as the standard surroundings. I took Menachem's hard work and handicraft as my birthright, as the ground substance of our written world, and immediately I saw how to improve it. There were mistakes–these I corrected. There were thoughtless generalizations–these I challenged. There was a rather pompous style–and this, in my strong-headed youthfulness, I could not tolerate. Why was Menachem not more like me? I thought. I am afraid, Rabbi, that I wrote in rather scornful terms about this man's fine work, and now I am sorry that I did. Old Menachem was a bold and thoughtful man; he was a great master of scholarship, and I hope that, in his eternal rest at the feet of the Greatest Master of the Word, he will forgive me my shallow criticisms."

And Dunash ben Labrat–also known as "Adonim"–remained silent for a long, long time.

Eventually, time passed, and Dunash's last words rang more and more quietly. Hours slid by, the light faded; then Rabbi Abraham heard the spirit saying, "There are things of which I am more proud, Rabbi, things of which I would rather talk–and one of those is poetry."

The spirit nodded its misty old head. "Yes, *poetry,* Rabbi, and specifically *poetic meter.* You see, poetry is verse. Verse means, literally, a furrow drawn by a plough. In other words, a verse is a line of words, planted evenly, arranged smoothly, and sown with deep-rooting and life-filled meanings in words that will grow of their own accord. Verse should be complete unto itself in form and content. It should feel natural–but it should also be inspired by God.

"I grew up in an Arabic culture, and I was struck by the rhythmic meter of the foreign poetry around me. As you know, old Hebrew poetry (poetry such as the Psalms) did not rhyme. We Hebrews built our poems with repetitions of words. Ah, but the Greeks and the Arabs used *rhymes,* word endings that ring in the ears in the same way for different words. Although the essence of verse is repetition–and old Hebrew verse had beautiful repetitions–a new and special joy is added when we can use rhyming verse too. Rhyme makes rolling verse, gentle verse, light verse, edged with rhyming words that we've heard–lulling words, ringing words, where striking sounds abound, rolling round off the tongue and far away beyond."

The spirit smiled. "That is how I would explain it to my students. . . . In any case, Rabbi, I grew up amidst fine poetry, for the local Cordovan verse has rhyming meter. Also, it is unique. Each great civilization, the Greeks, the Romans, the Arabs, has had its own special preferred kind of verse. Certain meters strike an especially resonant chord in the heart of a people. Certain themes capture particular times and particular geographic locations, places with their own special climes–warm and dusty or cool and misty or low and wild and damp. Verses are the music of a specific language and people and place–and just as language, people, and places come in an endless variety, so too come the verses.

"And, Rabbi Abraham, once I was let loose, I could not contain myself. Why were the synagogue hymns so gloomy, when poetry is so wonderful? Poetry shows us Heaven. It rings and sings straight to the heart by any route: it can bypass the eye when it is read aloud, and it can bypass the ear when it is read silently. I was overwhelmed by this rich, direct, and immediate joyfulness, even when still a child in my hometown of sunny Cordova.

"Here–let me tell you a bit of verse in the special Cordovan style. . . ."

The mystic Rabbi of Cologne smiled and nodded. His eyes were closed, and he heard the gentle, ancient voice of old Rabbi Dunash chanting a poem:

Even as the smallest child
I wondered and asked unreconciled:
"Who is this Divine Companion–
What is our God like in person?"

So in those young green childhood days
I stared into the sky which blazed
With stars, a powdered deep night haze:
For hours I gazed upon the heights.
And in the deep black star-filled nights
I was always very sad
For never once in all that cosmic place
Had I caught a glimpse of God's glorious face–
Instead, I saw thin fleeting wraiths
Wild creatures flying on high paths
In windswept clouds of wispy gray
That swirled and then dissolved away.

But in one wondrous nighttide dream
I finally saw the Lord agleam
In the distance far above the land
Yet as near as my childhood hand.
He smiled down with a contented eye
From a window in the sky;
He had a little old-man's face
And a curly beard that wisped in space.

Dunash's voice was low and very quiet. Although he did not actually move, and although his eyes were closed, nonetheless Rabbi Abraham felt that he himself was leaning forward to hear the old poet's gentle words:

He scattered golden yellow sand
From the window with His hand,
Showering glints and flashing traces
Falling through the nighttide spaces,
And then the sand exploded brightly
Becoming sparkling lightnings whitely
Shimmering teeming starshine rains
Dissolving powdery crystal grains.

Ah, a nightsky moonlit trace
Was that gentle old-man's face–
And afterward, in deep night dreams
I saw Him in light bits and gleams
Sitting in the sky again
And pouring down His golden grain
From His quiet windowed room
High up beside the glowing moon.

And once I saw Him cluck and hurl
His grain just like our servant girl
When she was throwing barley seed
To our barnyard hens for feed–
And then I saw the falling seeds
Explode like fluff from milkyweeds
And rain down gently below His knees
On misty nighttime childhood trees.

Softly, the ancient voice faded away. Old Rabbi Abraham opened his eyes. The specter was gone. It had vanished into a childhood Sabbath night, a night where the candles were pure and yellow and the bread was soft and warm. Yes, it was a childhood Sabbath. It was a Sabbath where even on the coldest winter night the house was a comforting blanket enwrapping the whole wonderful Night Tale world. It was a Sabbath of children who ever looked up at bearded white-haired old men scattering handfuls of misty crystal bubbles from Heaven's little window into the endless starry nighttime Sabbath sky again.

Good evening, Rabbi. Of course–please sit here by the stove. What a beautiful white robe! You look like a Jewish Pope. No, no, my friend. I mean no sacrilege, and of course there once *was* a Jewish Pope. You do not believe that story? Well, I have heard it many times, and also my grandmother said that it was true. Although early in the Dark Ages a number of important bishops were called "Pope," this man was not a bishop. I am referring to a later time: it was the Middle Ages, when there was only one Pope, the grand bishop of Rome, the successor of St. Peter, the primate of Italy, the patriarch of the western Catholic Church. When Issachar, the son of Rabbi Aaron the Great of Mainz, was the Pope, he was the one Pope and the ruler of Italy, politically as well as ecclesiastically.

Issachar was called Pope Anacletus. This was in the days just before Abraham ben Alexander was the Chief Rabbi of Cologne. Old Achselrad heard the details from a stranger, and he recorded the tale in one of his many manuscripts, just as it had been told to him one cold winter night. You see, Rabbi, a wanderer, a traveler, appeared one night after the last prayers in the Cologne yeshiva; he stamped the snow from his shoes in the anteroom and he rubbed his hands together. Rabbi Abraham heard the noise and looked up. Soon the stranger was standing in the doorway of the little back study room, shining from the glow of the winter candles.

"Good evening," said the Rabbi.

"Good evening to you, Rabbi," said the man. "May I come in and get warm by the stove?"

"Certainly," answered old Achselrad.

The man walked to the stove; he rubbed his hands and turned around and around a few times. Rabbi Abraham waited politely.

"That feels very good," said the man. "Already I am less frozen."

"You are not from around here, are you?" asked the Rabbi.

"No, I am from Mainz."

The stranger was a broker. He was alone in Cologne on business, and he was looking for a warm place to spend the night. Rabbi Abraham offered some blankets and a corner of the little back study room. "That would be wonderful," said the man from Mainz. He pushed his satchel over to a wall and sat down. Rabbi Abraham set out some bread. The two men talked of small matters. The stove warmed the stranger, and he talked more and more. The hour became late. The traveler was telling longer and longer stories, and eventually this is what old Achselrad heard:

"You may know, good Rabbi, that a recent Pope was Jewish. Well yes, it does sound incredible. But it is a fact. The Jewish Pope came from Mainz, and I heard the whole story from a woman who knew his mother. Mainz has always had many Jews, ever since the old Roman days. Not too many years ago–when I was a young boy–there lived in Mainz a pious sage named Aaron ha-Kohen. You have heard of him? *Exactly,* he is the same scholar now known as Rabbi Aaron the Great. He was a brilliant man. He could debate for hours–and he was also a fine chess player. And this wonderful Rabbi had one son, named Issachar."

The traveler from Mainz moved back a bit from the stove and stretched out his legs.

"Rabbi Aaron was a very busy man," continued the traveler. "And as for his wife? She was a member of the Burial Society, she ran the Jewish hospice, and she was responsible for the community charities. How could she possibly care for her household alone? She could not, so the Rabbi hired another woman, a Gentile, to help around the house. The cleaning woman was a very religious Christian. This woman needed the money, but every time she entered the Rabbi's house, she made the sign of the cross and said a protective prayer. 'It is such a shame,' thought the woman, looking at Issachar, 'that this beautiful little boy must grow up with the curse of the Hebrews.' She sighed and brushed his hair, and then she went about her chores.

"One Sabbath, everyone in the Rabbi's house had gone to the synagogue. The Gentile woman, the *Sabbath Goyah,* was all alone. She finished cleaning the kitchen. Young Issachar ran up to her and gave her a hug. She sat him on her lap and played with him and sang him a song. Then it was time for her to go. But how could she leave little Issachar alone? She took him by the hand, and together they left and went back to the Gentile part of the city.

"Issachar was excited. He held the woman's hand. But now what should she do? Perhaps she could protect Issachar from the sad heathen ways for which he was destined. Perhaps he could be baptized secretly. His inherited Jewish sins would be washed away, God would smile on him forever, and no one else would know but she and the great Lord God in Heaven, amen.

"The woman looked around her. They were near the grand Cathedral. They walked up the steps. Issachar's eyes were wide. What a beautiful building! Inside, the woman found the priest. "Father, let us baptize this child," she said. "Very well," said the priest. Issachar looked up at the woman. She smiled down at him. She squeezed his hand and he smiled back. Then the woman and the priest gently washed Issachar. They rubbed him with a light oil mixed with balsam. The priest said prayers, and he sealed the ceremony with the sign of the cross, so that Issachar's soul might be protected. Finally, Issachar was dressed in a clean white robe and given a drink of milk and honey.

"The priest patted the boy and he looked at the woman. 'Father,' said the woman to the priest, 'I must confess–this is a Jewish child. I want him to be freed from his peoples' sins: I want him to go to Heaven.' The priest nodded. 'He is now a Christian; he can be *your* son,' said the priest. 'But,' said the woman, 'the Jews will know where to find me.' The priest thought a moment, then he said, 'You and your new son can go and stay in the castle of St. Angelo. There the priests will protect you and take care of you and they will train this young man to be a priest also.'

"The priest went into his back room. He wrote out a letter of introduction for the woman and the boy, and he brought out five gold coins. 'Here, good woman,' said the priest, 'take these and go immediately to Johann Mathar the carter. He will take you to St. Angelo's. And God bless you both.' The woman thanked the priest, and she and the boy hurried off and were taken south from Mainz that very evening."

The traveler from Mainz nodded to himself a few times; then he continued:

"Meanwhile, Rabbi Aaron and his wife returned home. The house was clean, a meal was set out, but the *Sabbath Goyah* and Issachar were gone. What was this?! Had robbers come? Had there been some terrible accident? The Rabbi rushed around. His throat was tight. His back was chilled. He shivered. 'What has happened here?' he demanded, but there was no answer.

"The Rabbi's wife sat and cried. The Rabbi called in friends and neighbors. They searched. They called out. They hunted and asked everywhere through the entire town. No one knew about the boy or the Gentile woman. Then, a few days later, word came back that the *Sabbath Goyah* had packed her bags hurriedly and had left the city with a small child. The truth was out. This woman had kidnapped young Issachar–but no one knew where she had gone.

"The Rabbi and his wife went into mourning. For seven long sad days, they grieved and mourned the loss of their son. The Rabbi felt so helpless. Events had rushed him along and he had no control. It was as if he were a tiny man in a land of giants–giants who spoke far over his head and who disregarded him completely. His son had been swept off, carried away on the winds. Was Issachar still alive somewhere out there in the far and distant giant's land? The Rabbi shook his head, and then he shook his head again.

"Somehow days passed. Weeks came and weeks went, and life moved on about them. Rabbi Aaron became a quieter man, but life went on."

The candles were burning low. Rabbi Abraham stood and lit another candle on the side table. The traveler from Mainz stretched. "Shall I continue, Rabbi?" he asked.

Old Rabbi Achselrad sat down again. "Please do," he said.

"Let me see," said the traveler. "From the grand Cathedral in Mainz (where the famous Archbishop Boniface is buried) the boy went to the castle of St. Angelo in Rome. The priests of St. Angelo heard the whole story. They welcomed the woman as if she were Issachar's mother, and they named the boy Pietro Pierlioni. Pietro had the intellect of his father: he was a brilliant boy. Quickly he mastered everything the priests could teach him. When he grew up, he went from university to university, and then he returned to Rome. Pietro knew German, Italian, Spanish, Latin, and Hebrew. He became a priest and then a cardinal, and his fame spread far and wide.

"Then Pope Honorius the Second died. The cardinals voted. A minority supported Gregorio Paparesci del Guidoni, but the majority voted for Pietro Pierlioni. Pierlioni was declared the Pope of Rome; he took the name Anacletus the Second, and he ruled all of Italy. However, Paparesci also claimed the papacy; *he* took the name Innocent the Second, and he was supported by the kings of England, France, Germany, and Spain. Interminable political feuding followed, and this occupied much of both men's time.

"But Pope Anacletus also fulfilled his religious obligations, issuing papal proclamations and advising the priests and the other clergy. One day, the Pope was talking with the elder priests from St. Angelo's castle. As they talked, one old man said: 'Your Highness, I am nearing death, and I must now tell you an amazing story –' and the Pope finally learned the full details of his own childhood. The Pope was stunned. He could not remember his real father and mother. Was he actually a *Jew*?!

"For many days, the Pope sat alone in his small room. He fasted. He prayed. He stared at the blank walls. He knew that for all these years something strange and wonderful had been hiding in the back corners of his mind. Was it his tiny childhood days? Now all of his life felt like a cloud, a mist, a vapor. What firm things could he stand on? Pope Anacletus wanted a home and a childhood; he wanted a father, as tall as a tree and as strong as all outdoors. Had his own father been like that? And was he still alive?

"Pope Anacletus could not simply ask his councilors; he did not dare risk having anyone discover the truth. Innocent the Second wanted to be the sole Pope, and many local clerics supported him. If it were known that Pietro Pierlioni was actually a Jew, then he would be deposed and perhaps imprisoned or even killed. Moreover, Pope

Anacletus could not leave Rome to travel. His strongest supporter, King Roger of Sicily, protected southern Italy, but much of Europe was under the domination of Pope Innocent. How could Anacletus find out about his real father, Rabbi Aaron?

"Not long afterward, Archbishop Arnold of Mainz wrote to the Pope, requesting that the Jews of Mainz be forbidden to observe the Sabbath. 'The Jews refuse to work on their Sabbath,' said the Archbishop, 'and the entire economy of the city is disrupted. There is no reason that Jews cannot worship on Sundays, as do good Christians. In addition,' wrote the Archbishop, 'the Jews often fail to appear when called before the ecclesiastical courts; such disrespect for the Church and its officials is a bad example for the community at large.'

"Anacletus read the letter and nodded. 'Here,' he thought, 'is my chance.' The Pope instructed the Archbishop that he would grant this request in one month unless the elders of the Mainz Jewish community could present a compelling argument to maintain their Sabbath–and the Mainz Jews would have to send a delegation to Rome in person.

"The Pope's answer reached the Archbishop, and the Archbishop told the Jews. What choice did they have? The Jews of Mainz prayed and they fasted; then they chose a group of three rabbis to travel to Rome and to see the Pope. The representatives from Mainz were three well-known scholars: Rabbi Hayyim, Rabbi Samuel, and Rabbi Aaron."

Here, the traveler paused again and shifted his legs.

"So they came to Rome," said the man from Mainz, "where none of the three rabbis had been before. Two men from the local Jewish community in Rome accompanied the rabbis across the city to the Lateran basilica, where the Pope lived and presided. A guard at the front door ushered the delegation into a study. The room was old and holy, and the walls echoed. The cardinal bishop of Ostia formally presented the Jews to the Pope. 'Your Highness,' he said, bowing, 'here are the Jewish clerics from Mainz.'

"Pope Anacletus II looked up. He sat at a white stone desk. He wore white robes with thick red embroidered edges. The Pope was quiet for a moment; then he said, 'Let the oldest Jew remain. The others may leave.'

"Rabbi Hayyim and Rabbi Samuel left with the guards and the cardinal. Rabbi Aaron remained behind. He stood quietly. His white beard was thin. He looked old and weak. Was this bent old Jew really his father? The Pope stared. He tried to imagine Aaron as a young man as big as a tree and as strong as all of outdoors.

" 'Are you Rabbi Aaron?' asked the Pope.

" 'I am,' replied the old man.

" 'You have come about the Sabbath restrictions,' said the Pope. 'The Jews of Mainz will be free to follow their religion. When you leave I will give you a letter that instructs the Archbishop to leave you in peace.'

"Rabbi Aaron raised his eyebrows. Was this some miracle? Had God answered their prayers after all? The Rabbi remained silent, afraid that anything he would say might change the Pope's mind.

"The Pope looked strangely at the old Jew. 'Well, sir,' said the Pope after a moment, 'please sit down.' The Rabbi sat on the edge of a chair.

"Still the Rabbi said nothing. Finally, Pope Anacletus said, 'Tell me about yourself.'

"Rabbi Aaron hesitated, then he said, 'I am a Jew, an old Jew from Mainz. I am also a rabbi, and I have spent my life studying the Holy Scriptures.' The Rabbi stopped talking. The Pope waited quietly.

"A few minutes passed. The Pope said, 'I see . . . so, you are a scholarly rabbi. And do you have a family? Are you married? Do you have children?'

"Rabbi Aaron said, 'Well, Your Honor, I have a fine wife. We had a son, but he disappeared when he was very young.' Tears were in the old man's eyes, and tears were in the eyes of the Pope. After a moment, the Pope cleared his throat. 'What do you do with your spare time, when you are not studying?' he asked.

" 'There is always work to be done in the garden,' answered Rabbi Aaron. 'And sometimes I manage to play a game of chess with my friends.'

" 'Ah,' said the Pope softly, 'we will have to play a game together sometime.'

" 'What a strange conversation,' thought the Rabbi. The Pope was talking quietly and gently. He seemed so respectful of the old Rabbi. What was happening here? wondered Rabbi Aaron.

"The room was silent. The Rabbi looked down at his hands and feet. He felt small, as if he were a miniature person in a land of giants. When he looked back at the Pope, there were tears in Anacletus's eyes. Very quietly, the Pope said, 'Father–I am your son. I am Issachar.'

"Rabbi Aaron opened his mouth but said nothing. He just sat in his chair, staring at the man before him. 'Father,' said Anacletus, 'it is really me.'

"Many minutes passed. Finally, Rabbi Aaron said, 'How can this be?'

"The Pope leaned back in his chair. He felt weak and tired. He looked at the thin old Jew in front of him. 'Father, let me tell you what I only learned recently.' Anacletus told his whole story. Rabbi Aaron kept his hands on his knees. Things seemed to recede into the distance for old Rabbi Aaron. He heard the Pope's voice. He heard the story, but it was a tale that sounded far, far away. The Pope himself seemed to be just a vague white shape, a ghost, a specter, a wavering form. Then Anacletus was finishing: 'I have thought for long hours through sleepless nights,' he concluded. 'I want to come home . . . that is, if you will have me.'

"And the Rabbi only said, 'Yes.'

"Now the Pope hurried on: 'That is good. It is wonderful. I would like so very much to return home. But I must plan quietly and carefully. If I left suddenly, the European Christian kingdoms would be thrown into chaos. Also, Gregorio Paparesci would like nothing better than to have me killed; so I am in great danger outside Rome.'

"The Pope was tapping his chin. 'However, Father, I have a plan. If it works, then I should be back in Mainz within a year. Until then we have our secret, and I have hope. Now, let me write you that letter to the Archbishop.' The Pope took a pen and inscribed a formal declaration upholding the rights of the Jews of Mainz, and he affixed his papal seal. He handed the document to Rabbi Aaron. Suddenly, the Pope did not know what to say. He found that he could not stand and that he could not speak. The Rabbi waited a moment. He was an old man. He looked down at his son. 'Good-bye, Issachar,' he said. 'Good-bye, Father,' whispered the Pope.

"Rabbi Aaron turned and left the room. He walked slowly. Outside, he found the other two Rabbis waiting patiently on a bench. Rabbi Aaron gave them the proclamation, and they read it in disbelief. They smiled and patted old Rabbi Aaron on the back. 'Tell us everything,' they said as the three men walked from the Lateran palace. Old Rabbi Aaron only shook his head. 'I must lie down,' was all that he said.

"Rabbi Hayyim and Rabbi Samuel looked at each other. Something very strange was afoot. They returned to the house of the Jew with whom they were staying. Silently, Rabbi Aaron went to his room. He did not come out for dinner. The next day, the three Jews left for Mainz. Rabbi Aaron remained silent. He stared at the countryside on the long wagon ride back to Germany. He watched the windhovers wheeling far overhead in the sky. He saw the peasants bent in the fields. He heard wind and he felt rain. And then he was back in Mainz again. Perhaps it had been a dream, he thought. And now he felt very sad."

The stranger from Mainz sounded sad himself. He took a deep breath, and he closed his eyes. After a few moments, Rabbi Abraham asked, "And what happened after that?"

The traveler opened his eyes. "After that? Well, the Pope put his plan into effect. He wrote a short book, a pamphlet, condemning Christianity. He locked it in his desk drawer. It was a logical and damning document, but no one will ever read it because it was destroyed by his successor, Pope Innocent the Second. Then Anacletus took into his confidence one trusted servant. Late at night, a body was cut down from the Rome gallows. It was smuggled into the Lateran palace, it was dressed in the Pope's robes, and it was laid in the Pope's bed. The Pope had died, declared the servant, and he managed to keep the cardinals at a distance. The fake Pope was buried the next morning, and Gregorio Paparesci was immediately invited to a meeting, the second Lateran Council, in Rome. Thousands of clerics attended. The cardinals voted, and Paparesci was formally declared Pope Innocent the Second of Rome. As pope, Innocent's first act was to excommunicate King Roger of Sicily.

"Meanwhile, Issachar had dressed like a common merchant, and secretly he returned to Mainz. Rabbi Aaron ha-Kohen hugged him and kissed him. His mother cried, and she could not stop stroking his hand. Issachar had been kidnapped, said his parents to friends and neighbors, but he had managed to study abroad and now he had returned home as a great scholar. People marveled at Issacher's broad learning, his complete command of the Holy Scriptures, and his amazing facility with

Latin. Eventually Issachar succeeded his father as the head of the local yeshiva when Rabbi Aaron stepped down from the rabbinate.

"Then, old Rabbi Aaron would sit and talk and advise in the rabbi's room of the yeshiva. And one day he even wrote a poem. Rabbi Aaron the Great wrote a dream poem, a mystical poem that is still recited in Mainz on the second day of *Rosh Hashanah;* it begins":

Young Issachar, my son,
At long last night is done
And a golden dawn has now begun.

I dreamt I was a tiny man
In a giants' distant land
Among their feet, lost in the sand.

I stumbled on the smallest stones
Dirt tripped me, clawed my aching bones
Winds pushed me back with howling tones.

And, my boy, away you flew
Through the giants' skies of blue
Beyond all places that I knew

You were carried without a trace
From that distant giants' place
And into God's last warm embrace.

Now it was late. The traveler yawned. "I think I would like to lie down and sleep," he said. Rabbi Abraham nodded, but he remained in his chair. The traveler curled up on a blanket on the floor, while the Rabbi sat there late into the night, wondering at the wealth of details in this strange, strange tale.

What is that, Rabbi? Do I believe the story? Yes, I do – for this is how the actual poem begins. And how could anyone fabricate such a poem from nothing? Besides, originally I heard this tale from my grandmother, and she swore that this is what had really happened, once upon a time in the town of Mainz in medieval Europe when the world was very different, a long, long time ago.

Good evening again, Rabbi. It is hard to sleep when there is a new moon. Tonight is dark and cold – who knows what demons are abroad? Put your feet up on the side bench and I will open the stove door. Let me push the coals back; the bright white glow will keep the nighttide spirits at bay.

On a night like this, demons might simply walk in out of the dark, even into a holy place. Oh, it is true that most demons stay away from light and holy places, places filled with the golden glows of sacred candles. That is the case for *most* demons. But once upon a time, when the world was younger, a huge lumbering demon walked right in on Mathiah. It came into the golden light and glowing warmth from a cold black Rhineland night of long ago. This was in medieval Cologne along the wide and dark River Rhine. It was when Rabbi Abraham ben Alexander was the Chief Rabbi and when, in those distant days, there lived in Cologne a fine young man, a bright, brave, and warm spirit, named Mathiah ben Jekamiah.

Mathiah was a brave young man, but he became entangled in a sad, sad affair. I remember my grandmother recounting the story, and she kept her eyes closed during the entire tale:

It was *Hannukah,* said my grandmother, and in Cologne the Jews had a winter feast. Each winter, in the month of *Kislev* and halfway through the *Hannukah* holiday, there was a large meal in an inn owned by a wealthy Jew. People sang and danced. The fires were high. Greenery hung on the walls and over the doorways. Everyone ate and drank and laughed.

The women had baked and cooked for days. Tables were piled with breads – sourbread, chicory bread, fig cakes, and honey breads. There were meats and drink. Two deep fireplaces had roaring, crackling blazes, with boys pushing in new logs as soon as the old ones had burned to stumps. The room was always aglow, as befitted the great *Hannukah* "Festival of Lights." Green wreaths were on the doors. Dishes of ground spices were set in the corners of the room. Laughing and shouting men roamed about or sat telling stories and drinking. It was the middle of a happy *Hannukah.*

But one year, well after dark, when the children had curled up on rugs along the dark edges of the walls and when the women had collected near one of the fireplaces and when bright moonbeams shone through the west windows, in through the main door hunkered a stranger, a giant, rough barbarian. He was bearded and long-haired. His hands were dirty. His hat was a torn kerchief. From his belt hung the leg of a game bird, and over his shoulder he carried a tremendous cold, cold sword. There was a hush in the room. . . .

Yes, Rabbi, there was a hush. A stranger had walked in – a vast, threatening man, a formidable giant. He was a Gentile, or perhaps some demon. He came from far outside the city. But do you know what was the most disturbing and foreboding thing? It was his sword. Weapons were not permitted in the inn. It was absolutely forbidden during that joyous holy fest. Into the room lumbered this gigantic armed man, and he brought with him a strange feeling, a fearsome, Otherworldly feeling that lay dark and bleak on his shoulders and spread around the room. No wonder a hush fell thick within the inn. There was silence. People looked around at one another. And then Mathiah spoke up.

Mathiah ben Jekamiah ha-Levi was a brave young athlete. He had common sense and he was honest. Had there been a war in which he could win fame and glory and far renown, then there is no doubt that Mathiah would have made the German Jews proud. He was their strong, fair-haired young hero, he was a fine young man, and he was destined to be a champion of the Jews.

Why, perhaps he was a prince like one of the Maccabees, Rabbi–who can say? "Maccabee" means hammer: in the distant biblical days, the Maccabean family had struck a hammer's blow for religious freedom. They had fought king Antiochus of Syria. They had freed the Jews. They had established a family of priest-kings who ruled for one hundred and twenty years. So, when the gigantic churl stumped into the inn of medieval Cologne and when all the Jews inside fell silent, they immediately looked to Mathiah, their German Maccabee.

Mathiah felt a chill as he stared at the huge man, but he took a deep breath and said, "Good friend, you are obviously a stranger and you do not know the custom here. Tonight we leave our weapons outside."

The giant stared back at Mathiah and made no answer. The other men looked at their feet or at the fire, and the women shivered.

Mathiah looked away a moment. Then he said, "Stranger, do you not speak German? You must set your sword outside the door."

Only silence was the response.

Mathiah was thinking. He tapped a finger on the table. And, Rabbi, do you know what he was thinking? He was thinking of the Talmud: he was thinking of the talmudic story:

> After the good Lord God (blessed be He) had fashioned men, he instructed the archangel Gabriel to put intelligence into them. First, Gabriel made a special jug for measuring the intelligence. Then he carefully poured an equal quantity of intelligence into each man. The little men were filled to the brim with fine thoughtfulness. Unfortunately, the large men were not quite full. And as for the giants? They were so large that a vast empty space was left.

Mathiah ben Jekamiah remembered the old talmudic story, and he thought, "If I am to believe the Talmud, then this giant cannot be very smart. Let me see how I can salvage this situation, which is becoming embarrassing for me."

Mathiah stood up and said, "My good man, you are obviously attached to that sword of yours–and a fine and unusual sword it is. Perhaps you fear for its safety outside the door with no one to guard it.

Well, let me put your mind at ease: we are all honorable men here. No one will touch it. I give you my word."

Still, the giant remained silent, and everyone looked to Mathiah, so he said, "Stranger, if you will just hand the sword to me, then *I* will set it outside the door."

And then, Rabbi, do you know what happened? The giant spoke. He spoke in a thick, uncultured accent; he spoke as if there were a piece of meat in his mouth (which there very well may have been), but he spoke passable German, and he said, "Only the bravest of men touch this sword."

Mathiah was taken aback. What should he answer? He raised his eyebrows, and suddenly he had an inspiration–undoubtedly an evil spirit whispered in his ear. (Have you ever heard voices, Rabbi? . . . Ah, I know exactly what you mean: I too am always hearing voices when no one is about.) And this was what happened to Mathiah also. Some strange evil spirit hissed in Mathiah's ear, because Mathiah said to the giant, "Clearly, you are a brave man. Frankly, my friend, *I* am brave also. So let us just demonstrate our bravery, here and now. (*Then* I will set the sword outside the inn.)

"This is what I propose. We will each stand brave and tall and still, one first and then the other. As one of us stands, the other can strike a single blow with the sword. Now give me the sword, and I will hit you first. Then you can take a rest. Perhaps you can return later this evening. Of course then I will take *my* stand, and you will give me your best hit."

What is that, Rabbi? Yes, that *was* a rather bold proposal. It was the inspiration of an evil spirit, and it was met with stone-cold silence.

Mathiah stood a moment; then he said, "You must agree, my friend–this is a pact for brave men only." The giant remained silent, and Mathiah asked, "You are a brave man, are you not?"

Minutes passed. Finally the huge lout nodded his head slowly.

"Then," said Mathiah, "prove your bravery: hand me the sword."

And, Rabbi, you know how quiet it is late, late at night just before the dawn. All the insects finally have fallen asleep. You awaken confused and unsure where you are. There is a strange empty feeling in your stomach and, although your last meal was hours ago, it is the wrong time to eat again. It is a time when, if you step outside the house, you wonder whether anyone else is alive in the world. Well, that silent hour is loud compared to the silence in the inn while all the Jews awaited the giant's move.

And you know how quiet it is on a winter's night in the mountains. No people or animals are about. All the golden angels are far away, warmly wrapped in their heavenly beds. Well, even *that* nighttime is loud compared to the absolute stillness in Cologne on that sad feast night midway through the *Hannukah* holiday. All was completely and absolutely and entirely silent.

Then the giant demon moved. Slowly he took his sword–his cold, dark sword–from his shoulder. Evenly and gently he handed it to Mathiah, who had to reach up in order to take it in his hands. The sword was so heavy that Mathiah almost dropped it on the floor. But our young Mathiah was a well-muscled athlete. He managed the huge weapon, he swung the sword from side to side, and suddenly, quick as you please, he slashed and he cut off the giant's curly-haired head. The head rolled to the floor with its eyes open and its mouth gaping, and the crowd in the inn gasped.

Then, a most remarkable thing happened. Yes–a remarkable thing happened: the giant, headless as he was, calmly bent down and picked up his fallen head. He grabbed it by the curly hair, he took the sword from the stunned young hero Mathiah, and then that headless giant lumbered off, out of the inn and into the night. Slowly, he stalked away, and he left only his shadow and the blank, disbelieving silence of the inn on that night, the fourth day of *Hannukah*–a silent, cold, German winter night along the black medieval River Rhine long, long ago.

No one knew what to say. No one knew whether to leave or to stay. Mathiah tried to smile, but his lips were dry. Eventually there was weak talk, but it was broken and desultory and whispered. The fires burned low. The women shivered. Time crept by slowly. You can imagine, Rabbi, that Mathiah wanted desperately to leave and to go home. Mathiah wanted, more than anything, to disappear into his warm home, far on the other side of town. But what should he do? Dare he leave?

What, Rabbi? Dare he stay? Ah, it is a good question, my friend–but stay he did.

Mathiah was a hero in the Juden Viertels: he could not leave. He returned to his seat, and he waited. He did not eat. He did not drink. He sat with a full wine cup at his elbow, and he stared at the empty doorway. The doorway of the inn was like the doorway in the house of a dead man. It was black and thick and ominous. It was the door of death, and no one dared walk out through it. Everyone looked away, and they remained within the inn, quiet and weak and cold. Time passed more slowly, the fires burned lower–and then the demon returned.

At first it was just a shade, then it was a shadow, and then it was the giant himself, lumbering in through the doorway of the dead, walking down past the tables and straight through the clumps of people, who shivered and shrank back. Slowly the demon stalked up to Mathiah. There was a blank and disbelieving silence. It was the same gigantic lout: he was a lumbering, churlish clod of a tree trunk, a rude, crude ruffian with hairy arms, and his head was in place and his beard was knotted and his hat was a torn kerchief and over his shoulder he carried the heavy cold sword.

On both sides of Mathiah, men stood aside. The giant waited. Mathiah was frozen; his legs were weak. He could not look at anyone else. Why did his hands not work? Would his feet even hold him up? The giant waited, unmoving. Did hours pass, or was it only minutes? No one seemed to breathe.

Finally, our young, fair-haired Mathiah stood up. As he did, he knocked over his wine cup and the red wine spilled over the tabletop and onto the floor and into the cracks in the cold, dark bricks. Mathiah stood up. Still the giant waited. There was quiet, and the world narrowed. Then the gigantic demon–the lumbering, churlish clod of a tree trunk, the crude ruffian, this barbarian from the hinterlands, from somewhere far, far away in the mountains–slowly lowered the sword from his shoulder. The giant grasped the haft of the cold sword of death. There was a tear in his eye. Evenly and gently he raised the sword, like a toy or a stick or the lightest of knives, and suddenly he whipped it out and cleanly he slashed the head from poor Mathiah ben Jekamiah ha-Levi's shoulders. And then the huge black demon turned and lumbered off, out of the inn and into the night. Slowly he stalked away, and he left only his shadow and the blank, disbelieving silence behind. And ever since, at the end of the feast on the night of the public *Hannukah* celebration, the Jews of Cologne spill a cup of wine, and the red wine rolls down over the tabletop and onto the floor and into the cracks in the cold, dark bricks. Then all the Jews go home quietly, disappearing into the silent German Rhineland winter night.

Good evening, Rabbi. No sleep for the weary? Well, sit here on the bench and I will stoke up the oven. This stoker? It is one of the old iron shoe scrapers from the front hall. There are still two scrapers in the anteroom for dirty shoes, but I myself am of the old school: you should remove your shoes before coming into the building. Pray barefoot. Barefoot is holy. Why, when he arrives, the Messiah will walk barefoot into the city of Jerusalem.

Ah, but now Jerusalem is quite far from us, Rabbi, and it has always been far from Mainz, a cold city not often at peace with the spirit of the warm and dusty Holy Lands. Why do I mention Mainz? Well, I was thinking of old Simon ben Isaac ben Abun, a Jew from Mainz at the end of the Dark Ages.

In Europe, the Jews lived fairly quietly during the Dark Ages. Generally they were tolerated, but the feudal system did not allow them to hold land, so they were tenant farmers or merchants or bankers. In central Europe, the Jews kept a wary distance from the Christian culture before the Renaissance.

In contrast, in the Mediterranean regions Jews mixed freely with Christians and Arabs. The Mediterranean regions provided the Jewish teachers for Europe. First these teachers came from the Holy Lands and from northern Africa; later they came from Spain and southern France. In the Dark Ages, European Jews traveled to Provence to study, and then they returned to Bonn, to Coblenz, and to Cologne. But at the end of the tenth century, a brilliant young Jew, Gershom ben Jehuda, returned to Mainz from Provence and founded a school that became the first independent center of Jewish culture in Germany.

This was the famous Rabbenu Gershom, *Meor ha-Golah*—the "Light of the Dispersion." Along with Jacob ben Yakar and Moses ha-Darshan (the "Exegete") of Narbonne, Rabbenu Gershom established the European school of talmudic commentary that culminated almost a century later in the great scholar Rashi. Rabbenu Gershom expounded the Talmud to his pupils with a brilliance and a clear directness. Beside his commentaries, Rabbenu Gershom set forth a series of *takkanot,* or "improvements," approved at a consensus meeting of scholars. These regulations applied to every possible aspect of life: they included rules forbidding polygamy, requiring the consent of the wife for a divorce, establishing privacy for all personal mail (under threat of excommunication), and demanding that copyists be absolutely faithful and not change any manuscripts, even those portions that seemed wrong.

Mainz was an ancient fortress city on the River Rhine, and it had long been populated by Jews. At the end of the Dark Ages, Rabbenu Gershom's academy in Mainz produced Jewish scholars thoroughly schooled in the Holy Scriptures and in Jewish oral and written traditions. The Mainz talmudic scholarship was pacesetting, and the Mainz school remained the center of European Jewish studies for almost a century.

What? No, I was just resting my eyes. Let me see, now where was I? Oh yes, once upon a time in the town of Cologne on the wide River Rhine, there lived a fine old rabbi named Abraham ben Alexander. (Yes, yes, Rabbi, I will get to Mainz and Simon ben Isaac ben Abun in a moment. Just be patient.) In those medieval times, Cologne had strange dark nights, and it was on one of those mysterious nights that a thin traveler arrived in the back room of the yeshiva where Rabbi Abraham was hard at work.

It was a strange night, a dark night, a cold night. Still, it was nearing the springtime, and there was the hint, just a tiny hint, of the wonderful mysteries of new springtimes to come. Old Abraham

Achselrad had fallen asleep, but now he awoke. He could feel a slight tingling in his fingers. Had some spirit slipped into the yeshiva-synagogue, the *scholae Judaeorum* of Cologne, that night? The Rabbi looked up. A stranger stood in the doorway–or was it only the shadow of a late-night breeze?

The stranger in the doorway seemed to waver. The Rabbi winked and blinked and he rubbed his eyes. The stranger smiled. "Hello, Rabbi," he said in a light springtime voice.

"Hello to you," said Rabbi Abraham. "It is rather late to be out and about."

"Yes, it is," said the man,

The Rabbi continued to stare. Finally, he asked, "And who are you, my good man?"

"My name, Rabbi, is Simon ben Isaac ben Abun," said the spirit traveler. "I come from the town of Mainz, more than a century ago."

Old Achselrad nodded and stroked his beard. "Tell me your story, my friend," he said, sitting back in his chair. And this is what the Rabbi heard:

"Well, Rabbi," began the wanderer, "I lived once upon a time in the city of Mainz; it was almost two centuries ago. Originally, I was from Le Mans in France. When I arrived in Germany, I was young and energetic. I knew a thing or two about the Talmud, and immediately I became a staff member of Rabbenu Gershom's Academy. The great Rabbenu was a saint. He patted me on the back; he had kind words for me every single day. And with his encouragement suddenly I found myself writing a book–the *Yessod,* I called it. I also wrote poetry and hymns. I lectured and commented and argued. My business (I was an importer of silks) could not have done better. Soon, I was wealthy too. But then the storms began."

Rabbi Achselrad listened patiently, stroking his beard from time to time.

"Not long before I arrived," continued the spirit, "Mainz had become the local Church headquarters: by then, it was an archbishopric, as initially established by the legendary Archbishop Boniface. Moreover, Charlemagne had a palace in the neighborhood. He came once a year with vast troops of attendants. Just before the king arrived, the estate was opened and aired and the gardens were tended. Suddenly fancy people filled the markets and the surrounding countryside. Horses with embroidered shawls and saddles and all manner of decorative trappings were ridden by festooned ladies and beweaponed men, and they could be seen daily, even in the deep woodland gullies and along the distant bare mountain ridges.

"Charlemagne was fond of our region. To him it was a civilized place for a summer retreat. He gave special privileges to Mainz. Mainz merchants had priority selling goods throughout France. The young men of Mainz were invited into the ranks of court advisors and military leaders. Old-guard Mainz families talked of the splendors of the big European cities, where they now traveled frequently. Musicians, writers, and actors looked for Mainz patrons–in all ways, the city of Mainz became known as a place of wealth and importance. The Dukes of Mainz convened international councils attended by French, Italian, and Spanish officials, as well as those from Germany. Political initiatives and proclamations issued from Mainz. Mainz merchants took the lead in organizing the Guilds. Major political movements began there–and when, in my day, persecutions of Jews became widespread, Mainz was, unfortunately, in the fore also."

The spirit wavered and disappeared. Rabbi Abraham Achselrad sat up in his chair. Had he himself fallen asleep for a moment? The Rabbi rubbed his eyes; he blinked and he looked around. The spirit of Simon ben Isaac was sitting on a bench on the other side of the room. Calmly it continued its narrative:

"A conversion triggered the latest wave of anti-Semitism. A certain Duke Conrad–a cousin of the emperor–had a court chaplain named Wecelinus. One day, out of the blue, Wecelinus came to Rabbenu Gershom. 'I wish to become a Jew,' said the chaplain, and Rabbi Gershom opened wide his eyes. Wecelinus was welcomed into the fold of Judaism. On the second day of the cold month of *Adar,* Wecelinus was blessed and washed in the bathhouse and was given a Jewish name, Yehudi. Then he spent many weeks learning the Jewish traditions. Yehudi took to Judaism fiercely. He was angry with his past. In his free time, he wrote a scathing lampoon of Christianity. Needless to say, it was not well received in the Gentile community.

"The emperor was King Henry II. He supported Church reforms, but he was a serious and devout Catholic. He believed in the Church with all his soul. He observed all the Church rites strictly. King Henry

II was called 'King of the Romans' and he was a friend of the pope, Benedict VIII; I have heard, Rabbi, that King Henry has even been canonized now, more than a century after his death. In any case, when Yehudi published his diatribe, Henry was furious. He commissioned one of his own clergy to write a reply. But Yehudi was a fine writer. His manuscript continued to be widely read, and it was circulated secretly from the city of Mainz. How could the emperor tolerate such blasphemy? Simply put: he could not. Finally, King Henry II decreed that all Jews should be expelled from Mainz if they refused to be baptized.

"Ah, Rabbi, we had become complacent. Who in Mainz imagined such a catastrophe? The entire Jewish community was stunned and went into mourning. But I thought: we cannot take this lying down. 'Do not just pack your things,' I said to my friends. 'Somehow there must be a way to remain here, to keep our lives together, to maintain our heritage.' I gave speeches at the two yeshivas in Mainz. Young people joined me in activist groups. We collected and hid all of Yehudi's manuscripts. We petitioned the local officials. We tried to talk to the archbishop – who, unfortunately, refused to see us. Meanwhile, I kept up the energy level of the community. I wrote letters. I even composed dirges lamenting the expulsion. For example, I remember writing":

How can wide-eyed little children
Awaken every newborn morn
Among full strangers, different men
Who mock them with rebuffs and scorn?

How can Jewish employees
Earn sufficient salaries
To feed their hungry families
And warm them through the winter's freeze?

How can pious weak old men
Lift their graying heads again
As good and hopeful Jews and then
Pray to such a distant Heaven?

Will a bitter winter blast
Once more disperse the autumn sheaves,
The rootless Jews, again outcast
Like November's crumbling leaves?

"I started a fund for displaced Jews. I tried to give spirit to the disheartened community. I never gave in, Rabbi–I never let up. I talked to everyone who would listen. I turned my store into a meeting place. I gave away my belongings and my money. I tried to radiate energy into others, and with all of us in constant motion, the Jews and the friendly Gentiles of Mainz kept active.

"Of course there were setbacks. Many Jews became Christians in order to save their possessions and their lives. And I understand how hard it was on them: they had to live; many had no other place to go, no relatives to support them, and absolutely no future otherwise. Among the converts was the son of Rabbenu Gershom ben Jehuda. But when the son died a Christian, his father ignored the recent past and observed the full religious mourning ceremonials for him, just as if he had died a Jew.

"Meanwhile, I traveled to other cities–even as far as Cologne here. I spoke out. Sadly, I found that the forces unleashed by Emperor Henry were widespread. Landlords now had an excuse to confiscate Jewish belongings on their property. Merchants would not extend credit to us. Every city seemed to have instituted new Jewish taxes and fees and surcharges. Jews were arrested on trifling charges; then they were released only for large sums of money. In effect, we were being ransomed. So I spoke out. I went to court daily. I pleaded with the magistrates. I also used my personal funds to bribe officials.

"Then what happened? Well, it was a remarkable thing–the emperor rescinded his order! We had been so noisy and so time-consuming that finally he wanted to wash his hands of the whole matter. The Jews were permitted to return to Mainz. Neighbors who had been baptized now returned to the fold. In other times and in other places, the returning apostates would have been shunned: no one would have come within four paces of them, and they would be buried with stones on their coffins. In Mainz, however, in a formal ceremony, the Hebrew names were reaffirmed for returning Jews. Our long-lost brothers were readmitted to all their appropriate synagogue rights and honors. They were allowed to marry into the community with no restrictions. Their children were accepted unconditionally as full-fledged Jews. The protection of the returning Jews was ensured by Rabbenu Gershom: he threatened to excommunicate anyone who reproached them. The Rabbenu reminded his congregation, 'We welcome new converts "with outstretched arms beneath the wings of God's all-forgiving radiant *Shekhinah,*" so we should doubly rewelcome our old converts, our returning brethren, amen.' "

Simon ben Isaac's voice faded away. In the late hours of the night, Rabbi Abraham had closed his eyes. When he opened them again, the worn bench was empty, the room was empty, the doorway was empty. But the little back study room seemed large; it was old and timeless. The walls were far away and dim. The ceiling was as tall the tallest synagogue–it reached to the very heavens. Had the old Rabbi been dreaming? He rubbed his eyes; then he closed them again, and this time he fell fast, fast asleep. . . .

What is that, Rabbi? Well, my grandmother told me that when Simon ben Isaac ben Abun died, the people of Mainz wept and mourned. The Jewish community of Mainz wanted their children to remember Simon. They wanted to be certain that over the years, as other things crowded their minds, nonetheless Simon was still thanked somehow. Therefore, every Sabbath in the synagogue in Mainz they added to the end of the morning prayers: "We remember Simon ben Isaac ben Abun (may his memory be blessed) who exerted himself on behalf of us and our parents and through whom persecutions eased and finally have ceased." This same epitaph was carved into a stone bench along the east wall of the prayer hall. In addition, the men of the congregation lit a candle and recited a special *Kaddish* prayer for old Simon one night each summer, on the ninth of every *Av.*

However, this made no difference to Simon. By then, Simon ben Isaac ben Abun was far, far away, resting where

Snows and frost are never known
Warm breezes play, flowers lightly blown,
No torrents of rain e'er drench your home

With only a touch upon your door
Of western winds from far offshore
To hint of mortal life outwore.

And there he rested, in the *Gan Eden,* rocking eternally, warm, happy, and at ease, in the bosom of Abraham.

Back on earth, in the Jewish community of Mainz, people had instituted remembrances. But these no longer mattered to old Simon ben Isaac ben Abun. On the other hand, while he had lived and aged, certain things *had* been important. Over those years of graying hair, Simon often sat back and mused. He remembered how he had stood tall before angry city officials. He recalled recklessly selling a set of wagons and horses and giving the money as a bribe to the assistant magistrate of the ecclesiastical court of Mainz. Simon thought again of the time that he hid a young Jewish family in his barn. Simon remembered lecturing and praying. He remembered hours of arguing with old men in candlelit rooms. Pictures of old times flickered back and forth for old Simon, and when one day he died peacefully in his sleep, he was dreaming happy old-man dreams–and so it was that Simon died a happy old man, a man well contented with his life.

Good evening, Rabbi. Are you having difficulty sleeping? Let me open the stove door and tap the coals a bit. The white glow of the oven will wash away all the worries of a hard day. Are you too hot? Here, have a cup of water. There is magic in water, you know. Yes, yes–I am talking about plain water, plain cool, clear water: especially in a new clay cup, water has endless untold magical depths.

My grandmother always said, "Sit outdoors and drink fresh water, my golden young boy. Sunshine is the most healing of all radiances, and pure springwater is the most healing of all medicines." And, in His infinite beneficence–for the benefit of all mankind–God has distributed springwaters throughout the world. Springs sprout from the mountaintops and also from the ocean bottoms. (Oh yes, Rabbi, they actually gush up from the depths of the sea too.) There are two varieties of springwater. The warm mineral waters heal the outside of your body: mineral water baths tighten the skin, they ease aching muscles, and they cure joint pains, nervous disorders, and all other internal congestions. In contrast, the cool waters work inside the body: they reduce your temperature, they calm your heart, and they soothe your digestion. Both types of springwater strengthen sleep–

and the amazing bubbly waters produce a complete relaxation. And why do they work? It is through holy magic.

What? Well, I do not know how a holy man like you can be such a doubter. Certainly you would admit that springwater is holy. Water is the primal substance from which God created the Heavens and the Earth. Water is the essential nourishment for all the plants and creatures under Heaven. And think of the *Sukkot* holidays. Ever since the days of the Great Temple, a flask of springwater is poured out at the altar on *Sukkot* as we thank God for the rains and the waters. This is the deepest of mystical ceremonies. The Talmud declares: "He who has not witnessed the great *Sukkot* water-drawing and who has not shared in its powerful communion with God's water-founded universe has never in his life experienced the heights of joy."

Just speaking of it makes me thirsty: I could use some of the springwater's cool magic. I have heard of people adding fir oil, camomile, thyme, or oak extract, but it is the pure water itself that holds the magic. My grandmother could list all the cold springs of Germany that produce pure healing waters: the most famous are Kissingen, Kreuznach, Pyrmont, and Soden. In fact, it was Kreuznach springwater that helped the silversmith Seth ben Mordecai to escape execution. You do not know that story? Then let me tell you:

Once upon a time, said my grandmother to me, in the days when Abraham Achselrad was the Chief Rabbi for all the Rhinelands, there lived in the city of Bonn an outspoken and strange craftsman named Seth ben Mordecai ha-Levi. Seth was a silversmith and a wondrous engraver. As you know, Rabbi, silver represents the moon and other mysterious mystical nighttime matters. Perhaps it was for this reason that Seth was known as a mysterious mystical man. He was certainly strange and Otherwordly and fearless. He stared deep into your eyes when he talked, and he always spoke his mind. Everyone who knew Seth would shake his head and say sadly, "Someday Seth's bald honesty will cause him very serious trouble." Everyone said this – and so of course it came to pass.

Seth was known far and wide for his amazing metalwork. When he was young, he had spent many years in the northlands as an apprentice to a famous silversmith named Volund, and when Seth finally returned to Bonn, he himself had silvery gray hair. In Bonn, Seth set up his own smithy specializing in silver. Noblemen and wealthy people from all over the Rhinelands came to Seth for their finest silver pieces. One day, Duke Edmund of Bonn was visiting Seth's shop with his men to buy some of Seth's exquisite plates, pitchers, and pots.

In medieval Germany, there were all manner of dukes. The old-line dukes had inherited their titles for many, many generations, while newer dukedoms were created by kings and emperors to reward their best generals. Duke Edmund's father had been a famous warrior. He had been brave and successful, and now his family was new aristocracy. Edmund had grown up protected and pampered. "I will make my family the equivalent of any of the old-line dukes," he thought.

One day, Edmund decided to increase the family heirlooms. "We have the money," he said, "so I will buy the best silver in Germany." Of course, Duke Edmund went to Seth's shop. Seth demanded prices more than double that of any other local craftsman, and the Duke wanted to bargain. He picked up a goblet. "I have seen better," he said.

"I do not know where," answered the Jew. "This is the best *kesef.* It comes from the fabulous silver mines just recently discovered in Freiberg in Saxony. I use only the finest metal, and it is for that reason that my work is more expensive."

"*Kesef?*" asked Edmund.

"*Kesef* is silver," said Seth. "That is its Hebrew name–it means 'paleness.' "

The Duke smiled. "Yes, that is appropriate. Your Jewish silver *is* rather pale. A little more polishing would not hurt."

The Duke looked at some other pieces. He picked up a dish. He held it at arm's length and sighted along its edge. "This is a bit crooked, my friend," he said. He put the dish down and he picked up a candlestick. "Rather ordinary looking, I would say," he added.

The Duke pointed to some silver cups. "The sculpting, the engraving–I am afraid it is not very well done," he said.

Seth stood with his hands in his apron. "If you think you can do better, then make a pitcher yourself," he said.

The Duke's men were very silent. They stood motionless and

uncomfortable. Duke Edmund said, "I am taking this pot, and the price will be three gold coins." He picked up the silver pitcher he had been eyeing.

"You may get out of my shop," answered Seth.

The Duke of Bonn took the pitcher, he threw three coins onto the counter, and he left without another word.

When he returned to his house, the Duke still felt hot and tense. "How could I let a Jew talk to me like that?" he thought. "I should have had him arrested right then and there." Duke Edmund stood up and he walked around the room. Then he turned to his marshal and ordered that a group of soldiers bring the Jew to him immediately.

Four officers went to the silversmith's shop. Seth heard heavy knocking on the door. He heard angry voices. He heard the clank of steel weapons. Quickly Seth recited seven incantations and he put a holy amulet around his neck–a thin moon-white silver box engraved on the outside with mystical symbols. Seth lit a brazier with incense that made a sweet, dense mist. He said, "Blessed be You, O Lord our God, who has sanctified us and has commanded us to wrap ourselves in the fringes." Then Seth wrapped himself entirely in his holy *tallit,* which was a pure, spotless, silvery white, and he went on working as usual.

The soldiers burst in, but they could not see the Jew. Was the shop hazy, or was it just the warmth of the afternoon? The place felt thick with crowds of spirits, and yet it looked empty. The soldiers were dizzy. It felt as if someone was working nearby–it sounded as if silver was being shaped. But the guardsmen could see no one. The room spun. The soldiers stepped outside where the air was cool. They shook their heads, and they stood about uncertainly. Eventually, they went back to the Duke and reported that they could not find the Jew.

The Duke was angrier than ever. He sent the officers back again. "Wait outside the shop," ordered the Duke. "The Jew will appear eventually. Then grab him and bind him and bring him back to me." So, the guardsmen returned to the smithy. They surrounded the shop and the house, both front and back, and they set an extra guard at the cellar door.

The silversmith peeked from his window. He sighed: he was already in prison. He shrugged his shoulders. He unwrapped himself from his prayer shawl, and he walked calmly out the door. Immediately the soldiers grabbed him and bound him and marched him back to the Duke.

Duke Edmund sat behind a large oak table. "Well, my silversmith, you do not look so self-assured all tied up like that," he said. Seth remained silent. "I am afraid," said the Duke angrily, "that you must learn some manners. You need to have the proper respect for authority if you are to live in this community. You will have to remain in prison for one full year."

But Seth said, "Listen, Duke, this is not my fault. You would not admit that I am a fine craftsman. Then you refused to pay the true worth of the merchandise. Now you are just trying to look good in front of your men. This whole unpleasantness is your fault. In fact, *you* yourself are the one who should be in prison." The Duke was so angry that he sentenced the Jew to death, and Seth was dragged away to the prison. In one week's time, he was to be hanged.

Executions were examples; they were public demonstrations. The town crier made the announcement. "In one week's time," he said, "the Jew named Seth Mordecai is to be hanged at the town gallows, the Ravenstone." And when the appointed day came, a great crowd of spectators, young and old, stood whispering nervously in Ravenstone square.

In those days, there was a custom: a condemned man could have one last meal of his choosing. When he had been asked, Seth ben Mordecai tapped his chin and then he asked for a drink of water, a single drink of springwater. Specifically, Seth requested a newly made pottery cup filled with fresh, cold springwater. The guardsmen raised their eyebrows. "But," said Seth, "the water must be from the famous Kreuznach cold springs near Bingen south of Coblenz, and the cup must be newly made."

The soldiers reported to the Duke, and the Duke said, "Fine, fine, do as he asks–just hurry up!" The Bonn city officials and the Duke's guardsmen looked at one another and shrugged their shoulders. Fresh springwater was brought back from the Kreuznach spring. A new gray pottery cup was bought.

The next day was the execution. The cup was filled with springwater. Seth was led to the Ravenstone and he was untied. He put a finger into the cup. He tasted the water, and he nodded his head. Seth was wearing his *tallit,* which had a magical six hundred and thirteen fringes. He looked up into the sky. Far, far away he could see a windhover circling beyond the clouds. Seth smiled. He wrapped himself completely in the prayer shawl. Then he jumped, and he plunged into the water and he disappeared forever. The people wondered whether they had actually seen this happen. Had Seth really been standing there before them? And if so, was this a holy man, or was it a demon? My grandmother was uncertain, and frankly, Rabbi, so am I.

Good evening, Rabbi. I was resting my eyes. The white coals of the stove hold my eyes with their glow. If I stare at them, I can already see the Holy Land into which – the good Lord willing – I will roll someday smoothly like a round, round bottle beyond the grave. The stove door is the mouth of a cave, and I can look through it and into the bright warm sunshine of that golden land with its ancient, holy, suntanned hills. Do you know the story of the cave to the Holy Land, Rabbi? Dan ben Moshe the dairyman? No, this is another story. It is about Elkanan and the demon – but perhaps it was the same cave. My grandmother told this story to me when I was just a boy, and, as usual, it begins with her favorite rabbi, old Achselrad of Cologne:

You see, once upon a time, just south of the medieval city of Cologne, there lived a man named Elkanan ben Aleydis ha-Kohen. Elkanan had an upsetting dream. It remained with him vividly when he awakened the next morning, and it made him uneasy all day. So that night he went to consult with Rabbi Achselrad.

Elkanan came alone. He wandered through the nighttime city of Cologne, with its dark, winding, intricate byways. Finally he came to the alley that led to the synagogue in the Juden Viertels. Elkanan walked quickly through the main prayer hall, which was filled with wooden benches. He passed the twelve stained-glass windows with their colored lions and snakes, he looked up at the Holy Ark, the *Aron ha-Kodesh,* made of stone, and he walked to the door of the back study room. It was late at night; the Rabbi was bent over a book. Was he studying or was he asleep? It was very quiet.

After a moment, Elkanan asked, "Rabbi Abraham?"

The Rabbi looked up in the candlelight and he blinked his eyes. "Yes?"

"Rabbi, my name is Elkanan ben Aleydis. I live just south of here. Do you have a moment to talk?"

"Certainly," said the Rabbi.

Elkanan remained standing. "It is about a dream I had. I have always wanted to take a pilgrimage. I have wanted to be one of those pious free spirits who walk off to the warm southern regions and who end up at the Holy Land."

Elkanan smiled, but then he frowned. "Recently I had a dream about traveling south. I cannot get the dream out of my mind. I think it is telling me that now is the time to go to the land of our forefathers, but I am not certain. Do you have the time to interpret it for me?"

The Rabbi put down his book. "Tell me about your dream, Reb Elkanan," he said.

"Well, Rabbi," said Elkanan, settling down on a bench, "in my dream, I am out somewhere in the countryside and I meet a man. He is a stranger. I cannot see his face. He is waiting for me, just for me, and he offers to lead me to the Promised Land. This is wonderful. Of course, I am a bit frightened – who would not feel hesitant suddenly to walk off to parts unknown? But this is something I have always wanted to do. It is an answer to my prayers. I have always felt my life would not have been worth living if I do not make such a pilgrimage.

"Now, in my dream, I am packing my bags. Magically, all the belongings I need are right there by the side of the road. But they are so bulky that I can barely walk with them. Still, I stagger along after my guide. I cannot see where I am walking. I fall into a pit. My guide is gone. I fall and fall and fall, but fortunately I awake before I reach the bottom.

"When I awoke I was sweaty and warm and cold at the same time, and I shivered. I remembered the dream perfectly, and I have not been able to get the scenes out of my mind. So how does this sound to you? What do you think that this dream means?"

It was late at night. In the dim candlelight, Elkanan could not see the Rabbi clearly. Were the Rabbi's eyes closed? Yes, they were, and now the Rabbi's chin had sunk to his chest and he was breathing heavily and slowly. Elkanan was not certain what to do. Finally he said, "Rabbi?"

Old Achselrad opened his eyes. He stared at the ceiling. He said something very quietly. Elkanan bent toward the Rabbi. "What did you say, Rabbi?"

The Rabbi looked at Elkanan. Rabbi Abraham stared at Elkanan as if he were trying to see inside the man. Then the Rabbi said, "Elkanan, my good friend, listen to me carefully. It is ordained that you should not go to Jerusalem. I strongly advise against it."

"But Rabbi," said Elkanan, "I–"

The Rabbi held up his hand. "Just a moment," he said, and he reached into his desk. He took out a clean piece of kosher parchment and on one side he wrote the *Shema,* followed by seven mystical words. After the ink had dried, Rabbi Abraham wrote a special protective charm for Elkanan on the other side:

> Mighty is Yahweh of Israel. By all the virtues of these many holy signs and seals that are herein engraved, inscribed, and enumerated, may Elkanan the *kohan* be saved from every manner of demon, dybbuk, devil, and ghost. May the Holy Words protect Elkanan from illness, disease, and an early death. May You, O Lord, protect his going out and his coming in. May Your mighty right hand loosen any ties and bonds from him. May Elkanan live a long and quiet life, ever in the light of Your Law–for now and for ever more, eternally. Amen, *selah,* amen.

Then the Rabbi rolled the parchment into a tight scroll. Rabbi Abraham tied the paper with seven white threads, and in each thread he put seven neat knots. The Rabbi put the scroll into a small square silver box with magic numbers on it.

Rabbi Abraham ben Alexander handed the amulet to Elkanan ben Aleydis. The Rabbi said, "Keep this amulet with you at all times."

Elkanan took the amulet and stared at it. "I must warn you," continued Rabbi Abraham, "put all thoughts of travel out of your mind, Elkanan."

The little silver box felt heavy and cold. Elkanan's satchel was at his feet; he bent down, he put the amulet inside the satchel, and he tucked it into a woolen scarf.

Elkanan waited for more advice, but old Achselrad had closed his eyes, and again the Rabbi seemed to have fallen into a deep sleep. So eventually Elkanan ben Aleydis stood up, and he slipped quietly out of the Cologne yeshiva.

Elkanan kept the amulet with him at all times, and he tried to think of other matters. But, try as he might, travel remained close to his thoughts. Elkanan's wanderlust was always peeking out from around the corner. German hills became suntanned *holy* hills; German dirt became warm, ancient, and holy dust. And then one day, Elkanan met a stranger on the road near his home. The stranger had an old dirty coat and a floppy white hat. He had sandals and a walking stick. But, Rabbi, this stranger was actually a demon, a tempting traveling wraith; he saw the wanderlust in Elkanan's eyes, and he knew just what to say.

Elkanan raised a hand. "Hello, stranger," he said. "Where are you from?"

"Where?" repeated the demon. "Where am I from? My good man, I am from everywhere. I come from north and south and east and west. I have gone to there and I have come from here and I have passed all the places in between."

Elkanan looked down the road wistfully. "It sounds like quite a fine life," he said.

"Oh it is, it is," replied the demon. "You yourself look like a worldly man. I suppose you have traveled to far-off regions? Undoubtedly you have traded in Tripolis and bartered in Peiraeus. There is no mistaking your love of the exotic."

"Yes," said Elkanan, "I am completely captivated by the idea of foreign lands. But to tell you the truth, I have never been farther south than Bonn."

"Impossible!" said the demon. "How could you resist the urge to move about and to see new places and to talk with new people? I know that without travel, my life would not be worth living."

Elkanan sighed. "Exactly, my friend. It is just that I have never had the opportunity. I need a little guidance to start out, but once I get going, then I am sure that I will continue on and on until I find myself in the great and warm Holy Land with the good Lord's sunshine smile overhead and with my toes in the warm, warm sands, amen."

The demon smiled. "I know how you feel," he said. "A journey to the Holy Land is a blessed event. I have been there many times myself. In fact, that is where I am headed next."

"What?!" said Elkanan. "You are going to the Holy Land? If only I could come too."

"I do not see why you could not join me," said the demon. "The great and glorious Holy Land is at the end of all southern pilgrimages. And once you get there, God will reveal Himself to you, just as He did to the prophets. Ah, what a blessing it is to see the beauties of the Land of Israel! Each grain of sand and each pebble is holy. It is a warm and dusty place of ancient windswept joys." The demon sighed; then he looked around and lowered his voice. "Now, my friend, if you really wish to go there, and if you are very brave, then I will reveal to you a wonderful secret. God has shown me an underground cave. It is not far from here. It skirts the mountains, it runs under the seas, and it comes out directly in the Holy Land."

Elkanan felt a tingling when he heard this. He pictured the old and suntanned hills, hills walked upon by his most holy of forefathers. He could feel the dusty warm sand. He could taste the ancient waters. And he never looked carefully at this stranger, who was a demon through and through. "Let me pack my bags," said Elkanan. But the demon said, "There is no need, my friend. It is best to travel quickly and to travel lightly. We will leave now, and we can be back next week. Just follow me." And in a glow and a fog, Elkanan followed behind the demon stranger.

The two walked out into the country, away from the city of Cologne, away from the dark, cold River Rhine. They walked all morning and they walked all afternoon. Elkanan felt light and easy, and the road seemed downhill all the way. Eventually, the demon stepped from the road, and Elkanan followed. They walked through a small clump of oak trees until they reached an open field. They walked up beyond a ridge, past a meadow, and into the woods. Deeper and deeper into the woods they went. The trees were tall and the forest was dark and thick. Then, up ahead, Elkanan saw a large pile of rocks.

But it was more than just a pile of boulders: actually, it was the rocky opening to a cave. The cave was hidden in a ravine. Had it originally been an underground river? Was it once the channel of a raging torrent, one of the streams of the original Great Flood rushing to the foot of Mount Ararat far to the south? The mouth of the cave was only the width of a man. The demon went in, bending and twisting sidewise, and Elkanan followed behind.

Elkanan followed the demon. He went in, and never once did he consider how in the world he might get out again. The tunnel went straight on for some way. Then it dipped suddenly down, so suddenly that Elkanan had not a moment to think. He stumbled, but the ground was soft; he seemed to have fallen upon a heap of sticks and dry leaves, and he was not hurt at all.

Elkanan stood up, and he found himself inside a winding tunnel. He looked toward the ceiling, but all was dark overhead. Before him was another long passage, and far, far ahead, he saw the demon walking swiftly away from him. Elkanan followed the demon. All seemed dreamlike. As Elkanan went along, stones fell from the walls and water dripped along his right. And were there dybbuks in the shadows? Reremice and blanktees fluttered along the dark damp ceiling. The many recesses were gloomy places. Elkanan felt afraid. He walked on and on and on. The passage was endless. His faith in Heaven kept him from panicking, although he did not have the courage to look too closely into the many small side tunnels that he passed.

They walked all afternoon and through the night, down one winding passage and up another. The farther they went, the darker it became. The cave was more than just a single tunnel: it had side passages and cracks in the walls. But most terrifyingly, it had skulls of old animals–hyenas, rhinoceros, stag, and bison. It had refuse heaps where ancient tribes had left the bones of reindeer and the antlers of other long-gone animals. Charcoals and burnt stones littered the floors. Flakes of arrows and spears and harpoons were scattered about, and the walls had thin sketches of men hunting spiral-tusked mammoths.

"How much farther is it?" asked Elkanan, out of breath. "I am very tired; I would like to rest awhile."

"Have patience," answered his guide. "Soon we will be in the ancient Land of Israel. We have only to cross the final quicksands. See–over there is a log bridge. Just follow me."

And as he said this, the demon guide stepped on a slippery log. The quicksand beneath was bottomless, covering an edge of the Great Abyss of Gehenna. The demon stood with his hand out to help Elkanan. But would he really lend a hand? Of course not–he would push the poor Jew into the quicksand, where Elkanan would sink down forever and ever, far below the earth.

Steam rose from the quicksand, which bubbled and churned. Elkanan was tired and afraid. He clutched his amulet. He stepped onto the edge of the log, he reached out his hand to the demon, and he took a hesitant step. The demon stretched out his evil fingers, reaching closer and closer to Elkanan. Then from behind Elkanan there was a tug at his sleeve. He turned his head and he lost his balance, but a strong arm caught him from behind and pulled him back to the safety of the rocky ground. There stood an old, white-bearded man, a thin robed figure–it was the Prophet Elijah.

Elijah waved his arms and said the nine mystical Names of God. With a hiss and a raspy cry, the demon burst and crackled like a burning paper, and it fell into the quicksand and disappeared.

"Elkanan, Elkanan," said the prophet, shaking his head, "what *have* you been doing? Why did you not listen to old Rabbi Achselrad? And why ever did you follow this stranger? Could you not recognize a demon when you saw one?" Elkanan was still holding onto Elijah's hand. Elkanan felt the old thin skin. He felt the veins and the sinews, and he felt the ancient holy strength. A deep warmth came from the prophet–and Elijah was continuing: "Elkanan, this demon led you deeper and deeper into the earth. His only goal was to kill you. God will see to it that you find the great Holy Land–but you must be patient. All will come in its own due time."

Elkanan had tears in his eyes. So the Prophet Elijah said, "It is hard to wait, my friend–I know." And the old prophet took Elkanan by the hand, and slowly and quietly they walked together out of the cave and back up the road until they came to Elkanan's home south of the medieval city of Cologne.

Elkanan was tired. He sat in the dark that night, and he sat through the next day. "I must get up and get moving again," he thought. He did his chores. He ate some food, and later he slept the dreamless sleep of the dead.

Slowly, life resumed its quiet hues and its modest daily sounds.

Elkanan said his prayers, but he was afraid to face Rabbi Achselrad and he avoided going to the synagogue. One night, however, he had a special dream. Elkanan dreamt that he was small and round and fat and smooth. He was like a little glass bottle, and he rolled everywhere he went, and one cool evening he rolled into a hole. Elkanan rolled gently and smoothly, without a bump, and along he went, deep into the cold, rocky earth. On and on he rolled and rolled, evenly and smoothly. After a time there was a warm golden glow ahead; then he was rolling through sand, and soon he came out into an ancient dusty land with warm sands and suntanned hills and with the good Lord God's sunshine smile overhead. Elkanan stretched out his little smooth fingers and his little smooth toes, and gently he buried himself in the warm, warm sands – and Elkanan fell fast, fast asleep. And in the morning, Elkanan awoke refreshed and warm and happy, and he went to the synagogue and he prayed and prayed and prayed all day long.

Rabbi, let me ask you something: Do you believe in coincidences? I mean when two things happen together with no apparent connection. Perhaps you find a long piece of string on the street just as your bundle is ripping. Or a tree branch grows out perfectly to shade your window from the sun. Then there are the times when the wind blows from behind to help you up a steep hill. These things happen to all of us. But do they just *happen* to happen by themselves, or are they the thoughtful handwork of the all-seeing Lord God?

What, Rabbi? Well certainly God has *created* everything. Psalm 19 reminds us:

The skies ring out God's eternal glory,
His handwork sculpts each cotton-edged cloud;
The whole world shouts – it sings aloud
The craftsmanship of His creative story.

Creation's music rolls on and on
Through Heaven and the world below
As God's intricate ornate imbroglio
Sings each leaf in the grassy lawn.

God has done all. He has sculpted all. He has created all. Every complex byzantine thing is His, is His, is His. And of course He knows all – but has God *planned* everything? Has He bothered to organize each of the innumerable details of our intricate, ornate, multicolored world? Has every little thing and every single event been *foreordained* by God?

I myself am of two minds. You see, on the one hand, it is possible that every single item was thought out carefully in advance. On the other hand, some people say that God purposely built the world with unimaginable diversity. The Lord, they claim, desired a rich, thick, tangled variety. Perhaps the Almighty Lord God revels in the unpredictability that comes about when an incondensably complex world plays itself out. In this case, anything might happen – and sometimes it does. Now, could *this* be God's plan? Does He hope even to surprise Himself?

Ah well, Rabbi, whichever may be the case, the Lord certainly is ever-watchful. His *Shekhinah* shines over all. The great Lord God Almighty illuminates each of our daily lives, and He Himself protects us from difficulties and from our adversaries. Psalm 18 says:

> You, O Lord, make my lamp burn bright,
> You, great God, make the nighttime light –
> With Your help I have crystal clear sight
> And walk black alleys without fright.
>
> God's paths and Truths are perfect and right,
> His holy Word sustains the Israelite –
> He watches us, and with His arm of might
> He protects us from each menacing plight.

This, at least, we can have faith in: time and again, our adventures testify to God's protection. God reigns, He guards, He watches over us.

Our world is incondensably complex. No human can understand it fully. No mortal's book can hold its details between two covers. No simple laws or formulas can ever capture it; the universe cannot be summarized and abbreviated and carried about in one's pocket. But in this rich, rich complexity there is at least one eternal truth for man: God is a rock, a stronghold, and a protective shelter.

Yes, Rabbi, the good Lord God is always watchful, and He gives us divine protection. The Talmud says:

> Were it not for the shadow of the most Holy One, blessed be He, which protects each human being, then harmful spirits would slay him with a certainty–as it is said in the Book of Numbers: "The Lord is with us; therefore, you have nothing to fear from them."

The Talmud also reminds us:

> If a man performs a religious precept, then one angel is assigned to him. If he performs two precepts, then two angels are assigned to him. And if he performs *all* the rules, laws, and precepts, then many, many angels are assigned to him. Psalm 91 testifies that for a righteous man:
>
> No disaster, however slight,
> Shall befall you even late at night,
> For God has charged His angels bright
> To guard your paths through dark and light.
>
> Angelic hands will guide each trip;
> You shall walk safely without a slip,
> Stepping fearlessly on scorpions–
> Even deadly snakes will seem your friends.

These angels are a man's guardians–and they operate everywhere. I remember, for instance, how my grandmother told me a tale of God's protection against the wild cannibals south of the Holy Lands.

I do not know if there still are any such peoples, but once upon a time cannibals abounded. Grandmother's story took place long ago, in the Middle Ages. It began with Rabbi Asher ben Yehiel. You see, before he moved to Toledo in Spain, Rabbi Asher was the leading scholar in Cologne. Asher was a young man in those days. He spent most of his time writing and reading, continually studying the Torah and the Talmud in the little back room of the yeshiva. The study room was where the Cologne rabbis had passed endless hours, working and thinking and arguing with themselves–and above this room was a loft for storage.

It was a springtime day. The windows had been opened as wide as possible. The winds were cool and filled with the out-of-doors, and Rabbi Asher could not concentrate on his work. He leaned back in his chair. His feet were bare. Absently he tapped his fingers on a book filled with words that now seemed far, far away. Rabbi Asher shook his head slightly. He yawned and stood up. Slowly he walked to the corner of the room and climbed the ladder to the loft. "Perhaps," he thought, "I will straighten up the old papers." Rabbi Asher looked around. He pushed a few books aside and then he noticed a letter. It was from Rabbi Petahiah ben Jacob of Regensburg to one of Asher's predecessors, Rabbi Abraham ben Alexander, Achselrad of Cologne. Rabbi Asher sat on the cot in the loft and read the letter, and this is what it said:

"*My dear Rabbi Abraham*–

"I have just met a fine young man, a Jew from Gorlitz; he has agreed to carry this letter to my good friend, Rabbi Hillel of Dresden, who I am certain will then arrange to transport it to you. I write to wish you and your family well, to convey my fondest greetings to all the Jews of your blessed community in Cologne, and to praise the good Lord God (blessed be He) and His Almighty Name for ever and ever, amen.

"I will not trouble you with the details of my many wagon rides and my subsequent sea voyages. Suffice it to say that safely they brought me here to the Oriental regions, regions that are so near to the great Holy Land where someday the Messiah shall return and deliver us and resurrect all souls and rebuild the Temple on Zion, amen. I write now in order to record for you some details of the lands and the peoples that I have seen in these old and foreign realms. The bright and glorious hand of God is visible everywhere, if only we look–praise the Lord Yahweh-Elohim.

"As you might imagine, my old friend, I have had many, many adventures in arriving here. I hope–if the good Lord is willing–to relate more of these events to you in person. For now, let me just say that after touring the Holy Lands of Palestine, I turned south to find, in the middle of the desert, the famed trading center of Petra.

"Petra is a two-week journey south of the city of Amman. It is a fortress walled by towering rocks and watered by a perennial stream.

But, Abraham, Petra is more than a city or a stronghold–it is a monument, it is actually a sculpture. Petra is a complex architecture carved from the desert hillsides in a basin among the mountains. An ancient race called the Nabataeans began the sculpting in biblical times, and later the Romans continued. Temples and tombs and places of worship are all cut into the surrounding hillsides. It is truly an amazing spectacle.

"The major trade routes cross in Petra, and all caravans from the north and the south stop here. As we arrived we passed nomadic tribes, encamped along the routes to and from the city. The nomads travel by camel, they sleep in tents, and their campfires can be seen for miles at night. The main route to Petra crosses a number of steep valleys known as 'wadis.' My guide told me that these are dried riverbeds: they are winding canyons carved into the desert with hints of red rock and with an innumerable variety of brown hues.

"And then suddenly there is Petra. It is a rose-red city, half as old as time itself. Petra is a valley within dry desert hills. This valley can be entered only by a single cut in the eastern rock face. The entryway is known as the Siq; it is a narrow lane, a split in the huge sandstone rocks three kilometers long and sixty meters high, and in places the narrow gorge is less than four meters wide. As we walked through the Siq, our footsteps echoed. The leader of our caravan pointed out hangers chiseled beyond our reach along the rock walls, where earlier peoples had hung their oil lamps.

"Like an empty riverbed, the Siq winds down into a valley, which contains the city of Petra. Pink mountains wall Petra on all sides, and the walls are cut by deep black fissures and lined with rock tombs shaped like towers. Perched on the cliffs and ledges and peaks are great mausoleums which frown down at the dust bowl below. The whole valley is filled with temples carved into the hillsides.

"Inside this valley is the River Wadi Musa, and the city is built along both banks where the ground is flat. Roads with cobblestones radiate out in all directions. Just beyond the city is the capstone monument. It is called the 'High Place of Sacrifice,' and it sits on a hill that is a half-hour climb up a twisting stone staircase from the valley below. The 'High Place' has a hollow ringing silence and it was the site of holy ritual sacrifices.

"Originally, at the time of Ezra the Scribe, Petra was the central city of a nomadic tribe called the Nabataeans. All caravans traveling through the region were taxed, and Petra became quite wealthy. Trade flourished. Famous thieves hid treasure here. Next came the Romans: they built Petra into an architectural wonder and made it a provincial capital. Recently, the city has been held by the Crusaders, who are building a Christian citadel near the 'High Place' on Mount en-Nejr.

"With travelers from all parts of the world passing through, many exotic goods and much strange knowledge is available. In the marketplace, I met a small, dark man who spoke Hebrew, although he was not a Jew. We sat for many hours, and I listened to his fantastic tales. He claimed that in his travels he had seen dog-men – creatures with faces like men and bodies like dogs. They have, so he said, a third eye somewhere under their hair on top of their heads. From their heads to their waists they are shaggy dogs, but from the waist downward they are again like human beings. The dog-men talk with human voices that are rough and gravelly. Their backs and legs are hairy. Also, their feet are webbed – their toes have folds of skin between them – but, unlike ducks, these creatures cannot swim and do not dare to go into the water or they will drown.

"And what do these creatures eat? They prefer meat; in fact, Abraham, they are cannibals. They live in a land where pepper grows, and they trade their pepper for other goods with the merchants who come there. But the dog-men themselves eat no vegetables. Instead, when they catch a trading merchant alone, they throw him into a pit; then they keep him and fatten him. First, however, they give the man some sort of drink by which he loses his senses – next, they feed him honey and cakes to make him fat and tasty, and, in the end, they eat him.

"Humans are a delicacy for these dog-men, and they do not hurry the fattening process. When they think that a prisoner is ready to be eaten, the jailer first feels the thickness of his dinner's finger. Is it plump? If so, the dog-men slice off the tip of his little finger; then they fry it and taste it. And if the poor man has reached the peak of deliciousness, then the dog-men take him out of the pit and roast him and make a great feast.

"Now, Abraham, this story seemed utterly fantastic, but as my companion talked, other men collected in the space around us, nodding and gesturing and adding their own accounts. One thin and dirty traveler began to talk at great length. My companion translated, and this is the story that I heard:

"One time, two adventurous merchants were caught by these dog-men and they were thrown into the pit. For three days, the prisoners were given no food. Suddenly the dog-men brought a delicious meal. One of the men, named Salira, took the food and ate it immediately. With this dinner was a magical drink that the dog-men made from a plant by drying the milky sap of the seed pods and mixing this sap with sugar and water. The potion made Salira tired and warm. He felt happy and relaxed. A twisted ankle stopped hurting. The world seemed like a summery blanket. Salira took some of this drink with every meal, and he lived his days in a pleasant stupor. Soon, he got so fat that the cannibals took him out of the pit and roasted him and ate him.

"Salira's companion, Benaiah ben Solomon, was a Jew. He had guessed what was in store for him. Therefore, he refused to eat or to drink anything at all. Instead, Benaiah fasted and prayed. He said the *Shema* ten times each morning and ten times each afternoon, and he shriveled into a lean and withered man. However, the natives were patient: they continued to offer him food, hoping to fatten him up again.

"One night, Benaiah, who was now quite skinny and very weak, managed to climb out of the pit. He was breathing hard. His muscles ached. He stood uncertainly. Then he chanted the protective verse from the Book of Exodus":

> Terror and dread fell upon them
> And through the might of Your right arm
> They all stopped, stone-still
> While Your people passed safe from harm
> Through the danger, by Your will
> Amen.

"Benaiah felt stronger. Quietly, he entered the house of one of his captors. He stole a sword and he was about to kill the sleeping guardsmen, when there was a shout. Benaiah turned and he ran and ran and ran down to the river in order to save himself.

"When the dog-people heard what had happened, they ran after him, trying to catch him. But, no sooner did they get into the water than these strange half-people could not move: the water filled the spongelike webbing in their feet, which became as heavy as thick mud. The dog-men floundered about helplessly. They shouted. They barked. But they could not catch Benaiah.

"Benaiah ran and ran and did not look back. With all his strength, he sloshed through the mud. Vines grabbed his arms. Flies bit his legs. Crabs clawed his feet. He waded through the shallow water until he reached the mouth of the river. There he found the trunk of a huge cedar tree in the water. Benaiah was panting, exhausted. He climbed onto the floating tree and he fell asleep.

"The tide and current carried Benaiah safely downstream into larger river after river. The light waves rocked him gently, and when he awoke he found that God had been watchful and had protected him. Now he was in the open, rolling down a river with reedy summer banks. Benaiah saw children jumping and running in green lands under a shining, windswept, endless blue sky. Benaiah lay there, content. He floated on and on. And after a day, he came to the city of Cairo, the majestic Egyptian city on the eastern side of the great River Nile.

"Benaiah was a natural trader, and in Cairo he found himself quite at home. He sold his cedar log for a large sum of money. Then he ate a delicious meal and he found a place to live. Cairo was filled with diverse races, with distinctive faces, and with all manner of skin colors. People flowed everywhere through the narrow and tortuous streets. Shop noises and goods seemed to roll through the town, and Benaiah rolled along with them, past the merchants selling cotton, fruits, and gum, hides, indigo, and ivory, ostrich feathers, shawls, and sheep, sherbets, sugarwater, and woolens of all imaginable kinds. Benaiah became a regular fixture in the marketplaces. He bought and sold a succession of goods–spices, cloths, carpets, and gems–and with his easy business manner, he soon became quite rich. The teller of this tale had met Benaiah in Cairo, where the Jew had settled permanently. Benaiah ben Solomon had become a leader of the Jewish community. He was a pious man, and he attributed all his success to the good offices of the Jewish Lord our God, who in His own miraculous way, watches over all Jews wherever we may be, protecting us from strange and extraordinary troubles even in the most distant of regions, amen.

"Well, that is the whole strange story, Abraham, and now I will end my letter too. The good Lord God protected Benaiah from distant exotic evils, as He protects all the righteous, even from their small and ordinary daily troubles. I have tried to be a righteous man, and I am certain that the Lord God Almighty will watch over me. And if He should call me to the Great Hereafter before I return to Germany, if I slip away to the far-off celestial regions with their wispy cotton clouds, regions where angels fly and slide in the gentle spring winds of forever, then I will go smiling and thinking of you. For I know, dear Abraham, that we will meet again as children, the most wondrous and magical of beings. Yes, I will see you again on the grassy summer banks of a river in the sky. There, we will ever jump and roll and run in green and blue lands under the shining, windswept, endless dome of Heaven, amen. Yes, Abraham, hallelujah for our childhoods, and a warm, God-sheltered, and glorious amen.

"Your childhood friend,
Petahiah, the son of Jacob"

What is that, Rabbi? No, no – you did not wake me. I was just resting here happily by the stove. I was thinking of old Abraham Achselrad. He is my favorite of all the medieval rabbis that my grandmother would talk about. You know that he was a pupil of the visionary Eliazer ben Judah, the mystic of Worms, and Achselrad himself was forever having visions. I guess that is why I am so fond of him: now, in my old age, I seem always to be having visions. At least, I see things in the glow of the stove at night.

Now? Well, Rabbi, I see a sunny morning in those white coals. Yes, it reminds me of a sunny morning, when no one is about but when the clouds are high and white and when the sun is far and bright and when the sky is blue and light. Out in the countryside fields, the grasses are a misty sea. The first streams of sunlight from the great and rosy-fingered dawn have rolled across the marsh, the field, the hills, and the trees. It is just like one sunny dawn when, in the early morning glow, Abraham ben Alexander, Achselrad of Cologne, suddenly realized that he had been writing all night in his mystical tome, the *Keter Shem Tov*.

Old Rabbi Abraham set down his pen and he looked up. The candle had gone out. A gentle light filtered in from the main prayer hall, a prayer hall filled with wooden benches. The light had passed through the twelve stained-glass windows with their colored lions and snakes. It had been made holy as it rolled around the stone Ark, and then it had streamed into the door of the back study room. In this *ki tov* light of the good and radiant Lord God Almighty (blessed be He), Rabbi Abraham looked up, and he saw no one there. Yes, the Rabbi looked up, and there was no one standing in his morning doorway, amen.

It was very early in the morning, one day long, long ago. The sun was out, and no one was about at the old yeshiva. Rabbi Abraham stood up. He walked through the main prayer hall and he looked out the front door. It was the great *ki tov* dawning of the day. The morning colors glowed in the opposite order of the evening; first came the reds, next came the oranges, and finally God's brilliant golden yellows slipped up from behind the mountains east of the sky. The Rabbi looked up, and he looked down. Where were all the people? The Rabbi stood still for a moment. Then he stepped out into the courtyard. Was the world empty of all mankind? How could this be? It felt so bright and so warm.

Was there a young man walking up the alleyway? Rabbi Abraham blinked and rubbed his eyes. No, there was no one there. Perhaps the Rabbi was remembering his childhood friend, Petahiah ben Jacob. Petahiah was the brother of Rabbi Isaac ben Jacob ha-Lavan, Yizchak the White, of Prague. Petahiah himself was a wanderer: one day he set off on a trip to see the entire world. When he returned, he dictated a book about his travels to the mystic Judah he-Hasid of Regensburg; the book was called *Sivuv ha-Olam (Around the World).* As he traveled, Rabbi Petahiah had written many letters to his friend Rabbi Abraham, but the two men had not actually seen each other since their happy green days. Rabbi Achselrad thought many times of his friend. What did old Petahiah look like now? The morning was drifting by. Old Rabbi Achselrad stood musing about summers and rains and long scratchy grasses and warm afternoons of a long time ago.

Rabbi Abraham Achselrad shook his head gently and he stepped into the courtyard. Down the alleyway he walked toward Judengasse Street. He stopped, and who should be coming toward him? It was Dan ben Moses, a Cologne merchant recently returned from the south. And what was this? Reb Dan had a letter for Rabbi Abraham, and it came from Regensburg. Rabbi Abraham smiled and he took the letter back to his study. Old Achselrad recognized the handwriting on the envelope: it was the distinctive curly Hebrew script of Rabbi Petahiah ben Jacob. Rabbi Abraham patted the envelope but he did not open it.

Old Rabbi Abraham was now seventy years of age. He set the letter on his desk, he folded his hands on his stomach, and he leaned back in his chair. Abraham Achselrad rested his eyes for a moment. The morning drifted on. Was it only a moment or was it an hour? Who knows–for soon the Rabbi fell asleep, and as he slept he dreamt a dream, a great and wondrous childhood dream:

Abraham ben Alexander was walking and talking with his friend Petahiah ben Jacob. They were in a warm land where the nighttide had rolled in. All about them the town was empty of people, yet it was not lonely because the warmth of human spirits floated through the streets and the buildings. "I suppose," said Abraham, "that it would be different in the wilds or in the bare desolation at the edges of the world."

"The edges of the world?" repeated Petahiah. "You know, Abraham, that reminds me of a story my father used to tell. It was a tale about a wee bit of an angel who lived off at the far corner of the world. I have not thought of that Night Tale for years and years and years."

"Well, Petahiah," said Abraham Achselrad, "here I am, awake in the dead of the night, so perhaps you will tell me that old story."

"All right, Abraham. It begins long ago, when there once was an angel, a very small angel, and he lived on the edge of the world:

"There once was an angel, a very small angel, and he lived on the edge of the world. He lived alone in a tiny hut, and he gardened quietly for his food. The garden plot was bordered in jipijapa plants. And this garden was in front of the little angel's house, because the back wall of the house was right along the high cliff of the astral universe. In the mornings when he ate breakfast, the angel looked out and down into the deepest blue, where the clouds floated below as far as the eye could see. When he looked up, it was a golden gray. And straight out there was no horizon, but the stars and the moon and the planets rolled along in waves of the deepest blue far, far beyond.

"The little angel never talked, of course, for there was no one with whom to talk. He grew yams and he grew peas. And the days were all cool and fair, and his life was all ordered and fine. Each evening was like the early spring. A damp wind would come from a marsh nearby; it would roll over the fields and it was warmed by the grasses, the stackburs, and the field cedar. Growing so fast on a springtime night, the plants heated the dirt around them, and you could walk barefoot for miles and miles and miles.

"Nightly, the very small angel would sit on his porch, in front of the house. He would look out at his garden. He would watch the yams grow and he would follow the peas as they gently twisted about on the vines, under the patient jipijapa plants. The olive trees were old, and they grew slowly and quietly.

"The little angel had a chair and he had a rail for his feet, and he sat back and rocked gently. Late one night, along by the turn of the path, down as far as he could see in that cool, misty, moisty light in the back glow of the edge of the world past the black oaks, came a young man walking along. The small angel rocked quietly. The young man wore a brown coat and he carried a cloth sack. He walked up to the porch, and without a word he set the sack down on the ground. Then he turned and he left. The young man passed the weathered wood fence at the far edge of the garden plot rimmed with jipijapas, and he went up beyond the olive trees, along the beginning of the forest that lined the edge of the world. And then, he disappeared through the black oaks.

"Nothing stirred. No wind blew, no insects moved, the stars were frozen and watchful. The small angel stopped rocking; the peas stopped growing. The night deepened, and the sack sat silently.

"Now, after a while, a bit of mist accumulated at the corner of the world, there along the rim of the nighttime newborn world. Undoubtedly it was some damp stardust, blown in with the universal tides as the planets swept by; it was some wispy mystical cosmic wind from the edge of the heavens, a bit of galactic magic. The mist curled slowly, fraying and dissolving. Then it rolled up at the tip, and it flowed, ever so gently, toward the hut and the porch and the angel and the garden and the jipijapa plants and the sack.

"You would not have noticed that mist, if you had not been sitting for hours, if your eyes had not been accustomed to everything else. The mist was so fine that it was like the lightest foggy rain on a springtime day. It misted and it twisted slowly, past the house and the porch, past the angel and along the garden and through the jipijapa leaves. It touched the sack almost by accident. The mist curled slowly, fraying and dissolving and settling, and it slid and it sank, and the sack was misty for a moment.

"A little breeze arose. The insects cricked a bit. The stars marched. The angel rocked. The peas grew, and the night deepened. The wind rustled the sack–and out of the sack rolled a smooth, round stone, no bigger than your fist.

"Out rolled a rock no bigger than your fist. It was just a rock, smooth and round and creased. It was old and worn, and it rolled with a limp."

And Achselrad raised his eyebrows and he stroked his chin. "With a limp, Petahiah?" he asked.

"Well, Abraham," said Petahiah, "the rock rolled slowly and unevenly, bumping along. Not uncomfortably, mind you, but not quite smoothly. It rolled out of the sack.

"There in front of the rock was a small pebble; so the smooth old rock, rolling out from within the sack, opened its mouth and–"

"Its mouth?" asked Achselrad.

"Yes, its mouth. Please do not interrupt, Abraham."

"I am sorry, Petahiah; continue your tale," said Abraham.

"Very well, my friend," said Petahiah.

"The rock opened its mouth and it swallowed that little pebble. Then it rolled on, slowly and unevenly, bumping along until it had reached the border of the garden with its neat gray fence and with the jipijapas peeking through, watching the old worn rock.

"That old black rock was worn and creased through and through. It stopped at the edge of the garden, and then it opened its mouth and it swallowed the fence, post by post. It inhaled the neat gray fence, post by post by post. Then it rolled on into the garden. The peas were gently growing and twisting on the vines. The peppers were getting fat and thick. The old black rock just swallowed the peas and the vines and the peppers and the leaves and the stems and all. And then, the old black rock began to grow bigger and bigger and bigger.

"The wee small angel sat back, still and silent. His eyes grew wide. The black rock rolled on and on. It opened its black rocky mouth and it swallowed an olive tree. It gaped its stony jaws and the forest of black oaks slid down its craggy gullet. Its canyon chasm swallowed fields and grasses and stackburs and cedar; it swallowed knotroot grasses and rutabagas and crab apples and tangleberries. The old black rock was round and swollen – it looked like a great black hill. It sipped and it sucked the river beyond; it drank and it gulped the marshes, the lowlands, and all the wet places that lined the foresty woodlands, down past the hills on the edge of the world. That old black rock, from within the sack, had become a giant; it was stone-crushing, bone-breaking, and mountain-devouring. Relentlessly it ate, and it tore away at the lands and the towns and the great gray granite cliffs afar. The wee small angel sat very still indeed."

"Yes – very still indeed," thought Rabbi Abraham ben Alexander, Achselrad of Cologne. And Petahiah was continuing:

"With a ravenous intake of all that was around it, the rock devoured the earth. The oceans sank into its bottomless throat. As the waters poured down in a murky whirlpool, a small island floated toward the gaping black maw. On the island was a tiny yellow flower, a buttercup. In the daylight it would be a bit of golden sun, with five round petals newly painted, happy and bright. In the center of the buttercup was a little puff of yellow. It would be smiling there, that buttercup, standing on its one spindly leg with a few green shavings on its toes. That would have been in the day, of course. But now it was night, and the black rock swallowed the island, buttercup and all, clover fields and honey hives and gulls' nests and crab caves and all.

"Insatiable, the enormous rock devoured the islands and the seas. It ate the earth, and it ate the ocean's roaring streams. As the waters poured down its bottomless throat, an old ship was swept along. On its mast was a torn sail, on the sail was a frayed rope, and on the rope was a black bug. In the daylight the bug would be a glistening beetle; it would be a soldier dressed in glints and gleams, with shining wings and neat clicking feet. It would be standing there at attention on its sharp black legs, with not one speck of beetle dust, not one smudge of beetle dirt. That would have been in the day, of course. But now it was night, and the black rock blindly swallowed the ship, sail, rope, beetle and all – planks and flags, sailors and rigging, and rudder and all.

"With boundless appetite, the vast rock sucked in the seas; it drained the rivers, it emptied the lakes and the ponds and the bays, it dispatched the brown hills and the gray cliffs. And as the land broke away and crumbled into the grim gaping pit, a thatch-roofed home teetered on one of the massive rock teeth. In this home was a baby, just one month old. In the daylight that child would be opened-eyed, rosy-cheeked, and tousled-haired; it would wave its fists and it would roll its wrinkly neck. The tiny child would raise its eyebrows, surprised at every single thing around it – its crib, its mother, its blankets, its fist. The little baby would blink and tickle its tongue and hit its eye with its tight tiny hand. That would have been in the day, of course. But now it was night, and the black rock could not see and it could not hear and it could not smell or feel or taste – and it did not care. The home fell in, and the thick black mountain of a rock swallowed the home, baby and all, crib and blankets and mother and father, and cupboards and all."

"And all," whispered old Rabbi Aschelrad in his sleep.

"And now," said Petahiah, "the only thing that the little angel could see was a massive black shape, as tall as the sky and as wide as the earth. It was the back of the old black hungry rock.

"From within this rock, there came a deep rumbling and drumming sound, as the blocks and the chunks of the world fell upon one another. Inside the great rock, thunder echoed back and forth and waves crashed. The massive black shape grew larger and larger and larger. On the far side, the whole mortal earth was fast disappearing, and the wee small angel sat there, on the last remaining rim of the world, with the clouds and the stars and the vast cosmic spaces falling endlessly away behind him, with the deep blue sea of the Heavens rolling forever back. And the old black rock devoured the entire earth – and then it began to turn around."

"It began to turn around, Petahiah?" asked Abraham.

"Yes, Abraham," said Petahiah, "the old black rock – worn and creased, massive, swollen, mountainy, and thick – stopped, and it turned around. It turned back toward the wee small angel. The cold black breath of its chasm and gullet chilled the air as it rolled back toward the house at the edge of the world. Its stone jaws were wide; its stone mouth was empty.

"The wee small angel sat still as stone himself. He opened wide his bright, bright eyes, he listened well with his softest and tiniest ears. There was no marsh, no woods, no garden, no jipijapa plants. There was only the wee small angel on his rocking chair and porch, with blackness before him and with the endless Night behind. The old black rock was as full and as wide as forever. It was as cold as Death, and it moved and it rumbled and it drummed and it echoed, and the wee small angel just sat very still. The wee small angel sat still as stone – and then, Abraham, then the little baby angel jumped.

"The wee small angel – this little angel at the edge of the world, living on the rim of the fresh, clean, old world of before – he jumped. He jumped a little baby angel's leap, as only a little angel can jump. He bounced up, and he leaped around, and he tipped and he topped and he flipped right up and over that massive black mountain hole. The wee little angel jumped higher than the knotroot grasses; he jumped higher than the apple trees. The wee small angel jimped and he jumped, and he tickled the nose of the old black rock, the old worn nose, past the creased crevice and up and around. And that hungry rock stretched its black mountain chasm of Death, its gloomy black jaws, to snap and to gobble the last little angel from all this mortal earth. And it cracked.

"The ancient hungry rock reached its rocky jaws wide and it cracked and it split. The old black stone stretched and it gaped and it cracked, and great thundering fjords broke along its old worn face. Great thundering jagged rips of stone rent its sides, and in powdering spumes of dust and scrabbling skree, it dissolved – like a curtain of harsh rain at the end of a storm when it is suddenly ripped and blown away by the wind. Then the world tumbled forth again, and as the clouds and the rocks and the trees and the lands suddenly fell into place, there was a comforting nighttime silence once more across the world."

"For a moment," said Petahiah, "the wee small angel was lost. He found himself on the grass, in the corner of a woods. The angel looked around, and he saw the old oak trees and the low spicebush brush. He picked up two brown leaves and crumbled them and cracked them, and he kicked a little pebble.

"Then the little one walked back slowly to his house on the edge of the world. The little angel walked down the path, in the cool misty light, and he passed the sack sitting in front of his porch. A hint of mist curled about the brown canvas flap of that old sack. The little angel climbed onto his porch; he sat on his chair, and he watched the peas growing again on their summer-pea vines.

"The wee small angel sat back, and gently he rocked. The ancient olive trees continued to grow, slowly and quietly. And after a while, along by the turn of the path, down as far as you could see in that cool, misty, just-before-morning light, in the back glow of the edge of the world, past the black oaks, came the young man walking along. The small angel rocked quietly. The young man walked up to the porch. Without a word, he took the sack; without a backward glance, he turned and he left.

"The young man passed the weathered wood fence–now gray in the early light–at the far edge of the garden plot. The garden was rimmed with jipijapa plants, and the young man went up past the jipijapas and beyond the olive trees along the beginning of the black oak forest that lined the edge of the world. The very small angel looked away and then he looked back again, and he rocked a bit. The grass was a misty sea. The first streams of sunlight from the great and rosy-fingered dawn rolled across the marsh, the field, the hills, and the trees. It was the great *ki-tov* dawning of the day, and the colors appeared in the morning in the opposite order of the evening. The reds came first, oranges came next, and finally there were God's brilliant golden yellows. I looked up, and I looked down. Where was the young man? Was the world empty of all people? How could this be? It felt so bright and so warm. I looked down the road, but even in the morning glow, I could not tell whether I saw the young man with the sack and the old brown coat. Perhaps it was just one of the oaks that had stepped out into the dirt road–an oak that had decided to dig its rooty toes into a fine, cool, springtime morning road."

"*You* could not tell, Petahiah?" asked Abraham.

"Yes *I*, Abraham–for my father would say that it was a story about *me*, when I was just a very small angel, once long ago as I lived on the far edge of my fresh, bright, newborn baby world."

Thus said Petahiah to old Abraham Achselrad once upon a time, long, long ago, as the old man dozed in front of the stove in the rabbi's study room of his small yeshiva. It was in a medieval springtime along the dark, wide, medieval River Rhine. And that was many, many years ago, Rabbi Petahiah. Yes, it is a Night Tale remembered from a great many years ago.

The End

Scrivener with the writer's pen
Tell Petahiah's words again,
His dreams of an ancient Lord, amen.

And when beyond old age as must
This generation returns to dust
He shall endure anew, I trust.

ACKNOWLEDGMENTS

This is the last volume of ***The Night Tales Trilogy***, which began with:

Katz, M. J. (1988). *Night Tales of the Shammas.* Northvale, NJ: Jason Aronson.

Katz, M. J. (1990). *Night Tales Remembered: Fables from the Shammas.* Northvale, NJ: Jason Aronson.

Brief versions of some of the tales in the present volume can be found in:

Abrahams, I. (1896). *Jewish Life in the Middle Ages.* New York: Macmillan.

Aleichem, S. (1985). *From the Fair: The Autobiography of Scholom Aleichem.* Trans. C. Leviant. New York: Penguin Books.

Altmann, B. (1940). Studies in Medieval German Jewish History. Part I. *Proceedings of the American Academy for Jewish Research* (New York). Vol. 10, pp. 5–98. Philadelphia: Jewish Publication Society.

Ausubel, N., ed. (1948). *A Treasury of Jewish Folklore.* New York: Crown Publishers.

Bacher, W. (1911). Kimhi. In: *The Encyclopaedia Britannica,* 11th ed., vol. 15, p. 800.

Benisch, A., trans. (1861). *Travels of Rabbi Petachia of Ratisbon, who, in the latter end of the twelfth century, visited Poland, Russia, Little Tartary, the Crimea, Armenia, Assyria, Syria, the Holy Land, and Greece.* 2d ed. London: Longman and Co.

Bernstein, M. (1960). Two Remedy Books in Yiddish from 1474 and 1508. In: *Studies in Biblical and Jewish Folklore,* ed. R. Patai, F. L. Utley, and D. Noy, pp. 287–305. Bloomington, IN: Indiana University Press.

Bildersee, A. (1918). *Jewish Post-Biblical History through Great Personalities, from Jochanan ben Zakkai through Moses Mendelssohn.* Cincinnati: Union of American Hebrew Congregations.

Brewer, E. C. (1949). *Brewer's Dictionary of Phrase & Fable.* Rev. and enl. New York: Harper & Brothers.

Budge, E. A. W. (1930). *Amulets and Superstitions.* London: Oxford University Press.

Cohen, A. (1949). *Everyman's Talmud.* New York: E. P. Dutton & Co.

Dembitz, L. N. (1898). *Jewish Services in Synagogue and Home.* Philadelphia: Jewish Publication Society.

Gaster, M. (1924). *The Exempla of the Rabbis.* Reprint. New York: Ktav Publishing House, 1968.

____________ (1928). *Studies and Texts in Folklore, Magic, Mediaeval Romance, Hebrew Apocrypha and Samaritan Archeology*. Reprint. Vols. 1 and 2. New York: Ktav Publishing House, 1971.

Gollancz, H., ed. and trans. (1902). *The Ethical Treatises of Berachya, son of Rabbi Natronai ha-Nakdan, being the Compendium and the Masref.* London: David Nutt. Reprint. New York: Arno Press, 1973.

Graetz, H. (1894). *History of the Jews.* Vols. 2 and 3. Philadelphia: Jewish Publication Society.

Grayzel, S. (1968). *A History of the Jews.* 2d ed. Philadelphia: Jewish Publication Society.

Heine, H. (1835). Concerning the history of religion and philosophy in Germany. In: *Heinrich Heine: Selected Works,* ed. and trans. H. M. Mustard, pp. 274–420. New York: Random House, 1973.

Hertz, J. H., trans. (1945). *Sayings of the Fathers or Pirke Aboth.* New York: Behrman House.

Katz, M. (1989). *Socrates in August: From Incondensable Complexity to Myth.* American University Series, vol. 66. New York: Peter Lang Publishing.

____________ (1989). *Socrates in September: The Entanglements of Complexity.* American University Series, vol. 53. New York: Peter Lang Publishing.

Kober, A. (1940). *Cologne.* Trans. S. Grayzel. Philadelphia: Jewish Publication Society.

____________ (1944). Jewish monuments of the Middle Ages in Germany. Part I. *Proceedings of the American Academy for Jewish Research* (New York). Vol. 14, pp. 149–220. Philadelphia: Jewish Publication Society.

____________ (1945). Jewish monuments of the Middle Ages in Germany. Part II. *Proceedings of the American Academy for Jewish Research* (New York). Vol. 15, pp. 1–91. Philadelphia: Jewish Publication Society.

Kobler, F., ed. and trans. (1952). *Letters of Jews Through the Ages.* Pp. 156–165, 243–244. New York: East and West Library, Hebrew Publishing Co.

Leslau, W. (1944). Texts on Yemenite folklore. *Proceedings of the American Academy for Jewish Research* (New York). Vol. 14, pp. 221–251. Philadelphia: Jewish Publication Society.

Lonnrot, E. (1969). *The Old Kalevala and Certain Antecedents.* Cambridge, MA: Harvard University Press.

Maimon, S. (1888). *Solomon Maimon: An Autobiography.* Trans. J. C. Murray. Boston: Cupples & Hurd.

Millgram, A. E. (1971). *Jewish Worship.* Philadelphia: Jewish Publication Society.

Noy, D. (1963). *Folktales of Israel.* Trans. G. Baharav. Chicago: University of Chicago Press.

O'Crohan, T. (1935). *The Islandman.* Trans. R. Flower. New York: Charles Scribner's Sons.

Parry, M., collector (1954). *Serbocroatian Heroic Songs.* Vol. 1, *Novi Pazar: English Translations.* Ed. and trans. A. B. Lord. Cambridge, MA: Harvard University Press.

Robinson, J. H. (1903). *An Introduction to the History of Western Europe.* Boston: Ginn & Co.

Stevenson, R. W. Wishes. In: *The Oxford Book of English Verse,* ed. A. Quiller-Couch, p. 1035. New. ed. New York: Oxford University Press, 1940.

Straus, R. (1939). *Regensburg and Augsburg.* Trans. F. N. Gerson. Philadelphia: Jewish Publication Society.

Trachtenberg, J. (1939). *Jewish Magic and Superstition.* New York: Behrman's Jewish Book House.

Tutuola, A. (1953). *The Palm-Wine Drinkard.* New York: George Braziller, Grove Press.

North Sea
England
Cologne
Atlantic Ocean
Mainz
Rhine
Paris
Worms
German
France
Rhone
Leon
Toledo
Cordova
Mediterranean
N. Burgard